ADVERTISING AND MARKETING COMMUNICATION MANAGEMENT

John H. Murphy II
The University of Texas at Austin

▼

Isabella C. M. Cunningham
The University of Texas at Austin

The Dryden Press
Harcourt Brace College Publishers

Fort Worth   Philadelphia   San Diego   New York   Orlando   Austin   San Antonio
Toronto   Montreal   London   Sydney   Tokyo

Acquisitions Editor: Lyn Keeney Hastert
Marketing Manager: Lise Johnson
Production Manager: Trisha Dianne
Manager of Production: Diane Southworth

Project Management: Elm Street Publishing Services, Inc.
Compositor: The Clarinda Company

ISBN: 0-03-051069-4

Library of Congress Catalog Card Number: 92-43667

Printed in the United States of America
345-039-987654321

The Dryden Press
Harcourt Brace

We dedicate this book to our children—
Erin and Kristen M. and John C.

The Dryden Press Series in Marketing

Assael
Marketing: Principles and Strategy
Second Edition

Bateson
**Managing Services Marketing:
Text and Readings**
Second Edition

Blackwell, Blackwell, and Talarzyk
**Contemporary Cases in
Consumer Behavior**
Fourth Edition

Boone and Kurtz
Contemporary Marketing
Seventh Edition

Churchill
Basic Marketing Research
Second Edition

Churchill
**Marketing Research:
Methodological Foundations**
Fifth Edition

Czinkota and Ronkainen
International Marketing
Third Edition

Dunn, Barban, Krugman, and Reid
**Advertising: Its Role in
Modern Marketing**
Seventh Edition

Engel, Blackwell, and Miniard
Consumer Behavior
Seventh Edition

Futrell
Sales Management
Third Edition

Ghosh
Retail Management

Hutt and Speh
**Business Marketing Management:
A Strategic View of Industrial
and Organization Markets**
Fourth Edition

Ingram and LaForge
**Sales Management: Analysis
and Decision Making**
Second Edition

Kurtz and Boone
Marketing
Third Edition

Murphy and Cunningham
**Advertising and Marketing
Communication Management**

Oberhaus, Ratliffe, and Stauble
**Professional Selling:
A Relationship Process**

Park and Zaltman
Marketing Management

Patti and Frazer
**Advertising: A Decision-
Making Approach**

Rachman
Marketing Today
Second Edition

Rogers, Gamans, and Grassi
Retailing: New Perspectives
Second Edition

Rosenbloom
**Marketing Channels:
A Management View**
Fourth Edition

Schellinck and Maddox
**Marketing and Research:
A Computer-Assisted Approach**

Schnaars
MICROSIM
*Marketing simulation available
for IBM PC and Apple*

Sellars
Role Playing: The Principles of Selling
Second Edition

Shimp
**Promotion Management and
Marketing Communications**
Third Edition

Talarzyk
Cases and Exercises in Marketing

Terpstra and Sarathy
International Marketing
Fifth Edition

Tootelian and Gaedeke
**Cases and Classics in
Marketing Management**

Weitz and Wensley
**Readings in Strategic Marketing
Analysis, Planning, and Implementation**

Zikmund
Exploring Marketing Research
Fourth Edition

Preface

Advertising and Marketing Communication Management is designed to serve as the primary text for advanced undergraduate and graduate courses taught in either a communication or a business school environment. Our intention is to provide students with an applied understanding of the integrative planning of advertising and marketing communication efforts. This is accomplished by blending practical textual discussion of the planning process; short exercises that help students understand the concepts and issues involved; and cases that describe actual decision-making dilemmas and challenge students to apply the concepts presented.

This book is designed to be used as the cornerstone for a course whose objective is to provide students with broad insights into the managerial decisions involved in developing, planning, presenting, and implementing the advertising and marketing communication efforts of a broad range of enterprises. In order to accomplish this objective, we have placed the primary emphasis on students learning-by-doing. That is, students learn by making communication management decisions in the environment in which they occur, through the cases provided in the text.

The unique position of this text is its strong emphasis on applied decision making, supported by a foundation of conventional wisdom and academic insights. In addition, we provide a balanced mix of both textual treatment *and* actual cases.

The book is organized into four parts:

- Introduction to the case method (including how to develop and deliver effective presentations);

- Advertising management decision making;

- Other communication mix elements; and

- Additional considerations affecting advertising and promotion decisions.

Following a brief introduction, Part II includes six chapters that cover the following areas: the marketing context of advertising and promotion, establishing objectives, determining the advertising appropriation and budget, developing creative strategy, developing media stategy, and advertising research. Part III includes four chapters that focus on personal selling, sales promotion, .public relations, and direct marketing. Part IV consists of two chapters examining client/agency relations and ethical considerations.

Each chapter presents a concise discussion of the key management issues in that area followed by three to six cases which allow students to apply the concepts. In addition, each chapter concludes with a set of short exercises that illustrates the points discussed in the chapter and provides students with focused experience in applying these concepts before tackling the case assignments. The four major competitive advantages of this book are (1) text coverage and treatment; (2) range of actual cases; (3) classroom-tested text and cases; and (4) exercises.

Text coverage. The text provides coverage of the major areas of advertising and marketing communication management with an emphasis on an applied rather than a theoretical treatment. Each chapter presents a concise discussion plus clear, real-world illustrations of how to plan a firm's communication efforts.

Cases. The forty-eight cases included span a wide range of firms and were selected for their high interest value to students. Examples include a movie studio (Walt Disney Pictures), a commercial truck manufacturer (Peterbilt), a nonprofit conservation group (National Wildflower Center), a regional motel chain (La Quinta), and an international cosmetics company (Mary Kay). The cases provide a realistic range of marketing situations including consumer and business-to-business environments; local and international operations; large and small firms; and nonprofit, political, and service marketing. All cases are based on actual decision-making situations of real companies (note that the identities in fifteen of the cases have been disguised). The cases are supported by many photos, exhibits, illustrations, and a videotape of commercials, which helps bring the situations to life for students. The length and complexity of the cases varies, as does the size of the subject firms. As a result, the cases provide students with pragmatic exposure to a wide range of communication problems and opportunities across diverse settings.

Classroom tested. All of the text material and cases have been used in class at The University of Texas at Austin, and our classroom experience led to substantial revisions. We have used this process of trial and error in the classroom to clarify and strengthen the material and to enhance the learning experience for the student.

Exercises. At the end of each of the managerial decision-making chapters in this book is a set of short exercises that illustrates the points discussed in the text and exposes students to applied examples. These provide students with practical experience before tackling the case assignments.

We gratefully acknowledge the contributions of many people for their assistance during the development of this book. Our acknowledgments begin by recognizing the contributions of our students who patiently responded to drafts of both the text and the cases. Next, we thank the many practitioners who allowed us to develop case descriptions of their situations. Further, we want to extend our appreciation to our academic colleagues who supported the development of this book by contributing suggestions and recommendations regarding text content and cases.

A special thanks to Jayne Spittler at Leo Burnett Company for the use of Burnett's Media Cost Guide as an appendix. We also thank the following individuals for the use of their cases: Bob Anderson, Dick Beltramini, Ed Cundiff, Mark Desky, Morton Galper, George Franke, Debra Low, Chuck Patti, Bill Penczak, Don Schultz, Linda Scott, Bill Swinyard, and Paul Wang. In addition, the following individuals contributed by co-authoring cases in this book: George Franke, Cheryl Halpren, Owen Hannay, Gene Kincaid, Christi Myers, Leonard Ruben, Barry Smith, and Marshall Taylor.

In conclusion, we appreciate the strong support of Lyn Keeney Hastert, our editor at The Dryden Press; Phyllis Crittenden, JoAnn Learman, and Barb Bahnsen of Elm Street Publishing Services; and Anita Mote and Wendy Farajollahi of The University of Texas at Austin. Finally, we acknowledge that this book was made possible by the supportive environment which we have enjoyed for over twenty years at The University of Texas at Austin.

John Murphy
Isabella Cunningham
Austin, Texas
March 1993

Contents

CHAPTER **4**

Developing Advertising Objectives   86

CHAPTER **5**

Determining the Advertising Appropriation   128
and Budgeting

PART **III**

PERSONAL SELLING, SALES PROMOTION,   331
PUBLIC RELATIONS, AND DIRECT MARKETING

CHAPTER **9**

Personal Selling   333

CHAPTER **10**

Sales Promotion   380

CHAPTER **11**

Public Relations   407

INTRODUCTION

*T*he opening section of this book sets the stage for efficient student learning through the use of the case method. The first chapter describes the case method and stresses that a course utilizing cases requires different ground rules than do traditional lecture-based courses. For example, class discussion of cases requires a commitment from *all members* of the class to actively participate and to objectively consider the often conflicting opinions expressed by their classmates. In addition, Chapter 1 presents a decision-making framework for use in analyzing marketing communication management problems and opportunities. This systematic framework is recommended for analyzing all of the cases presented in the book.

The second chapter focuses on the development and delivery of effective presentations. In advertising and marketing communication, developing a brilliant recommendation or plan for utilizing advertising and other communication tools is often not enough. The recommendation or plan must also be persuasively sold to upper management personnel so they will implement it. Therefore, the chapter covers the basics of preparing and delivering effective presentations. The purpose of the chapter is to provide students with guidelines for planning and delivering their own case analyses/recommendations to the class. The valuable experience each student gains in making and observing such presentations should be an integral part of the course.✤

1

The Case Method

This book is designed to help students acquire decision-making skills through the study of a combination of advertising and marketing theory, short practical problems, and traditional cases. In this introductory section of the text, we explain the general philosophy of the book and stress the importance and use of case analysis in training managers.

This book does *not* contain elaborate and lengthy theoretical chapters. The text portion of each chapter provides a summary of selected, essential concepts and theoretical principles. These summaries function as a review tool for students preparing to handle the problems and cases that follow. The text material opening each chapter provides a general overview of the materials with which students should be familiar but is not intended to cover all aspects of the topics in detail. Students should be responsible for supplementing the material covered in the chapter openings with additional reading.

This book is designed to reflect advertising practice through use of specific examples. After students have read the chapters on each of the advertising and marketing communication management topics, they should be ready to analyze the exercises that follow. These were developed to encourage an orderly transition from theory to practice for those students who have not previously had a case-based course. As students become familiar with the general problem-solving procedures recommended, they will be able to progress from the simpler to the more complex cases on each topic. The following section explains the philosophy and purpose of case teaching. It also provides some simple guidelines for case analysis and discussion.

THE CASE DISCUSSION METHOD OF LEARNING

The management of advertising and marketing communication is a science that requires both basic knowledge and—above all—decision-making skills. Cases are designed to train students to develop those skills. Skills are best learned through practice, and cases that simulate decision-making situations allow students to role play and attempt to solve actual management problems as they occur.

Typically, cases do not afford simple solutions—as in most management situations, there may be no right or wrong answer. The heart of decision making is the ability to analyze the variables critical to the issue. By sharing this task in a group situation, students benefit from the group's insights as well as their own knowledge and experience.

There is no perfect formula or set of procedures for approaching a case analysis. Some general questions can, however, be asked in any decision-making situation: What is the problem we need to solve? What is the situation at this time? What factors are critical to a solution? What variables can be manipulated when devising a course of action?

A case study is simply a written description of a management problem. Analyzing a case study in administration can be thought of as the equivalent of providing a medical second opinion, with the student being the person asked to provide the second opinion. Like a consulting physician, the student must review the relevant facts described in the case, analyze them, reach some conclusion about the problem and its cause, and recommend some treatment or appropriate action.

Unlike medical cases, however, administrative cases are analyzed in a class of 20 or more students. Each student will have invested time outside of class working individually on the case before the class discusses it. The discussion will allow each student to benefit from all the other students' insights and to work toward a final decision or recommendation, which may differ from the one he or she reached individually.

The purpose of the case experience is to develop each student's ability to consider hard evidence, personal experience, and other factors in arriving at a sound decision and shaping a convincing recommendation. This process duplicates real-life situations in the best possible manner.

For both instructor and student, case-based learning requires sailing a very narrow channel between overcontrol and ambiguity. The promise of the case method, for those who successfully thread this course, is not that it will produce an excellent decision maker. Rather, with the instructor's aid, the student will be transformed into a more skilled decision maker through the experience. Therefore, to have a meaningful experience, students must have carefully studied each and every case used in the course, even though they may not be required to turn in a written assignment on most of the cases discussed. If they have not prepared carefully, the class discussion will be of little benefit to them.

Because management cases are dissected through discussion in a community of learners, each student should be an active participant, dynamically questioning the validity of his or her individual analysis continually as the group discussion unfolds. Thus, unlike in many classroom settings, the student spends much time *thinking* about his or her own point of view, which is constantly challenged by the other participants, who will have developed different views based on the same facts presented in the case. Therefore, the ability to present ideas and persuade others is also very important to case discussion.

In addition, case analysis teaches future managers to keep all options open and to listen carefully to information presented during the discussion. Because there are no right or wrong solutions to a case, information and discussion allow participants to develop an informed and logical way of making a decision.

The practical nature of the problems and opportunities presented in an advertising and marketing communication management case means students must be able to deal with such quantifiable concepts as costs, efficiency of messages as measured by exposures, expected results, profits, and sales. Students are expected to be able to handle calculations with skill and acumen. While personalities and human relations are important aspects of management, the bottom line is always a major consideration. Therefore, it is important to be able to handle appropriate mathematical calculations.

Many advertising and marketing communication management problems require the development of creative ideas and concepts. Others demand the ability to plan media schedules and budgets. Cases allow students to focus their energies and resources on one discrete issue at a time. More comprehensive issues dealing with the development of complete campaigns can also be examined using the cases in this book. Our overriding goal is to develop students' ability to deal with the issues involved in managing a firm's communications functions by projecting themselves in the role of company product manager, advertising agency account executive, or any other role pertaining to the management of advertising.

Several frameworks can be used in conducting a case analysis. The following section presents some suggestions and recommendations designed to aid students in analyzing cases.

CASE ANALYSIS FRAMEWORK AND OTHER GUIDELINES

A time-tested framework for organizing the analysis of a case is presented in Exhibit 1-1. This procedure can also be used as an outline for developing a concise written analysis of a case.

Exhibit 1-2 presents a decision tree, or flowchart, of the same case analysis process. This exhibit clearly indicates that a case analysis is a developmental process. For example, students may redefine the problem statement after evaluating alternatives. Students can glean many useful insights into conducting a case analysis by studying these two exhibits. In addition, several other general steps to analyzing a case and approaching its class discussion should be followed.

First, the students will enhance their understanding of the situation at hand by actively playing the role of the decision maker described in the case. This encourages them to commit themselves to a position and then actively defend it. Because management decisions consist substantially of analysis, choice, and

---

EXHIBIT 1-1   Framework for Case Analysis

The following framework is a logical and practical procedure to follow when analyzing decision-making situations. The approach is recommended for use in organizing your thinking and developing a recommended course of action.

1.   *Statement of the Problem.* Clearly define the central problem (or opportunity) posed in the case. The statement may mention symptoms and minor problems.

In analyzing a case with no stated emphasis, it is very easy to identify symptoms as the problem. In other words, what may at first appear to be the problem may, in fact, be a mere symptom or manifestation of a more central issue. For example, an advertising strategy may be identified by management as "ineffective" simply due to the misguided decision to advertise under unfavorable conditions.

2.   *List of Critical Factors.* Identify and list the critical factors related to the **solution of the identified problem,** as opposed to factors documenting that there is a problem. These should be listed in order of importance in developing a solution to the problem. Do *not* evaluate these factors or relate them to the problem or possible solutions at this point in your analysis. Simply list them in order of importance.

3.   *Definition of Alternatives.* In this section, state several alternative courses of action for coping with the identified problem and evaluate them using the critical factors. Some alternatives may be obvious from the material supplied in the case; others will require much analysis to formulate.

After each alternative has been concisely stated, a discussion of its pros and cons should be presented. *This balanced discussion is the heart of the analysis framework.* The critical factors are introduced into this discussion as appropriate. These are keyed as they are discussed, using the rank order numbers assigned in the Critical Factors section.

The most critical aspect of the analysis is the evaluation of alternatives. To engage in analysis is to separate parts of the situation so as to discover the nature, proportion, and function of and underlying relationships among a set of variables. Thus, to analyze is to dig into and work with the facts to uncover associations that may be used to evaluate possible courses of action. Also, *changes in the ordering and additions/deletions to the list of critical factors should occur during the analysis of alternatives.* At this point, it should become clear that the framework is a dynamic tool for analysis.

4.   *Conclusion.* Indicate the alternative(s) most appropriate for dealing with the problem. Briefly justify the recommended alternative(s) based on the previous discussion. Identify the recommended alternative(s) by number.

5.   *Additional Comments.* This section of the analysis is optional. Included are observations, recommendations, and so on, which are not necessarily directly related to the central problem. For example, students might indicate future problems that are likely to develop, areas that warrant future research, or suggested operational improvements. This section is particularly useful in demonstrating a grasp of the total situation.

Note: Unless otherwise noted, the cases in this text are listed under the major area of advertising and marketing communication management to be emphasized in their analysis. Thus, the problem statement should clearly reflect this emphasis.

---

persuasion, role playing realistically involves students in defending their positions.

Second, in preparing a case, students should begin by reading the case quickly in order to grasp the general problem, understand the position of the main character in the case, and develop an initial appraisal of the situation. After this first reading, it is imperative that students reread the case in detail, retracing their steps as many times as they feel necessary to absorb all the important details.

EXHIBIT 1-2   Case Analysis Process

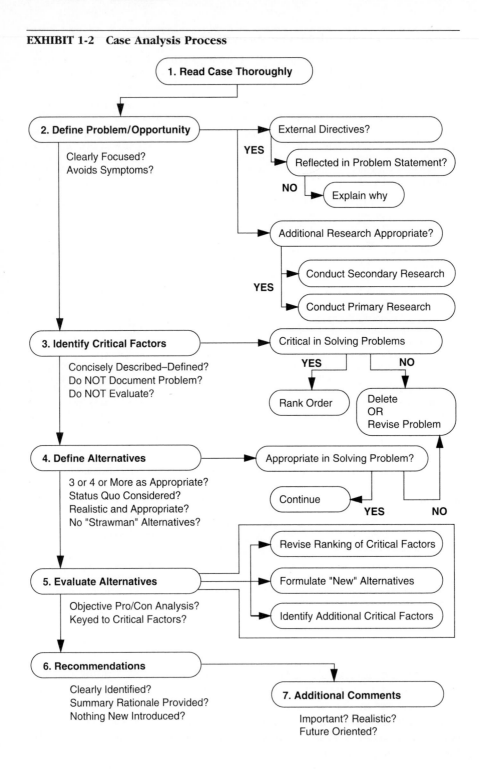

After the second reading is completed, students will be ready to begin isolating the main decision issues in the case. What is the best target for the promotional message? Is the salient issue scheduling media or developing and allocating a media budget? Such questions are at the center of the secondary phase in case analysis.

These decision issues may lead logically to questions about the specific case. At this point, students should go back to the case and single out the facts and numbers that they can analyze to answer their questions. Identifying costs and assessing their relative importance, ranking media vehicles according to their ability to reach specific target markets, and establishing the relative values of different target audiences are some of the many analysis tools that can be used to fully understand the problems at hand. Whenever complete information is not found in the case, research should be done or reasonable assumptions made. Logic, experience, and similar cases and situations can all be used to develop acceptable assumptions.

Once these tasks have been completed, students should be ready to identify the best course of action. This is perhaps the hardest step in the process of case analysis. Most of us dislike taking risks, and students tend to shy away from taking a specific stand, given the uncertainty surrounding a decision situation. Two of the most common objections raised by students faced with case analysis are that there is not enough time to gather needed information or that the case contains too much information. Yet such pressure is typical of all decision-making situations characterized by inadequate time and information.

It is helpful for students to try out their solutions in a group discussion prior to class discussion of the case. This allows them to justify their position, prepare for objections, or perhaps even reconsider their solution.

Finally, students should always be encouraged to culminate their analysis by recommending a specific course of action. In most cases, it is helpful for students to develop two or three feasible solutions to the case, analyze each alternative in depth, and finally, choose the best solution. Whether the instructor prefers to have students discern alternative solutions or immediately opt for one course of action, it is important that a student's case analysis result in a single decision.

THE ORGANIZATION OF THIS BOOK

This chapter has explored the purpose and usefulness of case analysis and has suggested a method for conducting that analysis. Case analysis is the heart of the book and its major teaching tool.

To further develop students' managerial skills, the instructor may request that they make individual or group presentations to the class or to an audience of classmates and professionals. Such presentations typically involve analyzing and solving a case or an exercise taken from this book. As an example, a student or a group of students might be asked to play the role of a consultant for St. John's Hospital and to design a research study to answer some of the planning questions asked by its management. On the other hand, the instructor might choose to ask two or three groups to make a speculative presentation, complete with alternative creative strategies, to a specific client—perhaps a hypothetical client described in one of the cases in this book.

Presentations are commonly given by advertising professionals, and they involve important skills, including the ability to approach an issue in a thorough, analytical manner. Such skills can be achieved by role playing, as well as by observing fellow students' presentations.

Presentation skills are as important to managers as effective speaking skills, interpersonal skills, and organizational ability. Managers are required to argue for budget allocations, defend competitive positions, and develop positive client relations. Presentations are a useful strategic tool in all these situations. Because guidelines for effective presentations are hard to find, we dedicate a full chapter to their discussion.

This book is organized to teach future advertising and promotion professionals the skills needed to make them effective. The text preceding each set of exercises and cases summarizes the background knowledge required to handle the decision-making challenge involved. The exercises are provided to help students visualize clearly stated problems, while the cases duplicate the real-life situations they will encounter when in a position to make strategic and tactical marketing communications decisions.

The first part of the book sets out some of the rules of the game, providing students with guidelines and blueprints for tackling the more complex tasks they will be asked to undertake. The second part of the book examines the main components of advertising and promotion decision making. It is divided into six chapters dealing with the relationship of advertising and promotion to the other marketing tasks, establishing advertising objectives, determining the advertising appropriation and budgeting, developing creative strategy, developing media strategy, and advertising research. After studying this section, students should have the analytical skills to approach any complex advertising and promotion decision problem.

The third part of the book focuses on specific advertising and promotion activities. While encompassing several general characteristics of typical advertising and promotion functions, these activities are unique in certain aspects and should be approached selectively. They were chosen for inclusion because of their timely importance in the overall spectrum of marketing communication in the United States. Students should be asked, therefore, to concentrate on the factors that make personal selling, sales promotion, public relations, and direct marketing special communication activities.

The last part of the book is dedicated to client/agency relations and ethical considerations. Such considerations are often an integral part of the managerial decision-making process. While managers' first obligation is to produce a positive bottom line for the firm, they must do so while acting in an honest, equitable, and fair manner, compatible with the basic values of our society. This section will raise questions about the type of relationship agencies and clients should have, the fairness of compensation practices, and the ethical responsibility of agencies in representing products that are considered harmful or unsafe to all or certain segments of society.

The answers to ethical dilemmas are not always clear-cut or easy to reach by consensus. At different times in our history, ethical questions have polarized public opinion, swayed customers, and occasionally made the difference between a successful business and an outright failure. Events such as the random poisoning of Tylenol capsules have required tremendous expenditures of time and resources and swift and courageous management action to avoid potential corporate disaster. There are many ethical and social issues in advertising and promotion; those addressed in this book were carefully chosen for their broad appeal and timeliness.

This book has been designed to touch broadly on all the vital areas of management decision making involving advertising and promotional issues. The exercises and cases in the last section of each chapter are important in developing an overall perception of how advertising and promotion are integral parts of business. A list of suggested readings has been added to each section to aid students in gathering necessary supplemental information. The book also allows instructors adequate flexibility to tailor the course to a diverse audience of students by choosing those problems which best fit their needs.

The next chapter provides a detailed outline for making presentations. It is the last portion of the introductory section.

How to Develop and Deliver Effective Advertising Presentations

It boils down to this: If you want to make it big in advertising (or any business), you'd better put "presentations" somewhere near the top of your list of required courses.[1]

Ron Hoff

The presentation is universally recognized as an extremely important part of business communication. It is not enough for the advertising manager to develop an excellent campaign plan for next year; she must also sell the plan to others via a presentation. Brilliant ideas will never reach consumers unless they are persuasively sold to management.

Further, it is rare for an agency to be awarded an account before several presentations have been made and evaluated by the prospective client. In fact, most important promotional and advertising recommendations are delivered in the form of a presentation to marketing or top management.

Nothing happens until someone sells something. Further, the bigger the stakes and the more important the decision, the more likely the selling job will be in the form of a formal presentation. The implications are clear: To be effective, an advertising person needs to know how to put together and deliver a winning presentation.

The purpose of this chapter is to outline a number of basic considerations useful in developing effective presentations. Reviewing and following the suggestions and conventional wisdom presented in this chapter will greatly improve your chances of developing successful presentations.

---

[1]Ron Hoff, "Make Your Next Presentation a Winner," in Schultz's *Strategic Advertising Campaigns* (Lincolnwood, Ill.: NTC Business Books, 1990), 568.

MAKING PRESENTATIONS: INITIAL CONSIDERATIONS

Common Shortcomings

In examining the issues involved in developing effective presentations, Ron Hoff suggests that a logical starting point is to identify common mistakes of other presenters and presentations. To accomplish this, Hoff interviewed top people in the advertising business in New York and Chicago and identified the following seven common complaints about presentations and presenters:

1. The failure to precisely state the problem and relevant factors.
2. The failure to stay within time allotments.
3. The failure to properly use props.
4. The failure to put oneself in the other guy's shoes.
5. The failure to inspire confidence.
6. The failure to properly prepare and rehearse.
7. The failure to have a sense of the theater; that is, a boring delivery.

To make these common shortcomings more memorable, Hoff condensed the seven failures into three cardinal sins. The most common and devastating failures to be avoided are presentations and presenters that are (1) imprecise, (2) unorganized, and (3) deadly dull.[2]

Presentation Strategy and Structure

A presentation is designed to accomplish one purpose—to persuade. The strategy behind every presentation is to persuade the audience of the reasonableness and appropriateness of the presenter's recommendation, plan, or program.

Presenting is *not* just an exercise in which the presenter holds up an ad and describes the illustration, reads the copy, and suggests how the target audience is likely to respond. Presenting should be an exercise in logic—like a lawyer pleading his case by laying a foundation, presenting evidence, marshaling arguments, and guiding the jury to a decision in his client's favor.[3]

The presentation should build a case by providing a logical explanation of why the recommendation makes sense. Therefore, it should unfold in a natural and logical sequence that leads the audience to agree with the recommendation. The strategy should be to get the audience in the habit of agreeing with the points made in the presentation. The audience should be nodding "Yes!" to what the presenters say, "Yes!" to the way the presenters think, "Yes!" to the way the presenters understand the client's business and problems, and then, "Yes!" to the presenters' recommendations. To accomplish this, the presenters must move carefully.

---

[2]Ron Hoff, "FCB Presentation Course" (Chicago: Foote, Cone & Belding, 1976), 3–11.

[3]Ibid., 15.

Experience shows that a standard sequence is most effective in building a logical case and leading the audience to the recommended position. The five segments of a standard business presentation are:

1. *Introduction.* The opening segment should outline the direction of the entire presentation and present a brief overview.

2. *Background or situation analysis.* This segment should present an insightful analysis of such relevant considerations as the competitive environment, consumer trends, and past and future sales trends. This analysis sets the stage for the following segments of the presentation.

3. *Problems and opportunities.* Growing out of the background analysis, this section concisely identifies the problems the recommendations are designed to solve and/or the opportunities to be capitalized on.

4. *Recommendations.* This segment presents the recommended solutions, along with supporting rationale.

5. *Summary.* This section includes a quick recap of key points, plus a clear directive to the audience to act.[4]

Audience Focus

All presentations should focus on the audience's needs and problems and show how the proposed program can help to meet these needs. Ultimately, the audience's perceptions, concerns, and priorities are most relevant to obtaining approval of a recommendation.

Mayer and Greenberg, in their classic *Harvard Business Review* article, "What Makes a Good Salesman," underscore the importance of the prospect's perspective in *any* selling situation. They stress that one of the basic characteristics of successful salespeople is empathy—the ability to understand the selling situation from the prospect's perspective and to relate the sales pitch to that perspective.[5]

The marketing concept suggests that, in order to succeed, you must see the world from the buyer's point of view. To be most effective, you must structure all marketing activities around the consumer or audience.

Clearly, a presentation is a marketing activity. Therefore, considerable attention should be devoted to focusing the presentation on the audience's concerns. You can work wonders if you relate everything in your presentation to the audience's problems and opportunities.

It is therefore important to find out as much as possible and practical about the decision maker(s) in the audience. What are their business and personal backgrounds and biases? The presentation should then be designed to "focus

---

[4]Sandra Moriarty and Tom Duncan, *How to Create and Deliver Winning Advertising Presentations* (Lincolnwood, Ill.: NTC Publishing, 1989), 24.

[5]David Mayer and Herbert Greenberg, "What Makes a Good Salesman?" in *Business Classics: Fifteen Key Concepts for Managerial Success* (Boston: *Harvard Business Review,* 1975), 51–57.

on the lion,"[6] or key person. What are the key individual's background characteristics and biases? The more you know about the key decision maker(s) and their business background, the easier it is to build tidbits into the presentation that will appeal to them. In the absence of such information, a presenter may be swimming upstream and not know it.

THE OPENING AND THE CLOSING

The opening and closing of a presentation are the most important parts. We will discuss these two segments of the presentation next.

The Opening

The opening of a presentation is crucial because most members of the audience decide during the first 90 seconds whether it is going to be worthwhile to listen! Therefore, the presentation must get off to a good start. The opening should be memorable and should provide an overview of the entire presentation.

Be Memorable   Kershaw suggests that a presentation is a serious business occasion to be treated with decorum and seriousness. The presenters should be polite and pleasant, but businesslike. Kershaw recommends that the presenter *avoid* opening with a funny story or with profuse thanks for the privilege of having been invited to present. Ideally, the opening should be memorable. As an example, he cites David Ogilvy's "Shell is strong!" opening, which focused on the underlying proposition for an entire campaign and effectively captured the audience's attention.[7] This opening initially puzzled the Shell Oil executives but captured their attention. As the presentation unfolded, Ogilvy explained how the recommended campaign capitalized on Shell's strengths.

Munter suggests four general possibilities for developing "grabber" openings:

- a vivid image
- an important statistic
- a rhetorical question
- a startling example or story.[8]

---

[6]Don Schultz, Dennis Martin, and William Brown, "How to Make Winning Presentations," *Strategic Advertising Campaigns* (Chicago: Crain Books, 1984), 468.

[7]Andrew Kershaw, "How to Make Agency Presentations" (New York: Ogilvy & Mather, 1976), pamphlet.

[8]Mary Munter, *Managerial Communications* (Englewood Cliffs, N.J.: Prentice-Hall, 1982), 84.

A key criterion for evaluating a possible memorable opening is its relevance to the entire presentation. Further, it is useful if the memorable opening can be referenced later during the presentation, especially in the closing.

An excellent example of a memorable and relevant opening was provided in a presentation to the marketing and general management of Chili's restaurant. Chili's had requested recommendations for an introductory advertising campaign to announce the opening of its first store in the Austin, Texas, market. After the audience was seated and attentive, the agency presenter opened with what at first seemed to be a strange set of questions:

"Who is Chili's?" (pause)

"What does Chili's serve?" (pause)

"Where is Chili's located?" (pause)

"You and I know the answers to these questions. But *your prospective customers* out there (gesture) in the Austin market don't know the answers to these questions! (pause) That is why we are here this evening. . . ."

The entire presentation was focused on the most effective and efficient way to communicate the answers to these basic questions to target customers. The conclusion emphasized how the recommended campaign would convey this information to the target audience in a meaningful way.

Although ideally the opening of a presentation should be memorable, such openings are often risky. If an appropriate grabber opening cannot be developed, the presenters would be well advised to use a less dramatic opening. It is essential to have a relevant opening that is in good taste—if it is not, scrap it.

Provide an Overview   In addition to being memorable, the introduction should provide an overview of the entire presentation geared to stimulate interest and establish confidence. Note that an overview will help to reduce some of the tensions inherent in any presentation situation.

Repetto has stressed that there is an inherent adversarial relationship between presenters and prospects. The presenters are challenging the audience's marketing knowledge and putting pressure on them to approve a recommendation. Also, the prospects do not know what to expect next. This open-ended feeling is unsettling to an audience.[9]

These audience tensions need to be reduced in the introduction. The presenters can accomplish this by telling the audience what to expect and by establishing themselves as problem-solving partners of the prospects. The first presenter should outline the presentation's agenda with a visual aid, making it clear what decision the prospects will be asked to make and when—"This is where we are going, this is how we'll get there, and when we get there, this is what we'll ask you to do"—thus eliminating any surprises.

---

[9]Schultz et al., "How to Make Winning Presentations," 468.

The Closing

In closing or summarizing, the presenter needs to accomplish three objectives: to provide a summary recap of key points, to end forcefully, and to ask for the order. In providing a summary recap, cover key views on the situation facing the prospect, the recommended course of action, and the rationale for the recommendation. This summary recap will serve to reinforce the overall selling message. The Greek rhetoric axiom definitely applies to a presentation: "Tell them what you are going to tell them (in the introduction), tell them, and tell them what you've told them (in the closing)."[10] Repetition is important; people remember little of what they hear only once.

The strongest presenter should wrap up with a strong ending. Never let the presentation taper off or end with a whimper. Finally, never forget to ask for action by the client or prospect. Make clear what you expect the prospect to do and make the requested action as easy as possible. For example, present the prospect with a contract appointing your agency or an authorization to proceed with a project, saying, "All we need is your signature authorizing us to begin implementing the exciting ideas we've outlined this afternoon!"

STAGE MANAGEMENT

Kershaw points out that if the stage management of a presentation is handled well, it will at least look professional. In addition, strong stage management may disguise some shortcomings in content. On the other hand, if the stage management is badly bungled, the audience will forget the content and recall most clearly that the slides were upside down and backwards, or the chart fell on someone's head, or someone forgot to bring the crucial videotape. Above all else, they remember the disaster![11]

Following are some basic suggestions for stage management:

- When appropriate and possible, make the presentation in your own office. There is a home field advantage—it's easier and more comfortable to make a presentation in a familiar setting.

- The most advantageous time for a presentation is 10:00 A.M. on a Tuesday, Wednesday, or Thursday.[12]

- Avoid using a microphone and presenting in total darkness.

- Do *not* distribute handouts before or during the presentation. This results in divided attention.

- Use props—for example, the physical product, competitive ads, a $50 bill.

---

[10]Moriarty and Duncan, *How to Create and Deliver Winning Advertising Presentations,* 24.

[11]Kershaw, "How to Make Agency Presentations," 12.

[12]Moriarty and Duncan, 20.

- Never exceed the assigned time limit.[13]

- Control the situation. Make it your show and do not let the audience take over. Discourage premature questions.

- Encourage questions *after* the presentation. Anticipate questions and have replies ready. Listen to each question carefully. Never bluff an answer. The questioner may know the answer and the fact that you don't and may be just checking your honesty. There is nothing wrong with responding, "That's a good question. I don't know the answer. I'll check and get back to you tomorrow."

- Make sure *someone* is clearly in charge of all props and equipment, such as easels, podiums, pointers, projectors, and flip charts. Never assume these items will take care of themselves. Murphy's Law states that anything that can go wrong will go wrong, and it often does for disorganized presenters.

- Dress is an important presentation variable. Molloy points out a truism, "The way we dress has a remarkable impact on the people we meet professionally or socially and greatly affects how they treat us."[14] An advertising wag observed, "If you can't put clothes together, why should they believe you can put an advertising campaign together?" You must look the part.

Visual Aids

Visual aids are a must for almost all formal presentations. They support the presentation and rivet attention on key points, in addition to making the presentation easier to follow. Most important, visual aids increase audience attention, comprehension, and retention.[15]

Choose a medium to fit the situation. For informal communication of a few simple facts to one or two individuals, several typed pages may be appropriate. For small groups, flip charts or boards work best. For large groups, slides are generally most appropriate. An overhead projector is also an option for small and large groups.

If you use an overhead projector, use it professionally.[16] To change a transparency, pause, step to the projector, change the transparency, step back, reestablish eye contact, and only then start talking. In fact, the presenter should never talk while doing something physical. Don't talk while advancing the slide projector or flipping boards. Pause, complete the physical activity, reestablish eye contact, and then continue talking. By following this advice, the presenter will look and sound more polished and in control.

---

[13]Charles Patti and Charles Frazer, "Making an Advertising Presentation," Appendix E in *Advertising: A Decision-Making Approach* (New York: The Dryden Press, 1988), 562.

[14]John Molloy, *Dress for Success* (New York: Warner Books, 1975).

[15]Munter, *Managerial Communications,* 890.

[16]Paul LeRoux, "Mastering the Art of the Winning Presentation," *Working Woman,* February 1985, 84–86.

The KISS principle (Keep It Simple, Stupid) applies to visual aids. By keeping it simple, presenters avoid uncomfortable situations spawned by complex staging or by switching back and forth from slides to videotape to flip boards. In addition, all numbers should be rounded to hundreds and all percentages to whole percentages (which add to 100 percent where appropriate).

Kershaw offers four sage suggestions for using visual aids:

1. Remember that the audience reads visual aids. When the words on the visual aid do *not* match the speaker's words, a problem exists. What the eye sees and the speaker says must march together.

2. The speaker should never turn his or her back on the audience to read a visual.

3. Learn to use a pointer. The audience will be riveted to it, and it enables the speaker to stay out of the audience's line of vision.

4. Inevitably, some charts or slides will contain misspellings or a wrong figure. To avoid this, proofread carefully prior to final production. If it's too late to correct a mistake, always point it out in advance. Never let the audience spot it first.[17]

ADVANCE PREPARATION

Rehearsal and Practice

It is crucial that presenters both rehearse and practice their presentation. Rehearsal is fine tuning, adjusting and rearranging the sections of the presentation. Practice is simply going over a presentation to become more comfortable with it.

It is important to have dress rehearsals with all participants, using all visual aids and props to practice the presentation just as it will be delivered, in the room where it will be made, if possible. Rehearse everything as it will be. It is most unprofessional to begin by asking, "How do you turn this thing on?" or to discover that it is impossible to read visual aids because of the lighting.

In addition to rehearsing the presentation, individual presenters should be encouraged to practice their parts alone. The more comfortable they are with the material, the more likely they are to be successful.

Visualization

The day or morning before a major presentation, it is useful to go through a visualization exercise. One member of the team describes what will happen just before, during, and after the presentation. Describing in some detail how

---

[17]Kershaw, 25–27.

the events surrounding and including the presentation will unfold generates a sense of confidence:

> *OK, after Jane closes with that line, there will probably be some applause. At that point, Jane will ask if there are any questions. Then Mr. Goldfish will most likely ask about our use of radio in the media plan. We're ready for that! Jack will tackle it by quickly reviewing three or four points as Mr. Goldfish nods in agreement. Next, we'll most likely be asked about the focus on older women. . . .*

Such an exercise helps to establish a sense of control and mastery of the situation, putting individual presenters more at ease. It is particularly recommended for less-experienced presenters operating in highly charged environments.

Work to Improve Your Delivery

The most efficient way to improve your ability to speak in public is to take lessons from a professional speech coach. The second best way is self-analysis of a videotape of your performance. Third best, you can listen to an audiotape of yourself. These are humbling but useful experiences.

Should you read or speak from notes? This is a personal decision, but play it safe. Most speakers are more effective if they script every word they want to say but practice so much that they almost know their script by heart. Then they can read their script, but it won't appear that they are reading.

Following are some basic considerations for improving delivery:

- The most important voice characteristics are energy and enthusiasm.

- Stand when you present, and make eye contact with prospects.

- Be especially careful with your first few sentences. It's crucial to get off to a good, smooth start.

- Don't indulge in such yahoo habits as leaning on the podium, rattling the change in your pocket, chewing gum, or putting your hands in your pockets.[18]

- Learn to read the audience and adjust the presentation when appropriate.[19]

- If you are nervous, don't apologize for it—this only draws attention to it. The best way to overcome nervousness is rehearsal, practice, and visualization. The better you know your material, the less likely nervousness will be debilitating. Arriving early to check out the room will allow you to feel in charge and ease your tension over the presentation.

Finally, review the checklist for evaluating presentations that appears in Exhibit 2-1 for a summary of many of the points stressed in this chapter. Learn

---

[18]Ibid., 44.

[19]Moriarty and Duncan, 99–101.

EXHIBIT 2-1   Checklist for Evaluating Presentations

1. *Professional Approach.* Tone, dress, preparation, strategy, style. Time:
2. *Introduction.* Memorable, appropriate, included an overview, set tone effectively.
3. *Delivery.* Smoothness, wording, pace, confidence, easiness to follow.
4. *Innovativeness.* Did the group do something that was *appropriate* and different that set them apart and added audience interest?
5. *Visual Aids.* Appropriate medium? Summary support of key points, large enough to read, complete coverage of major points, neat, made an impact.
6. *Audience Focus.*
7. *Conclusion.* Forceful ending, summary recap, clearly "asked for the order."
8. *Enthusiasm!*
9. *Division of Presentation.* Among members of the presentation team. For variety and effect.
10. *Coordination of Visuals and Positioning of Group.* In relation to the audience.
11. *Questions/Answers Handled Effectively.*

Overall Evaluation:

---

from your presentation successes and your failures. It's easy to be a gracious winner, much more difficult to be a good loser. Always take the high road and move on to the next challenge.

You should now be ready to tackle the problems and challenges that you will find in this book. As you proceed, you may find it useful to refer back to the first two chapters. Do so as often as you need, and add your personal observations and changes as you see fit. Each of us has a personal management style. Time and careful observation will help you develop your own. Good luck!

Suggested Readings

Hoff, Ron. "Make Your Next Presentation a Winner." In Schultz's *Strategic Advertising Campaigns.* Lincolnwood, Ill.: NTC Business Books, 1990.

Moriarty, Sandra, and Tom Duncan. *How to Create and Deliver Winning Advertising Presentations.* Lincolnwood, Ill.: NTC Publishing, 1989.

Munter, Mary. *Managerial Communications.* Englewood Cliffs, N.J.: Prentice-Hall, 1982.

II

ADVERTISING MANAGEMENT DECISION MAKING

*T*he second half of the twentieth century has seen a fantastic communication revolution. The explosion of information has affected every aspect of our lives. At home, at work, or while engaging in leisure activities, we can communicate with our immediate social groups and the rest of the world as well.

It is not surprising, therefore, that specific forms of communication are considered an end in themselves, rather than a means to a specific end. This has often been the case with advertising. Social scientists, educators, and regulatory agencies have frequently looked at advertising as an isolated phenomenon when considering the cultural and sociopsychological consequences of its messages on specific segments of our society, such as children. Advertising, however, is a marketing communication tool that does not exist in a vacuum. While advertising messages may be considered a form of entertainment by many, their objective is to inform and persuade consumers and to be an integral part of a marketing and promotion strategy.

We are distracted from the main purpose and function of advertising too many times. It is important, therefore, that the first section of this book focus on the decision-making process essential to the management of the advertising function.

Advertising decisions should be made as an integral part of the overall marketing strategy of the company or institution. As a communication tool, advertising must take into consideration the long-term and short-term goals of the firm and the nature of the product marketed, as well as the many other internal factors affecting the firm's relationships with its many publics. The firm's image, its sales goals, even its ability to recruit and retain human resources could be affected by its advertising strategy. This is true not only of corporate or institutional advertising but of any type of external communication initiated by the firm. As an example, Coors Brewing Company's advertising has stressed the purity of the beer it manufactures, while at the same time it has contributed to the environmentally responsive image of the company. The pure water and high mountains featured in the ads and their accompanying copy have supported the company's institutional goals.

As the general goals of a firm change over time, its communication strategy may have to change. This is why the management of the advertising function must take into consideration the overall marketing strategy of the firm. For example, the advertising strategy for the introduction of Crystal Pepsi into the market in 1992 had to take into consideration competing products, including the other soft drinks marketed by Pepsi. Whether Crystal Pepsi was expected to cannibalize a portion of the market share of Pepsi Cola affected the type of message and the media strategy selected for the new product.

The advertising management functions—determining advertising objectives, establishing the advertising budget, developing a creative strategy, and developing the media plan—are described in the next six chapters in detail. In addition, the advertising research function is discussed and analyzed, as it provides vital input to all other advertising decisions. The importance of the relationship between marketing and advertising strategies is stressed in Chapter 3, the first chapter of this section.

The six chapters in this section will concentrate on each managerial task vital to advertising. The cases in each chapter will help students understand the steps to advertising decision making and allow them to focus on each separately. Each building block will lead to a global view of advertising management and campaign development.❖

The Marketing Context of Advertising and Promotion

We are no longer in the business of advertising; our business is to help our clients, by whatever means, with the orderly management of change in the marketplace.[1]

Carl Spielvogel
BACKER SPIELVOGEL BATES

THE ROLE OF ADVERTISING

Advertising is a strong marketing force. It pervades our media and is noticed by audiences of all ages, economic profiles, and walks of life. Every consumer in a developed economy today knows about advertising, and, what is more, considers himself or herself an advertising expert.

Advertising is important to our economy. Expenditures on advertising and promotion have grown for the past century in steady proportion with our economic growth.

Such an activity, therefore, must be carried on with professionalism and a thorough understanding of its role in the economy and in society. In addition, the interaction of the advertising function with the other marketing functions performed by the firm must also be comprehended fully, so that advertising can be effective and efficient in achieving its purpose.

This chapter is concerned with advertising within the marketing environment. Its role as a marketing tool will be considered, as well as its contribution to the marketing of products and services.

---

[1]"The party's over," *The Economist,* February 1, 1992, 69.

Advertising as a Marketing Function

Advertising is one of many functions performed in the context of an overall marketing program. A marketing program is intended to plan how products or services are taken from the point of production to the point of consumption in such a way as to develop a positive relationship between consumers and producer that will foster additional or repeat usage. As such, marketing is concerned with both short-term and long-term results. The advertising function, therefore, must fit the marketing objectives set by the firm and cannot be effective if considered in isolation.

A marketing plan should contain a statement of *short-term* and *long-term* objectives. It should then spell out the particular strategies and tactics that will be implemented to achieve these objectives. Strategic objectives will be met by the use of marketing tools such as advertising, marketing research, product packaging and design, and personal sales. Authors have attempted to group the marketing functions into basic categories. One of the most common summaries groups the marketing functions into 1) product functions, 2) price functions, 3) distribution functions, and 4) communication functions. Advertising is one of the communication functions to be performed within the marketing plan.

Because products and services are very diverse, not all marketing plans use the same mix of marketing functions. As an example, advertising is a major element of the marketing mix for products such as breakfast cereals and soft drinks. On the other hand, the manufacturers of mainframe computers do not rely as heavily on advertising to move their products; instead, they invest considerable time and effort in personal sales functions. For some products or services, the use of advertising could generate negative, rather than positive, results. Medical doctors and health care organizations have found that large investments in advertising can be counterproductive. It is important, therefore, to understand fully just how advertising fits into the overall marketing program before proceeding with the actual planning and implementation of the advertising function.

The Marketing Process and Advertising

The marketing planning process generally starts with a thorough *situation analysis.* This enables a firm to recognize the challenges and opportunities that face it within the marketplace. A situation analysis is also necessary to understand the role to be performed by the advertising function. The situation analysis involves examining all the important factors operating in a particular situation. It invariably involves the use of research. A situation analysis will investigate consumer motivation and behavior with regard to the product or service at hand. In addition, it will consider the economic and competitive environment facing the firm and the changes that might affect market demand.

The second step in the marketing planning process is setting overall *marketing objectives* and goals for the firm. Objectives and goals are general and broad in nature. They may be concerned with obtaining a specific market share, securing repeat purchases, or increasing profits. In any case, it is important to know what the marketing objectives of the firm are because they will determine the marketing strategy and the communication objectives the firm will pursue.

The third step in the marketing planning process is to develop a *marketing strategy.* The marketing strategy deals with the use of all the elements of the marketing mix, of which communication is but one. This is the planning stage, in which the interplay and interdependence of the elements of the marketing mix can best be seen and understood. The marketing executive controls decisions affecting the marketing mix. Price setting, product design and packaging, distribution strategy, promotional objectives, and tactics can all be manipulated internally by the firm. While market forces may affect the direction(s) in which the firm chooses to act, the manager's actions will still be crucial in this phase of the planning process.

The marketing strategy utilized by the firm will be set with its *target market* in mind. This is the segment of the overall market to which the firm wishes to appeal. The identification of its target market is a very important step in the marketing planning process of the firm.

An example of how the different elements of a marketing mix may impact promotion decisions is the case of national brands versus generic products. The quality of generic products such as paper towels and canned vegetables is very comparable to that of several nationally advertised products in the same class or category. Nationally advertised products, however, command higher prices, have packages designed to attract shoppers' attention, and are featured in nationally advertised campaigns and sales promotions. Brand is an essential element of a nationally advertised product, and most of the communication campaign effort is designed to build brand loyalty and consumer recall and recognition for the product.

Generic products, on the other hand, are developed to compete primarily on the basis of price. They do not feature a brand name. Their package is not designed to call attention to the product, and usually they do not command a lot of shelf space. Generic products are not advertised; it is assumed that buyers will understand and opt for the price economy they represent.

It is clear from this example that advertising and promotion decisions must be developed as an integral part of the overall marketing strategy. The following section will consider the elements of an advertising and promotion strategy.

THE ADVERTISING AND PROMOTION PLAN

The promotion and advertising plan is an essential element of the marketing mix. It can be a small portion of the overall marketing strategy, as with some industrial products, or it can dominate the marketing program, as happens often with such products as cosmetics and soft drinks.

It is important to understand that advertising and promotion together are only one of the marketing tools employed to influence consumer decisions. Advertising by itself cannot close the sale of a product; rather, it should be used as a facilitator of the sale. Advertising decisions, therefore, must involve a clear understanding of the intended effects of advertising for the specific marketing situation at hand.

Any advertising plan will encompass three major decisions: establishing advertising objectives and the necessary budget allocation, determining the contents and structure of the message to be conveyed to the intended audience, and deciding which media to use when conveying the message to the audience. Therefore, budget, message, and media are the three main elements of an advertising and promotion plan.

When making such decisions, the advertising manager must always go back to the information gathered for the situation analysis. The evaluation of alternative courses of action will involve those factors which make each situation unique. Questions that must be part of the advertising planning process include: What is the competitive approach? How many new products are likely to be brought to the market? How have consumers' buying decisions changed?

The Establishment of Objectives

The central aspect of any management plan is the *development of objectives* that will direct operational decisions. Operational objectives serve as a standard of performance and as a tool to measure results. Advertising budget decisions are dependent on and tied to objective decisions. Only when the manager knows what advertising is supposed to accomplish can he or she allocate the necessary and appropriate budget to carry out the task. The advertising *budget,* therefore, should begin with a detailed specification of what a firm expects to accomplish with advertising. Then the specific amounts required to carry out each task can be determined.

An example of this specific management task is the 1992 change in Perrier's advertising campaign. Perrier, which was America's best-selling brand of sparkling water, suffered serious market share losses in 1990 when Source Perrier ordered a worldwide recall of over 70 million bottles of the product. The recall was caused by the discovery of traces of benzene in some bottles, and consumer confidence in the product was shaken considerably by it.

In 1992 the company engaged in an effort to position its product as an everyday drink. This objective was part of the overall marketing strategy that focused on increasing overall sales and market share. Perrier was perceived as a "country-club drink," according to James Caporimo, creative director at Waring & LaRosa, the company's advertising agency.[2]

To accomplish its objective and promote Perrier as a mass-market product, the advertising agency developed ads with the tagline, "Perrier. Part of the local color." The campaign showed a cross section of real people and real places across America, along with the product. In addition, because the message was designed to reach a much broader segment of consumers, the advertising budget was increased 60 percent over that of 1991. This boost in ad spending was combined with a shift from television to magazine advertising.

---

[2]Alison Fahey, "Perrier Ads Sell Common Appeal," *Advertising Age,* April 6, 1992, 38.

The 1992 Perrier advertising strategy shows the interdependence of marketing and advertising. It also demonstrates the importance of developing an advertising budget that allows the achievement of company objectives and goals.

The Development of Advertising Messages

Once the advertising and promotion objectives have been stated, the theme of the communication must be determined. The *message* is a very important component of the advertising and promotion decision. In many instances, the wrong message can jeopardize the whole communication plan.

The first step in developing a message is to decide which of several alternative central themes best serves the communication goals. The theme will then be used to develop specific advertising messages.

The advertising messages are often tested before being implemented in order to assess their relative effectiveness. The advertising manager must, therefore, understand both the creative process involved in writing advertising messages and the management goals that advertising must serve.

Sometimes the messages that appear most creative and potentially memorable are not received by all in a positive manner. The "socially aware" Benetton ads featuring dying AIDS patients, a rainbow of colored condoms, and a nun kissing a priest have met, at best, mixed reviews from consumers. The company and its agency claim that their ads are designed to bring people together and raise awareness of social issues, but a survey conducted by *Advertising Age* showed that only 38.9 percent of respondents perceived the ads as having a positive effect, while the other respondents felt they had a negative effect or no effect at all. Some Benetton customers said the ads were in bad taste and would actually keep them away from Benetton stores. An overwhelming majority of the survey respondents (72 percent) felt that the campaign was not an effective marketing strategy.[3]

The company's position concerning its advertising message poses important questions: How effective is the Benetton advertising? How can we measure the effectiveness of the advertising expenditures by Benetton? What criteria should be used for setting the advertising budget? These questions should be answered when establishing advertising objectives and determining an advertising budget. In the case of Benetton, however, management has stated its objectives in a vague and general manner. It would be hard to measure whether the campaign has succeeded in raising society's awareness of issues such as AIDS, safe sex, and illegal immigration, among others.

It is understandable, therefore, that such a campaign would meet with mixed reviews. It might even have a negative effect on sales of Benetton products. Management must be careful to develop *specific* and *measurable* advertising objectives and to set a budget that will allow it to accomplish these objectives.

---

[3]Adrienne Ward, " 'Socially Aware' or 'Wasted Money'?" *Advertising Age,* February 24, 1992, 4.

In addition, the firm must test its messages to verify that they are understood by consumers in a positive and productive manner. While controversial and strong messages may be memorable, they do not always produce the intended effects. The objective of the Benetton campaign—raising social consciousness—might have produced a favorable image for the company if its messages had been different. Research would have been helpful in determining the nature and content of the messages most likely to be received favorably by the intended audiences.

The Establishment of the Media Budget

The last component of the advertising decision process deals with the allocation of budgets to specific *media.* Media allocation is the task of determining which audiences to reach and the nature and effectiveness of specific media vehicles. Because it is such a complex task, mathematical models have been developed to aid managers in making media allocation decisions.

When developing a budget for a campaign, the advertising manager must take into account several factors in addition to the media expenditures themselves. Many companies have started to look at advertising and promotion budgets in a more integrated manner. Companies are increasingly concerned with *all* the marketing variables, which combined may produce a synergistic effect and increase the efficiency of their advertising expenditures.

An example of this integrated approach to advertising management is the successful use of cross-promotional efforts by Kmart. During the 1991 holiday season, Kmart was involved in joint programs with Walt Disney, Eastman Kodak, Chrysler, Coca-Cola, and Burger King. These cross-promotions involved the distribution of game cards, prize giveaways, sweepstakes, and other promotional tools. Since most retail advertising is intended to build increased store traffic, the development and advertising of cross-promotions should be even more effective than retail advertising alone. Kmart's holiday sales were up 10.6 percent over the previous year's sales, and management was happy with that performance.[4]

Marketers often use cross-promotions to maximize their advertising and marketing expenditures. Setting up cross-promotions is not a simple task, however. Managers must find compatible and strong partners who share similar target markets so that the cross-promotions will be beneficial to all. In addition, partners must be willing to commit adequate resources so that the promotions will result in a strong response.

Advertising budgets should also consider nontraditional media channels and technologically innovative ways to reach consumers. In 1992, General Motors sent out 250,000 promotional videocassettes to young, upper-income families featuring its new TransSport minivan. The families were also offered a $500 discount coupon along with the cassettes. The cost of this innovative and

---

[4]John Cortez, "Kmart happy with holidays," *Advertising Age,* February 3, 1992, 28.

targeted type of advertising should also be included in the development of a budget.[5]

It is clear, therefore, that setting the advertising budget is a task which must take into consideration all the other marketing variables. In the General Motors example, pricing and distribution were an integral part of the promotional campaign for the TransSport minivan. Advertising and promotion are not independent functions; they are one of the elements of the marketing strategy of a company.

These three elements—budget, message, and media—combine to form the advertising plan. Not all advertising plans are similar, however, because the external environmental factors facing each advertiser may vary a great deal. In addition, since the task assigned to advertising will depend in part on decisions made concerning other marketing elements, the interdependence of advertising and the other components of the marketing mix must be underscored. The elements in the marketing mix not only influence the task of the advertising manager, but also the amount of money available for advertising. The advertising manager's job, therefore, must be viewed as an important element of a complex team effort designed to achieve the overall marketing objectives of the firm.

DEVELOPMENT OF AN ADVERTISING PLAN WITHIN A FIRM'S MARKETING CONTEXT

The Case of High-Tech Sneakers

This section will provide a hypothetical example of an advertising plan. Its purpose is to show the importance of marketing variables in the development of an advertising plan. The data in this example are derived from existing figures and facts concerning the U.S. sneaker industry, which have been disguised for the purposes of this chapter.[6,7,8]

We will consider the development of an advertising plan by the fictitious Tiger sneaker company. The company is one of the six major competitors in the U.S. athletic shoe market, which has estimated total sales of $6 billion. Tiger sales are equivalent to 5 percent of the total market, or $300 million.

Situation Analysis The first step in the development of an advertising plan is a complete situation analysis. This includes an overview of the industry as a whole, an appraisal of the company's competitive position, and an

[5]"The party's over," 69.

[6]"Reebok: Pumping Up," *The Economist,* February 15, 1992, 78–79.

[7]Joseph Pereira, "From Air to Pump to Puma's Disc System, Sneaker Gimmicks Bound to New Heights," *The Wall Street Journal,* October 31, 1991, B1.

[8]David J. Jefferson, "Reebok Primes the Pump While Rivals Stress Value," *The Wall Street Journal,* February 3, 1992, B1.

examination of the firm's long-term and short-term marketing strategies for its products.

The U.S. sneaker market is divided among six major firms and several small firms. The two leading companies are Nike and Reebok, which account for 30 percent and 24 percent of total sales, respectively. Twenty-four percent of sales is accounted for by small producers and store brands, and the remaining 22 percent is divided among four other companies, including Tiger.

During the 1980s, U.S. sales of athletic shoes grew by 20 percent to 40 percent a year, but this growth slowed to about 1 to 4 percent for the first two years of the 1990s. Sales for 1993 are predicted to be flat, and the leading companies are considering major changes in their marketing strategies to maintain their market shares. While most companies are planning to concentrate on more economic, no-frills models at moderate prices, Reebok plans to introduce a very expensive "double-pump" line designed for "serious athletes" to be sold to more affluent consumers. It is a well-known fact that over 80 percent of sneakers are bought for style, not performance, reasons, and the "gimmicky" products have been very successful in the past in spite of their high prices. However, most market leaders feel the mood of the market has shifted, and they are emphasizing the lower-cost, simpler models for 1993.

Tiger has one line of medium-high-priced products—the "PAWS." These compete directly with the Reebok Pumps and Nike's Air Shoes. This line accounts for 15 percent of Tiger's total sales, down from 25 percent two years ago.

The Problem   Tiger management met to develop a long-range marketing and advertising strategy for the firm. The discussion centered around whether the firm should continue to promote primarily the high-end, high-tech sneakers or the no-frills, medium- to low-priced shoes. In the past, advertising expenditures had centered around the PAWS line. A shift in marketing strategy would involve an increase in the advertising budget and a change in the creative and media strategy.

The Solution   The management of Tiger should weigh all the information gathered in the situation analysis against the strengths and weaknesses of the firm and its products. Management should then develop a complete marketing plan for both the short term and the long term.

The advertising strategy should be developed from the marketing plan. The creative appeal, advertising budget, and media plan should take into account the market profile and the firm's best forecast of demand trends. This process will allow management to continuously monitor the firm's performance and to adjust to major market changes.

This integrated marketing approach will permit advertising managers to develop a sound strategy. The interaction of advertising and marketing decisions will benefit the firm's long-term planning and allow for a more efficient decision-making process.

Suggested Readings

Aaker, David A., and John G. Myers. *Advertising Management.* 3d ed. Englewood Cliffs, N.J.: Prentice-Hall, 1987.

Bauer, Raymond A., and Stephen S. Greyser. *Advertising in America.* Boston: Division of Research, Graduate School of Business Administration, Harvard University, 1968.

Burnett, John J. *Promotion Management.* 2d ed. St. Paul, Minn.: West Publishing, 1988.

Journal of Marketing (Spring 1983).

Lodish, Leonard M. *The Advertising and Promotion Challenge.* New York: Oxford University Press, 1986.

Nylen, David N. *Advertising: Planning, Implementation, and Control.* Cincinnati: South-Western Publishing, 1986.

Ries, Al, and Jack Trout. *Bottom-Up Marketing.* New York: Plume Printing, 1990.

Wensley, Robin. "Strategic Marketing: Bets, Boxes, or Basics." *Journal of Marketing* (Summer 1981): 173–182.

Exercises

1. Tom Thumb is a small grocery chain located in Texas. Its merchandising strategy is to appeal to the upper-middle- and upper-class shopper with quality products and a wide assortment of gourmet food labels. Tom Thumb's positioning strategy has distinguished it profitably from other grocery chains.

During the late 1980s and early 1990s, warehouse club stores such as Wal-Mart's Sam's Warehouse Club garnered an important share of all grocery sales. A study by Opinion Research Corp. found that nearly one shopper in five bought some groceries at either club stores or another type of mass merchandiser. The typical customers of those new retail outlets were larger families and people who spent greater than average amounts on groceries.

When club stores first appeared, high-quality grocers did not feel threatened. They assumed people who bought at such outlets were looking for bargains. However, later studies have shown that bargain shopping was not the only reason for joining a "club." Customers felt it was "fun" to shop at such a store, and more and more customers were

doing so. While they wished club stores offered a greater variety of goods, as well as fresh produce, bakery and dairy products, and meat, consumers were loyal club buyers of other packaged items.

Tom Thumb's management has decided it is time to consider the impact of club stores on its customers. The chain would consider developing any promotional tool that might increase customer loyalty to its stores. It wants to maintain a "quality" position but needs to give customers an incentive for repeat buying.

Develop a marketing strategy for Tom Thumb that would accomplish this objective. How can advertising and promotion be used to implement such a marketing strategy? Describe the interaction of marketing and advertising, as well as the function of promotional variables, in the development and implementation of Tom Thumb's strategy.

Source: Richard Gibson, "Marketing," *The Wall Street Journal,* April 6, 1992, B1.

2. Promotional videotapes are becoming an important marketing and advertising tool. Describe the types of

marketing strategies that would best benefit from the use of promotional videotapes. What types of products and services most likely would be sold using such a tool? How can promotional videotapes be integrated within the overall marketing strategy of a firm?

3. Traditional fast-food outlets' sales have faced a slump in recent years. In an effort to reestablish its position in the market, McDonald's Corp. has changed its marketing and advertising approach.

In 1992, the fast-food chain leased over 20,000 billboards across the United States, investing in outdoor media a large amount of the budget usually spent on network TV advertising. The message was the same for all billboards: "Great Food at a Great Value, at McDonald's." Combined with TV advertising, this campaign was intended to reach 98 percent of the U.S. population.

In addition, in June 1992 McDonald's started testing a limited dinner menu in two markets, featuring baked chicken, pasta, and pizza. This marketing move was an attempt to increase the chain's sales in the evening, traditionally its slowest time.

Do you think McDonald's is responding properly to market changes? Does the new advertising campaign fit in properly with its marketing strategy? Describe how the new McDonald's advertising strategy may impact its long-term marketing plans.

Source: Richard Gibson, "McDonald's Ads Will Combine Food and Board," *The Wall Street Journal,* March 26, 1992, B1, B3.

St. John's Hospital

St. John's Hospital is a multiunit, nonprofit corporation affiliated with a national Catholic health care services network. Charitable services are provided through direct medical care to patients with acute or critical conditions and free or low-cost community outreach programs. Located in a mid-sized southern city with a population of 465,622, St. John's provided more than $5.6 million in charity care to 935 patients with acute or critical medical conditions in fiscal year 1989. In addition to its acute-care hospital core units, St. John's offers health care services at community health centers and free health fairs, with the assistance of the diocese, city and county agencies, physicians, other health care providers, and neighborhood associations.

As a charitable institution, St. John's Hospital donates resources to causes at home and abroad. It conducts health screenings at many local outlying communities and is the only local hospital contributing to the city's food bank. Furthermore, St. John's donates supplies to medical missions in Africa, Central America, and South America. As St. John's moves into the 1990s, strategic decisions must be made in light of the growing population of local indigent patients and the hospital's competition, which consists of one city-owned hospital, one other private hospital, at least two suburban hospitals, and a growing number of private health care clinics.

Numerous methods have been employed to determine St. John's position in the local market. Consumer surveys and focus groups, among others, have been used to measure the public's perception of St. John's Hospital. In addition, research has been conducted to assess how it rates now and how it compares to the competition in several categories. Some of the categories measured include obstetrics, neonatal, cardiology, oncology, orthopedics, pulmonary, and emergency room services. Within each of these categories, attitudes about food, nurses, housekeeping, and other variables were rated.

The findings (see Tables 3-1-1 to 3-1-3) suggest that the three competing hospitals in this region are considered by the public to have different strengths and weaknesses. St. John's, which derives more than 90 percent of its revenue from acute-care services, leads the competition in the public's perception of "hospital of choice," "quality" care, cancer care, maternity care, care of women, and care of people over 55. The Riverdale city hospital, on the other hand, is perceived as the best for orthopedic care and emergency room

This case was written by Isabella C. M. Cunningham, The University of Texas at Austin, and is intended to serve as the basis for classroom discussion, not to illustrate the effective or ineffective handling of an administrative situation. Used by permission of Daughters of Charity Health Services of Austin.

TABLE 3-1-1   Comparison of Hospital Ratings by Northside Residents

Hospital	Top-of-Mind Awareness of Hospitals	Quality Care	Hospital of Choice	Cardiac Care
St. John's	39.6%	46.8%	44.3%	41.8%
Riverdale	25.5	20.6	19.3	35.7
Other				
Private	17.4	22.5	21.4	13.8

Note: Percentages do not total 100 percent due to incomplete responses to some questions.

TABLE 3-1-2   Comparison of Hospital Ratings by Southside Residents

Hospital	Top-of-Mind Awareness of Hospitals	Quality Care	Hospital of Choice	Cardiac Care
St. John's	27.4%	40.2%	36.5%	31.0%
Riverdale	33.9	25.0	21.7	42.4
Other				
Private	15.2	23.7	21.4	17.8

Note: Percentages do not total 100 percent due to incomplete responses to some questions.

TABLE 3-1-3   Comparison of Hospital Ratings by Central City Residents

Hospital	Top-of-Mind Awareness of Hospitals	Quality Care	Hospital of Choice	Cardiac Care
St. John's	38.1%	45.8%	44.0%	39.3%
Riverdale	38.8	29.8	28.3	37.2
Other				
Private	20.3	23.3	25.0	22.3

Note: Percentages do not total 100 percent due to incomplete responses to some questions.

services. While not taking the lead in any of the preceding categories, St. John's private competition does show strength in attracting those with annual incomes of less than $15,000—perhaps because of its location—and those between the ages of 45 and 64.

Several questions come to the minds of administrators when planning for the next five years. Given the present position of St. John's Hospital in the market and the changing health care needs of the community, how should St. John's position itself for the future? Trends affecting health care in the community include:

1. A move toward unbundled health care—a more fragmented delivery system in which different locations specialize in different services.

2. Increased pressures to keep total costs of health care down.

Orthopedic Care	Obstetric Care	Cancer Care	Most Convenient	Care for Ages 55$^+$	Care for Women
33.7%	43.2%	45.0%	28.9%	47.9%	47.4%
37.1	17.1	27.3	13.8	20.3	15.3
20.4	31.6	18.6	15.8	25.6	28.2

Orthopedic Care	Obstetric Care	Cancer Care	Most Convenient	Care for Ages 55$^+$	Care for Women
27.9%	36.7%	40.3%	8.9%	39.1%	37.6%
53.6	20.6	27.2	23.8	18.5	18.2
10.7	30.2	17.3	7.5	26.7	26.5

Orthopedic Care	Obstetric Care	Cancer Care	Most Convenient	Care for Ages 55$^+$	Care for Women
30.0%	44.4%	38.4%	46.3%	42.4%	48.9%
52.7	29.4	26.4	25.0	26.8	22.8
16.5	26.2	18.7	25.3	25.0	26.2

3. More control by managed care organizations over which health care providers patients are to use.

4. Increased competition from other institutions and physician groups.

5. Continued growth of area market, but at a more reasonable rate and perhaps in spurts, rather than smoothly.

6. Increased number of people not able to pay for health care.

7. Continued improvement of technology, bringing new options for diagnosis and treatment.

8. Continued decline of acute inpatient care use rates (amount of care used per person), but need for net additional beds due to area population growth.

St. John's can choose to proceed in several directions. One option (Option I) would be to continue in its present capacity, which emphasizes high-quality acute inpatient care while leading the community in technology. Another potential, though completely different, option (Option II) would be to develop a totally integrated, communitywide health care delivery system. This would include developing and operating all services not currently offered, implementing additional delivery sites convenient to all areas of the community, and offering total financial management capabilities. Table 3-1-4 compares the advantages and disadvantages of these two alternatives. A more probable alternative (Option III) is a compromise between Options I and II. Option III is the development of an areawide integrated network of health care services on a schedule determined by the competitive environment, the growth and economic condition of the community, and the development of additional skills and human resources in the organization. Within this framework, some services may be developed cooperatively with physicians or other providers, some may be developed by the network itself, and still others may be linked to the network through referral or contractual arrangement. The attractiveness of this option is that it would move toward achieving the advantages of diversification listed in Option II, while carefully managing the inherent risks.

To implement Option III, the following steps should be taken:

1. Determine the health care needs of the community and continue utilizing programmatic approaches to developing and providing needed services.

2. Determine the role of St. John's main campus in the integrated health care network.

3. Determine the roles of other network-affiliated community hospitals.

4. Determine the role of the network in the south and southwest areas of the community. Develop a plan for implementation of this role.

5. Develop closer ties with a mix of physicians to ensure a sufficient flow of patients through the integrated health care system. Continue to develop opportunities for cooperative ownership and operation of outpatient services.

6. Plan for development of managed care services. Begin implementation.

TABLE 3-1-4   System Features

	Option I	Option II
Human resources in place	Yes	No
Concentration of efforts/resources in one place	Yes	No
Capital investment	Low	High
Short-term financial return	High	Lower
Ability to provide charity care in the short term	Yes	Yes
Vulnerability to economic downturn in community	Low	Higher
Ability to contract with macrobuyers for total health care packages	Decreased	Increased
Vulnerability to development of other institutions	Increased	Decreased
Risk of loss of reputation and loss of capital and time during system implementation	Low	High

7. Determine the need for post−acute care services such as nursing, home health, rehabilitation, and respite care. Continue development as needed.

8. Determine the network's role in long-term care services such as nursing homes and retirement communities. Begin implementation of linkages or services development as needed.

9. Determine the network's role in psychiatric services. Begin implementation of linkages or service development as needed.

RIVERDALE: THE CITY

Riverdale is a mid-sized city. The total area population is over 760,000, while the urban area itself has a population of just under half a million people. There are 302,600 households in the city of Riverdale, and the average household size is 2.5 persons. The city's demographic profile is considerably different than that of other major cities. The population is more educated than the average city's population. Recent research indicates that approximately 33 percent of the city's adult population hold a college degree. In addition, more than 60 percent of all adults living in Riverdale have attended a college or university. The average age of the population of Riverdale is approximately five years below the national average. The median annual household income is $33,500, slightly above the U.S. average. It is also important to note that the average annual income in Riverdale has been rising sharply over the past five years. A median single-family home in the city of Riverdale is valued at over $85,000, and the city includes almost 30,000 commercial businesses. The city is considered the fifth fastest-growing metropolitan area among the 100 largest in the United States, with population growth during the period 1980 to 1987 estimated at 38 percent.

The industries in the area are primarily high-tech information industries. Because there are several universities in and around Riverdale, research and development is one of the most important economic activities in the city. The city enjoyed steady employment growth during the past seven years as a result of expanding industry and expanding numbers of professional and service workers. Population projections for the year 2000 range from 1 million to 1.2 million people. These figures would maintain Riverdale's status as one of the nation's fastest-growing cities.

Riverdale is located in a picturesque area surrounded by hills and lakes. The city has a large number of government employees and hosts many visitors every year. It has had a stable economy for a number of years and is considered an ideal location for people who want to retire while keeping an active social life and a dynamic life-style.

THE U.S. HOSPITAL INDUSTRY

The American hospital industry is a $200 billion industry that is approaching maturity. It is facing several major problems, such as declining margins, excess capacity, burdensome bureaucracies, and poorly planned and executed diversification moves, as well as major economic and health crises including funding cutbacks and epidemics such as AIDS.

Hospitals enjoyed record operating margins in 1985, in spite of an almost 20 percent decline in inpatient use. By the end of 1988, however, operating earnings had declined tremendously. In addition, hospitals seem to depend primarily on Medicare as their largest payment source. Recent Medicare cutbacks come at a time when the elderly are pressing for extended benefits and hospital costs are increasing. The hospital of the future will reach out into homes and residential communities as much as it depends on the sick to cross its threshold for help, in an effort to diversify its services so that it can survive.

One of the ways in which hospitals can stay alive is by cutting their costs. To do that, hospitals are looking for economies of scale. Scale economies in health care delivery have been confined mainly to the more efficient utilization of capital and fixed resources, such as buildings and equipment, but those represent only about 15 percent of total costs. Personnel represents the biggest cost item—60 percent or more of the total for most hospitals. So far, large hospital chains have been unable to achieve scale economies in the use of their key resource—skilled professionals and technicians. The chains that remained profitable in the past five years did so by adapting aggressive rate increases and offering psychiatric and rehabilitation services in order to diversify their portfolios and achieve other sources of revenue. The rate increases as well as the new psychiatric and rehabilitation services have been the target of recent investigations.

Another business strategy hospitals have recently undertaken is to bypass the middleman and deal directly with the consumer. Hospitals have engaged in an effort to retail their health services by circumventing the physician and advertising directly to patients. However, in most cases, such efforts have backfired. Experience has shown that doctors remain at the center of care delivery. Their share of the health care dollar rose in the 1980s in direct proportion to the hospitals' declining share. Organizations such as HMOs that set out to "tame" their physicians suffered bloody defeats in their initial skirmishes.

It is important to note that health care organizations cannot continue to be managed by a manipulation of revenues. Many of the strategies undertaken by hospitals to market their products have not worked in the past. Advertising campaigns or marketing campaigns have really not created additional markets for hospitals. In the 1980s, hospitals suffered from "marketing myopia," throwing dollars at a maturing, acute-care market as they lost sight of the changes in the demand for care. Demand for inpatient care has continued to decrease because of technological advances and new practice patterns, while the demand for outpatient care has increased. This has caused many hospitals to face spurts of empty beds, increasing their overall costs and decreasing their profits.

In the United States today, 80 percent of all deaths and 90 percent of all illnesses are related to chronic conditions, not to crisis situations. Despite the threat of viral illnesses such as AIDS and hepatitis, the demand for most hospital care is due to chronic illnesses. Our contemporary cure systems tend to ignore diseases until they reach life-threatening stages. In the future, hospitals must address the symptoms of chronic illnesses as one of their principal missions. Therefore, they must shift their focus away from crisis treatment and toward diagnosis and management of chronic diseases, bringing services to the patient as much as bringing patients to the hospital. This is why many experts feel that in the next 20 years many health care services will be concentrated in the home and the residential community rather than on the hospital campus. In addition, ambulatory services such as diagnostic imaging, laboratory testing, and emergency and unscheduled treatment will become principal products of the hospital. For these services, patients will stay in the hospital less than 24 hours and be classified as outpatients. From 1985 to 1987, radiology and laboratory use for elderly patients rose by more than 8 percent in U.S. hospitals.

Productivity needs to be improved in the hospital industry. Full-time employment per occupied bed rose more than 20 percent from 1980 to 1987. While this was a consequence of the prosperity of that period, it has increased hospital costs beyond those reflected in reimbursement schedules. In the next few years, hospitals will have to simplify their structures, eliminate layers of administration, and streamline their staffs.

The overall scenario for hospital administration in the 1990s is one of innovative management, good forecasting skills, and aggressive action to take advantage of existing trends. Hospitals can survive reduced help from federal and state subsidies, but only if they concentrate on serving the market and being flexible to accommodate market changes.

THE HEALTH CARE MARKET FOR RIVERDALE

Five major hospitals serve the city of Riverdale, as well as ten surrounding counties. The breadth of services of these hospitals has been made necessary by the closings of county hospitals in the ten-county region surrounding Riverdale. Until 1987, there were six hospitals in the city of Riverdale, but one has since closed. Market share for all hospital services in the area (excluding rehabilitation services) is shown in Table 3-1-5 and Figure 3-1-1.

Local trends are shaping the health care industry in the Riverdale area. The local hospitals have an inpatient overcapacity, except for St. John's, which has been working at 90 percent capacity for the past two years. In addition, the region shows changing demographics. More middle-aged and older people are

TABLE 3-1-5   Market Share for All Services

	1980	1981	1982	1983	1984	1985	1986	1987
St. John's	36.6%	38.4%	38.0%	38.4%	39.9%	37.8%	39.1%	39.7%
Riverdale	31.2	30.8	31.6	29.8	26.3	26.7	25.2	25.3
St. David's	24.7	24.6	24.1	21.5	20.8	22.3	21.7	22.3
Hotel Dieu	7.5	6.2	5.3	4.1	2.9	2.3	1.9	1.1
South Riverdale			1.0	5.4	7.1	7.1	7.5	7.4
North City Hospital				0.8	3.0	3.8	4.6	4.2
Total	100.0%	100.0%	100.0%	100.0%	100.0%	100.0%	100.0%	100.0%

FIGURE 3-1-1   Market Share of Total Admissions (excluding rehabilitation services)

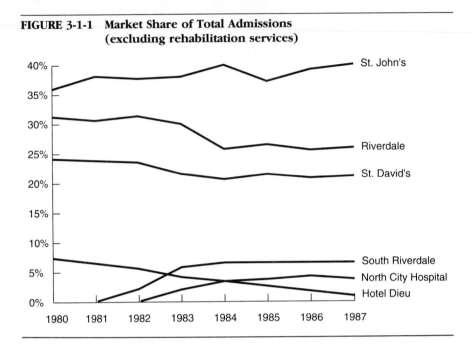

expected to be living in the area by the year 2000. A large number of people in the area live below the poverty level and are served by different charity organizations, but St. John's serves approximately 60 percent of poor residents in the area. Most of the population in Riverdale will be located north or south of the city in the year 2000. It is assumed that about 79 percent of the population of Riverdale will be located in suburban areas. By the year 2000, about 73 percent of the population of Riverdale will be under the age of 44, and the percentage of Hispanics in the population will grow from 20 percent to about 35 percent of the total. It is important to note that the fastest-growing segment of the population in Riverdale is those 45 years of age or older. A large percentage of these people suffer from one or more chronic conditions. Therefore, they are the segment of the population most likely to be served by local hospitals. In addition, minority population segments are growing at a faster rate than the white population in Riverdale. These segments have some additional propensity to develop certain chronic diseases, such as high blood pressure for blacks and diabetes for Hispanics, that will require specialized services from the local hospitals.

The ten-county area surrounding Riverdale has a population of approximately 400,000 that is expected to steadily increase at the rate of 4 percent per year. It is impossible to quantify just how many patients come to Riverdale from the outlying ten counties. St. John's officials estimate that about 25 percent of their patients are from these areas, but they don't know if the other four hospitals in Riverdale are experiencing a similar rate of out-of-town patients.

All the hospitals in Riverdale are privately owned, except for the Riverdale city hospital, which is owned and managed by the city government. While the

TABLE 3-1-6   Uncompensated Care in 1990

Charity medical care	$ 5,425,404
Other charitable services	510,087
Bad debt	4,607,880
Medicaid	3,398,418
Medicare	25,250,485
Total	$39,192,274

city hospital is expected to serve all the indigent patients of the city, several of the other hospitals also do so. Because of its Catholic and charity mission, St. John's also serves a large share of indigent patients, both from the city of Riverdale and from the ten-county surrounding area. With a total revenue of approximately $250 million, last year St. John's provided more than $6 million in medical care for patients who could not pay the cost of their health care. In addition, St. John's has also provided a considerable amount of uncompensated care. The total of charity and uncompensated care provided by the hospital during the last fiscal year was $40.5 million, or approximately 17 percent of total revenue.

Uncompensated care as a percentage of total revenue has been growing steadily during the past five years. That growth has burdened the balance sheet of the hospital and has worried its administrators. Table 3-1-6 and Figure 3-1-2 show that growth.

FIGURE 3-1-2   Uncompensated Care: 1986 to 1990 (in millions of dollars)

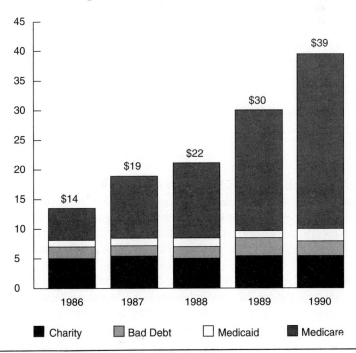

FIGURE 3-1-3   Forecasted Growth in Population for Ten-County Riverdale Area, by Age Group

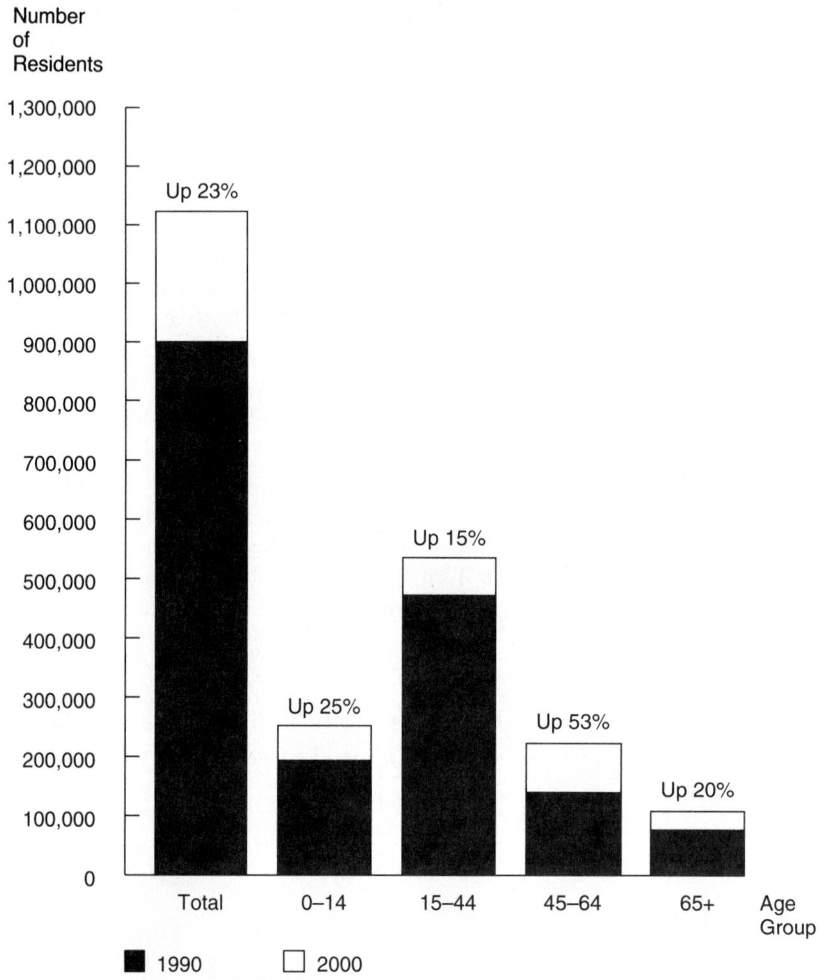

Number
of
Residents

■ 1990   □ 2000

Over 12 percent of all workers in the state do not have medical insurance for themselves or their families, and that percentage is growing. Researchers estimate that over 75 percent of these uninsured workers have family incomes under the poverty level. Administrators at St. John's consider this one of the greatest challenges in the future of hospital and health care administration.

A forecast of the general indicators of demand for St. John's Hospital shows that the total demand for the hospital services will increase steadily during the next ten years. In addition, certain acute-care areas are expected to face a higher demand than others. For example, the demand for cardiac and cancer

FIGURE 3-1-4   Growth Trends for Selected Hospital Services

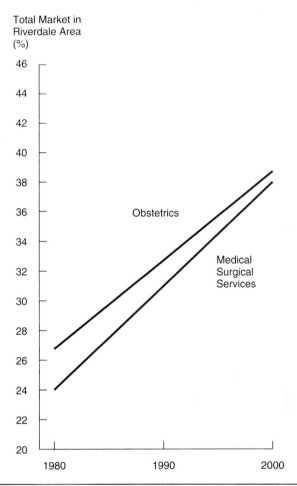

care is expected to increase at a higher rate than the demand for other services. In addition, St. John's is expected to continue to increase its market share in the Riverdale and surrounding ten-county area.

Some consideration must be given to the fact that the average patient's length of stay is decreasing. The hospital should investigate the possibility of changing its offering mix to adapt to such a trend. Figure 3-1-3 shows the forecasted growth in population for the Riverdale area, by age groups. Figure 3-1-4 indicates the different growth trends for selected hospital services, while Figure 3-1-5 is a projection of average length of inpatient stay for all hospitals in the United States.

These general trends will affect the planning decisions of St. John's administrators. They must be a major consideration when developing strategic marketing tools for the next five years.

FIGURE 3-1-5   **Average Length of Hospital Stay in the United States**

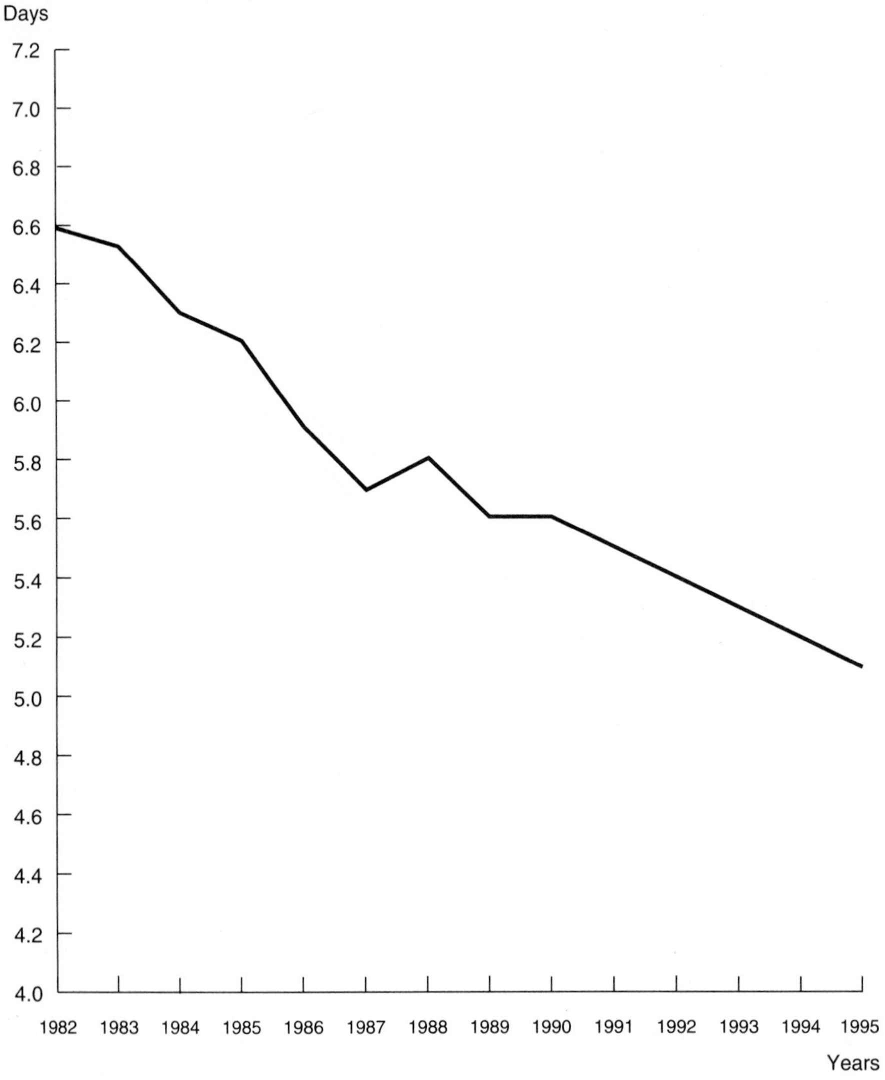

Days

ST. JOHN'S MARKET: A SITUATION ANALYSIS

St. John's Hospital has been steadily gaining market share in its market area. This gain has been achieved in all categories of hospital services. The largest gain was in the area of outpatient surgery services, with a 4.2 percent increase, and the smallest in the area of total admissions, with a 0.7 percent gain. Following are the market share gains for different categories for St. John's from 1989 to 1990:

	St. John's Share	Net Gain in Share
Total admissions	41.0%	0.7%
Medical/surgical, pediatric, ICU admissions	41.2	0.7
Deliveries	39.3	2.3
Surgery		
All surgery	27.9	2.5
Inpatient surgery	39.4	3.0
Outpatient surgery	19.0	4.2
Emergency room cases	19.0	1.0

The hospital was the market share leader in most categories. In outpatient surgery, however, a local clinic led the market with a 40.7 percent share of all cases. This, however, represented a drop in share for that clinic of about 4.5 percent. Another area in which St. John's did not lead was that of emergency room admissions. The city hospital, which specializes in trauma care, led with a market share of 43.7 percent of all cases. This represented a drop in market share in this category for the city hospital of about 3.4 percentage points. Table 3-1-7 illustrates the market shares for St. John's and the other hospitals in the Riverdale area of outpatient surgery cases for the seven years from 1980 to 1986. That trend away from inpatient procedures and toward more outpatient surgery has continued, and it is expected to affect all acute-care hospitals in the area. St. John's is considering including outpatient care as a major strategic part of its next five-year plan.

While the demand for health care in the Riverdale area has continued to increase steadily, hospitals have competed for their share of the market by diversifying their offerings and targeting different market segments. The administrators of St. John's are charged with developing a five-year plan for the hospital that will allow it to maintain or increase market share. This must be done by increasing the demand for services that generate greater marginal revenues, so that the hospital can continue to care for its share of the indigent and uninsured in the region. Presently, the hospital has almost reached a

TABLE 3-1-7 Market Share of Outpatient Surgery Cases

	1980	1981	1982	1983	1984	1985	1986
St. John's	12.6%	13.2%	12.7%	12.9%	12.8%	13.8%	17.7%
Riverdale	15.3	16.5	17.9	15.9	14.7	13.2	13.2
St. David	5.2	7.0	14.0	17.2	17.4	18.9	17.8
Hotel Dieu	4.3	2.8	2.2	1.7	1.1	1.0	1.3
South Riverdale	0.0	0.0	0.3	2.3	3.8	4.7	4.5
North City Hospital	0.0	0.0	0.0	0.5	2.4	3.3	4.8
Local outpatient clinic	62.6	60.5	52.9	49.5	47.8	45.1	40.7
Total	100.0%	100.0%	100.0%	100.0%	100.0%	100.0%	100.0%

break-even point, and it must not increase the percentage of charity and uncompensated care in the future.

The administrative team recognizes the urgency of such a task and intends to develop a plan that will define the target markets St. John's wishes to reach and a creative communications campaign capable of delivering the market share needed to satisfy its financial needs. Such a task will involve the establishment of communication objectives for the hospital, the determination and description of the target audience that must be reached, and finally the development of a complete creative concept and specific message to be conveyed in the most efficient media available to the hospital. While a complete advertising and communication budget is not needed, the administration must develop clear enough guidelines so that a consultant can develop a complete campaign. In short, the guidelines must include, along with the variables already mentioned, a determination of whether broadcast or print media should be used and the proposed combination of advertising and public relations that would best achieve the hospital's goals.

To achieve such a task, the administration can draw information from secondary market data and also rely on extensive market research conducted with hospital audiences over a period of four years. This research traced the awareness and perception of the hospital by patients and potential users, as well as its image relative to that of its major competitors. A summary of the results of that research is shown in Appendix 3-1.

THE PROBLEM

The administrative team of St. John's Hospital must include in its strategy considerations the market trends facing St. John's, the Riverdale region, and U.S. hospitals in general. With that knowledge, it must draw from the consumer survey data enough knowledge of people's perception of St. John's to be able to evaluate future marketing strategies for the hospital.

One can assume that St. John's will adapt its operation to serve any product-mix change its administration feels necessary. Capital needs can be satisfied through the national network. The task at hand is to consider only marketing and advertising decisions in the face of the changing health care environment.

Questions for Discussion and Review

1. Given future trends, what services mix must St. John's communicate to its publics?

2. How should St. John's be positioned among all other hospitals in the area, including private outpatient clinics?

3. What should be the main creative theme for St. John's marketing strategy for the next five years?

4. What mix of advertising, public relations, and promotional activities would best serve St. John's objectives?

Appendix 3-1

A summary of the awareness and perception of St. John's research among hospital patients and potential users.

Unaided recall of area hospitals (all mentions)	1987	1988	1989	1990
St. John's	77.5%	83.7%	78.0%	69.9%
Riverdale	83.1	79.3	79.7	69.0
St. David's	76.4	74.4	68.3	64.3
South Riverdale	18.8	16.3	18.4	17.9
North City	10.6	12.0	10.0	10.6
Hotel Dieu[a]	8.8	7.1	5.9	—
Other	5.9	3.7	5.8	5.5

If there were a need for major medical care for you or your family, which hospital would you choose?

St. John's	43.0%	39.9%	41.3%	40.4%
Riverdale	18.4	20.4	22.8	18.6
St. David's	25.5	24.3	22.4	23.6
South Riverdale	5.9	5.3	6.2	7.3
North City	3.4	4.9	4.6	3.5
Hotel Dieu[a]	—	—	—	—
Other	4.0	5.1	2.7	6.6

Which area hospital do you feel gives the best care for:

People 55 years or older?

St. John's	42.5%	41.5%	42.8%	45.0%
St. David's	26.1	26.8	25.9	24.7
Riverdale	23.3	24.7	21.5	20.8
Other	8.0	7.0	9.8	9.5

Orthopedic needs?

St. John's	35.1%	34.4%	30.5%	29.2%
St. David's	21.4	18.3	15.8	20.4
Riverdale	36.6	38.8	47.5	40.9
Other	6.9	8.5	6.2	9.4

Heart problems?

St. John's	45.9%	42.5%	7.0%	40.9%
St. David's	22.1	22.8	17.6	17.7
Riverdale	27.2	28.1	38.6	35.4
Other	4.8	6.6	6.7	6.1

Cancer?

St. John's	42.7%	39.4%	41.4%	43.0%
St. David's	21.3	20.4	18.2	21.1
Riverdale	17.1	14.9	27.0	21.9
Other	18.9	25.3	13.4	14.0

Maternity?

St. John's	42.1%	42.3%	41.1%	42.8%
St. David's	31.6	27.3	29.7	26.4
Riverdale	17.6	23.5	21.6	23.0
Other	8.6	6.9	7.6	8.0

Note: Not all percentages will add up to 100 percent because of multiple responses, or because of sample non-responses. For some questions, responses regarding St. John's, St. David's, and Riverdale were tabulated separately from all other responses.

[a]Hotel Dieu data not available after the hospital was closed in 1989.

C A S E   3 - 2

Rooster Andrews Sporting Goods, Inc. (A)

William E. "Rooster" Andrews's athletic career began in Dallas in the 1930s at Woodrow Wilson High School and continued at The University of Texas at Austin. In the early 1940s, Andrews achieved national acclaim as the first All-American Waterboy, as well as a degree of notoriety for his drop-kicking ability for the football team.

Beginning in 1943, Andrews converted his knowledge of sports and his friendship with athletes and coaches into a successful career selling sporting goods. In November 1970, after working for several sporting goods retailers, Andrews opened his own sporting goods company—Rooster Andrews Sporting Goods, Inc. (RASG).

Although RASG began by catering to team and institutional accounts, the firm later shifted its emphasis to retail sales. While the firm maintained its position as a primary supplier to institutional accounts, including The University of Texas and other universities and schools, retail sales to individuals accounted for 95 percent of volume.

RASG drew retail customers from a central Texas primary market area consisting of 30 counties, with the Austin SMSA providing the core. The firm served this market through three retail stores. The original Guadalupe Street store was located approximately ten blocks north of The University of Texas campus in central Austin. In the 1980s, RASG opened a northside store at Anderson Lane and Shoal Creek and a southside store at South Lamar and Ben White.

The depth and assortment of merchandise carried at the two branch locations was varied to fit their different markets, characterized as more blue-collar workers, Hispanics, and "Bubbas"[1] in the south and more yuppies in the north. This year RASG expected sales to reach approximately $6 million—up by about $1 million over last year. In planning for next year, management anticipated a 2 to 3 percent increase in sales. Roughly half of this

---

This case was written by John H. Murphy, The University of Texas at Austin, and is intended to serve as the basis for classroom discussion, not to illustrate the effective or ineffective handling of an administrative situation. Used by permission of Rooster Andrews Sporting Goods, Inc.

[1] Austin humorist Cactus Pryor describes a Bubba as follows: "Bubba is a good ol' boy. He likes the NRA (National Rifle Association) and Bubba dips snuff and Bubba likes Ollie North (the "super patriot" Marine officer of the Iran/Contra scandal fame) and Bubba likes to fish and hunt and eat barbecue and talk about women. . . . Bubbas are hard to not like because they're friendly. They hate Yankees. Bubba wears cowboy clothes." Elizabeth A. Moize, "Austin—Deep in the Heart of Texans," *National Geographic,* June 1990, 63.

volume would come from the original store and half from the combined total of the two branches.

Seasonality was extremely important in the sporting goods business. The bulk of all sales occurred during three selling periods: (1) the back-to-school period, during the month of September; (2) Christmas, concentrated in mid-December; and (3) all of March through mid-April.

THE COMPETITIVE ENVIRONMENT

RASG's merchandise consisted of sports equipment, shoes, and sportswear. The store carried equipment for badminton, baseball, basketball, cross training, darts, football, racquetball, rugby, running, soccer, softball, sports medicine, squash, swimming, tennis, track, volleyball, water skiing, and weightlifting. The store's distinctive mix was also notable for what it lacked. For example, RASG did *not* carry hunting and fishing equipment, camping gear, golf equipment, scuba gear, boating equipment, or snow skiing items.

Given RASG's mix, the firm had two major competitors in Austin— Academy and Oshman's. Academy had originally been established in Austin as an army/navy surplus store but had added a heavy emphasis on sporting goods in recent years. Academy competed on a price basis and used extensive newspaper and television advertising for its aggressive price appeals. In addition to athletic shoes and many other items carried by RASG, Academy offered a wide range of outdoor and sporting equipment not available at RASG. For example, Academy carried a wide range of outdoor, hunting and fishing, and other recreational equipment.

Oshman's was a national sporting goods retailer that competed most directly with RASG in terms of the lines of merchandise carried. Management of RASG was curious about what impact the opening of Oshman's new "SuperSports USA" store might have had on Austin sporting goods consumers. The opening of the new "super store," approximately nine months earlier, had been accompanied by heavy advertising support.

The new Oshman's store occupied a mammoth 80,000 square feet of space in Northcross Mall, roughly three blocks from RASG's north store, and offered "activity centers" for shoppers to try out equipment. Alvin Lubetkin, CEO of Oshman's, explained the thinking behind its new approach to marketing sporting goods in a local newspaper article:

> The concept is to provide the most complete and exciting selection and assortment of merchandise in any category, so anybody interested in an activity wouldn't think of shopping anyplace else. It makes shopping what it should be—not only rewarding but fun.

ADVERTISING AND MARKETING STRATEGY

Ron Habitzreiter, who had been with the firm from its inception, was RASG's general manager and legal counsel. In addition, he was responsible for all of RASG's advertising and marketing activities. In his judgment, the sporting goods industry operated in the Stone Age with respect to marketing. With only a few notable exceptions, sporting goods manufacturers and retailers paid little attention to customer wants and needs.

Habitzreiter believed RASG's "make-a-market" strategy had paid large dividends. This strategy consisted of identifying certain categories of sporting goods that the firm would carry in an extremely large depth and breadth. For example, RASG had followed this strategy in athletic shoes, knee braces, swimming goggles, and darts. In the main store, RASG had 23 brands and 150 styles of swimming goggles.

Athletic shoes accounted for 35 percent of the firm's overall volume. RASG carried 40 brands and roughly 400 styles of athletic shoes. This wide assortment provided the store with a major advantage over the competition. (Twenty percent of sales volume was from T-shirts and shorts; 10 percent, hard goods; 10 percent, sweats and other athletic clothing; 25 percent, miscellaneous goods.)

EXHIBIT 3-2-1

Note: RASG's quarter-page Yellow Pages ad appeared under both the "Sporting Goods—Retail" and "Shoes—Retail" classifications at a cost of $1,200 per month. Also included in this monthly charge were boldface listings in the White Pages and one-inch boxes under other sporting goods categories. Academy and Oshman's ran no ads in the Yellow Pages and had only a line listing under Sporting Goods—Retail.

EXHIBIT 3-2-2

Once exposed to RASG's giant assortment in one of these areas, the enthusiasts were hooked. They knew of no other retailer who handled anything approaching RASG's assortment. This draw brought them into the store consistently, where they made numerous purchases in other categories of sporting goods.

Through his own experience, Habitzreiter had come to a number of conclusions regarding which advertising approaches made the most sense (and money) for RASG. His views included the following:

> *Loyalty to a sporting goods retailer is zero. A price special on a brand name will take your best friend across town to your competitor. . . .*
>
> *Print works for us, broadcast doesn't. I rely on the* Austin American-Statesman *and the* Daily Texan *(The University of Texas student newspaper). Also, the Yellow Pages are important. . . . [see Exhibit 3-2-1]*
>
> *A two-column by six-inch ad size is effective [see Exhibit 3-2-2]. Price deals on brand names is what makes these ads cook [see Exhibit 3-2-3] . . . .*
>
> *One hundred percent of our print advertising is co-op driven. Most of the co-op programs are matching or 50/50, based on an allowance of 1 percent of brand sales [see Exhibit 3-2-4 for a typical co-op program]. We have a system which tracks our co-op allowances and usage, plus prints out a reimbursement request*

EXHIBIT 3-2-3

[see Exhibit 3-2-5]. In planning an ad, the first step is to check our
records of what co-op is available. I also have to check to make
sure that we have sufficient stock available at all three stores
before I run an ad featuring a shoe or whatever. There are about
ten manufacturers which account for most of our advertising:
Russell Athletic, Nike, and six to eight others are the big guns. . . .

I'm a tough sell when it comes to advertising. Especially,
image advertising. . . .

I measure the effectiveness of my advertising by how an item
sells. In retail, it's easy to know how your ads pull. . . .

We've never had much luck with an advertising agency.
They've talked us into running generic ads which didn't pull well

EXHIBIT 3-2-4

1991 NIKE CO-OP ADVERTISING PROGRAM

MAXIMUM ALLOWANCE

The accrual periods are first quarter (January–March), second quarter (April–June), third quarter (July–September) and fourth quarter (October–December). Funds are available at the following rates based on your net shipments:

> **FOOTWEAR:** 1% on all shipments of first-quality merchandise.
> **APPAREL:** 3% on all Future I and Future II shipments of first-quality merchandise.

Shipments of "B" grades, irregulars or close-out merchandise do <u>not</u> accrue funds.

Occasionally, special sales programs are offered that do <u>not</u> accrue Co-op funds at the rates listed above. Your Nike sales rep can explain these sales programs to you.

Nike reserves the right to terminate or amend any portion of the Co-op program within 30 days of written notice to all retailers eligible under the program.

TERMS OF REIMBURSEMENT

Media Advertising

- 100% on all qualifying advertising.
- Reimbursement will be in the form of a Nike credit memo.
- Reimbursement will be limited to the available qualifying balance at the time of claim submission. No further credit will be issued toward the short-paid claim. **To avoid short payment, you are encouraged to contact the Co-op Department prior to claim submission for your current Co-op balance.**

Point-of-Purchase Merchandise and Supershots

- Payment for most Supershot and Point-of-Purchase invoices will be automatically deducted from Co-op funds. If there are insufficient funds available, an invoice will be issued for the balance due, and a payment should be remitted to Nike. If an invoice is generated due to insufficient Co-op funds, a copy of the paid invoice can be submitted for Co-op credit within 90 days of the invoice date.
- The date that your POP or Supershot order is received at Nike will determine the quarter(s) that will be accessed for Co-op reimbursement. Payment will be deducted from the previous quarter's funds first, and if necessary, from the current quarter's funds.

USAGE TIMELINES

1991 Accruals

- Qualifying advertising run during any given quarter can access that quarter's accrual as well as any balance in the previous quarter's accrual.
- Unused funds accrued during any given quarter will expire at the end of the following quarter.
- Claims for Co-op reimbursement must be submitted within 90 days from the date of the advertisement.
- See Co-op Usage Timeline chart.

6836

[see Exhibit 3-2-6, which presents an ad for skiing equipment which has since been dropped]. Also, their production charges of $500 to $700 per ad didn't sit too well. Now, I do all our print production. I bought a camera, a developer, and a typesetter. Plus, I have a great collection of clip art from all the manufacturers' co-op programs. With my setup, I do it all right here and I just tell the newspapers when to pick up my ads. . . .

We've done one quality television spot. About six years ago, 3rd Coast [a production company] did a spot which showed quick cuts of a whole bunch of stuff we carried with the voice-over that we are specialists in all these areas. It cost $8,000

EXHIBIT 3-2-5

ROOSTER ANDREWS SPORTING GOODS, INC.
P.O. BOX 2163
AUSTIN, TEXAS 78768

MAY 8, 1990

RUSSELL ATHLETIC ACCOUNT MANAGER
% Advertising Checking Bureau, Inc.
P.O. Box 140334
Orlando, Florida 32814
  Attn: Maria Diamond

Re: Russell Coop Reimbursement
1990 Calendar Year Program
ACCOUNT NO. 5108

Gentlemen:

Our firm is, through this letter, submitting a claim for Cooperative
Advertising reimbursement under the Russell coop program. Accordingly,
we are asking for reimbursement for the following ads as specified:

(AAS = Austin American Statesman DT = Daily Texan TC = Third Coast)

Ad Description	Date(s) run	Medium	Column Inches	Cost
WINDSHORTS	4/18	AAS	24.0	671.28
		TOTAL		671.28

We understand that your participation up to our maximum program funds
to be 100% of advertising costs. Kindly remit payment in the amount of
$671.28 payable to Rooster Andrews Sporting Goods, Attn: Ron Habitz-
reiter.

Tear sheets and media invoices are attached. Please advise the remaining
coop balance in our fund for the previous year as well as current accruals.

Very sincerely yours,

Ronald Habitzreiter

RH:wp

---

*and we've run it over and over again for years. What's funny is
that I still get calls from people who say they love our* new *TV
spot! Unfortunately, some of the styles shown are not made
anymore, so we cannot continue to air the spot. [see Exhibit
3-2-7]*

EXHIBIT 3-2-6

A RESEARCH STUDY

To provide data useful in planning RASG's upcoming marketing communication efforts, a research study was conducted. The study was designed not only to be useful in campaign planning, but also to provide a benchmark against which to measure changes in target consumers' levels of awareness, knowledge, and attitudes at the conclusion of the campaign.

A sample of residential telephone listings was randomly drawn from the most recent Austin telephone directory. Telephone interviews were conducted between 6:00 and 10:00 in the evening, only with adults who reported that they had made a sporting goods purchase in the past six months. The interview was conducted using a structured questionnaire (see Appendix 3-2).

A total of 308 interviews was completed, 160 with women and 148 with men. The overall findings of the survey are presented as a part of Appendix 3-2. In addition, selected variables cross-tabulated against gender and age are presented in Table 3-2-1.

EXHIBIT 3-2-7

30-sec. TV spot

AUDIO: Fast paced music throughout.

VIDEO: Quick cuts of international sports symbols

AUDIO: Announcer: "Name your game. Any game and Rooster Andrews is ready to play with the biggest names in sports." Music under

VIDEO: Quick cuts of international symbols.

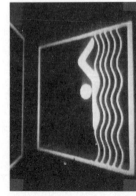

AUDIO: Fast paced music up and continues.

VIDEO: Quick cuts of brand name merchandise against a black background, some with sports symbols

AUDIO: Fast paced music continues.

VIDEO: Quick cuts to brand name merchandise plus some sport equipment in use.

AUDIO: Fast paced music continues.

VIDEO: Quick cuts to close ups of brand name on sporting equipment continues.

AUDIO: Announcer: "But, when it comes to sporting goods, we don't play games." Music under.

VIDEO: Rooster Andrews We don't play games superimposed on screen.

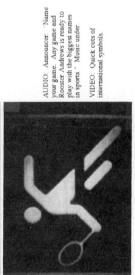

TABLE 3-2-1   Sporting Goods Study Findings Classified by Age and Gender Groups

	Total	18–24		25–34		35–49		50+	
		Men	Women	Men	Women	Men	Women	Men	Women
Sample size	308	32	42	55	52	36	45	25	21
First Mention, Top-mind Recall									
RASG	22%	28%	31%	16%	6%	22%	36%	12%	24%
Academy	6	0	7	7	8	17	0	0	10
Oshman's	61	62	55	71	79	39	53	72	48
Buy Most Past 3 Years									
RASG	13%	19%	5%	9%	6%	6%	24%	16%	38%
Academy	21	19	10	22	25	28	31	8	10
Oshman's	32	28	40	44	25	31	20	44	14
First Mention, Reason for Store Choice									
Location	31%	22%	41%	29%	37%	14%	33%	32%	38%
Price	21	28	14	20	27	28	20	12	14
Selection	21	22	17	27	17	22	16	20	29
Participate in Sports or Fitness at Least Once per Week									
Yes	76%	91%	90%	78%	71%	75%	73%	68%	63%
No	24	9	10	22	29	25	27	32	37

THE COMING MARKETING YEAR

At this point, Habitzreiter planned to carefully review the study findings and then plan a complete promotional program for the coming fiscal year (August 1 through July 31). During the present year, out-of-pocket advertising expenses are projected to be $260,000, with an additional $115,000 to $120,000 in rebate monies received through manufacturers' co-op programs.

For planning purposes, he began with the assumption of an overall, out-of-pocket advertising and promotional appropriation of 3 to 5 percent of forecasted sales. However, like all fiscally responsible business people, Habitzreiter appreciated an efficient, cost-conscious use of marketing dollars, along with a solid rationale justifying the recommended investment. (The National Sporting Goods Association reported that the national average advertising-to-sales ratio for larger sporting goods retailers was 3.2 percent.)

In addition to traditional media advertising, Habitzreiter was also interested in exploring the use of direct marketing, sales promotion, and publicity. In the past, RASG had made minimal use of these promotional tools. Note that management had decided not to sponsor any athletic events, such as a 5K run, because of liability considerations.

Questions for Discussion and Review

1. Which environmental factors would have the most significant effect on RASG's marketing communication plans?

2. What role would Habitzreiter's past experience and attitudes play in shaping any proposed marketing communication programs?

3. How can the data from the research study be used most effectively in planning and evaluating the marketing communication plan?

4. What advertising appropriation would you recommend? Why? How would you recommend that this appropriation be allocated across media and other expense categories? What role should co-op advertising rebates play in the program?

Appendix 3-2
Research Questionnaire—Sporting Goods Study

TELEPHONE # _____   QUESTIONNAIRE # _____

INTERVIEWER _____   NOTE TIME BEGIN: _____

3 CALLBACKS ON 2 DAYS BEFORE MOVING TO THE NEXT # ON EACH ROW.

Hello, my name is _____ and I work for CRP, a local market research firm. We're conducting a survey among selected Austin residents about their shopping patterns. We're only interested in your opinions and we're *not* selling anything.

1. First, I need to determine if you qualify for an interview. Are you 18 years old or over? IF YES, CONTINUE.

           IF NO, ASK: May I speak to someone in your household
                 who is 18 or older?

Second, have you purchased any sporting goods, such as athletic shoes, sporting equipment, or apparel, in the past six months?

           IF YES, CONTINUE.

           IF NO, ASK: May I speak to someone in your household who
                 is 18 or older and who has purchased sporting
                 goods in the past 6 months?

2a. When you think of sporting goods stores in Austin, what are the first three which come to mind?

	First Mention	Second Mention	Third Mention
ROOSTER ANDREWS	22%	27%	8%
ACADEMY	6	12	9
OSHMAN'S	61	20	4
HERMAN'S	0	4	3
SEA & SKI	0	0	0
REI	1	3	6
OTHER (SPECIFY)			

IF DO *NOT* MENTION ASK: *(Note that percentages are among those who did not id in 2a.)*

2b. Have you ever heard of Rooster Andrews? YES ....81% NO 19%
 Have you ever heard of Academy? YES ....96% NO 4%
 Have you ever heard of Oshman's? YES ....94% NO 6%

3. Where did you buy most of your sporting goods *in the past three years*?
 ROOSTER ANDREWS ....13% OSHMAN'S 32%
 ACADEMY ....21% OTHER 34%

4. Why did you select _____ (STORE FROM #3)?
 IF ONLY ONE OR TWO REASONS CITED, ASK: Are there any other reasons?

	First Mention	Second Mention	Third Mention
LOCATION	31%	8%	5%
PRICE	21	14	4
REPUTATION OF STORE	6	5	1
SALES PERSONNEL	1	2	0
SELECTION	21	10	4
QUALITY OF MERCHANDISE	3	5	3
STYLE OF MERCHANDISE	2	2	1
RECOMMENDED BY FRIEND	2	1	1
BOUGHT THERE BEFORE	4	0	2
OTHER (SPECIFY)	9	6	2

Next, we'd like to get your opinions about some local Austin sporting goods stores. For each one, I will read a statement which describes the store and I'll ask you to tell me the extent to which you agree or disagree with the statement.

5. First, I'd like for you to think about *Oshman's*. Would you please tell me if you strongly agree, agree, neither agree nor disagree, disagree or strongly disagree with the statement, Oshman's carries a wide selection of sporting goods.

(CONTINUE FOR ALL SCALES)	Strongly Agree	Agree	Neither Agree nor Disagree	Disagree	Strongly Disagree
Oshman's carries a wide selection of sporting goods	55%	32%	11%	1%	1%
Oshman's has knowledgeable sales personnel to assist customers	16	35	40	6	3
Oshman's carries high quality, brand name products	50	37	11	1	1
Oshman's offers everyday low prices on the brands of sporting goods they carry	6	25	48	17	4
Oshman's is a fun place to shop for sporting goods	27	33	30	6	4

6. Next, I'd like for you to think about *Academy.* Would you please tell me if you strongly agree, agree, neither agree nor disagree, disagree or strongly disagree with the statement, Academy carries a wide selection of sporting goods.

(CONTINUE FOR ALL SCALES)	Strongly Agree	Agree	Neither Agree nor Disagree	Disagree	Strongly Disagree
Academy carries a wide selection of sporting goods	18%	37%	33%	10%	2%
Academy has knowledgeable sales personnel to assist customers	10	30	39	17	4
Academy carries high quality, brand name products	9	36	39	13	3
Academy offers everyday low prices on the brands of sporting goods they carry	30	40	25	4	1
Academy is a fun place to shop for sporting goods	8	30	43	12	7

7. Next, I'd like for you to think about *Rooster Andrews.* Would you please tell me if you strongly agree, agree, neither agree nor disagree, disagree or strongly disagree with the statement, Rooster Andrews carries a wide selection of sporting goods.

(CONTINUE FOR ALL SCALES)	Strongly Agree	Agree	Neither Agree nor Disagree	Disagree	Strongly Disagree
Rooster Andrews carries a wide selection of sporting goods	25%	40%	31%	3%	1%
Rooster Andrews has knowledgeable sales personnel to assist customers	19	40	38	3	0
Rooster Andrews carries high quality, brand name products	25	43	30	1	1
Rooster Andrews offers everyday low prices on the brands of sporting goods they carry	3	20	55	16	6
Rooster Andrews is a fun place to shop for sporting goods	9	33	50	6	2

Thank you. Now all we need is some information to help classify this questionnaire.

8. First, we are interested in how frequently you participate in sports or fitness activities. On the average, do you participate in sports or fitness activities at least once a week? YES............76% NO............24% IF NO, SKIP TO Q. 10.

  IF YES, ASK: On average, how many days per week do you engage in sports or fitness activities?

  1.........11% 2.........15% 3.........24% 4.........14% 5.........9% 6.........2%
  7.........9% UNSURE..........16%

9. What is your age? Are you
  18–24.........24% 25–34.........35% 35–49.........26% 50–64.........10%
  65+.........5% REFUSED.........0%

10. How many people, including children, live in your household?
  1(20%) 2(35%) 3(22%) 4(14%) 5(4%) 6(2%) 7(2%)
  8 OR MORE (1%)

11. What is your ZIP Code?   787_____.

12. In case my office wants to check my work, may I have your name?

_____

13. NOTE SEX OF RESPONDENT: FEMALE........51%   MALE........49%

VERIFIED BY _____. DATE _____.

C A S E   3 - 3
Roy Cordes, Jr., Campaign

With only three weeks until election day, the fall 1990 race for county judge in Fort Bend County, Texas, did *not* look promising for Roy Cordes, Jr. At that point both Cordes, running as a Democrat, and his Republican opponent, John Knox, were making final adjustments in their campaigns to replace the popular Judge Jodie Stavinoha, who was retiring. (Stavinoha, a Democrat, had received 54 percent of the votes in the 1986 general election.)

FORT BEND COUNTY

Fort Bend County is one of 13 counties which make up the Houston/Galveston region (see Exhibit 3-3-1). Fort Bend County covers a total of 869 square miles. Twenty years ago, the county was largely rural, with four small towns—Richmond (the county seat), Rosenberg, Sugarland, and Missouri City/Stafford. However, in the early 1980s, the northeastern portion of the county had experienced tremendous growth (the county had experienced a 56 percent population increase overall between 1980 and 1990), and it now contained what had become several large, upscale, bedroom communities that identified closely with Houston.

Exhibit 3-3-2 presents a map showing the county's proximity to Houston's freeway system and landmarks. This map also indicates the geographic relationships among the five larger cities in the county —Missouri City, Richmond, Rosenberg, Stafford, and Sugarland. Table 3-3-1 presents a demographic profile of county residents, published by the Greater Fort Bend Economic Development Council, classified by age, race, income, and mobility with projections through 1993.

COUNTY JUDGE DUTIES AND RESPONSIBILITIES

In Fort Bend County, the position of county judge was largely administrative rather than judicial. The county judge was basically the business manager of the county. The judge was a member of, and presided over, the commissioners court, which was responsible for conducting the business affairs of the county. The commissioners court had fiscal responsibility for funding most of the appointed and elected officials of the county. Further, the court was responsible for supervising and funding the operation and maintenance of the

This case was written by John H. Murphy, The University of Texas at Austin, and is intended to serve as the basis for classroom discussion, not to illustrate the effective or ineffective handling of an administrative situation. Used by permission of the Roy Cordes, Jr., Campaign.

EXHIBIT 3-3-1   Houston/Galveston Region Map

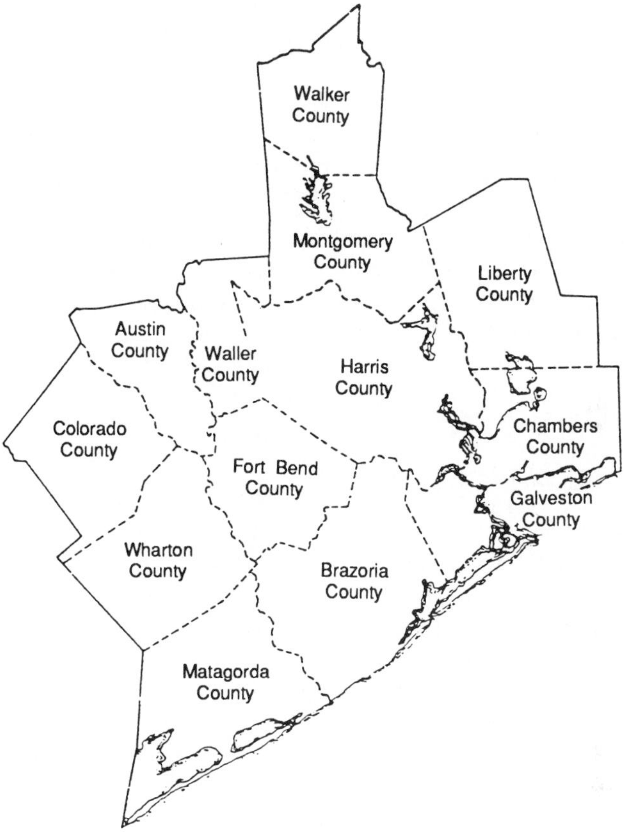

county's services and its sewage, road building, and other construction projects.

The county judge, with the assistance of the county auditor, prepared and submitted to the commissioners court an annual budget for the operation of the county. In 1990, Fort Bend County's budget was more than $54 million. Much of what the county judge did involved coordinating the activities of the 50-plus departments of county government.

In addition, the county judge in Fort Bend County had judicial authority under the constitution. The judge also had probate, mental commitment, and juvenile authority. Although not typically called to serve in this role, the judge could preside over misdemeanor criminal cases and sit as an administrative judge.

Finally, the county judge represented the county at the local, regional, state, and federal levels. The judge worked as a lobbyist in the state legislature in Austin and served as an advocate for the county in Washington.

EXHIBIT 3-3-2   Fort Bend County Map

TABLE 3-3-1   Fort Bend County Demographics: 1980, 1990, 1993

	1980 Census	1990 Estimate	% Change 1980 to 1990	1993 Projection
Total population	130,846	204,642	56.4%	254,369
Total households	39,840	65,522	64.5	83,930
Household population	127,356	201,152	57.9	250,879
Average household size	3.2	3.1	−4.0	3.0
Average household income	$29,011	$48,734	68.0	$60,615
Median household income	$25,668	$41,110	60.2	$50,806

TABLE 3-3-1   *(continued)*

	1980 Census		1990 Estimate		1993 Projection	
	Number	Percent	Number	Percent	Number	Percent
Population by Age						
Total	130,846	100.0%	204,642	100.0%	254,369	100.0%
0–4	12,986	9.9	20,142	9.8	23,610	9.3
5–9	13,129	10.0	19,061	9.3	23,244	9.1
10–14	12,365	9.5	17,723	8.7	21,136	8.3
15–19	10,943	8.4	16,674	8.1	19,522	7.7
20–24	10,301	7.9	16,786	8.2	21,542	8.5
25–29	14,401	11.0	18,259	8.9	24,105	9.5
30–34	15,081	11.5	19,337	9.4	22,189	8.7
35–39	10,239	7.8	18,497	9.0	18,541	7.3
40–44	7,151	5.5	15,353	7.5	19,367	7.6
45–49	5,657	4.3	10,955	5.4	16,862	6.6
50–54	5,101	3.9	8,225	4.0	12,095	4.8
55–59	4,055	3.1	6,828	3.3	8,934	3.5
60–64	2,950	2.3	5,597	2.7	7,189	2.8
65–69	2,412	1.8	4,151	2.0	5,882	2.3
70–74	1,670	1.3	2,933	1.4	4,157	1.6
75–79	1,152	0.9	1,996	1.0	2,779	1.1
80–84	694	0.5	1,214	0.6	1,793	0.7
85+	559	0.4	911	0.4	1,422	0.6
Median age total population	27.0		28.3		28.8	
Median age adult population	34.6		37.1		38.2	
Population by Race						
Total	130,846	100.0%	204,642	100.0%	254,369	100.0%
White	66,073	50.5	113,579	55.5	145,721	57.3
Black	20,420	15.6	28,004	13.7	33,922	13.3
Other	17,697	13.5	25,204	12.3	29,212	11.5
Hispanic	26,656	20.4	37,855	18.5	45,514	17.9
Household Income						
$ 0– 7,499	4,507	11.3%	3,745	5.7%	3,838	4.6%
$ 7,500–14,999	5,259	13.1	5,036	7.7	5,054	6.0
$15,000–24,999	9,577	23.9	7,750	11.8	7,334	8.7
$25,000–34,999	10,080	25.2	9,570	14.6	8,830	10.5
$35,000–49,999	6,849	17.1	16,347	24.9	16,223	19.3
$50,000–74,999	2,548	6.4	14,619	22.3	21,239	25.3
$75,000+	1,213	3.0	8,455	12.9	21,412	25.5

Neighborhood Mobility: Household Moved In	1990 Estimate
Most Recent Year	6,840
Last 5 Years	23,699
6–9 Years Ago	9,251
10–14 Years Ago	5,129
15+ Years Ago	3,544

Source: Donnelly Demographics and Greater Fort Bend Economic Development Council.

THE CANDIDATES

Exhibits 3-3-3 through 3-3-5 provide a concise description of the backgrounds of the two candidates. In addition, these representative campaign materials identify some of the issues each candidate perceived to be important in the campaign.

Knox, who had been mayor of Missouri City since 1979, had announced that he would run for the position before Judge Stavinoha indicated he would not seek reelection. On the other hand, Cordes had waited until after Judge Stavinoha's announcement to enter the race. This gave Knox a significant advantage in that he tapped a number of sources of campaign funds early and, hence, handicapped Cordes's efforts to raise money to conduct his campaign.

THE 1988 GENERAL ELECTION

Table 3-3-2 presents a breakdown of the results of the general election held on November 8, 1988. As indicated in this table, although Republican presidential candidate and Houstonian George Bush garnered a substantial majority of all votes cast in the presidential election in Fort Bend County in 1988, the strength of his majority varied considerably by areas of the county.

Ticket splitting across party lines was reasonably widespread in Fort Bend County in the 1988 election. For example, Democrat Lloyd Bentsen received a clear majority from the Fort Bend County voters in his race for a U.S. Senate

---

EXHIBIT 3-3-3

- Native of Fort Bend County
- Graduate of
    Fort Bend School System
    University of Texas - BBA Finance
    University of Houston - Law Degree
- Served in U.S. Air Force
- Self Employed, Law Practice
- Sugar Land City Council - 9 yrs
- Sugar Land Economic Development
    Council - Chairman
- Greater Fort Bend Economic
    Development Council - Member
- Fort Bend Senior Citizens Inc.
    Director
- Fort Bend Chamber of Commerce
    Past Director

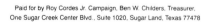
Pride in Yesterday, Planning for Tomorrow

Paid for by Roy Cordes Jr. Campaign, Ben W. Childers, Treasurer,
One Sugar Creek Center Blvd., Suite 1020, Sugar Land, Texas 77478

ROY CORDES JR.
for
COUNTY JUDGE

EXHIBIT 3-3-4

FORT BEND COUNTY JUDGE
ABOUT THE CANDIDATES
(based upon published material)

Roy Cordes, Jr.			John Knox
Second generation Fort Bend Native; Born Sugar Land; Father former Mayor of Sugar Land.	☐	**Background** ☐	Native of Beverly, Mass Raised in Boston area. Lives in Missouri City
Law Degree from University of Houston; B.B.A. in Finance, University of Texas.	☐	**Education** ☐	No degree; attended Boston University and the University of California at Berkley during 1960s.
U.S. Air Force, Intelligence Specialist in Electronics, Three years in Europe	☐	**Military** ☐	None reported Honorary Admiral, Texas Navy
Private law practice; former chief counsel and member of management committee, Sperry-Sun, Inc.	☐	**Business** ☐	Senior Systems analyst Shell Oil.
Chairman, Fort Bend Senior Citizens, Inc., past Director, Fort Bend Chamber of Commerce; Past officer East Fort Bend Kiwanis	☐	**Community** ☐	Honorary Member, Oyster Creek Rotary Club.
Sugar Land City Council 1981-1990	☐	**Government** ☐	Mayor, Missouri City 1979-present
Three Tax Rate DECREASES (from 1981-90)		**City Comparison**	35 Per Cent Tax Rate INCREASE (from 81-90)
Crime Rate 2.85% (1989 FBI Report)			Crime Rate 5.182% (1989 FBI Report)
Industrial Tax Base Business and Industry Pay 48% of 1990 Taxes			Industrial Tax Base Business and Industry Pay 10% of 1990 Taxes
Chairman, Sugar Land Economic Development Committee. (1987 to date) Trustee, Greater Fort Bend Economic Development Council	☐	**Economic Development** ☐	President, Fort Bend Industrial Development Board (Inactive); Director, Greater Fort Bend Economic Development Council
Does NOT favor increased tax support of EDC expenses.			Favors increased tax support of EDC expenses.
Direct involvement in bringing 788 jobs, $18.4 Million Payroll and $20 Million investment to Sugar Land alone. Assisted in expansion or relocation of such non-polluting companies as: Unocal, Henley International, Carton Sales. Three major corporate moves to be announced soon. Sugar Land, under his EDC committee, favors added industrial expansion in city.	☐	**EDC Results** ☐ (from Greater Fort Bend Economic Development Council)	An engineering company and a machine shop with 80 jobs and a $2.3 million payroll moved into city.

seat. Even in the heavily Republican community of Sugarland, Bentsen had received a majority of the votes in his Senate race despite a 73 percent vote for the Republican ticket of Bush and Quayle.

CORDES'S MARKETING COMMUNICATION STRATEGY

Up to the last three weeks of the race, the Cordes campaign had relied primarily on five activities: (1) "walking the neighborhoods"; (2) public appearances; (3) a phone bank; (4) "coffees for Cordes"; and (5) direct mail.

EXHIBIT 3-3-5

John Knox:
The Right Man for
The Business of
The County.

As Fort Bend's top administrator of county government, our County Judge must have the skills to manage a multi-million dollar budget and guide the efforts of more than fifty county departments. When it comes to the pressing business of county government, there's simply no time for on-the-job training.

For over a decade, John Knox has served as a government's top administrator. As Mayor of Missouri City, John has helped prepare and manage eleven city budgets. With his guidance, Missouri City has experienced a decade of planned growth, economic development, and enhanced quality of life.

One of John's greatest assets is his ability to bring people together and get things done. Whether as Mayor of Missouri City or as a director of the Greater Fort Bend Economic Development Council, John has demonstrated quiet, mature leadership.

Now, John needs your support in his bid to become your County Judge. After more than a decade as a top government administrator, John Knox has proven he's the right man for the business of the county.

- Mayor of Missouri City since 1979.

- Established public safety as a community priority: Missouri City has one of the fastest police response times in the state.

- President of the Fort Bend Industrial Development Corporation.

- Secured funding for Gessner Road extension and widening and improvement of FM 2234, FM 1092, and Cartwright Road.

- Acquired and developed over 200 acres of Missouri City park land.

- Served on steering committee supporting successful Fort Bend library bond election.

- Director of Fort Bend Economic Development Council.

- Twenty-eight years of management and technical experience with major oil company.

- Active member of the Fort Bend Republican Party since 1976.

- Co-founder and original director of the Fort Bend Republican Men's Club.

In "walking the neighborhoods," teams of campaign workers and the candidate and his wife canvassed as many neighborhoods as possible. If the team called on a residence where no one was home, it left a "push card" with Cordes's picture and background information. These cards had a short handwritten message printed in blue ink on the backside: "Sorry I missed you! If you have any questions, please call me at 491–2588."

As the underdog, Cordes attempted to attend as many public functions throughout the county as possible during the fall. If appropriate, Cordes delivered a brief speech tailored to the audience. Cordes's strategy of attending and speaking to even small gatherings *throughout* the county differed from that of his opponent. Knox concentrated on Republican strongholds and events held in his hometown of Missouri City.

A third means of contacting voters by the Cordes campaign was via telephone. Although the Cordes campaign phone bank of volunteer workers had fallen short of its original objectives, this means of direct contact with voters was considered crucial. Knox, on the other hand, benefited from a large

TABLE 3-3-2   1988 General Election Results

	County Total[1]	Missouri City/ Stafford	Sugarland	Richmond/ Rosenberg	Arcola/Beasley/ Needville
# of Registered Voters	90,079	25,004	23,660	16,255	2,914
Percent of county	100%	28%	26%	18%	3%
Total Turnout	71%[2]	73%	77%	64%	69%
President and Vice President					
Bush & Quayle (R)	62%	51%[3]	73%[4]	58%[5]	62%[6]
Dukakis & Bentsen (D)	37	49	27	42	38
U.S. Senator					
Beau Boulter (R)	43%	34%	48%	35%	39%
Lloyd Bentsen (D)	57	66	52	65	61
U.S. Rep. District 22					
Tom DeLay (R)	68%	57%	79%	64%	66%
Wayne Walker (D)	31	43	21	36	34
County Tax Collector					
Marsha Gaines (R)	64%	53%	75%	58%	60%
Mark Miller (D)	36	47	25	42	40
Straight-Party Vote					
Republican	12,374	2,089	3,811	892	201
Democrat	12,975	3,888	1,781	1,670	354

[1]There were 66 precincts in Fort Bend County.
[2]52,445 voted at the polls on election day; 10,205 voted absentee in person and 1,604 by mail.
[3]Nine of 18 precincts voted for Bush with a range from 5 percent to 80 percent.
[4]Eleven of 12 precincts voted for Bush with a range from 40 percent to 88 percent.
[5]Six of 9 precincts voted for Bush with a range from 16 percent to 80 percent.
[6]Three of 3 precincts voted for Bush with a range from 59 percent to 73 percent.
Source: Fort Bend County courthouse records.

and effective telephone operation actively supported by the Republican Party's aggressive Fort Bend County organization.

A fourth effective means of stimulating support for Cordes had been small parties held in supporters' homes. The hosts of the party would invite neighbors and friends to meet Cordes in their home. Parties had ranged in size from 3 to 50. These informal meetings had worked well, and many of the people who attended became active in working for the Cordes campaign.

Finally, direct mail advertising had been used effectively. The piece presented in Exhibit 3-3-3 had been mailed to every address in the county in early October. In addition, several promotional pieces addressing the concerns of specific neighborhoods had been mailed to targeted groups within the county. In this area, Knox's better-funded campaign dominated. His collateral materials and mailings had both been more extensive than those of Cordes. Further, the reproduction quality of Knox's mail pieces was superior to that of

Cordes's. Exhibit 3-3-5 presents an inside panel from an elaborate, multifold mailer printed on heavy stock.

Due to the limited funds available, little media advertising had been run during the race. In addition, efficient media coverage of Fort Bend County was difficult. While Houston newspapers and television stations reached a substantial portion of all voters in the county, using these vehicles resulted in massive waste coverage and costs were high. On the other hand, local community media such as the Rosenberg *Herald-Coaster* provided limited coverage of only a portion of all voters in the county. The open per-column-inch rate for the *Herald-Coaster* (circulation 7,000) was $6.74.

Table 3-3-3 presents expenditures made by the Cordes campaign during the period July 1 through mid-October. To cover these expenditures, the campaign received cash contributions totaling $16,079 during this period. These contributions broke down as follows: a number of contributions of less than $50, totaling $859; seven contributions of $50; fourteen contributions of $100; two contributions of $150; five contributions of $200; eight contributions of $500; five $1,000 contributions; and one $1,500 contribution. In addition, the campaign had received $870 in cash contributions in seven other amounts. Further, Cordes had loaned the campaign $19,776, and the campaign had received $3,896 in "in-kind" contributions.

In budgeting for the final three weeks of the campaign, it was anticipated that some additional contributions would be received, and Cordes was prepared to make an additional loan to the campaign of $5,000 maximum.

TABLE 3-3-3   Cordes Compaign Expenditures, July 1 through Mid-October

Expense Category	Amount
Postage	$11,000
Kwik Copy printing	7,471
Signs and banners	3,331
Mailing list company	2,419
Newspaper advertising	
Ford Bend Mirror	1,510
Gulf Coast Tribune	126
Herald Coaster	192
Southwest Star	1,136
The Advocate	696
Campaign manager	2,000
Reception expenses	1,414
Photography	876
Misc. advertising (football programs)	845
Telephone	838
Electricity	345
Miscellaneous	1,420
Total	$35,619

However, competition for funds from the Knox campaign meant funds were limited.

A RESEARCH STUDY

Methodology

To set the stage for planning Cordes's marketing communication efforts during the final three weeks of the campaign, a research consultant was retained to conduct a survey of voter preferences. Due to cost constraints, campaign volunteers who received a crash course in telephone interviewing were used to collect the data. The consultant agreed to supervise the project pro bono, and the study was conducted for less than $300.

Based on 1988 voter registration records, four areas containing 75 percent of all voters in the county were identified for inclusion in the study sample. The three major urban areas in the county—Missouri City/Stafford, Sugarland, and Richmond/Rosenberg—were included, plus a combination of three outlying rural precincts (Arcola/Beasley/Needville). The latter area was included to provide some data on how the more rural areas of the county might vote. A systematic, random sample of telephone households was drawn using a combination of the most recent telephone and city directories.

A brief structured questionnaire was developed to gather the desired information. Using a bank of telephones at the Cordes campaign headquarters, the volunteers conducted interviews with respondents who reported that they were registered voters and residents of Fort Bend County. All interviews were conducted between 6:00 and 10:00 P.M., and a total of 349 interviews was completed during one week in early October.

Findings

The results of the study are presented along with the questionnaire in Appendix 3-3. In addition, a cross-tabulation of the four sample areas by relevant variables is presented in Table 3-3-4.

What Next?

In light of their extremely limited budget and the findings of the survey, John Whitmore (the Cordes campaign manager), Roy Cordes, his wife Helen, and other campaign workers wondered what would be their most productive strategy during the last three weeks of the campaign. Despite the findings, which clearly indicated that Cordes trailed Knox by a substantial margin, two factors offered some hope. These two factors were the large group of undecided voters and the faltering campaign of Clayton Williams, the high-profile Republican candidate for governor. However, it was clearly time to play catch-up in the face of extremely tight time and money constraints.

TABLE 3-3-4   Voter Preference for County Judge by Selected Variables

	Likely to Vote for:			
	Knox	Cordes	Other	Don't Know
Governor's Race Preference				
Clayton Williams	55%	13%	3%	29%
Ann Richards	20	46	4	30
Other	29	18	11	42
Don't Know	18	16	4	62
Political Party Affiliation				
Democrat	10%	49%	6%	35%
Republican	57	11	2	30
Independent	34	19	6	41
None	8	8	0	84
Age				
18–24	46%	15%	5%	34%
25–34	29	19	6	46
35–49	37	24	4	35
50–64	42	27	1	30
65+	32	16	2	50
Gender				
Female	33%	22%	5%	40%
Male	42	21	3	34
Geographic Location				
Missouri City/Stafford	42%	15%	8%	35%
Sugarland	35	27	1	37
Richmond/Rosenberg	34	21	4	41
Arcola/Beasley/Needville	28	25	4	43

Source: Fort Bend County Political Attitudes Survey, Metropolitan Research Services, October 1990.

Questions for Discussion and Review

1. How does the development of a communication mix for a political candidate differ from that for a consumer product? A consumer service?

2. How can the data on past elections be most productively used by the Cordes campaign? How can the data from the survey be most appropriately applied?

3. In terms of their impact on the outcome of the county judge race in Fort Bend County, how important are the national and high-profile state-wide races?

4. What factors play the most important role in determining which communication tools and activities should be emphasized in Cordes's communication mix?

5. What potentially effective tactics should nevertheless be avoided in a political campaign, based on ethical considerations?

6. Should political advertising be banned? Why do authorities such as David Ogilvy (in his book *Ogilvy on Advertising*) and John O'Toole (in his book *Keeping the Deal*) argue against such advertising?

Appendix 3-3
Metropolitan Research Services—Fort Bend County Political Survey, 10/90

TELEPHONE # _____ QUESTIONNAIRE # _____

GEOGRAPHIC AREA: _____   INTERVIEWER ID _____

NOTE DAY & TIME OF CONTACT: _____ 2ND CONTACT _____ 3RD _____

Hello, my name is _____, and I am with M.R.S., a public opinion survey company. We're interested in finding out what Fort Bend County residents think about the upcoming general election. I am *not* selling anything or asking you to vote for anyone, we'd just like about 2 minutes to ask you a few questions.

1. First, are you a resident of Fort Bend County? IF YES, CONTINUE . . .

2. Are you registered to vote in the upcoming general election to be held November 6th?   YES.....................1   CONTINUE   NO.....................2

   IF NO, ASK: May I speak to someone in your household who is registered to vote?

   IF THE VOTER IS UNAVAILABLE, TRY TO ARRANGE A CALLBACK TIME.

3. How likely would you say you are to vote in the upcoming general election to be held on November 6? Would you say that you are very likely, likely, *un*likely or very *un*likely to vote in the upcoming general election?

1 =	67%
2 =	25
3 =	3
4 =	2
5 =	3

VERY LIKELY.....1 LIKELY.....2 *UN*LIKELY.....3 VERY *UN*LIKELY.....4
UNSURE.....5

4. If the election were held tomorrow, who would you vote for in the governor's race? Would you vote for Republican candidate Clayton Williams, Democratic candidate Ann Richards or for some other candidate?

1 =	44%
2 =	23
3 =	11
4 =	22

CLAYTON WILLIAMS................1 ANN RICHARDS................2 OTHER................3
DON'T KNOW, UNSURE................4

5. What about the Lieutenant Governor's race? If the election were held tomorrow, who would you vote for in the

1 =	28%
2 =	41

Lieutenant Governor's race, Democratic candidate Bob   3 = 4
Bullock, Republican candidate Rob Mosbacher or some   4 = 27
other candidate?

BOB BULLOCK...................1 ROB MOSBACHER..................2 OTHER..................3
DON'T KNOW, UNSURE...................4

6. What about the Ford Bend County Judge's race? If the   1 = 36%
election were held tomorrow, who would you vote for in   2 = 22
the Fort Bend County Judge's race, Republican candidate   3 = 4
John Knox, Democratic candidate Roy Cordes, Jr., or some   4 = 38
other candidate?

JOHN KNOX.....................1 ROY CORDES, JR.....................2 OTHER...................3
DON'T KNOW, UNSURE.....................4

7. Did you happen to vote this past spring in a 1990 primary   1 = 58%
election?   2 = 40
                                                                  3 = 2
    YES.....1   NO.....2   DON'T KNOW, UNSURE.....3

8. Did you happen to vote in the 1988 presidential election?   1 = 95%
                                                                  2 = 5
    YES.....1   NO.....2   DON'T KNOW, UNSURE.....3

9. Do you consider yourself a Democrat, a Republican, or an   1 = 22%
independent?   2 = 39
                                                                  3 = 33
    DEMOCRAT.......1 REPUBLICAN.......2 INDEPENDENT.......3   4 = 4
    UNSURE.......4 REFUSED.......5   5 = 2

Now all I need is a little more information on your household to help classify
this questionnaire.

10. Including yourself, how many registered voters now live in   1 = 17%
your household?   2 = 71
                                                                   3 = 12

        1   2   3   4   5   6   7   8 OR MORE

11. Will you tell me into which age group *you* fall? Are you   1 = 4%
between . . . ?   2 = 21
                                                                   3 = 43
    18–24...............1   35–49...............3   65 or older.......5   4 = 18
    25–34...............2   50–64...............4   REFUSED...........6   5 = 13
                                                                   6 = 1

12. What was the last grade of school *you* completed? (DO NOT   1 = 15%
READ LIST.)   2 = 4
                                                                   3 = 25
GRADUATE DEGREE.............................1 HIGH SCHOOL GRAD...6   4 = 21
SOME GRAD STUDY.............................2 SOME HIGH SCHOOL...7   5 = 2
COLLEGE GRAD (4 YEARS)...............3 8TH GRADE OR LESS....8   6 = 24

SOME COLLEGE...4 NO SCHOOLING.............9   7 = 5
VOCATIONAL OR TECH SCHOOL....5 REFUSED.............................0   8 = 4

May I have your name please, in case
my office wants to check my work?   NAME:_____

1 = 63%
2 = 37

Thank you very much!   INTERVIEWER NOTE: FEMALE...1   MALE...2

VERIFICATION: BY: _____   DATE: _____

C A S E   **3 - 4**

National Wildflower Research Center

INTRODUCTION

The National Wildflower Research Center, a nonprofit organization dedicated to the conservation, propagation, and use of wildflowers, native grasses, shrubs, and trees in this country's wild and planned landscapes, was facing the beginning of its tenth year of existence. At a retreat, the staff pondered some of the accomplishments of the past and challenges of the future.

Louise Wilkinson, the director of marketing, was particularly worried about the future of the marketing campaign for the Center. In her mind, the Center had not reached the hoped-for level of awareness among the general public. Also, she felt that most people misunderstood its functions and mission. During the retreat, she brought up that point several times.

At the end of the retreat, the director and management staff of the Center concluded that it would be of paramount importance to consider renaming the Center and developing an easily recognized logo. It was felt that the name "National Wildflower Research Center" was too long and too hard to memorize and so did not bring recognition to the nonprofit organization. The following is an analysis of the events and circumstances that prompted that decision.

This case was written by Isabella C. M. Cunningham, The University of Texas at Austin, and is intended to serve as the basis for classroom discussion, not to illustrate the effective or ineffective handling of an administrative situation. Used by permission of the National Wildflower Research Center.

Wilkinson was asked to submit a marketing and advertising program for the Center for the next five years. After being approved by the executive committee, this plan would be submitted to the board for its approval.

DESCRIPTION OF THE CENTER

The National Wildflower Research Center was founded in 1978 by Lady Bird Johnson, who endowed it with a gift of land and money to support its operation. Johnson was dedicated to increasing Americans' awareness of the beauty and value of native flowers, grasses, shrubs, and trees. She felt that they not only contributed to the beauty of the landscape but also were very important factors in the ecological conservation of our country. The goal and objectives of the Center, as well as its statement of mission, are shown in Appendix 3-4A.

Research

The Center started with a staff of three people in 1978 and developed quickly into a unique and successful nonprofit organization. Its most important function was research. The Center had as its goal the increased use of wildflowers and native plants in planned landscapes, and, as such, it needed to experiment with different native plants in different climatic and environmental conditions. For that purpose, the Center had an on-site laboratory and greenhouse, as well as a facility that allowed field planting of different kinds of regional mixes of wildflowers and plants. The Center wanted to eventually develop research projects throughout the country to obtain parallel information on wildflowers and native plants for each region. The overall purpose of the Center was to publicize the importance and potential of native wildflowers, shrubs, and grasses for year-round cover and control of soil erosion and as minimum maintenance choices for highway right-of-ways, parklands, and public places. The Center had been very successful in its research. It had developed several papers and information leaflets, published several articles, and informed its members and interested others about these developments as they were accomplished.

Membership

Another goal of the National Wildflower Research Center was to establish a constituency of members. The purpose of the membership program was to serve and educate the members and establish grass-roots support for the Center's activities.

Membership was obtained by dues of $25 or more. The dues allowed members to receive direct mailings and publications of the National Wildflower Research Center, specific on-site programs on education, and access to the library of the Center. The members contributed dues ranging from the minimum of $25 to over $1,000 per person. The Center counted over 15,000 members. The members were recruited through direct mail campaigns as well as personal solicitation, speaking engagements, publicity, and local and national publications. The membership of the National Wildflower Research Center was largest in, but not limited to, Texas. It is important to notice that the membership renewal rate was not as high as expected. The renewal rate after ten years of existence was about 50 percent. This implied that a yearly effort had to be made to identify potential new members and solicit their contributions and support for the Center. This was a cumbersome and expensive procedure. Wilkinson hoped that membership turnover would not be so great once a new marketing program had been established. In addition, she hoped to more than triple membership over the next five years.

Publications

The Center maintained several publications, some available to all members and some available by request for additional payment. One of its publications was the members' newsletter, the *Wildflower,* which kept members informed of current wildflower research, published practical information for gardening, listed the dates of conferences across the nation, and described the Center's social activities. In addition, the *Wildflower Journal* was published. This journal was written by professionals in fields ranging from landscape architecture to horticulture and botany but directed to a lay audience. In addition to these two publications, Wildflower Center personnel had written several articles for national magazines and assisted with the publication of several wildflower books sold by different publishers across the nation.

The Center had plans for increasing the number of its publications and was particularly interested in publishing a wildflower sourcebook, a seedling identification book, and other educational materials. The lack of resources was delaying these particular projects.

Education

One of the most important tasks of the Center was to provide educational programs and materials to people of all ages and income levels. The Center sponsored major conferences and held on-site programs and workshops for children, teachers, and the general public. Additionally, guided tours of the Center facility were given every spring to large numbers of visitors.

Along with its ongoing educational programs, Center management wanted to produce materials that could reach audiences throughout the nation. One such educational product would be a children's videotape on wildflowers to be used in classrooms. Center management also wanted to provide other educational materials for both schools and adult groups.

The educational activities of the Center also included the management and development of a Speakers' Bureau. The Speakers' Bureau was made up primarily of volunteers who were provided with videotapes and other materials by the Center whenever possible. This particular activity left a lot of room for improvement.

Clearinghouse and Library

The final function of the Center was to establish an on-site clearinghouse and a complete reference library to answer inquiries from people all over the nation. The clearinghouse would serve as a nationwide network for people requesting information about native plants. The number of inquiries to the clearinghouse had been growing annually, with a current average of 20,000 per year. To answer such inquiries, the Center was responsible for maintaining a data base, a slide library, a reference library, and several fact sheets to be distributed to interested callers. The library's size and content clearly depended on the Center's ability to attract gifts or special funds.

BUDGET AND FUNDING

The National Wildflower Research Center's basic budget can be seen in Appendix 3-4B. The Center had been controlling its expenditures in order to function within the restrictions of the monetary gifts it had received. As the Center expanded its services beyond the state of Texas, more staffing and capital investments were needed, and the Center was now facing the prospect of raising additional funds to support these expenses.

The Center was funded in several ways. First, the endowment of the Center, which had started with the gift from Lady Bird Johnson, had to be continually increased by major gifts from other individuals. To develop the endowment program, a subcommittee of the members of the board of the Center had developed the Founders' Fund, which was designed to appeal to donors who might be interested in giving monies for restricted endowment purposes. The total endowment of the Center was in excess of $3 million, but this amount was only sufficient to manage its present activities. Additional endowments were needed if the Center were to expand its scope. In addition to the endowment, the Center engaged in several other fund-raising activities.

Annual Giving

The annual giving program involved soliciting money from trustees and special friends, and it had been growing steadily each year.

Special Events

Another program for raising monies was the development of special fund-raising events. Some examples of these events were "An Afternoon In the Country," held in Washington, D.C., "Hearts and Wildflowers Victoriana," held in Galveston, Texas, and the "Garden Tour of England." Special committees were in charge of these events, and the money they raised was added to the operating income of the Center.

Special Mail Appeals

Special mail appeals were made to members, potential members, and selected donors for particular purposes. Such appeals were made when additional land was needed for experimental planting or to support field researchers and interns.

Memorial Program and Other Fund-Raising

Other fund-raising programs were the memorial program, initiated to encourage support through remembrance of special friends and loved ones, and the solicitation of foundations for funds for library materials, greenhouses, and other capital projects. In addition, the income from memberships represented about 10 percent of the annual budget of the Center, and it was hoped that the membership would start representing an increasing percentage of the annual budget. Corporate and business prospects were asked for in-kind gifts as well as other kinds of donations, and the Center was also engaged in selling products such as notecards, aprons, T-shirts, sweatshirts, tote bags, and so on. The proceeds from such sales accrued to the operating income of the Center. Last but not least, the Center had entered a number of licensing and royalty agreements with publishers of books and developers of products such as wallpapers and botanical sculptures.

The imagination of the development staff was the only limitation to the type and number of projects in which the Center became involved. Although every project added to the overall operating income of the Center, it is important to underline that Wilkinson worried about how diverse and fragmented the development program was. She felt that a more standardized development program, perhaps with fewer publication materials used for solicitation, would be more effective. She stressed in her report that each mailing developed for a specific program differed slightly, using different logos or names for the Center, as well as different packaging designs and colors. She felt that the diverse appearance of the materials used by the Center could only confuse the public as to what the Center was and what its purpose was.

THE PROBLEM

Although the National Wildflower Research Center was a unique organization, Wilkinson pointed out in her report that more than 150 environmental organizations throughout the United States competed with the Center for memberships and donations. Many conservation organizations felt that they had similar missions and should join together in one major group. The Center's executive committee did not feel this was a good idea. It was probably true that once a person became a member of one environmental organization, he or she might feel that it was not necessary to join another similar organization. Among the competing organizations were groups like Greenpeace, the Sierra

Club, and the Audubon Society, all active for many years longer than the National Wildflower Research Center. All of those organizations had national recognition and a national membership. In addition, local and national garden clubs and beautification societies had the advantages of being closer to their members throughout the United States than the Center and providing them with a sense of local civic pride.

Membership was probably the most stable source of income for the Center. According to the latest membership survey, the average member of the Center was about 60 years old with an average household income of more than $65,000 per year. Most members were well educated, and 41 percent had some type of post-college education. They were concerned about environmental protection and the maintenance of our country's natural beauty. Those were the primary reasons indicated by the members for joining the National Wildflower Research Center. Yet research showed that national awareness of the Center was extremely low. Wilkinson attributed that low awareness to the fact that the Center had done very little, if any, advertising. The name of the Center and its logo were not easily recognized and were not memorable.

When asked what benefits the members felt were important, 60 percent mentioned the clearinghouse fact sheet, 45 percent mentioned the membership newsletter, and 43 percent mentioned the journals. Gift benefits, gift items, and travel opportunities were rated as the least important reasons for joining. Free wildflower information from the clearinghouse and the support of environmental causes were the most important factors for remaining members of the Center. However, only 28 percent of the members of the Center had requested copies of the fact sheets published through the clearinghouse. This may seem surprising, until one realizes that about 73 percent of the members mentioned they did not know such a service was available to them.

The members stated they were interested in seminars and would be willing to pay to attend them. Most of the members (82 percent) had never visited the Center, but many believed that wildflower trips and other local activities were good ideas.

To the members, the most important activities of the Center were research on wildflowers and native plants (93 percent) and the cooperative research with universities and botanical gardens nationwide (80 percent). Dissemination of research knowledge gained was also important to those polled. Members felt that research should be disseminated through articles in national publications and through Center publications.

Of the members who responded to the survey, 41 percent belonged to other conservation or gardening organizations. Thirty-seven percent belonged to the Nature Conservancy and 22 percent to the World Wildlife Fund. However, only 25 percent belonged to a garden club or a civic beautification organization.

Among other results, the respondents mentioned their most popular leisure activities: driving through areas of natural beauty (82 percent), active gardening (74 percent), and reading about gardening (61 percent). The general age group of the respondents was 45 and older, and 73 percent were female. Twenty-one percent of respondents were aged 45 to 54, 25 percent were 55 to 64, and 23 percent were 65 or older. The average annual income of the respondents was over $65,000, and their occupations included professional manager (27 percent), homemaker (25 percent), and various others. The average respondent owned a house (87 percent), lived in the suburbs (37 percent), and had no children under the age of 18 (83 percent).

The National Wildflower Research Center felt it was not competing successfully with conservation organizations or other nonprofit organizations. As an example, the Nature Conservancy received nearly $170 million per year, the Sierra Club $40 million, and the National Audubon Society about $35 million per year, while the Center's income was not nearly in that range.

Wilkinson listed the main challenges that she felt should be addressed by the new marketing program. First, she felt it was important to realize that the name "National Wildflower Research Center" was too long and complicated to recall. In addition, the name was not indicative of the true function of the Center, which included education, repair, and restoration, as well as research. Further, wildflowers were not the only emphasis of the Center; the Center was interested in studying all native plants. Even though the name contained the word "national," it was often perceived as a Texas organization because of its location and its relationship with Lady Bird Johnson.

In addition to the problems with the name, Wilkinson pointed out that the Center had a history of inconsistency regarding its logo. She felt it was absolutely necessary to the marketing program to develop a logo that could be used in all publications to increase recall and awareness of the Center. Last but not least, Wilkinson was worried about the multiplicity of programs, mailings, and other development activities of the Center. She felt the Center should concentrate its efforts on some basic activities and then perhaps add one or two special programs per year. Membership was, in her mind, the most important fund-raising activity of the Center; however, she was concerned about the demographic characteristics of the present membership. She felt that if the organization were to become national in scope, it must acquire a more diversified membership by reaching out to more men and people of different income and education levels.

To solicit bids and proposals from private advertising agencies, Wilkinson developed a call for a proposal to design an overall campaign for the National Wildflower Research Center that would meet the following goals:

1. To develop a new name and logo that meet the desired criteria stated in the mission and purpose of the Center and that would be easily remembered and recognized by members and potential members.

2. To increase awareness of the Center from 1 percent to about 8 to 10 percent of the total population polled.

3. To broaden the membership base and the overall income it represented.

4. To increase awareness of the organization among foundations and corporations in order to generate grants and major gifts as well as endorsements from major organizations.

5. To standardize the promotional material so as to increase memorability and recognition for the Center.

6. To develop an overall marketing program for the next five years that would include a budget of approximately $500,000 per year, to be increased by the fifth year to about $1 million per year. Publicity, press releases, and other promotional activities would not be included in that overall budget.

Questions for Discussion and Review

1. What should be the major strategic goals of the National Wildflower Research Center's five-year advertising and marketing campaign?

2. Do you agree with the goals for the national advertising and marketing campaign as stated by Wilkinson? Why or why not?

3. What target market should the National Wildflower Research Center consider to increase its: a) national membership, b) annual giving, and c) endowment fund? If these three target markets are not the same, please explain the differences among them and why they differ.

4. What kind of an advertising and promotional campaign can you develop for the National Wildflower Research Center within a budget of $500,000 a year?

5. If you feel Wilkinson is correct in stating the National Wildflower Research Center's name and logo are major obstacles to its achieving a higher level of recall and recognition, suggest an alternative name and a possible logo for the Center.

6. Provide an overall outline for the National Wildflower Research Center's marketing and advertising campaign for the next five years.

Appendix 3-4A
National Wildflower Research Center Goals

Introduction

The purposes of the National Wildflower Research Center, established in December 1982, are as follows:

- To stimulate, underwrite, and research the propagation, cultivation, conservation, and preservation of wildflowers and native grasses, shrubs, and trees in cooperation with universities, botanic gardens, arboreta, other research institutions, and private industry throughout the United States;

- To provide a site for studies, lectures, seminars, and other endeavors relating to wildflowers, including other wild flora;

- To serve as a clearinghouse for research and educational programs throughout the United States and to establish a library to serve these needs more effectively;

- To assemble and disseminate information that will encourage the cultivation, conservation, and preservation of wildflowers throughout the United States;

- To analyze alternative landscaping options which would allow improvements in water conservation, labor costs, and maintenance costs by using wildflowers and native landscapes;
- To encourage botanical research of wildflowers for pharmacological, industrial, forage, and food uses.

Within the framework of its charter, the Center's trustees, officers, and staff are committed to the foregoing purposes and declare the following goals for the National Wildflower Research Center:

Research

- *Advisory council:* To establish an advisory council of scientific personnel to advise on research and related matters.
- *Industry outreach:* To collaborate with landscape architects, urban planners, land managers, and other organizations that share our interests.
- *Facilities development:* To develop facilities such as laboratories, greenhouses, and study plots in order to accelerate the research program.
- *Regional research programs:* To generate plans for the development of regional research in various parts of the United States, including the Northeast, Midwest, Northwest, West, Southwest, and Southeast. These programs will be initiated with universities, botanic gardens, arboreta, and other institutions having appropriate facilities and expertise.

Education

- *Library:* To establish a scientific library that will fulfill our needs and enable us to share information with interested groups and individuals.
- *Films and slide shows:* To develop appropriate films and slide shows that will serve to familiarize the public with the Center and function as educational tools.
- *Internships:* To establish internships that will supplement the work of the permanent scientific and educational staff.
- *Exhibits and displays:* To develop exhibits and displays that can be shown at the Center and that are designed to be shared with other institutions throughout the country.
- *Speakers' bureau:* To establish a bureau of trustees and staff to meet requests for speakers from various institutions and other sources.
- *Visitor tours:* To mount a program of visitor tours that will communicate the activities of the Center in various ways.
- *Bus tours:* To sponsor tours to various parts of the country to educate and encourage those interested in wildflowers.
- *Symposia:* To sponsor or cosponsor symposia at the Center and other regions to share information that advances our goals and objectives.

Membership

To develop a national membership program that is substantial—the objective being to fund the educational and related research purposes of the Center.

Newsletter

To publish a newsletter that will communicate the activities of the Center and its purposes.

Management/Administration

- *Budget:* To prepare and keep current a "needs list" of capital equipment items and projects so that budget requirements are presented in an orderly, systematic, and realistic manner.
- *Personnel and staff:* To foster employees' growth and development by increasing their capabilities and opportunities through training, rotating assignments, special duties, and other means, and to plan staffing needs as the scope and activities of the NWRC change.
- *Organization:* To study our staff and organization and make such adjustments as may be necessary to ensure the proper fulfillment of our mission, always remembering our obligation to those who support our purposes and objectives.

Development

To undertake appropriate fund-raising activities to enhance the work of the Center, including special events and grant proposals to appropriate foundations and funding entities.

Founders' Fund

To build an endowment, the proceeds of which will be used to fund the activities of the Center.

Merchandising

To engage in the marketing of products that complement the purposes and objectives of the Center, always being mindful that they must be representative of its mission and must be tasteful and appropriate from every point of view. Formation of a for-profit corporation will be considered a mechanism to accomplish this goal.

Public Relations

To develop a public relations and public information program that will communicate the Center's activities, programs, goals, and objectives in a manner that will engender understanding of our mission and purpose.

General

- To seek ways to conserve on energy consumption, including gasoline, electricity, and water, and to promote and encourage others in their conservation, educational, research, and commercial activities, so long as they serve to further the message of the NWRC.

- To seek new ways to further the purposes of the NWRC and to effectively work with others to understand and conserve our natural resources, so long as such endeavors further the message of the NWRC.

Appendix 3-4B
National Wildflower Research Center 1992 Unaudited Balance Sheet

Assets	
Current Assets	
Cash and CDs	$4,356,084.44
Stock	365,305.60
Inventory	103,265.74
Other receivables	3,565.36
Total Current Assets	$4,828,221.14
Fixed Assets	
Land	$1,000,000.00
Equipment	13,100.00
Total Fixed Assets	1,013,100.00
Total Assets	**$5,841,321.14**

Developing Advertising Objectives

As I see it, this is where we stand. We measure the sales effectiveness of ads or commercials on their ability to attract attention and communicate, or on their ability to affect attitudes, or on some combination of these and we hope, and have some evidence to indicate, that we are really measuring the sales effects of the advertising.[1]

**John S. Coulson, Vice-President of Research,
LEO BURNETT COMPANY**

THE CONTEXT AND SCOPE OF ADVERTISING OBJECTIVES

The first step in the advertising and promotion management decision-making process is to conduct a careful situation analysis. This analysis is designed to provide information useful in making decisions about how to most effectively communicate with the firm's market(s). After the situation has been evaluated and some initial decisions made about the most appropriate mix of communication tools, and assuming that advertising is included in that mix, the next step is to establish clear, measurable objectives specifying what advertising is to accomplish.

Advertising objectives are simply statements describing what is to be accomplished by advertising to capitalize on opportunities and/or overcome problems facing the advertiser during the planning period.

---

[1]"Ads Can Change Attitudes, Hike Sales; Effects Measurable," *Marketing News,* February 16, 1976, 5.

Determining appropriate objectives to assign to the firm's advertising efforts is a key part of advertising campaign planning. Objectives set the basic direction for the entire advertising program or campaign. Furthermore, clear, measurable objectives are required for managerial evaluation and control of the firm's advertising efforts. Without measurable objectives established prior to the beginning of an advertising campaign, it is impossible to evaluate whether these efforts succeeded and plan the most effective use of advertising in future periods.

In specifying what advertising is to accomplish, the planner faces perhaps the most intriguing and frustrating characteristic of advertising: its link to sales. Typically, businesspeople invest money in advertising in the belief that stimulating demand for their brand through advertising will create additional sales, and the revenue generated by these added sales will more than cover the cost of the advertising investment. However, in most situations, two major considerations make the use of sales as a criterion for evaluating the success of advertising inappropriate: (1) advertising is only one of many factors that determine whether a sale occurs, and (2) advertising has a carryover, or delayed, effect that extends beyond a calendar or fiscal year.[2]

Only in those product/market situations where these two considerations do *not* apply is it appropriate to use sales as an advertising objective. A sales objective may be appropriately assigned to advertising in direct-response situations—those where immediate action is called for in the ad, the merchandise is sold directly to consumers, and advertising alone plays *the* dominant role in the marketing program. Further, sales objectives apply to some retail advertising that focuses on promoting a limited-time sale or special promotional event. Even in these situations, however, it may be more logical to evaluate advertising based on the number of inquiries received, or the number of prospects who called an 800 number for more information, or a traffic count of the number who attended a sales event.

Therefore, while overall marketing objectives are stated in terms of sales volume and market share, in most situations it is *not* appropriate to assign such objectives to advertising alone. Rather, advertising objectives should be stated in terms of those variables that advertising communication *can* measurably influence, whether or not sales are consummated.

WHAT SHOULD BE INCLUDED IN A STATEMENT OF ADVERTISING OBJECTIVES?

In practice, statements of advertising objectives vary widely. Some advertisers are content with vague objectives such as "to increase awareness of the brand," "to stimulate trial," or "to enhance the brand's image." Unfortunately, such statements handicap efforts to develop effective and efficient advertising and preclude precise evaluation of the firm's advertising efforts. In developing

---

[2]Donald S. Tull, "The Carry-over Effect of Advertising," *Journal of Marketing* (April 1965):46–53.

statements of advertising objectives, spending the time and effort to develop thorough and specific objectives makes the work that follows easier and the advertising more focused and productive.

In his classic work sponsored by the Association of National Advertisers, Colley suggests that an advertising objective should be defined as "a specific communication task, to be accomplished among a defined audience to a given degree in a given time period."[3] Later, Britt expanded Colley's definition by suggesting that four components must be clearly covered in a statement of advertising objectives. These are: (1) what basic message is to be delivered, (2) to what audience, (3) with what intended effect(s), and (4) what specific criteria will be used to measure the success of the campaign. Britt maintained that unless each of these areas is specified in a statement of advertising objectives, it is impossible for an advertiser to know if advertising efforts succeeded or failed.[4]

Britt's four components provide a solid foundation on which to build and evaluate an advertising program. If these four areas are clearly specified, the direction of the firm's advertising efforts can be communicated to all the individuals who will be involved in their development, and sound evaluation of their success is possible. Therefore, these areas are a recommended outline of what should be covered in statements of advertising objectives. Note that these decisions should be made in sequential order, beginning with a definition of the target audience. Next, the message should be identified, and then intended effects and measurement criteria should be specified. These four components are described and illustrated in the sections below.

Target Audience

The single most important decision the advertising planner makes is what group(s) of consumers to target with promotional messages. All other advertising decisions follow from this basic decision. Is the budget sufficient? Is the media mix right? Is the creative execution appropriate? All such questions are evaluated considering the target audience's size, perspective, concerns, and so on.

A definition of a target audience begins with a concise statement of key demographics. For example, the following audience was defined for a national chain of day-care centers: female household heads aged 25 to 34 employed outside the home who have one or more children under age 6 at home and who live in the top 50 Areas of Dominant Influence markets.

This target audience definition makes it clear on whom the advertising should be focused by defining the audience in terms of gender, age, employment status, parental status, and geographic location. These factors are

---

[3]Russell H. Colley, *Defining Advertising Goals for Measured Advertising Results* (New York: Association of National Advertisers, 1961), 6.

[4]Steuart H. Britt, "Are So-called Successful Advertising Campaigns Really Successful?" *Journal of Advertising Research*, Vol. 9, 1969, 2:3–9.

important in identifying women who are attractive prospects for the day-care center's services.

Such a target audience definition is useful in focusing the advertising; however, it fails to provide insights into consumers' motivations and how the product or service fits into their lives. Life-style and psychographic profile data attempt to fill this void by painting a more three-dimensional picture of consumers. Based on its research, SRI International suggested a nine-group VALS classification scheme based on consumers' attitudes, needs, and beliefs that has proven useful in segmenting many consumer markets.[5]

Adding such data to a demographic definition of the target audience provides everyone involved in the development of the advertising with a more realistic and useful understanding of how the selling problem may be best attacked. For example, the following VALS and attitude data gathered through primary research add important additional insights to the demographic profile of working mothers referred to earlier.

The target segment of this demographic group aspires to have both a successful career and family. These women are serious about their child-rearing responsibilities and are avid readers of books and articles on the subject. They are primarily Outer-Directed Emulators and Achievers in terms of VALS categories. They are concerned about where and with whom they leave their children. Their child's "experience" is of crucial importance, while cost of the service is an important, but secondary, concern.

Message Content

The second component of a statement of an advertising objective is a clear description of the competitive benefit to be focused on in the advertising. The message statement presents a concise statement of the key benefit the advertiser promises the consumer if he or she will buy the brand.

A consumer benefit is based on product features. The message component should specify how using the brand will benefit the target consumer. For example, a large rear seat is a feature of an automobile; the benefit is that the automobile can seat five adults comfortably.

A solid example of a concise statement of the message component is provided by J. Walter Thompson's successful "Sword" campaign for the Marines. Thompson's primary target audience for this advertising was male high school seniors or graduates of good character, ages 17 to 21, who were uncertain about their future. The message of the award-winning "Sword" campaign was captured in 16 words, "The Marine Corps offers a respected career for a young person about to finish high school."[6]

In describing DDB Needham's approach to developing effective advertising strategy, Wells suggests that the special meaning of the consumer benefit

---

[5]James Atlas, "Beyond Demographics," *Atlantic Monthly,* October 1984, 49–58.
[6]W. Keith Hafer and Gordon E. White, *Advertising Writing—Putting Creative Strategy to Work* (New York: West Publishing, 1989), 42, 47–48.

can be appreciated by filling in the blanks in the following statement: "When I _____, I will _____."[7] In this sentence, a typical member of the target audience is the "I," the first blank describes the purpose of the advertising—what the advertiser wants the consumer to do—and the second, the benefit. Wells provides the following examples:

- "When I take Amtrak instead of the plane from New York to Washington (purpose), I will be more comfortable, better treated, and more valued (benefit)."

- "When I buy insurance from State Farm instead of from some other insurance company (purpose), I will know that a friendly State Farm agent will be at my side if I need help (benefit)."

- "When I invest in a holiday in Mooréa instead of some other destination (purpose), I will bring romance back into my life (benefit)."

Effects

This component of a statement of advertising objectives specifies what the advertising is to accomplish—the end result or change stimulated by the target audience being exposed to the advertising message.

As pointed out in the opening section of this chapter, in most situations sales is not an appropriate effect to assign to advertising. In arguing against the use of increased sales as an advertising objective, Colley stressed that advertising should be regarded as a communication force and so assigned only communication tasks.[8] Broadly, advertising as a communication force can affect three variables: awareness, knowledge, and attitudes.

The relationship between advertising as a communication force and awareness, knowledge, and attitudes, plus their link to sales, is outlined in Lavidge and Steiner's hierarchy-of-effects model of the consumer decision-making process. These authors suggest that a consumer typically proceeds through a standard set of information-processing and reasoning steps or stages in moving from being unaware of a brand's existence to purchasing the brand. These sequential stages are: (1) awareness, (2) knowledge, (3) liking, (4) preference, (5) conviction, and (6) action.[9]

Briefly, the first step in moving toward a purchase is "awareness"—the consumer is made or becomes aware of the existence of the brand. The second stage is "knowledge"—the consumer learns something about what the brand has to offer. The next three stages—"liking," "preference," and "conviction"—represent the attitude field of the model. Liking represents the assignment of a favorable predisposition to the brand on one or more

---

[7]William D. Wells, *Planning for R.O.I.: Effective Advertising Strategy* (Englewood Cliffs, N.J.: Prentice-Hall, 1989), 12.

[8]Colley, *Defining Advertising Goals,* 10–12.

[9]Robert J. Lavidge and Gary A. Steiner, "A Model for Predictive Measurement of Advertising Effectiveness," *Journal of Marketing* (October 1961):59–62.

dimensions. In the preference stage, the consumer's favorable predisposition has developed to the point of preference over other brands in the category. Conviction signals that preference has been coupled with a desire to buy, plus the belief that the purchase would be wise. This final attitude stage of conviction then stimulates the behavioral step in the process—purchase.[10]

Although more elegant models of this process have been suggested, most are patterned on Lavidge and Steiner's steps. Further, because of its commonsense qualities, Lavidge and Steiner's model provides the basis for most marketing managers' view of the purchase decision-making process.[11] For these reasons, the Lavidge and Steiner model provides a sound basis for establishing measurable advertising objectives.[12]

In most situations, the marketer's objective in using advertising is to facilitate the movement of target consumers up the hierarchy, which will ultimately lead to purchases of the desired brand. That is, the marketer aims to move consumers from unawareness to awareness, to convey information about the brand and its performance (knowledge), and to favorably affect the consumers' attitudes regarding the brand. Hence, the general intended effects of advertising are to *increase* the target audience's levels of awareness, knowledge, and favorable attitudes toward the brand. For example, the intended effects of advertising for a hypothetical product called Zippies could be stated in the following form:

- To increase unaided awareness of Zippies from 20 percent to 30 percent (awareness).

- To increase the percentage of the target audience who believe that Zippies contain "the lowest levels of fat" of any brand in the category from 0 percent to 10 percent (knowledge).

- To increase the percentage of the target audience who strongly agree with the statement, "Zippies are environmentally safe" from 15 percent to 30 percent (attitude).

Specific intended effects are required for measurable objectives. The strategist must clearly specify how much of an increase is planned—note that this requires establishing a pre-advertising, or benchmark, level against which the post-advertising level will be compared. "To increase unaided awareness among the target audience" is vague; "To increase unaided awareness from 10 percent to 15 percent of the target audience" is specific. In the second objective, 10 percent is the pre-advertising level of unaided awareness among target consumers, and 15 percent is the post-advertising level. Also, note that while the intended effect represents an absolute increase of only 5 percent of the target audience, it represents a 50 percent increase in the pre-advertising level of unaided awareness ($15 - 10 = 5$; $5 \div 10 = 50\%$).

---

[10]*Ibid.*, 60.

[11]Richard Vaughn, "The Consumer Mind: How to Tailor Ad Strategies," *Advertising Age,* June 9, 1980, 45–46.

[12]Don E. Schultz, *Strategic Advertising Campaigns* (Lincolnwood, Ill.: NTC Business Books, 1990), 226.

Determining how large an increase to specify as an intended effect involves considerable uncertainty. This task is made easier when benchmark data are available for more than one year. For example, the results of a research survey on top-of-mind awareness of hospitals among adults in Austin, Texas, are presented below. With three years' data and experience, the planner for St. David's Hospital is in a much better position to factor in likely changes in competitors' budgets, creative executions, market growth, and so on when developing a realistic and aggressive targeted increase in "first mention" awareness for the coming year.

"When you think of Austin area hospitals, which ones comes to mind?"

Percentage Identifying Each Hospital "First Mention"

	St. David's	Brackenridge	Seton	Others
Year 1	38%	33%	18%	11%
Year 2	39	26	25	10
Year 3	47	23	29	1
Year 4	?	?	?	?

Measurement

As Britt stressed, sound advertising objectives should specify how the intended effects will be measured after the advertising has appeared.[13] That is, the measurement component must be described (and a research budget set aside) *before* the advertising runs. This ensures the accountability of advertising and, since pre-advertising or benchmark measures are necessary, makes research findings an integral part of planning both present and future advertising efforts.

An outline of the Lavidge and Steiner model, along with examples of the types of measurement appropriate at each stage, is presented in Exhibit 4-1. This exhibit is designed to serve as a practical guide to the data collection techniques that may be used in measuring intended effects.

A wide range of data collection, measurement, and analysis techniques may be utilized in determining if the intended effects were achieved. For example, a pre- and post-campaign survey research project may be conducted using telephone interviews with members of the target audience. A series of open- and closed-ended questions, rating scales, adjective checklists, and multiple-choice questions may be used to gather the necessary data. In addition, Chi-square analysis, T-tests, analysis of variance, and other techniques may be used to determine if differences between the pre-campaign and post-campaign data are statistically significant.

[13]Britt, "Are So-called Successful Advertising Campaigns Really Successful?" *Journal of Advertising Research*, Vol. 9, 1969, 2:3–9.

Hierarchy-of-Effects Model of the Consumer Decision-Making Process (Measurement at Each Stage)

Stage in the Process	Appropriate Measures	Examples of Measurement
(1) Awareness	• Unaided recall	"Thinking about toothpastes, which brands come to mind?"
	• Aided recall	"Have you ever heard of XQB toothpaste?"
(2) Knowledge	• Direct questions	"Which brand of toothpaste has Z-82 added?"
	• Playback	"Which brand of toothpaste claims that 'it was invented by the tooth fairy'?"
(3) Liking	• Ranking	"What are your three favorite brands of toothpaste?"
	• Rating scales	"On a scale of 1 to 5, with 1 = effective and 5 = ineffective, how does XQB rate on 'cleans my breath'?"
(4) Preference	• Likert scales	"Please tell me whether you strongly agree, agree, neither agree nor disagree, disagree, or strongly disagree with the following statement: 'I believe XQB is a pleasant-tasting toothpaste.'"
(5) Conviction	• Semantic differential scales	"Please describe XQB toothpaste using the following adjectives scales: Pleasant to Use ... Unpleasant to Use 1__ 2__ 3__ 4__ 5__ 6__ 7__"
	• Projective techniques	"Tell me about the brands of toothpaste teenagers who just left home to attend a university are likely to use and why. Which brands would they like to use if money were not a factor? Why?"
(6) Purchase	• Self-report	"Which brand(s) of toothpaste have you purchased for yourself or your family in the past four weeks?" "Which brand of toothpaste do you usually use?" "Which brands of toothpaste are presently available in your home?"

ADDITIONAL SUGGESTIONS FOR DEVELOPING STATEMENTS OF ADVERTISING OBJECTIVES

The purpose of this section is to provide some insights into the practicalities and value of developing the type of advertising objectives described in this chapter. The section begins with some basic considerations that apply to most business objectives. It then provides advice for developing useful advertising objectives and discusses the potential value of such objectives.

Advertising objectives, like other promotional objectives, must be consistent with marketing and overall corporate objectives. They must be in writing, and they must be understood and subscribed to by the people involved in the development of the advertising. The objectives should also specify a time frame.

The objectives should be internally consistent. The message should fit the targeted prospects. The areas or dimensions identified in the message section should be covered by the intended effects. The measurement method recommended should be appropriate for generating data to evaluate the success of the advertising.

It is important to recognize that advertising objectives are always based on many assumptions. These include, for example, assumptions about how effective the creative execution will be, the adequacy of the advertising appropriation, the effectiveness of the accompanying media plan, and the actions of competitors. Because some educated guesswork is involved in establishing appropriate increases in the intended effects section, experience is the best teacher.

Further, despite the fact that measurable objectives are set, in the final analysis, judgment and intuition play an important role in evaluating the performance of advertising. For example, a major increased investment, plus innovative creative by a competitor, may mean it is appropriate for a marketer to conclude that a campaign was successful, despite the fact that it did not achieve the specified intended effects.

Adoption of advertising objectives following the guidelines suggested in this chapter can help other members of the firm's management team understand the proper role of advertising within the overall promotional and marketing mixes. Finally, complete objectives, coupled with a realistic appreciation of advertising's role in the marketing mix, protect advertising from becoming a "whipping boy" when sales fall below levels specified in the marketing plan. Too often advertising that effectively delivers its communication message is blamed for other marketing shortcomings.

SAMPLE STATEMENT OF ADVERTISING OBJECTIVES FOR A PROFESSIONAL BASKETBALL TEAM

This section illustrates a complete statement of advertising objectives that covers the four components discussed earlier in the chapter. The data presented in this example have been disguised. The professional basketball franchise city is disguised as Boxworth, and the team as the ThunderBolts.

As part of the situation analysis, a research firm was employed to conduct a study of the sports interests and attitudes of male household heads aged 25 to 64 who resided in five key ZIP codes in the Boxworth market. Management believed these adults were an attractive target audience for its upcoming marketing efforts. One of the purposes of the study was to provide benchmarks against which advertising objectives could be set for the upcoming 19XX season.

A statement of advertising objectives based on the research findings is presented in Exhibit 4-2. Selected data from the study are included in this statement and keyed to the questionnaire. Exhibit 4-3 presents selected portions of the questionnaire used to collect the information used in the advertising objectives statement.

Advertising Objectives: Boxworth ThunderBolts' 19XY–19XX Campaign

Audience. The target audience is male household heads aged 25 to 64 who reside in the five highest-income ZIP codes in the Boxworth SMSA. Many of these men are latent "jocks" who enjoy the vicarious excitement of pro sports. They appreciate the opportunity for camaraderie with other fans, both at the games and in other social encounters. Most are not serious students of the game but enjoy identifying with their team and individual players.

Message. The primary message is that the ThunderBolts players, as individuals, are concerned about the quality of life and general well-being of the local community, and, hence, merit fan support. The secondary message is that the ThunderBolts games provide an excellent sports/entertainment value—fans can relax, forget personal troubles, and enjoy active support of their team.

Effects. The effects of the campaign are to increase and strengthen awareness, knowledge, and favorable attitudes toward the team and toward attending games among members of the target audience. Specifically, the effects *among members of the target audience* are as follows:

- To increase *awareness* of the team's name from 85 percent to 90 percent (see Question 3 of the Boxworth Sports Attitudes Study in Exhibit 4-3).
- To increase correct *knowledge* of the price of single-game tickets from 5 percent to 15 percent (see Question 6a).
- To increase correct *knowledge* of the price of season tickets from 4 percent to 10 percent (see Question 6b).
- To increase the percentage who identify the ThunderBolts as their favorite Boxworth area team from 26 percent to 32 percent (see Question 4) *(attitude change)*.
- To increase the percentage who identify the ThunderBolts as their favorite NBA team from 48 percent to 58 percent (see Question 5) *(attitude change)*.
- To change *attitudes* regarding the ThunderBolts' concern for the local community from an average of 2.25 to 4.0 (see Question 9).
- To change *attitudes* regarding the relative value of ThunderBolts' games from an average of 1.70 to 3.10 (see Question 10).

Measurement. In order to evaluate the campaign's success, pre-campaign data were collected from a random sample of the target audience. Selected portions of the questionnaire appear in Exhibit 4-3. A second set of data will be gathered using the same data collection instrument and a different random sample after the campaign has run. The criteria for success will be achieving the awareness, knowledge, and attitude changes indicated in the "Effects" section above.

Data were collected using telephone interviews with members of the target audience. Two hundred and fifty interviews will be completed in both the pre- and post-campaign phase of the research. A professional research and interviewing service was used to gather and analyze the data.

Boxworth Sports Attitudes Study

ASK TO SPEAK TO THE MALE HEAD OF THE HOUSEHOLD. Hello, my name is _____; I work for Metropolitan Research Services. We're conducting a brief study of the attitudes of men about sports. I'd like to ask you a few questions. I'm not selling anything. First,

1. What is your favorite participation sport?
   _____ Baseball _____ Basketball _____ Tennis _____ Football _____ Golf _____ Bowling
   _____ Swimming _____ Running _____ Other: _____

2. What is your favorite spectator sport?
   _____ Baseball _____ Basketball _____ Tennis _____ Football _____ Golf _____ Bowling
   _____ Swimming _____ Running _____ Other: _____

3. What is the name of Boxworth's National Basketball Association team? _____

4. What is your favorite sports team in the Boxworth area?
   _____ Boxworth Bombers _____ Boxworth Rascals _____ State University Tigers
   _____ Boxworth ThunderBolts _____ Other: _____.

5. Which team in the National Basketball Association is your favorite?
   _____ Boxworth ThunderBolts _____ Chicago Bulls _____ Detroit Pistons
   _____ Boston Celtics _____ L.A. Lakers _____ Other: _____

6. a. How much do the cheapest single-game tickets to attend a Boxworth ThunderBolts basketball game cost? $_____ per ticket.
   b. What does a season ticket cost? $_____ per ticket.

Next, I'd like for you to indicate the extent to which you agree or disagree with several statements by telling me if you Strongly Agree, Agree, Neither Agree nor Disagree, Disagree, or Strongly Disagree with each. The first statement is, "I regularly engage in strenuous participation sports." Would you say that you:
Strongly Agree, Agree . . . (continue pattern for all statements).

Strongly Agree	Agree	Neutral	Strongly Disagree	Disagree

7. I regularly engage in strenuous participation sports.

5	4	3	2	1

8. I frequently swim for exercise.

5	4	3	2	1

9. The Boxworth ThunderBolts players are concerned with the local community.

5	4	3	2	1

10. All things considered, Boxworth ThunderBolts basketball games are one of the best sports/entertainment buys in the Boxworth area.

5	4	3	2	1

11. The key to a winning basketball team is teamwork.

5	4	3	2	1

12. I would enjoy going to more State University Tigers football games.

5	4	3	2	1

13. The Boxworth Bombers baseball team has produced more major-league players than any other triple-A franchise.

5	4	3	2	1

14. What is your age? _____

15. What is the ZIP code of your home? _____

Thank you very much for your help!

Suggested Readings

Britt, Steuart H. "Are So-called Successful Advertising Campaigns Really Successful?" *Journal of Advertising Research* (Vol. 9, 1969): 3–9.

Campbell, Roy H. *Measuring the Sales and Profit Results of Advertising.* New York: Association of National Advertisers, 1969.

Colley, Russell H. *Defining Advertising Goals for Measured Advertising Results.* New York: Association of National Advertisers, 1961.

Lavidge, Robert J., and Gary A. Steiner. "A Model for Predictive Measurement of Advertising Effectiveness." *Journal of Marketing* (October 1961): 59.

Schultz, Don E. *Strategic Advertising Campaigns.* Lincolnwood, Ill.: NTC Business Books, 1990. Chapter 7.

Wells, William D. *Planning for R.O.I.: Effective Advertising Strategy.* Englewood Cliffs, N.J.: Prentice-Hall, 1989.

Exercises

1. The 1992 Mazda sedan was introduced to the market in late 1991. The car features a new design, technical improvements, and a unique solar-powered ventilation system to keep the car cool while parked. Solar cells are imbedded in the glass roof of the sedan; these cells power two fans that ventilate the interior. The system operates constantly while the car is sitting in sunlight and shuts off automatically minutes after one starts driving. The system also responds to cold-weather conditions. If the temperature drops below 59° F, a sensor hidden in the back bumper automatically switches the current to recharge the car's battery while the car is parked.

In what ways would this unique improvement influence the company's statement of advertising objectives for the 1992 sedan? Why?

Source: "Smart Car," *Fortune,* December 16, 1991, 125.

2. During the past decade, U.S. manufacturers have witnessed an erosion of brand loyalty among consumers. Branded packaged goods were once the foundation of marketing in this country. Polls by the Roper organization found that in 1991, only 46 percent of all consumers interviewed said they knew what brand they wanted to buy when they entered a store—a drop from 56 percent three years before.

Several factors are blamed for this trend. First, the number of new products or new brands arriving on the stores' shelves each year lead consumers to view brands as transient. Second, marketers are not successful in differentiating their brand from those of competitors. Third, there has been an erosion of ad dollars and an increase in the amount marketers spend on price promotions, coupons, and special promotions. Fourth, the quality of products has declined. Last but not least, private and store labels are increasingly important.

The success of discount and mass merchandisers such as Wal-Mart, Phar-Mor, and Drug Emporium reveals a shift of market power from manufacturers and chain stores to mass merchandisers.

Do you think American packaged goods manufacturers can recapture the brand loyalty of their customers? What advertising strategies would benefit them and restore their ability to control the flow of packaged goods? How might these strategies be reflected in advertising objectives?

Source: Julie Liesse, "Brands in Trouble," *Advertising Age,* December 2, 1991, 16–20.

3.   The new Eastern European countries have joined the free world with a mind-boggling burden of economic problems. Demand for packaged and durable goods is very high and supply almost nonexistent. In addition, distribution channels are very old-fashioned and scarce. The consumers do not have a lot of disposable income and have not been exposed, until now, to any traditional advertising. Opportunities for new business ventures are many, but entrepreneurs must cope with many market inadequacies.

Assume Procter & Gamble decided to market a full line of packaged goods in the Eastern European countries. Should it use a push or pull marketing strategy? Why?

4.   ComputerLand, the world's biggest computer-retailing chain, with $3 billion in sales, has gotten the attention of some computer manufacturers in recent months. ComputerLand managers and some industry experts argue that survival in the future of computer mass marketing will favor large computer superstores and cost cutting. The small specialty stores, they argue, will be forced out of business.

There is another current of thought in the industry as well: Some believe that consumers will be willing to buy from a store that will provide them with complete technical support and assistance, even if this means having to pay a higher price. They argue that the purchase of a computer is but a first step in a long process, and consumers rely increasingly on technical advice and software support as they become more intensive users of computers. These people feel that computer companies should invest in offering consumer support, either on their own or through agents or retailers equipped to do so.

Which of these two groups do you feel is forecasting correctly the future of the personal computer industry? How would an integrated marketing and advertising approach help computer manufacturers fight competitive inroads? Explain.

Source: "ComputerLand—Cheaper by the Ten Dozen," *The Economist,* November 23, 1991, 76.

Lack's Furniture Centers

Management of Lack's, a regional chain of furniture and appliance stores located in a number of markets in Texas, develops marketing programs tailored to the characteristics of each market in which it operates. In planning an advertising/marketing program for the coming fiscal year in San Antonio, management was concerned with developing the most effective and efficient efforts to target Mexican-Americans.

Mexican-Americans made up more than 50 percent of the San Antonio market and had contributed a significant portion of Lack's business in the past. Although Lack's did well in comparison to competitors in selling furniture to Mexican-Americans, management believed that appliance sales to Hispanics were far below potential. Exhibit 4-1-1 presents a map indicating the locations of Lack's and three major competitors (Levitz, Sears, and Montgomery Ward).

To aid the development of complete advertising and marketing plans for next year, Lack's and its advertising agency commissioned a marketing research firm to profile the attitudes of Mexican-Americans toward furniture and appliance stores. A description of the study and findings is presented below.

THE RESEARCH STUDY

The research firm collected data using telephone interviews conducted with a randomly selected sample of female and male household heads with Spanish surnames drawn from the most recent San Antonio telephone directory. In addition, only those potential respondents who described their ethnic background as Mexican-American were included in the study.

Four hundred interviews were completed. Half of the respondents were surveyed regarding their furniture shopping behavior; half were asked about their appliance shopping patterns. Exhibit 4-1-2 presents sampling variations associated with a sample size of 200.

The interviews were conducted by bilingual interviewers employed by a professional interviewing service. The interviewers utilized either an English or Spanish version of the questionnaire as needed, based on the language of the respondent.

This case was prepared by Isabella C. M. Cunningham and John H. Murphy, Department of Advertising, The University of Texas at Austin, to serve as the basis for class discussion, not to illustrate either the effective or ineffective handling of an administrative situation. Note that some data have been disguised.

EXHIBIT 4-1-1   Map of San Antonio, Texas

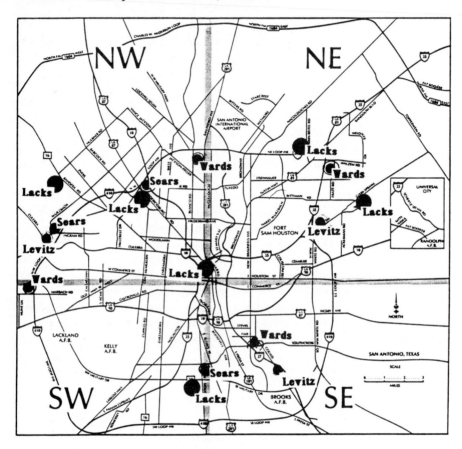

Lacks Furniture Centers
6838 Bandera, Perrin Beitel at 410,131 San Pedro,
6351 Rittiman, 4545 Fredericksburg Rd., 930 S.W. Military Dr.

Levitz Furniture
5430 Greatfare Dr., 6707 N.W. Loop 410, 3002 Goliad Rd.

Sears
Central Park Mall, Ingram Park Mall, 735 S.W. Military Dr.

Montgomery Ward
Crossroads Mall, Windsor Park Mall, Westlakes Mercado Mall, McCreless Mall

The questionnaire was developed to collect information from the respondents on their furniture and appliance attitudes and shopping preferences. The questionnaire was carefully pretested prior to final data.

EXHIBIT 4-1-2 **Probable Deviation (+ or −) of Results Due to Size**
(*n* = 200) of Sample Only[a] (safety factor of 20 to 1)

Survey Result Is:	Probable Deviation:
1% or 99%	1.4
2% or 98%	2.0
3% or 97%	2.4
4% or 96%	2.8
5% or 95%	3.1
6% or 94%	3.4
8% or 92%	3.8
10% or 90%	4.3
12% or 88%	4.6
15% or 85%	5.1
20% or 80%	5.7
25% or 75%	6.1
30% or 70%	6.5
35% or 65%	6.8
40% or 60%	7.0
45% or 55%	7.0
50%	7.1

[a]This exhibit presents the range of variation in survey results around the true value in the population being sampled that is due to sampling error. For example, with a sample size of 200 and a survey result of 25 percent, you may be reasonably sure (odds 20 to 1) that this result is no more than 6.1 percent off, plus or minus. That is, the true value is between 18.9 percent and 31.1 percent. *Note that other values apply to other sample sizes.* Larger samples reduce the range of sampling error.

THE FINDINGS

The major findings of the study related to planning Lack's advertising and promotional efforts for the next year are presented in Tables 4-1-1 to 4-1-9. Table 4-1-1 presents the respondents' top-of-mind awareness of furniture and appliance stores; Table 4-1-2 indicates at which store the respondents shop most often. Table 4-1-3 indicates whether the respondents had ever shopped at Lack's; Table 4-1-4 lists the reasons why stores were selected. Table 4-1-5 indicates the sources used to gather information about stores; Table 4-1-6 presents data on the respondents' perception of how Lack's and three major competitors compare on ten selected attributes. Table 4-1-7 presents data on respondents' overall rating of Lack's versus three major competitors; Table 4-1-8 provides insights into how knowledgeable respondents were regarding Lack's San Antonio operation. And finally, Table 4-1-9 provides a profile of respondents based on selected demographic variables.

After an initial examination of the data, three variables appeared to hold potential as segmentation criteria for further analysis. These variables were

TABLE 4-1-1   Top-of-Mind Awareness: Percentage Citing Each Store

	Furniture Stores		Appliance Stores	
	First Mention	Any Mention	First Mention	Any Mention
Joske's	8%	22%	11%	30%
Lack's	29	46	2	4
Levitz	14	34	a	a
Penney's	2	11	5	24
Sears	14	38	41	78
Montgomery Ward	9	34%	16	64
All others	24	b	25	b
Total	100%		100%	

[a]Less than 1 percent.
[b]Multiple responses by each respondent cause "Any mention" percentages on "All others" to be meaningless.

TABLE 4-1-2   Store at Which Respondents "Bought Most" in Past Three Years

	Furniture	Appliances
Lack's	17%	2%
Sears	12	41
Montgomery Ward	11	16
Levitz	9	a
National	8	a
Joske's	3	6
Plaza	2	a
Toudouze	2	a
Penney's	2	4
All others	34	31
Total	100%	100%

[a]Less than 1 percent.

TABLE 4-1-3   Ever Shopped at Lack's for Furniture or Appliances?

	Furniture	Appliances
Yes	51%	26%
No	49	74
Total	100%	100%

TABLE 4-1-4 Reasons Store Selected

	Furniture Stores		Appliance Stores	
	First Mention	Any Mention	First Mention	Any Mention
Location	10%	34%	11%	33%
Price	32	59	22	54
Store reputation	4	16	3	11
Salespeople	2	11	3	12
Selection	9	27	11	24
Quality	6	28	13	40
Recommended by friend	5	12	2	6
Services offered	6	19	9	26
Type or style	5	8	4	9
Other reasons	21	[a]	22	[a]
Total	100%		100%	

[a]Multiple responses by respondents cause "Any mention" percentages on "Other reasons" to be meaningless.

TABLE 4-1-5 Sources of Information about Stores

	Furniture Stores		Appliance Stores	
	First Mention	Any Mention	First Mention	Any Mention
Television	14%	56%	13%	57%
Magazines	4	18	3	17
Radio	1	18	1	15
Newspapers	57	80	63	83
Circulars or catalogues	4	23	4	22
Friends	10	27	5	29
Shopping	8	14	8	18
Salespeople	1	5	1	4
Other sources	1	[a]	2	[a]

[a]Multiple responses by respondents cause "Any mention" percentages on "Other sources" to be meaningless.

age, household income, and whether the respondent had shopped at Lack's. Cross-tabulations using these variables revealed that only age provided a clear and useful division of the sample. The significant findings using age (18 to 34/35+) as a segmenting variable for each of the two samples will be discussed next. In addition, data from a national study of variations in purchasing behavior by age groups are presented in Table 4-1-10.

TABLE 4-1-6   Respondents' Perception of Lack's versus Major Competitors

	Furniture				
	Lack's	Levitz	Sears	Ward	Don't Know
Highest quality	30%	21%	25%	12%	12%
Friendliest personnel	16	8	31	25	20
Most services	14	8	42	20	16
Most convenient locations	16	5	48	24	7
Widest selection	30	29	20	12	9
Most brands	28	28	16	9	19
Best-known brands	28	24	20	10	18
Lowest prices	23	13	19	16	29
Most modern stores	22	24	18	13	23
Most formal stores	25	14	26	12	23

TABLE 4-1-7   Overall Best Place to Shop

	Lack's	Levitz	Sears	Ward	All	Don't Know
Furniture	27%	23%	23%	15%	4%	8%
Appliances	6	3	58	27	2	4

TABLE 4-1-8   Knowledge of Lack's Operations

	Correct	Incorrect	Don't Know/ Unsure
Do you know the number of Lack's locations in San Antonio?			
Furniture stores	15%	15%	70%
Appliance stores	12	16	72
Do you know the number of years Lack's has operated in San Antonio?			
Furniture stores	8	12	80
Appliance stores	9	10	81
Do you know any brand names of furniture (appliances) available at Lack's?			
Furniture[a]	54	11	35
Appliances[b]	15	3	82

[a]In response to the question, "Do you know any brand names of furniture carried by Lack's?" 65 percent responded "yes" and 45 percent, "no." Those who responded "yes" were then asked to specify brands available at Lack's. (If any were correct, the response was counted as "correct.")

[b]In response to the question, "Do you know any brand names of appliances carried by Lack's?" 18 percent responded "yes" and 82 percent, "no." Those who responded "yes" were then asked to specify brands available at Lack's. (If any were correct, the response was counted as "correct.")

		Appliances		
Lack's	**Levitz**	**Sears**	**Ward**	**Don't Know**
10%	6%	53%	21%	10%
7	4	40	24	25
2	1	61	28	8
5	2	54	28	11
5	2	51	24	18
11	8	37	20	24
7	5	45	21	22
4	7	36	23	30
8	13	36	22	21
13	8	33	22	24

Furniture Sample

Cross-tabulation of age against top-of-mind awareness of furniture stores revealed that a much larger percentage of the younger group than the older group (41 percent versus 19 percent) identified Lack's. Levitz was also identified more strongly by the younger than the older group (22 percent versus 8 percent). Sears, on the other hand, was much more frequently mentioned by the older group (23 percent, versus 1 percent for the younger group).

Variations between the two age groups on the reasons mentioned for store selection were significant. Price was considerably more important to the younger group. Younger Hispanics appeared to be much more price oriented than older Hispanics when making furniture store selection decisions.

Cross-tabulation of age against the series of comparisons of the four stores across ten dimensions revealed several significant differences. It is important to note that, in each case, a larger proportion of the older group fell into the "Don't Know" category. On the "highest quality" furniture dimension, a larger percentage of the younger than the older group chose Lack's (40 percent versus 22 percent), and more older Hispanics identified Sears (29 percent versus 20 percent). On the "widest selection" variable, Lack's and Levitz were much stronger among the younger group, while Sears was identified by a significantly larger percentage of the older group. Finally, a significantly larger proportion of the under-35 group chose Lack's on the "most brands" and "best-known brands" dimensions. These last two general findings also apply to Levitz.

On the important "overall best place to shop for furniture" question, Lack's was stronger among the younger than the older group (31 percent versus 24 percent), as was Levitz (31 percent, versus 18 percent for the older group). Further, Sears was significantly more frequently identified by the older group (27 percent, versus 16 percent for the younger group).

TABLE 4-1-9 Demographic Profile of Respondents

	Furniture Sample	Appliances Sample
Age		
18–24	15%	14%
25–34	28	25
35–49	26	32
50–64	19	19
65 and over	12	10
Total	100%	100%
Marital Status		
Married	76%	82%
Single	10	8
Divorced, widowed, separated	14	10
Total	100%	100%
Household Size		
1–2	27%	20%
3	20	25
4	26	29
5 or more	27	26
Total	100%	100%
Education		
Elementary or less	21%	22%
Some high school	25	21
High school graduate	22	24
Some college	20	19
College graduate	12	14
Total	100%	100%
Total Household Income		
Under $10,000	16%	10%
$10,000–$14,999	19	21
$15,000–$24,999	20	21
$25,000 and over	18	17
Don't know	23	24
Refused	4	7
Total	100%	100%
Sex		
Female	62%	60%
Male	38	40
Total	100%	100%

Appliance Sample

Cross-tabulation of age against top-of-mind awareness of appliance stores revealed that a much larger percentage of the under-35 group identified a store classified as "other" when compared to the older group (37 percent versus 18 percent). The older group, on the other hand, had a much stronger awareness of Sears and Joske's than the under-35 group.

TABLE 4-1-10 Proportion of Purchases Made in America, by Age Group

	Purchases Made by Consumers Aged:		
	18 to 34	35 to 54	55+
Distribution of sample	34%	33%	33%
Index	[100]	[100]	[100]
Women's wear	37%	39%	24%
Index	[109][a]	[118]	[73]
Men's wear	42%	36%	22%
Index	[124]	[109]	[67]
Furniture, furnishings	33%	42%	25%
Index	[97]	[127]	[76]
Major appliances, TVs	38%	36%	25%
Index	[118]	[109]	[76]
Small appliances	34%	34%	32%
Index	[100]	[103]	[97]
Hardware, tools	37%	41%	22%
Index	[109]	[124]	[67]
Automotive supplies	44%	38%	18%
Index	[129]	[115]	[55]
Garden supplies	32%	38%	30%
Index	[94]	[115]	[91]

Source: *How America Shops and Buys* (New York: Newspaper Advertising Bureau, 1983).
[a]This index was calculated by dividing 37, the percentage of all women's wear purchases made by women aged 18 to 34, by 34, the percentage of all adult women in the 18 to 34 age group.

On the "overall best place to shop for appliances" measure, Sears was identified by a majority of both age groups. However, Montgomery Ward was identified by a significantly larger proportion of the younger respondents (37 percent versus 21 percent). Cross tabulations on other variables revealed no significant differences.

PLANNING THE ADVERTISING PROGRAM

In developing a complete advertising program for Lack's in San Antonio for the next fiscal year, management turned to the research findings for insights and guidance. The first step was to clearly define advertising objectives for next year. Key issues to be resolved included the identification of the most appropriate target audience(s) within the Mexican-American market and the relative amount of attention to devote to advertising furniture versus appliances.

The levels of awareness, knowledge, attitudes, and preferences presented in the tables would be used as benchmarks that the upcoming advertising campaign would be designed to impact. At the end of the campaign, the same study would be repeated, using another randomly selected sample of Mexican-Americans. Changes in the percentage of responses to key questions would be used to evaluate the advertising campaign's effectiveness against the pre-campaign objectives which were to be developed.

Questions for Discussion and Review

1. What are the most significant findings presented in the tables? Why are they the most important?

2. What are the major contrasts between Lack's relative position among furniture shoppers and among appliance shoppers? Between younger and older shoppers?

3. Given Lack's stronger position in the furniture market, what *risks* is the firm likely to run by shifting a larger proportion of its advertising to support appliance sales? What *opportunity costs* might Lack's incur by not expanding its advertising support of appliances?

4. Should Lack's advertising appeals be directed to younger or older shoppers? Why? How would the attractiveness of a comparative ad format be affected by which age group was targeted?

5. What is a realistic statement of advertising objectives for Lack's? How would your objectives vary depending on whether you focused on younger or older Hispanics as your target audience? How would your objectives vary depending on whether you focused more heavily on appliances or furniture?

C A S E   **4 - 2**

Wainright Chevrolet

Whenever a new Chevrolet automobile dealership is opened, a thorough amount of planning is required. The Wainright Chevrolet (WC) dealership established in Bloomfield several years ago was no exception. The new dealership was located in the growing northwest section of Bloomfield, with over ten acres of cars and 900 feet of frontage on a major traffic artery.

The two principals who established the dealership, Harold Wainright and Jack Burke, were extremely pleased about the prospects for their new dealership. They were confident that despite heavy competition, the widespread consumer acceptance of the Chevrolet product line, coupled with the healthy Bloomfield market, would produce a winning combination. The success the dealership enjoyed during its first few years seemed to justify their confidence, and prospects for even greater success in the future appeared bright.

THE AUTO INDUSTRY

No motor vehicle manufacturer has control of any part of the market. There are striking variations in customer acceptance of each manufacturer's

---

This case was prepared by John H. Murphy, The University of Texas at Austin. The case is intended for use in generating class discussion and not to illustrate the effective or ineffective handling of an administrative situation. The identity of the actual firm has been disguised.

products—variations by product groups, car lines, and geographic area. Although repeat sales are highly prized, the evidence has been overwhelming that customer loyalty must be earned anew with each sale.

Motor vehicle producers also face competition from the large stock of used vehicles in the United States. The great reservoir of unused mileage and the fact that motor vehicles can be repaired give customers the option of continuing to use existing vehicles rather than purchasing new ones. This interaction between new and used vehicles is an integral part of competition in the industry. Since motor vehicles are durable and their purchase represents a major family decision, cyclical swings in employment and in consumer confidence create amplified swings in new-car demand.

THE BLOOMFIELD MARKET

According to published estimates, the Bloomfield Standard Metropolitan Statistical Area (SMSA) ranked in the top 100 markets in terms of population, while the city of Bloomfield ranked in the top 50 of the U.S. Commerce Department's ranking of cities by population. Automobile dealer sales per capita for the Bloomfield SMSA were estimated to be at or slightly above the national average.

Over the past few years, Bloomfield had been breaking records for population increases, although the tide of immigration had eased from its peak period. The city's economic picture for the near term continued to be bright. Given its almost recession-proof economy firmly rooted in government, education, tourism, and a growing industrial complex, Bloomfield officials were optimistic about the city's continued growth.

BLOOMFIELD AUTO DEALERS

Two other Bloomfield Chevrolet dealers in competition with WC were Cannon and Star Chevrolet. Star led in sales, with Cannon at an estimated 85 percent of Star sales and WC at 80 percent of Star sales. Cannon had been in Bloomfield for over 60 years, and it tended to use more newspaper and TV advertising than Star or WC. Cannon called itself "Your Chevrolet Place."

Star Chevrolet had been located in a nearby town for 30 years before moving to Bloomfield more than a decade ago. Star tended to advertise heavily in newspapers, and its slogan was "Bloomfield's Favorite Dealer."

Bloomfield also had Toyota, Buick, Cadillac, Oldsmobile, Lincoln-Mercury, Ford, Chrysler-Plymouth, Nissan, Saturn, Dodge, Volkswagen, Lexus, Mercedes, Honda, and Pontiac/GMC dealers. In addition, dealers in surrounding communities provided a fair amount of competitive pressure on the Bloomfield auto market.

WC'S PAST ADVERTISING EFFORTS

Since opening, WC had changed advertising agencies twice. For approximately its first three months, the dealership had used an out-of-state agency, but it quickly became apparent that this arrangement was unsatisfactory. Next, an

---

EXHIBIT 4-2-1   Representative Radio Spots

Jingle

Chorus: Pick a Wainright Chevrolet—you can do it today—with a Wainright Chevrolet.

Take it from the folks who save. Pick a Wainright Chevrolet. The dealer who will help keep your car new. It's waiting here for you to help you keep your car new. Wainright's waiting here for you. Wainright Chevrolet.

"Crazy Day Sale"

Announcer: Time is running out at Wainright Chevrolet. Chevy's national sales campaign ends April 5, and we are desperate to meet our goal. So we've gone a little crazy. We want to move cars more than make profits. So this is your chance to save big on a beautiful new Chevrolet car or truck. We're forgetting the sticker price—it's what you can buy it for. Now that's what really counts. Come on out—we've got hundreds in stock. Wainright Chevrolet, on 183 North at Eleven Four Hundred Research. *Chorus:* (SINGS JINGLE)

"Door Slammer Sale"

Announcer: Chevrolet is slammin' the door . . .
Sound effects: (DOOR SLAMS)
Announcer: . . . on inflation with a door slammer sale. Because all new Chevies coming in are factory priced one hundred dollars higher than those now in stock, the cars and trucks we have at the old price will go fast, so hurry in now. New Celebrities are priced from $_____.
Sound effects: (DOOR SLAMS)
Announcer: Berettas from $_____.
Sound effects: (DOOR SLAMS)
Announcer: Come to Wainright's door slammer sale for your best deal in Bloomfield.
Chorus: (SINGS JINGLE)

"Image Trucks"

Announcer: The trucking life in Bloomfield starts at Wainright Chevrolet. Wainright knows what folks want in a pickup and handles the trucks at the prices to fit that life-style. Chevy pickups are built to stay tough, and tough in the right places. Wainright has the Chevy truck to fit your needs, whether it's rugged ranch work, or comfortable in-town cruising. For your best truck deal in Bloomfield, come to Wainright Chevrolet.
Chorus: (SINGS JINGLE)

---

agency based in Bloomfield was hired to facilitate communication and to add a new creative punch to the firm's advertising. Exhibit 4-2-1 presents representative radio spots produced by this agency.

Two major reasons were cited for the decision to drop the second agency in favor of another local agency. These reasons were: (1) The WC owners felt that the agency had failed to produce advertising with creative flair on behalf of their dealership, and (2) they believed that the agency's casual attitude toward research resulted in a failure to properly initiate and utilize research in planning WC's advertising efforts.

RESEARCH PROJECT

To provide continuous research input for use in advertising planning and evaluation, the dealership and the new agency commissioned a series of ongoing research studies. A local advertising and marketing research firm was retained to conduct an initial benchmark study and additional follow-up surveys. After a series of meetings with the client and the agency, the research firm developed the following research plan to collect the necessary data.

The ongoing research project was titled "Awareness, Knowledge, and Attitudes toward Automobile Dealers among Adults Residing in Selected Areas of Bloomfield." Phase I had just been completed. This initial study provided a benchmark measure of the awareness, knowledge, and attitudes of target prospects concerning WC and the competition. Such measures, repeated at regular intervals, were to be used in establishing objectives and as a control device for evaluating the effectiveness of the promotional activities of the dealership.

In each phase, a random sample of target prospects who live in a selected geographic area of Bloomfield reasonably close to the dealership were to be interviewed. In addition to being relatively accessible to the dealership, this targeted area contained the best prospects for the dealership, based on socioeconomic considerations.

Telephone interviews were used to collect the data. Three hundred male and female adult household heads were contacted using a random sampling procedure. A structured questionnaire was used to measure respondents' unaided and aided recall of automobile dealerships and of Wainright Chevrolet.

Identification of slogans, attitudes toward automobile dealerships, factors considered in making automobile purchase decisions, and several demographic variables were also included in the questionnaire. Selected portions of the research instrument are presented in Appendix 4-2. Tables 4-2-1 to 4-2-8 present the findings of Phase I of the continuing research project.

Phase II of the research program was to be conducted 12 months after a new advertising campaign had been launched. During the time between Phase I and Phase II, the advertising slogan and theme used by WC in its campaign were to be modified. Other changes would include different advertising time slots, an increased budget for the campaign, and a greater emphasis on location, service, or price in WC's advertising.

TABLE 4-2-1   Top-of-Mind Awareness, All Car Dealers (see Question 1)

	First Mention	Any Mention[a]
Cannon	13%	28%
Buick dealer	4	0
Star	18	29
Ford dealer	13	22
Lincoln dealer	7	15
Oldsmobile dealer	10	22
Toyota dealer	5	17
Wainright	5	11
Other	25	47
Don't know	0	
	100%	

[a]Multiple responses (first three mentions recorded).

TABLE 4-2-2   Why Dealership Was Selected (see Question 2)

Reason	Percentage Mentioning
Offered "best deal," cheapest, best price	32%
Only dealer in town	15
Had car, model wanted, etc.	15
Convenient location	8
Friends with owner or employee	8
Dealt with dealer before	5
Reputable, honest	4
Service	4
Friend or relative recommended	3
Sales personnel	2
Good trade-in	2
Easy credit	1
Advertising	1
Others	—
Work there	—
No reason	—
	100%

TABLE 4-2-3   Most Important Qualities of Car Dealers— Any Mention (see Question 3)

Qualities	Percentage Mentioning
Service	77%
Location	5
Reputation	13
Price	33
Sales staff	13
Personal attention	13
Other	32

TABLE 4-2-4   Top-of-Mind Awareness, Chevy Dealers (see Question 4)

	First Mention	Any Mention[a]
Cannon	44%	65%
Star	37	66
Wainright	15	33
Other	4	21
	100%	

[a]Multiple responses (first three mentions recorded).

TABLE 4-2-5   Slogan Identification (see Question 5)

	Percentage Who Correctly Identified Slogan	Percentage Who Incorrectly Identified Slogan	Percentage Who Didn't Know Slogan
Cannon	50%	9%	41%
Star	27	13	60
Wainright	0	2	98

TABLE 4-2-6 Awareness of Wainright Chevrolet (see Question 6)

(A) Ever heard of Wainright?

Yes	66%
No	34
	100%

(B) Do you know what make of car Wainright handles (among those who had heard of Wainright)?

Chevrolet	90%
Other	3
Don't know	7
	100%

(C) Do you know Wainright's location (among those who had heard of Wainright)?

Correct ID	82%
Incorrect ID	3
Don't know	15
	100%

TABLE 4-2-7 How Respondents Compare Wainright with Other Chevrolet Dealers[a]

(A) "Best" service department (Question #7)

Cannon	9%
Star	12
Wainright	8
All same	1
Don't know	70
	100%

(B) "Best" prices (Question #8)

Cannon	9%
Star	7
Wainright	9
All same	3
Don't know	72
	100%

(C) "Best" selection (Question #9)

Cannon	8%
Star	10
Wainright	15
All same	4
Don't know	63
	100%

[a]The three dealers compared were Cannon, Star, and Wainright.

Phase II would use the same data-collection methodology as Phase I, although a new random sample would be drawn and interviewed. The purpose of the Phase II study would be to evaluate whether potential buyers perceived local dealers—specifically WC—differently. Also, other attitudinal and demographic measures made in Phase I and repeated in Phase II and later phases would provide a longitudinal study of the effectiveness of WC's campaign and would be useful in monitoring other changes in the market.

TABLE 4-2-8   Sample Demographics of Respondents

(A) Household size (Question 12)

1	9%
2	37
3	18
4	23
5+	13
	100%

(B) Age (Question 13)

Under 18	0%
18–24	8
25–34	27
35–49	32
50–64	18
65+	12
Refused	3
	100%

(C) Annual household income (Question 14)

Under 20,000	9%
$20,000–$34,999	13
$35,000–$49,999	26
$50,000 and over	28
Don't know/refused	24
	100%

(D) Race (Question 15)

White	95%
Other	5
	100%

(E) Sex

Male	55%
Female	45
	100%

Phase II would indicate both past successes and future directions for changes in advertising by WC. In addition, information from the study would help management to determine whether current advertising expenditures were sufficient, given the firm's objectives.

FUTURE DIRECTIONS FOR WAINRIGHT'S ADVERTISING

Against the background of this research project, the new agency's task was to develop a complete advertising campaign for the upcoming fiscal year, September 1 through August 31. For initial planning purposes, the agency was told to make any reasonable assumptions about the level of the advertising appropriation for the coming year. It was noted that, in past years, WC had invested between $450,000 and $600,000 in its total advertising budget.

In developing campaign recommendations, the agency's first step was to develop a set of specific, appropriate, and realistic advertising objectives. More specifically, the agency was asked to prepare a written statement of advertising objectives for WC that met Britt's four criteria for sound advertising objectives: (1) what basic message is to be delivered, (2) to what audience, (3) with what intended effects, and (4) what specific criteria are to be used to measure the success of the campaign.

Wainright and Burke both firmly believed that developing advertising objectives consistent with Britt's philosophy and comparing Phase I and II research findings would lead to some valid conclusions regarding the effectiveness of the new advertising campaign. Both of the dealership principals were eager to confer with the agency regarding its proposed statement of objectives. Individuals at the agency realized how important this task of formulating objectives was, not only in terms of directing all other decisions in the campaign planning process, but also in proving to the owners of WC that they could handle the account properly.

Questions for Discussion and Review

1. What are the limitations and strengths of Phase I of the WC research study? What modifications or additions would be appropriate? Why?

2. What additional data from the Phase I study beyond that presented in the case would be useful?

3. How can the data presented in Tables 4-2-1 to 4-2-8 be used to develop a statement of advertising objectives?

4. Which of the four component parts of advertising objectives identified by Britt is most important? Why? Which involves the most uncertainty? Why?

Appendix 4-2
Questionnaire for Wainright Chevrolet: Capitol City Research Services Auto Dealers Attitudes Survey

Telephone # _____
Questionnaire _____
Census Tract _____
Interviewer _____
2nd contact _____
Note day and time of contact _____
May I speak with the male or female head of household? (If neither is available, call back).

Hello, my name is _____. I work for Capitol City Research Services, a public opinion survey firm. We are interested in finding out what selected Bloomfield residents think about automobile dealers.

1. When you think of new car dealers, what are the first three that come to mind?

	Cannon	"X"	Star	"Y"	"Z"	"A"	="B"	Wainright	Other	D.K.
1st mention	1	2	3	4	5	6	7	8	9	0
2nd mention	1	2	3	4	5	6	7	8	9	0
3rd mention	1	2	3	4	5	6	7	8	9	0

2. Have you ever purchased a new car?   Yes   No (skip to Question 3)
   From what dealership did you buy the car?
   Write name of dealership in blank.
   Why did you select _____ (name of dealership)?

3. What do you feel are the three most important qualities of a good new car dealer?

	Service	Location	Reputation	Price	Sales Staff	Personal Attention	Other (specify)
1st mention	1	2	3	4	5	6	7
2nd mention	1	2	3	4	5	6	7
3rd mention	1	2	3	4	5	6	7

4. When you think of Chevrolet automobile dealers, what are the first three that come to mind?

	Cannon	Star	Wainright	Other
1st mention	1	2	3	4
2nd mention	1	2	3	4
3rd mention	1	2	3	4

5. Now I'd like to know if you recall which specific new car dealer uses the following slogans? First, what about "The Tradin' Place." Which new car dealer uses "The Tradin' Place" as its slogan?

	"B"	Star	"Z"	Cannon	Wainright	Other	Don't Know
"B's" slogan	1	2	3	4	5	6	7
Star's slogan	1	2	3	4	5	6	7
"Z's" slogan	1	2	3	4	5	6	7
Cannon's slogan	1	2	3	4	5	6	7
Wainright's slogan	1	2	3	4	5	6	7

6. Have you ever heard of the Wainright car dealership?

Yes	1
No (skip to Question 10)	2

If yes, what make of new cars does Wainright handle?

Chevrolet	1
Other	2
D.K.	3

Where is the Wainright dealership located?

Correct ID	1
Incorrect ID	2
D.K.	3

7. Now thinking about the service department of the three Bloomfield Chevrolet dealers, which of the three—Cannon, Star, or Wainright—do you feel would have the best service department?

Cannon	1
Star	2
Wainright	3
All same	4
Don't Know	5

8. Again, thinking about the three Bloomfield Chevrolet dealers, which one of the three do you feel would have the lowest prices on new cars?

Cannon	1
Star	2
Wainright	3
All same	4
Don't Know	5

9. Now thinking about the selection of cars on hand at the three Bloomfield Chevrolet dealers, which one of the three do you feel would have the largest selection of cars on hand?

Cannon	1
Star	2
Wainright	3
All same	4
Don't Know	5

Now, a few questions to help classify this questionnaire.

10. Do you own or rent your home?

Own	1
Rent	2

11. How long have you lived at your present address?

Less than 1 year	1
1–2 years	2
3 years	3
4–9 years	4
10 years or more	5
D.K., unsure	6

12. Counting yourself, how many persons now live in your household, including babies?

Number _____

13. What is your age?

Under 18	1
18–24	2
25–34	3
35–49	4
50–64	5
65 and over	6
Refused	7

14. What was the approximate annual income for all members of your household before taxes last year . . . would it be $35,000 or more or would it be less than that?

(continued)

$35,000 or more. Ask:		Less than $35,000. Ask:	
Would it be		Would it be	
Under $50,000 or	3	Over $20,000 or	2
Over $50,000	4	Under $20,000	1
Don't know	5		
Refused	6		

15. Finally, would you please tell me your race?

White	1
Black	2
Mexican–American	3
Other	4

May I have your name, please, in case my office wants to check my work?
Name _____

Note sex:

Male	1
Female	2

Thank you very much!
Verification: By _____ Date _____

C A S E   **4 - 3**

Jefferson Savings

Jefferson Savings (JS) was founded in Stanfield, a medium-sized midwestern city, in 1960. The institution had grown steadily since its establishment and now operated a central downtown office and a number of suburban branches located throughout the metropolitan area.

Five major savings and loan associations competed for the Stanfield market, along with a large number of smaller savings and loan associations. Besides JS, the four other major savings and loan associations were First Federal Savings, University Savings, Franklin Savings, and First State Savings. JS ranked fourth in terms of total deposits, behind University, First Federal, and First State. Local savers could also choose to open their savings accounts in one of sixteen major commercial banks or one of twenty credit unions, all located in the market. To grow and maintain a prominent position in such a competitive market, JS had to devote a great deal of thought and effort to developing its promotional programs.

This case was prepared by John H. Murphy, The University of Texas at Austin. The case is intended for use in generating class discussion and not to illustrate the effective or ineffective handling of an administrative situation. The identity of the actual firm has been disguised.

PAST PROMOTIONAL STRATEGY

JS had been committed to an objective of increasing its market share and deposits steadily during the past five years. To continually expand its market share and deposits, JS had invested approximately $500,000 in media advertising last year and $400,000 the preceding year.

JS's basic media budget for the past two years was broken down roughly as follows:

- 60% television
- 20% radio
- 10% newspaper
- 10% regional magazines

In addition, outdoor advertising had been used on a seasonal basis to supplement these basic media expenditures.

In buying television time, JS purchased both 30- and 60-second spots on three major commercial stations. JS ran a fairly consistent schedule of 60-second radio spots on four major stations. A number of newspaper ads of varying sizes were run in the *Gazette,* Stanfield's major daily. Magazine advertising was placed in local editions of *Newsweek, U.S. News and World Report, Time,* and *Sports Illustrated.* These magazine ads were all one full page and in full color.

JS had also utilized a number of specialty advertising items during past years. These items included matchbooks, lifesavers, buttons ("Think Happy with Jefferson Savings"), balloons, pens, and suckers. The firm also sent out "Welcome to Stanfield" letters to new residents.

A central theme of JS's promotional program was portrayed by its logo, which depicted a family holding hands, and the motto "Jefferson Savings: Your Family Financial Center." Emphasis was given to promoting the idea of using JS to meet all the family's financial needs. Along with this central theme, several other appeals had been used in JS's advertising program during the past two years. The first was "Be Better Off Next Year Than You Are Now," accompanied by promotional gifts that coupled the "happy" idea with financial betterment. This theme was deemphasized when economic conditions declined. The second theme, "financial security," was used as a basic selling proposition during the depressed economy. Finally, JS's growth and its strong financial situation were made known by publicizing its total dividends payments.

ACCOUNTABILITY THROUGH RESEARCH

JS had recently given the responsibility for creating and placing its advertising to a local ad agency. The agency selected, Crystal Advertising Concepts, had an excellent reputation built around its ability to develop successful campaigns for diverse clients. In securing the JS account, Crystal Advertising had emphasized the need to base any advertising/promotional decisions in the highly competitive Stanfield market on a solid foundation of marketing research.

Initially, the new agency developed ads that differed only slightly from past efforts believed by JS management to have been effective. Crystal Advertising planned to delay any significant change in JS's advertising until after a thorough marketing research study could be conducted. A local marketing research firm, SRM, was employed to develop a research study that could serve as the basis for all strategic decisions concerning JS's advertising/promotional efforts during the upcoming fiscal year.

After several planning sessions involving the three parties, a methodology was developed for collecting the desired information. During a two-week period, SRM conducted 301 personal interviews with Stanfield residents to gather what was believed to be the necessary information for developing JS's future advertising strategy.

SAVINGS PREFERENCES STUDY

SRM collected the desired information using a questionnaire survey approach. After pretesting the research instrument, SRM collected data through personal interviews. A random sample of households was drawn from within the primary trading areas located in close proximity to the branch locations of JS. Thus, the sample was not necessarily representative of the total Stanfield market. Male or female household heads were asked to respond to a questionnaire administered by trained interviewers in the respondents' home. To qualify for an interview, the household had to presently have a savings account.

Data were gathered in five major areas of interest. First, data were collected on respondents' top-of-the-mind awareness of savings institutions and level of recall of selected financial institutions' symbols and slogans. Second, quantitative and qualitative information about savers such as the number and types of savings accounts they held and the frequency of their account usage was obtained. Third, respondents' reactions to a series of attributes considered to be important when choosing a savings institution were obtained. Fourth, data related to the respondents' perceived image of each of the five major Stanfield area savings and loan associations were collected. (Each respondent profiled JS and one of the other four major savings and loan associations, which was selected at random.) Finally, demographic information about the respondents was collected. These data included the education, age, income, employment status, and profession of the head of the household, as well as other descriptive data.

All data collected were verified. The verification procedure involved first selecting a random sample of approximately 15 percent of each interviewer's completed questionnaires. The subjects selected for verification received a telephone call thanking them for their cooperation and inquiring as to the performance of the interviewer. If any irregularities were found in the interviewing procedure, all of the questionnaires handled by that interviewer were verified. If appropriate, the interviewer's work would be eliminated from the sample. In addition, all questionnaires were checked for completeness and logical relationships by both a verifier and a coder prior to data entry.

Frequency distributions and cross-tabulation were used to verify the importance of some variables, and subjects were also cross classified according to specific characteristics. Mean values of the attitudinal variables used by respondents to describe their image of savings and loan associations were subjected to an analysis of variance. A factor analysis was conducted on the variables used to determine the important factors in the choice of a savings institution. Chi-square analyses were employed to compare the distribution of savers based on demographic variables.

One of the objectives of the research was to obtain a balanced number of responses from both the male and female heads of households in the sample. To achieve this purpose, the interviewers were instructed to try to conduct an interview with the male head of the household. If the male household head was not available, the female head was interviewed. In the final sample, 45 percent of respondents were male and 55 percent were female.

Tables 4-3-1 to 4-3-8 present some of the major findings of the investigation conducted for JS by SRM.

TABLE 4-3-1   Saver Profile

Question	Response	Percent
More than one account?	Yes	55%
	No	45
Among those with more than one account, with which type of institution largest amount saved?	Bank	27%
	Savings and loan	37
	Credit union	36
Who selected specific institution(s) where save?	Husband	48%
	Wife	19
	Both	29
	Other	4
Automobile or mortgage loan?	Auto only	15%
	Mortgage only	38
	Both	19
	Neither	28
Excluding interbranch changes, now save anywhere did not a year ago?	Yes	14%
	No	86
Among those with only one savings account, where?	Bank	40%
	Savings and loan	31
	Credit union	29
Frequency with which savers make deposits and withdrawals?	Once a week or more	12%
	Two or three times a month	13
	Once a month	43
	Less than once a month	32

		Average Number of Accounts
Among those with more than one account, the average number of accounts at financial institutions?	Banks	1.50
	Savings and loans	1.87
	Credit unions	1.45

TABLE 4-3-2   Financial Institutions Used by Savers

Financial Institutions	Percentage of All Savers ($n = 301$)	Percentage of Savings and Loan Savers ($n = 156$)
Savings and Loan Associations		
None	55%	—
University Savings	13	30%
First Federal Savings	9	19
Franklin Savings	5	11
Jefferson Savings	16	36
First State Savings	10	23
All other S&Ls	6	14
Commercial Banks		
Have an account	46%	31%
Do not have an account	54	69
Credit Unions		
Have an account	47%	48%
Do not have an account	53	52

TABLE 4-3-3   Determinant Attributes in the Selection of a Savings Institution

Attributes	Mean Importance[a]
Security	1.78
High interest rates paid	1.83
Friendly, personal service	2.03
A convenient location	2.07
Reputation of the institution	2.09
Credit reference	2.19
Interest rate compounded daily	2.26
Cash personal checks and pay checks	2.42
Single monthly statement of all accounts with institution	2.44
Ease of acquiring loan	2.46
Checking account available	2.46
Hours open	2.58
Free parking	2.92
Travelers' check service	3.03
Drive-in window	3.06
Free save-by-mail service	3.17
Trust services	3.23
Credit card available	3.46
Safety deposit boxes	3.53
Recommended by a friend	3.77
24-hour automated services	3.81
Night depository	3.85

[a]Respondents evaluated each attribute on the following scale: 1 = Extremely important, 2 = Very important, 3 = Important, 4 = Slightly important, and 5 = Not important at all.

TABLE 4-3-4 Factor Loading of Determinant Attributes in the Selection of a Savings Institution

Factors	Factor Loadings
Factor #1: Financial Services	
Checking account available	.73
Cash personal and payroll checks	.69
Credit reference	.69
Credit card available	.67
Single monthly statement of all accounts	.61
Ease of acquiring loans	.59
Drive-in windows	.56
Factor #2: Stability and Interest	
High interest rates paid on savings	.73
Security	.70
Interest compounded daily on savings	.64
Reputation of the institution	.54
Factor #3: Convenience	
Free parking	.73
Hours open	.73
Convenient location	.70
Factor #4: After-hours Convenience	
Free save-by-mail service	.76
Night depository	.56
24-hour automated services	.52

Note: Attributes with a loading of less than .50 were omitted.

TABLE 4-3-5 Savers' Images of Savings and Loans (Mean Values)

	Jefferson Savings ($n = 253$)	University Savings ($n = 56$)	First Federal Savings ($n = 68$)	Franklin Savings ($n = 51$)	First State Savings ($n = 45$)
Easy/hard to get loan[a]	2.7	2.7	2.7	2.5	2.6
Family/business oriented	2.7	2.7	2.8	2.5	2.7
Low/high interest on loans	3.0	2.9	3.0	2.9	3.0
Low/high interest on savings	3.2	3.1	3.1	3.3	3.2
Much/little advertising	2.5	2.6	2.5	2.3	3.0[b]
Personal/impersonal	2.6	2.4	2.6	2.4	2.8
Cooperative/uncooperative	2.4	2.5	2.4	2.4	2.4
Progressive/backward	2.4	2.4	2.4	2.4	2.4
Reputable/disreputable	1.9	1.9	1.9	2.1	2.0
Women-oriented/not women-oriented	2.9	2.9	3.0	2.8	3.1[b]

[a]Respondents reacted to each variable by marking one of five scale positions separating the bipolar phrases. For example, easy 1 2 3 4 5 hard to get a loan.

[b]A comparison of respondents' perception of Jefferson Savings against respondents' perception of each of the other four S&Ls individually on each of the 18 variables revealed six significant differences (those indicated by a[b]).

(continued)

TABLE 4-3-5 *(continued)*

	Jefferson Savings (n = 253)	University Savings (n = 56)	First Federal Savings (n = 68)	Franklin Savings (n = 51)	First State Savings (n = 45)
Friendly/unfriendly personnel	2.3	2.4	2.4	2.3	2.4
Well-known/unknown	1.9	1.9	1.8	1.9	2.3[b]
Convenient/inconvenient hours	2.4	2.5	2.6	2.4	2.8[b]
Many/few services	2.5	2.4	2.5	2.5	2.5
Convenient/inconvenient locations	2.1	2.4	2.3	2.0	2.4[b]
Professional/unprofessional	2.3	2.3	2.2	2.4	2.3
Convenient/inconvenient pricing	2.3	2.5	2.3	2.4	.5
Concerned/not concerned about local community	2.5	2.5	2.6	2.2[b]	2.6

TABLE 4-3-6 Top-of-Mind Awareness of Savings and Loans

	First Mention (percent)	Second Mention (percent)	Third Mention (percent)	Any Mention (percent)
Jefferson Savings	23%	21%	17%	47%
University Savings	22	20	13	43
First Federal Savings	18	22	15	42
Franklin Savings	14	17	23	40
First State Savings	13	12	14	29
All other S&Ls	10	8	18	26
	100%	100%	100%	a

Note: Respondents were asked, "When you think of savings and loan associations, what are the first three that come to mind?"

[a]Percentages add to more than 100 percent because of multiple responses.

TABLE 4-3-7 Identification of Slogans and Symbols of Financial Institutions

	Percentage Identifying with Correct Institution	Percentage Identifying with Wrong Institution	Percentage Who Don't Know
An S&L ad theme	1%	4%	95%
A bank slogan	39	13	48
"Your family financial center" (Jefferson slogan)	2	7	91
A bank ad theme	30	11	59
Franklin logo	78	3	19
University Savings logo	22	16	62
First Federal logo	16	8	76
Jefferson logo	3	5	92
First State logo	7	8	85

TABLE 4-3-8 Demographic Profile of Savers

	All Savers (*n* = 301)	Jefferson Savers (*n* = 48)	All Other S&Ls Combined (*n* = 103)	Bank Savers (*n* = 42)	Credit Union Savers (*n* = 137)
Total	100%	16%	34%	47%	46%
Savings account at					
Bank	47%	45%	35%	100%	43%
Credit union	46	45	43	32	100
S&L	45	100	100	31	48
Education[a]					
Graduate study	29%	41%	26%	31%	30%
College graduate	25	25	22	27	23
Some college	25	17	27	22	29
High school education or less	21	17	25	20	18
Age (chief wage earner)[b]					
18–24	8%	2%	7%	8%	6%
25–29	21	10	16	23	20
30–34	15	15	13	17	15
35–39	14	14	13	14	14
40–44	10	16	8	9	13
45–54	17	27	19	14	16
55 and over	15	16	24	15	16
Income[c]					
Less than $15,000	14%	6%	13%	14%	10%
$15,000–$24,999	19	15	12	18	21
$25,000–$49,999	32	42	35	25	36
$50,000 or more	27	33	32	35	26
Refused, don't know	8	4	8	8	7
Value of savings account[d]					
Less than $2,000	21%	15%	12%	24%	16%
$2,000–$4,999	19	10	19	18	22
$5,000–$9,999	16	15	16	14	19
$10,000–$14,999	12	19	10	13	11
$15,000–$24,999	6	8	4	7	6
$25,000 or more	12	23	23	13	15
Refused, don't know	14	10	17	11	11
Tenure[e]					
Own	73%	83%	85%	72%	76%
Rent	27	17	15	28	24
Time at present address[f]					
Less than 1 year	23%	10%	17%	20%	20%
1–2 years	27	21	22	34	26
3–6 years	26	23	27	23	28
7 or more years	24	46	34	23	26
Marital status					
Married	87%	90%	90%	84%	91%
Single	7	4	5	6	6
Divorced, widowed	6	6	5	10	3
Chief wage earner					
Male household head	82%	86%	88%	80%	82%
Female household head	13	10	8	14	12
Other	5	4	4	6	6
Chief wage earner employed in downtown Stanfield					
Yes	31%	33%	33%	30%	33%
No	69	67	67	70	67

(continued)

TABLE 4-3-8 *(continued)*

	All Savers (n = 301)	Jefferson Savers (n = 48)	All Other S&Ls Combined (n = 103)	Bank Savers (n = 42)	Credit Union Savers (n = 137)
Household size					
1–2	35%	28%	36%	36%	31%
3	21	23	21	23	18
4	25	30	29	20	27
5 or more	19	19	14	21	24
Type of dwelling					
Single unit	77%	78%	83%	79%	80%
Apartment	19	20	15	18	15
Other	4	2	2	3	5

[a]Chi-square comparison of "All Savers" and "Jefferson Savers" significant at the $p = .12$ level.
[b]Chi-square comparison of "All Savers" and "Jefferson Savers" significant at the $p = .06$ level.
[c]Chi-square comparison of "All Savers" and "Jefferson Savers" significant at the $p = .14$ level.
[d]Chi-square comparison of "All Savers" and "Jefferson Savers" significant at the $p = .05$ level.
[e]Chi-square comparison of "All Savers" and "Jefferson Savers" significant at the $p = .13$ level.
[f]Chi-square comparison of "All Savers" and "Jefferson Savers" significant at the $p = .001$ level.

FUTURE DIRECTIONS FOR JEFFERSON'S ADVERTISING

After the study results were presented to Crystal Advertising, the agency's task was to develop a total advertising program for JS for the coming fiscal year (July 1 to June 30). In developing this program, the agency hoped to draw heavily on the SRM research findings. Before it could develop an advertising program, however, the agency first had to interpret the results of the study.

In addition to providing data useful in planning JS advertising/promotional strategy, the Savings Preferences Study would also serve as a benchmark against which the results of the new campaign would be evaluated. At the end of the one-year campaign, another study following the same methodology would be conducted. Many of the same questions would be asked, and changes or shifts in respondents' levels of awareness, attitudes, and preferences would be used to evaluate the success of the campaign against previously established objectives.

Questions for Discussion and Review

1. Were the procedures followed in conducting the Savings Preferences Study sound from a methodological standpoint? What changes in the study's design would strengthen it?

2. What are some of the major conclusions that can be drawn from the data presented? Which of these conclusions are most important and useful in planning Jefferson's promotional programs?

3. How can the data presented be used to establish advertising objectives for the coming campaign?

4. What are some realistic advertising objectives for Jefferson to consider in guiding its advertising efforts and in evaluating the campaign's effectiveness? What are the strengths and weaknesses of alternative statements of advertising objectives?

Determining the Advertising Appropriation and Budgeting

No company that markets products or services to the consumer can remain a leader in its field without a deep-seated commitment to advertising.[1]

Edwin L. Artzt
CHAIRMAN AND CEO,
PROCTER & GAMBLE

INTRODUCTION

Determining an advertising budget is an old challenge. But, as media choices have become more numerous and the "noise" in the marketplace has increased, the budgeting decision has grown increasingly difficult. This chapter explores some traditionally popular advertising budgeting techniques as well as the new challenges facing advertising managers when dealing with the allocation of budgets for advertising efforts.

The relationship between advertising objectives and budget decisions is a vital one. It is important, therefore, to review some of the principles set forth in Chapter 4 to better understand the rationale behind advertising budget allocation models. This chapter will consider long-term and short-term advertising objectives as major criteria for budget decisions. The effectiveness of advertising expenditures will also be examined, as budgeting should be considered a control tool as well as a planning ingredient.

---

[1]Edwin L. Artzt, "Grooming the Next Generation of Management," *A.N.A./The Advertiser* (Spring 1992):69.

TRADITIONAL METHODS OF SETTING ADVERTISING BUDGETS

The advertising budgeting decision can be divided into two major components: (1) how much money should be spent on advertising and promotion within a specific time period, and (2) how the total advertising and promotion budget should be earmarked for different media, different products/services, and different geographic areas or target markets.

Determining the size of the advertising budget is a very important decision because it will affect the future impact of all of the firm's marketing efforts and be instrumental in determining the firm's future marketing strategy. In addition, an advertising and promotion budget is generally a major financial commitment of the firm and will be closely scrutinized by top management. It is crucial, therefore, that such a decision be made with a careful and thorough consideration of its potential effects, along with its constraints and limitations.

Some budgeting methods have been popular among advertising managers for many years. While all such methods have some shortcomings, they have allowed managers to plan and control the performance of the advertising and promotion functions by comparing against results within their industry or against the performance of major competitors. Such methods will be discussed next.

The Percentage-of-Sales Method

There are two ways of establishing an advertising budget according to the percentage-of-sales method. The first is to calculate advertising allocations as a fixed percentage of *past sales.* This calculation is done by applying a specific percentage number to the previous year's total sales revenue for a product, a line of products, or the whole company. The formula for this calculation is

$$A_2 = f(S_1)$$

where:
A_2 is the total advertising budget for next year (or period 2)
f is a percentage figure
S_1 is sales for period 1 (or last year's sales).

Advertising-to-sales ratios are computed by industry every year by professional advertising organizations. An example of such calculations can be seen in Table 5-1.

The reason for this practice is to provide a general overview of whether total advertising expenditures change over time by industry in response to market or competitive conditions. Year-to-year comparisons are also reported to provide another measure of relative growth for specific industries. For example, an article interpreting the advertising-to-sales figures of Table 5-1 stated that 11 of the business sectors reported had shown an increase in their advertising-to-sales ratio. The relative increase or decrease in advertising expenditures is also considered in light of economic conditions, since it

TABLE 5-1 Advertising-to-Sales Ratios, 1991, Computed by Industry Sampling

Industry	SIC no.	Ad Dollars as Percent of Sales	Ad Dollars as Percent of Margin	Annual Growth Rate (%)
Abrasive, asbestos, misc minerals	3290	1.1	3.9	(0.4)
Adhesives & sealants	2891	2.7	5.9	9.4
Agriculture chemicals	2870	0.7	3.1	7.4
Agriculture production-crops	100	2.2	7.1	14.3
Air cond, heating, refrig equip	3585	1.7	6.5	(0.9)
Air courier services	4513	1.2	9.9	11.7
Air transport, scheduled	4512	1.9	65.5	5.0
Aircraft & parts	3720	0.6	3.1	3.9
Aircraft parts, aux equip, NEC	3728	0.8	3.1	2.8
Apparel & other finished prods	2300	4.3	11.3	10.1
Apparel & accessory stores	5600	1.9	5.0	5.0
Auto & home supply stores	5531	2.2	8.9	9.2
Auto rent & lease, no drivers	7510	2.4	3.6	6.7
Automatic regulating controls	3822	3.3	11.5	5.8
Bakery products	2050	8.0	47.6	17.8
Beverages	2080	8.6	14.6	8.6
Bldg matl, hardware, garden-retail	5200	4.9	12.9	4.4
Books: publng, publng & printing	2731	2.9	6.0	3.8
Broadwoven fabric mill, cotton	2211	4.3	21.7	(1.5)
Btld & canned soft drinks, water	2086	3.0	6.6	6.2
Business services, NEC	7389	2.7	6.5	9.8
Cable & other pay TV services	4841	2.9	6.0	17.7
Can fruit, veg, presrv, jam, jelly	2033	2.6	8.4	14.4
Can, frozen presrv, fruit & veg	2030	7.7	18.9	8.8
Catalog, mail-order houses	5961	6.9	17.7	6.7
Chemicals & allied prods-whsl	5160	4.2	18.0	7.7
Chemicals & allied products	2800	2.3	6.1	12.1
Cigarettes	2111	3.9	6.6	(3.0)
Computer & comp software stores	5734	0.6	3.1	12.3
Computer integrated system design	7373	1.5	4.1	6.2
Computer processing, data prep svc	7374	1.5	2.9	8.4
Commercial printing	2750	2.7	10.4	11.0
Communications equipment, NEC	3669	2.1	4.9	11.3
Computer & office equipment	3570	1.6	3.3	7.1
Computer communication equipment	3576	1.9	4.0	13.1
Computer peripheral equip, NEC	3577	1.9	4.1	13.1
Computer storage devices	3572	1.4	4.8	18.9
Computers & software-wholesale	5045	0.6	5.2	14.4
Construction, mining, matl handle equip	3530	4.4	12.9	7.4
Convert paper, paperbd, ex boxes	2670	2.3	5.2	5.8
Cutlery, hand tools, gen hardware	3420	9.6	18.8	8.7
Dairy products	2020	4.1	11.2	22.9
Department stores	5311	2.8	14.3	4.5
Drug & proprietary stores	5912	1.6	5.6	7.4
Durable goods-wholesale, NEC	5099	3.6	7.6	32.4
Eating places	5812	3.4	17.9	7.8
Educational services	8200	6.9	15.7	11.5
Electrical measure & test instruments	3825	2.6	5.4	4.1
Electr, other elec equip, ex compuJtrs	3600	2.2	5.6	6.2

Sources: Schonfeld & Associates, 1 Sherwood Drive, Lincolnshire, Ill. 60069. (708) 948–8080.

Legend: SIC = Standard industrial classification. NEC = Not elsewhere classified.

Ad dollars as percent of sales: Ad expenditures/net sales. Ad dollars as percent of margin: Ad

Industry	SIC no.	Ad Dollars as Percent of Sales	Ad Dollars as Percent of Margin	Annual Growth Rate (%)
Electric lighting, wiring equip	3640	2.5	8.5	9.0
Electromedical apparatus	3845	1.3	2.2	11.2
Electronic comp, accessories	3670	0.7	2.3	9.6
Electronic computers	3571	3.6	7.2	10.3
Electronic parts, equip-whsl, NEC	5065	2.0	7.5	5.7
Engines & turbines	3510	1.3	6.6	(13.2)
Engr, acc, resrch, mgnt, rel svcs	8700	1.4	6.7	2.0
Equip rental & leasing, NEC	7359	0.7	2.4	4.5
Fabricated plate work	3443	1.0	3.7	10.2
Fabricated rubber products, NEC	3060	0.7	3.9	41.8
Facilities support mgmt svcs	8744	1.9	11.6	14.6
Family clothing stores	5651	2.3	6.8	12.8
Farm machinery & equipment	3523	1.1	4.5	6.6
Finance-services	6199	0.8	6.9	3.6
Food & kindred products	2000	6.3	14.9	9.6
Footwear, except rubber	3140	4.6	11.9	8.9
Functions rel to dep banking, NEC	6099	6.0	55.8	8.5
Furniture & home furnish-wholesale	5020	6.6	22.9	(14.6)
Furniture stores	5712	7.6	15.8	6.3
Games, toys, child veh, ex dolls	3944	16.3	33.5	9.9
Gen med & surgical hospitals	8062	0.3	1.7	(2.4)
Gen industrial machine & equip	3560	1.9	6.6	12.4
Glass, glassware-pressed, blown	3220	1.7	3.9	12.5
Grain mill products	2040	9.4	19.6	6.8
Greeting cards	2771	5.3	8.7	7.9
Groceries & related prods-whsl	5140	1.3	8.8	7.4
Grocery stores	5411	1.2	4.7	4.4
Guided missiles & space vehc	3760	1.3	7.4	(3.1)
Hardware, plumb, heat equip-whsl	5070	1.8	14.3	6.3
Help supply services	7363	1.7	7.5	10.1
Hobby, toy & game shops	5945	1.8	5.5	10.0
Home furniture & equip stores	5700	4.4	13.4	13.1
Hospital & medical svc plans	6324	0.9	5.4	13.3
Hospitals	8060	5.2	34.7	8.9
Hotels, motels, tourist courts	7011	3.9	13.8	6.0
Household appliances	3630	2.1	11.1	11.8
Household audio & video equip	3651	5.1	12.2	14.0
Household furniture	2510	3.8	13.9	11.2
Ice cream & frozen desserts	2024	5.6	21.1	13.4
Industrial inorganic chemicals	2810	19.4	44.2	7.6
Indl trucks, tractors, trailers	3537	0.9	3.8	7.4
Industrial measurement instr	3823	1.9	4.9	6.4
Industrial organic chemicals	2860	1.6	5.6	0.9
Investment advice	6282	8.0	21.6	5.3
Iron & steel foundries	3320	1.6	5.8	8.3
Jewelry stores	5944	2.8	8.2	11.4
Jewelry, precious metals	3911	2.3	5.5	8.7
Knit outerwear mills	2253	1.3	3.8	7.6
Knitting mills	2250	5.8	17.2	7.7

expenditures/(net sales − cost of goods sold). Annual growth rate of advertising dollars. Reprinted with permission from the September 16, 1991 issue of *Advertising Age.* Copyright 1991 by Crain Communications, Inc.

indicates the private-sector reaction to projected increases or decreases in sales.

This first budgeting model of advertising-to-sales ratio has some shortcomings. First, the use of past sales to determine future advertising allocations does not seem logical. Advertising is assumed to influence a firm's sales performance, yet the use of past sales to determine future advertising allocations will not take that interdependence into consideration. In addition, such a method would not allow the advertising manager to adjust the budget to meet emerging changes in the marketplace because the only criterion used is the past sales performance of the firm.

The second advertising-to-sales method attempts to eliminate these drawbacks. Instead of basing advertising expenditures on past sales, a forecast of *future (next year) sales* is made, and the advertising budget is calculated as a fixed percentage of that amount. The formula for this model is

$$A_2 = f(S_2)$$

where:

A_2 is the total advertising budget for next year (or period 2)
f is a fixed percentage
S_2 is the total sales forecasted for next year (or period 2).

This second model is an improvement over the previous one because it bases its budget calculation on the sales period that will theoretically be affected by the advertising expenditures to be budgeted. However, the model still reflects only one of the possible effects of advertising—its relationship to sales. It ignores all other possible variables that may be influenced by advertising, mainly some of its long-term effects.

The advertising-to-sales ratio is as good a method of budgeting advertising expenditures as a firm makes it. If used to develop a base allocation, which can be modified as the market or firm objectives change, then it is a very good initial yardstick for budget considerations.

The Competitive-Parity Method

Another popular method for setting advertising budgets is the competitive-parity method. This method establishes an advertising budget as a proportion or share of the product or service's market share. The expenditure on advertising for the product is expressed as a share of the total advertising expenditures for all products in that category. As an example, if the total advertising expenditure for athletic shoes is $100 million, and the expenditure for Nike is $30 million, Nike would have a 30 percent share of advertising, or a 30 percent *share of voice.*

The formula for the calculation of the "share of voice" for a specific product/service is as follows:

$$A_{SV} = \frac{A_F}{A_C + A_F}$$

where:

A_{sv} is the firm's advertising share of voice

A_F is the firm's advertising expenditures for the period in question

A_c is all competitors' advertising expenditures for the period in question.

The reason for using share of voice as a method for setting advertising budgets is the belief that, in a stable market, a firm's share of voice should ideally be the same as its share of market. If a firm were attempting to gain market share over its competition, its share of voice should be greater than its share of market. This would commonly be the case for new products entering a competitive marketplace.

The competitive-parity method also focuses on only one of the many variables affecting advertising. The fact that competitors' actions should be one of the variables considered when establishing advertising expenditures is undeniable. However, this method ignores other important factors that may affect advertising allocation. Changes in consumer habits, economic conditions, and the strategic objectives of a firm are some of the forces that should be taken into account.

This method does have some advantages. It provides a yardstick for comparing results whenever a product faces a very stable market and enjoys a mature competitive position. As such, it is a useful planning and control tool.

An example of the use of competitive-parity spending can be seen in the recent move by some automobile companies. In an article appearing in *Advertising Age* on October 28, 1992, Ford Motor Company and the Chrysler Corporation stated that they planned to increase their advertising spending to try to reclaim market shares lost to Japanese competitors. Japanese auto manufacturers had advertised very heavily in 1991, and domestic manufacturers believed that in order to recapture their market share they would have to fight back with an increased budget. The advertising expenditures of General Motors and Toyota, for example, appeared to be very different for the first six months of 1991. General Motors had spent 6 percent less than the previous year, while Toyota had spent 11 percent more. Sources from the companies indicated that they felt Toyota's increased advertising expenditure was responsible for the relative market share of the two companies. In this specific example, the competitive-parity method appears to have been the main motivation behind the domestic manufacturers' reaction to competitive spending.

The competitive-parity method also takes into consideration the long-term effects of advertising. To establish a stable market share, the competitive-parity method suggests that a firm should maintain a share of voice over a certain period of time. Many leaders in industry believe likewise. Edwin Artzt, chairman and CEO of Procter & Gamble, stated that "advertising is a longer-term investment, and it shouldn't be intruded upon by short-term needs." This statement supports continued expenditures in advertising in spite of changes in profits and sales. The expenditures should continue to reflect a firm's competitive position as opposed to a concentration on immediate results.

The Objective-and-Task Method

The objective-and-task method of setting advertising budgets is used by the majority of the largest advertisers in the United States.[2] According to this method, a firm will first set objectives for its advertising task. These objectives may include reaching a certain percentage of the population or of prospective customers, creating awareness of the product among a percentage of the individuals within a specific market or geographical area, and so on. After these objectives have been set, the firm calculates which media to purchase and at what cost. That cost may be arrived at by deciding what percentage of the total population should be reached by the advertisement and how many times each individual in that population should be exposed to the advertising message. The cost of obtaining this advertising reach and frequency will then be translated into an advertising budget.

This approach is more logical than the previous two approaches because it relates specific tasks of advertising to the amount of money being spent to accomplish those tasks. It also relates the theory of advertising effect to the budget decisions. For example, if the main goal of advertising is to develop awareness among the public, then fewer exposures per person will be needed than if the objective is to achieve customer preference for the product.

The major problem with this approach is that it doesn't fully consider the relationship between short-term and long-term effects of advertising or translate them immediately into a budgeting decision. In addition, although a certain number of exposures may produce a specific effect on the audience, that relationship is not always constant or measurable. Nevertheless, the objective-and-task method is an improvement over the percentage-of-sales method and the competitive-parity method. This method has been refined using different mathematical models. Large advertising firms have developed their own internal models which they use to formulate budgets in specific product and service categories. This practice illustrates the belief that the memorability and efficiency of advertising will differ by product categories or according to geographic or demographic factors.

An example of the application of the objective-and-task method is a recent decision by Anheuser-Busch to advertise its products to female consumers. At the end of 1991, Anheuser-Busch kicked off a sharply different campaign, directed primarily at women. Its purpose was to try to cut through the typical sexism of beer advertising and to treat women as equals. The previous advertising appeal used by Anheuser-Busch was the "Nothing beats a Bud" campaign—a two-year-old campaign that the manufacturer believed was no longer timely and was perceived as arrogant by women.

The chairman of Anheuser-Busch stated when unveiling the campaign that the company wanted to portray both men and women as healthy and vital individuals. It did not want to be perceived as using women as sex objects. The

---

[2]Charles H. Patti and Vincent Blasko, "Budgeting Practices of Big Advertisers," *Journal of Advertising Research* 21 (December 1981): 23–29.

budget for this campaign was considerably higher than for the previous campaign because the advertiser was focusing on a specific target market and trying to obtain particular results from the advertising.[3]

Although there are many other ways to establish an advertising budget, the three methods discussed in this portion of the chapter are the ones most commonly used by advertising firms and agencies. Another method frequently mentioned is the "all-you-can-afford" method, meaning a firm will decide to spend as much money as it can on advertising without regard to specific objectives, to competitive parity, or even to the level of sales. In addition, economic models are used to try to achieve a level of expenditure that will bring a positive marginal gain to the company. Examples of such methods abound in specific studies made for classes or even brands of products over the years. As marketing factors change drastically and as the number of variables affecting marketing decisions increases, economic models to develop advertising budgets and to assess advertising effectiveness are becoming increasingly complicated. Nevertheless, in the future it is expected that more and more firms and advertising agencies alike will resort to such models because advertising expenditures are increasing and the accountability of advertising is becoming more of an issue, at least among U.S. advertisers. The next section will consider recent changes in advertising budgeting methods.

RECENT TRENDS IN ADVERTISING BUDGETING DECISIONS

The late 1980s and the early 1990s witnessed a major change in consumer responses to advertising in the United States. Following a period of economic growth caused by massive defense spending by the federal government, U.S. producers found themselves trying to reach a market faced with slowed income growth and higher unemployment. The American recession and the increase in foreign and domestic competition produced a market situation that advertisers had not faced before. One of its immediate effects was an increase in the number of appeals that proposed immediate results for the consumer. Coupons, price cuttings, discounts, and special promotions became more common in the marketplace, with varying market reactions. One such reaction was the perception that brand advertising no longer worked. Brands are insubstantial things that signal differences between products. Good brands are supported by large amounts of advertising expenditures. Despite the evidence of the value of brands, in the early 1990s, creating and sustaining brands became increasingly difficult. Manufacturers were under pressure to make big short-run gains in sales, and a lot of brand managers gave up long-term advertising expenditures on behalf of short-term promotional tools such as sweepstakes, price cutting, and price promotions.

---

[3]Ira Teinowitz, "This Bud's for Her—Women to Get 'Equal Roles' in New A-B Campaign," *Advertising Age,* October 28, 1991, 1 and 49.

One of the focuses of advertising budgeting has to be deciding just how important specific brands are for a given firm or market. Advertisers should weigh the relative importance of price, the product itself, or the brand name before deciding how to allocate advertising expenditures. As consumers become more discriminating and as they perceive products to be more and more similar, the importance of brand advertising may decrease.

Firms have tried to attack the problem of the declining importance of brands in different ways. Manufacturers have tried to steer consumers' attention away from promotion by developing a stronger image for some of their specific products rather than developing an image for a product class. Campbell's Soup, for example, has emphasized in its advertising soups with less salt or soups developed for consumption by children. This steering away from the previous umbrella strategy of brand advertising is one of many attempts to reestablish the long-term importance of brand image in the marketplace.

Another trend of the early 1990s is the focus on environmental, political, or controversial issues. Some corporations have developed campaigns dealing with such issues; an example is the Benetton campaign mentioned in Chapter 3. When the topic was so controversial that a specific corporate sponsor might not want to be identified with it, a nonprofit organization of sorts established by interested corporations was used as the campaign spokesperson.

Corporate critics have argued that it is unfair for companies to campaign in their own interest while hiding behind fictitious foundations. An example is the campaign against the animal rights movement by Americans for Medical Progress, an "educational foundation" largely funded by U.S. Surgical Corp. U.S. Surgical is a medical company with annual sales of more than $800 million that kills thousands of dogs each year so that its customers—physicians—can practice surgery using U.S. Surgical products. The campaign features print advertisements with a picture of a white rat and the caption, "Some People Just See a Rat. We See a Cure for Cancer."

Several organizations of this kind provide a public relations front for corporations to campaign for causes that benefit them. The American Council on Science and Health, which counts among its contributors Anheuser-Busch, Philip Morris, and Dow Chemical, is another example of this type of entity.[4]

In addition to these two trends, advertisers are groping for new ways to cut through the clutter of advertising messages and enrich the consumer in an effective manner. This effort is not confined to media advertising but also incorporates such promotional tools as coupons and direct response advertising. For example, in an attempt to cut through the clutter of coupons reaching Americans every year, a Connecticut supermarket promotion firm named Actmedia worked out a different technique. In an average year, over 280

---

[4]Laura Bird, "Corporate Critics Complain Companies Hide Behind 'Grass-Roots' Campaigns," *The Wall Street Journal,* July 8, 1992, B-1 and B-6.

billion coupons are distributed in the United States. This means that every U.S. household will receive about 3,000 coupons. The redemption rate of coupons is very low, however; only 1 in every 50 coupons is actually redeemed by consumers. Actmedia asserts that the use of coupon machines that dispense coupons at the supermarket is more effective than the media distribution of coupons. It contends that consumers who pick up the coupons as they shop in the aisles of the supermarket are actually interested in the specific product that is being featured and are therefore more likely to purchase it. The Actmedia theory is supported by some of its corporate customers. Such companies include Hormel, Procter & Gamble, and Great Atlantic & Pacific Tea. Grocers do not pay anything for the machines, and an average store will obtain about ten machines. Actmedia receives a monthly fee from the marketers, and the advertiser takes full responsibility for the cost of coupon redemption. Whether this promotional technique is more valuable than the traditional distribution of coupons still has to be proven; nevertheless, this innovative move shows one more way in which advertising budgets are being adjusted to meet the changing times.

CONCLUSION

Advertising budgeting is a very important management function. The advertising budget is a planning tool in that it allows the advertiser to develop both short-term and long-term objectives and to allocate a specific allowance of money to accomplish them. At the same time, budgeting is a control tool in that it allows the advertiser to verify which advertising techniques best serve their intended purposes.

In recent years, advertising budget decision makers in the United States have faced a changing environment. In an effort to adapt to that environment, advertisers and advertising agencies alike have come up with different techniques yet to be proven effective. This experimentation has led to the view that advertising expenditures should be integrated more directly with all other marketing functions of the firm, thereby strengthening their interdependence.

As our markets become more global, the clutter of advertising messages increases, and consumers become more educated and more discriminating, advertising budgets will have to adapt to these changing conditions. More innovative ways of spending advertising allocations will have to be devised by advertising agencies and by manufacturers. In addition, new and innovative media channels are continuing to appear, allowing advertisers to experiment with different ways of conveying their messages to the public. Interactive media and sales channels are but a few that are changing the world of advertising today. An advertising manager should keep in mind that adapting to change is essential to survival, and the ability to adapt and to devise effective advertising methods is crucial to the long-term survival both of the firm and of advertising as we know it today.

Suggested Readings

Aaker, David A., and James M. Carman. "Are You Overadvertising?" *Journal of Advertising Research* 24 (June–July 1984): 37–44.

Aaker, David A., and John G. Myers. *Advertising Management.* 3d ed. Englewood Cliffs, N.J.: Prentice-Hall, 1987, 61–84.

Colley, Russell H. *Defining Advertising Goals for Measured Advertising Results.* New York: Association of National Advertisers, 1961, 1.

Green, Charles P. "A Model for Evaluating Individual's Behavior When Influenced by Advertising." *Journal of Media Planning* (Fall 1989): 16–19.

Levin, Gary. "It's Tough Not to Work by the Numbers—Agencies Grow Frustrated by Hard-to-Quantify Ad Systems." *Advertising Age,* August 27, 1990, S-2 and S-4.

Patti, Charles H., and Vincent Blasko. "Budgeting Practices of Big Advertisers." *Journal of Advertising Research* 21 (December 1981):23–29.

Premier, Gus. "A Better Media Model Starts With Understanding of How Advertising Works." *Journal of Media Planning* (Fall 1989): 29–32.

Exercises

1.   During the late 1980s, frozen yogurt became one of America's favorite desserts and snacks. Sales of frozen yogurt reached an all-time high during 1988 and 1989.

At the beginning of 1992, total consumption of frozen desserts started to fall. In 1992, frozen yogurt showed the largest market loss among all frozen desserts. During early 1991, 44 percent of the respondents in a market study stated that they had eaten frozen yogurt in the previous four weeks; in 1992, that same study showed that only 38 percent of respondents had done so. This represented a 15 percent decrease in frozen yogurt consumption.

The vice-president of marketing for a large franchise chain of frozen yogurt outlets is concerned about this problem. She believes that a good advertising campaign can increase people's awareness of her brand and their overall consumption of frozen yogurt. Total sales of yogurt for the chain had been $50 million per year. Last year, total sales were $43 million. In the past, the chain had spent 7 percent of sales on advertising, on average.

Indicate what variables should be considered when planning an advertising campaign for this frozen yogurt chain. How should the vice-president of marketing establish a budget for the campaign? What total budget would be appropriate to achieve her intended goals?

Source: Valerie Reitman, "For Frozen Yogurt a Chill Wind Blows," *The Wall Street Journal,* June 3, 1992.

2.   The two major competitors in the sneakers market in the United States are Nike and Reebok, with 30 percent and 25 percent shares, respectively. In 1991, Nike spent $100 million on U.S. advertising, while Reebok spent $76 million.

In 1992, the athletic shoe market appeared to have flattened out. It was estimated that the $5.8 billion athletic shoe market was growing at just 4 percent a year. In view of sluggish sales, Nike announced that its 1992 advertising expenditures would be increased to $115 million. Reebok also decided to increase its commitment to advertising and announced an 18 percent hike, or a total projected advertising expenditure for 1992 of $90 million.

Are Reebok and Nike spending enough on advertising, assuming the two companies adopt the competitive-parity method of advertising budgeting? In your judgment, will the increase in advertising for both competitors' budgets stimulate an increase in consumption of athletic shoes in general? Will the budget increases benefit Reebok and Nike only? Explain your thoughts.

Source: Joanne Lipman, "Sneaker Ads Fail to Put a Bounce in 1992 Profits," *The Wall Street Journal,* June 12, 1992, B-1 and B-6.

3. An advertiser of children's toys set advertising expenditures for the current year at $250,000. Sales for the same period were $7.5 million. The marketing manager for the company was convinced, however, that an increase in the advertising budget would cause much greater sales. The president of the firm disagreed, arguing that advertising expenditures were excessive and a large portion of advertising dollars were, in fact, wasted.

To test which of the two theories was correct, the company divided its sales territory into four portions with similar sales potential. The following year's sales were expected to reach $10 million, and each of the four submarkets was expected to contribute 25 percent of total sales revenue.

The advertising budget for the following year was set at $83,500 for two of the four submarkets. One of the remaining submarkets was given an advertising allocation of $125,000, while the remaining submarket received only $41,750.

Sales increased by 40 percent in the market with the largest advertising budget. The two submarkets that received $83,500 each in advertising registered an increase of 20 percent in sales over the previous year, while the submarket with the smallest advertising budget registered a drop of 60 percent in sales.

Which one of the two executives was right? Plot on a graph the advertising expenditures and corresponding sales for all four territories. What level of advertising would be most desirable for this particular toy manufacturer, based on the results of the experiment?

4. Suppose that a company sets its advertising budget utilizing the percentage-of-sales method. Sales for last year were $1 million, and next year's sales are projected to reach $1.2 million. If the percentage-of-sales allocation used is 6 percent, what will be the advertising budget for next year? What other variables would you suggest the company consider when making its advertising allocation decision? Discuss.

Bernard's Entrée for Two

Bob Bernard, president of Bernard Foods, Inc., of Lafayette, Louisiana, believed he had an exceptional opportunity to establish his brand in an exciting new category—chilled foods. To capitalize on this opportunity, Bernard needed a marketing and advertising program that would persuade consumers to try his brand—Bernard's Entrée for Two (BE). Six years of experience with the brand had indicated that once consumers tried the product, a significant proportion would adopt it for continuing use. For example, 2,000 returned in-pack response cards indicated an overall "excellent" rating of 8.3 on a 9-point scale and a 93.8 percent repurchase intent.

THE CHILLED FOODS CATEGORY

While chilled foods were recognized as a major growth area in supermarkets, the category had been a trouble spot for several manufacturers. At least five major players and several smaller companies had marketed entries in the category with mixed results. Both Campbell's Fresh Chef and General Foods' Culinova had been pulled after test marketing because of pricing problems and mishandling at the retail level. Three other major entries—Nestlé's FreshNes, Carnation's Contadina, and Kraft's Chillery—were alive but had experienced problems, and only Contadina appeared to be even close to fulfilling its promise. Another smaller company, Culinary Brands, had pulled its chilled foods product after a prolonged test.

The problems experienced by each of these brands were similar. First, a short shelf life, usually five to fourteen days, necessitated an expensive store-door delivery system and resulted in high returns due to out-of-code product. Second, the cost of the product was relatively high. The more expensive distribution system and greater waste increased the product's price point well above that of frozen foods. Prices were often $5 to $9 per meal, versus $1 to $4 for frozen meals. Third, the new category lacked a clear position in the supermarket. Chilled food items usually ended up in the deli area and were forced to compete for space with higher-margin items.

This case was written by Owen Hannay, The Richards Group, Dallas, Texas, and John H. Murphy, The University of Texas at Austin, and is intended to serve as a basis for class discussion, not to illustrate either the effective or ineffective handling of an administrative situation. Used by permission of Bernard Foods, Inc.

BERNARD'S CHILLED FOODS PRODUCT LINE

Bob and Lynn Bernard had developed a proprietary process for packaging fresh seafood entrées at the peak of readiness for shipment to supermarkets refrigerated, not frozen. This process enabled the Bernards to "create entrées which taste exactly like the Creole recipe we serve at home in Lafayette." Each entrée was made from high-quality Louisiana seafood such as gulf shrimp and crab, freshly chopped vegetables, real aged cheddar cheese, and authentic seasonings and spices. Entrées were microwavable, and each was packaged along with a pouch of rice, both of which could be ready to eat within ten minutes since they were not frozen.

The BE product line included seven entrées: Shrimp Creole, Seafood Gumbo, Shrimp Etouffée, Crabmeat Au Gratin, Shrimp Marinara, Shrimp Orleans, and Chicken & Sausage Gumbo. BE items were packaged in an attractive plastic tub (see Exhibit 5-1-1) and sold in the fresh seafood department of supermarkets. The tub contained separate packets of rice and pour-over entrée. Any leftovers could be stored in the same container. BE items sold for $4.99 per package, which served two people. This price compared favorably with premium frozen entrées, which cost almost as much but served only one person.

BE differed from other ventures in the chilled foods category in five significant ways. First, Bernard's preparation process allowed for a 45-day shelf life—much longer than that of other entrées. This enabled Bernard's to use existing distribution systems. Second, the line was primarily seafood, which provided both a stronger reason for the fresh meal ("Seafood doesn't freeze well") and a potential problem of consumer acceptance ("Seafood can't stay fresh for more than two to three days"). Third, Bernard's entrées were

---

EXHIBIT 5-1-1 Bernard's Entrée for Two Product Packaging

TABLE 5-1-1   Bernard Foods, Inc., Distribution and Sales Analysis

Markets	Percentage of U.S. Television Households[a]	Estimated Current Percentage Distribution	Development Index
Core Market			
New Orleans	.65%	90%	100
Baton Rouge	.27	80	90
Austin	.41	90	75
Underdeveloped Markets			
Lafayette	.20%	70%	60
Lake Charles	.09	70	60
Atlanta	1.59	50	20
Birmingham	.55	50	10
Columbus, Ohio	.75	50	15
Dallas	1.92	75	30
Houston	1.58	40	40
San Antonio	.64	75	20
Memphis	.65	50	10
Mobile	.45	50	10
Nashville	.79	50	10

[a]Source: 1991–1992 Arbitron Universe Estimates Summary.
[b]Sales and spending figures have been disguised.

packaged to serve two; this made them a better overall value but created a higher overall price point for trial than that of typical single servings of frozen entrées. Fourth, BE items were distributed through the fresh seafood/meat department, which made them unique items for the seafood manager but difficult for consumers to find. Managers were enthusiastic about the product because they believed that BE meals provided "plus business" — that is, added sales to their section of the supermarket without taking sales away from their other items, such as fresh fish and crab. Finally, the Bernards' Louisiana heritage made their product unique.

THE PRESENT SITUATION

BE meals were introduced in New Orleans in February 1986. More than six years later, they were distributed through a number of major supermarket chains in New Orleans, Baton Rouge, Lafayette, and Lake Charles, as well as in other parts of Louisiana. BE items were also available in major supermarket chains in Atlanta, Austin, Birmingham, Columbus (Ohio), Dallas, Houston, Memphis, Mobile, Nashville, and San Antonio. These chains also had made the brand available in other locations they serviced. For example, in Houston, BE meals were available only in Randall's and AppleTree; hence, while significant, distribution in Houston was limited. In Austin, on the other hand, BE meals were available in Albertson's, AppleTree, H.E.B., and Tom Thumb for a 90 percent distribution based on grocery volume. Table 5-1-1 presents data on

Sales per Thousand Households[b]	Percentage Sales Growth History		
	Year X	X + 1	X + 2
$1,250	+50%[cd]	+150%[c]	+100%[c]
1,125	+20[d]	+100[c]	+200[c]
750	—	+20	+100[c]
$ 500	+20%	+20%	+20%
500	+20	+20	+30
100	—	—	+30[d]
50	—	—	+40
75	—	—	+30
163	—	+20	+30
200	—	+20	+20
100	—	—	+60[d]
63	+10	+10	—
50	—	—	+30
50	+10	+15	—

[c]Advertised in the market during that year.
[d]Growth attributable primarily to increased distribution.

the distribution and sales of Bernard's Entrée for Two by market. Sales varied significantly by months, with Lent having an index of roughly 120, and July, August, and September having an index of roughly 80. The remaining months had an index of approximately 100.

Mediamark Research, Inc. (MRI) data on the "Frozen Main Courses" category indicated a concentration of users among the 25 to 54 age group with household income of $35,000+, and heavier use in the larger A and B sized counties. BE had targeted Stouffers, Healthy Choice, Le Menu, and others in this category as primary competitors.

Bernard's sales and spending as a percentage of sales for the three core markets are presented in Table 5-1-2. Bernard's had typically invested heavily

TABLE 5-1-2 Bernard Foods, Inc., Sales and Advertising Spending Last Year in Core Markets

Market	Sales[a]	Advertising as a Percent of Sales
New Orleans	$750,000	10%
Baton Rouge	300,000	17
Austin	350,000	28

[a]Note: Sales and spending figures have been disguised.

in newer markets and then lowered spending levels considerably in years two, three, and four. None of the markets outside of the core had ever received advertising support.

In addition to advertising, BE had been promoted in many markets using in-store sampling. The success of in-store sampling stemmed from the fact that once prospective consumers tried a sample, they realized the quality of the product and were likely to make a purchase. The results of in-store sampling indicated that, on average, 43 meals were sold per day, 217 customers sampled meals, labor expenses were $66.53, and 10.5 samples were used. In the past, BE had used cross-promotions with rice, wine, and bread companies. For example, a Gallo wine promotion offered $1 off a Bernard's entrée with the purchase of a bottle of wine. BE coupon response rates had not been high in markets with low product penetration/awareness. Promotions to the trade had been limited to a "Win a trip to New Orleans" contest, and BE had never paid a slotting allowance to gain distribution. In fact, Bob Bernard had resisted distribution offers from some supermarket chains because he believed it could be a mistake to stock the brand in locations without adequate marketing support to drive sales.

To realize BE's potential, Bernard believed that three major barriers to awareness and trial would have to be overcome. These barriers were summarized as follows:

1. *New form and location for prepared entrée.* BE offered the first refrigerated seafood entrée. While BE meals were sold in the seafood department, other competitive prepared entrées were sold in the frozen food section of the supermarket. This resulted in confusion among consumers about where to find BE items.

2. *Poor retail visibility.* Merchandising in the seafood department varied from store to store. "Shelf" locations included ice bins in front of the full-service counter, a small section in the meat case, and upright refrigerated coolers. BE items were shelved together with a hodgepodge of unrelated items, such as shrimp cocktail and packaged oysters.

3. *High-ticket item.* The quality and convenience of BE meals contributed to an attractive value. However, $4.99 represented a high price point for an initial purchase.

TEST-MARKET DATA

Austin had been used as a test market for BE. A television commercial (see Exhibit 5-1-2) had been airing heavily in Austin for six months. The stated objective of the test was "to test the ability of an advertising-oriented marketing program to significantly establish the brand as a viable business." In addition to the television advertising, BE had been supported in Austin with promotions to the trade ("Win a Trip to New Orleans"), an in-store sampling program, public relations efforts, and couponing.

To determine the Austin market's acceptance of BE products, a survey research project was conducted. The purpose of the study was to provide insights useful in planning future advertising efforts and to serve as a

EXHIBIT 5-1-2   TV Storyboard for Bernard's Entrée for Two "Ice Bombs"

BERNARD FOODS, INC.   :30 TV   "FRESH/NEVER FROZEN"

SFX: Arctic wind/freezer "roar"

Introducing Bernard's Entrees For Two. Guaranteed fresh, never frozen.

SFX: "Kaboom" as competitor's product hits counter

Just minutes in the microwave, and they come out full of the flavor of Louisiana.

Upbeat Zydeco music up and under

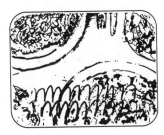

New Bernard's Entrees For Two.

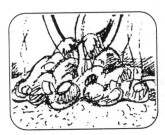

Super: Bernard's Shrimp Creole

Look for them in the fresh seafood and meat case.
SFX: "Kaboom"
But not the freezer.

TABLE 5-1-3   Bernard Foods, Inc., Selected Survey Research Findings

	Top-of-Mind Awareness[a]		Aided Awareness	Ever Tried?	Tried in Past 30 Days?
	First Mention	**Any Mention**			
Stouffers	23%	30%	84%	54%	17%
Healthy Choice	8	18	76	40	12
Bernard's Entrées	—	2	36	12	3
Lean Cuisine	12	21	89	53	14
Contadina	—	1	42	9	1
Le Menu	2	7	82	37	7
Swanson	9	15	84	52	10
Budget Gourmet	3	6	55	34	8
Weight Watchers	3	8	88	30	9
Night Hawk	4	7	72	38	8
Banquet	3	6	77	40	9
Others	3	23	—	—	—

[a]The question was: "When I mention pre-prepared meals or entrées that you heat up at home, what brands come to mind?"

benchmark against which to evaluate the impact of the upcoming campaign. (It was assumed that the Austin findings could be adjusted appropriately based on past sales to approximate findings in other markets.) A telephone survey was conducted using a random sample of Austin residents aged 25 to 64 who reported they were the male or female household head. A total of 217 interviews was completed by a survey research organization using a structured questionnaire. All interviews were conducted under close supervision in the firm's facility, and all interviewers' work was verified for accuracy.

The final sample in the study had the following profile: 59 percent female; 77 percent employed; 55 percent married; 29 percent aged 25 to 29, 36 percent aged 30 to 39, 35 percent aged 40 to 64; 57 percent college graduates; and 26 percent living in households with total income over $50,000. Selected relevant findings are presented in Table 5-1-3. In addition, the study revealed that *among those who had heard of BE:*

- 74 percent remembered having seen the commercial.
- 60 percent indicated BE meals were sold in the meat/seafood section of the supermarket.
- The vast majority rated BE meals as "excellent" in terms of "overall flavor," "value," and "ease of preparation."

PLANNING FOR THE NEXT SIX MONTHS

Bob Bernard requested that BE's agency, The Richards Group, develop a six-month campaign with two thrusts. First and most important, the agency was asked to develop a campaign to support and expand BE's franchise in the three "core markets" where the brand was established—New Orleans, Baton Rouge, and Austin. The overall marketing objective the campaign was to support was to increase sales in these markets 75 percent over sales achieved during the first six months of the previous year. The second objective was to develop a parallel campaign to expand trial and build BE's franchise in 11 other major markets where the company had distribution but had not firmly established itself. These 11 markets, which were considered "underdeveloped" in terms of their potential, were Atlanta, Birmingham, Columbus (Ohio), Dallas, Houston, Lake Charles, Lafayette, Memphis, Mobile, Nashville, and San Antonio. The overall marketing objective established for the underdeveloped markets was a 50 percent increase in total sales over sales during the first six months of the previous year.

The agency was instructed to use its own judgment in identifying the best target consumers, allocating the appropriation between core and underdeveloped markets, determining the appropriation for each market (possibly no investment in some markets), and tackling media planning and budgeting. The Richards Group's objective was to stretch limited dollars by making the most efficient trade-offs among markets, targets, media, and other factors. Finally, the agency was asked to build research into its recommendations in such a way that the advertising was accountable.

In developing a recommended appropriation and tentative budget for presentation to Bernard, the agency noted that in past years BE had invested between 10 percent and 30 percent of sales in advertising. In analyzing the cost efficiency of advertising across the 14 markets, the agency began by examining SQUAD cost information. These estimates are presented in Table 5-1-4. The media cost per rating point estimates in Table 5-1-4 were used to create Table 5-1-5, which approximates the average ratings of TV shows by dayparts. In addition, Table 5-1-5 provides media planning guidelines used by The Richards Group concerning the *minimum* number of rating points acceptable per week by dayparts.

Questions for Discussion and Review

1. What factors play an important role in determining how much money BE should invest in advertising? In other forms of marketing communication?

2. How does BE's low distribution in some markets impact the decision of which markets to emphasize during the upcoming six-month marketing effort? How can media costs be most appropriately factored into the decision as to which markets to advertise in?

3. What would be a reasonable trade-off between core and underdeveloped markets in terms of advertising investment? Why?

4. How could the various elements in BE's communication mix be coordinated?

TABLE 5-1-4 Bernard Foods, Inc., Estimated TV and Radio Costs per Rating Point for Adults 25 to 54, Plus Newspaper Costs and Circulation

	Prime	Prime Access	Daytime	Early Fringe	Late Fringe	Early News	Late News	Radio	Newspaper per col. inch + circulation			
									Daily	Sunday	Daily (000)	Sunday (000)
Atlanta	$221	$100	$ 68	$102	$102	$ 88	$144	$ 80	$207	$258	499	722
Austin	52	41	28	40	37	37	49	28	79	98	181	237
Baton Rouge	34	30	25	26	21	29	30	10	47	51	107	146
Birmingham	52	33	23	31	33	28	44	41	92	88	235	222
Columbus (OH)	103	61	56	55	76	66	78	56	97	140	276	414
Dallas	442	212	140	153	162	190	343	122	184	204	414	649
Houston	334	159	165	161	146	152	274	124	172	147	427	653
Lafayette	35	27	18	22	20	25	28	12	18	19	32	32
Lake Charles	20	12	11	10	10	13	11	14	16	17	39	40
Memphis	56	48	29	29	28	38	51	46	163	173	188	296
Mobile	37	34	33	45	36	42	41	15	37	37	106	116
Nashville	80	71	48	53	69	64	76	48	112	151	207	279
New Orleans	89	55	33	43	49	64	84	44	95	98	278	336
San Antonio	77	62	41	59	47	75	67	57	113	125	197	292

Source: Spot Quotations and Data, Inc., April 1992.

TABLE 5-1-5 Bernard Foods, Inc., Daypart Ratings, Minimum Point Levels, and Average TV Home Ratings

Daypart[a]	Average Household Rating	Average Rating Among Those Aged 25 to 54	Approximate Minimum Level/Week[b]
Early morning: 6–9 A.M.	3.0	1.8	9
Daytime: 9 A.M.–3 P.M.	5.5	3.3	20
Early fringe: 3–5 P.M.	5.0	3.0	15
Early news: 5–6:30 P.M.	9.5	5.7	17
Prime access: 6:30–7 P.M.	9.0	5.4	20
Prime time: 7–10 P.M.	16.0	9.6	30
Late news: 10–10:30 P.M.	10.5	6.3	20
Late fringe: 10:30 P.M.–1 A.M.	4.0	2.4	9

[a]Daypart times are for the central time zone.

[b]The minimum levels recommended here should be considered guidelines only; for example, if prime time is used as a daypart, 30 points (or three spots per week) should be considered a minimum level.

C A S E   5 - 2

Barbara's Flower Market

Barbara's Flower Market, owned and operated by Gregory Berry, was a full-service florist shop that had operated in Austin, Texas, for more than ten years. Barbara's primarily sold cut flowers, arrangements, and plants. The store was a member of a number of wire services, including the FTD national network of florists. Barbara's offered a no-minimum-charge home delivery service through which it made any delivery, from single to multiple items. The store stocked a line of gift items ranging from greeting cards to potpourri baskets. The gift cards could be described as a bit off-the-wall.

Barbara's stressed its ability to handle large weddings, religious ceremonies, and funerals. The store employed one full-time designer and four part-time designers to meet seasonal demands. All the designers and Gregory

This case was written by John H. Murphy, The University of Texas at Austin, and is intended to serve as the basis for class discussion, not to illustrate either the effective or ineffective handling of an administrative situation.

Berry performed sales duties, and for the past five years the day-to-day operations had been overseen by the general manager, Nina Castro. The staff of Barbara's all had considerable expertise with the flowers and plants they handled.

Barbara's imported most of its fresh-cut flowers and all of its roses from California, Florida, or outside the United States. Last year Barbara's instituted a unique pricing policy of undercutting other florists. In fact, almost two-thirds of Barbara's stock sold for less than a dollar per stem. Lower prices were believed to have increased the volume of sales and helped differentiate Barbara's from other florists.

FLORIST INDUSTRY TRENDS

Most florists nationwide were small businesses, but this did not mean that they were struggling financially. On the contrary, the industry was in good health despite a reasonably prolonged period of tight money, inflation, and cost consciousness by consumers.

As an industry, florists had experienced steady growth over the past five years, and sales were projected to increase in the neighborhood of 15 percent during the coming year. Florists had done particularly well in the growing market for fresh-cut roses. Roses accounted for 20 percent of total industry sales, and the growth of this segment was expected to continue to be strong.

A threat of some concern to the florist industry's growth was the entrance of supermarkets, nurseries, and discount stores into the fresh-cut flower market. These new entries had in the past concentrated on selling green plants and had met relatively little success because of the overall weakness of this market. However, many of the larger retailers had begun carrying fresh-cut flowers at lower prices than florists could match. Although at the present time approximately 88 percent of the purchases of cut flowers were from a florist, the new entries introduced some long-run uncertainty into this market.

Historically, florists had higher sales in the months of April, May, and December (see Table 5-2-1). Further, roughly 80 percent of all floral items were purchased for gifts and 20 percent for personal use. Flowers and plants were generally considered a "safe" gift because they were emotionally appealing and the vast majority of people appreciated receiving them.

National FTD data indicated that flowers were purchased as gifts for the following reasons: get well (15 percent); funeral (14 percent); anniversary (13 percent); Mother's Day (11 percent); surprise (10 percent); birthday (9 percent); holiday (8 percent); and other occasions (20 percent). (Note that inclusion of non–FTD sales by local FTD members would change these estimates somewhat.) Further, most flower purchases were singular in nature; that is, they were bought on a cash-and-carry basis exclusive of other flower purchases. The most frequently purchased items were arrangements, which accounted for slightly less than 50 percent of all flower purchases nationwide from florists.

TABLE 5-2-1 Percentage of Retail Sales by Month

	All Retail Stores	Florists
January	7.0%	6.7%
February	6.9	8.2
March	8.2	7.5
April	8.0	10.0
May	8.4	13.7
June	8.5	6.3
July	8.2	6.2
August	8.8	5.8
September	8.2	6.4
October	8.6	6.7
November	8.9	7.0
December	10.3	15.5

Sources: U.S. Department of Commerce and Florists' Transworld Delivery Association.

TARGET MARKET

In organizing the firm's marketing efforts, Barbara's management identified its target market. The market consisted of businesses in a ten- to fifteen-block radius of the store. This geographic market area included downtown Austin, student neighborhoods, and some very affluent residential areas west of downtown. Barbara's management decided that obtaining business accounts first would lead to a greater chance of procuring personal accounts. Not only would Barbara's get the one new business account, but there would be the potential of developing a personal account with every individual who worked in the business.

COMPETITION

Barbara's competed in a market that was highly fragmented, with no truly dominant florist competitor. Most of the 97 local firms listed in the Yellow Pages under "Florists—Retail" could be classified as reasonably small businesses grossing under $100,000 per year. Eighty-nine percent of Austin's florists had only one location. Freytag's had the most locations (five), and another large florist, Connely-Hillen, had three locations. The bulk of the other multiple-outlet florists had two locations.

CURRENT SALES AND ADVERTISING

During the current year, Barbara's had projected average monthly sales of $17,500. It is important to note, however, that Gregory Berry believed the business climate for florists, though not erratic, was not solid enough to project sales for the upcoming year. Sales of flowers and plants at Barbara's fell into this general pattern: individual cut flowers (10 percent); arrangements (60 percent); plants (10 percent); and gift items (20 percent). The only advertising that Barbara's expected to undertake during the current year was a direct mailing during the holidays and a listing in the Yellow Pages.

NEXT YEAR'S ADVERTISING BUDGET

Barbara's management wanted to increase awareness in its target market and was considering an increase in advertising for the coming year. As part of this campaign, management had approved a new series of print ads for the coming year. Exhibit 5-2-1 presents three representative ads from the upcoming campaign. Management felt these ads were appropriate and would do much to sharpen Barbara's image. Management's task now was to determine the advertising appropriation for the upcoming year and a supporting rationale. Industrywide, florists used the percentage-of-sales method to set advertising appropriations, and Barbara's was willing to invest a percentage of sales in this manner. After identifying an appropriate total amount to invest in advertising, management would develop a budget allocation and supporting rationale.

Several questions needed to be answered before the budget could be created. Would the campaign be continuous or seasonal in nature? What media vehicles should be used? Should the target market be divided into business and personal accounts? Should there be a contingency fund to allow for flexibility, and if so, how large should it be? At this point, it became clear that budgeting and media planning decisions were interrelated. Representative media costs are presented in Appendix 5-2.

**EXHIBIT 5-2-1   Barbara's Flower Market Print Advertisements,
Approved for New Campaign**

Make it crystal clear
that you care.

barbara's
florist

477-1153 835 W 12th at Lamar

The dinner party
place setting.

barbara's
florist

477-1153 835 W 12th at Lamar

Bring the summer
inside your home.

barbara's
florist

477-1153 835 W 12th at Lamar

Questions for Discussion and Review

1. In planning the advertising appropriation for the coming year, how large a role is the current level of investment likely to play? How might the new advertising campaign (see Exhibit 5-2-1) impact the decision as to how much to invest in advertising?

2. How realistic is the sales increase forecasted for the coming year? How should this forecast be related to the level of advertising investment?

3. What major considerations should be evaluated in establishing an amount to invest in advertising? What factors are most important in allocating the advertising investment across budget categories, such as target markets and months of the year?

Appendix 5-2

REPRESENTATIVE MEDIA COSTS

AUSTIN AMERICAN-STATESMAN
Monthly Earned Rate
Per-Column Inch

Inches per Month	Daily	Sunday
Open-transient rate	$38.98	$47.33
1 to 14	32.21	39.60
15	29.01	35.70
35	26.79	32.96
65	25.90	31.84
350	25.34	31.16
650	25.02	30.80
1,300	24.65	30.31
3,300	24.28	29.87
4,500	23.10	28.38
6,500	22.24	26.87
7,500	21.38	25.34

AUSTIN CHRONICLE

	1×	3×	6×	13×	26×
Full page	$1,150	$1,025	$965	$910	$790
¾	925	835	785	735	640
⅔, or junior page	850	770	720	680	590
½	650	585	550	525	450
⅜	550	485	460	435	375
⅓	485	435	410	385	335
¼	365	325	310	290	250
⅙	270	250	235	220	190

(continued)

AUSTIN CHRONICLE

	1×	3×	6×	13×	26×
⅛	$220	$200	$185	$170	$150
1/12	165	145	140	135	115
1/16	125	115	110	100	90

Color advertising is available upon request. Add $160 per standard color per page to the black-and-white rates.

AUSTIN BUSINESS JOURNAL
Display Rates (ROP)

Black & White	1×	4×	7×	13×	26×	39×	52×
Full page	$1,290	$1,225	$1,155	$1,095	$1,030	$970	$900
¾ page	1,120	1,060	1,015	950	900	840	780
½ island	970	920	870	820	775	730	675
½ page	885	820	775	730	695	650	605
Magazine ⅔	730	695	655	620	590	550	520
¼ page	580	545	520	490	465	435	410
Magazine ⅓	485	465	435	415	390	365	340
⅛ page	385	370	350	330	310	290	270
1/16 page	200	190	180	170	160	150	140

Color Rates:

One process color:	$250
Full color:	$350
Two color:	$300
One PMS color:	$300

OUTDOOR ADVERTISING
AUSTIN MARKET[a]

		Coverage		
		Posters		Cost per
Population	GRP/Show	Non Illuminated	Illuminated	Month
732,900	100	12	32	$14,008
	75	9	24	10,626
	50	6	16	7,064
	25	3	8	3,562

[a]Travis, Hays, and Bastrop counties.

BROADCAST

Radio: Cost same for :30 and :60 spots

KBTS-FM B-93	Time	Cost
AMD	6–10a	$95
MID	10–3p	85
PMD	3–7p	95
NITE	7p–12a	45
TAP	6a–7p	92

(continued)

BROADCAST

Radio: Cost same for :30 and :60 spots

KBTS-FM B-93	Time	Cost
KLBJ-FM		
AMD	6–10a	$90
MID	10–3p	82
PMD	3–7p	90
NITE	7p–12a	50
TAP	6a–7p	88
KLBJ-AM		
AMD	6–10a	$75
MID	10–3p	45
PMD	3–7p	65
NITE	7p–12a	25
TAP	6a–7p	50

Television Cost Per :30 Spot

Austin Cablevision	ESPN	CNN	Headline News	MTV
TAP (⅓, ⅓, ⅓)	$ 40	$ 40	$28	$38
6a–12 noon	25	25	20	20
12 noon–6p	45	45	25	40
6p–12 midnight	70	70	35	55
Prime fixed position	100	100	42	75
ROS (6a–12 midnight)	25	25	20	20
Overnight: 12 midnight–6a	10	10	5	10

KXAN-TV Channel 36 (NBC) M-F

6:45–7a	KXAN News at Sunrise	$ 50
7–9a	Today	60
9–12p	AM rotation	60
12–3p	Afternoon rotation	75
3–4p	A Current Affair/Inside Edition	125
4–5p	Oprah	200
5–5:30p	Jeopardy	300
6–6:30p	Evening News	300
6:30–7p	Wheel of Fortune	400
10–10:30p	Late News	400
10:30–11:30p	Tonight Show	225
11:30p–12:30a	Late Night	175
12:30–1a	Later	50

The Slick Stick

INTRODUCTION

David Jones had finally completed the first working model of his team roping simulator machine. He had spent many hours observing roping teams and perfecting the techniques handled by his machine. Now that the first prototype was successfully completed, Jones faced the task of developing a marketing plan and an advertising campaign that would reach all those potentially interested in it.

David Jones, 44, was a riding and roping instructor who raised quarter horses on his Rockin' J Ranch in Round Rock, Texas. The Slick Stick Team Roping Simulator consisted of a mechanical fiberglass horse and steer mounted on an eight-by-ten-foot steel deck. According to Jones, the machine could be a trainer or a plaything. It could be used by team ropers for rodeo training, or it could be an attraction at a bar, an entertainment park, or a state fair.

The device, said Jones, gave ropers an accurate perspective on their position and that of the steer. Previously, team ropers trained by standing on the ground and tossing a rope at a set of horns stuck in a hay bale. The machine was valuable because it saved the time that would be spent learning the correct distance and movements of a real roping situation. Jones also pointed out that his machine was safer than a mechanical bull, since the horse did not buck.

Jones had spent over a year working on the machine before he was satisfied with the results. He then obtained a patent for the Slick Stick and proceeded to think of ways to market this new invention. He felt that the market for the Slick Stick went well beyond the rodeo; he expected interest from entertainment centers, sophisticated bars, and even private ranchers willing to allow their help and their guests to train as ropers.

Jones needed to capitalize on the Slick Stick quickly, since the previous two years he had invested all of his revenue in the project. He had also obtained a major loan from the local bank to finance his operating expenses and the first capital outlays necessary to build the prototype, and the loan would come due during the next 12 months.

His usual source of income was the breeding, training, and selling of quarter horses to pleasure riders. Since the Texas economy had been in a slump, Jones's business had suffered a major decline in sales. His family was dependent upon the horse business income, and therefore Jones had also had

---

This case was written by Isabella C. M. Cunningham, The University of Texas at Austin, and is intended to serve as the basis for classroom discussion, not to illustrate either the effective or ineffective handling of an administrative situation. Used by permission of Ropro Company.

to draw from the bank loan to maintain his family's minimum living requirements.

David Jones was faced with having to make several decisions quickly. He needed help determining the size and type of market most likely to be attracted to the Slick Stick, and then he needed to develop a marketing and promotional plan that would bring enough sales for him to repay his debt and finance his budding business. To do this properly, Jones decided to hire a small but strong advertising agency: Cunningham, Smith, and Forte. Its task was to analyze the market potential for Slick Stick, make recommendations as to the desired level of production and sales for the first five years, and develop a promotional plan for the product.

The account executive for Slick Stick, René Smith, had two weeks to get back to David Jones with a detailed proposal. She worked on the problem long and hard because she knew that the financial future of her client depended on how quickly he could sell several Slick Stick units.

THE PRODUCT

The Slick Stick Team Roping simulator was an idea ahead of its time. The mounted fiberglass horse and steer were designed to facilitate the training of team ropers. Team roping is a popular rodeo sport in which two mounted riders with ropes catch a steer by the head and heels. The event requires precise timing, muscle memory skills, and a quick horse. The Slick Stick gave the roper the ability to practice with a coach guiding and scrutinizing every move. It showed the rider exactly what position the horse should occupy in relation to the steer before the rider threw the rope. The machine was not meant to replace practice with livestock; it was meant to enhance that training by allowing the roper to develop a specific technique when throwing the loop. The physics involved in throwing the rope could be discussed and studied without the distraction of the horse and steer movement. The rider could concentrate on maintaining a correct riding position while throwing the rope. The machine removed all the uncontrollable variables, so the rider could perfect all the basic roping movements.

The construction of the Slick Stick was impeccable. A novice could climb on the machine and learn to rope in a matter of hours. The fiberglass horse and steer were mounted on steel posts and controlled by electric motors, which were safely powered by two 12-volt car batteries. The product was meant to last whether it was used inside or outside, and in any weather condition.

The horse's movement simulated getting into position for either the header or the heeler. The steer movement was confined to its kicking back legs. The steer's kicking had variable speed for different levels of expertise.

Besides being used in rodeo training and for entertainment, the product could be an attraction for western clothing stores, saddle manufacturers, and the like. Also, it could appeal to arena owners, roping schools, rodeo managers, and horse trainers. The promotional opportunities for Slick Stick were unlimited, according to Jones.

The machine could be sold either as a freestanding unit or on a trailer that could be moved to different locations. Jones priced the freestanding unit at $5,000 and the trailer model at $7,500.

To develop a forecast of expected sales according to different levels of promotion, Smith wanted to first have some idea of how many units Jones needed to sell to break even. She made a list of all the costs of producing the unit and developed estimates of net income for different sales volumes. Exhibit 5-3-1 explains the different break-even formulas she used. In addition, a list of the costs of producing the Slick Stick can be seen in Exhibit 5-3-2.

Smith estimated total revenue and profits for a period of five years, considering 100-unit increments in production and sales for the sake of simplicity. The next task was to estimate the promotional costs of different potential campaigns. First, however, Smith wanted to take a serious look at the potential market for the product. Information about that market is given in the following section.

THE MARKET FOR SLICK STICK

Smith conducted an interview with David Jones to ask him what he felt were the most likely targets for the purchase of Slick Stick. Jones listed several known potential markets, such as college rodeo programs, high school rodeo

---

EXHIBIT 5-3-1   Break-even Calculations

Formula used to calculate break-even point in units:

$$\frac{\text{Fixed Cost}}{\text{Sales Price} - \text{Variable Cost/Unit}}$$

Break-even point in dollars:

$$\frac{\text{Fixed Cost}}{\text{Sales Price} - \text{Variable Cost/Unit}} \div \text{Sales Price}$$

1. Hiring one bookkeeper and one worker:

Fixed Cost = Total Fixed Cost + Fixed Advertising Costs + Salaries (bookkeeper + benefit compensation).

$$\text{Variable Cost} = \frac{\text{Total Variable Cost}}{\text{Sales Unit}} + \text{Other Variable Expenses}$$

2. Hiring one bookkeeper:

Fixed Cost = Total Fixed Cost + Fixed Advertising Costs + Salaries (bookkeeper + benefit compensation − $5,000 [benefit compensation of worker])

$$\text{Variable Cost} = \frac{(\text{Total Variable Cost} - \$30,000)}{\text{Sales Unit}} + \text{Other Variable Expenses}$$

3. Break-even point without hiring anyone and without Jones's salary:

Fixed Cost = Total Fixed Cost − Fixed Salaries − Fixed Benefits + Total Advertising Cost

$$\text{Variable Cost} = \frac{\text{Total Variable Cost}}{\text{Sales Unit}} - \text{Direct Labor} + \text{Other Variable Expenses}$$

EXHIBIT 5-3-2   Costs of Producing the Slick Stick

- Patent cost: $7,800 (to be amortized in 17 years).

- Organization cost to establish corporation: $7,500, including lawyers' fees, etc. (to be amortized in 5 years).

- Direct materials costs:

Trailer	$ 750
Fiberglass	440
Motor	375
Other	500
Total:	$2,065

- Direct labor costs: Salary plus benefits for one employee = $30,000/year.

- Plant depreciation: The initial cost of the plant, $45,000, to be depreciated in 10 years. After the third year, a second plant costing abut the same is expected to be built. The depreciation scale for the second plant is also 10 years.

- Equipment depreciation: $3,750 per year.

- Supplies depreciation: $5,000 per year.

- Labor accounted for is one person for every 100 units produced per year.

- A fixed salary for David Jones should be added in the amount of $50,000 per year.

- A contingency provision of 15 percent should be added to total costs.

- Fixed costs should also include estimated costs of electricity, telephone, insurance, the salary of a bookkeeper, and benefit compensation for all employees of about 17 percent of total salary.

---

programs, county youth extension programs, team roping instructors, professional rodeo cowboys, roping trainees, military rodeo teams, and the like. In addition, Jones felt that a large untapped potential market could be found within the recreation industry and perhaps even in foreign markets attracted to the allure of the U.S. western life-style.

The task of finding and listing all the rodeo programs Jones felt were important potential clients was long and laborious. Such clients would be best reached through direct mailings and demonstrations. Smith was sure she would have to earmark some of the budget for the final promotional plan to reach these organizations. She estimated that about 500 college and high school programs included serious rodeo concentrations; in addition, the military was an important but not large market.

In addition to these schools and professional groups, Smith wanted to quantify the portion of the total U.S. population that might be interested in the sport of roping as a leisure activity. These people might be serious users of the Slick Stick even though they would not pursue roping as a serious profession.

In estimating the size of that market, Smith concluded that the target individuals would be those male adults who wore western boots, chewed tobacco and/or used snuff, participated in some kind of horse-riding sport, drove pickup trucks, and had access to horse trailers. Additional variables to be considered would be the use of western wear, country music radio station listenership, and a total family income of at least $40,000 per year.

Smith concluded her study by assessing that the total potential market for the Slick Stick included from 1 million to 1.8 million male adults, depending how many variables were included in the criteria used to select prime prospects. It was important to settle on a specific audience and then establish their media habits, so that Smith could recommend a total promotional plan and budget that would allow Jones to reach a realistic production goal, given his financial condition. This was the final task facing Smith.

THE PROBLEM

On Monday, January 23, Smith and Jones had a meeting at the Cunningham, Smith, and Forte agency headquarters. Jones appeared very nervous, and Smith asked him whether he was worried about something in particular. Jones told her that the note he owed the bank would come due within the following 12 months and he was in a hurry to start marketing his product. He was sure that he could sell several million dollars worth of Slick Stick products within the following ten years, and he did not want to try to raise capital by selling interests in his newly established corporation. The money would have to come from the sale of products. It was Smith's job to suggest how to best accomplish the sales goals Jones wanted to reach.

Jones also said he firmly believed that the endorsement of a prominent rodeo figure would be vital to marketing the product successfully. Smith was not sure of the importance of product endorsement for sales, but she was not familiar with this specialized market, so she reserved judgment as to the type of appeal that would be most appropriate for the campaign. She was more concerned now about making sure that Jones understood and approved an adequate promotional budget.

Questions for Discussion and Review

1. What is the break-even point for Slick Stick if an equal number of trailer and nontrailer units are sold?

2. Was Smith correct in her estimation of the total male adult market for the Slick Stick?

3. What combination of media do you feel would best reach the leisure consumer market for Slick Stick?

4. If you were Smith, what kind of promotional plan would you propose for the product?

5. Do you feel that Jones will eventually become a millionaire entrepreneur as a result of his invention? Explain why or why not.

J. Westfahl

BACKGROUND

In September 1981, James Westfahl opened a men's clothing store in the center of downtown Austin, Texas, at 617 Congress Avenue. Westfahl's background in the clothing business was extensive. His experience in retail clothing prior to opening his own store ranged from stock boy to store manager. Westfahl had worked his way through college as a salesman at a clothing store. In addition, he had been on the road for 11 years as a manufacturer's representative for various lines of traditional men's clothing.

The store, J. Westfahl (JW), carried a full line of traditional clothing and accessories. Westfahl estimated that traditional clothing accounted for roughly 10 percent of all clothing sales.

JW handled Southwick, Corbin, and Norman Hilton lines of slacks, sportcoats, and suits. These were premium-priced, high-quality lines. The prices of men's and women's suits ranged from $185 to $435 for spring fashions and $245 to $600 for fall fashions. Further, the store sold a number of other high-quality lines, such as Alden shoes, Gitman Brothers shirts, Robert Talbot neckwear, and the Gurka line of luggage.

JW added women's clothing and accessories in September 1983. Westfahl added women's lines in response to the trend of major manufacturers of men's clothing diversifying into women's lines. He saw this as an opportunity to substantially increase his potential market. The women's clothing carried by JW was considerably better made and more durable than most women's clothing.

Women's clothing and accessories made up roughly 25 percent of JW's sales. About 25 percent of total sales were men's suits, 10 percent sportcoats, 10 percent slacks, 10 percent dress shirts, 10 percent ties, 5 percent shoes, and 5 percent miscellaneous items such as belts and wallets.

JW had six employees including James Westfahl and his wife, Jane. The other four employees included an experienced male salesperson, a tailor, a seamstress, and a shoeshine man. The downtown Austin location provided easy access for a large group of professional people who worked in the immediate vicinity, and considerable foot traffic passed the store each day.

Westfahl believed that although all clothing retailers were competitors, JW competed directly with only a small number of stores specializing in

---

This case was written by John H. Murphy, The University of Texas at Austin, and is intended to serve as the basis for classroom discussion, not to illustrate either the effective or ineffective handling of an administrative situation.

TABLE 5-4-1 Percent of Total Retail Sales by Month and Type of Store

	January	February	March	April	May
Total (all stores)	7.2	7.0	8.0	8.2	8.7
Men's and boy's clothing	6.7	5.8	6.9	7.9	8.3
Women's clothing	6.2	6.1	7.9	8.0	8.2

Source: U.S. Department of Commerce, 1985.

traditional clothing. These stores included The Haberdashery, The Texas Clothier, Chasnoff's Ltd., and Britton's Clothiers.

The retail clothing business was seasonal. The peak buying seasons were spring (March, April, and May) and fall (October, November, and December). December was by far the biggest month (see Table 5-4-1 for national sales data). JW followed a policy of having only two sales per year—one after each of the peak seasons. These two sales of men's clothing were scheduled just after Christmas and Father's Day. JW's sales of women's clothing were even more seasonal than men's, with women's sales occurring earlier in the season.

ADVERTISING APPROPRIATION AND BUDGET

Westfahl viewed advertising as a necessary evil. Mixed success had caused him to approach advertising with caution.

As a rule of thumb, he had used 6 to 7 percent of forecasted sales for advertising. This approach resulted in a planned appropriation of $45,000 for the present year. (The Menswear Retailers of America reported that the national average percentage of sales earmarked for advertising by menswear stores was 3.1 percent.)

Westfahl had used most of the major media in past years, with mixed results. Most recently, JW had used television and radio commercials, plus magazine ads in *Texas Monthly* (see Exhibit 5-4-1) and the Southwest edition of *The Wall Street Journal*. In addition, JW utilized direct mail targeted to both past and prospective customers (see Exhibit 5-4-2).

In addition, Westfahl had signed a one-year contract for $10,000 with a local radio station (KASE). The contract ran January 1 through December 31 and allowed almost complete flexibility in selecting air times. Westfahl had opted primarily for Monday through Friday drivetime positions. Each 30-second spot cost $26. Westfahl anticipated that 40 percent of the contracted radio time would have been purchased by the beginning of his next fiscal year (June 1).

In planning his advertising efforts for the upcoming fiscal year, Westfahl based his appropriation on the following plans and assumptions:

1. *JW's primary target audiences were:* (a) professional men and women aged 35 to 54 with high levels of education and household income who worked in downtown Austin (an area bounded by Martin Luther King

June	July	August	September	October	November	December
8.3	8.4	8.8	8.3	8.4	8.6	10.1
8.0	6.8	7.7	7.2	8.3	10.2	16.2
7.4	7.5	8.6	8.1	8.7	9.7	13.6

Boulevard on the north, Interstate Highway 35 on the east, the Colorado River on the south, and Lamar Boulevard on the west); and (b) 1,200 MBA students at The University of Texas.

2. Based on planned, aggressive marketing efforts, *a 10 percent increase in JW's sales was forecasted.*

EXHIBIT 5-4-1   Representative Magazine Ads for J. Westfahl

EXHIBIT 5-4-2   Representative Postcard Mailers for J. Westfahl

*J. Westfahl cordially invites you to a
special showing of the* **ALDEN SHOE** *line
of dress and casual shoes.*

Mr. John Sherrow of **ALDEN** *will be on
hand to help you make your selections.*

*During the showing you will be able to
special order any* **ALDEN** *shoe at regular
in-store prices.*

*Wednesday, April 10
9:30 to 5:30*

J. **Westfahl**

AUSTIN

617 Congress Avenue   *477-5656*

*J. Westfahl cordially invites you to a
special showing of the* Norman Hilton
*clothing line of suits, sport coats
and slacks.*

Mr. Biv Hendrix of Norman Hilton *will be
on hand to help you make your selection.
During the showing you will be able to
special order any* Norman Hilton *garment
in stock sizes and have it tailored in your
choice of fabrics all at regular in-store
prices. Made to measure is available
upon request.*

*Wednesday, April 10
9:30 to 5:30*

J. **Westfahl**

AUSTIN

617 Congress Avenue   *477-5656*

3. *Media costs were forecasted to increase 4 percent.* (See Appendix 5-4 for representative media costs for the present year.)

4. *Co-op advertising programs were available.* However, this source of advertising dollars had been drying up. (As Westfahl observed, "They provide lots of slicks but few dollars.")

5. *Advertising and promotional activities by competitors were not expected to increase significantly* during the planning period.

6. *A planned image campaign* with the theme line, "Fine Traditional Clothes for Men and Women" *plus clever promotions were expected to leverage JW's marketing efforts.*

7. *Approximately 15 percent of the total advertising and sales promotion appropriation should be earmarked for sales promotion* (if sales promotion offers with a high probability of successfully reaching either or both target audiences could be identified).

8. A modest proportion of the appropriation should be included as a *contingency fund.*

9. Through careful selection of media vehicles, *a more efficient and effective advertising effort could be initiated.*

With these considerations in mind, Westfahl contemplated the important decision of identifying a reasonable total amount to invest in advertising and sales promotion during the next fiscal year. At the same time, he wanted to budget the total advertising appropriation across broad media categories, by target audiences, by months, and for the men's versus women's departments.

Questions for Discussion and Review

1. What factors beyond those James Westfahl specifically identified are important in recommending a rational advertising appropriation?

2. What is the relationship between identifying a reasonable appropriation and media planning?

3. How should the plans and assumptions identified be factored into the process of recommending an appropriation and budget?

4. Ideally, how should forecasted sales for the planning period be related to the advertising appropriation and budget? Is this typically done by small retailers? By marketers of national consumer products? By business-to-business marketers?

5. What should determine the relative sizes of the advertising appropriation and the sales promotion appropriation?

6. What alternative sales promotion programs might be attractive to JW's two target audiences? How important would it be to have sales promotion offers be unique to the two targets?

Appendix 5-4
Representative Media and Production Costs

Television:

KTBC (CBS affiliate) and KVUE (ABC affiliate): approximately $60 per 30-second spot on a rotating schedule without control over when the commercials appear.

KBVO (Fox affiliate showing old movies and reruns): $30 per 30-second spot without control over when commercials appear.

Print:

Texas Monthly (regional magazine): $190 per inch (black & white).

The Wall Street Journal (Southwest edition): Texas, Oklahoma, Louisiana, Arkansas, southern Kansas, Mississippi, and western Tennessee: $68.60 per column inch.

Austin American-Statesman (newspaper): $38.98 per column inch morning and evening; Sunday, $47.33 per column inch open rates.

Direct Mail:

Five mailings of 1,500 5.5″ × 4.25″ postcards, printed both sides on heavy stock. Total cost including postage, addressing, and creative charges: $1,888.

Production Charges:

Television: two 30-second commercials at local station, including shooting, editing, and duplication. Total: $2,850.

Radio: three 30-second commercials produced at local production house, including talent and dubs. Total: $246.

Print: three black & white, nonbleed ads in various sizes, including artist fees, typesetting, and veloxes. Total: $530.

C H A P T E R

6

Developing Creative Strategy

*In the past, we have had a strategy, but our agencies
didn't stick to it. But they did make good commercials
and they did win awards. This may surprise you,
though. I don't care about awards; I want to sell
product.*[1]

James W. Harralson, CEO
ROYAL CROWN COLA COMPANY

THE PURPOSE AND CONTEXT OF CREATIVE STRATEGY

As stressed in the preceding chapters of this book, to be most effective,
advertising must be based on a careful consideration of the environment
within which the brand is being marketed. The first step in the advertising
management process is a careful situation analysis designed to provide the
decision maker with information useful in making all of the advertising
management decisions. After the situation has been evaluated, the next steps
in the process are to establish clear, measurable advertising objectives and
then to determine the advertising appropriation.

After these decisions have been at least tentatively made, the planner
focuses on developing a statement of creative strategy. Ideally, the development of a statement of creative strategy should be a team effort involving both
management and the creative individuals who will use the statement as a guide
in developing specific ads or otherwise executing the strategy.

*The purpose of developing a statement of creative strategy is to make the
advertising more effective by channeling the efforts of the creative individ-
ual(s) in the most productive direction.* As Bill Bernbach so aptly pointed out,

---

[1]Philip Dougherty, "Advertising," *The New York Times,* April 5, 1988, D23.

"A good strategy gives a good creative person something to be creative about."[2]

Bernbach also stressed that management has a responsibility to establish the boundaries or "lay down the tracks" within which the creative specialists should work. This discipline of following an appropriate creative strategy statement sharpens the creative person's work and multiplies its value. In the absence of the discipline and focus provided by a clear statement of creative strategy, there is a danger of misdirected creativity, which can be dysfunctional.[3] In fact, undisciplined creativity can lead to destructive results—prospects who are exposed to such advertising may be less likely to try the brand or to want to find out more about it than those who are *not* exposed!

Once the strategy has been agreed upon and clearly communicated in writing, management should withdraw from the creative process, leaving the creative specialists alone to work their magic. In fact, management interference typically will destroy rather than help build good advertising.[4] Management reenters the process at the approval level after the creative team has developed its ideas. Typically, example executions will be presented by the creative team to management for discussion and approval. These example executions may be roughs or they may be more highly finished.

After the creative team has developed some tentative executions, copy-testing research is often used to provide an outside, objective evaluation of the target audience's reaction to the tactical executions. If the creative team has suggested three alternative tactical executions of the creative strategy, ads based on these three executions would then be tested on separate samples of the target audience to measure their reactions. Based on the research findings, an execution would be selected, or modifications and further research might occur.

Management's key role in supervising the creative process involves two steps:

- Developing a clear statement of creative strategy.

- Evaluating proposed tactical executions to ensure that they are "on strategy."

Management is responsible for ensuring that a statement of creative strategy is established and clearly communicated to the creative specialists. Once this statement has been turned over to the creative team, management moves out of the creative process. Ideally, management then reenters at the approval level by reviewing the proposed executions of the strategy.

At the approval level, management's responsibility is to be sure that the executions are consistent with the previously developed strategy statement. If

---

[2]"A Conversation with Bill Bernbach," videotape produced by the American Association of Advertising Agencies, 1976.

[3]*Ibid.*

[4]John Leckenby and Nugent Wedding, *Advertising Management* (Columbus, Ohio: Grid Publishing, 1982), 340.

the execution or translation of the strategy into advertising does *not* conform to the strategy, management should be firm in rejecting it. Management must determine whether the execution is consistent with the other elements in the brand's marketing plan and the agreed-upon positioning, whether it fits the desired image or personality of the brand, and whether other criteria considered in developing the strategy have been met. It may be brilliant, innovative advertising, but if it is off-strategy, management should reject it (or modify the strategy).

In evaluating proposed creative executions, management reviews the rationale provided by the creative team explaining how the executions fit the strategy. This rationale is obviously crucial in determining approval of the tactical executions as consistent with the strategy. Hence, the creative team is advised to have developed a concise written explanation of how the executions fit each of the strategy points. This rationale must be sold to management. Typically, it is not enough to come up with great advertising ideas. These ideas must be presented in a way that will enable them to clear the hurdle of account management and client approval, as discussed in Chapter 2.

CREATIVE STRATEGY AND TACTICS

Mary Wells Lawrence points out that creativity in advertising involves a two-stage process. The first stage is formulating a "way to sell the brand." The second stage consists of "putting the words together," or actually writing the advertising.[5] The first stage involves strategy; the second, tactics.

In a broad sense, a creative strategy statement is simply a general outline of what is to be communicated in accomplishing advertising objectives. A tactical execution, on the other hand, is a specific approach, technique, or device employed to effectively convey the message. Strategy comes first and provides a framework within which tactical executions are developed.

In reality, too often this process is reversed. That is, the advertising execution is developed first, and then a strategy statement is fashioned to fit the execution, or no strategy statement is developed at all. An "execution first" approach runs the risk of overlooking substantial opportunities that could be identified through the process of carefully developing the strategy first. The human tendency to jump in and start generating executions first should be avoided.

Note that advertising's impact comes from creativity in advertising execution. The tactical translation of the strategy into advertising provides the spark that stimulates the desired response among the target audience. It is possible for a brilliant strategy to fail due to a weak execution or for a brilliant execution of a weak strategy to fail to produce acceptable results. On the other hand, a brilliant execution of a solid strategy is the formula for advertising success.

---

[5]Mary Wells Lawrence, "Creativity in Advertising," *Marketing News,* February 13, 1976, 5.

WHAT SHOULD BE INCLUDED IN A STATEMENT OF CREATIVE STRATEGY?

There is considerable variation in what authorities suggest should be included in a statement of creative strategy. Each expert and agency recommends a slightly different list of points that should be included. In recommending one from among the many approaches suggested, Roman and Maas present a solid set of components for guiding the development of advertising. These authors suggest that statements of creative strategy should include concise coverage of four major components:

- Target audience
- Objectives
- Key consumer benefit/support
- Personality (Roman and Maas use "Tone and manner").[6]

Target Audience

What group of consumers represents the firm's best prospects during the planning period? This is perhaps the single most important decision management must make. A multitude of considerations can be relevant to identifying and describing the most appropriate target audience(s). A demographic profile of the key prospects is a basic starting point, but a more in-depth understanding of consumers is necessary to develop the most effective advertising. Qualitative profiles of consumers that provide insights into their motivations and how products fit into their lives are of great potential value.

DDB Needham suggests that sterile descriptions of the target—"women 18 to 34 with children 12 years of age"—should be avoided.[7] Such a description tells the creative team nothing about the people they are selling to—what they are like, how they feel about brands in the category, and what values they have that are relevant to advertising the brand.

Life-style and psychographic profile data paint a more three-dimensional picture of consumers, enabling marketers to develop more effective programs. For example, SRI's VALS (values and life-styles systems) categories are widely utilized to classify consumers into groups for purposes of designing marketing programs. The VALS groups are based on a composite of attitudes, values, and life-style considerations.[8]

One of the dangers in defining a target audience is attempting to reach too many consumers with a single strategy. Stretching a benefit or the way the benefit is communicated in an attempt to appeal to a broad target audience can

---

[6]Kenneth Roman and Jane Maas, *The New How to Advertise* (New York: St. Martin's Press, 1992), 2–3.

[7]*Strategic Planning Guide* (Chicago: Needham, Harper & Steers, 1982), 11.

[8]Charles Patti and Charles Frazer, *Advertising* (New York: The Dryden Press, 1988), 198–201.

be a costly mistake.[9] The purpose of segmentation analysis is to identify *smaller,* more homogeneous subsets of consumers among whom the brand may develop an advantage. Aiming at broad target audiences potentially squanders the advantage or leverage segmentation is designed to create. The planner should consider developing separate statements of creative strategy for secondary or tertiary audiences.

Objectives

What effect is the advertising to have on the target audience? In a statement of creative strategy, management is *not* concerned with specificity or measurements. For guiding the creative team, general statements are appropriate. Here are some examples:

"To create awareness of _____ ."
"To convey the fact that _____ ."
"To reinforce the fact that _____ ."
"To generate leads from qualified prospects."
"To build distributor or retailer enthusiasm for _____ ."
"To increase the depth of awareness that Acme Products is a supplier of a wide selection of quality sports and recreation products."

Key Consumer Benefit

Why should the consumer buy the brand? This is also referred to as the "copy platform" or "purchase proposition." It should be stated in a concise, straightforward fashion. Sound statements of the key consumer benefit represent substantial research, experience, projections, and intuition, all boiled down into 25 words or less.

One of the dangers of defining the key consumer benefit is the temptation to include too many key benefits. Cramming too many benefits into a strategy runs the risk of confusing the target consumer and failing to clearly differentiate the brand from the competition. The strategist should avoid including a laundry list of benefits in the creative strategy statement. Experience indicates that the most effective, memorable advertising usually consists of *one clear, concise benefit,* directed to a single target audience.[10]

Support

Why should the consumer believe in the benefit? It is important that advertising be based on an underlying foundation of truth. The best long-run interests of everyone involved are then served, regardless of whether the support is specifically mentioned in the advertising.

---

[9]Don Schultz, Dennis Martin, and William Brown, *Strategic Advertising Campaigns* (Chicago: Crain Books, 1984), 248.

[10]*Ibid.*

Support may come from independent laboratory tests of brands in the category, consumer survey data, testimonials from experts, or any of a variety of sources. The American Dental Association's endorsement of Crest's cavity-prevention claim is a classic example. Other examples of support include the following:

- R.L. Polk automobile resale values, used to support a claim that one brand of automobile performs better than another.

- An article in the *New England Journal of Medicine* that evaluates the ingredients in pain relievers.

- A price comparison survey conducted by a supermarket of 25 commonly purchased items at five different chains on the same day.

- A United States Department of Agriculture study of the vitamin content of fruits and vegetables.

Personality

What image or personality should be projected through the advertising? Advertising messages project obvious and subtle information about the character and personality of the brand. These cues are reflected in the mood, tone, manner, and overall atmosphere of the advertising.

Wells suggests that the personality or image of a brand makes it stand out. A brand with a vivid, appealing image or personality is perceived by consumers as different from and better than other brands in the category, and consumers expect to have favorable experiences with it.[11] Through its tone and manner, advertising can play a key role in forming and maintaining a brand's perceived personality.

Although Wells provides a checklist of over 1,000 words that can be used to describe the personality of a product or service, he suggests that "less is more" when choosing adjectives to describe a brand's personality.[12] Wells presents the following examples of the personalities of brands advertised by DDB Needham:

- Microsoft (Germany)—Friendly, trendsetting, innovative

- CHEE-TOS—Childlike, messy, young at heart, traditional but not old-fashioned

- Moorea—Mysterious, exotic, colorful, warm, and friendly.[13]

The advertiser must consider carefully how the brand's personality should be portrayed through advertising. Does the advertiser want an image of being breezy or businesslike? Simple or complicated? Home-oriented or cosmopolitan? Exacting or forgiving? In developing a description of the brand's

---

[11]William D. Wells, *Planning for R.O.I.: Effective Advertising Strategy* (Englewood Cliffs, N.J.: Prentice-Hall, 1989), 31–35.

[12]*Ibid.,* 59–73.

[13]*Ibid.,* 34–35.

TABLE 6-1 Adjectives Useful in Describing Personality

Affectionate	Energetic	Mysterious
Alluring	Friendly	Polite
Authoritative	Generous	Romantic
Believable	Genteel	Sensuous
Clever	Home-oriented	Sexy
Conventional	Idealistic	Sophisticated
Considerate	Impeccable	Sympathetic
Deliberate	Intelligent	Unabashed
Effervescent	Jovial	Venturesome
Enchanting	Kindhearted	Zany
Exciting	Logical	Zesty

Source: William D. Wells, *Planning For R.O.I.: Effective Advertising Strategy* (Englewood Cliffs, N.J.: Prentice-Hall, 1989), 59–73.

TABLE 6-2 Categories of Television Commercial Tone or Atmosphere

Cute/adorable	Hard sell
Warm and caring	Modern/contemporary
Wholesome/healthy	Technological/futuristic
Conservative/traditional	Old-fashioned/nostalgic
Happy/fun-loving	Cool/laid-back
Somber/serious	Uneasy/tense/irritated
Relaxed/comfortable	Glamorous
Humorous	Suspenseful
Rough/rugged	

Source: Stewart and Furse, *A Study of 1,000 Commercials* (New York: Lexington Books, 1986).

personality, the planner uses adjectives that describe the personality of a person. See Table 6-1 for a partial list of such adjectives and Table 6-2 for a set of commercial tone/atmosphere categories.

SAMPLE STATEMENTS OF CREATIVE STRATEGY AND TACTICS

Three statements of creative strategy and sample executions of each strategy are presented in Exhibits 6-1 through 6-3. The three advertised items—a tourist destination (Bermuda), a wine (Blue Nun), and a public utility (TU Electric)—were selected to illustrate a range of marketing situations.

THE PERSONAL PROFILE

A statement of creative strategy should be supplemented by a personal profile. A personal profile is a hypothetical description of a typical consumer who is a member of the target audience. Based on statistical data, focus group

---

EXHIBIT 6-1   Bermuda Statement of Advertising Creative Strategy

Target Audiences	*Primary* — Adults 45 and over, household income $75,000+, attended or graduated from college, live in northeastern region of the United States. *Secondary* — Adults in same age, income, and education categories who live in Chicago, Dallas, Houston, Atlanta, San Francisco, and Los Angeles.
Objectives	1. To reinforce *awareness* that Bermuda is a class destination with great weather where the vacationer can relax and unwind. 2. To increase *knowledge* that in addition to sun, sea, and sand it offers a variety of good restaurants, sightseeing, and sports facilities. 3. To change the targets' *attitudes* regarding Bermuda's value-for-the-money as a tourist destination. 4. To stimulate a stronger, immediate, "do-it-now" attitude toward requesting information *(action)*.
Key Consumer Benefit/Support	*Benefit.* Bermuda is a warm, beautiful island for upscale vacationing year-round. It is populated by friendly, English-speaking natives and offers a range of accommodations and a wide variety of vacation experiences that give visitors their money's worth. *Support.* Bermuda, a British Crown Colony, is semitropical and has an ideal resort climate with two seasons — spring and summer. The average seasonal temperature is mild with rain during only a low percentage of all days. There are more than 100 places to stay on the island, ranging from large resorts through cottage colonies to guest houses. Ministry of Tourism activity lists indicate a complete range of events each month. Past airport and cruise studies among visitors document Bermuda's high rating on key considerations that influence the selection of a vacation destination, and Bermuda's high perceived value vis-à-vis the Bahamas and the Caribbean islands.
Personality	The personality and image of the island to be projected is that of a class destination. Bermuda's personality reflected in the advertising should key around the island's British heritage and style — the place is a little foreign but friendly. The tone of the advertising must be upscale, sophisticated, and border on being snobbish.

Source: Materials provided by Foote, Cone & Belding, New York.

interviews, and other appropriate information, the typical consumer is given a name, and his or her interests, media exposure patterns, and so on are described.

The personal profile is similar to the fictitious but representative individual journalists sometimes invent to dramatize the effect of an event on an average person. The purpose of this profile is to provide the creative team with a human being to whom it can communicate — a "person" the admakers can address in the spirit of genuine person-to-person communication.[14]

The personal profile is a wonderful device for sharpening the creative team's and the planner's understanding of the target audience. The person

---

[14]Keith Hafer and Gordon White, *Advertising Writing: Putting Creative Strategy to Work,* 3d ed. (New York: West Publishing, 1989), 42–43.

EXHIBIT 6-2   Blue Nun Statement of Advertising Creative Strategy

Target Audience	Heavy users of wine among adults 21–34 who live in urban areas. Heavy users concentrate in married-couple households with high income who attended or graduated from college. Major psychographic or life-style considerations are that heavy users entertain in their home and dine out frequently. In typical heavy user households, women are becoming more dominant in the wine purchase, deciding when to serve, when to buy, and what to choose. Selection is based upon price, the advice of friends, and having tasted the wine in the past.
Objectives	1. To further establish brand *awareness* and product identity. 2. To convey that Blue Nun is **an imported white wine** (*knowledge*). 3. To reinforce the belief that Blue Nun is a white wine that people can be comfortable with and sure about because it **goes well with any food** (*attitude*).
Key Consumer Benefit/Support	*Benefit.* The product is a delicious, imported wine that is appropriate with any food or meal in any setting. *Support.* The product is a premium Rhine wine, pale golden in color, with an excellent balance of sugar and acid, making it a round and extremely pleasing wine. It is a Liebfraumilch made from carefully selected Riesling, Sylvania, and Miller-Thurgau grapes. It is a refreshing wine that combines elegance with body, fruitiness with charm, and it is quite low in alcohol (10 percent by volume).
Personality	The personality of the product as reflected through the advertising should be light-hearted, unconventional, and humorous. This tone should represent a departure from usual wine advertising, which features price, brand superiority, or education.

Source: Materials provided by Della Femina, Travisano & Partners, New York.

described in the concise, three-dimensional, composite profile could be real since he or she is based on demographics, psychographics, and other relevant information. Coverage of activities and experiences relevant to the product category should be included. In addition, an appropriate photograph of the hypothetical consumer should be included along with the profile.

Exhibit 6-4 presents an example of a personal profile for the following target audience: female, 18–24, from a middle- to higher-income household, attending college, and moderately fashion conscious.

FAMOUS CREATIVE APPROACHES AND STYLES

This section presents a brief summary of some suggestions for developing and executing creative strategy recommended by four famous practitioners—Leo Burnett, Rosser Reeves, Bill Bernbach, and David Ogilvy. These individuals' thoughts have been widely discussed and generally accepted as useful. Keep in mind, however, that each man's ideas may be more or less appropriate, depending on the product/market situation facing the advertiser.

EXHIBIT 6-3   TU Electric Statement of Advertising Creative Strategy

Target Audience	All adults in TU Electric's service area. The most critical segment of customers is young families with children, mid-to-low household income.
Objectives	1. To improve *name recognition* and build positive *awareness* of the newly established TU Electric name and logo. 2. To reinforce positive customer *attitudes* toward the company, its personnel and services. 3. To reestablish employee identity and company unity following the recent consolidation.
Key Consumer Benefit/Support	*Benefit.* The electric company provides dependable power, and when a storm, high winds, or any other occurrence interrupts electrical service, the company responds promptly. *Support.* Electric company employees are on duty 24 hours a day, 365 days a year, to make sure power is available. A call to the emergency repair service number will promptly bring a crew to restore power as quickly as possible.
Personality	The personality and image of TU Electric to be projected through the advertising is that of a dependable, dedicated, professional friend. The ads should convey that employees, although they are ordinary folks, are experienced and serious. In addition, the ads should project determination, honesty, and strength.

Source: Materials provided by Evans/Dallas, Dallas, Texas.

Leo Burnett: Inherent Drama

Leo Burnett believed that there is what he called "inherent drama" in almost every product or service. The task of the admaker is to identify this drama and capitalize on it through advertising. Burnett commented on inherent drama:

> *In some cases . . . it is relatively easy to find. In other cases . . . you often have to dig for it and for ways to interpret it which will lay it before the reader or viewer with great simplicity and directness and . . . of course, with great believability, without tricks or obvious borrowed interest. It is what the manufacturer had in mind in the first place when he conceived the product. It is the most direct route to the mind of the reader or viewer.*[15]

Advertising that draws on this drama, Burnett suggested, "gives the effect of news, even in an old product, and has about it a feeling of naturalness which gives the reader an emotional reward and makes him feel good about it."[16]

It is worth noting that Burnett's agency is famous for keeping long-running ideas for mature brands fresh. Essentially, the Burnett agency has used inherent drama to romanticize and personalize its clients' products. Examples of its inherent drama strategy and execution include "The loneliest man in the

---

[15]Leo Burnett, *Book of Leo* (Chicago: Leo Burnett Co., 1971), 77.
[16]*Ibid.*

EXHIBIT 6-4   Hypothetical Consumer Profile: Mary Elise Abrams

Hypothetical Consumer Profile:

Mary Elise Abrams

"Female, 18–24, middle- to higher-income household, attending college, and moderately fashion conscious."

Mary Elise Abrams

Mary Abrams is a 19-year-old college freshman. Before she graduated from high school last year, Mary lived at home with her parents and worked part-time as a clerk for a regional mass merchandiser. That's not to say she didn't study, because she did. In fact, she had made a deal with her parents. If she studied and got decent grades, they'd pay her essential college expenses, starting in the fall. She decided to go to college, not just to get ahead but also because most of her friends were going.

Mary's parents were both working and combined earned over $45,000 a year. Because her parents were often busy, Mary would do the household shopping as well as cook dinner for her family. Mary made nearly all her own decisions about what clothes to buy. And even though she worked last year, her parents paid for most of her clothes. Before she went to college she was saving most of her earnings to be used during her first year away from home. She had a savings account at the same bank her parents used.

In her last year of high school she had gotten together with her friends a couple of times a week, very informally, just to have fun and listen to rock music or watch MTV. A very social animal, Mary was always on the go at home and away.

Now Mary goes to State University, about 150 miles from her parents, and lives on campus in an old but comfortable dorm. Socially, she is more active now than she was last year at home with her parents. She goes out to parties much more often than she used to, to concerts with friends who live in the dorm, to football games, and she goes to the movies regularly. She goes to classes and studies, and she recently got a part-time job off campus. Tomorrow she plans to open a checking account near campus so that her money will be more accessible.

One of the things Mary likes to spend her money on is clothes. When she goes out partying, she likes to look good and she knows that little details can make all the difference. On campus she dresses very casual and usually just throws on a pair of jeans. When she goes shopping, she looks for quality and value. She keeps up with the latest fashions, reads several fashion magazines, but she has her own style. She won't buy something just because a magazine says it's "in." She talks to her girlfriends about clothes, what they like and what looks good. Mary is now more concerned with her appearance in general than she was last year.

In many respects, Mary's life is still similar to what it was like when she lived at home, except now she has much less "homebound" responsibilities. This gives her more opportunity to get together with newly acquired friends; they all live close-by and someone always has something to do.

world" campaign for Maytag washers, "Sorry Charlie. Only the best tuna get to be Star Kist," and "You're in good hands with Allstate."

The Burnett agency is also known for inventing "critters" to utilize (or perhaps more accurately to create) inherent drama. It has created, for example, Morris the Cat for 9-Lives cat food, the Pillsbury Doughboy, the

Keebler Elves, the Jolly Green Giant, and the Snap, Crackle, and Pop characters for Kellogg's Rice Krispies.[17]

Rosser Reeves: Unique Selling Proposition

Rosser Reeves maintained that the most effective basis for selling a brand was a creative strategy built around what he labeled a "unique selling proposition," or USP. A USP—a distinctive claim that sells the brand—is based on some physical differentiation of the brand. Once an important physical differentiation point is identified, the brand's advertising is used to present this difference in a meaningful and persuasive way to the target audience.[18]

Reeves maintained that a brand could *not* be effectively advertised unless the consumer was offered a distinctive reason to buy the product or service. He felt that it was the job of the advertising team to examine the product in order to find and then articulate a reason for the consumer to buy. In his view, a USP could not be developed for all brands, and those brands without a USP were doomed to failure in the marketplace.

Reeves suggested three rules for developing a USP strategy: (1) the claim must be specific—"you buy this brand and you get this specific benefit"; (2) the claim must be unique, a benefit that the competition cannot or does not offer; and (3) the claim must be regarded by consumers as important, and thus, one that will sell the brand. Once a strong USP has been identified, all that remains to be done is to use advertising to drive the point home with consumers through repetition.[19]

One of the most significant advantages of the USP, according to Reeves, is that once an advertiser identifies and effectively associates its brand with the advantage, it almost never wears out. Hence, long-running campaigns that capture a USP offer the advertiser a substantial advantage. Examples of USPs expressed in taglines are Colgate's "It cleans your breath while it cleans your teeth"; Dove's "It's one-quarter cleansing cream"; Ivory's "It's 99 and 44/100 percent pure"; Woolite's "It safely soaks sweaters clean in just five minutes"; and Mars M&M candy's "It melts in your mouth, not in your hand."

Bill Bernbach: Appeal to the Passions

One of Bill Bernbach's most famous quotes is, "Advertising doesn't work unless you feel it in the gut." This statement expresses Bernbach's fundamental belief that the most effective advertising appeals to underlying motivations. He

---

[17]While Rice Krispies' advertising used the terms, "It crackles and it snaps," long before the Leo Burnett Agency handled the account, the agency created the three cartoon characters Snap, Crackle, and Pop that we see in today's advertising.

[18]Rosser Reeves, *Reality in Advertising* (New York: Alfred Knopf, 1961).

[19]*Ibid.*

pointed out that the average person does *not* reach a decision on a purely intellectual or rational basis. Therefore, it is necessary to appeal to both the head and the heart (ration and emotion), realizing that an appeal to underlying emotional drives is by far the more important.[20]

Bernbach's analysis of human nature and advertising led him to the conclusion that human behavior is motivated by a set of basic drives or ruling passions that are unchanging. "When you burrow deep enough into any fashionable, carefully rationalized, socially approved proposition, you'll always find one of these Neanderthal drives lurking at the bottom . . . which is why an appeal to logic so seldom works. The brain is not an instrument of logic at all. It's an organ of survival, like fangs and claws."[21]

Bernbach was also a champion of the view that research plays an essential, but limited, role in the process of developing outstanding advertising: "Research tells you what to say, but not how to say it." He rejected conventional rules of advertising in developing executions and emphasized the importance of developing a unique personality for his clients' advertising, believing "without one you won't get very far."[22]

David Ogilvy: Brand Image

David Ogilvy politely stresses that, although he is credited with popularizing the importance of brand images, Claude Hopkins described it much earlier. Just as people have images or personalities, so do brands. Ogilvy emphasizes that a key part of framing a creative strategy is deciding what image or personality would best serve the brand. Then, every advertisement should be designed to contribute to the desired brand image.[23]

Ogilvy suggests that it is wise to associate most brands with an image of quality. As he expresses it, "Give the brand a first-class ticket." This is particularly true for products consumed or used in a visible social setting. As examples of the successful application of the brand image concept, he cites Schweppes, Jack Daniel, and Marlboro.[24]

Projecting a personality through advertising is accomplished by surrounding the brand with symbols or contexts that create the desired aura, image, or association. Brand image advertising often focuses on the users of the brand rather than on the product itself. It seems to be a particularly viable strategy for product categories characterized by little physical differentiation among competing brands.

---

[20]"A Conversation with Bill Bernbach," Videotape produced by the American Association of Advertising Agencies, 1976.

[21]Carl Hixon, "The Bernbach Fantasies," *Advertising Age,* August 11, 1986, 24–29.

[22]"A Conversation with Bill Bernbach."

[23]David Ogilvy, *Ogilvy on Advertising* (New York: Crown Publishers, 1983), 14–16.

[24]*Ibid.*

Suggested Readings

Bogart, Leo. *Strategy in Advertising.* Chicago: Crain Books, 1984.

Hafer, Keith, and Gordon White. *Advertising Writing: Putting Creative Strategy to Work.* 3d ed. New York: West Publishing, 1989.

Jewler, Jerome. *Creative Strategy in Advertising.* 4th ed. Belmont, Calif.: Wadsworth Publishing, 1992.

Leckenby, John, and Nugent Wedding. *Advertising Management.* Columbus, Ohio: Grid Publishing, 1982, Chapter 10.

Levenson, Bob. *Bill Bernbach's Book: A History of Advertising That Changed the History of Advertising.* New York: Villard Books, 1987.

Ogilvy, David. *Ogilvy on Advertising.* New York: Crown Publishers, 1983.

Reeves, Rosser. *Reality in Advertising.* New York: Alfred Knopf, 1961.

Ries, Al, and Jack Trout. *Positioning: The Battle for Your Mind.* Rev. ed. New York: McGraw-Hill, 1986.

Roman, Kenneth, and Jane Maas. *The New How to Advertise.* New York: St. Martin's Press, 1992.

Schultz, Don, Dennis Martin, and William Brown. *Strategic Advertising Campaigns.* Chicago: Crain Books, 1984, Chapters 9 and 10.

Wells, William D. *Planning for R.O.I.: Effective Advertising Strategy.* Englewood Cliffs, N.J.: Prentice-Hall, 1989.

Exercises

1. a. *Develop a statement of creative strategy.* Using the information provided in the Rooster Andrews television commercial (see Case 3-2, Exhibit 3-2-7), develop a statement of creative strategy which logically could have guided the person who created the commercial. Your statement should clearly address each of the four components of creative strategy separately (target audience, objectives, key consumer benefit/support, and personality). Roughly one to four sentences should be used to describe each component.

b. *Create a new execution.* Following the statement of creative strategy that guided the admaker, create a completely different execution of the Rooster Andrews strategy. Your new and completely different execution of the same strategy is to be executed in a quarter-page newspaper ad.

c. *Explain your rationale.* In separate paragraphs, explain both how your execution follows the statement of creative strategy and why your newspaper ad would be effective in communicating with the target audience. Take care to clearly explain your reasoning on both points.

Your response to this exercise is to be expressed in a typewritten, single-spaced memorandum that does not exceed one 8½″ × 11″ page. Develop a rough layout of your newspaper ad and staple it to your memo.

2. Buy a current issue of any magazine. Select a full-page advertisement and use this ad instead of the Rooster Andrews commercial to complete the exercise described above.

3. Develop a hypothetical personal profile of a married couple representative of Columbia Savings' primary target audience (see Case 6-3). Your personal profile will be used by a creative team in developing ads to be directed toward the target and should provide a three-dimensional, composite profile of this couple. *Note:* Be sure that your profile clearly relates the targets' lives to the choice of a financial

institution. A major section of your report should focus on this area plus other relevant considerations such as media exposure and attitudes about advertising. Also, attach a photograph or picture of your hypothetical consumers to your one-page (maximum) description.

4. Buy one or more current issues of any magazines. Select different full-page advertisements that illustrate the application of:

- Burnett's "inherent drama" concept

- Reeves's "unique selling proposition" concept

- Ogilvy's "brand image" concept.

Develop a concise discussion of how each ad illustrates the application of the appropriate concept.

5. An important part of advertising management is the ability to persuade, describe, and explain—in short, to communicate effectively through spoken and written words. Being creative also helps. This exercise provides an opportunity to illustrate both your communication skills and your creativity.

Your task is to carry out one of the following four assignments. There are no correct approaches or right answers.

a. Introduce yourself using the format of a 30-second television or radio commercial.

b. Buy a current issue of any magazine. Select a full-page advertisement you like. Briefly explain why you like it (one page only). Attach the ad to your comments.

c. Invent a new product and create a full-page magazine advertisement for that product. (No science fiction, please. There must be a market for the product now, and the technology for producing it must be readily available at present.)

6. As new members of the large marketing staff of a major consumer packaged goods company, you and the other new employees are required to develop detailed descriptions of yourselves to be distributed to all other members of the department. These descriptions allow everyone to get acquainted with each others' qualifications, personality characteristics, and backgrounds. The idea is to quickly and creatively give everyone some idea of who you are and what to expect from you as an employee and a member of the team.

The self-description must follow some explicit guidelines. While you should feel free to use creative copy, you must do the following:

a. Attach a passport-sized photo of yourself. This must be clear and recent.

b. Include your full name and any nicknames.

c. Indicate your relevant background experience, your aspirations, and what you see as your role in the organization.

d. Indicate what you think are your best attributes and your shortcomings, if any, relevant to your role in the department.

e. Do not exceed the front of one 8½″ × 11″. Use single spacing, a double space between paragraphs, and at least a one-inch margin.

Walt Disney Pictures (A)

The products of the movie business are all *experiments.*

A.D. Murphy, Film Industry Analyst

In the early 1980s, corporate raiders proposed to buy the struggling Walt Disney Company and sell off its assets. In 1984, Roy Disney (Walt's nephew) helped form a group of investors, which included the wealthy Bass brothers of Fort Worth, in an attempt to save the company. The investors restructured the company and hired Michael Eisner away from Paramount Pictures to reverse the fortunes of the "new" Disney.

Disney's successes under Eisner's leadership included:

- A string of box office hits under the Touchstone logo—*Down and Out in Beverly Hills, Ruthless People, Stakeout, The Color of Money,* and *Good Morning Vietnam.*

- The revitalization of animation with the release of all-new, full-length animated features.

- A revamped Disneyland and Walt Disney World with new hotels and attractions, and the construction of Euro Disneyland outside Paris.

- Continued vigorous growth of The Disney Channel.

- The release of one or two cartoon classics per year on videocassette.

- The production of network TV series such as "The Golden Girls" and an all-new weekly "The Disney Sunday Movie," plus syndicated series such as "Siskel & Ebert At The Movies," "Ducktales," and "Win, Lose or Draw."

THE MARKETING OF FEATURE FILMS

In 1986, the average movie cost $17.5 million to make and $7.5 million to market. To break even at the domestic box office, ignoring the financing and overhead costs to run a studio, a movie needed to generate $66 million in

---

This case was written by Robert B. Levin, President, Worldwide Marketing, Walt Disney Pictures, and John H. Murphy, The University of Texas at Austin. The case is intended for use in generating class discussion and not to illustrate either the effective or ineffective handling of an administrative situation. Used by permission of Walt Disney Pictures.

ticket sales. During 1986, only 9 movies out of the 236 widely released made $66 million in domestic box office.

The nine films that reached this hypothetical break-even point from domestic box office in 1986 were *Top Gun, Crocodile Dundee, Karate Kid Part II, Back to School, Star Trek 4, The Color Purple, Alien 2, Ruthless People,* and *Ferris Bueller's Day Off.* For the 227 other films, the break-even point, if it ever came, resulted from videocassette sales, foreign box office, and cable TV sales. Of these remaining 227 films, only 19 grossed $40 million or more in domestic box office, and only 31 grossed over $30 million. Fifty-seven grossed less than $1 million.

The Life Cycle of a Feature Film

There are four distinct stages in the life of a successful feature film. First, a film is placed in domestic theatrical exhibition. Local theaters are typically located in the suburbs, often as key tenants in an area's high-volume shopping mall. Since many more films are released than there are theaters to show them, competition for the limited screens available is brutal.

A movie stays in a market only as long as its weekend business is competitively strong. The weekend is important during nonvacation periods, since the vast majority of a movie's volume occurs on Fridays, Saturdays, or Sundays.

A film's opening weekend is critical. A weak opening weekend results in independently owned theaters dropping the film in favor of the next picture looking for a home. Further, for most pictures, the opening weekend offers the best volume the picture will ever achieve. An important rule of thumb in the industry is that the bigger the opening weekend, the slower the rate of decay, and the bigger the hit (and the potential profits). Hence, a major portion of a film's total marketing appropriation will be devoted to generating awareness of and interest in the film for opening weekend. For the most part, after opening weekend, the marketer attempts to slow the rate of decline from the opening weekend volume.

Second, roughly four months after a movie's original domestic theatrical opening date, the film may be released into the airline and military markets. Third, approximately six months after original release, the film is staged for release into the pay cable, domestic home video, and foreign theatrical exhibition markets. Finally, a few years after domestic theatrical release, the movie is released on network TV and/or syndicated television. In foreign markets, the move from theatrical exhibition to home video to TV is usually more condensed.

The Revenue Stream

Major changes in the revenue stream of the feature film industry have occurred in the past few years. The approximate data that follow indicate the nature of these changes.

Revenue Source	1978	1986
Domestic theatrical release	54%	28%
Foreign theatrical release	29	12
Worldwide TV	13	8
Home video royalties	2	40
Pay TV fees	2	12
Total	100%	100%

Although from these data one might conclude that the domestic theatrical market is slipping in importance, this is not at all true. Without success in the domestic market, there will be no ancillary market stream.

MOVIE ATTENDANCE

Younger Age Groups

A recent study conducted by the Opinion Research Corporation revealed that over half of all people aged 12 to 17 went to the movies at least once a month, compared to only 20 percent of the population 18 and over. Teenagers were by far the age group most likely to attend movies frequently.

While those aged 12 to 24 represented only 27 percent of the population aged 12 and over, they accounted for 54 percent of all movie admissions. Adults aged 40 and over represented 44 percent of the 12 and over population, but they accounted for only 13 percent of movie admissions. Adults 25 to 39 were only slightly more likely to go to the movies than their share of the population.

In this research, the frequent moviegoers (who are skewed toward youth) were extremely important to the movie industry in total. While these individuals constituted only 22 percent of the population 12 and over, they accounted for 84 percent of all admissions.

Adults

Another study conducted by the Newspaper Advertising Bureau ("Movie Going in the United States") indicated that while 24 percent of all adults (individuals 18 and over) reported that they go to the movies once a month or more often, these frequent moviegoers represent 83 percent of adult movie admissions. Of these adult frequent moviegoers, roughly four out of ten are 18 to 24, and almost 70 percent are under 35. By contrast, 72 percent of all adults over 50 reported that they had not been to a movie in the past year. Table 6-1-1 presents a demographic profile of adult moviegoers.

TABLE 6-1-1 Adult Movie Patronage by Demographics

	Total	Frequent Moviegoers[a]	Infrequent Moviegoers[b]	Adults Who Hadn't Been to a Movie in the Last Year
Male	48%	50%	48%	46%
Female	52	50	52	54
	100%	100%	100%	100%
18–24	18%	40%	18%	6%
25–34	26	30	33	18
35–49	27	19	28	23
50+	29	11	21	53
	100%	100%	100%	100%
Married	62%	41%	60%	72%
Single	22	47	23	8
Divorced/Separated Widowed	16	12	17	20
	100%	100%	100%	100%
College grad+	17%	17%	22%	12%
Some college	17	26	19	11
High school graduate	39	39	38	40
Some high school or less	27	18	21	37
	100%	100%	100%	100%

[a]Those who had attended a movie one or more times in the past month.
[b]Those who had attended a movie three or four times in the last six months or less often, but had attended in last year.
Source: "Movie Going in the United States" (New York: Newspaper Advertising Bureau, 1986).

RESEARCH STUDIES: *THREE MEN AND A BABY*

To serve as the basis for developing an advertising and marketing plan for the Touchstone release *Three Men and a Baby,* several research projects were conducted. All of the projects were conducted by The National Research Group, Inc. (NRG) of Los Angeles, California. Two of these projects— "Advertising Strategy Survey" and "Recruited Audience Survey"—will be described next.

Advertising Strategy Survey

The purpose of the study was (1) to determine the level of interest in the movie based on title and stars only and based on two alternative concept descriptions; (2) to determine the most likely audience for the movie; and (3) to identify those elements which give the movie its best advantage in the marketplace and will maximize the potential audience.

NRG conducted telephone interviews with 602 moviegoers aged 12 to 49, half male and half female, who had seen at least one movie in the past two months. Respondents were interviewed in eight geographically dispersed markets.

In evaluating the results, it is important to note that the research techniques used were designed to assess the movie's *marketability* rather than *playability*. Marketability refers to moviegoers' interest when they hear a concept description but before they see the movie. On the other hand, playability is moviegoers' response to the movie when they see it. While these two concepts are closely related, they are not the same.

The respondents were asked about their awareness of the movie's three stars and how popular each star was with them personally. The findings are presented in Table 6-1-2. Respondents were then asked how likely they would be to go see the movie based strictly on the title and the stars. The data generated by this question are presented in Table 6-1-3.

Next, respondents were read one of two concept descriptions of the movie and then asked to indicate how likely they would be to go to see the movie based on the description. The two concept descriptions, titled "Funny Human Nature" and "Action with Comedy," are presented in Exhibit 6-1-1. A photograph made during filming is presented in Exhibit 6-1-2. Table 6-1-4 presents the respondents' level of interest in seeing the movie based on concept descriptions cross-classified by gender and age. Finally, respondents were asked how much selected elements added to their interest in the movie (see Tables 6-1-5 and 6-1-6).

Recruited Audience Survey

To gain further insights into the moviegoing public's likely responses to the movie, a recruited audience screening was conducted. Two hundred and ninety-nine moviegoers aged 15 to 49 viewed the movie at the Topanga Cinema in Woodland Hills, California. No walkouts occurred, and 97 percent of the viewers completed questionnaires probing their reactions to the movie. After the screening, 14 audience members participated in a focus group session to obtain additional insights into their reactions to the movie. Selected research findings are presented in Table 6-1-7.

When asked if there was anything confusing about the movie that was not cleared up by the end, the vast majority said no. However, some members of the audience wondered who the black man and the white man who followed the leads were. A few were confused about the drug deal and wanted to know what happened to the drug dealers.

Audience members were also asked what they would tell their friends about the movie. Audience members said they would mainly tell their friends that the movie was a funny comedy with a good story and a good cast. Secondarily, they would tell their friends the movie was entertaining, touching/emotional, and cute.

TABLE 6-1-2 Awareness and Popularity of Stars

	Total	Males		Females	
		Under 25	25+	Under 25	25+
Awareness[a]					
Tom Selleck	98%	98%	100%	97%	99%
Ted Danson	66	62	68	64	74
Steve Guttenburg	53	58	56	46	54
Popularity Rating[b]					
Tom Selleck	41%	36%	38%	44%	47%
Steve Guttenberg	33	37	25	39	28
Ted Danson	26	27	20	32	25

[a]NRG norm is 50+.

[b]Response of "one of my favorites" or "very good," NRG norm is 40+.

Source: "Advertising Strategy Survey—*Three Men and a Baby*," National Research Group, Inc., May 1987.

TABLE 6-1-3 Interest Based on Title and Stars

"How likely would you be to go see the movie?"

	Base	Definitely[a]	Probably[b]	Might or Might Not	Probably Not	Definitely Not	Total Positive[c]
Total	602	16%	41%	22%	17%	4%	57%
Sex:							
Male	300	13	41	25	18	4	54
Female	302	20	41	19	16	4	61
Age:							
12–17	121	15	46	20	16	3	61
18–20	120	18	42	25	14	1	60
21–24	120	18	42	20	15	4	60
25–34	144	15	39	24	19	3	54
35–49	97	16	33	21	20	10	49
Sex/Age:							
M/−25	180	16	45	23	14	3	61
M/25+	120	8	34	28	24	6	42
F/−25	181	18	42	20	17	3	60
F/25+	121	23	39	17	15	6	62

[a]NRG norm is 10 percent.

[b]NRG norm is 35 percent.

[c]Total Positive is the sum of "definitely" and "probably." NRG norm is 45 percent for total positive.

Source: "Advertising Strategy Survey—*Three Men and a Baby*," National Research Group, Inc., May 1987.

EXHIBIT 6-1-1   Two Alternative Concept Descriptions

"Funny Human Nature"

Three Men and a Baby, starring Ted Danson, Steve Guttenberg, and Tom Selleck, is a very funny movie about Michael, an architect, Peter, a commercial artist, and Jack, an airline pilot—three carefree bachelors who share a luxury apartment and never think about the future because they are having such a good time. However, their lives change forever when Michael discovers a baby on their doorstep. A note asks the men to babysit for a while until the mother returns from Europe. Baby Mary's presence throws Peter and Michael into shock, as they know nothing about babies and are totally inept at baby care. Jack has an even greater surprise when he returns from an overseas flight and finds out that the note also says that Jack is the father. The three men reluctantly work out baby-sitting schedules around their jobs, and women become a thing of the past as motherhood takes priority. Before long, Mary begins to grow on the guys, and they actually begin to have a feeling of responsibility for the first time. However, they still think they want their old life-styles back and are only too happy to give Mary to her mother when she returns from her temporary job in Europe. The men set out to party but suddenly do not know what to do with themselves, as their life is empty without Mary. In the surprise ending, the guys and the mother decide that the mother should move in as a fourth tenant, and they can share raising the baby.

"Action with Comedy"

Three Men and a Baby, starring Ted Danson, Steve Guttenberg, and Tom Selleck, is a new action-filled comedy about three happy bachelors, Peter, Michael, and Jack, who find themselves living a comic nightmare when a baby is left at their doorstep. A note explains that Jack is the unsuspecting father of baby Mary and that the mother has gone to work temporarily in Europe. Jack is out of town, so Peter and Michael become reluctant nannies. That same day, a mysterious package is accidentally delivered to the apartment. When punks arrive to pick up the "package," Peter and Michael assume they mean the baby and give baby Mary to them. When the punks leave, Michael sees the real package and finds drugs inside. Michael snatches Mary from the punks, but undercover cops watching the punks now incorrectly suspect the guys of being involved with the punks. Jack returns to town in the middle of this craziness and the three guys plot to get the cops and the creepy punks out of their lives. In a hilarious chase through Central Park, the guys outsmart the cops and the punks to get rid of the package. The men become full-time mothers but are thrilled when the mother finally returns to take Mary home. However, the guys find themselves wanting the baby back so much that in the end they convince the mother to move in as their fourth tenant so they can be one big happy family.

DETERMINING A CREATIVE STRATEGY

With the media appropriation for the pre-opening and a five-week advertising effort set at $15 million and the NRG research completed, attention focused on the development of advertising objectives and a creative and media strategy. While the planning process involved fashioning these crucial components of the advertising plan for *Three Men and a Baby* simultaneously, the most immediate concern was creative strategy.

Based on past experiences, it was clear that decisions regarding the creative direction of a film's advertising played a major role in determining its opening weekend and long-term success. In clearly and concisely specifying the target audience, objectives, key consumer benefit/support, and personality to project, the planner faced a unique opportunity in advertising a film. This opportunity stemmed from the fact that the audience's expectations about the film plus the context within which they viewed it were both strongly

EXHIBIT 6-1-2   Publicity Photograph: *Three Men and a Baby*

TABLE 6-1-4   Interest Based on Concept Descriptions

| | Total | Males | | Females | | NRG Norms |
		Under 25	25	Under 25	25	
"Funny Human Nature"						
Definitely interested	33%	25%	20%	45%	41%	25%
Probably interested	38	48	34	35	32	35
Total positive	71%	73%	54%	80%	73%	60%
"Action with Comedy"						
Definitely interested	32%	32%	18%	37%	39%	25%
Probably interested	37	38	30	47	29	35
Total positive	69%	70%	48%	84%	68%	60%

Source: "Advertising Strategy Survey—*Three Men and a Baby*," National Research Group, Inc., May 1987.

influenced by exposure to advertising prior to deciding to see the movie. Hence, the next step in planning the advertising efforts for *Three Men and a Baby* keyed around specifying the most appropriate and effective creative strategy.

TABLE 6-1-5 Interest in Elements: *Three Men and a Baby* "Funny Human Nature" Concept

| | | Adds "a Lot" to Interest in the Movie | | | |
| | | Males | | Females | |
	Total (401)	Under 25 (120)	25+ (80)	Under 25 (121)	25+ (80)
This movie stars Tom Selleck	46%	37%	49%	48%	54%
Michael, Peter, and Jack share an apartment, but their lives change drastically when they find a baby left on their doorstep	44	38	34	51	50
Jack arrives home only to surprisingly discover that the baby is his	37	36	30	47	40
The men know nothing about babies or baby care, but they work out a schedule around their jobs so each man takes his turn with the baby	37	30	31	40	49
They find themselves missing the baby and, in the surprising ending, the guys take the baby and her mother in as their fourth tenant	36	28	30	44	45
Three Men and a Baby is a funny movie about three carefree bachelors who are having such a good time that they never think about the future	31	28	24	38	35
This movie stars Ted Danson	30	26	30	29	39
This movie stars Steve Guttenberg	27	32	20	27	26
They become so involved with being mothers to the baby that women become a thing of the past	26	24	22	26	35
They miss their old ways and are only too happy to return the baby to her mother when she returns	18	18	18	14	22

Source: "Advertising Strategy Survey—*Three Men and a Baby,*" National Research Group, Inc., May 1987.

TABLE 6-1-6 Interest in Elements: *Three Men and a Baby*
"Action with Comedy" Concept

| | | Adds "a Lot" to Interest in the Movie | | | |
| | | Males | | Females | |
	Total (240)	Under 25 (60)	25+ (80)	Under 25 (60)	25+ (40)
This movie stars Tom Selleck	48%	45%	35%	55%	56%
The three happy bachelors' lives become a comic nightmare when an old girlfriend of one of the men leaves her baby on the doorstep	41	38	30	53	39
With keystone cop police and goony punks after them, the men pull off a hilarious switcheroo in Central Park and get the cops, the package, and punks out of their lives	40	48	30	42	37
Later, punks come by for the "package," which the men assume is the baby, and give the baby to the punks. But then one of the men sees the real package and finds dope inside	40	45	25	47	39
Three Men and a Baby is a new action-filled comedy about three bachelors and a baby	33	25	22	42	42
While the men are busy becoming reluctant "mommies," a mysterious package is delivered to the apartment	32	40	20	33	29
This movie stars Ted Danson	32	30	25	35	37
Undercover cops trailing the punks see the men snatching the baby from the punks and assume they are involved with the punks	31	40	22	30	27
The men happily return the baby to her mother when she gets back into town, but they find themselves missing the baby and convince the mother to be their fourth tenant	28	15	15	43	37
This movie stars Steve Guttenberg	19	17	22	20	20

Source: "Advertising Strategy Survey—*Three Men and a Baby*," National Research Group, Inc., May 1987.

TABLE 6-1-7   Selected Findings: Recruited Audience Survey

		Males		Females		
	Total	**Under 25**	**25+**	**Under 25**	**25+**	**NRG Norms**
Movie Ratings						
Excellent	62%	55%	44%	73%	67%	25%
Very good	28	24	40	26	26	30
Total highly positive	90%	79%	84%	99%	93%	55%
Word-of-Mouth Definite Recommend	83%	74%	67%	92%	88%	45%
Performances[a]						
Tom Selleck (Peter)	77%	67%	51%	86%	90%	35%
Guttenberg (Michael)	70	65	48	83	72	35
Ted Danson (Jack)	57	55	34	68	60	35
Elements[b]						
The comedy	69%	53%	46%	87%	72%	30%
The story	60	51	38	74	63	25
The setting	57	52	32	67	64	25
The ending	54	45	31	69	55	25
The music	48	32	36	58	52	25
The pace	44	36	29	56	43	25
Adjective Selection[c]						
Entertaining	93%	88%	94%	93%	96%	
Humorous	79	62	67	87	89	
Well-acted	69	58	58	74	76	
Funny	67	52	54	76	72	
Scenes Liked Most (number mentioning)						
Changing the baby	121	20	17	40	44	
Men singing to baby	58	4	8	22	24	
Ending (unspecified)	29	7	5	12	5	
Finding baby	28	0	5	9	14	
Park scene	28	5	2	7	14	
Baby—pink hard hat	25	3	4	9	9	
Ted/baby in shower	24	2	3	10	9	
Scenes Liked Least (number mentioning)						
Baby crying	18	2	8	1	7	
Party scene	14	2	4	0	8	
Beginning (unspecified)	11	1	3	5	2	
Drug scenes	11	0	2	4	4	

[a]Percentage of respondents rating the actor's performance as "excellent."

[b]Percentage of respondents rating the elements as "excellent."

[c]Percentage of respondents selecting the adjectives as descriptive of the movie.

Source: "Recruited Audience Survey—*Three Men and a Baby,*" National Research Group, Inc. August 1987.

Questions for Discussion and Review

1. In developing a statement of creative strategy, what are the most important conclusions that can be drawn from the two research studies?

2. What unusual characteristics of advertising and marketing a movie are important in formulating a creative strategy for introducing *Three Men and a Baby?*

3. Is a statement of creative strategy more important for a movie than for a consumer durable product? Why or why not?

4. Which component of a statement of creative strategy is most difficult to develop for *Three Men and a Baby?* Why? Which component is the most important? Why?

C A S E   **6 - 2**

Women's Athletics (A)

Sports marketing has become a major business. Top Madison Avenue sports media buyers have dealt with contracts in the billions of dollars. Major TV sports contract expenditures in 1990 varied from network to network, but CBS, for example, had a contract expenditure of over $3 billion just for sports. While the marketing of sports may vary from year to year to respond to audiences' differences and preferences, it has become a major concern, not only in professional sports but also in collegiate sports. College sports have become more popular with the advent of ESPN and cable. Through these new media, college sports have reached much larger audiences and, as a result, have become a big business.

College football is probably the most popular of college sports and, therefore, the one that commands more money and more advertising. Men's college basketball follows right behind, now involving media exposure at the level of major networks in some cases.

The newcomers on the media scene in college sports are women's sports. Women's sports are not very popular at the professional level, but they now command respectable audiences at the college level. As women's involvement in sports has become more popular, the attitudes of Americans toward this particular segment have become more favorable. Spectators have

---

This case was written by Isabella C. M. Cunningham, The University of Texas at Austin, and is intended to generate classroom discussion, not to illustrate the effective or ineffective handling of an administrative situation. Used by permission of Intercollegiate Athletics for Women, The University of Texas at Austin.

swelled arenas for women's basketball and volleyball games and shown support for other sports as well. At large state universities, women's sports are still not major money-makers, but it is important to the universities to cultivate audiences and potential donors who might identify with women's sports.

SOUTHWEST UNIVERSITY WOMEN'S ATHLETICS

At a large southwestern university, both men's and women's sports were classified in Division I. Men's athletics had been a large operation for a long time and was a big money-maker. The attendance at football games averaged 50,000 to 60,000 per game, and attendance for men's basketball games averaged about 10,000. These two sports were able to support all the other men's sports as well as contribute to women's sports.

In the early 1970s, Southwest University made the decision to develop and support a full-fledged Division I women's athletics department. This involved the promotion and maintenance of six different sports. It was decided that in order to help support women's sports it would be necessary to develop a large number of donors for the women's athletics operation, as well as to build consistent audience numbers for the more popular sports.

Basketball and volleyball were the two most popular women's sports. Several promotions made it possible to attract large audiences to basketball games and a sizeable audience to volleyball games. In the late 1980s, the average audience for basketball was about 6,000 to 8,000, and the average audience for volleyball was about 3,000.

Additional revenue for sports could be achieved by selling advertising in both broadcast and print media as well as the programs sold at sports events. Local and national advertisers were potential buyers of space and time. In order to develop advertising sales for its media coverage of sports, the women's athletic department felt the need to develop a media package. A basic requirement for selling advertising was to have consistently large audiences. The department set out to tackle that challenge first.

Two major goals were set for Southwest University's women's athletics department for the 1990s. The first was to develop advertising and promotional appeals that would bring consistent and loyal audiences for both basketball and volleyball. In addition, the department wanted to increase average attendance at these games by 10 percent per year for the next five years.

One of the major factors in attracting audiences is the performance of the teams. The department knew how fickle sports audiences can be; after just a couple of bad games, the women's basketball audience dropped drastically. However, both the basketball and volleyball teams had been ranked in the top ten in the nation for the previous five years, and the development experts in the department felt that such a record would be very helpful in building loyalty and consistency among game-goers.

It was also felt that loyal attendance was a first step toward consistent giving to and participation in booster clubs. The department had started a giving program patterned after successful small donor programs used by other Southwest University departments. Several levels of membership were available, and the benefits of membership included choice seating, parking facilities, and halftime talk clubs, among others.

To achieve these first two goals, the department decided to gather relevant information about the audiences for both sports. The results of this research would then be used by the development specialists and an advertising consultant to identify the target audience(s) for a campaign to spur and maintain sports attendance. Details about the research study follow.

THE RESEARCH STUDY

Two large survey research studies were conducted with audience members at a major basketball game and a major volleyball game. The audience members were given a general questionnaire and asked to complete it during the game and return it to specific boxes at the exit. The results were tabulated and analyzed. Among the variables included in the questionnaire were the following:

1. Demographic characteristics such as gender, place of residence, marital status, household type, age, education, occupation, and income

2. Participation in and attendance at both women's and men's collegiate sports events—particularly, frequency of attendance at women's sports events

3. Affiliation with the university

4. Ticket-buying behavior

5. Media usage, such as the use of newspaper, radio, television stations, and cable television

6. Some life-style variables, such as shopping habits and credit card usage, and some life-style patterns that might be significant in determining which market segment the respondents belonged to and how willing they would be to buy products advertised in the program.

Tables 6-2-1 and 6-2-2 report some of the results of the research.

Because the first task was to identify target audiences and develop advertising and promotional appeals that would increase attendance at games and develop loyalty among fans, only a portion of the results was analyzed. Table 6-2-1 shows a tabulation of the demographic characteristics of volleyball and basketball audiences.

Some additional variables were also investigated, including attendance practices, ticket-buying behavior, and some life-style characteristics felt to be important in identifying those people most likely to become loyal followers of and potential donors to the volleyball and basketball teams. Table 6-2-2 shows the tabulation of some of these selected variables.

TABLE 6-2-1   Demographic Characteristics of Volleyball and Basketball Audiences

	Percentage of Volleyball Audiences	Percentage of Basketball Audiences
Gender		
Male	53.9%	36.3%
Female	46.1	63.1
Marital Status		
Single	55.2%	30.0%
Married	36.4	57.4
Divorced	4.6	7.0
Other	3.8	5.6
Dwelling Type		
House/Condo	62.6%	89.3%
Apartment	25.3	9.9
Dormitory/Other	12.1	0.8
Age		
18 and younger	11.2%	2.5%
19 to 24	23.1	4.8
25 to 34	24.1	18.3
35 to 49	23.7	35.2
50 to 64	12.7	24.2
65 and older	5.2	15.0
Employment Status		
Employed	65.3%	73.8%
Full time	69.8	74.8
Part time	30.2	25.2
Occupation		
Professional	46.0%	52.1%
Managerial	7.4	10.8
Clerical	8.2	10.4
Student	29.5	5.8
Other	8.9	20.9
Income		
Under $15,000	16.7%	6.1%
$15,000 to $30,000	19.4	20.5
$30,001 to $50,000	25.5	28.8
$50,001 to $75,000	21.9	28.3
Over $75,000	16.5	16.3
Education		
Some high school/high school graduate	12.4%	14.0%
Some college	37.0	27.2
College graduate	23.0	28.0
Post-graduate	27.6	30.8

(continued)

TABLE 6-2-1 *(continued)*

	Percentage of Volleyball Audiences	Percentage of Basketball Audiences
Children at Home?		
Yes	18.8%	24.4%
One child	53.9	53.3
Two or three children	44.9	43.0
Four or more children	1.1	3.6
Age of Oldest Child Living at Home		
6 and younger	17.4%	13.6%
7 to 12	17.4	21.0
13 to 17	30.4	31.8
18 and older	34.8	33.6
Number of People in Household		
One	23.9%	18.4%
Two	42.5	52.8
Three	15.8	15.4
Four or more	17.8	13.2
Affiliated with University?		
Yes	60.5%	40.0%
Student	51.3	11.0
Staff/Faculty	15.7	15.8
Alumnus	27.9	43.5
Other	5.1	29.7
Member of Booster Group?		
Yes	23.1%	31.2%
No, but friend of one	10.0	11.4
Other	66.9	57.4

TABLE 6-2-2 **Sports Attendance, Ticket-buying Behavior, and Selected Lifestyle Variables of Volleyball and Basketball Audiences**

	Percentage of Volleyball Audiences	Percentage of Basketball Audiences
Season Ticket Holders for Selected College Sports[a]		
Men's basketball	16.4%	14.5%
Men's football	19.4	16.0
Other men's sports	13.5	7.0
Women's basketball	34.1	68.4
Women's volleyball	38.8	8.0

(continued)

TABLE 6-2-2   *(continued)*

	Percentage of Volleyball Audiences	Percentage of Basketball Audiences
Attendance at Athletic Events (any frequency)[a]		
Men's football	52.1%	49.4%
Men's basketball	45.0	34.0
Other men's sports	39.8	30.0
Women's basketball	57.2	100.0
Women's volleyball	100.0	28.0
Other women's sports	37.4	18.5
Activities Enjoyed		
Basketball	5.9%	3.8%
Golf	7.9	10.3
Baseball/Softball	4.2	4.1
Tennis	7.7	4.8
Volleyball	16.4	2.4
Watching other teams	2.8	1.9
Water sports	10.1	8.8
Biking	5.7	4.3
Hunting	1.8	3.5
Fishing	2.2	5.1
Other outdoor sports	5.0	9.6
Indoor sports	2.2	4.4
Aerobics	2.4	19.8
Games	4.0	3.6
Crafts	5.0	8.8
Reading	15.6	23.2
Collecting	0.8	0.8
Other hobbies	4.0	6.7
Listening to music	4.2	3.9
Watching TV	1.4	3.0
Using computer	1.0	0.8
Watching sports	18.0	15.1
Attending music performance	2.2	1.6
Attending movies	4.4	6.5
Social activities	3.2	2.8
Caring for animals	1.0	1.6
Gardening	2.4	4.8
Relaxing	1.8	1.9
Traveling	2.8	4.6
Shopping	1.4	1.4
Other	6.7	4.6

[a]Percentages do not add to 100 percent because some respondents held season tickets for more than one sport or attended more than one sport.

THE PROBLEM

The development specialists in the women's athletics department at Southwest University and the advertising consultant were struggling with several questions. First, they were debating whether one advertising and promotional campaign could appeal to both volleyball and basketball fans. The data from the research seemed to be very helpful in making such a decision.

The second question dealt with the type of appeals to be used in reaching the two women's sports audiences. The consultant knew they must emphasize education and the value of sports, but they had not decided just what creative strategy would most effectively achieve the goals defined by the department.

The director of women's athletics had scheduled a meeting with top administration personnel to present a plan of action. Her task: To draw on the team's expertise and the research findings to identify target audience(s) for both basketball and volleyball and to determine the most appropriate creative strategy to reach them.

Questions for Discussion and Review

1. Develop a statement of advertising objectives for attracting audiences to (a) women's volleyball home games and (b) women's basketball home games, respectively.

2. If only one campaign were developed for all women's sports, what types of appeals should it emphasize?

3. Describe the target audience for women's basketball and volleyball. How can they be reached effectively?

4. Prepare a creative strategy to reach the audience for women's sports. If appropriate, provide a rough sketch of the advertisement(s) you propose to use.

C A S E **6 - 3**

Columbia Savings (A)

For many years, Columbia Savings (CS) had been a successful savings and loan association, with six branches in a large and growing metropolitan market (Ourtown) located in the southwestern United States. Management of CS had been content to coast along, paying savers low interest rates that were set by law. CS's marketing efforts, aimed at attracting new customers and increasing its deposit base, were relatively weak and ineffective. Despite its lack of

This case was written by John H. Murphy, The University of Texas at Austin, to generate class discussion and not to illustrate either the effective or ineffective handling of an administrative situation. The identity of the firm involved has been disguised.

aggressiveness, CS had consistently made a very handsome return on investment for the firm's owners.

In recent years, however, the financial environment in CS's market had changed substantially. Deregulation of the financial industry had increased the flexibility of product offerings. New technology, coupled with deregulation, had made the battle for customers increasingly competitive as the distinctions among banks, S&Ls, credit unions, brokerage firms, and other financial institutions blurred. CS had largely chosen to ignore these changes and opportunities.

Further, as the market had grown over the past ten years, a number of large and relatively sophisticated banks and S&Ls based in other markets had established a position in CS's market either by opening branches or through mergers. These newcomers were innovative and aggressive marketers and paid considerably higher rates on money-market accounts, certificates of deposit, checking accounts, and other accounts than did CS.

These and other changes had resulted in a declining deposit base for CS. This situation continued for many months, and the atmosphere at CS went from conservative smugness to the worry and insecurity of an old, downtrodden loser. At that point, the board of directors realized that radical surgery was in order if CS was to regain its position as a leader in its market. To perform the surgery, the board hired a new president, David Woburne. Woburne had a very strong marketing success track record with a regional department store and several financial institutions.

Woburne was given a free hand to make wholesale changes in the operations of CS. After a period of evaluation lasting several months, he began to take action. He implemented a number of key personnel changes, including the hiring of a new senior vice-president of marketing, David Carlyle. Branch locations were evaluated, and fixtures and furnishings were updated and coordinated to project a more progressive image for the firm. Applications were submitted to the state regulatory agency for new branch locations in growth areas of the market. A training program for all cashiers and other branch personnel was designed and begun. Perhaps most significantly, the firm adopted a new strategy of shopping competitive rates via telephone each week on the popular money-market accounts and certificates of deposit and setting CS's rates to equal or exceed the competition's.

In addition, Woburne felt that advertising should not be handled in-house by CS's marketing department, as in the past. To remedy this situation, he hired a full-service advertising agency (Boyton & Dodds) based in a major metropolitan market in another state to develop a new campaign to communicate what the revitalized CS offered to customers and potential customers. Woburne had worked with the agency before and was good friends with both its principals.

THE AGENCY'S PROPOSED ADVERTISING STRATEGY

After a careful evaluation of the situation, CS's account executive at Boyton & Dodds recommended that a consistent newspaper advertising campaign be launched after the branch training had been completed, new brochures were ready, the branch locations had been refurbished, and other changes had been made. The agency recommended that ads be run in the business sections of both major daily newspapers in the market on Tuesdays and Sundays. Further, the agency suggested that a quarter-page size (6 $\frac{7}{16}''$ × 10½ ″) would be the most efficient size for all ads in the campaign.

During the process of developing a recommended advertising campaign, agency personnel met with Woburne and Carlyle on numerous occasions. One of the most important topics discussed was the development of a statement of creative strategy around which the campaign would be structured. This guideline was crucial since it clearly established the boundaries within which creative ideas and executions must fall. Woburne and Carlyle reviewed and approved the following creative strategy:

- *Target Audience:* Aged 55+, demographically upscale, with a small household size, and relatively well educated. Security and stability oriented. Many of these individuals developed their social, moral, and other values in the 1930s and 1940s. They are concerned about and spend a good deal of time thinking about their savings and investments. In terms of motivation, the Unidex Report (a specialized commercial research service) on "high-balance depositors" indicates that rate is the paramount reason cited for opening an account at a new institution.

- *Objective:* To stimulate target prospects to contact CS for additional information regarding CS's money-market and/or certificate of deposit accounts. The desired response is a telephone or mail inquiry or a visit to a CS branch location.

- *Key Consumer Benefit* (Generic): To assist consumers in achieving their financial accumulation needs, plus serve protection and transaction needs to some extent.

   (Specific): CS pays the highest average rate on money-market and certificate of deposit accounts in the local market. In addition, deposits are safe and insured by a federal agency. Further, CS has financial strength and a track record of performance.

- *Support:* CS has a commitment to paying the highest rate to depositors on money-market and certificate of deposit accounts. CS has demonstrated this commitment over the past five months by paying higher rates than any bank or S&L in the market.

   Every day management receives a report on the rates paid by all major competitors in the market, and once a week CS adjusts its rate to be above the competition's. Money deposited with CS is insured by the FSLIC, and CS has total assets of over $200 million.

- *Personality:* The advertising should project the character and personality of a straightforward friend. The ads should be light and conversational in tone yet serious and businesslike. A light, even humorous headline and visual should be balanced by a traditional layout and serious copy. It is important that the advertising project the image of speaking from a position of strength. Further, there must be an underlying foundation of stability and consistency projected in the advertising.

PROPOSED CREATIVE EXECUTIONS

The agency presented its proposed creative executions for the campaign to the president, the vice-president of marketing, and other members of CS's management team. Exhibit 6-3-1 presents three roughs from the proposed campaign. The following summary of key aspects of the agency's rationale for the recommended campaign was presented by the Boyton & Dodds account executive:

> *In developing a proposed campaign format for CS, we focused careful attention on the creative executions of present competi-*

EXHIBIT 6-3-1 Three Print Executions from the Proposed Columbia Savings Campaign

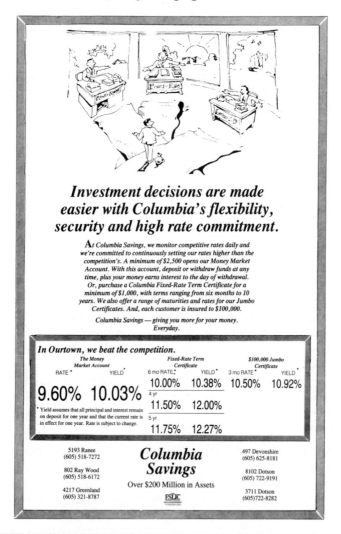

(continued)

EXHIBIT 6-3-1 *(continued)*

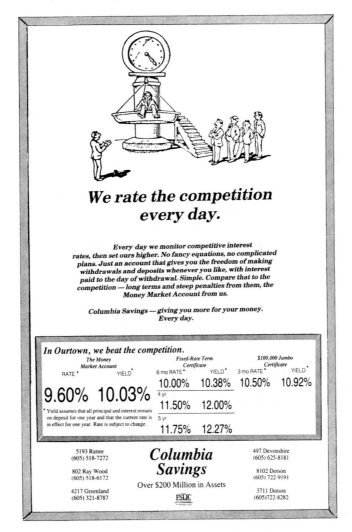

We rate the competition every day.

Every day we monitor competitive interest rates, then set ours higher. No fancy equations, no complicated plans. Just an account that gives you the freedom of making withdrawals and deposits whenever you like, with interest paid to the day of withdrawal. Simple. Compare that to the competition — long terms and steep penalties from them, the Money Market Account from us.

Columbia Savings — giving you more for your money. Every day.

In Ourtown, we beat the competition.

The Money Market Account		Fixed-Rate Term Certificate		$100,000 Jumbo Certificate	
RATE *	YIELD *	6 mo RATE *	YIELD *	3 mo RATE *	YIELD *
		10.00%	10.38%	10.50%	10.92%
9.60%	**10.03%**	4 yr			
		11.50%	12.00%		
* Yield assumes that all principal and interest remain on deposit for one year and that the current rate is in effect for one year. Rate is subject to change.		5 yr			
		11.75%	12.27%		

5193 Ranee (605) 518-7272	*Columbia*	497 Devonshire (605) 625-8181
802 Ray Wood (605) 518-6172	*Savings*	8102 Dotson (605) 722-9191
4217 Greenland (605) 321-8787	Over $200 Million in Assets FSLIC	3711 Dotson (605)722-8282

(continued)

tors. A review of current advertising revealed a mix of approaches but a category that, by and large, lacked fresh and insightful creative approaches. The vast majority of financial institution advertising is very dry and unimaginative.

In an effort to differentiate CS from the pack of plodding, "me-too" bank and S&L advertisers, we strongly recommend the fresh, mildly humorous campaign we have presented today. Mildly humorous is appropriate in that, while the target audience is serious about its money and dealing with a solid, safe, established firm, it can appreciate some humor being associated

EXHIBIT 6-3-1 *(continued)*

with selecting the appropriate financial institution for its savings/investments.

You've seen three roughs from the proposed campaign, and the finished versions will be even stronger! These ads all reflect the statement of creative strategy we agreed on. *All are distinctive, friendly, straightforward, and speak with confidence.*

The ads in the campaign focus on these consistent elements:

1. Message—*comparing CS rates with the competition using a dominant headline as a lead-in*
2. Layout—*consistent placement of headlines, art, copy, information box, locations, logo, and FSLIC bug*

3. Art—line drawings with strong visual appeal, executed in a finely rendered, almost whimsical style and presenting small characters as the players in CS's message (note that identification with these characters is the key to tying the campaign together)

4. Box—useful for last-minute changes and for display of rate comparisons

5. Screened border—creates a delineation between CS and other ads plus creates a sense of perspective (an optical illusion that happens when grays are introduced into a black-and-white medium).

Together, these elements will set CS's message apart from the other S&L and bank ads with which they will be seen in the business section. The light approach is eye catching and clever, which will serve to distinguish CS from the crowd in the minds of our target audience.

After the account executive finished presenting the proposed executions, Carlyle thanked agency personnel for their efforts and asked that they return in two days to discuss the matter further. He explained that he wanted some time to reflect on how closely the proposed executions fit the statement of creative strategy and to discuss the ads with the other members of CS's management team.

Questions for Discussion and Review

1. What factors should play a prominent role in the development of a statement of creative strategy?

2. Does the statement of creative strategy agreed on by CS and its agency seem appropriate in light of the situation facing the firm? Why or why not?

3. Are the proposed executions "on strategy"? Why or why not?

4. What other factors or aspects of CS's operations and market offerings will have an impact on the effectiveness of the proposed advertising campaign? Which of these factors seems to be most important? Why?

5. What alternative executions of the creative strategy statement would be appropriate?

C A S E   6 - 4
Peter Piper Pizza

"C'mon over to Peter Piper Pizza" waves the rotund pizza cook whose face is familiar to most of us. This familiar chef who appears in his striped apron and chef's hat is Anthony Cavolo, chairman and chief executive officer of Peter Piper Pizza. It was in November 1973 that Cavolo and his son-in-law, Steven Herrgesell, opened the first Peter Piper Pizza restaurant in Glendale, Arizona. Currently there are 90 restaurants throughout eight southwestern states, of which 32 are company owned and 58 are franchised.

Upon retirement from the restaurant business in New York in 1973, Cavolo moved to the Phoenix area and went to work for a pizza company there. By November of that same year, Cavolo decided to use his many years of restaurant experience to open a pizza restaurant of his own.

In 1974, Cavolo began to experience some difficulties. Faced with limited financial resources, he changed his concept to "lower prices and quality pizza." With this new concept, Cavolo invested his final $3,000 and went before the public on television. "Good pizza at low, low prices" was all Cavolo had to say in order to turn his pizza business into the success that it is today!

Peter Piper Pizza is one of the fastest-growing restaurant chains in the nation, selling approximately seven million pizzas a year. In 1985, sales were $42 million, with 1986 sales expected to reach $60 million. Due to the success of the first Peter Piper Pizza restaurant in Glendale, Cavolo decided to open a second in the East Valley. This was the first franchised restaurant, and it opened in Tempe in 1977. Currently, 64 percent of all Peter Piper Pizza restaurants are franchised. This seems to be fairly consistent with the franchising activity of the restaurant industry as a whole.

Franchising has become the wave of the future for the restaurant industry.[1] The number of franchisee-owned restaurants increased from 47,544 in 1984 to 56,259 in 1986. The corresponding sales also increased from $27 million to $33.5 million. Among the top franchised restaurants in the United States, four are pizza chains (see Exhibit 6-4-1). The estimated total number of pizza restaurants is 16,259, of which 10,959, or 67 percent, are franchisee-owned.[2] Pizza sales commanded 11.4 percent of the total industry's sales in 1984 (see Exhibit 6-4-2).

This case was prepared by Richard F. Beltramini, associate professor of marketing and advertising at Arizona State University, as a basis for classroom discussion and not to illustrate the effective or ineffective handling of an administrative situation. Copyright 1986 Richard F. Beltramini. Used by permission from Richard F. Beltramini.

[1]John Naisbitt, "2001: A Franchising Odyssey," *Nation's Restaurant News*, March 3, 1986, F13.

[2]Jacque White Kochak, "New products deliver quality and freshness," *Restaurant Business*, September 20, 1985, 104–114.

EXHIBIT 6-4-1 Systemwide Sales by Company and Franchise[a]

Franchise System	1984 Sales (in thousands of dollars)	1985 Sales (in thousands of dollars)	1984–1985 Percentage Change
McDonald's	$10,000	$11,000	10%
Burger King	3,420	3,990	17
Kentucky Fried Chicken	2,850	3,100	9
Wendy's	2,420	2,700[b]	12
Hardee's	1,900	2,200	16
Pizza Hut	1,700[b]	2,100	24
Dairy Queen	1,390	1,572	13
Taco Bell	925[b]	1,140[b]	23
Big Boy	1,000[b]	1,135[b]	14
Domino's Pizza	626	1,097[b]	75
Arby's	757	814	8
Church's	634	739[b]	17
Ponderosa	585	681	16
Long John Silver's	602	637	6
Jack in the Box	588[b]	612[b]	4
Dunkin' Donuts	532	577	8
Shoney's	516	576	12
Roy Rogers	443[b]	507[b]	14
Sizzler	384	443	15
Baskin-Robbins	389[b]	423[b]	9
Bonanza	401	421	5
Western Sizzlin'	428	420[b]	(2)
Popeyes	304	355[b]	17
Chi-Chi's	273	334	22
Little Caesar's	227	300	32
Sonic Drive-In	283	292	3
Rax Restaurants	216	280	29
Perkins	281	276	(3)
Captain D's	239	280	13
Godfather's Pizza	304	268	(12)
Total	$34,390	$39,258	

[a]Includes international operations.
[b]Estimated.
Source: *Restaurant Business,* March 20, 1986, 182.

U.S. RESTAURANT INDUSTRY TRENDS

Americans have less time to prepare meals, but they have more money to spend. About half of all American households consist of one or two persons, and 50 percent of all households have two wage earners. All this, coupled with the fact that about 60 percent of women age 20 to 44 work outside the home, explains the increase in disposable income and the decrease in leisure time. In 1984, Americans allocated 15.1 percent, or $390.1 billion of their disposable

EXHIBIT 6-4-2   Sales by Product Group

Product Group	Number of Companies	Sales (in thousands of dollars) 1984	Sales (in thousands of dollars) 1985[a]	Percentage of Total Industry 1984	Percentage of Total Industry 1985
Hamburgers, franks, roast beef, etc.	105	$22,043,955	$24,058,881	50.1%	50.0%
Steak, full menu	111	7,767,393	8,413,997	17.9	17.5
Pizza	104	4,932,329	5,721,265	11.4	11.9
Chicken	33	3,891,165	4,402,558	9.0	9.2
Mexican food	36	2,113,104	2,403,653	4.8	5.0
Seafood	12	1,074,426	1,202,950	2.5	2.5
Pancakes, waffles	13	985,350	1,065,430	2.3	2.2
Sandwiches and other	51	626,060	739,839	1.4	1.5
Total	465	$43,433,782	$48,008,573	99.4%	99.8%

[a]Data estimated by respondents.
Source: *Restaurant Business,* March 20, 1986, 174–175.

income, to food purchases. The amount of money spent on food purchases away from home was 29 percent, of which 40 percent was generated by the fast-food segment. The remaining 71 percent of Americans' food dollars was spent in grocery stores.[3] These trends seem to indicate that Americans will continue spending more of their disposable income for the consumption of food away from home.

Convenience stores are beginning to compete in the fast-food segment. Food-service volumes at convenience stores rose from 4 percent in 1980 to about 10 percent in 1984. This area has become a great opportunity and a big competitor of the restaurant industry and is projected to reach 15 percent in the next few years. The advantage of convenience stores is the variety of products that they have available. One cannot go to a fast-food restaurant and purchase a meal along with beer, cigarettes, gas, and diapers, for example. Also, fast-food restaurants have become more restaurant oriented by placing more emphasis on menu variety than fast service.[4]

The issues of nutrition and calories are continuing to be of concern to those eating out, influencing their eating decisions. Those who are nutrition and calorie conscious tend to eat those foods that they believe are nutritious and low in calories.[5] However, although consumers are asking for nutritious, low-calorie foods, restaurants tell us that what consumers order are "perceived" healthy foods: high-quality, light, fresh foods. The fast-food industry is responding to these trends and offering "lite" menus. For example, McDonald's

---

[3]"Food industry is steady as she goes," *Standard and Poor's Industry Surveys,* F13–17.

[4]Howard Shlossberg, "Time on their side: Convenience stores have groceries, gas, banking machines—and a quick meal," *Restaurants & Institutions,* April 2, 1986, 13.

[5]"Continued growth likely for restaurant industry," *Standard and Poor's Industry Surveys,* R139–141.

EXHIBIT 6-4-3   Most-Patronized Pizza Restaurants

	Rank	
Pizza Restaurant	1983[a]	1984
Godfather's	1	1
Pizza Hut	2	2
Pizza Inn	4	3
Shakey's	5	4
Pizza Time Theatre	7	5
Straw Hat Pizza	6	6
ShowBiz Pizza	3	7

[a]Adjusted to reflect the deletion of chains with less than a 100-person patronage base.
Source: *Restaurants & Institutions,* December 19, 1984, 111.

EXHIBIT 6-4-4   How Americans Decide Where to Eat

Source/Influence	Percent Identifying
Recommendation of a friend	65.0%
Reputation of the restaurant	39.8
Suggestion of a family member	39.0
Price discount	24.6
Coupons	23.9
Newspaper advertisement	21.3
Restaurant review in newspaper	19.9
Advertisement on TV	10.3
Advertisement on radio	6.7
Magazine dining guide	5.9
Restaurant review on radio	3.9

Source: *Restaurants & Institutions,* December 5, 1984, 105.

has introduced the McDLT hamburger that has fresh lettuce, tomatoes, and onions, and Wendy's has added multigrain buns and a "Light Side" menu featuring baked potatoes and salads.[6]

Also of concern, especially to the Yuppie segment, is a trend toward preferring comfort, service, and status. These concerns have brought about a new trend featuring the "gourmet" eating experience. This new trend is evidenced by gourmet hamburgers on freshly baked rolls, croissants, and even gourmet pizza.[7]

Finally, the trend toward ethnic foods has grown within the restaurant industry. Mexican food has been among the most successful, with the popularity of Japanese, Chinese, and Indian foods growing.[8] Exhibits 6-4-2 through 6-4-4 illustrate the growing competition in the restaurant industry and

---

[6]Rona Gindin, "The healthy food phenomenon," *Restaurant Business,* March 20, 1986, 127–142.
[7]Andrew Kostecka, "Restaurant franchising in the economy," *Restaurant Business,* March 20, 1986, 172–182.
[8]*Ibid.*

the trends in consumer preferences. Exhibit 6-4-4 also illustrates influences in selecting a restaurant.

THE PHOENIX PIZZA MARKET

In general, Peter Piper regards all fast-food restaurants as competitors. Peter Piper Pizza is geared toward getting the order out fast, and it can have a pizza ready in 15 minutes or less. Also regarded as competition are a number of "ma and pa" stores. These are the single- or double-unit pizza restaurants that are often small and family owned. However, Peter Piper's most direct competition are the various other pizza chains that compete within the same markets. Among these chains within the Phoenix market are Domino's (32 units), Pizza Hut (30 units), Little Caesar's (14 units), Godfather's (10 units), Pizza Inn (10 units), Gino's (10 units), Village Inn (5 units), Round Table (3 units), and ShowBiz Pizza Place (2 units). On a national level, Pizza Hut has continued to be the market leader, with Domino's at the number two spot (see Exhibit 6-4-5).

Of all of these leading pizza chains, Pizza Hut and Domino's are considered most threatening to Peter Piper Pizza. These two chains are considered to be Peter Piper's top competitors because they are the two top-selling pizza chains. However, in the Phoenix market, Peter Piper Pizza is the market leader, holding a 33 percent market share, with Pizza Hut and Domino's trailing close behind.

A recent study by the Gilmore Research Group revealed that Phoenix residents are more likely to be experienced with Peter Piper Pizza or Pizza Hut

---

EXHIBIT 6-4-5   National Pizza Leaders

Restaurant	Units	1984 Sales[a]	Market Share	Average Unit Volume
Pizza Hut	4,332	$1.9	19.4%	$450,000
Domino's	2,300	625	6.4	416,000
Godfather's	900	312	3.2	450,000
ShowBiz Pizza Place	364	n/a[b]	—	950,000
Pizza Inn	720	252	2.6	415,000
Little Caesar's	600	230	2.3	383,000[c]
Shakey's	318	200	2.0	520,000
Round Table	430	162	1.7	440,000
Mr. Gatti's	350	135	1.4	450,000
Ken's Restaurant Systems	240	130	1.3	936,000 (Mazzio's) 500,000 (Ken's)

[a]In millions of dollars, except Pizza Hut, which is in billions of dollars.
[b]The merger of ShowBiz and Pizza Time Theater created a much larger chain than in 1984.
[c]Estimated by *Restaurant Business.*
Source: *Restaurant Business,* September 20, 1985, 104.

EXHIBIT 6-4-6   Pizza Restaurant Experience among Phoenix Residents

Percentage of Residents	Visited in the past year?
60.0%	Peter Piper Pizza or Pizza Hut
33.3	Village Inn, Pizza Inn, or Godfather's
25.0	Gino's, Domino's, or Chuck E. Cheese's

Source: Gilmore Research Group, "Dining Preferences Among Phoenix Arizona Residents," 1984, 28.

than any other pizza restaurant in the area (see Exhibit 6-4-6). This study also revealed pizza restaurant preferences among Phoenix residents. Overall, once pizza diners try Peter Piper Pizza, they are most likely to prefer it. However, approximately three out of ten pizza diners visit Peter Piper Pizza most often, and almost twice as many visit its major competitor, Pizza Hut.[9]

The same study conducted by the Gilmore Research Group found that Phoenix residents enjoy a variety of restaurants when dining out. Closely following the national trend, Mexican restaurants have been the most popular. Approximately nine out of ten Phoenix residents will dine at a Mexican restaurant. Eight out of ten Phoenix residents will eat at either a hamburger or pizza restaurant, and seven out of ten will dine at seafood restaurants.[10]

PETER PIPER PIZZA'S MARKETING COMMUNICATIONS APPROACH

"Coupons, coupons, coupons!!! At Peter Piper's you don't need any coupons," quips Cavolo. Since Cavolo opened his first Peter Piper Pizza restaurant, coupons and promotions such as those used by the competition (see Exhibit 6-4-7) have been against his philosophy. Cavolo keeps his prices low so that consumers do not have to wait for a coupon to come out before going out for pizza. However, there are exceptions. Occasionally, Cavolo will run a back-to-school coupon to help attract students at the start of the school year. Also, coupons are used when entering into new markets to encourage trial. Cavolo has found that consumers sometimes tend to equate his low price with low quality. By using the coupons, Cavolo hopes to get the consumer who is unfamiliar with Peter Piper Pizza into the restaurant to try his high-quality pizza. Then, consumers tend to return on their own, because they like the pizza.

Peter Piper recently tested its first store promotion. For every large Coke that was bought, the consumer received a plastic tumbler with the Peter Piper Pizza logo on it. The objective of this promotion was to thank the customer for

---

[9]Gilmore Research Group, 1984, 9–38.

[10]*Ibid.*

EXHIBIT 6-4-7   Competitors' Promotions

Competitor	Promotion
Restaurant A	A large pizza for the price of a medium.
Restaurant B	Buy a pizza at regular price and get a second pizza of equal or lesser value free.
Restaurant C	A 12-inch, one-item pizza for $5.99 and two free Cokes.
Restaurant D	Buy one pizza and get another pizza of the same size free.
Restaurant E	$3 off any large, thin-crust pizza or $2 off any large, original-crust pizza.
Restaurant F	$2 off any large pizza or $1 off any medium pizza.
Restaurant G	Free quart of Coke with the purchase of a large or medium pizza.

supporting Peter Piper Pizza and to differentiate Peter Piper Pizza from the competition. Cavolo believes that it is not enough to offer quality pizza for a low price anymore. To compete successfully with the competition, restaurants need to get their names into the consumers' households.

Cavolo believes that community awareness is what has made Peter Piper Pizza a strong competitor. Therefore, he wants Peter Piper to get out into the community and work with it. Participating in a number of charitable promotions has been a positive way for Peter Piper to accomplish this. The majority of these promotions included donating 50 cents on every pizza purchased to various nonprofit organizations, including, for example, the Special Olympics, Phoenix Children's Hospital, and the Epilepsy Foundation. Also adding to these successes was the Bowl-a-Thon that Peter Piper Pizza sponsored to benefit the Muscular Dystrophy Foundation. All of these promotional activities represent Peter Piper's public relations work. They have proven to be great opportunities to add to Peter Piper Pizza's positive image within the Phoenix community.

"No coupons. No gimmicks. No Tuesday night specials. Just good pizza at a low, low price," continues Cavolo. Price and quality pizza are the major themes in Peter Piper Pizza's advertising campaigns. As a matter of fact, Cavolo will give customers their money back if they are not fully satisfied with their pizza at Peter Piper's.

Cavolo feels he can guarantee quality and low price for a number of reasons. By taking advantage of all volume discounts, Peter Piper Pizza can pass these savings on to the consumer. Peter Piper employs high-volume production techniques that allow for greater efficiency than if skilled labor were employed. This minimizes the extra labor costs that would be incurred if skilled labor were to be used. Also, by limiting the menu selection to pizza, salad, beer, and soft drinks, Peter Piper minimizes paid labor costs that would be required if the menu were expanded. Most Peter Piper Pizza restaurants are located along main streets or strip malls where rent costs are lower. Finally, all management at Peter Piper Pizza restaurants is well trained and closely supervised in regard to cost and production controls. Cavolo believes that this is vital in order to minimize unnecessary spending. All of the above are employed in order to keep Peter Piper's costs low, passing the savings on to the consumer by way of lower prices.

Cavolo believes in using nothing but fresh, quality ingredients in his pizza. Therefore, he uses only 100 percent mozzarella cheese, the finest California tomatoes, dough made fresh daily with the finest grade of flour, and quality toppings.

Selling prices at Peter Piper Pizza are up to 50 percent less than what the competitors normally charge. By continuing to keep the menu selection limited to pizza, salad, beer, and soft drinks, Peter Piper is able to keep the prices low. Adding more variety to the menu would increase labor costs. Although 60 percent of Peter Piper's business is take-out, delivery will not be added to Cavolo's concept due to the added insurance costs involved. All of these extras would mean added costs to Peter Piper, and ultimately added costs to the consumer, too. Cavolo would like to continue his quality pizza/low-price concept.

During Peter Piper's first year in business, approximately $7,000 was spent on advertising. In 1986, $800,000 was allocated toward the advertising budget for the Phoenix market alone. Typically, the budget totals approximately 5 percent of sales (see Exhibit 6-4-8). According to Cavolo, this is what has worked best for Peter Piper, and there have been no thoughts regarding any changes in this area.

In the past, Cavolo believed in handling all advertising in-house. During this time, Peter Piper Pizza was not as big or as competitive as it is today. Therefore, Cavolo felt that Peter Piper's advertising did not need the creative talents, production technology, or planning expertise that an agency would provide. In addition, Cavolo did not feel that the extra finances involved in hiring an agency would have been justified. However, Peter Piper Pizza recently hired an agency to work on creative strategy and production. Cavolo felt that to continue to be competitive, better quality commercials were needed. The production quality of the commercials can be upgraded substantially through the use of an agency. Cavolo and his in-house personnel work side by side with the agency to continue the same general flavor in Peter Piper Pizza's advertising.

EXHIBIT 6-4-8 Peter Piper Pizza's Advertising Budget, Company-owned Stores

Year	Sales (in thousands of dollars)	Advertising Budget
1986	$16,000 (estimated)	$800,000
1985	14,200	710,000
1984	11,100	555,000
1983	7,900	395,000
1982	5,700	285,000
1981	3,400	170,000
1980	2,300	115,000
1979	1,600	80,000

Source: Company records.

Currently, Peter Piper is utilizing four media: spot television, spot radio, newspaper, and outdoor advertising. The majority of the budget (90 percent) is devoted to television. Cavolo believes that Peter Piper's success in the beginning was a result of advertising on television, and therefore, he remains loyal to it. Also, Cavolo's friendly face has become familiar to many through the use of television and adds a personal touch. The remaining portion of the budget is allocated to radio, newspaper, and outdoor advertising.

As mentioned earlier, newspaper is utilized only rarely, capturing about 2 percent of the budget. It was not until recently that radio was introduced into the media schedule. Therefore, Cavolo is currently observing how radio will affect his level of sales. This medium currently only commands 3 percent of the budget. Two outdoor billboards rotate throughout the Phoenix area, accounting for the remaining 5 percent of the budget. This overall media mix used by Peter Piper is fairly consistent with that of some of the top pizza chains in the nation (see Exhibit 6-4-9).

Peter Piper's radio and television advertising runs for three weeks each month. By doing so, Peter Piper can achieve the high level of frequency that is desired. As a company representative remarked, "We want to blast them for GRPs (gross rating points)." The television spots are run during the first and third weeks of each month, with the radio spots also running every third week of each month. The advertising appears all through the year, with the heaviest periods corresponding with the heaviest monthly sales (see Exhibit 6-4-10).

With the production needs for Cavolo's commercials being minimal, five or six television commercials are produced in an hour. This schedule enables Cavolo to keep his production costs down to about $200 per commercial, or $1,000 per hour as compared to the thousands spent by Peter Piper Pizza's competitors.

EXHIBIT 6-4-9   Competitors' Advertising Budgets

Competitor	Ad Budget (in thousands of dollars)	Media
Pizza Hut	$64,456.7	NSOC
Domino's	18,205.4	NSOC
Godfather's	8,749.8	SO
Round Table	2,821.5	SO
Little Caesar's	2,174.9	SO
Pizza Inn	2,126.2	SO
ShowBiz Pizza	2,108.0	SO
Shakey's	1,294.4	SO
Gino's	18.5	O

Note: N = Network TVB
  S = Spot TV
  O = Outdoor
  C = Cable TV networks

Source: *Leading National Advertisers Ad Dollars Summary,* 1985, 111–347.

**EXHIBIT 6-4-10   Peter Piper Pizza: Phoenix Area of
Dominant Influence Sales**

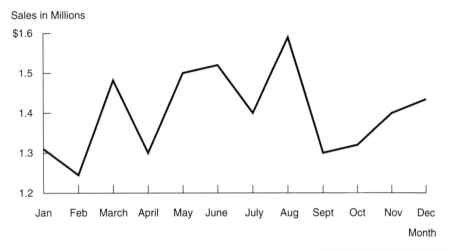

Cavolo as the main attraction in Peter Piper's commercials is what has worked best. Each 30-second spot features Cavolo as the spokesperson. In front of the camera stands Cavolo with his chef's hat, white shirt, striped apron, and that all-familiar friendly smile, telling his viewers of his good-quality pizza at low, low prices. For each flight, the copy for the commercials changes, but Cavolo remains in the spotlight.

The 30-second radio spots also feature Cavolo as the spokesperson. As in the television spots, the radio spots emphasize Cavolo's two main benefits— price and quality (see Exhibit 6-4-11). Cavolo's approach is simple and straightforward, but it has helped make Peter Piper the success that it is today.

EXHIBIT 6-4-11   Peter Piper Pizza Television and Radio Spots

Television Spot

"You see a lot of commercials for pizza: This one tastes great, that one looks delicious, but there's one thing they keep leaving out . . . the price. Peter Piper Pizza tastes great, looks delicious, and costs less than the others. Our large special six-item pizza's only $5.95; all our others are even less. Try a great combination . . . Peter Piper Pizza with an icy cold Coke. So come on over to Peter Piper Pizza."

Radio Spot

"Can we talk? I'm Tony from Peter Piper Pizza, and I know that most of you are pizza lovers. And I also know that some of you are paying as much as $9 or $10 for a pizza! Now that's silly. At Peter Piper Pizza our large six-item special is only $5.95. All our others are even less. Try your next Peter Piper Pizza with an icy cold Coke. So for all the pizza lovers, stop paying those high prices. For a good pizza at low, low prices, come on over to Peter Piper Pizza."

Cavolo attributes the majority of his success to the believability of his simple and straightforward approach. Several years ago, Peter Piper tested a cartoon character of Cavolo, but this was very unsuccessful. This experience proved to Cavolo that there was no substitute for the real "him." He believes that he creates a positive image for Peter Piper Pizza, and that is what has made it a success.

CHALLENGE FOR THE FUTURE

Cavolo is very confident in his concept of quality pizza at a low price. Although trends will come and go, Cavolo has no plans for adjusting his concept to meet these new demands. He feels that pizza will always be a favorite among Americans, and that his concept will always be attractive to a good many of these pizza lovers.

Cavolo will always keep his pizza top quality. However, there is no way that he can get around price increases when there are increases in the price of his ingredients. The fact that the economy may change, leaving even more disposable income available in the hands of the consumers, would not influence Cavolo to increase his prices, he claims.

Cavolo has two main advertising objectives for the future: to sell the quality product at a low price and to serve as a reminder to consumers. As the yearly sales continue to rise, so will the advertising budget. However, he seems adamant that the budget will always remain at 5 percent of sales.

The recent hiring of an advertising agency may be the beginning of a long-term plan. As Peter Piper becomes more competitive, Cavolo believes that a better quality commercial will have to be produced. He feels that this will be best achieved through the use of an agency. Therefore, the agency will become part of the picture more and more. Currently there are no plans to change the creative approach of Tony under the spotlight. It is a concept that has worked well and Cavolo plans to keep it, unless the concept proves otherwise.

Unlike various other pizza chains, Cavolo does not believe in setting specific goals toward expansion activities. "We're a one-step-at-a-time business, not 127 stores by 1987," remarks a company representative. Peter Piper seems to stand alone on this philosophy. Exhibit 6-4-12 indicates that many of the other pizza chains include plans to expand greatly in the future. Currently, Cavolo would like to limit expansion in the Phoenix market to company stores only. In other markets, however, there are no specific plans for the future. Currently, Peter Piper has just penetrated the California market. To enter big markets such as this, Cavolo has learned that one must have a number of stores to open at once to be successful. This means that where there are future expansion plans, there must also be those interested in franchising to open enough units to be successful. This further challenges Peter Piper Pizza's marketing communications programs for the future.

EXHIBIT 6-4-12   Competitors' Outlooks

Competitor	Outlook
Domino's	Beginning international expansion with units planned in Germany and other European countries.
Godfather's	"Wait-and-see" strategy following acquisition of Diversifoods by Pillsbury.
Pizza Hut	Two hundred units a year for next five years. Emphasis on urban areas such as New York, Chicago, Los Angeles.
Pizza Inn	Expansion resumed after four years of retrenchment. Expanding on military bases and overseas, among other places.
Round Table	Planning to build 60 new units this year, with majority in southern California.
Shakey's	With revamping, expansion picking up. Close to 100 new franchised locations now under contract.
ShowBiz	Concept revamping could give ShowBiz a shot in the arm. Marginal units have been closed but owner Brock Hotels Corporation remains confident.

Source: *Restaurant Business,* September 20, 1985, 104.

Questions for Discussion and Review

1. What statement of creative strategy could have provided the basis for Peter Piper's current advertising?

2. What statements of creative strategy could realistically be considered as possible extensions of or replacements for Peter Piper's current strategy? How could executions of these strategies be handled most efficiently?

3. What changes, if any, would you recommend in Peter Piper's current overall marketing communication program?

C A S E   **6 - 5**

Bowen Tools: Peck-O-Matic Division

Bowen Tools, Inc., is a large, diversified manufacturer of oil field equipment and supplies. Bowen is based in Houston, Texas, but operates worldwide. The firm has an outstanding reputation established after many years of manufac-

---

This case was written by John H. Murphy, The University of Texas at Austin, and Mike Brown, advertising manager of Bowen Tools, Inc. The case is intended for use in generating class discussion and not to illustrate either the effective or ineffective handling of an administrative situation. Used by permission of Bowen Tools, Inc.

turing and servicing high-quality oil field equipment. Last year Bowen purchased the Peck-O-Matic Company and converted the acquisition into a new operating division. Bowen has been a leader in the field for many years and hopes to effectively transfer its strong reputation to the new operating division.

The Peck-O-Matic Division manufactures power tongs, which are used in the oil patch to take apart and put together sections of drilling pipe. As simple as it sounds, this is a crucial task conducted on the rig platform under time pressure. Durability, ease and speed of operation, service, and other operating characteristics are the basis on which various power tong manufacturers compete.

The original Peck-O-Matic model of power tong was developed in 1963. After five years of testing and refinement, it was sold commercially on a wide scale. Until last year, the Peck-O-Matic Company was privately held by the Peck family.

All oil field equipment sales are currently depressed, as demand and prices have slumped over the past few years. In 1981, sales of Peck-O-Matic power tongs were at an all-time high as the oil industry boomed. Several years later, sales had declined so badly that a decision to sell out to Bowen became the best alternative. At the present time, few companies are buying power tong equipment. However, it is believed that a big turnaround for the industry may be just around the corner.

Peck-O-Matic power tong equipment is marketed to approximately 800 well-servicing companies. These companies range in size from very large divisions of the major oil companies (such as Exxon, Gulf, Texaco, and Shell) to major independent well-servicing companies, to small operators.

The major manufacturers of power tongs are B.J. Hughes, G.H. Foster, Peck-O-Matic, and Hilman Kelly. Peck-O-Matic ranks as the third largest power tongs manufacturer, behind Hughes and Foster but ahead of Hilman Kelly. All of these competitors advertise in general oil industry journals such as *Oil & Gas Journal* and *World Oil*. In addition, power tongs are advertised in specialized publications such as *Well Servicing, Drilling Contractor,* and *Drilling: The Well Site Publication.*

Peck-O-Matic power tongs are priced competitively; the 631 model, for example, sells for $12,992. The line has a very good reputation for performance in the field. Further, Bowen's sales force now actively sells the new lines.

Bowen has 28 sales divisions in the United States and Canada centered in the major oil-producing areas. Further, Bowen has three international offices with their own sales forces. Each office has a sales force of from one to four individuals.

As in most other types of industrial marketing, personal selling plays the key role. Advertising supports the efforts of the sales force by keeping the firm's name before prospects, building an image for the manufacturer, and generating sales leads. In both its advertising and selling efforts, Bowen can be characterized as *conservative.* Bowen prefers to take a somewhat low-key marketing approach, relying on the quality and reputation of its products to do a substantial portion of the selling job.

BOWEN/PECK-O-MATIC ADVERTISING

To guide the development of introductory advertising to announce the acquisition of Peck-O-Matic by Bowen, the following decisions were made:

- *Target Audience:* Purchasing agents and regional managers of major well-servicing companies and the owners and presidents of smaller independent well-servicing companies.

- *Message:* Bowen now owns, distributes, and services Peck-O-Matic power tongs under the new name Bowen Peck-O-Matic. Bowen's high-quality reputation, dependable service, and technological research now stand behind Bowen Peck-O-Matic. Finally, the basic specifications of the 631 and 781 models should also be communicated.

- *Objective:* To create awareness of Bowen's acquisition of Peck-O-Matic and the fact that Bowen now stands behind its new division. To stimulate inquiries and sales leads from the target audience. To contribute to Bowen's image as a leading supplier of oil field equipment.

Based on these guidelines, Bowen's advertising agency suggested that a finished ad (see Exhibit 6-5-1) be run in several trade journals to announce the addition of the Peck-O-Matic Division. After an initial meeting with agency personnel to discuss the proposed ad, Mike Brown (the advertising manager for Bowen) reacted positively. However, he stated that he would *not* be comfortable recommending the ad to top management at this point.

Brown was concerned that the agency's rationale for the appropriateness and effectiveness of the ad was weak in three key areas. First, he believed that, as in most situations, new advertising should be based on past campaigns. Therefore, it was important for the agency to examine ads utilized by the Peck-O-Matic Company prior to the Bowen acquisition and perhaps build on them. Second, he was also convinced that any advertising for the new division should be compatible with the overall Bowen "For Your Special Needs" advertising campaign. Finally, he was concerned about how any new ads for the division stacked up against the ads of direct competitors. Exhibit 6-5-2 presents a representative ad run by the Peck-O-Matic Company. Exhibits 6-5-3 presents an ad from the current Bowen campaign.

In addition, Brown felt that a more complete statement of creative strategy was in order. Therefore, he asked the agency to develop a new and expanded statement of advertising creative strategy that addressed his three key areas of concern, divided the present advertising message into key consumer benefit and support sections, and added a concise description of the "personality" to be reflected in the advertising.

Finally, he suspected that this review and new statement of creative strategy might result in some changes in the ad the agency proposed. Brown asked that the agency develop a rough of any such changes rather than presenting a finished ad. Brown concluded the meeting by stating:

> *People, we simply haven't covered our bases carefully enough. We've jumped in and sunk a lot of money on production charges for an ad that we* cannot *adequately justify to the folks upstairs. . . . Our rationale is* not *complete enough. It's my fault*

**EXHIBIT 6-5-1   Proposed Ad Announcing the Addition of
Peck-O-Matic Division**

EXHIBIT 6-5-2 Representative Ad Run by the Peck-O-Matic Company

Just like the members of our crew above, Peck-O-Matic's new model 78-S sucker rod tong is compact, lightweight and loaded with desirable features.

Weighing just 175 lbs., our lightweight power tong minimizes crew fatigue, while assuring correct torque throughout the string.

By combining the directional control valve and relief valve, we've reduced the length of our original compact model by one-third, to 24". And we've eliminated troublesome hoses and fittings.

No jaw changes are necessary from ⅝" to 1⅛", and changeover from make-up

Interested in a "Pecker Power" cap, t-shirt or sticker of your own? Ask us for details.

to break-out takes only seconds. No hammers, wrenches or wrestling is required.

Except for occasional greasing, you can forget about maintenance, too.

Before you decide on your next rod tong, check out the new Peck-O-Matic. The crews that use it are looking better than ever. **Circle Number 041**

peck·O·matic
TUBING & SUCKER ROD TONGS

10077 Wallisville, Rd., Houston, Tex. 77020, (713) 675-8686. Inquiries from overseas representatives welcome. Telex 792-920.

PECK-O-MATIC POWER TONG, PARTS AND SERVICE REPRESENTATIVES

WEST TEXAS	SOUTH TEXAS	OKLAHOMA	NEW MEXICO-FOUR CORNERS	WILLISTON BASIN	CANADA
Juaco Sales & Service, Odessa	Alice Hydraulics, Alice	Bynum & Co., Stonewall	Hopper Specialty, Farmington	Reten, Inc., Dickinson, N.D.	Petroleum Supply, Inc. Edmonton
EAST TEXAS	LOUISIANA	NEW MEXICO-EAST	WYOMING	Hickman Sales & Service, Williston, N.D.	CARIBBEAN
Well Servicing Equip. & Supply, Kilgore	Power Tong Service & Rental, Lafayette	Watson Truck & Supply, Hobbs	Watson Truck & Supply, Mills		Neal & Massey, San Fernando, Trinidad

EXHIBIT 6-5-3   Bowen Campaign

DRILLING TOOLS FOR YOUR SPECIAL NEEDS

Bowen's versatile and rugged line of drilling tools are designed to provide operators with more efficient drilling techniques. The Hydromechanical Drilling Jar Cushion Sub, Pressure Balanced Drilling Bumper Subs were all developed after extensive study and testing to solve specific problems encountered during drilling operations.

Our delivery time can't be beat
The Bowen *Hydromechanical Drilling Jar* is built to withstand the abuse and demand that a drilling jar must endure. Its two section design makes it easy to maintain and handle, and its powerful upward and downward blows can be controlled by the operator.

The Bowen *Cushion Sub* is designed to eliminate the variable dynamic loading conditions on the bit thereby ensuring the highest possible drilling penetration rate. Its extremely long stroke and very low spring rate provide a soft impact absorption system that greatly extends the life of the bit and drill string.

Bowen's *Pressure Balanced Drilling Bumper Sub* is specifically designed for offshore drilling from floating rigs. It eliminates bit weight fluctuations relative to vertical movement and also overcomes pressure differential extension or contraction problems. All of these Bowen tools have been developed and proven over many years of meritorious service. When you want state of the art tools that are rugged and dependable, you need Bowen.

Call or write for technical bulletin or general catalog.

Bowen is meeting the demand with tools of merit.

Our delivery time can't be beat

BOWEN Bowen Tools, Inc.   A ⬛ INDUSTRY
Call or write for more information.
P.O. Box 3186 Houston, TX 77253 713 869-6711 Cable: ITCO Telex 762-484

Boone Advertising Job No. - 583-9

more than yours, but we need to be more buttoned-up on this introductory advertising. To make matters worse, we still must present our recommendations to the folks upstairs next week as originally scheduled. I know I can count on all of you for a big push now. Too much is riding on this not to refine what we have done already. Let's go get 'em!

Questions for Discussion and Review

1. In what ways does the industrial or business-to-business advertising environment differ from the consumer advertising environment? In what ways are the environments similar?

2. What criteria should be used to compare the proposed ad with past ads, the present Bowen campaign, and competitors' ads?

3. What other considerations should impact the evaluation of the appropriateness of the agency's proposed ad?

4. Is Brown being fair with his agency in asking it to do considerably more work to develop and support its proposed ad? How might this additional work have been avoided? How typical is this situation?

7

Developing Media Strategy

For marketers, however, the mass media are no longer the sole choice. Traditional media retain an important advantage: the "rub-off" credibility that accrues from being part of a broadcast or publication invited into the home. But for many marketers, media advertising is a shotgun. The new technologies provide rifles, which can target prime prospects.[1]

Stanley E. Cohen

INTRODUCTION

Once a market analysis has been conducted and a total advertising budget established according to the overall objectives set for the advertising efforts, two tasks must be performed: a creative message must be developed and a media plan established that will efficiently and effectively reach the target audience selected for the advertising. This chapter will explore some of the key factors involved in developing that all-important media plan.

The first part of this chapter will deal with the steps needed to select traditional media for an overall advertising plan. The second part of the chapter will focus on nontraditional media sources and their overall importance for future advertisers.

---

[1]Stanley E. Cohen, "The Dangers of Today's Media Revolution," *Advertising Age,* September 30, 1991, 18.

DEVELOPMENT AND SELECTION OF A MEDIA PLAN

The advertising media plan starts with the development of *media objectives.* Media objectives are used to help implement the marketing objectives and strategy. There is no set formula or process to develop or create media objectives. In many cases the media objectives are stated in terms of reach and frequency—the percentage of the potential audience to be reached and the frequency with which that audience should be exposed to the advertiser's message. In addition, the continuity or consistency of advertising placement in the media could be a consideration in setting media objectives. Using media objectives to develop a media plan involves the following decisions:

1. What target audience should be reached by the media?
2. To which geographic market or markets should the message be directed?
3. How far into the target audience can the advertising reach, given budget constraints?
4. With what frequency should the message reach the target audience during the campaign?
5. At which times should the message reach the intended audience?
6. What type of media and/or specific vehicle provides the best match between the intended market and the actual audience?
7. Which support functions will best ensure the effective performance of the selected media plan?

This portion of the chapter will examine each of these decisions in detail. They are all integral parts of effective media planning.

Identifying the Target Audience

The advertising for a product must be directed to all those audiences that represent prospective or existing customers. Advertising messages are also sometimes intended for a larger audience: the general public, prospective employees, potential investors, other businesses, and many others. The identification of the target audience to be reached by an advertising campaign must therefore be the first step in the overall media planning process. Media planners will look for the similarities between the target market and the media audience.

It is not easy to reach effectively only the intended audience. Advertising campaigns often reach unintended audiences, sometimes with disastrous results. A survey of students prepared by BKG Youth, a research and marketing company, suggested that the R. J. Reynolds Tobacco Company's controversial campaign for Camel cigarettes was highly effective at reaching kids under the age of 13. The U.S. Surgeon General and the American Medical Association repeatedly criticized the company for using the Joe Camel cartoon to advertise its cigarettes because they felt the campaign enticed children to smoke. RJR repeatedly countered this criticism, stating that there was no evidence to substantiate such claims. The research results, however, showed that when asked to recall cigarette brands, 90 percent of the kids aged 8 to 13 named Camels, and 73 percent cited Marlboro. This evidence of such an effective reach of the campaign and such high brand awareness among the very young could potentially have a very negative effect on Camel, RJR Tobacco, and, ultimately, any kind of advertising.[2]

Selecting the Geographic Market to Be Reached

As the demand for and sales of products and services vary across areas and markets, it often becomes necessary to use different levels of advertising in different geographic locations. One way to overcome this diversity and plan adequately is to use a system of index figures that portray the relative weight of each geographical submarket. Once the overall objectives of the plan have been stated, they are translated into media goals for each geographic area. This usually corresponds to the distribution of advertising dollars across locations.

The advertising media plan, therefore, can strengthen exposure to advertising in those areas with greater potential or where, for some reason, sales are lagging. Brand management goals will be reflected in media allocations and selections, so as to complement the overall marketing strategy.

Determining the Desirable Level of Reach, Based on Budget Constraints

Reach is the percentage of the target market that is exposed to the advertising message within a specific time period. The objectives of reach and frequency are usually addressed at the same time, because they must be set within the same budgetary constraints.

The advertiser may choose to distribute messages widely, allowing as many prospects as possible to receive at least one message. On the other hand, the advertiser may decide that its objectives would best be served by exposing a small number of prospects to multiple repetitions of the same message.

An example of a shift in reach goals for a campaign is the advertising plan used by Universal Pictures to promote its 1992 film, *Fried Green Tomatoes.* Initially, the campaign was designed to reach an older audience and to feature a greater number of ads directed at such an audience. A few weeks after its release, however, research showed interest in the film among younger audiences. Universal Pictures restructured its advertising strategy, focusing on broader audiences including younger women. Media choices were increased and less emphasis was placed on frequency of messages. The results of this shift were very positive; the movie's revenues increased substantially. [3]

---

[2]Gary Levin, "Poll Shows Camel Ads Are Effective with Kids," *Advertising Age,* April 27, 1992, 12.

[3]Thomas R. King, "Little Film Shifts Its Aim to Big Audience," *The Wall Street Journal,* January 31, 1992, B1 and B5.

It should be noted that reach levels are often based on statistical estimates. It is harder to accurately estimate reach for narrowly defined audiences than for broad, general audiences. Also, reach levels should be determined to be compatible with all the other variables in the campaign.

Determining the Frequency with Which the Message Should Reach the Target Audience

The degree of repetition of an advertising message is a very important component of the media plan. As the media environment becomes more cluttered and audiences' attention becomes harder to capture, advertisers are concentrating on increasing the frequency with which their target audiences are exposed to advertising messages. The increase in advertising clutter has resulted in an increase of "zapping," or channel switching, by television audiences, according to a 1992 study by Bozzell, a New York advertising agency. The research points out that an increase of 10 percent in advertising clutter resulted in a 7 percent increase in channel switching.[4]

It is easy to understand, therefore, why advertisers would be concerned with increasing the number of times the same audience is *potentially* exposed to an advertising message. There is still little knowledge, however, as to what is a sufficient number of advertising exposures. The answer to this question varies by type of product advertised, level of consumer knowledge of and involvement with the product, and type of appeal used, among other factors. It is, however, a commonly accepted practice to assume that a minimum of four exposures is sufficient to create an acceptable level of awareness among the intended audience. Future research will be needed to refine and perfect this assumption.

Determining the Timing and Continuity of the Campaign

The nature of the product advertised influences the decision of where and when mass media should be used to reach potential consumers. Some products and services experience an even demand throughout the year. Examples are sugar or financial services. For these products, advertising media selection may be constant throughout the year, and the number of messages at any given period will also be stable.

Many products and services, however, face varied demands at different time periods. For example, the demand for toys is highly seasonal, and so is the demand for tourism services. A media plan for products/services with seasonal demand may concentrate advertising expenditures at specific times throughout the year. Also, the number of messages to which the intended audience is exposed may vary in intensity within these periods. As an example, advertisers may choose to concentrate the majority of messages in a specific medium, or at the end of each week.

---

[4]"Clutter Suffers Zap Attacks," *Advertising Age,* March 30, 1992, 38.

Choosing the Media and Vehicles That Provide the Best Match with the Intended Market

The effect of different media on the impact of a specific advertising message is known as the *source effect.* It is possible, for example, that exposure to a television commercial will have more impact on the intended audience than exposure to a magazine advertisement. By the same token, a full-page color advertisement may have a greater effect than an identical half-page black-and-white ad. Finally, exposure to an advertisement in one media vehicle might have more impact than exposure to the same advertisement in another vehicle. An advertisement for toothpaste in *Playboy* magazine may cause a very different audience response than exposure to the same ad in *Good House-keeping.*

Advertising managers, therefore, should carefully consider the media choices at their disposal as they develop a media plan. The media types and vehicles should be compatible with the overall objectives of the advertising strategy, and they should provide a positive environment for the product and service advertised. This environment should parallel the image of the brand, product, or service itself, rather than provide a contrast that might change its perception by intended audiences.

Some media vehicles have more loyal audiences than others. For example, craft/hobby magazines' circulations revenue accounts for between 65 percent and 70 percent of total revenue, indicating that their readers are highly devoted to that medium. Advertisers have taken notice of this, and when the intended market for a product is matched closely by the audience of a craft/hobby magazine, they are quick to secure media purchases from it.

New television formats have been developed to segment audiences in a cleaner and more discrete manner. The new Fox show "Jane" was designed to appeal to 18- to 34-year-old women, a segment practically ignored by other afternoon shows.[5]

Advertisers should respond positively to the availability of such targeted audiences. Media schedules should attempt to increase the efficiency of ad dollars by targeting closely their intended prospects.

Selecting the Appropriate Support Functions

A media plan is often not complete unless it is monitored and complemented with other functions to ensure it will meet its intended objectives. Sometimes such support functions are provided by direct-response vehicles such as postcards, requests for information, and the like. Such a complement allows the advertiser to monitor differences in responses to advertising in different vehicles, geographic regions, and media types. Other common support functions are provided by toll-free 800 numbers with automated information systems, split copy placements, and free sample redemption promotions.

---

[5]Kevin Goldman, "Sassy Talk Show Targets Young Women," *The Wall Street Journal,* March 9, 1992, B1 and B3.

As technology changes, more support functions will be developed to complement and reinforce advertising messages conveyed in mass media vehicles. Constant control of advertising effects and consequent modifications of media plans are important, as they allow the advertiser to pursue its goals in a flexible and highly efficient manner. The next section will consider some innovative media vehicles and their potential impact on traditional media.

TECHNOLOGICAL INNOVATIONS AND NEW MEDIA VEHICLES

The media revolution that has taken place during the past two decades had its beginning in the development and subsequent popularity of cable television. The growth in the personal computer market and the increasing sophistication of electronic communication tools such as the videophone, portable phone, and many others opened the door to the development of new media vehicles to serve the needs of advertisers.

Cable Television

When the first cable systems were installed in the United States, advertisers and agencies alike were very reluctant to purchase media time on such vehicles. Audience services such as Nielsen did not provide data about cable audiences, and most cable revenue originated from subscribers' fees. Today cable television appeals to many advertisers. In 1991, Procter & Gamble spent almost $68 million on cable TV network advertising, an increase of 17 percent over its previous year's expenditures.[6] The same can be said for several other major advertisers—General Motors, General Mills, and Anheuser-Busch, to mention just a few. The reason for such a change is the increased household penetration of cable. Now reaching a majority of all U.S. households, cable is a formidable competitor for the networks, offering segmented audiences and diversified services.

One such service just starting to grow is Pay-Per-View. The Pay-Per-View network (PPV) allows viewers to choose what they want to watch and to be billed accordingly. The major advantage of PPV is that it delivers very specific audiences, providing advertisers with a very efficient vehicle for penetrating narrow markets.

The potential of cable is still largely untapped. Shopping channels have enjoyed increasing attention and success, allowing direct marketers another choice besides direct selling and magazine advertising. International and multilingual formats and the use of infomercials have all been pioneered by cable, thereby broadening the number and quality of message choices available to advertisers.

---

[6]Alison Fahey, "Spending Shift Sends P&G Soaring Atop Cable List," *Advertising Age,* April 6, 1992, S-2.

Perhaps the most intriguing and least well-known option available to cable operators is interactive television. A tool that has been introduced experimentally in many formats, initially as Qube, interactive television has not yet been developed sufficiently to attract advertisers. However, because it offers consumers the ability to customize programs to their preferences and to respond immediately to polls, surveys, and sales pitches, interactive television provides an infinite array of options for the future.

Magazines

Technological innovations have also affected other media. Desktop production facilities have allowed magazines and newspapers a flexibility never known before. Production times have been reduced to hours, and some media firms have customized editions to satisfy geographical and cultural market diversity. Newspapers and magazines of the future will have less text but more variety and graphics. Illustrations and visual aids will replace text and provide consumers with more information. Magazine audiences have also changed over the past 20 years, and there has been a marked increase in per capita magazine readership.

Product Placement

Existing media have also provided additional outlets for advertising. Recently, increased attention has been given to product placement in films and made-for-television programs. After the sales success of Reese's Pieces as a consequence of its placement in the movie *E.T.*, advertisers have paid increasing attention to the benefits of product placement. This new vehicle provides an alternative with less clutter than television and is therefore a sought-after solution for competitive exposures.

The effects of product placements are not yet well known. The widespread distribution of movies through VCR tapes has allowed films to reach a much wider audience than that composed of traditional theater goers. In the future, home videos will become increasingly affordable, thereby contributing to their popularity.

Personal Computers

The increase in the use of personal computers at home has fostered the development of on-line entertainment services, allowing advertisers to explore another way to effectively reach a segmented audience. Services such as Prodigy, America-On-Line, and CompuServe all carry news items, mail services, and a myriad of other services. The number of computers with full-color screens is increasing, thereby making them an attractive vehicle for advertisers. In addition, automatic on-line shopping services transform personal computers into an addictive and exciting version of electronic catalogs. As such, they provide a successful way of advertising impulse purchase items, among others.

As with cable television, the future of personal computer on-line services is limitless. As hand-held computers become more popular and satellite telephones are added to our automobiles, briefcases, and airplanes, the combination of all those technologies opens a new world of media to advertisers. This, along with the progress made by direct-response media, points to a future in which consumers will do a lot of their shopping at home, in the car, or at the office instead of at traditional retail outlets. Such changes will cause a rethinking of the content and format of media, as well as the frequency and timing of message exposures.

AN EXAMPLE OF INNOVATIVE MEDIA

The number of ideas generated by media increases on a daily basis. In 1991, the firm Actmedia, in partnership with Turner Broadcasting Corporation, started to market a Check-Out Channel. This channel, an in-store network, was tested in 13 stores in September 1991. Monitors situated at supermarket checkout lanes broadcast Cable News Network and Headline News programs, along with 60-second and 30-second commercials. Turner sells the advertising for the new Check-Out Channel. In addition, several silent TV monitors are located in the stores' aisles. These monitors carry 10-second spots and a two-minute loop of general-interest and community news.

In addition to serving as an advertising medium, the Check-Out Channel, coupled with a store's scanners, provides vital data about the effectiveness of advertising messages as a sales tool for specific products. This network is not confined to use by supermarket chains. It is estimated that it might be a welcome addition to other retailing and services organizations.[7]

There is other evidence of changes in audiences' media habits. A 1992 study by the three television networks and Nielsen showed that as many as 20 million viewers a week watch TV out of their homes.[8] The increase in out-of-home viewing should be an incentive for innovative media like the Check-Out Channel.

CONCLUSION

The media planning function is a vital element of the advertising plan. Traditionally, media planners followed a series of sequential steps to develop an efficient and effective way of conveying advertising messages to intended audiences. The world of media is changing, however. New technology has opened a number of alternatives to traditional media vehicles. These innovative media have not yet been fully tested by advertisers; however, they provide more flexibility in communicating with consumers and, in some cases, the excitement of direct feedback.

---

[7]Michael Burgi, "Turner, Actmedia Roll In-Store TV," *Advertising Age,* May 20, 1991, 40.
[8]Joe Mandese, "Network Study Tracks Out-of-Home Viewing," *Advertising Age,* April 27, 1992, 40.

Future choices of media will present an exciting challenge for media planners and advertisers. Targeting narrow audiences will be increasingly possible, making media decisions more complex. This specific area of advertising management will be responsible for major changes in the decision-making process of advertisers and agencies.

Suggested Readings

Banks, Seymour. "Considerations for a New ARF Media Evaluation Model." *Journal of Media Planning* (Fall 1989): 8–10.

Barban, Arnold M., Steven M. Cristol, and Frank J. Kopec. *Essentials of Media Planning: A Marketing Viewpoint.* 2d ed. Lincolnwood, Ill.: NTC Business Books, 1989.

"Beam me up, Scottie." *The Economist,* March 28, 1992, 69–70.

Jugenheimer, Donald W., Arnold M. Barban, and Peter B. Turk. *Advertising Media—Strategy and Tactics.* Dubuque, Iowa: William C. Brown Communications, 1992.

Landler, Mark. "The Infomercial Inches toward Respectability." *Business Week,* May 4, 1992, 175.

Leckenby, John, and Kuen-Hee Ju. "Advances in Media Decision Models." *Current Issues and Research in Advertising* 12, nos. 1 and 2 (1990): 312–357.

McGann, Anthony F., and Thomas J. Russell. *Advertising Media.* 2d ed. Homewood, Ill.: Irwin, 1988.

Spaeth, Jim. "Advertising Effects and Media Planning." *Journal of Media Planning* (Fall 1989): 40–44.

"Special Report: Cable TV." *Advertising Age,* April 6, 1992, S-1 to S-15.

"Special Report: Magazines." *Advertising Age,* March 9, 1992, S-1 to S-18.

TABLE 7-1   ScanAmerica versus Nielsen

Top 10 programs	ScanAmerica		
	Nielsen rank	Network	ScanAm. rating
1 Roseanne	2	ABC	21.1
2 60 Minutes	1	CBS	19.8
3 Full House	4	ABC	18.8
4 Home Improvement	9	ABC	18.7
5 Family Matters	—	ABC	18.6
6 A Different World	12	NBC	18.4
7 Monday Night Football	11	ABC	18.3
8 Cheers	3	NBC	17.9
9 The Cosby Show	16	NBC	17.8
10 Step by Step	—	ABC	17.6

Source: Nielsen Media Research, Arbitron Co. Reprinted with permission from the February 24,

Exercises

1. Tiffany Thompson, the media planner for a large manufacturer of fruit juices that markets to the public in supermarkets and through vending machines, was trying to decide which TV network should receive the bulk of the firm's media expenditures for 1993. According to a recent report, Nielsen Media Research and ScanAmerica, a new network rating service, differ markedly as to their ranking of the three networks. Table 7-1 shows the differences in the rankings of the two rating services.

How should Thompson evaluate this information in view of the product she is advertising? Assuming Thompson had $50 million to allocate to network television, should she divide it between two of the three major networks? Why or why not?

Source: Joe Mandese, "Rival Ratings Don't Match Up," *Advertising Age,* February 24, 1992, 1 and 50.

2. A major fast-food chain is considering its media expenditures for next year. John Cunningham, vice-president for advertising, just read an article describing the recent growth in coupon redemption by consumers. In 1991, marketers distributed 292 billion cents-off coupons in the United States; coupon redemption was up 5 percent that same year. It was estimated that consumers saved more than $4 billion in 1991 by redeeming coupons. Most advertising consultants were very bullish on the use of coupons for spurring consumer sales, and so was Cunningham.

However, Madonna Jones, the assistant vice-president for advertising, disagreed with Cunningham. She argued that coupons led to price wars and that consumer loyalty would be enhanced by tie-in promotions such as the "Batman Returns" McDonald's venture. Results from tie-in promotions were not always positive, however, and some of the fast-

Top 10 programs	ScanAm. rank	Nielsen Network	Nielsen rating
1 60 Minutes	2	CBS	22.6
2 Roseanne	1	ABC	21.3
3 Cheers	8	NBC	19.5
4 Full House	3	ABC	19.4
5 Murphy Brown	15	CBS	19.1
6 Coach	11	ABC	18.0
7 Designing Women	24	CBS	17.2
8 Major Dad	29	CBS	17.2
9 Home Improvement	4	ABC	17.2
10 Murder, She Wrote	14	CBS	17.2

1992 issue of *Advertising Age.* Copyright 1992 by Crain Communications, Inc.

food chains were planning games and sweepstakes that offered cash prizes to consumers. The proponents of this latter type of promotion believed that cash was a greater incentive than toys and other tie-ins.

The fast-food chain was planning to spend about $50 million on some type of promotion. John and Madonna had their work cut out. What type of promotion would best serve a fast-food chain if its goal were to increase sales? Do you feel coupons are an effective tool to promote fast-food sales? How do you suggest John and Madonna spend their promotion dollars?

Sources: Scott Hume, "Will Travelers Eat Up Summer Promotions?" *Advertising Age,* June 15, 1992, 29; Scott Hume, "Couponing Reaches Record Clip," *Advertising Age,* February 3, 1992, 1 and 41.

3.   The advertising executive for a global investment banking company was considering placing some advertising for the company in international print media. He was given a budget of $15 million, and his goal was to obtain the highest possible audience reach for a minimum of four full-page exposures during each of 10 four-week periods. He did not feel that advertising would be effective during the summer months, as in several European countries business almost stood still during that period. A recent report by *Advertising Age* ranked the highest-circulation dailies, weeklies, and monthlies (see Table 7-2), and he

felt that would give him sufficient information to make a choice.

Develop a media schedule for this investment banking company. Indicate clearly your total expenditures, media vehicles chosen, and number of exposures.

Source: "Global Media and Marketing," *Advertising Age,* October 28, 1991, S-1 to S-16.

4.   An advertiser is selling accounting software and is attempting to decide whether she should include in the media schedule a group of PC users' magazines or a group of business magazines. The PC magazines have a combined circulation of 200,000, and about one-third of their readers are middle- and upper-level managers. Another one-third are professionals who may or may not be users of accounting software. The business magazines have a combined circulation of 150,000, and about two-thirds of their readers are middle- and upper-level managers.

The cost of an advertising page in the PC magazines group is $3,000, while an advertising page in the business magazines costs $6,000. Which of the two magazine groups would be a better buy for the advertiser of accounting software, assuming the intended target market is middle- and upper-level managers and the secondary target market is professionals?

TABLE 7-2 *Advertising Age*'s 1991 Global Media Lineup

| 6-2 | GLOBAL MEDIA & MARKETING | Advertising Age, October 28, 1991 |

Advertising Age's 1991 global media lineup

Title / Publisher / Headquarters	Worldwide 1990	% chg	North America 1990	% chg	By foreign region — Region	1990	% chg	Ad page costs 1990 b&w/4-color	% chg	1991 b&w/4-color	Global cpm 1990	% chg	Top worldwide in 1990
Dailies													
Financial Times of London / Financial Times Ltd. / London	290,368	0.0	23,770	1.2	Europe:	256,154	(1.1)	$45,696 / $57,400	22.9	NA / NA	$157.37	9.7	British Airways
					Middle East/Africa:	3,354	(2.2)						British Gas
					Asia/Pacific:	6,407	64.6						Toshiba
					Latin America:	682	(3.4)						Daimler-Benz / Renault
International Herald Tribune / New York Times & Washington Post / Neuilly, France	195,688	3.1	5,834	10.0	Europe:	140,369	2.8	44,958 / 65,126	8.9	48,616 / 70,493	229.74	5.5	AT&T
					Middle East/Africa:	6,865	2.4						MCI
					Asia/Pacific:	39,547	3.2						American Airlines
					Latin America:	3,073	5.7						IBM / Siemens Nixdorf
USA Today / Gannett Co. / Arlington, Va.	1,901,538	0.7	1,841,538	0.7	Europe:	46,000[1]	2.2	63,255 / 82,233	10.5	63,255 / 82,233	33.27	9.6	AT&T
					Asia/Pacific:	14,000[1]	0.0						General Motors Corp. / MCI / Sheraton Hotels / Apple Computer
The Wall Street Journal / Dow Jones Co. / New York	2,002,169	(1.0)	1,913,443	(11.6)	Europe:	51,608	7.9	131,655 / NA	7.0	NA / NA	65.76	3.9	AT&T
					Asia/Pacific:	37,118	(3.2)						IBM / Dreyfus Corp. / Fidelity Mgt. & Research / Hewlett-Packard Co.
Weeklies													
Business Week / McGraw-Hill / New York	1,009,226[2]	(1.2)	896,803	(1.6)	Europe:	59,592	4.8	48,985 / 74,460	7.5	49,340 / 74,680	48.54	9.6	General Motors
					Asia/Pacific:	33,211	1.9						AT&T
					Latin America:	19,620	(7.4)						Digital Equipment / Fujitsu Ltd. / Compaq Computer
The Economist / The Economist Newspaper / London	475,535	11.8	213,109	17.4	Europe:	189,704	7.1	11,400 / 35,500	15.6	12,880 / 40,115	23.97	3.4	Singapore Airlines
					Middle East/Africa:	14,756	(2.7)						Bank of America
					Asia/Pacific:	50,468	14.0						RTZ
					Latin America:	7,498	3.3						Boeing Co. / AIG
The Guardian Weekly / Guardian Publications / Manchester, England	76,849	6.1	27,729	2.5	Europe:	16,821	1.4	3,045[3] / NA	16.7	3,045[3] / NA	39.62	(13.5)	Barclays Bank
					Middle East/Africa:	4,044	(0.7)						Jardine Fleming
					Asia/Pacific:	19,273	18.3						Britannia Build. Soc.
					Latin America:	1,388	0.4						Abbey National
					Caribbean:	7,594	7.4						Standard Chartered Bank
Newsweek / Newsweek Ltd. / New York	4,177,445	5.9	3,420,167	6.0	Atlantic:	353,725	7.7	111,615 / 179,120	9.6	NA / NA	26.72	3.5	Rothmans International
					Asia:	234,589	9.3						Singapore Airlines
					Latin America:	66,191	8.1						Rolex
					Australia:	102,773	(8.2)						Thai International / Philip Morris Cos.
Paris Match International / Publications Filippachi / Paris	244,314	1.4	37,192	(6.4)	Europe:	143,441	4.5	10,200 / 16,000	(4.1)	10,900 / 17,100	41.75	(5.4)	Philip Morris Cos.
					Middle East/Africa:	33,915	(1.8)						Benson & Hedges
					Asia/Pacific:	2,155	17.0						Renault
					Latin America:	2,611	19.8						Peugeot
					Other:[4]	25,000	3.1						Citroen
Time / Time Warner / New York	5,756,618	3.1	4,663,076	1.5	Europe/Middle East/Africa:	613,403	15.8	163,774 / 246,254	12.3	173,600 / 261,025	28.45	8.8	Rothmans Group
					Asia/Pacific:	450,071	5.2						Kingdom of Spain
					Latin America:	90,068	(0.3)						Govt. of Singapore / Toyota / Philip Morris Cos.
Monthlies													
Cosmopolitan / Hearst Corp. / New York	5,880,471	3.2	2,679,000	(2.4)	Europe:	1,823,481	4.2	NA / NA	NA	NA[5]	NA	NA	Revlon
					Middle East/Africa:	108,622	(9.5)						Nestle S.A.
					Asia/Pacific:	650,979	13.2						Procter & Gamble Co.
					Latin America:	618,389	21.3						Unilever / Philip Morris Cos.
National Geographic / National Geographic Society / Washington	9,918,479	(2.6)	8,510,155	(3.1)	Europe:	801,242	1.6	136,725 / 180,480	0.0	142,194 / 187,699	13.78	9.2	Canon
					Middle East/Africa:	64,995	(8.9)						Mazda
					Pacific:	393,783	(2.2)						NEC
					Latin America:	99,618	4.0						State of Illinois
					Military Overseas:	48,686	15.9						NA
Reader's Digest / Reader's Digest Association / Pleasantville, N.Y.	28,204,598	(0.2)	17,968,009	(1.3)	Europe:	7,010,509	3.3	303,785 / 403,495	14.6	NA / NA	10.80	14.0	Unilever
					Middle East/Africa:	350,331	(3.5)						NV Philips
					Asia/Pacific:	1,725,195	(0.8)						Kraft General Foods
					Latin America:	1,150,554	(2.2)						Franklin Mint / Mazda
Scientific American / Scientific American / New York	638,129	20.0	527,068	2.6	Europe:	75,103	(0.8)	21,800 / 32,700	0.0	22,850 / 34,250	34.16	4.8	Hughes Aircraft
					Middle East/Africa:	3,924	(6.1)						Textron Lycoming
					Asia/Pacific:	23,923	0.2						NEC
					Latin America:	5,888	1.0						Ameritech
					Military Overseas:	2,223	(3.8)						Italtel
WorldPaper[6] / World Times / Boston	901,100	(1.3)	58,000	NA	Europe:	10,000	0.0	35,865 / NA	(6.2)	NA / NA	39.80	(4.6)	AT&T
					Middle East/Africa:	10,000	0.0						Delta Air Lines
					Asia/Pacific:	271,800	4.2						Visa International
					Latin America:	286,300	(20.3)						Gold Star Ltd.
					E. Europe/Soviet Union:	265,000	(1.8)						Sheaffer
Other													
Fortune / Time Warner / New York	802,848	1.1	681,850	0.7	Outside North America:	120,998	3.1	38,550 / 58,980	8.0	NA / NA	48.02	6.9	American Intl. Group
													Bank of America
													Astra Business Jets
													Gulfstream American / Samsung
World Link[7] / World Link Publications part of World Economic Forum / Geneva, Switzerland	44,282	16.1	18,043	65.2	Europe:	15,988	(5.0)	9,300 / 12,000	0.0	9,300 / 12,000	210.00	(13.9)	Audi
					Middle East/Africa:	2,100	3.3						Swissair
					Asia/Pacific:	6,413	(2.5)						Du Pont
					Latin America:	1,738	(1.3)						Asea Brown Boveri / Montres Breguet

Notes: 1. Second half '91 projection. 2. Not included in Business Week International world total are the following foreign-language editions, published locally as a joint venture: BW/China:53,000; BW/USSR:50,000; BW/Hungary: 8,000. 3. Full page b&w figure of pounds sterling 1,750 converted to dollars using the October 1991 rate of 1.74. B&w rate for 1991 and 1990 are the same in pounds sterling, but the dollar figure varies due to exchange fluctuations. 4. Other circulation includes data for French-speaking territories and airlines. 5. No figures available for b&w and color pages since rates are given on a case-by-case basis for 24 different editions. 6. Distributed as a newspaper supplement. 7. Published bi-monthly. See "How to read these rankings," Page S-13.
AA chart: Ilse Cermak

La Quinta Motor Inns

A La Quinta Inn is probably a familiar sight to the traveling businessman or family. A lodging chain found in 28 states, La Quinta Motor Inns, Inc., has more than 200 inns across the Sunbelt, Midwest, and Rocky Mountain areas. Typical La Quinta Inns are conveniently located near office complexes, universities, medical centers, and regional malls with good airport and highway access. Its customers are frequent travelers on business or vacation who appreciate the reasonably priced, "no-frills" but high-quality lodging found consistently at La Quinta Inns. Guests can expect clean, quiet, and well-maintained rooms with color TVs and AM-FM radios, as well as free local calls, swimming pools, and a quality of management made possible by the smaller size of the inn.

La Quinta Inns usually contain 106 to 138 guest rooms and have 24-hour front desks and message service, convenient parking, same-day laundry service, a swimming pool, color television with HBO/cable and AM/FM radio, free local telephone calls, wall-to-wall carpeting, and air conditioning. All La Quinta Motor Inns are of similar design, with Spanish Colonial architecture and complementary furnishings. Telephone reservations for accommodations at any La Quinta Motor Inn can be made free of charge through La Quinta's nationwide "teLQuik" reservation system, as well as through reservation telephones in the lobbies of all La Quinta Motor Inns.

In metropolitan areas, La Quinta effectively penetrates the market by what it calls "clustering"—building several inns to serve separate market areas rather than building a single 1,000-room inn. This reduces financial risk and maximizes chances for high occupancy.

Since Sam Barshop, CEO, founded the company in 1968, the company has been expanding, and it is now moving toward whole ownership of at least 70 percent of La Quinta Inns. Expansion plans are expected to bring a 15 to 20 percent annual increase in number of rooms. Table 7-1-1 shows some of the locations of La Quinta Inns. The La Quinta organization includes over 4,500 people located at the various inns, over twelve regional offices, and the home office in San Antonio, Texas.

The hotel and motor inn business is highly competitive, and the company is in direct competition with other motor inns and hotels in all the areas where it operates. The motor inn industry may be adversely affected by general

---

This case was written by Isabella C. M. Cunningham, The University of Texas at Austin, and is intended to generate classroom discussion, not to illustrate the effective or ineffective handling of an administrative situation. Used by permission of La Quinta Motor Inns.

TABLE 7-1-1   Major Markets in Which La Quinta Inns Are Located

City	Number of Inns
Atlanta	5
Austin	4
Chicago	3
Corpus Christi	3
Dallas/Ft. Worth	15
Denver	5
Houston	10
Indianapolis	2
Jacksonville, Miss.	3
Little Rock, Ark.	4
Memphis	2
Nashville	2
New Orleans	5
Phoenix	2
San Antonio	10
Tampa	2

economic conditions and government regulations that influence or determine wages, prices, construction procedures and costs, interest rates, availability of credit, and the cost of utilities. In addition, the demand for accommodations in a particular motor inn may be affected by changes in travel patterns, relocation of airports, construction or relocation of highways, availability or cost of energy supplies (including gasoline), and other factors.

The demand for motor inn accommodations for business travel is generally higher Monday through Thursday than on the weekend. Demand also varies by normally recurring seasonal patterns. Room occupancy in most company-owned motor inns is higher in the spring and summer months (March-August) than in the balance of the year. Overall occupancy levels may also be affected by the number of newly opened motor inns and by the length of time they have been in operation.

Approximately 95 percent of motor inn revenue is derived from room rentals. Other revenue sources include charges to customers for long-distance telephone services and restaurant and club revenues. Table 7-1-2 shows selected financial data for La Quinta Motor Inns from the period 1980 to 1984, and Table 7-1-3 shows a breakdown of La Quinta Motor Inn revenue from 1982, 1983, and 1984.

La Quinta is one of the most profitable and well-managed chains of motor inns in the United States. It has shown continued strength and growth for the past decade. In spite of the problems faced by the lodging industry in the United States, La Quinta has continued to show a profit during the past ten years.

TABLE 7-1-2   Selected Financial Data for La Quinta Motor Inns[a]

	1984	1983	1982	1981	1980
Revenues	$136,802	$113,378	$102,656	$ 82,765	$ 61,825
% Change	+20.7	+10.4	+24.0	+33.9	+28.2
Operating income	39,305	36,590	34,646	27,498	20,415
% Change	+7.4	+5.6	+26.0	+34.7	+33.6
Net earnings	12,815	13,456	12,291	8,611	6,412
% Change	−4.8	+9.5	+42.7	+34.3	+31.6
Earnings per share	.88	.93	.90	.69	.54
% Change	−5.4	+3.3	+30.4	+27.8	+28.6
Working capital provided by operations	40,917	38,825	31,590	23,187	17,910
% Change	+5.4	+22.9	+36.2	+29.5	+32.7
Additions to property & equipment, and motor inns under development	100,264	74,757	78,267	48,906	49,434
% Change	+34.1	−4.5	+60.0	−1.1	+31.1
Total assets	504,012	404,201	324,370	229,462	178,545
Shareholders' equity	108,760	93,746	79,324	49,369	29,390
Partners' capital	39,213	26,348	20,030	14,851	10,785
Long-term debt, excluding current installments	296,611	243,451	189,717	139,694	119,054
Return on shareholders' equity[b]	13.7%	17.0%	24.9%	29.3%	28.1%
Effective profit margin[c]	11.7%	14.8%	15.2%	13.2%	13.3%
Combined effective debt-to-equity ratio[d]	2.0	2.0	1.9	2.2	3.0

[a]Dollars in thousands, except per share data.

[b]Net earnings as a percentage of shareholders' equity at the beginning of the year.

[c]Net earnings plus tax-adjusted partners' equity in earnings and losses as a percentage of total revenues.

[d]Ratio of long-term debt excluding current installments to partners' capital plus shareholders' equity at year end.

THE HOTEL AND MOTEL BUSINESS IN THE UNITED STATES

U.S. Department of Commerce figures show that total receipts for the lodging industry for 1983 totaled $30 billion. This amount was up from $23.6 billion in 1980. These receipts came from 2,466,000 available rooms in 35,560 lodging establishments. In the United States, 41 percent of the industry's total establishments are franchised, whereas the rest are wholly owned.

TABLE 7-1-3   Revenue Distribution for La Quinta Motor Inns

	1984	1983	1982
Motor inn revenue (000)	$131,087	$108,281	$98,127
% Increase over prior year	21.1	10.3	24.2
Number of available room nights (000)	5,339	4,633	3,966
Percentage of occupancy	72.9	71.1	80.0
Occupied room nights (000)	3,889	3,295	3,174
% Increase over prior year	18.0	3.8	12.6
Average daily rate per occupied room	$32.10	$31.09	$29.01
% Increase over prior year	3.2	7.2	10.9

TABLE 7-1-4   Occupancy Rates for La Quinta Motor Inns[a]

Location		Region		Size (Number of rooms)	
Airport	68.3%	Northeast	69.5%	Under 150	64.9%
Suburban	62.2	North-Central	61.7	150–299	64.9
Highway	66.6	South	59.8	300–600	63.1
Downtown	63.1	West	69.0	Over 600	68.6

[a]Industry average occupancy rate is 61.6 percent.

Two-thirds of all rooms are filled on an average day in the United States. Occupancy rates vary based on location, region, and the size of the motel. Table 7-1-4 shows a general summary of occupancy rates distribution based on these three factors.

The table shows that occupancy rates are highest in lodgings near airports, followed by those on highways, downtown, and in suburban locations. The Northeast is where occupancy rates are highest, followed by the West, North-central, and South regions. Another factor affecting occupancy is the hotel type; hotels with 600 or more rooms have the highest occupancy rates.

In all but resort hotels, single occupancy constitutes the majority of business in the lodging industry. For all hotels, the occupancy rate is more than 60 percent; double occupancy as a percentage of the total is about 47.2 percent. Resort hotels, however, have an average occupancy rate of about 66.4 percent, and 80.3 percent of their occupancy is double occupancy.

While 95 percent of all La Quinta Motor Inns revenues come from room rental, the same is not true of the hotel industry as a whole. Table 7-1-5 summarizes the sources of revenue for the hotel and motel industry in the United States.

La Quinta's percentage of revenues coming from room rentals is higher than the industry average for motels with no restaurant (92.4 percent). Therefore, La Quinta appears to be a very efficient chain that maximizes room turnaround—a necessary condition for a profitable organization.

Nationwide, 12 percent of hotel and motel guests stay in deluxe or first-class accommodations. Seventy-five percent stay in average, middle-priced

TABLE 7-1-5   Sources of Revenue

	All Lodgings	Transient Hotels	Resort Hotels	Motels with Restaurant	Motels With No Restaurant
Rooms	60.5%	60.3%	53.5%	63.5%	92.4%
Food	23.5	24.0	26.7	22.5	
Beverages	8.9	9.0	9.0	9.6	
All other	7.1	6.7	10.8	4.4	7.6

accommodations, and only 13 percent stay in economy/budget-type accommodations. La Quinta competes for the average, middle-priced accommodation with the rest of the industry.

The travel market is divided into three major categories: business, pleasure, and vacation. Since some people travel for both business and pleasure, simultaneously, there is some overlap in the different travel segments. Sixty-eight percent of the travel market comes from business travel, 32 percent from pleasure travel, and 37 percent from vacation travel. While 43 percent of the travel market seeks lodging during weekdays, 34 percent occupies hotels and motels on weekends. Most of the travel (56 percent) is through airline trips, while 35 percent of travel involves automobile or truck trips. Almost all hotel guests (88 percent) arrive with reservations, most of which are made by travel agents. Forty-one percent of the business and 33 percent of the pleasure hotel bookings are made by travel agent systems.

Among business travelers, 65 percent make their own decision about where they want to stay, and 50 percent place their own reservations. According to research, the most important factors influencing the decision to stay at a specific hotel or motel are as follows: location (25 percent), recommendation from business associates (24 percent), image of the hotel (24 percent), cost (8 percent), and travel agent's recommendation (7 percent).

It is clear, therefore, that the lodging industry in the United States is a very diversified one, appealing to different types of customers under different conditions. The characteristics of customers using hotels and motels are important for marketing managers in this industry to understand.

THE HOTEL/MOTEL CUSTOMER

A profile of the hotel/motel customer would reveal that most are male, 35 to 54 years of age (56 percent), with an income of over $35,000 (67 percent). Most hotel/motel guests are professionals or middle- and top management (63 percent). Sixty percent of the guests usually occupy hotels or motels while on business, while 34.4 percent are tourists. Nearly 89 percent are U.S. residents, and about 40 percent of hotel/motel occupancy is made up of repeat trade.

Ninety-two percent of people participating in meetings or conventions stay at a hotel or motel. Most of the time, the decision to stay at a motel or hotel for a vacation is made by the male head of the household (51 percent). Only 30 percent of the time is the decision made by the female head of the household. The remainder of the time, the decision is made by a travel agent or by other adults or children in the family. Most people pay for their hotel with a credit card (52 percent), while over 22 percent pay with cash and another 23 percent pay with other credit, such as corporate accounts or trade.

Research shows that 52 percent of business travelers avoid high-priced motels. Thirty-one percent of the problems guests encounter are room related, such as noisy or dirty rooms, rooms that aren't ready, or early check-out times. Twenty-five percent of the problems with hotels/motels are service oriented. Twenty-six percent of the guests complain that there is no restaurant, 25 percent complain of unfriendly personnel, 26 percent complain of delays at check-in, and 18 percent complain of room unavailability or unconfirmed reservations. Service, therefore, is extremely important to hotel/motel customers.

Most La Quinta customers are younger, wealthier males who travel frequently and stay weekday nights at the hotel. Furthermore, a majority of La Quinta guests make their own reservations and arrive by car, and 73 percent are repeat customers and a source of loyal business. According to the firm's research, La Quinta customers are frequent travelers. Over 60 percent take more than one trip a month, and 25 percent take one trip per week. Almost 63 percent of visits to La Quinta are for business and only 22 percent for vacation or pleasure. Other reasons for lodging there are personal reasons and conventions. Of people who go to La Quinta, 54.2 percent use a single-occupancy room, and 38.5 percent use double occupancy.

The professional profile of La Quinta occupants is very similar to that of the industry as a whole. The average age of the La Quinta occupant in 1984 was 45, or younger than the average hotel/motel customer. Most La Quinta visitors (55.6 percent) are married, while only 13.7 percent are single, and their average income is about $47,000 in 1984 dollars.

Most of the business for La Quinta comes from residents of the south-central states. Therefore, La Quinta has unique customers with distinct characteristics, making them easier to segment and reach through a coordinated advertising program.

THE MARKETING PLAN

A recent five-year plan developed by La Quinta top management maps out the company's growth strategy. The plan contemplates the addition of new inns at an annual rate of 17 percent. This rate of growth would increase the number of owned inns from 125 to 300 by the end of the five years. Approximately 70 percent of all new inns are expected to be wholly owned and 30 percent owned by joint ventures in which La Quinta is half-owner. This expected ownership mix and the fact that new inns should average 130 rooms—somewhat larger than the current average—should result in an annual increase of about 20 percent in the equivalent number of rooms available.

At the end of the current fiscal year, 60 out of 125 company-owned La Quinta Motor Inns were located in Texas, 2 in California, and 5 in Florida. The five-year plan contemplates adding 14 new inns in Texas, 43 in California, and 19 in Florida. If this plan is carried out, the percentage of company-owned La Quinta Motor Inns in Texas would be reduced from 48 percent to 27 percent. Texas, California, and Florida together are expected to represent about half of La Quinta's expansion over the next five years. These three states accounted for more than 40 percent of the nation's population growth in the past decade and are expected to continue as big population gainers. In addition, the five-year plan emphasizes continued development throughout the Southeast and Southwest and entry into the east-central region of Virginia, Maryland, and Washington, D.C. Exhibit 7-1-1 shows present and planned locations of La Quinta Motor Inns.

La Quinta presently owns all properties except 13, which are franchised. This allows management control over operations necessary to ensure a high degree of consistency in both quality and pricing. In a recent survey of hotel/motel customers, La Quinta was rated highest in terms of overall quality, chain consistency, and value.

The profile of the business traveler is changing, and although La Quinta seems capable of responding readily to that change, top management is concerned with continuing to lead the industry in innovative marketing policies. More women are entering the business ranks, making women an increasingly larger share of the hotel/motel business. While these women are also likely to become weekend pleasure travelers, their choice of pleasure or vacation accommodations may not involve the same decision considerations used by their male counterparts. Thus, La Quinta wants to ensure that its

EXHIBIT 7-1-1   Present and Planned Locations of La Quinta Motor Inns

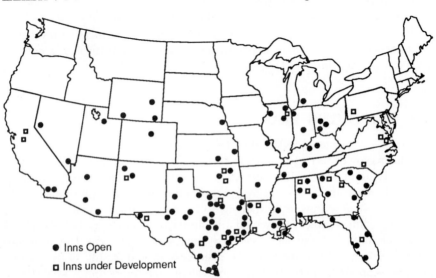

● Inns Open

□ Inns under Development

services will be as popular among female business travelers as they are among male business travelers.

In addition, La Quinta management is concerned that the chain appears to be more popular among travelers who reside in Texas than among travelers residing in other states. Although this is not too surprising a finding, since a majority of La Quinta motels are located in Texas, the chain hopes to expand nationally and achieve a broad coverage in the next ten years. To do so effectively, the chain will need to increase national awareness of its services and expand its popularity/usage among residents of other states.

At a top management meeting in June of 1990, it was decided that La Quinta would invest in a major advertising campaign in an effort to increase awareness of La Quinta among business travelers on a national basis and communicate an image of La Quinta that would appeal equally to male and female business travelers without targeting women specifically, since the total advertising budget would not allow such specific targeting. It is important also to underscore that, at the time of this decision, the majority of La Quinta customers were male, and the chain did not want to risk losing its present customer base in an effort to attract women.

The management of La Quinta decided to invest a total of $5 million in national and regional advertising during the following fiscal year. The vice-president of marketing, Martin Tollert, was directed to contact the chain's advertising agency, Tracy-Locke/BBDO, to request that it submit an advertising plan within that budget. A summary of the advertising plan submitted by the agency follows.

THE ADVERTISING PLAN

The proposed advertising plan recommends the following objectives for La Quinta Motor Inns:

- Increase awareness of the benefits of La Quinta Motor Inns, primarily among adults 25+ (male skew) who are business travelers.
- Provide optimal coverage of key source markets of greatest volume and potential. These markets account for 53 percent of La Quinta source dollars and have high/medium "BDIs." BDI (Brand Development Index) is defined as the individual market's contribution to brand sales. It is calculated as follows.

$$BDI = \frac{\text{Market X's Share of Total Brand Sales}}{\text{Market X's Share of U.S. Population}} \times 100$$

- Provide emphasis in primary key source markets. These markets account for 37 percent of La Quinta source dollars and have high "BDIs."
- Schedule advertising to establish presence/maximize continuity throughout the January–May 1991 period.

Table 7-1-6 describes the La Quinta key source markets.

Based on these objectives, the advertising agency recommended allocating the advertising budget as shown in Table 7-1-7. The rationale for the

TABLE 7-1-6   La Quinta Motor Inns' Key Source Markets

Primary Markets	Secondary Markets	Potential Markets
Corpus Christi	Oklahoma City, Okla.	Chicago
San Antonio	Shreveport, La.	
Lubbock	Atlanta	
Dallas/Fort Worth	Denver	
Odessa/Midland, Tex.	Kansas City, Mo.	
Austin	New Orleans	
Waco/Temple, Tex.	Phoenix	
Houston	Memphis	
	Tulsa, Okla.	

**TABLE 7-1-7   Recommended Media Allocation for La Quinta
Motor Inns' Advertising**

Media	Total Period: Adults 25+			Approximate Number of Weeks
	Reach	Frequency	GRPs[a]	
Spot TV	93%	11.1×	1,040	12
Regional magazines	34%	3.2×	109	20

[a]GRP (Gross Rating Points) is a measure of the total ratings for the individual sponsor programs. A rating point is equal to one percent of the potential audience of a medium, therefore: 150 gross rating points means 1.5 messages per average home.

Source: Jack Z. Sissors and E. Reynold Petray, *Advertising Media Planning,* Chicago, Ill.: Crain Books, 1976, 311.

**TABLE 7-1-8   La Quinta Motor Inns' Recommended Market
Area Expenditure Analysis**

La Quinta Market Area	Percentage of U.S. TV Households	Percentage of La Quinta Source Dollars	Expenditure by Market (thousands of dollars)	Percentage of Spending by Market
Primary	5%	37%	$1,704.4	73%
Secondary	11	16	625.6	27
Total key source markets	16%	53%	$2,330.0	100%
Remainder of U.S.	84	47	—	—
Total U.S.	100%	100%	$2,330.0	100%

Note: The remainder of the advertising budget was spent on production costs, print point-of-purchase displays and leaflets, promotions, and training for La Quinta personnel.

spending allocation was based on a study of American Express charges of lodgings by markets which showed that the primary markets for La Quinta were responsible for 37 percent of its dollar revenues, while its secondary and potential markets were responsible for 16 percent of the revenue dollars for the chain. The intended media allocations for each market, as stated in the advertising agency plan, are shown in Table 7-1-8.

Tollert was not fully satisfied with the agency's plan. He was not sure that it provided adequate reach and frequency of exposure to ensure the success of the five-year expansion plan. On the other hand, he did not feel qualified to critique the plan or suggest alternative media allocations. Among his considerations were the findings of a recent market survey, which reported the state of residence of La Quinta customers, along with the percentage of La Quinta sales by state. Tables 7-1-9 and 7-1-10 show the results of the market survey.

Tollert decided it was important to have the agency take a second look at the advertising plan. Most of all, he was concerned with increasing the

TABLE 7-1-9   La Quinta Customers by State of Residence

State of Residence	Percentage of All La Quinta Customers
Texas	36.4%
Oklahoma	2.3
Louisiana	2.3
Arkansas	2.5
Georgia	3.8
Illinois	3.3
California	4.8
New York	2.2
Colorado	3.2
Arizona	2.5
Florida	4.3
Kansas/Missouri	2.9
Other	29.5

TABLE 7-1-10   Percentage of Total La Quinta Dollar Sales by State

State	Estimated Percentage of La Quinta Dollar Sales
Texas	16.60%
Oklahoma	1.83
Louisiana	1.76
Arkansas	1.02[a]
Georgia	2.89
Illinois	6.19
California	5.59
New York	8.50
Colorado	1.89
Arizona	1.10
Florida	1.21
Kansas/Missouri	2.92
Other	48.50

[a]Estimated share.

advertising reach to gain more national coverage. In addition, he had been intrigued recently by the success of some cable stations, particularly the Cable News Network and ESPN. He knew that the majority of his friends and acquaintances were regular viewers of CNN and that a good portion also watched ESPN at least twice a week. While this group could not be considered heavy television viewers, it certainly mirrored the demographic characteristics of the higher-income La Quinta customers. Should cable TV have been considered in the media plan? The question was a valid one, and he hoped to get some answers.

The agency responded to the questions raised by Tollert with a complete report, which can be seen in Appendix 7-1.

Upon receipt of the proposed advertising plan and the subsequent report, Tollert and Sam Barshop, the company's CEO, met at length. At the end of the meeting, Sam Barshop said:

> *Martin, I am aware that you still feel we should give cable a chance. Why don't you make your own analysis of the agency's recommendations? I trust your instincts and your judgment. I'll recommend to the board the course of action you feel is most appropriate for La Quinta's future. Go ahead, give it a try, and be ready to present your recommendations to the full board next week.*

Tollert was flattered by his boss's confidence and intimidated by the task ahead. Nevertheless, he set out to undertake his new mission in an objective and comprehensive manner.

Questions for Discussion and Review

1. Should La Quinta accept the advertising agency's proposed media plan?

2. Why do you think Tollert is eager to examine cable television advertising as an alternative to the agency's plan?

3. Do you agree with Barshop's appraisal of Tollert's knowledge? Do you feel the agency would resent Tollert making a separate recommendation to the board? Would this incident cause a strain in the relationship between La Quinta and Tracy-Locke/BBDO?

4. What type of media strategy would be most appropriate for La Quinta? Why?

Appendix 7-1
Tracy-Locke/BBDO Report to La Quinta

Question #1:   *Would the audience composition of the recommended spot TV buy be as demographically qualitative as that of a cable buy?*

Answer: Yes, by advertising in the dayparts recommended for La Quinta in the FY 1985 spot TV buy, the audience composition would be almost as demographically selected as for a cable buy.

	Adults 25+ Audience Composition	
	Business Travelers	Stayed in Paid Accommodations
Recommended buy	4%	44%
Cable buy	5	53

For example, in the primary markets, the recommended spot TV buy would provide the following:

- More adult 25+ business traveler impressions/spot
- ESPN spot: 14,530
- ABC Sports spot: 54,488
- Greater cumulative reach potential
- Cable schedule: 44%
- Network schedule: 95%

Question #2: *Would a cable/regional magazine plan or a total cable plan be more effective than the recommended plan in reaching our target audience in the primary markets?*

Answer: No. In the primary markets, the recommended plan would have far more impact than either cable alternative in reaching not only total adults 25+, but also heavy business travelers.

Question #3: *Would either cable plan spend media dollars as effectively as the recommended plan against market areas of greatest potential?*

Answer: Fifty-three percent of La Quinta's source dollars come from key source markets, which comprise only 16 percent of the U.S. population. Neither cable plan would spend media dollars as effectively as the recommended plan against key source markets, which represent greatest potential for La Quinta.

Question #4: *How would a cable plan affect message delivery against a secondary, nonbusiness traveler audience?*

Answer: Both "cable only" and "cable/regional magazines" plans deliver significantly less reach and total GRPs against the total adult 25+ target audience, thereby reducing overall awareness within key source market areas. Both plans also deliver fewer "heavy business traveler" impressions within key source markets, especially primary markets.

The "cable only" plan delivers 3 percent more adult 25+ "stayed hotel/motel/other paid accommodations" impressions in key source markets than the recommended plan.

La Quinta Motor Inns
Recommended versus Cable Plans:
Target Audience Delivery Analysis
for Primary Markets

Plan Alternative	Total Period A25+			A25+ Heavy Business Traveler Impressions (in thousands)	Approximate Number of Advertising Weeks
	Reach	Frequency	GRPs		
Recommended Plan					
Spot TV	93%	11.1×	1,040	3,098	12
Regional magazines	34%	3.2×	109	1,346	20
Total	95%	12.1×	1,149	4,444	20
(Index)	(100)	(100)	(100)	(100)	(100)
Cable/Regional Magazine					
Cable	20%	9.8×	196	783	14
Regional magazines	34%	3.2×	109	1,346	20
Total	47%	6.5×	305	2,129	20
(Index)	(49)	(54)	(27)	(48)	(100)
Cable Only					
Cable	26%	12.5×	325	1,299	23
(Index)	(27)	(103)	(28)	(29)	(115)

La Quinta Motor Inns
Market Area Expenditure Analysis:
Recommended versus Cable Plans

La Quinta Market Area	Percentage of U.S. TV Households	Percentage of La Quinta Source Dollars[a]
Primary	5%	37%
Secondary/ Potential	11	16
Total Key Source Markets	16%	53%
Remainder of U.S.	84	47
Total U.S.	100%	100%

[a]Source: 1983 American Express Charges Lodging Market Analysis.

La Quinta Motor Inns
Recommended versus Cable Plans:
Target Audience Delivery Analysis
for Primary and Key Source Markets

				Total Period Estimated A25+ Impressions	
	Total Period A25+			Heavy Business Traveler[a] (in thousands)	Stayed Hotel/ Motel/Other Paid Accommodation[a] (in thousands)
	Reach	Frequency	GRPs		
Primary Markets					
Recommended plan	95%	12.1×	1,149	4,444	35,850
Cable/Regional magazines plan	52%	7.5×	389	2,129	10,002
Cable-only plan	26%	12.5×	325	1,299	12,514
Key Source Markets					
Recommended plan[b]	54%	8.2×	442	9,269	44,504
Cable/Regional magazines plan	52%	5.1×	265	9,026	38,777
Cable-only plan	22%	11.8×	259	4,743	45,702

[a]Source: 1983 Simmons Market Research Bureau.
[b]Includes spot TV weight, which covers primary markets only.

Expenditures/Percentage of Spending by Market

Recommended Plan		Cable/Regional Magazine Plan		Cable-Only Plan	
$ 852.2[b]	73%	$ 211.1	18%	$ 63.5	5%
312.8	27	351.8	30	105.8	9
$1,165.0	100%	$ 562.9	48%	$ 169.3	14%
—	—	599.2	52	993.6	86
$1,165.0	100%	$1,162.1	100%	$1,162.9	100%

[b]All expenditures are in thousands of dollars.

La Quinta Motor Inns
Cable Penetration:
Key Source Markets

	Primary Markets			Secondary/Potential Markets	
	Percentage of Cable Penetration	Number of Cable Households (in thousands)		Percentage of Cable Penetration	Number of Cable Households (in thousands)
Corpus Christi	51%	86.1	Oklahoma City	48%	284.4
San Antonio	56	289.2	Shreveport	46	209.1
Lubbock	51	76.8	Atlanta	37	422.2
Dallas	35	532.0	Denver	34	328.5
Odessa-Midland	70	95.3	Kansas City	45	317.5
Austin	53	152.6	New Orleans	46	292.0
Waco-Temple	58	133.6	Phoenix	35	286.1
Houston	42	591.9	Memphis	40	218.7
Weighted average	44.4%	1,957.5	Tulsa	51	232.9
			Chicago	22	674.0
			Weighted average	35.1%	3,265.4

Weighted average key source markets penetration	38%
National cable penetration	42%
Index	(90)

Source: A. C. Nielsen TVHH Estimates, September 1984.

C A S E   **7 - 2**

Peterbilt Motors Company

The Peterbilt Motors Company (PMC) was founded in 1939 by T. A. Peterman after he had became frustrated at not being able to find a truck to suit his needs. Peterman was a lumberman who needed a truck to haul logs from Morton, Washington, to his mill in Tacoma, Washington. To produce a truck to fit his

This case was written by John H. Murphy, The University of Texas at Austin, and is intended for use in generating class discussion, not to illustrate either the effective or ineffective handling of an administrative situation. Used by permission of Peterbilt Motors Company.

needs, he purchased the Fageol Truck and Coach Factory in Oakland, California, and renamed it Peterbilt Motors.

The company prospered during World War II as a result of government contracts to build nonmilitary trucks. Ida Peterman ran PMC after her husband's death, until she sold the company in 1947. In 1947, PMC had sales of $4.5 million. In late 1949, PMC introduced the cab-over-engine truck. This innovation was instrumental in increasing sales to approximately $7 million in 1950.

In 1958, PMC was purchased by PACCAR. PACCAR manufactured heavy-duty on- and off-road Class 8 trucks sold around the world under the Kenworth, Foden, and now Peterbilt nameplates. PACCAR also marketed Class 6 and 7 trucks in North America and was a leading supplier of industrial winches and mining equipment. Further, PACCAR facilitated the sale of its products through finance and leasing subsidiaries in the United States, Canada, Mexico, the United Kingdom, and Australia.

From the beginning, and continuing as a separate operating division of PACCAR, PMC's overriding philosophy was to offer its customers a wide range of options, enabling them to specify trucks to meet their exact needs for high performance and lower operating costs. PMC manufactured a variety of premium Class 8 trucks designed for long-distance, pickup and delivery, and on/off highway hauling. The company also marketed a line of Class 6 and 7 vehicles. Peterbilt trucks and parts were sold and supported through an independent dealer network of 132 outlets.

PMC was headquartered in Newark, California, with regional sales offices in Denton, Texas; Madison, Tennessee; Fremont, California; Itasca, Illinois; King of Prussia, Pennsylvania; and Surrey, British Columbia. The company had two manufacturing facilities located in Denton, Texas; and Madison, Tennessee.

PETERBILT CLASS 8 TRUCK SALES AND MODELS

Data on recent unit sales of Class 8 diesel trucks in the United States and PACCAR's market share follow. Note that Peterbilt accounted for approximately 48 percent of PACCAR Class 8 diesel truck sales and Kenworth accounted for 52 percent in 1986.

	Total Unit Sales	PACCAR Market Share
1986	112,000	19%
1985	130,000	18
1984	130,000	21

Based on 1986 R.L. Polk data, the market was dominated by 13 nameplates. Navistar had the largest market share with 23 percent. Mack and Freightliner each garnered a 15 percent share. Ford and Kenworth each had 10 percent shares, and Peterbilt and Volvo White each had a 9 percent share.

Peterbilt offered a range of six models of Class 8 trucks for a variety of duties. Five of the models utilized the classic long-nosed styling; these came in size ranges 379 (largest), 377, 375, 357, and 353. The 362 was a cab-over-engine design.

Peterbilt emphasized its commitment to design flexibility and choice of models. Each truck was custom designed to meet the purchaser's personal preferences. The average cost of a Peterbilt truck (cab only) was $65,000 to $80,000.

PETERBILT DEALER SALES NETWORK

All sales of Peterbilt trucks were made through authorized dealers. Peterbilt had approximately 125 dealers in the United States and Canada. Ninety-five percent of these were full-service dealerships; that is, the dealer sold trucks and parts and serviced trucks. The average size of the dealerships' sales staff was five persons. The classic 80/20 rule of marketing applied to sales generated by Peterbilt's dealerships—80 percent of sales was generated by only 20 percent of the dealerships.

The dealerships were supervised by six regional sales offices: five in the United States and one in Canada. Each regional office had a regional sales manager and an average of three district sales managers.

PETERBILT ADVERTISING

Donald Herbers, president of PMC's advertising agency (Pinne, Garvin, Herbers & Hock), characterized Peterbilt's major campaigns in recent years as "emotional imagery advertising." Herbers stressed that the word "class" and all that it connotes had been associated with Peterbilt through advertising for over 20 years: "The word 'class' is so closely tied to our trucks in the minds of our audience that no competitor would ever use the word in any of their advertising."

Ed Klar, Peterbilt's marketing services manager, believed the campaigns were successful because they promoted the high status of the Peterbilt truck among drivers and owners. The underlying assumption behind the campaigns was that "it's every owner/operator's dream to own a Peterbilt." Exhibit 7-2-1 presents a representative example of past "Class" campaigns.

In addition to the continuing "Class" campaigns, Peterbilt had run more conservative spread ads addressing technical subjects (see Exhibit 7-2-2 for an example) and an ad promoting its trucks as wise investments for fleet owners (see Exhibit 7-2-3). Although the bulk of Peterbilt's advertising appeared in specialized business publications such as *Owner/Operator* and *American Trucker*, the wise investment ad had run in *Business Week* and *Forbes*. Other publications utilized by Peterbilt included *Fleet Owner, Heavy Duty Trucking,*

EXHIBIT 7-2-1 Representative "Class" Advertisement for Peterbilt Trucks

Diesel Superintendent, The Wall Street Journal, and *Engineering & Mining Journal.*

To be consistent with Peterbilt's "Class" theme and image, each print ad was painstakingly developed with a generous production budget. The average production cost of a full-page, full-color ad was approximately $15,000.

In business-to-business advertising of a capital good, Peterbilt utilized a soft-sell approach and relied heavily on its dealers' sales force to make the sale. In general, advertising was used to (1) keep present and potential customers

EXHIBIT 7-2-2   Representative "Technical" Advertisement for Peterbilt Trucks

254

EXHIBIT 7-2-3 Representative "Investment" Advertisement for Peterbilt Trucks

Peterbilt.
The standard
for fiscal responsibility.

When it comes time to consider your next capital commitment in transportation, the trucks you select must satisfy your company's performance standards completely. Efficiently. For a meaningfully long period of time. For the right cost.

Fiscal responsibility demands nothing less.

But determining the true affordability of one vehicle versus another requires probing beyond the basics of face value.

Which is exactly why you should consider Peterbilt.

With a product and organization structured to help you maximize the return on your investment, Peterbilt offers you the added value that can make your purchase decision pay off again and again — well after your initial capital outlay.

Consider that no other manufacturer offers more design flexibility — enabling you to formulate a performance equation precisely tuned to meet your company's particular transportation needs.

The accessibility of our sales, marketing, manufacturing and engineering professionals is unrivaled in the industry. Which means you'll benefit from a level of personal involvement that just isn't found with most other manufacturers.

As for quality engineering, industry statistics demonstrate that Peterbilt consistently delivers the longest service life — and highest resale value — of any Class 8 truck available.

And the commitment to service and support provided by our network of independent Peterbilt dealers can only be likened to that of your own determination for success — simply because the financial prosperity of their privately-owned dealerships depends on it.

The cumulative effect of these, and many other critical elements enables Peterbilt to deliver a decidedly attractive union of quality and affordability. Which, in the final analysis, combine to make Peterbilt truly the soundest investment on the road today.

To help make your inspection of these claims more thorough, we invite you to write us for the Peterbilt Management Folio, which logically examines the issues pertinent to the ultimate success of your truck purchase decision — and why Peterbilt is particularly worth your consideration.

Or better still, visit or call your nearby Peterbilt dealer today for a consultation regarding your company's transportation needs.

A DIVISION OF PACCAR

Peterbilt Motors Company
38801 Cherry Street
Newark, CA 94560

255

informed of product introductions and changes and (2) communicate the quality/value of the product.

A tentative advertising appropriation for next year had been established at $1.5 million. This appropriation was earmarked to cover both media and ad production charges. Management anticipated that key competitors' investments in media advertising alone would be roughly as follows: Navastar, $2.5 million; Mack, $2.0 million; Freightliner, $2.0 million; and Kenworth, $1.5 million.

Peterbilt advertising had focused on five target audiences:

1. *A corporate and financial management market.* These individuals were often involved at the approval level in decisions regarding which trucks to purchase.

2. *An operational market.* This segment consisted of people in the trucking business, such as fleet managers, fleet maintenance personnel, and directors of transportation. In the past, this segment had accounted for about half of Peterbilt's sales.

3. *An independent owner/operators market.* This segment accounted for roughly 20 percent of past Peterbilt sales.

4. *A construction market.* This segment accounted for roughly 15 percent of past Peterbilt sales.

5. *A refuse market,* which accounted for an average of about 15 percent of sales.

SRI RESEARCH STUDY

To better understand its market, evaluate the effectiveness of its advertising, and plan future marketing activities, PMC commissioned a survey research study. The study, entitled "Class 8 Truck Market Survey," was conducted by SRI International of Menlo Park, California.

Methodology

The first step in conducting the study was to develop a self-administered questionnaire. To accomplish this task, an outline of potential survey issues was constructed and used for 16 in-person interviews with private and for-hire carriers. Based on the information gathered, a self-administered questionnaire was drafted. The draft was carefully pretested with a small sample of carriers.

The population of interest was defined as all companies in the United States that owned 100 or fewer Class 8 trucks and were in the following primary Standard Industrial Classifications (SIC) categories: (1) construction, (2) forestry, (3) mining, (4) petroleum, (5) manufacturing, (6) retail, (7) services, (8) lease/rental, or (9) for hire. These firms were considered to be PMC's primary target audience. Appendix 7-2A lists the primary SIC numbers in each category.

Next, a sampling frame (list) of these companies was obtained. The list was obtained from Trinc Transportation Consultants, a company that maintained a data base of all companies in the United States that owned five or more commercial trucks (Classes 1 to 8) or at least one truck-tractor. Approximately 28,000 companies were in the SIC categories of interest and owned from 1 to 100 Class 7 or 8 trucks.

To ensure an adequate representation of each group of interest, a stratified sample of 998 companies was drawn from the list. This sample was stratified based on the number of trucks owned, SIC category, and region of the country. (In the analysis phase of the study, responses were weighted to reflect the actual distribution in the population.)

Since PMC was only interested in Class 8 trucks, each of the firms from the sample list was contacted via telephone to determine whether the company owned/leased any Class 8 trucks. If the company did use Class 8 trucks, the interviewer asked who was the most appropriate person to receive the questionnaire (that is, who makes the Class 8 truck purchase/lease decision).

Of the 998 firms drawn into the study, 674 owned/leased at least one Class 8 truck. The appropriate individual at each of these 674 companies was mailed a questionnaire. One week after the initial mailing, each person was sent a reminder postcard. Two weeks after the postcard, all nonrespondents were sent a second questionnaire. A month after the initial mailing, nonrespondents were telephoned and encouraged to respond. Completed questionnaires were returned by 505 companies, for a 75 percent response rate.

Findings

To assist in planning PMC's marketing efforts, the Class 8 truck market was divided into segments based on fleet size, SIC category, and geographic region. Each of the resulting segments was a candidate for possible target advertising/marketing programs. Selected findings from the study are presented in Tables 7-2-1 through 7-2-3 and will be discussed next.

TABLE 7-2-1 Percentage of Markets Segmented by Fleet Size That Own/Lease One or More Peterbilts

	Total Market	Percentage That Own/Lease One or More Peterbilts
Small Fleets[a]		
(Companies that own or lease 1–5 Class 8 trucks)	62%	8%
Medium Fleets		
(Companies that own 1–6 Class 8 trucks and also lease 6–25 trucks, or companies that own 6–25 Class 8 trucks and lease 1–26 Class 8 trucks)	27	21
Large Fleets		
(Companies that own or lease 26+ Class 8 trucks)	11	16

[a]Survey did *not* include owner/operators who are not incorporated.

TABLE 7-2-2   **Percentage of Markets Segmented by SIC Category
That Own/Lease One or More Peterbilts**

SIC Category	Total Market	Percentage That Own/Lease One or More Peterbilts
Construction, forestry, mining and petroleum	45%	6%
Manufacturing, retail and services	26	10
For hire	25	25
Lease/Rental	4	20

TABLE 7-2-3   **Percentage of Markets Segmented by Region
That Own/Lease One or More Peterbilts[a]**

Region	Total Market	Percentage That Own/Lease One or More Peterbilts
Midwest	36%	8%
South	27	9
East	19	4
West	18	32

[a]See Appendix 7-2B for a list of states by region.

In response to a series of questions asking respondents to rate the importance of 22 variables in Class 8 truck selection, "availability of parts and service" was ranked most important. Other considerations ranked relatively important were "long operating life," "operating costs," "maintenance costs," and "reputation for good performance."

In evaluating sources of information companies rely on in making Class 8 truck purchases, "truck dealers" and the company's own "drivers" were rated highest. "Truck shows," followed by "advertisements," were rated least important.

Respondents were asked to rate their familiarity with Peterbilt and seven other makes of Class 8 trucks on a four-point scale. Peterbilt ranked last in terms of familiarity. Only 12 percent indicated that they were "very familiar" with Peterbilt; 14 percent were "quite familiar," 28 percent "somewhat familiar," and 46 percent indicated that they were "not at all familiar" with Peterbilt. Respondents were most familiar with International Harvester (Navastar), followed by Mack, Ford, GMC, Kenworth, Freightliner, and White.

Familiarity varied by region and fleet size. Respondents in the West and operators of medium-sized fleets reported that they were more familiar with Peterbilt than did other market segments.

Next, respondents were asked to describe how frequently, if at all, they read 21 trade magazines. Table 7-2-4 presents data on readership of trade

TABLE 7-2-4 Readership of Selected Trade Magazines
(Magazines listed in descending order of mean rating)

	Percentage Who:					
	Have Never Read	Rarely Read	Read 1 of Last 4 Issues	Read 2 of Last 4 Issues	Read 3 or More of Last 4 Issues	Mean Rating[a]	Number of Respondents
Fleet Owner[b]	23%[c]	19%	20%	14%	24%	2.96	498
The Wall Street Journal[b]	32	21	13	13	23	2.74	499
Business Week[b]	30	31	18	10	11	2.42	493
Heavy Duty Trucking[b]	48	12	11	9	19	2.40	498
Construction Equipment[b]	45	15	15	10	16	2.37	496
Owner/Operator[b]	54	18	12	6	10	2.01	496
Commercial Car Journal[b]	69	12	6	6	8	1.74	494
Fortune	62	18	8	6	5	1.74	497
Diesel Superintendent[b]	78	6	5	7	5	1.54	491
Engineering News Record[b]	77	7	7	4	5	1.53	494
Southern Motor Cargo[b]	84	4	2	3	8	1.48	497
Industry Week	77	10	8	2	4	1.45	495
Overdrive[b]	78	12	5	3	3	1.41	498
Modern Concrete	88	2	1	2	6	1.35	497
Forest Industries[b]	91	2	2	2	3	1.25	494
Go[b]	91	3	2	1	4	1.25	495
Traffic World	89	6	2	1	2	1.23	495
Solid Waste Management[b]	89	5	2	2	2	1.22	498
Engineering & Mining Journal[b]	91	6	2	1	2	1.17	496
Coal Age[b]	93	5	1	1	1	1.11	494
Waste Age[b]	96	2	1	1	1	1.09	496

[a]Readership calculated on a 5-point scale where 0 = never, 1 = rarely, 2 = read one of last four issues, 3 = read two of last four issues, 4 = read three or more of last four issues.
[b]Magazines in which Peterbilt has advertised in past years.
[c]That is, 23 percent of respondents have never read *Fleet Owner.*

magazines by the total sample. Tables 7-2-5 and 7-2-6 present data on readership of trade magazines cross-classified by relevant SIC and region of the country.

FUTURE PETERBILT MEDIA STRATEGY AND PLANNING

As Klar and Herbers began to discuss the development of a marketing plan for PMC for next year, they were confronted with a number of questions. How well had their past advertisements performed? What changes in Peterbilt's creative strategy might be appropriate? What segments of the Class 8 truck market represented PMC's best prospects? What sales support materials should be updated or retained?

TABLE 7-2-5   Readership of Selected Trade Magazines (Percentage of relevant SIC categories[a])

	Percentage Who:						
	Have Never Read	Rarely Read	Read 1 of Last 4 Issues	Read 2 of Last 4 Issues	Read 3 or More of Last 4 Issues	Mean[b]	Number of Respondents
Construction Equipment[d]	6%[c]	10%	28%	21%	35%	3.68	63
Fleet Owner[d]	15	12	19	12	42	3.56	231
Heavy Duty Trucking[d]	27	13	11	14	34	3.15	229
The Wall Street Journal[d]	32	21	13	13	23	2.74	499
Owner/Operator[d]	38	20	11	11	20	2.53	229
Engineering News Record[d]	42	16	16	10	16	2.42	63
Business Week[d]	30	31	18	10	11	2.42	493
Commercial Car Journal[d]	59	12	8	7	13	2.03	229
Overdrive[d]	54	25	10	5	7	1.86	229
Fortune	62	18	8	6	5	1.74	497
Diesel Superintendent[d]	75	6	8	6	5	1.62	292
Traffic World	78	8	4	3	6	1.52	229
Go[d]	85	1	3	2	10	1.50	229
Southern Motor Cargo[d]	85	4	<1	2	9	1.47	206
Industry Week	77	10	8	2	4	1.45	495
Coal Age[d]	Too few cases in relevant SIC categories						
Engineering & Mining Journal[d]	Too few cases in relevant SIC categories						
Forest Industries[d]	Too few cases in relevant SIC categories						
Modern Concrete	Too few cases in relevant SIC categories						
Solid Waste Management[d]	Too few cases in relevant SIC categories						
Waste Age[d]	Too few cases in relevant SIC categories						

[a]See Appendix 7-2C for a listing of relevant SIC categories for each magazine.

[b]Readership calculated on a 5-point scale where 0 = never, 1 = rarely, 2 = read one of last four issues, 3 = read two of last four issues, 4 = read three or more of last four issues.

[c]That is, among companies in SIC categories related to the subject matter of *Construction Equipment,* 6 percent have never read this magazine.

[d]Magazines in which Peterbilt has advertised in past years.

There were many issues to be resolved. In organizing their approach to planning a campaign for next year, Klar and Herbers each agreed to develop proposals in specific areas. Klar stated that he had a special interest in media planning for next year and would like to work directly with the media planner at Pinne, Garvin, Herbers & Hock in "making sure we get maximum leverage out of our media dollars."

Given an advertising appropriation of approximately $1.5 million for media and ad production costs during the coming year, Klar was particularly concerned about the efficiency and effectiveness of Peterbilt's media strategy and plans. In making decisions regarding Peterbilt's media strategy and tactics, Klar also wanted to make sure that the SRI survey results were utilized to their

TABLE 7-2-6 Readership of Selected Trade Magazines by Region (Percentage of relevant SIC categories[a])

	Percentage Ever Reading:					Number of Respondents
	East	South	Midwest	West	Overall	
Business Week[b]	76%[c]	73%	66%	69%	70%	493
Coal Age[b]	Too few cases in relevant SIC categories					
Commercial Car Journal[b]	45	20	53	40	41	229
Construction Equipment[b]	91	100	93	92	94	63
Diesel Superintendent[b]	16	9	34	34	25	292
Engineering & Mining Journal[b]	Too few cases in relevant SIC categories					
Engineering News Record[b]	88	70	44	43[d]	58	63
Fleet Owner[b]	80	69	95	93	85	231
Forest Industries[b]	Too few cases in relevant SIC categories					
Fortune	32	41	38	38	38	497
Go[b]	7	1	3	64[d]	15	229
Heavy Duty Trucking[b]	74	58	78	79	73	229
Industry Week	22	13	29	26	23	495
Modern Concrete	Too few cases in relevant SIC categories					
Overdrive[b]	35	41	56	46	46	229
Owner/Operator[b]	41	48	81	64	62	229
Southern Motor Cargo[b]	14	51	2	4[d]	15	206
Solid Waste Management[b]	Too few cases in relevant SIC categories					
Traffic World	36	11	26	13	22	229
The Wall Street Journal[b]	64	70	70	68	68	499
Waste Age[b]	Too few cases in relevant SIC categories					

[a]See Appendix 7-2B for a listing of states in each region and Appendix 7-2C for a listing of relevant SIC categories for each magazine.
[b]Magazines in which Peterbilt has advertised in past years.
[c]That is, among companies in the East that are in SIC categories related to the subject matter of *Business Week,* 76 percent have read this magazine.
[d]Percentages in this row reliably different from one another ($p < .01$).

full potential. He believed that a major portion of the study's findings had direct implications for the media area. At the same time, he wanted to be sure that the individual owner/operator market received careful consideration despite the fact that it was not included in the SRI data.

Questions for Discussion and Review

1. Peterbilt's prospects were defined initially as all firms in the United States that are classified in one of nine SIC categories and own or lease 100 or fewer Class 8 trucks. Based on the sample data, how many such firms are there?

2. Assuming that Peterbilt was considering narrower target markets, how many firms make up each of the following?

   a. Firms with small fleets in the "For hire" SIC, and located in the Midwest

b. Firms with medium-sized fleets, in the "Manufacturing, Retail and Services" SIC, and located in the Midwest.

3. What percentage of prospects in the "For hire" SIC read the average issue of *Fleet Owner?*

4. Estimate the net reach of two magazines. For example, what percentage of prospects in the "For hire" SIC is reached by the combined average issues of *Fleet Owner* and *Heavy Duty Trucking?*

Appendix 7-2A
SIC Code Numbers by Categories[a]

Construction: 1511-1799, 3273
Retail: 5211-5982, 5992-5999
Forestry: 0811-0851, 2411, 2421
Lease/Rental: 7512, 7513, 7394
Mining: 1011-1213, 1411-1499
For Hire: 4212-4214
Petroleum: 1311-1389, 2911, 2992, 2999, 4612-4619, 5092, 5171, 5172, 5983, 5984
Manufacturing: 2011-2399, 2426-2899, 2951, 2952, 3011-3272, 3274-3999
Services: 4111-4172, 4221-4231, 4511-4583, 4712-4789, 7011-7393, 7395-7399, 7519-8899

[a]The Standard Industrial Classification (SIC) system was developed by the federal government to facilitate the collection and analysis of data pertaining to all industries involved in economic activity in the United States. Within the system, each major area of activity, referred to as a Division (A, B, C, etc.), is first assigned a range of two-digit classification codes. For example, the manufacturing division (Division D) includes SICs 20 to 39, with each two-digit designation denoting a Major Group, such as SIC 20—Food. These, in turn, are subdivided into more than 150 three-digit Industry Groups, such as SIC 208—beverages. At the next level of detail, four-digit Specific Industries are identified (SIC 2082—malt beverages, or SIC 2086—bottled and canned soft drinks). This four-digit level of detail is widely used by marketers to plan their efforts. For a detailed listing of all industries, their codes, and their definitions, the *Standard Industrial Classification Manual* is available at libraries or may be purchased from the U.S. Government Printing Office, Washington, D.C. 20402.

Appendix 7-2B
States Classified by Region

Midwest: Illinois, Indiana, Iowa, Kentucky, Kansas, Michigan, Minnesota, Missouri, North Dakota, Nebraska, Ohio, South Dakota, and Wisconsin

South: Alabama, Arkansas, Florida, Georgia, Louisiana, Mississippi, North Carolina, Oklahoma, South Carolina, Tennessee, and Texas

East: Connecticut, District of Columbia, Delaware, Maine, Maryland, Massachusetts, New Hampshire, New Jersey, New York, Pennsylvania, Rhode Island, Virginia, Vermont, and West Virginia

West: Alaska, Arizona, California, Colorado, Hawaii, Idaho, Montana, New Mexico, Nevada, Oregon, Utah, Wyoming, and Washington

Appendix 7-2C
Relevant SIC Codes for Selected Magazines

Business Week, Fortune, Industry Week, and *The Wall Street Journal:*
Same as population—readership is spread across all SICs.
Commercial Car Journal, Fleet Owner, Go, Heavy Duty Trucking, Overdrive, Owner-Operator, and *Traffic World:*
4200-4299, 4700-4789, 7513
Solid Waste Management and *Waste Age:*
1000-1099, 1100-1112, 1200-1213, 1400-1499, 4950-4959, 8910-8999
Coal Age:
1111-1112, 1211-1213, 3532, 3535-3537
Construction Equipment:
1500-1542, 1600-1629, 1760-1761, 1770-1771, 1780-1781, 1790-1799, 3530-3537
Diesel Superintendent:
1500-1542, 1600-1629, 1700-1799, 4170-4172, 4200-4231, 4700-4789, 7513
Engineering and Mining Journal:
1010-1010, 1020-1021, 1030-1031, 1040-1044, 1050-1051, 1060-1061, 1111-1112, 1212-1213, 1400-1499, 3530-3537, 8910-8999
Engineering News Record:
1500-1542, 1600-1629, 1700-1799, 8900-8999
Forest Industries:
0821, 0843, 0849, 0851, 2610-2631
Modern Concrete:
3270-3275
Southern Motor Cargo:
1500-1542, 1600-1629, 1700-1799, 3713-3715, 4200-4231, 4710-4712, 4789

---

[a]See Appendix 7-2A for an identification of broad industries by SICs.

C A S E   **7 - 3**

Walt Disney Pictures (B)

In developing a media plan to support the introduction of *Three Men and a Baby* (see Case 6-1: Walt Disney Pictures [A]), the major focus was on the first weekend, with the picture opening the Wednesday night before Thanksgiving. As indicated in the Disney (A) case, the opening weekend was crucial for a number of reasons, and all introductory advertising and publicity was scheduled to deliver a peak audience at that point.

A total media appropriation of $15 million had been established to cover advertising through the first five weeks of the movie's run, including any pre-opening activity. This five-week period held the potential for delivering the highest box office volume of the year, since it included the Christmas and New Year's Day holidays. Of this total, $13 million had been earmarked for the top 50 markets in the United States and Canada. Major media planning issues to be resolved centered around:

- Defining the target audience(s).
- Determining the flighting strategy to be followed.
- Deciding how many weeks in advance to begin advertising.
- Deciding how to vary the timing and allocation of funds across the top 50 markets in the United States and Canada. Given past differences in these markets' responsiveness, variations in media dollar allocations and vehicles in each of the top 50 markets offered an important means of leveraging advertising supporting a film.

In approaching these and other media planning decisions, management began by reviewing past experience with other Touchstone and Disney movies. Table 7-3-1 presents information on the relative effectiveness of advertising investments in six movies across 10 markets. Table 7-3-2 details concentrations of grosses and advertising expenditures across the 50 markets.

Table 7-3-3 presents data on 1986 total advertising appropriations and media breakdowns for five Touchstone and five Disney films. Table 7-3-4 includes household and media costs data on the top 50 U.S. markets.

This case was written by Robert B. Levin, President, Worldwide Marketing, Walt Disney Pictures, and John H. Murphy, The University of Texas at Austin, and is intended for use in generating class discussion, not to illustrate either the effective or ineffective handling of an administrative situation. Used by permission of Walt Disney Pictures.

TABLE 7-3-1 Return on Advertising Index for Six Films in 10 Markets[a]

Los Angeles	288.6
Philadelphia	268.1
Top 50 market average	265.9
Detroit	251.4
Washington, D.C.	240.7
Dallas/Fort Worth	237.4
San Francisco	234.2
Cleveland	233.4
Boston	232.5
New York	225.4
Chicago	223.8

[a]Return on advertising is an index calculated by dividing box office gross by advertising expense times 100. The six films were *Ernest Goes to Camp, Benji the Hunted, Adventures in Babysitting, Snow White, Can't Buy Me Love,* and *Stakeout.*

TABLE 7-3-2 Walt Disney Pictures Marketing: Motion Pictures Concentration of Grosses and Advertising Expense, Average of Six Summer Films

Designataed Market Areas (DMA)	Percentage of All DMA Grosses	Cumulative Percentage	Percentage of All DMA Ad Expenses	Cumulative Percentage
New York	9.5%	9.5%	12.7%	12.7%
Los Angeles	7.3	16.8	7.6	20.3
San Francisco	3.4	20.2	4.3	24.6
Subtotal, Top 3 Markets	20.2%		24.6%	
Boston	3.0%	23.2%	3.9%	28.5%
Chicago	3.0	26.2	4.0	32.5
Philadelphia	2.8	29.0	3.1	35.6
Washington, D.C.	2.4	31.4	3.0	38.6
Dallas/Ft. Worth	2.3	33.7	2.9	41.5
Detroit	2.0	35.7	2.4	43.9
Seattle/Tacoma	1.7	37.4	1.8	45.7
Subtotal, Top 4–10 Markets	17.2%		21.1%	
Toronto	1.7%	39.1%	1.6%	47.3%
Miami	1.6	40.7	2.1	49.4
Houston	1.5	42.2	1.6	51.0
Denver	1.4	43.6	1.4	52.4
Atlanta	1.4	45.0	1.8	54.2
Minneapolis/St. Paul	1.4	46.4	1.6	55.8
Phoenix	1.3	47.7	1.2	57.0
San Diego	1.3	49.0	1.4	58.4
Sacramento/Stockton	1.3	50.3	1.0	59.4
Tampa/St. Petersburg	1.1	51.4	1.2	60.6
Cleveland	1.1	52.5	1.4	62.0
St. Louis	1.0	53.5	1.0	63.0
Orlando	1.0	54.5	1.1	64.1
Kansas City	1.0	55.5	1.2	65.3
Vancouver	1.0	56.5	0.8	66.1
Subtotal, Top 11–25 Markets	19.1%		20.4%	

(continued)

TABLE 7-3-2 *(continued)*

DMA	Percentage of All DMA Grosses	Cumulative Percentage	Percentage of All DMA Ad Expenses	Cumulative Percentage
Indianapolis	1.0%	57.5%	1.0%	67.1%
Pittsburgh	0.9	58.4	1.0	68.1
Salt Lake City	0.9	59.3	0.6	68.7
Portland	0.9	60.2	0.7	69.4
Baltimore	0.9	61.1	1.1	70.5
Hartford/New Haven	0.7	61.8	0.7	71.2
Cincinnati	0.7	62.5	1.1	72.3
Columbus, Ohio	0.7	63.2	0.8	73.1
Providence	0.7	63.9	0.5	73.6
Milwaukee	0.6	64.5	0.8	74.4
Buffalo	0.6	65.1	0.7	75.1
Oklahoma City	0.6	65.7	0.6	75.7
Grand Rapids/Kalamazoo/ Battle Creek	0.6	66.3	0.3	76.0
Norfolk/Portsmouth/ Newport News	0.6	66.9	0.5	76.5
Albany/Schenectady/Troy	0.6	67.5	0.5	77.0
San Antonio	0.5	68.0	0.6	77.6
New Orleans	0.5	68.5	0.5	78.1
Harrisburg/Lancaster/Lebanon	0.5	69.0	0.5	78.6
Nashville	0.5	69.5	0.4	79.0
Wilkes-Barre/Scranton	0.4	69.9	0.2	79.2
Charlotte	0.4	70.3	0.4	79.6
Raleigh/Durham	0.4	70.7	0.5	80.1
Memphis	0.3	71.0	0.4	80.5
Louisville	0.3	71.3	0.4	80.9
Greenville/Spartanburg/Asheville	0.3	71.6	0.2	81.1
Charleston/Huntington	0.3	71.9	0.2	81.3
Birmingham	0.3	72.2	0.2	81.5
Subtotal, Top 26–50 Markets	15.7%		15.4%	

Note: The six films were *Ernest Goes to Camp, Benji the Hunted, Adventures in Babysitting, Snow White, Can't Buy Me Love,* and *Stakeout.*

TABLE 7-3-3 1986 Film Advertising Expenditures by Media

	Percentage Newspaper Expenditures	Percentage Broadcast Expenditures
Touchstone:		
Down and Out in Beverly Hills	55%	45%
Off Beat	25	75
Ruthless People	47	53
Tough Guys	45	55
The Color of Money	51	49
Total Touchstone	48	52
Disney:		
Sleeping Beauty	43%	57%
The Great Mouse Detective	52	48
Flight of the Navigator	36	64
Song of the South	44	56
Lady & The Tramp	48	52
Total Disney	45	55

Questions for Discussion and Review

1. What additional information is necessary to develop a media plan?

2. What major trade-offs are made in media planning for the introduction of a movie?

3. How does media planning for a movie differ from that for a consumer durable good?

TABLE 7-3-4   Household and Media Costs Data for the Top 50 U.S. Markets

Rank	Market	1986 Total Households (in thousands)
1	New York	6,705
2	Los Angeles	4,380
3	Chicago	3,017
4	Philadelphia	2,518
5	San Francisco	2,065
6	Boston	1,960
7	Detroit	1,662
8	Washington, D.C.	1,551
9	Dallas/Ft. Worth	1,540
10	Cleveland	1,424
11	Houston	1,391
12	Pittsburgh	1,230
13	Atlanta	1,187
14	Seattle	1,178
15	Tampa/St. Petersburg	1,163
16	Miami/Ft. Lauderdale	1,163
17	Minneapolis/St. Paul	1,157
18	St. Louis	1,045
19	Denver	993
20	Sacramento	890
21	Baltimore	874
22	Indianapolis	868
23	Phoenix	843
24	Hartford/New Haven	802
25	Portland, Ore.	781
26	San Diego	764
27	Orlando/Daytona	715
28	Cincinnati	709
29	Kansas City	704
30	Milwaukee	695
31	Nashville	670
32	Charlotte	643
33	New Orleans	635
34	Buffalo	615
35	Greenville/Spartanburg/Asheville	614
36	Columbus, Ohio	603
37	Oklahoma City	600
38	Birmingham	588
39	Raleigh/Durham	584
40	Salt Lake City	582
41	Grand Rapids/Kalamazoo/Battle Creek	577
42	Providence	573
43	Memphis	560
44	Harrisburg/Lancaster/York	522
45	San Antonio	518
46	Wilkes-Barre/Scranton	516
47	Louisville	515
48	Norfolk	508
49	Charleston/Huntington	500
50	Albany/Schenectady/Troy	483

[a]Excluding prime.

[b]Tabloid.

Percentage of U.S. Households	Cost for 100 Household GRPs[a]	Cost for Full-page Friday	Number of Newspapers
7.76%	$27,500	$25,500	1
5.07	21,100	14,300	1
3.49	12,800	11,974	2[b]
2.91	13,700	7,410	1[b]
2.39	14,300	19,825	1
2.26	14,400	18,144	1
1.92	8,000	25,081	2
1.79	8,600	12,740	1[b]
1.78	11,300	10,160	2[b]
1.64	5,500	3,918	1[b]
1.61	11,400	18,982	2[b]
1.42	5,900	10,306	2[b]
1.37	8,300	8,325	1
1.36	6,200	7,655	1[b]
1.34	6,300	2,189	1[b]
1.34	8,400	13,382	1
1.33	7,000	6,832	1
1.20	5,000	6,473	1
1.14	7,000	5,444	2[b]
1.02	5,700	6,872	2
1.01	6,300	11,970	2
1.00	4,200	5,741	1
.97	8,400	6,966	1
.92	6,200	8,709	2
.90	4,700	3,940	1
.88	6,900	8,904	1
.82	3,900	6,923	1
.82	3,400	7,214	1
.81	3,700	14,508	2
.80	3,300	14,913	2
.77	4,300	4,580	1
.74	4,800	3,988	1
.73	2,800	4,736	1[b]
.71	3,400	3,686	1[b]
.71	2,600	2,129	1
.69	4,100	4,052	1[b]
.69	3,100	7,666	1
.68	2,500	3,743	1
.67	3,600	2,419	1
.67	3,000	3,496	1
.66	2,400	2,236	1
.66	3,000	6,824	1
.64	2,000	3,444	2[b]
.60	2,800	5,261	2
.59	4,200	3,751	2[b]
.59	3,100	5,049	2
.59	2,100	7,272	1
.58	3,200	5,459	1
.57	2,300	2,434	1
.55	3,200	3,246	1[b]

Women's Athletics (B)

After reviewing the attendance data for women's basketball and volleyball games, the department developed a creative strategy that would allow it to increase audience attendance at the games as well as develop loyalty among game goers. The task now facing the development officer was one of developing a media package that would positively contribute to sales of both broadcast and print advertising for media carrying women's sports. Specifically, the department would have to sell advertising space in the women's basketball program for 14 home games and time on the ESPN cable channel for 15 games. Any leftover money would be used to develop athletic scholarships. It was very important, therefore, to put forth a good effort so that advertising sales would exceed production costs.

Because this was the first attempt by the women's athletics department to sell advertising, the development officer used research data obtained through a survey to compile the media package. The research covered audience demographics (as described in Case 6-2: Women's Athletics [A]) and the shopping and media habits of the audience. Such information would also be used to develop a list of prospects on whom the sales force should call.

The price of advertising space and time was set at a very reasonable level to compete favorably with other local media. The purchase of one ad or one spot would guarantee 14 print or 15 broadcast exposures in a ten-month period—a level of repetition that would be considered excellent by most advertisers.

It was felt that salespeople should spend a considerable amount of time carefully picking their prospects and educating them about the program. They should stress the importance of the audience's size and its loyalty to women's athletic events. In addition, they should emphasize the importance of the audience's shopping patterns. These patterns were likely to make the audience for women's sports a very good prospect for several local businesses. While other media might deliver larger audiences, women's athletic events would deliver a homogeneous segment of prospective customers. Creative appeals and the high repetition level of advertising could certainly deliver a good response for the businesses willing to buy space or time. A good match between the audience and the advertisers was, therefore, necessary to foster good results.

This case was written by Isabella C. M. Cunningham, The University of Texas at Austin, and is intended to generate classroom discussion, not to illustrate the effective or ineffective handling of an administrative situation. Used by permission of Intercollegiate Athletics for Women, The University of Texas at Austin.

   The development officer for women's athletics called a meeting of her staff. The staff requested that Mrs. Gossett, who was in charge of advertising and marketing, prepare a report regarding advertising sales. She was to decide whether the same media package should be used to sell advertising in the volleyball and in the basketball programs. The same decision had to be made regarding television time for both sports. In addition, Gossett should prepare an outline of the media package(s) she wanted to develop. Also, a list of prospective advertisers for both sports was needed, so that they could be discussed at the following meetings.

   Table 7-4-1 summarizes the audience data available to Gossett. This data should be used as a basis to develop the media package(s).

TABLE 7-4-1   Demographic Characteristics of Women's Volleyball and Basketball Audiences

	Percentage of Volleyball Audiences	Percentage of Basketball Audiences
Gender		
Male	53.9%	36.3%
Female	46.1	63.1
Marital Status		
Single	55.2%	30.0%
Married	36.4	57.4
Divorced	4.6	7.0
Other	3.8	5.6
Dwelling Type		
House/Condo	62.6%	89.3%
Apartment	25.3	9.9
Dormitory/Other	12.1	0.8
Age		
18 and younger	11.2%	2.5%
19 to 24	23.1	4.8
25 to 34	24.1	18.3
35 to 49	23.7	35.2
50 to 64	12.7	24.2
65 and older	5.2	15.0
Employment Status		
Employed	65.3%	73.8%
Full time	69.8	74.8
Part time	30.2	25.2
Occupation		
Professional	46.0%	52.1%
Managerial	7.4	10.8
Clerical	8.2	10.4
Student	29.5	5.8
Other	8.9	20.9

(continued)

TABLE 7-4-1   *(continued)*

	Percentage of Volleyball Audiences	Percentage of Basketball Audiences
Income		
Under $15,000	16.7%	6.1%
$15,000–$30,000	19.4	20.5
$30,001–$50,000	25.5	28.8
$50,001–$75,000	21.9	28.3
Over $75,000	16.5	16.3
Education		
Some high school/high school graduate	12.4%	14.0%
Some college	37.0	27.2
College graduate	23.0	28.0
Post graduate	27.6	30.8
Children at home		
Yes	18.8%	24.4%
One child	53.9	53.3
Two or three children	44.9	43.0
Four or more children	1.1	3.6
Age of Oldest Child Living at Home		
6 and younger	17.4%	13.6%
7 to 12	17.4	21.0
13 to 17	30.4	31.8
18 and older	34.8	33.6
Number of People in Household		
One	23.9%	18.4%
Two	42.5	52.8
Three	15.8	15.4
Four or more	17.8	13.2
Affiliated with University		
Yes	60.5%	40.0%
Student	51.3	1.0
Staff/Faculty	15.7	15.8
Alumnus	27.9	43.5
Other	5.1	29.7
Member of Booster Group		
Yes	23.1%	31.2%
No, but friend of one	10.0	11.4
Other	66.9	57.4
Credit Cards		
Gas companies	84.2%	63.4%
Department stores	22.2	67.8
Visa	17.0	61.8
Mastercard	7.3	58.7
American Express	49.3	18.1
Discover	26.5	28.0
Other	1.0	9.4

TABLE 7-4-1 *(continued)*

	Percentage of Volleyball Audiences	Percentage of Basketball Audiences
Frequently Purchased Products/Services		
Restaurant food	77.3%	93.3%
Fast food	59.4	92.2
Toiletries/grooming aids	78.9	87.4
Clothing/shoes	85.6	77.3
Entertainment	37.8	76.2
Gasoline/motor oil	65.0	71.6
Dry cleaning/laundry	40.2	70.5
Alcoholic beverages in restaurant	32.5	61.4
Film/photo finishing	31.9	58.8
Records/tapes	36.4	52.2
Campus entertainment	75.3	52.0
Beer from a store	45.6	44.8
Sports equipment	82.3	43.8
Wine in a store	12.6	39.6
Hard liquor in a store	8.7	30.6
Shopping Habits		
South Mall	54.3%	67.7%
Downtown Mall	60.2	66.0
North Mall	47.2	49.2
Galleria Mall	62.5	41.7
Airport Shopping Center	43.7	41.4
Westgate Mall	32.1	26.5
East Mall	15.2	25.1
Local Stores Patronized		
I. Magnin	46.3%	75.1%
Dubonnet	41.2	68.5
Target	30.1	66.2
Sears	24.6	55.7
Bedford's	13.3	50.1
J. C. Penney	15.4	46.5
Stratton	11.7	41.8
KMart	8.7	39.3
Sam's	29.0	35.0
Frills	1.6	32.2
Mervyn's	14.7	31.7
Montgomery Wards	8.3	28.9
Highland	2.6	27.9
Audience Media Habits		
Television viewing (per day)		
0–1 hour	35.2%	20.8%
1–2 hours	32.3	31.8
2–3 hours	21.7	12.0
4 or more hours	3.2	6.0
Regularly read local newspapers	84.2	80.2

Questions for Discussion and Review

1. Should Gossett develop one media package to be used to sell advertising for both women's basketball and women's volleyball programs? Why?

2. Prepare an outline for the media package(s) to help Gossett in her task.

3. What type of businesses do you feel would be the best advertising prospects for the volleyball and basketball programs?

4. Do you feel that advertising during TV broadcasts of volleyball and basketball games should be sold using the same media package? Should the same prospects be approached by salespeople for both sports? Why?

5. What format would be most appropriate for the media package(s)? Develop a mock-up for it.

8

Advertising Research

*Advertising people who ignore research are as
dangerous as generals who ignore decodes of enemy
signals.*[1]

David Ogilvy

The objective of this chapter is to (1) emphasize the potential value of
research in all areas of advertising decision making and identify some of the
most widely used research techniques; (2) discuss the use of secondary
sources; and (3) briefly examine basic considerations in assessing the validity
of focus group research.

This chapter emphasizes the use of secondary and focus group research for
three reasons. First, secondary and focus group research are widely used forms
of advertising research. Second, as the cost of conducting primary research
increases and access to and richness of secondary information also increase,
secondary research will grow in importance. Third, a discussion of primary
research techniques is beyond the managerial scope of this text.

THE ROLE, SCOPE, AND SIGNIFICANCE OF
ADVERTISING RESEARCH

The potential value of research-generated information to decision making in all
areas of advertising and marketing communication management is substantial.
Information generated through research provides decision makers with the
power to make better decisions.

---

[1]David Ogilvy, *Ogilvy on Advertising* (New York: Crown Publishers, 1983), 158.

Ramond stresses that research information is useful in making more intelligent decisions in all areas of advertising. He suggests that the six key areas of advertising where research information is useful are as follows:

- What to say?   (Theme, copy platform)
- To whom?   (Target audience)
- How to say it?   (Copy, execution)
- How often?   (Frequency)
- Where?   (Media exposure)
- How much to invest?   (Budget)[2]

In addition to these six areas, research should be used to evaluate the effectiveness of the firm's advertising. As discussed in Chapter 4, by specifying specific, measurable objectives, the planner enables an assessment of the impact of an advertisement or an advertising campaign. As stressed in that chapter, in most product/market situations, advertising can be more appropriately evaluated by measuring its effectiveness against communication objectives rather than sales objectives.

At the same time, research information should be viewed as an aid to decision making and *not* a substitute for judgment. It is unrealistic to expect research findings to make decisions. The findings of even the best designed and conducted survey, test market, or experiment requires interpretation. Often the data and resulting recommendations do *not* clearly indicate which course of action is most appropriate.

Exhibit 8-1 identifies a cross section of sources of advertising research information. The exhibit is organized into two sections: secondary data and primary data. The top portion of this exhibit cites several examples of secondary sources. As a rule, primary data collection should be considered only after a thorough search of existing secondary sources has been conducted. Typically, valuable insights into a problem or issue can be developed based on secondary information. Or secondary data can be used to shape the extent and type of primary research ultimately conducted.

Six major sources of primary data are identified: survey research, qualitative research, experimentation, laboratory measures, syndicated services, and sales results. Exhibit 8-1 includes a brief description of a wide and representative range of advertising research techniques. The sources indicated in this exhibit illustrate the diverse range of research approaches available to the planner.

Although the design, execution, and report writing involved in primary research projects is typically completed by research specialists, the communication manager must exercise sound judgment in applying recommendations based on research. The manager must avoid blindly accepting data or

---

[2]Charles Ramond, *Advertising Research: The State of the Art* (New York: Association of National Advertisers, 1976), 3.

EXHIBIT 8-1 Examples of Sources of Advertising Research Information

Secondary Sources

Examples of secondary research include information obtained from published sources such as the trade and popular press; the firm's internal accounting records; U.S. Bureau of the Census and other U.S. government reports; *Sales & Marketing Management's Survey of Buying Power;* commercial suppliers such as Simmons Market Research Bureau (SMRB) volumes and Mediamark Research, Inc. (MRI); and reports and studies conducted by trade associations.

Primary Sources

Survey Research: measures of target consumers' levels of recall, knowledge, and attitudes and/or other information gathered using a representative sample and a structured questionnaire. Conducted by the firm or research suppliers on a project basis.

Qualitative Research

- Focus groups—qualitative data are obtained through informal discussion of the topics of interest led by a moderator. Typically eight to twelve consumers are guided through a discussion outline during an approximately two-hour session.
- Depth interview—one-on-one interview using unstructured probes of underlying motivations.
- Projective techniques—means of tapping underlying feelings through projection situations.

Experimentation: research studies that attempt to demonstrate causation.

- Experimental designs—various plans for controlling conditions related to an experiment.
- Test markets—use of comparable markets to test different levels of exposure to variables of interest.

Laboratory Measures: examination of responses to stimuli under controlled conditions.

- Eye camera—device used to determine what attracts attention, layout impact, etc.
- Tachistoscope—device that varies exposure time of ad to audience and notes what they can identify.
- Galvanic skin response—test that measures involuntary, physiological reactions to ad stimuli.

Syndicated Services

- Burke Day-After Recall—telephone interviews to evaluate TV commercials' impact.
- Starch Readership Studies—in-home interviews to determine impact of print ads.
- Tele-Research, Inc.—service that uses shoppers and forced exposure ads, tracks coupon redemption.
- Maples & Ross—on-air test of TV commercials' effect on brand preferences.
- Gallup-Robinson Impact Test—test that measures ad recall among magazine readers the next day.

Sales Results

- Internal company records.
- Selling Areas Marketing, Inc. (SAMI) warehouse product movement data.
- BehaviorScan—split cable TV exposure to commercials linked to brand sales using UPC data from supermarket data link.

---

conclusions suggested by research specialists. Healthy skepticism is often a valuable management trait.

In assessing the validity of a primary research project, management should evaluate a number of factors. For example, in reviewing a survey, the size and composition of the survey sample used must be evaluated. Further, the data collection instrument, measurement scaling, and sampling and nonsampling error all must be considered. For a thorough discussion of the basic considerations to be used in evaluating primary research projects, see the texts cited in the "Suggested Readings" at the end of this chapter.

The remainder of this chapter examines the importance and application of secondary and focus group research. Advertising and marketing communication managers need to have a solid understanding of these two valuable and widely used sources of advertising planning information. The material presented on each of these techniques is intended to inform and stimulate the reader to learn more about these important information sources.

SECONDARY INFORMATION RESEARCH

Secondary information is available and applicable information that has been reported by an organization or individual other than the person using the information. Astute marketing communication planners recognize the tremendous value of secondary information. Therefore, they are constantly reviewing and using available secondary information. (Smart players know how to capitalize on other people's work.)

There are two types of secondary information—internal and external. Internal secondary information may be available from such sources as sales invoices, sales staff reports, distributors' reports, warranty card returns, reports to shareholders, and corporate annual reports. An analysis of potential internal sources may reveal significant useful information and, hence, should be carefully conducted.

Examples of useful external secondary information abound. For example, an advertiser might find the following secondary information useful in developing a statement of creative strategy:

- estimates of market share reported in the trade press
- a profile of users and nonusers of a product category presented in a report available from a trade association
- truck registrations reported by a state bureau of motor vehicles
- vitamin content of ready-to-eat cereals reported by the FDA.

In many cases, useful secondary information is readily available at little or no cost. For example, the U.S. Bureau of the Census *Census of Business* reports statistics on business firms classified by SICs by regions and states, and technical information on product performance may be reported by an independent laboratory. Such information can be extremely valuable in developing advertising and marketing communication plans.

McDaniel and Gates provide a 16-page appendix titled "Published Secondary Data" that provides a thumbnail description of widely available secondary information sources.[3] This appendix is an excellent guide to published sources of secondary information available in most libraries.

---

[3]Carl McDaniel and Roger Gates, *Contemporary Marketing Research* (St. Paul, Minn.: West Publishing, 1991), 146–161.

In locating pertinent secondary information, a reference librarian is a valuable resource. Consulting reference librarians can save time and locate information that might be overlooked or unavailable without their assistance. These specialists' job is to help individuals make the best use of the library's resources, and you should not hesitate to request their assistance. (Smart players know how to enlist appropriate people's assistance to help them find what they need.)

On-line data bases offer the researcher a quick, thorough, and efficient (though often costly) means of locating potentially useful secondary information. These data bases provide information ranging from references to published sources to complete text coverage of topics (based on descriptors such as key words or topics input by the user) to complete raw data from massive survey research projects such as MRI's national study of 20,000 adults' product usage and media exposure patterns.

Individual on-line data base vendors provide access to an incredible range of information sources. Such vendors assist researchers by helping determine which data bases are most likely to meet their needs. Four of the most popular on-line data base vendors are Dow Jones News/Retrieval, The Source, Dialog, and CompuServ.[4] For information on the contents of the various vendors' data bases, see the most current edition of the *Directory of On-Line Databases*. Often, an initial step in conducting a thorough review of potential secondary information is the preparation of a list of potential sources generated by scanning an appropriate on-line data base.

Finally, although there are obvious benefits to the use of secondary information, such information is often limited in several ways. First, many advertising decisions are situation specific and do *not* lend themselves to the application of secondary research. For example, "Which of three specific executions of a creative strategy should be used?" can best be answered only with primary research. Second, secondary information, though useful, often fails to provide all the information the decision maker needs to make a decision. Third, information quickly becomes outdated. Fourth, there is always the danger of obtaining inaccurate information.[5] Therefore, the users of secondary information must beware of its limitations.

FOCUS GROUP RESEARCH

The Nature of Focus Group Research

In an advertising research context, the term *focus group* refers to a group discussion during which a leader or moderator guides a small group of consumers through a consideration of relevant marketing topics. In an informal environment, individual participants are encouraged to spontaneously express their opinions amid the security of a peer group and encouraged

---

[4]*Ibid.,* 128.
[5]*Ibid.,* 123–125.

by a supportive moderator. A transcript of what was said by participants is later analyzed, and tentative ideas related to the attitudes or behaviors of interest are formulated. This information is used to contribute to the formulation of additional research and/or more appropriate advertising.

Focus groups are used in an attempt to gain insights into "why"-type questions that underlie motivations for behavior and attitudes. The technique is based on group dynamics: individuals are more willing to talk about a subject amid the security of a group of other individuals sharing their thoughts on the same subject. The validity of the technique also stems from the synergy and spontaneity that can be created in an informal group discussion.

Unfortunately, focus groups inherently involve some troubling trade-offs. First, while focus groups are relatively cheap, quick, and easy to set up and conduct, they are difficult to moderate effectively and analyze definitively. Second, since focus groups are qualitative in nature and *not* based on a representative sample, they do *not* support generalizations. Ignoring this fact, users too often generalize their results. Third, focus groups are subject to multiple interpretations, depending on who evaluates the data. Finally, the role of the moderator is difficult to perform and exerts a major influence on the validity of the technique. As Calder has pointed out, "there is concern about the subjectivity of the technique, and a feeling that any given result might have been different with different respondents, a different moderator, or even a different setting."[6]

These trade-offs led one advertising wag to refer to focus groups as "hocus groups." Certainly controversy surrounds all aspects of the technique and there are no accepted guidelines for its use.[7] Critics of focus group research suggest that the findings are simply creative ideas of the analyst and should not even be considered research.[8]

Focus groups are subject to two major misapplications. First, focus groups can be used merely as evidence to support preconceived opinions. In evaluating verbal comments, there is always the danger of selectively interpreting what is said and deciding whose opinions to weigh most heavily. Second, definitive conclusions are sometimes drawn from focus group research even though the technique does not produce projectable data. Unfortunately, this is too often done, as when a product manager concludes, "Listen to what Linda just said—I knew it was a good idea!"

The legitimate application of focus group research is limited. In advertising and marketing research, focus groups may appropriately be used to (1) provide useful background information on consumer attitudes and the language consumers use when they discuss products' performance, (2)

---

[6]Bobby J. Calder, "Focus Groups and the Nature of Qualitative Marketing Research," *Journal of Marketing Research* 14 (August 1977): 353–364.

[7]Dan Bellenger, Ken Bernhardt, and Jack Goldstucker, *Qualitative Research in Marketing,* monograph series no. 3 (Chicago: American Marketing Association, 1976), 7.

[8]Harper Boyd, Ralph Westfall, and Stanley Stasch, *Marketing Research—Text and Cases* (Homewood, Ill.: Richard D. Irwin, 1985), 46.

generate ideas for new products, (3) gather consumers' preliminary evaluations of new advertisements and new product concepts, (4) structure a consumer questionnaire, (5) generate hypotheses to test quantitatively, and (6) interpret previously obtained quantitative research findings.[9] The user of focus group research information should beware of applications stretching beyond these areas.

Conducting Focus Group Research

As indicated earlier, one of the dangers of focus groups stems from the fact that they are relatively easy to set up and conduct. Therefore, it is relatively easy for an inexperienced person or firm to abuse the technique.

Exhibit 8-2 presents an outline of the steps to be followed in conducting a focus group session. The seven steps described represent a typical protocol for such research. Note that the procedure described in each step is simply one approach to conducting the session; other procedures may be equally or more appropriate given the nature of the topic or group. For example, step 6 *(Analyzing the data)* describes only one of many valid means of analyzing the data.

Evaluating Focus Group Research

A focus group that is poorly planned, moderated, or analyzed can result in misleading conclusions. To avoid being misled, the potential user of information based on a focus group session should evaluate the validity of the session. This means that the user needs to understand the basic mechanics of conducting a focus group session.

Exhibit 8-2 was developed to serve as a guide for evaluating the thoroughness and validity of a focus group research project. Comparing the procedures outlined in Exhibit 8-2 with those of a specific project may expose major gaps or problems related to careless or inappropriate procedures. This exhibit provides a realistic model against which to compare focus group sessions.

In addition, Exhibit 8-3 presents twelve specific areas that should be considered prior to accepting and applying the findings drawn from a focus group research project. While there are exceptions to the guidelines presented in Exhibit 8-3, these rules of thumb are valid criteria for evaluating most focus group situations.

Note the importance of the moderator as indicated by the number of considerations in Exhibit 8-3 directly related to this individual's background, interpersonal skills, and so on. There is universal agreement that the moderator's role is the crucial factor in determining the validity of a focus group research project.[10]

---

[9]Bellenger, Bernhardt, and Goldstucker, *Qualitative Research in Marketing,* 18–19.
[10]*Ibid.,* 11.

EXHIBIT 8-2   Steps in Conducting a Focus Group Session

1. *Establish objectives for the session.*

2. *Construct the discussion outline.* Cover all the topics to be discussed by the group, in sequence. The exact wording must be carefully developed to avoid bias. The moderator should work from the discussion outline, allowing roughly five questions per page with space for notes under each.

3. *Develop the screening questionnaire.* Given the objectives of the session, identify a small set of criteria to ensure that the most productive group is formed. The rule of thumb is that the more homogeneous the group, the better. Productive screening criteria are sex, age, household income, education, marital status, and parental status.

4. *Recruit participants.* Ideally, qualified potential participants are contacted via mail and then by telephone. Do *not* reveal the exact topic of discussion—only the general area. Offer money ($20 to $50) as an incentive for "about two hours of your time to participate in a small group discussion." If you indicate that the session will begin at 7:00 P.M., realize that it will actually start at around 7:20. Recruit a maximum of a week and a half to two weeks in advance. After potential participants agree to attend, send them a thank-you letter that includes a map showing how to find the room. Call the night before the session to remind them. To make sure 8 to 12 attend, recruit 20 who say that they will definitely attend (they won't if anything else comes up). If more than 12 come, pay the extras and send them on their way. Use a flowchart to keep on top of recruitment.

5. *Start and close the session appropriately.*
   a.   Use name cards with the participants' first names only.
   b.   Have the moderator introduce himself or herself and briefly explain the purpose of the discussion, stressing the importance of obtaining everyone's opinion.
   c.   Explain that the purpose of the two tape recorders (in case one doesn't work) is to help the moderator later (he or she can't remember everything).
   d.   Tell the subjects that this will be an informal discussion and they should feel free to get refreshments at any time.
   e.   Stress the importance of everyone's opinion.
   f.   Have the moderator ask everyone to introduce himself or herself, moving around the table.
   g.   The moderator should begin the session with a general question or subject for the group's reaction.
   h.   In closing the session, thank the participants for their help and do any appropriate debriefing.

6. *Analyze the data.* Ask the moderator to write up his or her conclusions immediately after the session is over or by the next morning. The moderator can tape impressions if this is easier. The expert doing the analysis should review the moderator's report *after* completing a draft of his or her conclusions. The expert should begin by listening to the tape once to get a general idea of what was said. In drawing qualitative conclusions, one procedure is for the expert to write each idea expressed on a small slip of paper and then arrange the ideas into categories. Multiple groups asked about the same topic can be analyzed at the same time using this procedure. Have the moderator review and discuss the expert's analysis before it is final.

7. *Report the results.* The data are soft and *not* projectable. Do *not* report any numbers. Use language such as "tends to indicate," "impressions," "observations," or "hypotheses for further examination."

Suggested Readings

Aaker, David, Rajeev Batra, and John Myers. *Advertising Management.* 4th ed. Englewood Cliffs, N.J.: Prentice-Hall, 1992, 406–438.

Bellenger, Dan, Ken Bernhardt, and Jack Goldstucker. *Qualitative Research in Marketing.* Monograph series no. 3. Chicago: American Marketing Association, 1976.

Calder, Bobby J. "Focus Groups and the Nature of Qualitative Marketing Research." *Journal of Marketing Research* 14 (August 1977): 353–364.

EXHIBIT 8-3   Checklist for Evaluating Focus Group Research

Evaluation Areas	Guideline Considerations
Moderator's background	Needs formal training in social psychology and group dynamics. Experience is crucial—how many focus groups has moderator handled? In what product categories? With what types of groups?
Moderator's handling of group	How many times does moderator ask why? The more whys, the better. Does moderator really listen to what members are saying? Is questioning directed? Does moderator look members in the eye when they speak? Handle any problems effectively?
Moderator's traits exhibited	Was the moderator kind but firm? Permissive without allowing chaos? Involved? Able to request clarification and expansion where appropriate? Encouraging? Flexible? Sensitive?[a]
Interaction between members	The more group interaction, the better. The less the moderator is involved in the discussion, the better.
Moderator's approach to project	Ideally, the moderator should be involved in planning the session. Does moderator seem to understand the problem and be excited about working on it? Is moderator flexible or rote in conducting multiple sessions?[b]
Homogeneity of group	The more homogeneous, the better. Members should be balanced socially and intellectually. Do not mix men and women. Want members who are comparable in terms of age, stage in life cycle, and psychographics. No relatives, friends, or established relationships. No repeat participants.
Moderator's match with group	Same sex, age, and so on encourages more open discussion.
Group size	Eight to twelve is best. Less than eight can be a burden on each member; more than twelve reduces member participation.
Recruitment and compensation	Must be handled professionally and in an unbiased manner.
Length and number of sessions	One and a half to two hours is typically long enough to build rapport without taxing member participation. Depending on the project, three to four sessions are usually sufficient; fewer is suspect.
Physical environment	Informal, relaxed, living room–type setting is best. Serve refreshments to relax atmosphere.
Appropriate conclusions	Remember the qualitative nature of the technique. Data are only directional in nature, not projectable. No statistics on responses should be presented due to the small, unrepresentative sample.

[a]Dan Bellenger, Ken Bernhardt, and Jack Goldstucker, *Qualitative Research in Marketing,* monograph series no. 3 (Chicago: American Marketing Association, 1976), 12–16.
[b]Donald Chase, "The Intensive Group Interview in Marketing," *MRA Viewpoints,* 1973.

Kinnear, Thomas C., and James R. Taylor. *Marketing Research: An Applied Approach.* 4th ed. New York: McGraw-Hill, 1991.

McDaniel, Carl, and Roger Gates. *Contemporary Marketing Research.* St. Paul, Minn.: West Publishing, 1991.

Ogilvy, David. *Ogilvy on Advertising.* New York: Crown Publishers, 1983:158–166.

Ramond, Charles. *Advertising Research: The State of the Art.* New York: Association of National Advertisers, 1976, 3.

Zikmund, William. *Exploring Marketing Research.* New York: The Dryden Press, 1989.

Exercises

1.   A new product was introduced in the United States in 1987: the cardboard, or disposable, camera. The camera, produced and marketed by Eastman Kodak Co. and the U.S. unit of Fuji Photo Film Co., was greeted with skepticism by consumers. The general public did not think the camera could take decent pictures.

Since 1987, "single-use" or "one-time" cameras have experienced a growth in sales. In 1990, U.S. consumers bought about 15 million of them. The sales of this product were solely responsible for the increase in film sales in this country during the past three years.

The cardboard cameras were at first positioned in the market as second cameras—an alternative to expensive cameras their owners might not want to take to the beach or ski slopes. The disposable cameras' prices range from $9 to $17, depending on whether they have a built-in flash. Kodak presently has 80 percent of the cardboard camera market, while Fuji has the remaining 20 percent. Recently, Konica entered this market with a basic model priced at $8.35.

The cameras have been advertised mainly to the general user using appeals such as Kodak's headline: "This picture was taken by someone who didn't bring a camera." Lately, however, both Fuji and Kodak have made attempts to target specific groups of camera users. At the 1992 Super Bowl game, Kodak introduced a telephoto model designed for sports fans, which sells for $16.95. In addition, both Kodak and Fuji sell basic flash, underwater, and panoramic or wide-angle disposable cameras. There are plans for a camera designed to allow skiers to take pictures while wearing gloves and for a model designed for people who have arthritis.

U.S. sales of disposable cameras from 1987 to 1991 were as shown in the following graph:

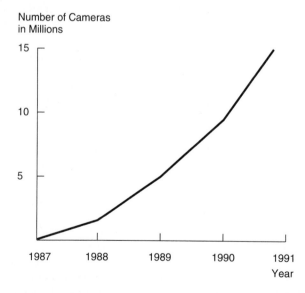

Number of Cameras in Millions

Executives in the photography industry feel that these sales represent only the tip of the iceberg; 1991 sales alone generated 2.1 percent of all film sales. The potential for growth is enormous, and companies would benefit from a more in-depth knowledge of the potential markets for the product. Research so far has been limited to focus groups and retailing shelf space surveys. Some new products have been test marketed, but response is always overwhelmingly positive. Therefore, it would be unwise to use these tests as a relative measure of potential sales to different consumer targets.

You have been asked by Kodak executives to prepare a proposal for an advertising campaign that would target specific groups of potential users of uniquely designed models of cardboard cameras. The campaign would run concomitantly with Kodak's general advertising campaign, which stresses the quality of the pictures and introduces the product to nonusers. You must select the two or three *niche* markets most likely to attract a large number of users. To do so, your agency has decided to conduct a study to gather the necessary information. It is your responsibility to design a study that will best pinpoint the niches with greatest market potential for this product.

Design a short research proposal to be submitted to your agency's management. Underline the specific goals of the research and the methodology to be used, and develop a budget. Note that total advertising expenditures in 1991 were estimated to be $4 million. Fuji plans to increase its budget in 1992 by 30 percent, and Kodak may well consider a similar increase. The research budget, therefore, should be kept reasonable, based on the overall advertising expenditures earmarked for the product.

Source: Joan E. Rigdon, "For Cardboard Cameras, Sales Picture Enlarges and Seems Brighter than Ever," *The Wall Street Journal,* February 11, 1992, B1–B2.

2. The marketing vice-president of a major airline was worried about the recent decline in air travel in the United States. She was convinced that more consumers could be enticed to use the airlines if different appeals were used in the company's advertising campaigns.

The vice-president, Deborah Soars, had just read an article that indicated that ads featuring children or the prices/values of products or services were most likely to be recalled by consumers. Conducted by Video Storyboard Tests, Inc., the study asked 22,000 people to name outstanding ads. A third of the top 25 most-mentioned commercials harped on low prices. Most of the others used cute kids to get their message across.

Soars did not feel that price advertising was an option for her company. Domestic airlines had been able to attract fliers with price promotions and frequent-flier deals. Yet Soars believed that the lower margins of and operations costs pressures on airline companies made additional rebate schemes economically unjustifiable.

Instead, she wanted her advertising agency to consider including cute little kids in the airline's commercials. If kids had been effective in increasing recall for Du Pont rugs and McDonald's hamburgers, why wouldn't they work for airlines? Business fliers accounted for a large percentage of total demand for airline tickets, but the remainder of the market was chiefly composed of leisure or vacation fliers. Surely commercials showing families with kids would appeal to such an audience!

1. What do you think of Soars's idea?

2. How could such an idea be tested through the use of research?

3. What type of research study would be most appropriate to answer Soars's questions?

Source: Joanne Lipman, "Consumers' Favorite Commercials Tend to Feature Lower Prices or Cuddly Kids," *The Wall Street Journal,* March 2, 1992, B1.

Big Brothers/Big Sisters of Austin

Big Brothers/Big Sisters of Austin is an organization founded on the belief that "Little people need big people." By matching children aged five to seventeen from single-parent households with adult volunteers, BB/BS of Austin helps bring about long-term friendships that support Little Brothers' and Sisters' academic, social, and emotional growth. Big Brothers and Big Sisters (and occasionally Big Couples) commit themselves to spending a few hours every week with their Little Brother or Sister for only one year, but formal matches often last many years and the friendships formed sometimes last a lifetime.

The congressionally chartered Big Brothers/Big Sisters of America (BB/BSA) traces its roots back to 1903, when a young Cincinnati businessman befriended a boy from a fatherless home and encouraged friends and associates to do the same. Founded in 1971, Big Brothers/Big Sisters of Austin is one of over 500 such agencies across the country affiliated with the national organization. Local agencies have their own boards of directors, set their own policies, and are responsible for their own funding. Headquartered in Philadelphia, BB/BSA assists local agencies by setting standards of practice, conducting on-site evaluations, and providing information on recruiting volunteers and raising funds. National fund-raising and public relations campaigns help at the local level by creating a broad base of public recognition and support.

The program does more than pair children with adults. Professional caseworkers provide counseling services for unmatched children and their families, help match children and adults with similar interests, and offer continuing guidance and support for the duration of the match. BB/BSA states that the program is cost effective in both human and economic terms. Because the friendship with an adult role model helps prevent juvenile delinquency, the annual cost of a match is money well spent compared to the much higher cost if that child were to enter the juvenile justice system.

The most recent annual budget for BB/BS of Austin totaled $406,487. About 46 percent of this amount was provided by various local fund-raising activities, such as the annual "Bowl for Kids' Sake." The United Way contributed 22 percent of the total, the city of Austin provided 21 percent, and Travis County gave the remaining 11 percent.

This case was written by George R. Franke, Virginia Polytechnic Institute and State University. It is intended for use in generating classroom discussion and is not meant to illustrate either the effective or ineffective handling of an administrative situation. Used by permission of Big Brothers/Sisters of Austin.

THE PROGRAM

Becoming a Big Brother or Sister is not a casual process. In Austin, the first step is attending a one-hour orientation meeting, held during a weekday evening every two weeks at a convenient downtown Austin location. Interested volunteers complete an application form that takes BB/BS of Austin two to four weeks to process. (The nature of the adult-child relationship means that careful checking of references and a police clearance are important parts of the screening process.) Applicants who meet basic eligibility requirements are interviewed by a caseworker. If approved, the applicant is matched with a child who enjoys similar activities and has age, race, or other characteristics preferred by the applicant. The applicant, parent, and child must all agree to the match.

Big Brothers and Sisters are asked to spend about four hours every week with their Little Brother or Sister doing such ordinary activities as going to a park or shopping mall, washing the car, mowing the lawn, going bowling, or seeing a movie. BB/BS of Austin discourages spending much money on outings because the adult's time and attention are much more valuable to the child. As Mark Wieland, director of public relations for BB/BS of Austin, puts it, "We're trying to provide friendship. We're not substitute parents, not authority figures, not a taxi service, and not Santa Claus."

PROGRAM PARTICIPANTS

Statistics on the number of inquirers, applicants, and participants in the program in the first half of a recent fiscal year, taken from the BB/BS of Austin *Quarterly Report,* are shown in Table 8-1-1. Careful screening ensures that volunteers meet a number of criteria before becoming Big Brothers or Sisters. They must be mature and emotionally secure, must have lived in Austin and been employed at least six months, must have transportation and insurance, and must be able to make a one-year commitment to the program. Applicants who expect changes within the year in their marital status, employment, or place of residence are advised to delay becoming Big Brothers or Sisters until their lives have stabilized.

Austin Big Brothers and Sisters have typically been between 20 and 33 years old, single, and middle to upper-middle class. About 80 percent of the volunteers are white, and roughly 55 percent are male (see Table 8-1-2).

Little Brothers and Sisters are also "volunteers"—they are never forced into the program. Often, applying to the program is the child's own idea. Other times, a parent, teacher, or friend suggests that the child apply. In all cases, though, both the parent and the child must approve of the child's participation. Children are not in the program because they are poor, emotionally troubled, or juvenile delinquents; their common denominator is that they are children from single-parent households who want a lasting relationship with an adult friend.

Though children aged 7 to 15 are eligible for the program, the typical Little Brother or Sister is from 8 to 12 years old. There are somewhat more

TABLE 8-1-1   Six-Month Participation Statistics for BB/BS of Austin

	October through December	January through March	Total
Applications from children	30	48	78
Children accepted	37	43	80
Volunteer call-ins	222	237	459
Volunteers attending orientation meetings	111	102	213
Applications from volunteers	36	50	86
BB/BS/Big Couples accepted	40	41	81
New matches	25	31	56
Matches ended	21	23	44
Average length of finished matches (in months)	25.7	25.4	25.5
Active matches	229	237	237
Children waiting to be matched	174	157	157
Children waiting to be interviewed	125	138	138

TABLE 8-1-2   Sex and Race of BB/BS of Austin Participants

	Percentage Who Are:			Total Number
	White	Black	Hispanic	
Big Brothers	85%	3%	12%	121
Big Sisters	80	4	16	100
Little Brothers	44	34	22	128
Little Sisters	23	44	33	101

Note: Big Couples are not included in the data for Big Brothers and Sisters.

boys than girls in the program and relatively equal numbers of blacks, whites, and Hispanics (see Table 8-1-2). Unmatched children are less evenly balanced, though. About 75 percent are male, and the racial breakdown is roughly 55 percent black, 25 percent white, and 20 percent Hispanic.

A GROWING PROBLEM

In Austin and across the country, the demand for the services of Big Brothers/Big Sisters organizations is growing. BB/BS programs serve roughly 100,000 children nationwide, but another 100,000 are on waiting lists hoping to be matched. BB/BSA estimates that nearly three million children in the United States are growing up without support from an adult of the same sex, and could therefore benefit from having a Big Brother or Sister. The problem is especially severe for boys. In Austin, more than 75 boys are unassigned, with another 85 on a waiting list, whereas only about 37 girls are unassigned. Boys also tend to have a longer wait for a match—typically six to twelve months, versus only three to nine months for girls.

One reason for the lengthy waiting lists is the growing number of single-parent families in the United States. More than 7.5 million U.S. households were headed by a lone male or female in 1989, a 25 percent increase over the number in 1980. Though the growth rate was higher for male-headed households than female-headed households (73 percent versus 20 percent), most single-parent families are still headed by women. Of the single-parent families with children under eighteen, 6.5 million were headed by women in 1989 and only 1.1 million headed by men. Female-headed families tend to be slightly smaller than male-headed families, with average sizes of 3.2 and 3.4 members, respectively.

Single-parent families are not uncommon in Austin. Of 191,049 total Austin households, the 1990 census showed that almost 14,654 families were headed by women with children under eighteen, including 7,604 white, 4,312 black, and 2,517 Hispanic families. A disproportionate number of black households in Austin have a female head. Of black families with children under eighteen, 42 percent are headed by females. This figure is more than double the 16 percent of white families with children under eighteen headed by women and almost double the 24 percent of families of Spanish origin headed by women.

Other factors also contribute to the problem. For example, a recent broad decline in the Austin economy helped reduce attendance at orientation meetings 30 percent in one year. The economy also caused some volunteers to withdraw their applications after taking part-time jobs to help make ends meet.

PROMOTIONAL ACTIVITIES

National promotional activities for the Big Brothers/Big Sisters program are created and coordinated by BB/BSA. BB/BSA prepares a national public relations campaign for release through print and broadcast media, designs national promotions in which affiliates can participate, and encourages corporate sponsorship of national programs. In 1986, for example, many national magazines carried public service announcements based on cartoons donated to BB/BSA (Exhibit 8-1-1). Another example of corporate support is Arby's donation of $240,000 to Big Brothers/Big Sisters of America and Canada, $1,000 for each run-batted-in hit by the American and National League RBI leaders.

Because resource limitations preclude most forms of paid advertising, BB/BS of Austin uses public service announcements, tie-ins with corporate sponsors, and brochures in its promotional efforts. Locally prepared PSAs are run without charge by Austin TV stations (see Exhibit 8-1-2 for a current example). Advertising for such activities as the Pepsi-Cola—sponsored Bowl-

EXHIBIT 8-1-1 Sample Magazine Ad for Big Brothers/Big Sisters of America

for-Kids'-Sake Super Strikes competition, which raised $70,000 for BB/BS of Austin, and the Chuy's Restaurant five-kilometer fun run, in which 2,500 runners participated, appears in various media as well (see Exhibit 8-1-3). Brochures are distributed to local social service agencies, at the biweekly orientation meetings, and at presentations to local organizations such as the Jaycees.

BB/BS of Austin also makes effective use of publicity. Articles on the program and on children looking for Big Brothers or Sisters appear occasionally in the *Austin American-Statesman,* and the "Wednesday's Child" feature on the local ABC-TV affiliate profiles a child on the waiting list during every second Wednesday's 10:00 news. Newsworthy happenings, such as a $100,000 gift to start a Big Brothers/Big Sisters scholarship fund and the gift of a car as a prize in the Bowl for Kids' Sake tournament, also are given local media attention.

RESEARCH EFFORTS

In reviewing its policies and strategies, the BB/BS of Austin board of directors realized it needed more information to set goals and evaluate past programs. Accordingly, it commissioned a local research firm to conduct focus groups and do an inexpensive telephone survey of adult Austin residents. The focus groups were intended to provide background information to the research firm and suggest problems and opportunities to the board. The ultimate purpose of the telephone survey was to help the board devise strategies for stimulating

**EXHIBIT 8-1-2   Sample Public Service Announcement for
Big Brothers/Big Sisters of Austin**

VIDEO: Young girl

Audio: Instrumental: "What the world
needs now"

VIDEO: Boy with fish bowl

Audio: VO: The world is full of kids
who need a ···

VIDEO: Girl in window

Audio: VO: grownup for a friend.
Become a Big Brother or Big Sister.
Because little people need big
people.

VIDEO: Boy with baseball

Audio: VO: Like you.

Boy: We sure do.

VIDEO: Super with phone number

Audio: VO: Look up Big Brothers/Big
Sisters in the phone book today,
or call this number.

**EXHIBIT 8-1-3   Sample Fund-Raising Activity Advertising for
Big Brothers/Big Sisters of Austin**

interest in becoming a Big Brother or Sister by quantifying perceptions of the program, its promotional efforts, and its participants. Because of the large number of boys waiting for a Big Brother, the board was also interested in determining perceptions of cross-sex matches—matching Little Brothers with Big Sisters.

The research firm conducted three focus groups during May: one male-only, one female-only, and the third combining males and females. Each group had eight to twelve participants and a moderator. The mixed male-female group was observed by two members of the board of directors. The participants encompassed a variety of demographic characteristics, though most were white, under 30, single, and college educated. An overview of the focus group findings is contained in Appendix 8-1A.

The research firm developed and pretested a questionnaire during the month of June. After approval of the final questionnaire, a random-digit-dialing procedure was used to call 684 adults in the Austin telephone exchanges in early July. Interviews were completed with 506 of the people contacted. The questionnaire used and the distribution of responses are shown in Appendix 8-1B, and other selected results of the survey are presented in Table 8-1-3.

Among other things, the research results helped BB/BS of Austin identify misconceptions people had about the program. These misconceptions were addressed at subsequent biweekly orientation meetings and in individual discussions with volunteers. Also, based on the research, the informational brochure was modified to provide more detail about the type of children in the program and what is expected of volunteers. Due to budgetary constraints, though, no new PSAs were made for distribution to the local TV stations. Although the board of directors felt that the research provided valuable information, they were not convinced that it provided sufficient justification for discarding their current ads.

At a board of directors meeting the following April, the advisability of conducting further research was discussed. A number of questions were raised at the meeting, including the following:

- What would be gained by conducting further focus groups? Why should another survey be conducted only one year after the first?

- Were there problems or opportunities suggested by last year's study that should be investigated in more depth? If so, how?

- Should a telephone survey be used again, or should other methods be considered? Could BB/BS volunteers serve as interviewers in a telephone survey to reduce the costs?

- Should the same questionnaire be used, or should it be modified? If so, what changes should be made?

- Was last year's sample size sufficient to represent the more than 600,000 people living in the Austin metropolitan area, or should it be increased? What would be the effect of reducing the sample size?

A committee was formed to study the merits of conducting further research. It was agreed that the committee would make a recommendation to the board at its next meeting, in May.

Questions for Discussion and Review

1. What conclusions can be drawn from (a) the focus group discussions and (b) the findings of the telephone survey? What changes are indicated for the promotional efforts of Big Brothers/Big Sisters of Austin?

2. How would you answer the questions raised at the board meeting?

3. What are the advantages and disadvantages of focus groups and telephone surveys as methods of gathering information?

4. What steps might BB/BS of Austin take to generate more publicity? To stimulate greater corporate sponsorship and support of its program? To raise more funds?

Appendix 8-1A
Big Brothers/Big Sisters of Austin
Focus Group Results

The focus group moderator wrote a report that was presented to the BB/BS board of directors. Highlights of the report are summarized below.

- *Awareness of the program* among the focus group participants was high, mostly from television but also from radio and outdoor advertising and word of mouth.

- *Understanding of the program's purpose* was mixed. Some participants thought the purpose of the program was to keep hoodlums off the streets

("The kids are rebellious and can't get along with their parents, so be their Big Brother and see if you can get them straight"), others knew that the program provides adult friendship to children from single-parent homes, and others perceived a more demanding mission ("It's more than just giving your spare time. It's almost like being a surrogate parent").

- *The rewards of participating* focused on "the emotional satisfaction you feel knowing that you're doing something special for this kid's life." "You could really make a big influence on a child, get a good feeling from being looked up to." Participating is also fun: "You get to do things you never had a chance to do when you were a kid."

- *Perceptions of adult volunteers* were varied. Some people thought ideal volunteers were college students or young adults—"35- to 40-year-olds are too old to be a 'brother' figure." More common was the notion that college students did not have enough time to participate or were not mature enough. Singles and "empty nesters" were seen as ideal volunteers by some—"It's hard enough to make time for your own children. Get people whose kids have grown up and moved away. . . . There are a lot of old people who don't have companionship." More generally, there was a daunting image of the Big Brother or Sister as a "model citizen," a "caring, social work–type," "a Phil Donahue kind of guy."

- *Perceptions of children in the program* were generally negative. Most focus group participants characterized the typical Little Brother or Sister as a minority member, problem child, or juvenile delinquent who was poor or from a broken home. One participant noted, "If the typical kid isn't a little ten-year-old boy from a broken home in the ghetto, they (BB/BS of Austin) need to change that perception. Because that's what I think of."

- The major *reasons for not volunteering* were the time, money, and emotional commitments involved. "Takes too much time" was the overwhelming deterrent. Money was a less important factor, though participants were surprised that spending money on Little Brothers and Sisters is discouraged. A few participants mentioned the emotional risk of high involvement or the guilt of having to quit the relationship before the child was ready.

- *Public service announcements on TV* were seen by many as too vague and uninformative—"The ads don't really tell you anything about the program, like who are these kids and what do they want volunteers for. All you know is that it's a good thing to do." "They don't say what a Big Brother program can offer you." However, some discussants thought the PSAs were effective: "They tell what the program is about. They're good at attempting to get the message across that they need volunteers." Other participants favored emotional commercials: "They should make commercials that make you want to cry—with chill bumps." Also, many participants thought the announcements should run more often, and some suggested supplementary media, such as billboards, to deliver the message to more people.

- The idea of *cross-sex matching* drew strong responses. Some thought "Any attention is better than none at all," though most disapproved of matching girls with Big Brothers because of the risk of molestation. (A rebuttal was that "a pervert is a pervert—you just have to be careful who you give the kids to.") Matching boys with Big Sisters also drew mixed reactions, some positive ("It's better to match a boy with a Big Sister than to leave the kid alone") and some negative ("There would be a conflict of interests; a Big Sister might want to go shopping, but the Little Brother wouldn't." "Being with a woman might make the kid turn out more feminine").

- *Ideas for increasing the number of volunteers* centered on increasing the amount and informativeness of advertising, reducing the time requirements, and focusing on narrower target audiences, such as church groups and college students. The University of Texas was suggested as a good source of volunteers. ("Make it a course assignment for education majors.") Campus organizations were seen as especially promising. ("I remember when I was in a sorority, we got extra points for doing stuff like that. It would be pretty fun to get all of your friends together with their little kids and do stuff on the weekends.")

Appendix 8-1B
Big Brothers/Big Sisters of Austin Survey Questionnaire and Responses

Questionnaire _____   Interviewer _____

INSTRUCTIONS: Unless stated otherwise, read each list of responses, except for yes/no questions. Don't read the number before the alternative. Circle or check the answer(s) given.

Hello, my name is _____, and I'm doing a short survey for Big Brothers/Big Sisters of Austin. We've chosen phone numbers at random to call and would like to include you in our sample.

(If they say it's not a convenient time) Should I call back later this evening or would tomorrow be better? (If they refuse, thank them and terminate; otherwise, note phone number and call back.)
First, are you 18 or over?
    Yes (go to Question 1)
    No: Is there someone there I can talk to who is 18 or over?
    Yes (start over with new person—read intro, then go to Q.1)
    No (thank and terminate)

1. Have you ever heard of the Big Brothers/Big Sisters program in Austin?
    89%   1. Yes (go to Question 1a)
    11%   2. No/don't know (go to Item 2)

1a. How did you hear about it? (Let them answer and check all that apply, then ask, "Did you ever hear about it from _____" and read the remaining items on the list.)

   65%[a]   commercials on TV
   19%   "Wednesday's Child" on TV news
   10%   the radio
   19%   a Big Brother or Big Sister volunteer
   21%   someone else
   15%   anything else _____
    5%   don't know/don't remember (DO NOT READ)

1b. What do you think the purpose of BB/BS is? Would you say that it's (read list)

   16%[a]   1. to help delinquent children,
   14%   2. to provide a substitute for a child's real parent,
   62%   3. to provide adult friends for children from single-parent homes,
    8%   4. or something else.

2. (Start description as appropriate, depending on whether they described it right or wrong or hadn't heard of BB/BS)

[Right,/Actually,] What the program tries to do is give children from single-parent households a chance to become friends with an adult volunteer. The adults are called Big Brothers or Sisters, and the children are called Little Brothers or Sisters. I want to ask you a few questions about what you think being a BB/BS volunteer might involve.

2a. First, when people volunteer to be a Big Brother or Sister, how long do you think they might have to commit themselves to staying in the program?

   10%   1. 3 months or less,
   21%   2. 4 to 6 months,
   31%   3. 7 months to a year, or
   28%   4. more than 1 year.
   10%   5. Don't know/no opinion (DO NOT READ)

2b. About how often do you think Big Brothers or Sisters would get together with their Little Brother or Sister?

   54%   1. 1 or more times per week,
   35%   2. 2 or 3 times per month, or
    7%   3. once a month or less.
    4%   4. Don't know/no opinion (DO NOT READ)

2c. About how many hours at a time do you think Big Brothers or Sisters would spend with their Little Brother or Sister?

   24%   1. Less than 3 hours,
   55%   2. 3 to 5 hours,
   14%   3. 6 to 8 hours, or
    3%   4. more than 8 hours.
    4%   5. Don't know/no opinion (DO NOT READ)

2d. And how much money do you think Big Brothers or Sisters normally spend on their Little Brothers or Sisters when they get together?

8% 1. Nothing,
20% 2. $1 to $5,
32% 3. $6 to $10, or
27% 4. over $10.
13% 5. Don't know/no opinion (DO NOT READ)

3a. The BB/BS program usually has more children applying than adult volunteers to match them with. What do you think are some reasons people might have for not volunteering? (Check relevant categories below. Do not read list. When person stops, ask, "Anything else?" until he/she is through.)

27% Not interested in participating
11% Don't think they're qualified to participate
23% Unsure of what's required
71% Takes too much time
11% Costs too much
12% Worried about type of children in program
8% Don't want to do the parent's job
2% Takes too long to get processed by BB/BS
3% Don't know/no opinion
22% Other (specify) _____

3b. What do you think children in the program might be like? (Do not read list. Check all that apply, then ask, "Anything else?" till through.)

25% Behavioral problems/delinquent
19% Emotional problems
38% Lonely/ignored
28% Poor/underprivileged
3% Physically handicapped
15% Mostly: 1. White [5%] 2. Black [5%] 3. Hispanic [4%]. Other [0%]
8% Don't know/no opinion
20% Other (specify) *"Normal"* 12% *"Minority"* 3%

3c. If it would increase the number of children who could be matched with an adult in the program, do you think it would be OK to put a Little Brother with a Big Sister, if they both were willing? (Do not read list)

77% 1. Yes
10% 2. No
11% 3. Maybe/not sure
2% 4. Don't know/no opinion

3d. What about matching a Little Sister with a Big Brother, if they both were willing? (Do not read list)

58% 1. Yes
19% 2. No
21% 3. Maybe/not sure
2% 4. Don't know/no opinion

4. If you became a volunteer in the program, what are some things you might

like to do with your Little Brother or Sister? (Check all that apply. Do not read list. Probe—"Anything else?")

45%   Sports—playing or watching.
62%   Outdoor things—camping, bicycling, gardening, etc.
47%   Indoor things—reading, movies, going to the mall, etc.
21%   Hobbies and games—photography, collecting things, etc.
29%   Eating out—hamburgers, ice cream, etc.
 5%   Don't know/no opinion
21%   Other (specify) ————————————

5. I have just a question or two on BB/BS advertising. Can you recall any commercials or announcements on TV about the Big Brothers/Big Sisters program? (Do not read list.)

60%   1. Yes
28%   2. No
10%   3. Maybe/not sure
 1%   4. Don't know/no opinion

5a. (If yes) What do you think about their advertising? Would you say that it's (read list)

 9%[b]   1. Very good
37%   2. Pretty good
41%   3. OK—not good or bad
10%   4. Pretty bad
 2%   5. Very bad
 2%   6. Don't know/no opinion (DO NOT READ)

5b. Why do you feel that way? (summarize) ————————————————
——

6. I need to ask these last few questions so that I can group your answers with similar people I've talked to.

6a. Are you (read list)

22%   1. 18–22 years old,
40%   2. 23–34 years old,
26%   3. 35–50 years old, or
11%   4. over 50 years old?
 1%   5. Refused (Do not read)

6b. What is your occupation? (Do not read list, check appropriate category.)

20%   1. Professional/technical
11%   2. Manager/proprietor
 8%   3. Office/clerical
 9%   4. Sales
11%   5. Service
 8%   6. Housewife
20%   7. Student
 8%   8. Retired/unemployed

4%   9. Other (specify) _____

1%   10. Refused (Do not read)

6c. Would you classify yourself as (read list)

73%   1. White

10%   2. Black

12%   3. Hispanic

3%   4. Other (Ask, "Would you mind saying how you would classify yourself?")

2%   5. Refused (Do not read)

6d. And my last question is, what is your ZIP Code where you live?

_____   Refused   _____

6e. Record sex:

43%   1. Male

57%   2. Female

That's all! Thank you very much for your help.

Phone number   _____

Interviewer   _____

Date   _____

Verified by   _____

---

[a]Among percentage of those aware, not total sample.

[b]Among percentage who recall advertising, not total sample.

TABLE 8-1-3 Big Brothers/Big Sisters of Austin Survey Results (see Appendix 8-1B)

	Age				Race				Employment Status				Sex	
	18–22	23–34	35–50	51+	White	Black	Hispanic	Other	Employed	Unemployed	Student	Homemaker	Male	Female
Total	113	200	132	55	369	50	63	13	321	38	102	40	202	268
Q1														
Aware[a,b]	103 (91%)	174 (87%)	119 (90%)	47 (85%)	342 (93%)	36 (72%)	52 (83%)	9 (69%)	289 (90%)	33 (87%)	90 (88%)	35 (88%)	170 (84%)	246 (92%)
Q1a[c]														
TV commercials	63 (61%)	115 (66%)	81 (68%)	29 (62%)	211 (62%)	27 (75%)	38 (73%)	6 (67%)	189 (65%)	22 (67%)	57 (63%)	21 (60%)	112 (66%)	157 (64%)
Wednesday's child[d]	19 (18%)	31 (18%)	22 (18%)	13 (28%)	62 (18%)	9 (25%)	11 (21%)	1 (11%)	53 (18%)	12 (36%)	13 (14%)	8 (23%)	34 (20%)	48 (20%)
Radio	11 (11%)	16 (9%)	11 (9%)	4 (9%)	31 (9%)	1 (3%)	8 (15%)	1 (11%)	24 (8%)	4 (12%)	10 (11%)	4 (11%)	13 (8%)	28 (11%)
Volunteer[e]	27 (26%)	37 (21%)	16 (13%)	6 (13%)	73 (21%)	5 (14%)	9 (17%)	0 (0%)	56 (19%)	3 (9%)	23 (26%)	5 (14%)	33 (19%)	46 (19%)
Nonvolunteer	25 (24%)	60 (21%)	22 (18%)	15 (32%)	72 (21%)	8 (22%)	9 (17%)	2 (22%)	63 (22%)	6 (18%)	19 (21%)	8 (23%)	33 (19%)	59 (24%)
Other source	12 (12%)	28 (16%)	17 (14%)	9 (19%)	54 (16%)	1 (3%)	7 (13%)	2 (22%)	49 (17%)	5 (15%)	10 (11%)	3 (9%)	22 (13%)	38 (15%)
Don't know	2 (2%)	9 (5%)	9 (8%)	4 (9%)	20 (6%)	2 (6%)	1 (2%)	0 (0%)	17 (6%)	3 (9%)	1 (1%)	2 (6%)	9 (5%)	13 (5%)
Q1b[b,c]														
Help delinquents	22 (22%)	30 (17%)	17 (14%)	3 (6%)	55 (16%)	8 (22%)	6 (12%)	2 (22%)	46 (16%)	3 (9%)	19 (21%)	7 (20%)	42 (25%)	31 (13%)
Substitute parent	8 (8%)	23 (13%)	19 (16%)	10 (21%)	42 (12%)	5 (14%)	11 (21%)	2 (22%)	43 (15%)	5 (15%)	8 (9%)	5 (14%)	31 (18%)	26 (11%)
Adult friend	67 (66%)	104 (60%)	72 (61%)	29 (62%)	213 (63%)	21 (58%)	32 (62%)	5 (56%)	172 (60%)	21 (64%)	58 (65%)	21 (60%)	84 (49%)	164 (67%)
Other	5 (5%)	17 (10%)	10 (8%)	5 (11%)	30 (9%)	2 (6%)	3 (6%)	0 (0%)	27 (9%)	4 (12%)	4 (4%)	2 (6%)	13 (8%)	23 (9%)
Q2a														
0–3 months	15 (13%)	21 (10%)	8 (6%)	4 (7%)	34 (9%)	6 (12%)	8 (13%)	0 (0%)	32 (10%)	2 (5%)	13 (13%)	2 (5%)	26 (13%)	22 (8%)
4–6 months	28 (25%)	42 (21%)	22 (17%)	11 (20%)	74 (20%)	7 (14%)	16 (25%)	6 (46%)	61 (19%)	11 (29%)	25 (25%)	8 (20%)	42 (21%)	58 (22%)
7–12 months	38 (34%)	61 (30%)	40 (30%)	17 (31%)	115 (31%)	19 (38%)	19 (30%)	2 (15%)	99 (31%)	8 (21%)	31 (30%)	18 (45%)	59 (29%)	89 (33%)

Over 1 year	25 (22%)	61 (30%)	40 (30%)	17 (31%)	110 (30%)	14 (28%)	14 (22%)	2 (15%)	95 (30%)	11 (29%)	27 (26%)	10 (25%)	58 (29%)	77 (29%)
Don't know	7 (6%)	15 (8%)	22 (17%)	6 (11%)	36 (10%)	4 (8%)	6 (10%)	3 (23%)	34 (11%)	6 (16%)	6 (6%)	2 (5%)	17 (8%)	22 (8%)
Q2b[a,d,e]														
1 or more/week	72 (64%)	114 (57%)	55 (42%)	31 (56%)	211 (57%)	16 (32%)	37 (59%)	8 (62%)	166 (52%)	19 (50%)	66 (65%)	23 (58%)	103 (51%)	151 (56%)
2–3 times/month	31 (27%)	72 (36%)	43 (40%)	19 (35%)	130 (35%)	24 (48%)	16 (25%)	4 (31%)	126 (39%)	13 (34%)	29 (28%)	10 (24%)	76 (38%)	91 (34%)
1 or less/month	7 (6%)	12 (6%)	14 (11%)	2 (4%)	20 (5%)	5 (10%)	8 (13%)	0 (0%)	22 (7%)	1 (3%)	5 (5%)	5 (12%)	16 (8%)	18 (7%)
Don't know	3 (3%)	2 (1%)	10 (8%)	3 (5%)	8 (2%)	5 (10%)	2 (3%)	1 (8%)	7 (2%)	5 (13%)	2 (2%)	2 (5%)	7 (4%)	8 (3%)
Q2c[e]														
< 3 hours/visit	34 (30%)	44 (22%)	31 (23%)	12 (22%)	85 (23%)	14 (28%)	13 (21%)	6 (46%)	75 (23%)	8 (21%)	32 (31%)	7 (18%)	92 (31%)	57 (21%)
3–5 hours/visit	64 (57%)	113 (56%)	66 (50%)	29 (53%)	211 (57%)	22 (44%)	33 (52%)	4 (31%)	174 (54%)	20 (53%)	53 (52%)	26 (65%)	97 (48%)	151 (56%)
6–8 hours/visit	10 (9%)	26 (13%)	26 (20%)	10 (18%)	51 (14%)	11 (22%)	10 (16%)	1 (8%)	53 (16%)	4 (11%)	10 (10%)	10 (15%)	27 (13%)	43 (16%)
> 8 hours/visit	1 (1%)	12 (6%)	1 (1%)	1 (2%)	8 (2%)	1 (2%)	4 (6%)	0 (0%)	9 (3%)	2 (5%)	3 (3%)	0 (0%)	6 (3%)	7 (3%)
Don't know	4 (4%)	5 (2%)	9 (7%)	3 (5%)	14 (4%)	2 (4%)	3 (5%)	2 (15%)	10 (3%)	4 (11%)	4 (4%)	1 (2%)	10 (5%)	10 (4%)
Q2d[d,e]														
Spend $0	14 (12%)	16 (8%)	7 (5%)	4 (7%)	34 (9%)	3 (6%)	5 (8%)	0 (0%)	27 (8%)	3 (8%)	12 (12%)	0 (0%)	19 (9%)	22 (8%)
Spend $1 to $5	21 (19%)	44 (22%)	25 (19%)	12 (22%)	76 (21%)	10 (20%)	11 (17%)	1 (8%)	61 (19%)	12 (32%)	19 (19%)	10 (25%)	38 (19%)	55 (21%)
Spend $6 to $10	43 (38%)	54 (32%)	37 (28%)	14 (25%)	122 (33%)	14 (28%)	20 (32%)	3 (23%)	98 (31%)	7 (18%)	38 (37%)	17 (42%)	61 (30%)	92 (34%)
Spend over $10	27 (24%)	56 (28%)	40 (30%)	12 (22%)	93 (25%)	17 (34%)	20 (32%)	4 (31%)	99 (31%)	8 (21%)	23 (23%)	7 (18%)	64 (32%)	62 (23%)
Don't know	8 (7%)	19 (10%)	23 (17%)	13 (24%)	44 (12%)	6 (12%)	7 (11%)	5 (39%)	36 (11%)	8 (21%)	10 (10%)	6 (15%)	20 (10%)	37 (14%)
Q3c LB with BS—yes[a,b]	91 (81%)	160 (80%)	92 (70%)	44 (80%)	291 (79%)	37 (74%)	49 (78%)	8 (62%)	244 (76%)	28 (74%)	85 (83%)	31 (78%)	144 (71%)	213 (79%)
Q3d LS with BB—yes[a,b,c]	72 (64%)	125 (63%)	64 (48%)	30 (55%)	228 (62%)	20 (40%)	33 (52%)	9 (69%)	187 (58%)	18 (47%)	67 (66%)	21 (52%)	114 (57%)	155 (58%)

TABLE 8-1-3 (continued)

	Age				Race				Employment Status				Sex	
	18–22	23–34	35–50	51+	White	Black	Hispanic	Other	Employed	Unemployed	Student	Homemaker	Male	Female
Q5														
Recall TV ad— yes	74 (65%)	126 (63%)	76 (58%)	27 (49%)	230 (62%)	29 (58%)	35 (56%)	5 (38%)	191 (60%)	20 (53%)	67 (66%)	26 (65%)	114 (57%)	166 (62%)
Q5a,b,e,f														
Ad quality— very good	5 (7%)	7 (6%)	9 (12%)	6 (22%)	17 (8%)	3 (11%)	4 (11%)	2 (40%)	18 (10%)	1 (5%)	3 (4%)	5 (21%)	4 (4%)	21 (13%)
Ad quality— good	27 (37%)	54 (43%)	20 (27%)	13 (48%)	86 (38%)	11 (39%)	13 (37%)	2 (40%)	68 (36%)	11 (55%)	26 (39%)	9 (38%)	36 (32%)	71 (44%)
Ad quality— OK	30 (41%)	56 (45%)	31 (42%)	6 (22%)	98 (61%)	10 (36%)	12 (34%)	1 (20%)	84 (45%)	6 (30%)	29 (43%)	5 (21%)	55 (49%)	53 (33%)
Ad quality— bad	11 (15%)	8 (6%)	13 (18%)	2 (7%)	25 (11%)	4 (14%)	6 (17%)	0 (0%)	18 (10%)	2 (10%)	9 (13%)	5 (21%)	17 (15%)	18 (11%)

[a] Responses vary significantly ($p < .05$) by race.
[b] Responses vary significantly ($p < .05$) by sex.
[c] Percents based on number aware of BB/BS.
[d] Responses vary significantly ($p < .05$) by employment status.
[e] Responses vary significantly ($p < .05$) by age.
[f] Percents based on those with an opinion about advertising quality.

Morning Treat Coffee

The petite Morning Treat Company based in Baton Rouge, Louisiana, was attempting to battle the giants of the coffee industry by building a national market and franchise for the coffee bag. Although the company had sold over one million bags per month during the previous year in foreign markets such as Japan and through specialty retailers like Neiman-Marcus, management was keenly interested in expanding distribution and sales through supermarkets.

The company's product was marketed under the name "Morning Treat Coffee Bags." Like the familiar tea bag, the coffee bag allowed an individual to brew a single serving of fresh ground coffee with the ease of using instant coffee. The bags were available in ten roasts including dark, coffee with chicory, regular, and decaffeinated. Each bag was sealed in a foil pouch (see Exhibit 8-2-1), which permitted maximum freshness for nine months. Designed for convenience, the coffee bag seemed especially suited for the traveler, office worker, student, and one- to three-cups-per-day coffee drinker, although the retail price was almost a third more than that for regular coffee on a per cup basis.

EXHIBIT 8-2-1   Morning Treat Coffee Bag and Individual Foil Package

This case was written by Marshall Taylor of Young & Rubicam, New York, and John H. Murphy, The University of Texas at Austin. It is intended for use in generating classroom discussion and is not meant to illustrate either the effective or ineffective handling of an administrative situation. Used by permission.

According to Sam Gallo, developer and president of the Morning Treat Coffee Company, the coffee bag concept was not new. Almost 75 years ago, tea merchants invented the tea bag. These bags consisted of silk sachets full of tea leaves. Naturally, coffee was also put into the sachets, but the bags went stale and rancid since the oils and acid contained in the ground coffee spoiled them.

For decades various individuals tried unsuccessfully to make a coffee bag. Then, in 1960, an American engineer, Earl Hiscock, began working to solve the coffee bag dilemma. He tried sealing the bag in a vacuum within a container. This kept the coffee from going stale, but the bag still became discolored and spoiled. Hiscock discovered that the cellulosic structure of the bags was responsible for the spoilage. Seven years later he patented an inert, noncellulosic filter-like material and the pouch design to hold the coffee. However, these were only theoretical patents since Hiscock never produced coffee bags.

That task was left to Sam Gallo. He obtained the patents from Hiscock and made the coffee bag practical by patenting several processes that made mass production feasible. Although the coffee bag became a practical and workable reality, General Foods and Procter & Gamble—the nation's largest coffee manufacturers—had chosen not to venture into this product line extension.

Gallo approached some of these coffee marketers but found that they were not interested in coffee bags. Gallo felt that because these companies had a virtual monopoly over the coffee industry, there was no reason why they should produce a coffee bag unless a competitor threatened a significant share of their market. At the same time, Gallo believed that if General Foods were to market a coffee bag, Procter & Gamble would have one on the market within 90 days. However, unless Gallo's company gained a significant share of the coffee market, the giant companies would probably ignore him and the coffee bag.

THE COFFEE MARKET AND THE PRODUCT'S POSITIONING

More coffee was consumed in the United States than in any other country in the world. Industry sources estimated that more than seven out of ten adults in the United States drank coffee. Further, on a typical winter day, Americans consumed approximately 400 million cups of coffee. Retail sales of coffee in supermarkets were a multibillion-dollar business.

The light and medium users (those who drank one to three cups per day) accounted for roughly three-fourths of all coffee consumption. Coffee consumption was spread fairly evenly among various age groups. The southern and north-central parts of the United States accounted for almost 60 percent of coffee usage.

Gallo realized that to garner even a fraction of the huge potential market for his firm's coffee bags, Morning Treat would need an effective introductory advertising campaign. In considering the use of advertising, he also was aware that Morning Treat faced the very difficult task of convincing consumers not only to break with traditional means of preparing coffee and try a new concept, but also to buy an unfamiliar brand.

On the other hand, Gallo felt Morning Treat was fortunate in that it was significantly different from the other products in its category. Thus, he believed it could potentially carve a niche for itself in the coffee market. Its competitors were regular and instant coffee marketers, not other coffee bag manufacturers.

Morning Treat's main benefit was convenience. Therefore, Gallo believed it should be marketed to those consumers who did not like or need to make a pot of coffee but who would rather drink fresh-brewed coffee than instant. This uniquely positioned Morning Treat somewhere between regular ground coffee and instant. Gallo was convinced that this positioning should apply only to its common coffee types: regular and decaffeinated. Other types and roasts of coffee, such as Louisiana dark, Colombian, and Santos, were specialty items. Morning Treat's efforts should focus on the regular and decaffeinated coffee markets.

In order to develop an effective advertising campaign for the coffee bag, Gallo hired an advertising agency. The agency developed a number of recommendations, which are described in the following section.

THE AGENCY'S RECOMMENDATIONS

First, the agency recommended a new name for the product—"Java." The agency pointed out that a simple and short name was preferable to Morning Treat (which in itself was limiting). "Java" was descriptive and suggested exotic, romantic experiences.

Most important, "java" was a slang term for coffee. According to the dictionary, "Java" could also refer to the main island of Indonesia, where a large amount of coffee was grown, or to the coffee bean or plant. Therefore, "Java" should make the product instantly recognizable as some sort of coffee product.

To specify the product even more, the agency recommended that the words "coffee bags" be used in conjunction with the new name Java to produce immediate recognition that the product was more than a new brand of coffee. Thus, the new name under which the product would be advertised was "Java Coffee Bags."

Before designing a package or advertising, the agency designed a logo for the product (see Exhibit 8-2-2). The typeface Korinna Heavy was chosen because it is bold and easy to read. The use of serif type helped to create a pleasing visual effect. The upper case "J" was elongated to increase the uniqueness of the logo. The letters were spaced closely together to reflect the current style of setting type, and the coffee bag was hung from the "J" to allow the product to be visible every time that the logo was displayed. This mnemonic device created an intriguing effect. The agency believed that the logo had a simple, posterlike quality that would easily stand out against the clutter and competition on the grocery store shelf.

EXHIBIT 8-2-2 Proposed Java Logo

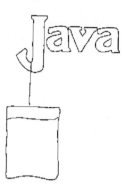

Following the development of a logo, the agency created a new package design (see Exhibit 8-2-3). The agency stressed the importance of having an aesthetically pleasing package, since the visual impression the brand made on the consumer through advertisements and in the store was a crucial factor in determining consumer acceptance.

The package for Java Coffee Bags was designed to give the product a specific identity and color as well as provide a quick description of the contents. The colors used were light and dark brown tones that conveyed a feeling of richness—a very important attribute for a coffee. The package design consisted of the logo over a photograph of coffee beans spread over a neutral-colored wooden butcher block. The white letters and coffee bag showed up very well against the dark brown coffee beans. The butcher block added an appropriate texture and contrast to the photograph.

In addition to a new name, logo, and package design, the agency proposed a campaign series of print, outdoor, and broadcast ads. Sample roughs from the introductory print campaign are presented in Exhibits 8-2-4 and 8-2-5 (visuals are indications of photographs). All the headlines for the introductory print ads

EXHIBIT 8-2-3 Proposed Java Package Design

EXHIBIT 8-2-4   Layout for Introductory Print Advertisement (1)

EXHIBIT 8-2-5   Layout for Introductory Print Advertisement (2)

were written to announce news to the consumer. Each headline offered a distinct benefit: the coffee bag is small, quick, convenient, easy, and neat. Each headline positioned the coffee bag against brewing regular coffee and also offered the instant coffee drinker an alternative. Copy in these introductory ads

EXHIBIT 8-2-6 Layout for Print Advertisement (1)

told lovers of the taste of brewed coffee that they could have brewed flavor with the convenience of instant. It also told those who drank instant that fresh brewed coffee was now just as easy. Phrases like "Meet the world's smallest coffee maker" implied that the product was "new" without employing the overused word itself.

The tag line "fresh ground coffee by the cup" was used throughout the entire campaign. This signature line served to remind the consumer that Java Coffee Bags contained real fresh ground coffee and could be brewed conveniently by the cup.

The second phase of the print campaign followed naturally from the first. Exhibits 8-2-6 and 8-2-7 present ads designed for use after the initial

EXHIBIT 8-2-7 Layout for Print Advertisement (2)

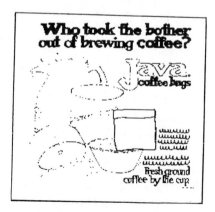

introduction of the product. In this series of ads, the major benefit stressed was the convenience of not having to deal with the complications of making regular ground coffee (whether in an automatic coffee maker, drip pot, or percolator). The headline questions were immediately answered with the logo. The product was the hero of these advertisements as it hung from the "J" of the logo. In the background were visuals that reinforced the headline (visuals are indications of photographs).

Layouts for Java outdoor boards were also presented to the client. These boards were simple. They consisted of a single phrase and employed the device of a coffee bag hanging from the J on the board. The bag extended off of the board. This embellishment created a visual surprise for the viewer. The headline on each board played off the bag concept, thus reemphasizing the packaging convenience of the product.

In addition to the print and outdoor ads, the agency suggested a number of specific radio and television commercials. All of these spots employed music and stressed many of the same copy points used in the print ads.

A FOCUS GROUP EVALUATION OF THE COFFEE BAG AND THE PROPOSED CREATIVE STRATEGY

After presenting an analysis of the situation facing the Morning Treat Coffee Company, as well as its recommendations for advertising and promotion, the agency suggested conducting a small research project to get a reading on consumer reactions to the product and the advertising. The agency proposed that a focus group interview be conducted prior to even regional introduction of the coffee bag through a mass media campaign. Gallo agreed that such a project would be useful.

To assess consumer reactions to the coffee bag and the proposed creative strategies, the agency conducted a focus group interview using female coffee drinkers. Following discussions with Gallo and as a first step in conducting the research, the agency developed a set of six objectives for the focus group interview. These objectives were as follows:

1. To assess acceptability of the coffee bag concept.
2. To discover apprehensions, negative feelings, or uncertainties concerning the coffee bag.
3. To examine perceptions of taste compared with that of regular and instant coffee.
4. To assess likeliness of use.
5. To evaluate potential product names.
6. To have the group evaluate and critique proposed creative campaign strategies.

A random sample of adult females was selected from the Baton Rouge telephone directory and contacted regarding possible participation in the group interview. Women who were not coffee drinkers were eliminated. Those who agreed to participate were sent a sample of the product along with a letter thanking them for their cooperation. Eleven women agreed to participate in the group interview. Of these, six actually attended the session. The entire session, which lasted about an hour and a half, was recorded on audiotapes.

The session was held in the evening at the agency's office. The agency's conference room was set up with living room–type chairs, a low coffee table, and other tables for refreshments. The session was moderated by a male principal of the agency who had considerable experience in moderating focus groups.

At the conclusion of the session, a short demographic questionnaire was administered to the six participants (see Exhibit 8-2-8).

The day after the focus group session was held, the agency reported to Gallo that the results of the session were encouraging. Gallo immediately indicated that he did not want to discuss the project prior to receiving a formal written report and analysis of the session. In addition, he requested a transcript of the session, which he wanted to read prior to evaluating the agency's formal report on the outcome of the research project. Gallo emphasized that all discussion of the results of the session should be postponed until he had had ample time to study the transcript and the agency's formal report.

The agency submitted a complete transcript of the session and its formal report to Gallo for his consideration. Gallo was particularly concerned with the group's reactions to the proposed product name, Java, and its evaluations of the proposed creative strategies. Appendix 8-2 presents the segments of the focus group session most relevant to these issues. A meeting was arranged at

---

EXHIBIT 8-2-8   Java Coffee Bags Focus Group Respondent Profile

Occupations

Retired teacher, high school counselor, program director, office manager, product planner for IBM, and personnel employment manager

Marital Status

Married (4); single (1); widowed (1)

Number of Children under 18

Zero (5); two (1)

Education

Bachelor's degree (1); Master's degree (5)

Average Number of Cups Consumed Each Day

Average = 4 cups
(1 cup [1]; 2 cups [1]; 3 cups [2]; 7 cups [1]; 8 cups [1])

Approximate Household Income

$15,000–$24,999 (1)
$25,000–$39,999 (4)
$40,000+   (1)

Ages

30, 31, 31, 34, 56, 66

the Morning Treat Company office a week later to discuss the conclusions that could be drawn from the focus group project.

Questions for Discussion and Review

1. Why are focus groups so popular among advertising researchers?

2. What are the major advantages and disadvantages of the focus group data collection methodology?

3. What major criteria should be used in evaluating the procedures followed in conducting a focus group?

4. What specific conclusions can be reached from reviewing the transcript of the session? What changes in the agency's recommendations do the findings suggest?

5. What changes in the procedures followed in conducting the focus group interview session described in the case would you recommend?

Appendix 8-2

Moderator: I thank you for coming tonight and your help is greatly appreciated. What we intend to do is to explore a new concept in the coffee industry—coffee bags—and this will take place as a group discussion. And we will consider several questions about the product. The tape recorder here will be used only to transcribe what we say. No names or anything like that—everybody's anonymous. And I urge everybody to express your opinions. Anything you want to say, positive or negative. I'm not selling these bags. I don't get any commission off of them, and so I don't have any interest in them. And feel free to serve yourself refreshments. You can get up, move around, and the rest rooms are down the other end of the hall down there. So, we probably should start out with everybody introducing themselves, and give a short history of what you do. You can start, Carol.

Carol: I'm Carol _____, and I work as an office manager with a large association, and I'm in charge of setting up and coordinating the association.

Linda: I'm Linda _____, and I'm manager of a personnel office. I've been there about 13 years. I spend a lot of time at my job.

Dianne: I'm Dianne _____, and I work for Product Planning—I work in Product Planning for IBM.

Jean: My name is Jean _____, and I work part time as a free-lance graphic designer or advertising person, but the biggest part of my day is spent working as a program director for a psychological testing company.

Katherine: I'm Katherine _____, and I'm a retired schoolteacher. I'm having a good time now. I don't miss the paper grading at all.

Vivian: I'm Vivian _____, and I'm a high school counselor.

Moderator: Okay. Well, I'm Mike, and I'm your discussion leader. The first question I want to deal with tonight is what do you think of the coffee bag concept. I guess all of you have tried it by now, and just what are your comments?

Katherine: I think it would be a handy thing to have, myself. I can think of times that I would have loved to have had a coffee bag with me.

Linda: It would be a lot easier to carry around than a jar of instant coffee, that's for sure. It's nice that it's premeasured, too.

Vivian: I would find an instant coffee that was packaged that way of more use, because this really has to be—you have to have boiling water to really dissolve it, and it takes two or three minutes, where instant coffee is ready as soon as you put the water on it. And I didn't think this was as good as most of the instant coffees.

Jean: I think as a concept it's really good—I mean, certainly it's parallel to tea —you know, put a tea bag in and pour the water over it. But personally it's not something I would really use. But I think the concept is good for many cases.

Moderator: Okay. If you had to pick one aspect—just one—what do you like most about the coffee bag?

All: Convenience.

Moderator: Okay. What do you like least about the coffee bag?

All: Taste.

(At this point the group continued to discuss the product itself, apprehensions and uncertainties toward the coffee bag concept, perceptions compared with regular and instant coffee, and the likelihood of use. This lengthy discussion is omitted from this transcript.)

Moderator: Okay, let's change directions just a little bit now. Let's talk more about—other than taste and all—let's talk about maybe a name for the coffee. If you were to name this product—let's say you haven't seen the package, you don't know what's on the package—if you just knew about this product, what names would you come up with to sell it?

Carol: I'd keep it simple, like tea bag coffee bag. Because somebody at work—I said I have to go to this silly thing to test coffee or something—no offense, but, you know— and I was showing—I said, here, I need to test this. She said, what is it? I said it's a coffee bag like a tea bag. I said you have to keep it simple when you're comparing them.

Dianne: The first thing that came to my mind when you asked that question was something with which I could identify—the bag. Which is a tea bag. Like flow-through coffee bags.

Moderator: Well, the company itself is called Morning Treat. Do you think that just calling it coffee bags is too generic a name?

Linda: It might well be if other manufacturers come out with the same product. Then you have "*The* Coffee Bag," or something like that. But I think Morning Treat in some ways gives the wrong impression, because it's for convenience.

Moderator: Anybody else think of any names?

Dianne: You know, you think of other products that came on the market as firsts that I think of, like Kleenex. I mean, how many of us say, "May I have a tissue, please." They always say, "Do you have a Kleenex?"

Moderator: But that's a brand name that's become a generic name. Coffee bags is a generic name to begin with.

Dianne: That's right. I mean, I think of those things as firsts on the market, and it would be a name that would be a catchall for it.

Moderator: Do you think that they would be disadvantaged if, let's say, some other competition came out and if they were coffee bags—just coffee bags—I don't know as far as copyright how it would be considered. Like Procter & Gamble can come out with it and call it "Sanka Coffee Bags." Do you think that would pose any problems as far as if you called your product just coffee bags?

Jean: I think it would.

Linda: You think about radio advertising. You don't have a product or an image to identify with. So you're advertising coffee bags. That's not going to—you know, how do you differentiate between this coffee bag and another manufacturer's coffee bag?

Moderator: So you're saying you might need a brand name to associate it with.

Linda: Right. To identify it.

Moderator: Any names that come to mind?

Jean: Are you saying that you need a name instead of coffee bags, or some catchy thing to go with it?

Linda: I think it needs something more than just coffee bags.

Moderator: Vivian, were you going to say something?

Vivian: Well, a lot of those brand names that have come out and become generic names like Kleenex and so forth, the sound of that name doesn't have that much to do with the product.

Dianne: That's right, all it is is a catch name.

Vivian: So I don't think you need to necessarily have something that says coffee bags. You need some catchy name and once that's established—

Dianne: Like Sanka. Sanka has nothing to it that suggests coffee, lack of caffeine, or anything.

Linda: But something like Easy Time would convey the simpleness of using it. Maybe it's too simple.

Moderator: Any other names?

Dianne: Bean Bags.

Carol: Something like One at a Time.

Moderator: One Bag at a Time? I couldn't resist.

Dianne: If it were a one-word—just like we were saying, like Sanka, Kleenex, Xerox. Where did the word Sanka come from, though?

Jean: Turn it around: Bag of Coffee or something. Initials usually don't work.

Moderator: P.D.M. Coffee Company.

Katherine: We aren't very creative, are we?

Moderator: Okay. The next question. Somebody did—I think it was Jean —mentioned something about this. What do you think about the current name of the product—Morning Treat Coffee Bags?

Jean: Well, I just thought it made people think just of in the morning, when in fact coffee can be had at night or anytime.

Linda: Maybe Coffee Treat.

Jean: I don't think Morning Treat is good. It seems to limit it in your mind.

Vivian: Quick Coffee.

Katherine: Presto.

Linda: Isn't there something?

Moderator: It's a cooker. Okay, I'll tell you a name someone has come up with. If you hate it, that's fine. I mean, don't—my feelings are nothing, because I don't care. What do you think about the name Java?

Jean: Isn't that the name of a kind of coffee?

Moderator: Okay. It is the name of a kind of coffee.

Jean: I'm not talking about Kava, I'm talking about—

Moderator: You're right, a roast. It is a particular roast, you're right. But what do you think about making it the brand name and calling it Java Coffee Bags?

Linda: It gives you a coffee association and gives you sort of an exotic —that gives me an exotic feeling.

Katherine: Well, I think it's repetitious to have Java and Coffee Bags.

Vivian: Yeah, because Java is sort of a slang term that means coffee.

Linda: I think it might raise your expectations, particularly on this brand. To me, that gives it a real rich, mellow connotation, and I think on this particular line the expectations—

Katherine: It indicates real roast coffee.

Linda: It's got a nice—sounds good—nice and short. You know, sort of sticks with you.

Katherine: But I'd call it just Java Bags.

Moderator: Just Java or Java Bags or Java in a Bag, maybe.

Dianne: What's the Spanish term for coffee, café?

Vivian: Café.

Moderator: French is café. I don't know about the Spanish.

Jean: But still, if you were to do your specialty coffees, would that form sort of a conflict?

Moderator: You would have to advertise it with some sort of label on the box that says the different roasts that they have, which they do have. I will now show you some preliminary layouts for an introductory creative campaign for coffee bags using the name Java. Please comment on whether or not you like the approaches taken and why. Be honest. Also, remember that these are only roughs and not finished layouts. The drawings represent indications of photographs. I would first like to get your impressions of some package designs. Here is the package design currently used by the Morning Treat Coffee Company, and on the back is a proposed design using the name Java. The same basic design is used on package boxes of eight, sixteen, and forty-eight individual bags. (See Exhibits 8-2-1 and 8-2-3.)

Carol: I really like the colors used in the Java package. The browns remind me of coffee—a rich-tasting coffee.

Linda: These are coffee beans, but what is the background?

Moderator: A butcher's block.

Linda: Oh, I agree with Carol. I like the brown tones very much. I think it's appealing, but I wonder if the bright orange of the original package might stand out better on the grocery shelf.

Katherine: I don't know. Personally the orange package with the yellow and white lettering scares me off. It's not very aesthetically pleasing.

Dianne: It really doesn't make any difference to me. I don't think the design of a package affects my purchases.

Jean: Oh, sure it does.

Dianne: Well not consciously, at least.

Katherine: "Java" coffee bags bothers me. Isn't that redundant?

Linda: Grammatically, maybe, but I think it's got a nice flow to it. I wouldn't think that it would bother the average consumer.

Vivian: I like the simpleness of the Java package. It's not cluttered like the Morning Treat package. To me that's very important in getting a consumer to notice the package on the shelf—simple design.

Moderator: Now I would like for you to look at a couple of layouts that are representative of series of layouts for an introductory print campaign for Java Coffee Bags. (See Exhibits 8-2-4 and 8-2-5.) Look at the ads briefly and then comment on them.

Vivian: As I said about the package design, I like the simple, uncluttered appearance of these ads. They are very appealing. A lot better than those old Folger's ads. I get so tired of Mrs. Olson or Cora or whatever her name is.

Jean: For me, the one that says "The world's quickest coffee maker" is the most appealing. For me "quick" is an important benefit. I hate to take time to make coffee. I've got more important things to do.

Vivian: Do you really think it's quicker than some of those automatic coffee makers? They're pretty fast.

Linda: If you count the time that it takes to measure the coffee and all that, it would be. All you have to do with the coffee bag is drop it in the water.

Katherine: I like the headline that emphasizes small. For me that's convenient. You can drop it in your purse and take it anywhere with you. Saying "The world's smallest coffee maker" and having the coffee bag over the cup of coffee is eye-catching. It sort of makes you say, "That's a clever little product."

Moderator: Carol, you were going to say something.

Carol: Oh, well, I was just going to say that I agree with Vivian about the appearance of the layouts. I think it was a good idea to use coffee mugs. They always make me think of rich coffee more than a coffee cup.

Moderator: Any other comments?

Linda: Oh, the "Fresh ground coffee by the cup." Is that going to be on all the ads?

Moderator: Yes. It's called a tag line.

Linda: Well, it's a good idea. It sums up what the coffee bag is.

Katherine: I think you should put it on the package, too. If not on the front then on the back or side somewhere.

Moderator: Now I want to look at a second series of ads that would be a continuation of the introductory ads that you have just seen. (See Exhibits 8-2-6 and 8-2-7.)

Linda: Oh, that first one was written for me. I always make a mess when I make coffee. I don't know what it is, but I inevitably spill a little. I'm really not that messy all the time. This ad really hits home.

Jean: The second one was written for me. I hate making coffee. This ad describes it perfectly. Any coffee that will take the bother out of brewing coffee I'll buy.

Vivian: Well again, I like the appearance of the ads. It's good that the coffee bag is displayed prominently. I think they go well with the first advertisements that you showed us. I can relate with the bother of making coffee, too. It's a good idea.

Dianne: What are these things right here?

Moderator: It's an indication of coffee grounds in a filter.

Dianne: Things you have to dump out and throw away.

Moderator: Right.

Dianne: I can relate to that. It's so much easier just to throw away the coffee bag when you're finished.

Linda: Those grounds are messy. Especially when you spill some on the floor. Yuk.

Katherine: Is there any copy that goes with these ads?

Moderator: Yes. These lines here indicate where the copy will go. However, I have not included the actual copy because I just want your immediate opinions on the ad concepts. If you're lucky, 6 percent of your readers will read the body copy. It's really secondary. Any other comments? If not, that will bring the session to a close. I do thank you all for coming tonight; you have been extremely helpful. I'll be glad to answer any questions that you may have. Feel free to help yourself to more coffee and cookies.

C A S E **8 - 3**

El Rancho Grande, Inc.

James Martinez, president of El Rancho Grande, was confident that he had an idea that would enable his company to become less than totally dependent on the national supermarket chain under whose private label his firm's output was marketed. Although he was satisfied with his firm's arrangement with the supermarket chain, the even modest success of a product under his own label was important to him from a psychological standpoint.

This case was written by John H. Murphy and Leonard Ruben. It is intended for use in generating classroom discussion and is not meant to illustrate either the effective or ineffective handling of an administrative situation. The identity of the firm has been disguised.

El Rancho Grande was a relatively small food-processing and canning company located in south Texas. The firm produced three basic types of canned products— tomatoes, peppers, and Mexican sauces. These products were packaged in a variety of can sizes ranging from seven ounces to six pounds.

The El Rancho Grande contract with the supermarket chain did not preclude the canning, labeling, and selling of products under the El Rancho Grande label. Realistically, however, Martinez was well aware of the formidable obstacles to his firm's achieving distribution in retail food stores, much less a respectable sales volume. In light of these obstacles, he proposed to distribute a food specialty item eventually through gift, gourmet, and other specialty stores. At the present time he felt the product could be sold on a mail-order basis. The whole proposal hinged to some extent on the Texas mystique.

THE TEXAS MYSTIQUE

Martinez felt that the time was right to capitalize on an apparently sustained wave of national interest in the cowboy mystique in general and the state of Texas in particular. Fueled by considerable national media attention, Texas chic seemed to have captured an enduring place in the national consciousness. Within the state, this same trend was reflected in a marked increase in state pride and a closer identification with people, places, and things uniquely Texan.

A number of consumer products had successfully utilized their Texas heritage in their marketing efforts. In addition to Texas beers, boots, cowboy hats, and Western wear, a large number of novelty items were available. These items included Texas ties, a wide variety of T-shirts, belt buckles, jigsaw puzzles, cookbooks, kites, and beer mugs. Three of the more unusual of these products are briefly described below.

- *Artesia:* A mineral water promoted as 100 percent pure and sparkling from the Texas Hill Country. The product was retailed in supermarkets in quarts and in six-packs of 12-ounce bottles by a firm based in San Antonio. The water, taken from the famous Edwards aquifer, was advertised in full-page magazine advertisements as a stand-alone healthful drink or as a mixer and was positioned against Perrier.

- *The Ice of Texas:* Ice trays that produced cubes in the shape of the state of Texas. This product was advertised as the state's "official" ice tray that made cubes with a distinctive flair. The product was sold through mail orders and a range of gourmet, kitchenware, and specialty stores.

- *Texas Cutting Boards:* A 1¼-inch-thick maple butcher block board shaped like the state of Texas. These cutting boards were available in two sizes and promoted as being individually handcrafted in Texas. The boards were expensive and available through mail order and gourmet, specialty, and department stores.

THE PRODUCT

Martinez's product idea, to be marketed under the El Rancho Grande label, was a sauce for use as an appetizer or snack, with chips or in preparing Mexican food. The new product was a slight variation of a product produced for the supermarket chain. The chain's product was branded under the chain's private label and identified as "Home Style Mexican Sauce."

By substituting jalapeño peppers for serrano peppers and adding carrots to the recipe for the chain's sauce, Martinez created a product he named "Texas Style Jalapeño Sauce." The ingredients as listed on the can were fresh tomatoes, onion, jalapeño peppers, carrot, iodized salt, and coriander. Variations in the proportion and variety of jalapeño peppers produced three versions of the sauce—mild, warm, and hot.

To get some feedback on likely acceptance of the new sauce, Martinez had some of his employees offer samples to adult shoppers as they exited supermarkets in a nearby community. Shoppers were offered a choice of tortilla, corn, or potato chips and three bowls of sauce marked mild, warm, and hot. After trying one or any combinations of the chips and sauces they wished, the shoppers were asked several questions to gauge their reaction to the sauce.

Although extremely informal, the results of this test were encouraging. Over 70 percent of the adults sampled reported they liked the product and would consider purchasing it, assuming it was competitively priced.

Encouraged by the shoppers' reaction, Martinez began to make plans to market the sauce. He decided that the sauce would be promoted as a specialty/gift item with a very high price relative to the cost of the ingredients and processing. The product would be placed in seven-ounce cans or glass containers and sold only in six-packs.

PACKAGING AND ADVERTISING

Martinez employed the services of an advertising design studio to produce the product's label and packaging (see Exhibits 8-3-1 and 8-3-2). In addition, the design firm was asked to produce several different creative approaches for direct-response advertising to be placed in print media.

A subjective evaluation of four alternative approaches narrowed the number of treatments to two. Three different-sized magazine ads ($\frac{1}{3}, \frac{1}{6}$, and $\frac{1}{12}$ page) using each of the two strategies are presented in Exhibits 8-3-3 and 8-3-4.

AN ADVERTISING TEST

Martinez was reluctant to commit to anything beyond very modest production or promotion of the new sauce without conducting some empirical research. He felt that before he proceeded, an advertising test should be designed to gain insights into several basic questions regarding the product.

EXHIBIT 8-3-1 Label Design for El Rancho Grande Texas-Style Japaleño Sauce

EXHIBIT 8-3-2 Six-pack of El Rancho Grande Texas-Style Jalapeño Sauce

First, it was necessary to determine what level of demand the new sauce would generate through direct-response advertising. Second, the test should be designed to evaluate the alternative creative treatments. Finally, there were the important issues of which individual magazine's audience would be most responsive and whether residents of Texas were better prospects than nonresidents.

Martinez suspected that some combination of state, regional, or city magazines would be best for the test. Although he was aware of the availability

EXHIBIT 8-3-3 El Rancho Grande Advertisements: Creative Strategy A

of regional and single-market editions of several national magazines, he wondered how many of these magazines might have split-run capabilities for testing the two creative treatments, and if this type of test would be appropriate.

Total media costs for the test could not run above $12,000; Martinez felt that any test should be as inexpensive as possible. Naturally, he felt the larger ads would pull best, but he was not sure he could afford to pay for these versions. He realized trade-offs would probably be necessary in conducting any research that sought to answer some or all of the basic questions he wanted answered.

EXHIBIT 8-3-4   El Rancho Grande Advertisements: Creative Strategy B

Questions for Discussion and Review

1. Are there any additional evaluations or reviews that Martinez should conduct prior to designing a formal test?

2. In light of financial constraints, should Martinez attempt to answer so many questions through a single test?

3. What general form should a test designed to provide data useful in answering Martinez's questions take?

C A S E   **8 - 4**

Hi-Power Beverage Company

Hi-Power Beverage Company produced and marketed several carbonated and noncarbonated lines of canned fruit- and cola-flavored soft drinks. Charles Iverson was the product manager for Upper C, a vitamin-enriched fruit drink line sold in the canned juice sections of grocery stores. The key promotional tool for the line was network television advertising, supplemented with spot TV in seasonally appropriate markets.

Iverson's usual procedure in the development of campaign strategy was to simply turn the problem, with relevant market data, over to the agency. The agency's account person, Katherine Cordaro of Cordaro, Oritt, and Harmon, Inc., would review the data, consult with Iverson in deciding upon a selling proposition, and then become somewhat reclusive until she returned with a "winning" campaign idea.

Ultimately, this single idea (along with an obviously poorer idea) would be developed into a storyboard and then presented to Iverson and the group product manager, Paul Waters. The presentation was usually supported by impressive multimedia techniques. In this way, even a relatively mediocre concept could be made to look good. After a few minor changes, Iverson and Waters would ordinarily decide upon the better of the two ideas. The agency would then move quickly to production and scheduling, where the media commission structure would begin generating revenue.

Now Iverson was beginning to question the procedure. He felt that there must be a better approach toward developing advertising campaigns for his company.

DEVELOPING ADVERTISING TACTICS

Over lunch one day, Iverson stumbled into a conversation between two members of Hi-Power's marketing research department. They were discussing some intriguing ideas from a study done by a researcher named Irwin Gross. As Iverson left the lunch, his head was swimming with the possibilities suggested to him. In approaching ad strategy, an advertising agency could either (1) move quickly through the creative execution stages and on to scheduling, thus maximizing the company's media expenditures, or (2) spend

---

This case was written by William R. Swinyard, Brigham Young University. It is intended for use in generating classroom discussion and is not meant to illustrate either the effective or ineffective handling of an administrative situation. The identity of the firm has been disguised. Used by permission.

TABLE 8-4-1   Consumer Perceptions of Enriched Fruit Drinks

Attribute	Attribute Importance (Weight)[b]	Consumer Evaluations[a]			
		Hi-Power	Brand A	Brand B	Brand C
Taste	.40	8	9	7	4
Calorie content	.18	7	5	7	4
Price	.15	6	8	6	10
Color	.02	6	7	7	6
Nourishment	.25	9	6	8	5

[a]On a 10-point scale, where 10 is the preferred rating.
[b]Refers to the relative salience of each attribute to consumers in discriminating between the purchase of one brand versus another.

far more time and money in the development and production of three or four solid alternative creative executions, copy test them, pick the highest-scoring execution, then move to media placement.

"Maybe if we spent more money in developing and testing alternative ideas," Iverson reasoned, "we could come up with a better campaign."

Iverson discussed his views with Waters, who agreed that this method promised much. They were certain, however, that the agency would resist. The men were not disappointed, for Cordaro marshalled all of the agency's political clout to squash the proposal. Finally, virtually under duress, Cordaro agreed to try the idea on a one-time basis.

Iverson and Waters instructed the agency to develop at least three alternative executions for a new campaign for Upper C. "We don't just want three ideas or storyboards," the agency was told, "we want three finished commercials." Only by having the finished commercials to test did the two men believe that a copy-testing organization could give them worthwhile feedback about which execution performed best.

Hi-Power's marketing research department provided recent survey data about the relative importance of product attributes for Upper C's product class. Iverson and Cordaro examined a summary table of these data (see Table 8-4-1) and concluded that the product's nourishment offered the most potential for positioning the brand. They translated this attribute into the selling proposition of "vitamin enrichment."

CHOOSING AMONG ALTERNATIVES

Five months and $90,000 later, the agency presented three finished commercials, each 30 seconds, and each having a completely different theme (see Exhibit 8-4-1). "These are all solid campaign concepts," Cordaro said. Iverson had to agree, but he did feel that "Pantomime Man" was an especially effective execution.

EXHIBIT 8-4-1   Summary of the Three Upper C Commercials

Pantomime Man

A 30-second commercial in which the video depicts the silhouette of a gymnast jumping on a trampoline doing rolls, flips, and other intricate maneuvers. The trampoline is not seen—the video is cropped well above it.

A voice-over speaks about Upper C's energy power, vitamins, and minerals, which combine to provide energy for and a pick-me-up after physical activity.

The camera closes on a slow zoom-in on a can and glass of Upper C.

Saturday Afternoon

A 30-second commercial in which the video and audio portray a plot line in which a grade-schooler comes into the kitchen, tosses his mitt on the table, screen door slamming. He and his mother exchange delighted phrases about his baseball victory while she makes a display of getting the Upper C from the refrigerator, opening the can, and pouring him a large glass. Label is in constant view.

Final scenes show boy drinking from glass, mother saying, "It makes me happy that you like things that are so good for you as Upper C."

Close on slow zoom-in on a can and glass of Upper C.

Show Girls

A 30-second commercial in which video and early audio depict the parade walk of show girls in Las Vegas costume.

Voice-over on low-level audience noises speaks of the wear and tear of a tough day and how refreshing a pick-me-up would be. . . that even adults need a full supply of vitamins.

Final scene in dressing room of show girl where she pours a glass of Upper C, samples it, looks at the camera, and says, "It sure helps out after a tough day."

The next step was to submit the commercials to a copy-testing organization. Although Hi-Power had used one such organization from time to time, Iverson wanted more information about what services were available. He went to the company's marketing research department for advice.

He thought that he would have to ask only, "Which advertising copy-testing service is best?" but he found that the answer was not at all straightforward. As the senior researcher put it, "That all depends on what you mean by 'best' and on which hierarchical model of behavior change you believe characterizes your product." Three popular services were described to him (see Exhibit 8-4-2 for details). It was also suggested that he study some papers by Krugman and by Ray, which Iverson dismissed as being too esoteric. The researchers shrugged and suggested that he might start with copy-testing service A.

Two weeks later, when the Firm A test scores had come in, Iverson looked at them with some dismay (see "Firm A" column of Table 8-4-2). They simply did not confirm his expectations of the performance of the commercials. Waters, too, was disturbed, for his personal favorite, "Show Girls," came in well below "Saturday Afternoon," which he felt was a relatively mundane commercial. Neither of the two men was satisfied. They decided to have the three commercials tested by another copy-testing agency. "We have spent over $90,000 on the production costs of these commercials," Iverson said, "so a few thousand extra for testing is hardly consequential." They set up a test with Firm B. When the results came in (see "Firm B" column of Table 8-4-2),

EXHIBIT 8-4-2   Description of Three Copy-Testing Techniques

Copy-Testing Service A

Firm A's technique is an in-theater viewing by local groups (from churches and other organizations). Respondents view a TV pilot, interspersed at expected intervals with commercials. Among the commercials is the test commercial.

Respondents, who believe that they are at the theater to evaluate the TV pilot (in fact, they sometimes are), complete a questionnaire about the pilot at the conclusion of the show.

Twenty-four hours later an interviewer from the firm telephones each of the respondents "to collect some additional information." At this point the interviewer questions the respondent about recall of commercials shown with the pilot, using open-ended questions such as, "I'm going to read you a list of products, some of which were advertised last night and some of which were not. Please think about each product and tell me whether you recall seeing that product advertised last night. Do you recall a commercial for. . . ."

Respondents who claim recall are asked the brand advertised. The percentage of respondents recalling correctly form an awareness "score" for the test commercial, which can be evaluated against a "norm," or average, for the product class.

Copy-Testing Service B

Firm B used pupilometric techniques, supplemented with attitudinal responses. One respondent at a time is exposed to several commercials, viewed by peering in a light box. While respondents watch the ads, a motion picture camera continuously photographs their left eye, recording changes in pupil size throughout the "control" commercials and test commercial. Firm B has experimentally established that pupils respond to emotional activity.

Up to 100 respondents participate in each test, and the pupil response, along with some paper-and-pencil attitude measurements for the brand, are combined for the entire sample of respondents. These are then transformed into an indexed score, which is compared with a norm for the product class.

Copy-Testing Service C

Firm C's technique involves a behavioral response measure. The copy-testing technique involves moving a well-equipped viewing room (contained in a motor home) to the parking lot of a large supermarket.

Shoppers are invited to participate in the test as they leave their cars and approach the store. In the van, they are shown a series of commercials. In some cases (test condition), the test commercial is included in those shown. In other cases (control condition), the respondents would see all commercials except the test commercial.

After viewing, all respondents are given a complimentary booklet of cents-off coupons for specific grocery products. Among the coupons is one good for cents-off on the test product. The respondents then proceed with their shopping.

At the close of the day, Firm C people collect all redeemed coupons, which had been coded to reflect whether they were given during the test condition or control condition. A comparison of the differential redemption rates of test versus control coupons is then made.

The differences between test condition redemption and control condition redemption are transformed into a percentile score, in which the norm for the product class is 50 percent.

Iverson and Waters were simultaneously delighted and puzzled. On the one hand, the test results confirmed their own expectations—both "Pantomime Man" and "Show Girls" were highly evaluated—but these results directly contradicted the scores from Firm A. In addition, the previously high-scoring "Saturday Afternoon" now scored quite low.

Their feelings of confusion turned to bewilderment when they tested the commercials a third time—this time with Firm C (see "Firm C" column of Table 8-4-2). Waters turned to Iverson and said: "'Saturday Afternoon' is getting scores like a yo-yo, and 'Show Girls' is back near the bottom again.

TABLE 8-4-2   Test Scores from Three Organizations

Commercial	Firm A Score	Firm A Norm[a]	Firm B Score	Firm B Norm	Firm C Percentile[b]
"Pantomime Man"	3	10	5.4	3.8	34%
"Saturday Afternoon"	17	10	1.5	3.8	73%
"Show Girls"	4	10	6.5	3.8	20%

[a]Scores above or below the norm reflect above- or below-average performance, respectively.
[b]50 percent is an "average" score.

Surely our friends in the marketing research department will help us understand what's happening here." "I hope so," Iverson replied, "or we'll be forced right back into our old system of one idea, one commercial. We just have to reconcile this dilemma."

Questions for Discussion and Review

1. What are the strengths and weaknesses of each of the three testing procedures?

2. What additional information would be useful in evaluating the testing procedures?

3. What action should Hi-Power take based on the results of the three research tests of the three executions?

4. Was the decision to use the "vitamin enrichment" proposition a wise one? Could this decision have exerted an influence on the outcome of any of the testing procedures? Would the nature of the executions have any possible effect on test results?

C A S E   **8 - 5**

Sports Trading Cards Focus Group

Marcie Anthone, vice-president and associate research director for the New York office of Bozell, Inc., was interested in what information could be gleaned from a focus group session that had just been completed. Bozell had

This case was written by John H. Murphy, The University of Texas at Austin. It is intended for use in generating classroom discussion and is not meant to illustrate either the effective or ineffective handling of an administrative situation. The author gratefully acknowledges the support of David Bell and Marcie Anthone in the development of this case. A videotape of the focus group session is available to adopters of the textbook by contacting The Dryden Press. Used by permission of Bozell, Inc.

commissioned a focus group with boys aged eight and nine to explore the sports trading cards phenomenon.

The research was conducted for a new business presentation and was entirely exploratory in nature, since Bozell had never worked with a client marketing sports trading cards. The primary purpose of the session was to help management and creative personnel at the agency better understand the dynamics of the category. The session was designed to provide insights into the following: (1) trading cards purchase behavior; (2) collecting/trading behavior; (3) determination of the value of a card; (4) motivation for enthusiasm about a card(s); (5) emotional relationships with cards; (6) brand awareness/imagery; and (7) reactions to current advertising.

A marketing research consultant was hired to moderate the group. Potential participants were recruited from New York City, primarily Queens, Manhattan, and the Bronx. To qualify, they had to actively participate in collecting cards. Eight boys participated in the group, which was conducted on a Tuesday evening after school. The group was provided with snacks and soft drinks during the session, which was held in a conference room in Bozell's office at 40 West 23rd Street. Microphones, a television camera, and technical people were clearly in view during the session. As compensation for their participation, the boys were each paid $40 and given two packs of trading cards.

Exhibit 8-5-1 presents a discussion guide developed for use by the moderator in leading the session. The moderator had five years' experience conducting a wide range of focus groups. Her background included working in three different advertising agencies during the course of the past ten years, conducting qualitative as well as quantitative research.

The lively focus group session lasted approximately one hour and 40 minutes. In addition to a general discussion, participants were asked to complete two written exercises, act out a role-playing exercise, and view and evaluate current television advertising by sports trading cards companies. Table 8-5-1 presents the group's evaluations of the three brands of cards,

---

EXHIBIT 8-5-1 **Sports Trading Cards Focus Group Discussion Guide**

Warm-up

- Hello, my name is Carolyn and I talk to different people about all kinds of different products. Has anyone ever been to a focus group before?

- Do you know that we are going to talk about trading cards—baseball, football, and hockey? You are our experts, and I would like you to tell me everything you can about trading cards. We really need your help, so please don't be afraid to speak up.

- The rules today are that there are no rules. There are no right or wrong answers, and if you disagree with anything said or have a different experience, it is very important that you let me know.

- Before we start, I'd like to go around the room so we can introduce ourselves. I'd like you to tell me your name, age, grade, where you live. What activities are you involved in after school? What other hobbies are you involved in?

(continued)

EXHIBIT 8-5-1   *(continued)*

Usage/Purchase Patterns

- You all mentioned that you trade baseball cards and other cards. What is so much fun about trading cards? *Probe:* earning money, owning the best players, having better cards than your friends? What is the one best thing about trading cards? What is the one worst thing about trading cards?

- Where do you buy trading cards? Do you usually buy single cards or buy them in packs? How much do packs usually cost? Do you trade one card for another? Do you sometimes trade more than one of your cards for one of someone else's?

- Who do you trade cards with? Do a lot of your friends also trade cards? Do you take them around to shows or stores and try to trade them that way? How often do you go to trade shows? Does your father get involved with you and take you to different shows?

- After you have purchased or traded for a card, what do you do with it? *Probe:* Do you put it in an album/box? Does it stay there long or do you try to trade it again?

- In a typical school week, how much time do you think you spend trading your cards or putting them in an album, etc.? Do you spend more time working on your cards than other activities?

- *(Written Exercise)* I would like you to make believe that you are the best baseball card that you own. I would like you to write a story about your life as a baseball card: where you were bought, how much you cost, what your new owner did with you when he bought you, how he felt about owning you, and what he plans to do with you in the future.

Trading and Brand Dynamics

- Do you buy mostly new cards or trade for older cards? How do you know if a card is valuable or not? *Probe:* Do you read magazines? Which ones? Does someone tell you? Who?

- Which cards are more valuable: baseball, football, or hockey? Which of these do you trade most often? Why?

- What makes a card valuable? Are there cards you are not willing to sell for any price? Which ones are they (name specific athletes)? Why is that?

- *(Verbal Exercise)* Since I don't know how to trade for a card, I would like you to help me understand by making believe that (choose respondent) is interested in getting a card owned by (name someone else in the group). I would like you to show me how a deal is made. (Try to get at least two pairs of respondents to make a deal in front of the group. Ask about certain language used or try to determine if there is specific terminology used in making the deal.)

- How many cards do you have? Do you have cards made by the same company? Are they made by different companies? What are the names of the companies that make trading cards?

- Do you like certain cards made by certain companies better than others? Which companies? What is special about them? *Probe:* Do certain companies feature more popular/better ball players than others? Which companies? Does one company show the stats on the back of the card better than another?

- *(Written Exercise only if brand awareness exists)* Rate "Tops," "Score," and "Upper Deck" on a scale of 1–10 on overall rating; featuring popular/good ball players; making a good-quality card (that doesn't tear); featuring clear, interesting stats; and being the best trading card.

- Did you know that bubble gum used to come in the packs? Would you like to buy card packages with bubble gum in them? Why? Why not?

---

which were collected using a written exercise. Exhibit 8-5-2 presents verbatim comments from the "make believe you are your own best trading card" task, which was also a written exercise.

After reviewing the tape and the moderator's interpretation of the highlights of the session and studying the written comments of the participants presented in Table 8-5-1 and Exhibit 8-5-2, Anthone began to formulate her final report. Her report was to be made the next week in the form of a

TABLE 8-5-1 Focus Group's Rating of Sports Trading Cards Brands[a]

	Tops	Score	Upper Deck
Overall rating	a—8	a—6	a—10
	b—9	b—7	b—10
	c—8	c—10	c—10
	d—6	d—9	d—10
	e—5	e—7	e—10
	f—9	f—5	f—10
	g—8	g—9	g—10
	h—6	h—7	h—9
Features great players	a—10	a—9	a—10
	b—6	b—2	b—10
	c—5	c—10	c—9
	d—5	d—8	d—9
	e—7	e—7	e—10
	g—7	g—6	g—9
	h—7	h—8	h—10
High-quality card	a—10	a—10	a—10
	b—9	b—3	b—10
	c—7	c—10	c—10
	d—7	d—10	d—7
	e—9	e—9	e—10
	f "waxed"	f "none"	f "none"
	g—6	g—9	g—8
	h—5	h—10	h—7
Good stats	a—9	a—6	a—7
	b—10	b—6	b—10
	c—3	c—10	c—10
	d—8	d—9	d—2
	e—10	e—9	e—7
	g—8	g—5	g—10
		h—7	h—8
Will become valuable	a—10	a—10	a—10
	b—7	b—1	b—10
	c—9	c—10	c—10
	d—10	d—10	d—10
	e—8	e—9	e—10
	f "yes"	f "yes"	f "no"
	g—9	g—8	g—10
	h—7	h—5	h—8
Best trading card	a—10	a—9	a—10
	b—9	b—1	b—10
	c—10	c—10	c—10
	d—7	d—10	d—8
	e—10	e—8	e—10
	g—7	g—9	g—10
	h—7	h—8	h—10

Verbatim Comments:

Tops—(a) "Best." (b) "Very good." (c) "good." (d) "good excellent good." (e) "good quality." (g) "It's Okay but their good." (h) "A lot of cards to trade. Also, has been around for a long time."

Score—(a) "O.K." (b) "not good." (c) "very great." (e) "good photo." (g) "I don't really like this brand." (h) "Lots of All-Stars and weird names."

Upper Deck—(a) "excellent." (b) "great." (c) "great." (e) "good quality." (g) "Upper Deck, I think is the greatest." (h) "Has a hologram in every pack. Has a lot of cards in the collection."

[a]Respondents were told to use a scale of 1 to 10 to evaluate the brands, with 1 being the worst and 10 the best. Each respondent is identified by a letter designation. Where no information was provided, no entry is included above.

**EXHIBIT 8-5-2   "Make Believe You Are Your Best Card" Exercise: Verbatim
Comments**

8– 9-Year-Old Group

- "Baba Ruth by Tops. I brought the baseball card at a Baseball card show. If I was the person who owned it I would sign my singherture on the card."

- "*Score.* My name is Frank Thomas in 1990 I was a good rookie. I am on the White Soxs. I have a good average. I was bought in a card shop. I was sold for $15–$20. My owner put me in the safe and is waiting for the card to go up in value or gets better Home Runs and R.B.I.s."

- "The Card. I have my best card they made of me. I bought myself in a candy store. When I saw myself I ran to my sports value guide and looked up how much I was I was worth. It said I was worth $70.00. I was so happy."

- "The Babe. I was bought in a candy store. I thought no one was going to buy me. I was stuck in between Micky Mantle and Pete Rose. Finally I was bough by myself. I don't"

- "Teddy Bergin. I was bought in a comic store he was suprised when he saw me in the furture he wants to trade me in because I am worth alot of money."

- "I was bought at a store called Comicmania. I'm worth $3.00. I am a wrestling card hologram. I was born in a card factory. My owner wanted to trade me for a baseball card worth the same. My owner would save me until I went up 20$ in value. The all hologram form of me is worth eight dollars. Adam."

- "Randy Kamintzky I Am the Baseball Card. He was born in Queens New York. I didn't no I'd be a great baseball, but when I new it, I was bout and put in a binder. It was tite but I was all whright. When I took me out I was on top of a guide and saw me worth $85.00/ That was the happiest time of my life."

- "Joshua. Roger Clemens, Rockey. I was bought at mint condition. I was put in a plastic case, and in a safe. My owner will keep me for a long time. Now I am worth $20.00."

---

presentation to the new business team working on the project. As she began,
she was concerned about capturing the essence of the bond that clearly
existed between the boys and their cards.

Questions for Discussion and Review (Answer after viewing videotape of focus group session.)

1. Were the mechanics of the session (size of group, physical setting, and so on) handled in a way conducive to generating valid findings? How effectively did the moderator handle the group?

2. What special procedural and other problems did the age of the participants present for the moderator? How did the moderator handle these problems? Are there any ethical issues related to using children aged eight and nine as participants in focus group interviews? If yes, what are they and how can they be satisfactorily resolved?

3. How useful were the role-playing exercises in which two members of the group participated in a mock trade? How useful was the "make believe you are your own best trading card" exercise? What about the written exercise in which each group rated three card companies?

4. What changes would you recommend to make the session more productive?

5. What useful conclusions can be drawn from the session? How would this information be used by the management and creative team working on a new business pitch?

III

PERSONAL SELLING, SALES PROMOTION, PUBLIC RELATIONS, AND DIRECT MARKETING

*T*his section of the book reviews four marketing communication mix elements that often work in partnership with advertising—personal selling, sales promotion, public relations, and direct marketing. In designing an effective and efficient marketing communication program, an advertiser seeks to strike an appropriate balance between advertising and these other elements.

Each element in the firm's communication mix is used for the same objective—to facilitate a brand purchase decision. Yet the optimum blend of mix elements varies across product/market situations. For example, business-to-business marketers typically rely more heavily on personal selling than do packaged goods manufacturers, who tend to invest the bulk of their marketing communication dollars in consumer advertising or sales promotion. A start-up company with an innovative product may rely exclusively on publicity and other forms of public relations to achieve initial visibility and sales. Later, as finances allow, it may hire a sales force and launch an advertising program to support its marketing communication efforts.

Even in situations where advertising, personal selling, or one of the other mix elements dominates the firm's promotional activities, the planner must constantly evaluate the cost and benefits of possible shifts in the firm's communication mix. The planner continually seeks the most efficient and effective means of accomplishing communication and overall marketing objectives.

As the marketplace changes, the importance of the individual elements in the firm's marketing communication program may shift. To effectively adapt the firm's promotional efforts to change, the decision maker must integrate all promotional decisions. For example, the activities of the sales force and development of its collateral support materials must be planned in concert with the firm's media advertising, public relations, sales promotion, and direct marketing activities.

In short, practicing integrated marketing communication means that the person in charge of the communication mix makes sure that all elements speak with a consistent voice and aim to accomplish the same objectives. This integration leverages the impact of each individual element and enhances the net impression of the overall program. To achieve such integration, the planner designs a mix consistent with the firm's long-run strategic marketing plan. This document along with the annual marketing and advertising plans should provide the framework for the development of an integrated communication mix.

In addition, the communication mix must be coordinated with the other elements in the firm's marketing mix — that is, the brand's pricing, distribution, and product strategy. The brand's price compared to competitors', product design features, packaging, and so on all communicate information to consumers. Hence, to be most effective, all aspects of the firm's market offering must convey a consistent message and be in sync with all the firm's marketing communication efforts.

The four chapters in this section of the book briefly examine the management of important marketing communication elements other than advertising and their coordination with the firm's advertising efforts. Chapter 9 provides an overview of personal selling and Chapter 10 focuses on sales promotion. Chapters 11 and 12 deal with public relations and direct marketing, respectively.✤

9

Personal Selling

*I don't know who you are. I don't know your company. I
don't know your company's product. I don't know what
your company stands for. I don't know your company's
customers. I don't know your company's record. I don't
know your company's reputation. Now—what was it
you wanted to sell me?*

McGraw-Hill Publications

THE IMPORTANCE OF PERSONAL SELLING

Selling is an integral part of the marketing program. Modern day salespeople
are problem solvers, and their activity is customer oriented. Sales personnel
are the company's personal link to its customers and clients. They are the
company's personification, providing an image with which the firm is often
identified. It is crucial, therefore, that they represent the company as efficiently
and flawlessly as possible.

In order to achieve their marketing and sales goals, companies must tailor
their marketing communication mix to the needs and wants of their
customers. They must also use marketing communication as a tool to
distinguish themselves from competitors.

Personal selling is a very effective marketing communication tool. It is
particularly powerful when used at certain stages of the buying process; for
example, personal selling is most effective when customers are building
preference for a product, developing knowledge and conviction about the
product, and, finally, deciding to buy the product.

Selling is the most expensive of all marketing communication functions.
Highly trained professionals engage in a personal interaction with customers;
therefore, the unit cost of each sales call far exceeds the individual costs of
advertising and sales promotion. For this reason, selling should be used

selectively. Criteria for using personal selling as opposed to, or in addition to, other marketing communication tools must be set and weighed carefully. For example, personal selling should be used for very complex and/or high-ticket items, as opposed to perishable packaged goods.

Competitive position, the types of goods sold, the stage in the life cycle of the product, and several other factors will determine whether an expenditure on personal selling is needed. This chapter will explore the conditions conducive to the use of personal selling.

THE ROLE OF A SALESPERSON

Salespeople perform several vital tasks that contribute to the success of the marketing strategy of a firm.

Salespeople are first of all a very important source of information for a firm's customers. This is especially true for industrial or institutional buyers, because they need more complete and detailed information about products. As an information source, salespeople help their customers by explaining the advantages and disadvantages of their products and by fitting their offerings to their customers' needs.

This problem-solving ability of salespeople allows them to develop a long-term relationship with their customers. The goodwill of a firm rests on the loyalty of its customers, hence salespeople are a vital element in building such goodwill. Also, because of their problem-solving ability salespeople are skilled professionals, able to answer sophisticated management questions. The stereotypical image of the salesperson—a good talker who does not offer much—could not be farther from reality. Modern salespeople are important contributors to the firm and to their clients.

Salespeople are the representatives of the whole company, and at the same time they provide the company with vital feedback about its customers. In such a role, salespeople are intelligence gatherers and researchers. They keep management informed about market trends and major changes in the marketplace. In addition, they provide management with information useful in improving the quality of the firm's products and services. Reporting on customers' difficulties in using the products, shipment delays, billing problems, and other causes of customers' discontent is an essential role of salespeople. This type of feedback would not be provided to management by any other source, and without it a company might not be able to maintain its customer base. Salespeople, therefore, provide market research insights and high-quality internal feedback to the firm.

SALES AND THE MARKETING CONCEPT

Firms that practice the marketing concept as their management philosophy believe in integrating all their efforts toward satisfying customers as a means of accomplishing their long-term strategic goals.

The idea that the entire firm focuses on the satisfaction of customer needs implies that the firm will attempt to determine what it can offer its customers that would meet their needs as closely as possible. Since no one company can completely satisfy all its potential customers and markets all the time, companies must strive to satisfy specific markets and specific customer needs.

Salespeople must keep in mind the need to keep the customer satisfied. This means that they will have to integrate their efforts with those of all of the other departments of the firm. Salespeople can adapt the company's marketing mix to the needs of each target market; therefore, they have more flexibility in responding to their customers' demands.

The three basic objectives of marketing communication are to *inform, persuade,* and *remind* target customers about the company and the products and services it offers. Most firms use a combination of communication tools to reach their intended audiences: advertising, public relations, and personal selling. The appropriate mix of communications is determined by several variables, among them the type of customers to be reached, type of product or service being sold, number of competitors, complexity of the product or service being sold, stage in the product life cycle, and overall competitive strategy adopted by the firm. Some of these variables will be discussed briefly.

Type of Customers to Be Reached

A firm that sells its products and services to industrial or institutional buyers will invest more money in its sales force than a firm that appeals directly to final consumers. Industrial and institutional buyers generally follow stricter directives when placing an order. Sometimes there are very technical questions to be answered and the need for knowledgeable and trained assistance. Final consumers, on the other hand, may respond to the emotional appeals of television advertising. A firm selling to industrial and institutional buyers, therefore, may decide to concentrate its communication efforts in the sales force while spending a smaller portion of the budget on advertising. The reverse would be true for a firm appealing primarily to final consumers.

Type of Product or Service

A firm selling a very complex product or service, or one requiring specific training for usage, will have to concentrate its efforts on personal communication so as to be able to answer questions and handle specific problems that may arise from the complexity of the product. This would be the case with, for example, personal computers and technologically complex products. While some advertising could be used to cause awareness of and interest in the product among potential buyers, only in a personal sales situation can information be given that will allow the customer to develop a preference for the product.

On the other hand, in the case of a cake mix, for example, the one-way communication provided through advertising may be sufficient to generate interest and enough preference for a product to motivate its purchase. While personal interaction with a salesperson might also be helpful, consumers' familiarity with the product and its technological simplicity may cause potential consumers to rely solely on emotional appeals to reach purchase decisions.

Another product characteristic relevant to determining the importance of personal selling is the perceived risk of the purchase decision. The more expensive the product or service, the greater the perceived risk of the purchase. A greater investment in personal selling would be best when selling high-cost items such as automobiles and insurance, while more emphasis on advertising might be advisable when selling packaged goods or personal care products.

Stage in the Product Life Cycle

When a product or service is in the early stages of its life cycle, it is important to provide customers with sufficient and relevant information about it. This can best be done through personal interaction with a salesperson. For example, when introducing videophones into the market, AT&T and its competitors would be well advised to spend a significant portion of their marketing communication budget on sales. The same is not the case when selling traditional touch-tone phones, which are now at the maturity stage in their life cycle. Advertising, coupled with product availability and self-service, could provide sufficient information for prospective customers.

Competitive Strategy

The type of marketing communication used could be instrumental in differentiating a product or a service from the offerings of competitors. For example, the heavy investment in personal selling made by Amway has developed a loyal and significant market for that product line. While Amway detergents and other cleaning products could be considered parity products, the marketing communication and sales techniques used by the firm are unique and give it a differential advantage. By the same token, when Southwest Airlines promoted its automatic ticket-vending machines, it was a major departure from the traditional selling and marketing communication techniques used in the airline business. This alone differentiated Southwest Airlines from its competitors.

It is important to recognize the interaction of personal selling with all the other elements in the marketing mix. The type of product and service sold, the customers targeted, the stage in the product life cycle, and the competitive environment of the firm are all important variables when determining the amount and extent of personal selling efforts required to achieve the firm's long-term goals and objectives. The following section will investigate the major steps in developing a personal selling effort.

THE MANAGEMENT OF PERSONAL SELLING

Once the decision is made to employ personal selling to communicate effectively with potential customers, a number of steps must be followed to manage the sales efforts. Sales managers must be able to develop a plan, assess the market potential for personal sales, forecast a sales level, and establish a budget for the sales functions. In addition, they must organize and staff the sales force, train and direct it, and, finally, assess the effectiveness of the sales effort. This portion of the chapter will elaborate on the various management tasks to be accomplished in order to successfully implement a personal selling program.

Developing a Plan and Assessing Sales Potential

A manager of sales must establish a long-range and a short-range plan for the firm that can be realistically achieved through the efforts of the sales force. The first step in planning is that of setting objectives and goals for the firm's sales force. These may vary from firm to firm: in some cases objectives will be translated into dollar sales; in other cases, they will consist of developing awareness and knowledge of a product or service among potential customers.

The objectives and goals stated in a sales plan will be determined by assessing the sales potential of a firm. A survey of the market situation and an assessment of the product's relative strengths and weaknesses with regard to competing products are essential inputs for establishing sales levels. Establishing the share of market a firm wishes to obtain, as well as evaluating possible variations in the demand for the product or service of the firm must be the first steps of the planning process.

Creating a Sales Forecast

A sales forecast may include seasonal or territorial estimates of sales. Because markets are never completely homogeneous, in order to efficiently allocate sales personnel, accurate forecasts of sales must be made.

Quantitative and qualitative forecasting techniques such as trend analysis or focus groups of potential customers may be used to achieve an accurate estimate of future sales. Among some of the models used for sales forecasting are the Delphi technique and the survey of expert opinion. In addition, sophisticated statistical methods may also be used for the same purpose. Whatever method is employed by a firm, it is essential that the results be evaluated in light of logical criteria such as past sales performance and common sense. The resulting estimate will be used to set territorial quotas or other sales goals for the firm.

Budgeting the Sales Effort

A budget expresses a company's goals and operational strategies in specific numerical terms. The sales budget takes into account the anticipated revenues for the period under consideration and the expenditures necessary to achieve such revenues.

Budgets improve and specify the planning goals by describing them in quantities or dollars. They therefore allow a firm to evaluate the sales effort by comparing its performance with the budgeted objectives.

Budgets are essential planning and organizational tools. In addition, they allow firms to exercise control and to evaluate the performance of their salespeople.

Organizing, Staffing, and Training the Sales Force

This function must take into account the human resources available to the firm and other variables such as the type of product sold, the type of potential customer targeted, and the overall objectives set for the sales force.

Sales training is a very specialized function. Salespeople are in general independent and entrepreneurial in nature. Sales managers train their employees in several ways, including by providing instruction at the sales office and by assigning trainees to experienced salespeople in the field for several weeks.

Sales managers also perform periodic training services for experienced salespeople. These consist of regular meetings held to discuss mutual sales problems. Also, new products and promotional campaigns are explained in periodic sales training sessions.

Evaluating the Performance of Salespeople

Sales managers are also responsible for evaluating sales personnel. Because sales is such a unique and independent function, evaluating sales efforts is not an easy task. Also, because each salesperson faces unique economic and buying conditions in his or her territory, sales managers must maintain flexibility in applying standards for the evaluation of sales performance.

Sales managers must also keep open lines of communication with managers in all the other departments of a firm. They must provide leadership and stress cooperation among their employees. These tasks must all be accomplished despite environmental factors over which managers have little or no control.

AN EXAMPLE OF THE DEVELOPMENT OF A SALES STRATEGY: THE CASE OF THE LCD PROJECTORS

The following is a hypothetical example of the type of decisions that must be made when a firm is evaluating the appropriateness of using personal sales as one component of its marketing mix. The information in this example is purely fictitious and is used solely for the purpose of illustration.

TechPro is a small high-technology company that has developed an LCD screen for use with computers. This product will make presentations a lot easier and more flexible. The projector will allow managers and teachers to develop slides for group presentations and lectures directly on a computer, with the aid of specialized software. The slides will then be ready to be projected on a screen, using specialized software and the LCD projector.

The potential markets for such a product are many. The firm has decided that since it has a very competitive and technologically advanced product, it must concentrate its efforts on developing a marketing plan that will allow it to cope with the growth of its markets.

Users of the LCD projectors can be found in many groups. One such group is that of public relations agents and/or consultants. Other users are personnel training specialists, corporate audiovisual departments, and educational institutions. This technology allows presentations to be produced economically and, when used with advanced software, is capable of handling multimedia presentations.

The manufacturer of this product competes with two large high-technology firms and a number of other small manufacturers.

The firm is satisfied with the quality of its product. The challenge confronting management now is that of deciding how to best reach potential buyers of the product.

The Marketing Communication Plan

The first step in the development of a marketing communication plan for the LCD projector is the assessment of the market potential for the product. Management must consider all the target segments it wants to reach and decide how many projectors could be purchased by each. Then it must decide what percentage of the total market it wants to secure for itself. In our example, the company felt it could obtain 10 percent of the total market potential in its region.

After the firm's potential sales revenues have been forecasted, management must determine the appropriate communication mix to achieve these goals. In this case, the firm's competitors used mass mailings and catalogs to reach potential users. Advertising in professional and business journals was also very prevalent among high-tech manufacturers.

The management of TechPro felt that an innovative communication campaign would best differentiate the company from its competitors. If a unique method of reaching potential buyers could be implemented, perhaps TechPro could penetrate the market more aggressively.

Personal sales was more expensive than mail promotions and catalog selling, but management felt that such a new and complex product would benefit from the personal interaction and immediate feedback that would result from using personal salespeople.

Another important consideration was the financial cost of establishing a sales force for TechPro. The company's managers determined that, over a period of five years, the overall profits of TechPro would be higher if personal sales were used. They felt that customer loyalty and the overall company image would benefit from the positive relationship that could be established between their sales force and their clients.

The final step in the planning process was the hiring and training of the sales force, the determination of sales territories, and the establishment of periodic means of assessing the sales force's performance. TechPro management was able to handle this final step in the process successfully within a six-month period. The results of the marketing communication plan were implemented within the first fiscal year.

Conclusion

This example is an attempt to walk students through the important steps in deciding to establish a personal selling plan. While no figures were discussed or analyzed in this example, such considerations would be an integral part of the final decision. The example provides an overview of the main variables to be considered when establishing a sales plan. Students must attempt to follow such steps when dealing with similar problems.

Suggested Readings

Clark, William A. "Where to Get Information from Your Competitor." *Marketing Times* 30, no. 2 (March-April 1983): 19–22.

Dubinski, Alan J., Thomas A. Barry, and Roger A. Kerin. "The Sales-Advertising Interface in Promotion Planning." *Journal of Advertising* 10, no. 3 (1981): 35–41.

Jackson, Donald W., Jr., William H. Cunningham, and Isabella C. M. Cunningham. *Selling—The Personal Force in Marketing.* New York: John Wiley and Sons, 1988.

Kotler, Philip, and Ravi Singh. "Marketing Warfare in the 1980s." *Journal of Business Strategy* 1, no. 3 (Winter 1986): 30–41.

Rogers, Everett M. *Diffusion of Innovations.* 3d ed. New York: Free Press, 1983.

Stumm, David A. *Advanced Industrial Selling.* New York: Amacom, 1981.

"When Sales Meets Marketing." *Sales and Marketing Management,* May 13, 1985, 59–65.

Exercises

1.   Describe the different variables a firm must analyze when it decides to make a major switch from using an intensive and broad-based advertising program to a personal selling program. What marketing factors would be most conducive to using personal selling as opposed to advertising? Explain.

2.   Videophones are the newest telephone technology on the market. Two people equipped with the $1,499 VideoPhone 2500 can watch moving images of each other on small screens. After dialing as usual, the user presses a "video" key to display himself/herself to the party at the other end of the line, and vice versa. Users can also avoid being seen by pulling a shield over the camera lens.

Two different sales appeals are being used to sell videophones. One is the emotional "keep in touch" appeal that implies the ability for generations to stay in touch with each other. The other appeal is of a corporate nature. Videophones are touted as a cheap one-

on-one alternative to audio conferencing.

Prepare a sales presentation using one of the two appeals discussed above. Be sure to provide a thorough and detailed description of the product's attributes.

Sources: Kate Fitzgerald, "AT&T Pictures Big Interest in Video Phone: Hits Market This Summer," *Advertising Age,* June 29, 1992, 33; John W. Verity, "Bits & bytes," (Industrial Technology Edition) *Business Week,* May 18, 1992, 130E.

3.   You are a sales manager for a furniture manufacturer that sells primarily to furniture leasing outlets. About 20 percent of your sales are made to traditional furniture retailers and 80 percent to furniture leasing companies or large real estate leasing companies. You are in the process of determining whether you should allocate your sales force by geographic territory or by type of customer. Indicate which of the two methods you would use to allocate your sales personnel. Explain your rationale.

Mary Kay Cosmetics, Inc.

Most women across the country recognize the name "Mary Kay Cosmetics." What many may not realize is that beyond the pink Cadillacs and glitzy award ceremonies is a dynamic company that has experienced phenomenal growth in terms of both sales (Table 9-1-1) and the size of its independent contractor direct sales force (Table 9-1-2) since its inception in 1963.

COMPANY BACKGROUND

Mary Kay Ash started her dream company in 1963 with $5,000 and plenty of determination and perseverance. Since 1953, she had been using a skin care system developed by a hide tanner. He believed that if you could turn stiff, large-pored hide into soft, small-pored leather, you should be able to achieve the same results on human skin. He began to experiment with his own skin, using a modified form of some of the same principles used in tanning hides. Mary Kay bought the formulas and started her company. She based Mary Kay Cosmetics on the golden rule ("Do unto others as you would have them do unto you") and the idea that women deserved unlimited opportunities for success.

The management team at Mary Kay Cosmetics has become a dynamic force in American business. The company is led by president Dick Bartlett and chairman of the board Richard Rogers. Mary Kay Ash, chairman of the board emeritus, remains the leading lady and master motivator of the company.

TABLE 9-1-1 Sales Growth for Mary Kay Cosmetics

Year	Gross Sales (millions of dollars)
1986	$245.0
1987	303.3
1988	376.2
1989	412.1
1990	442.1

This case was prepared by Cheryl R. Halpern and Christie Myers Pyle, Mary Kay Cosmetics, Inc., and John H. Murphy, The University of Texas at Austin. The case is intended for class discussion only and not to illustrate either the effective or ineffective handling of an administrative situation. Some figures have been changed to protect confidential information. Used by permission of Mary Kay Cosmetics, Inc.

TABLE 9-1-2   Size of Mary Kay Cosmetics Sales Force

Year	Average Number of Consultants
1986	121,000
1987	129,100
1988	152,700
1989	171,300
1990	189,200

Together, all 1,500 employees of the company aim for preeminence in the manufacturing and marketing of personal care products by providing personalized service, value, and convenience to Mary Kay customers through the independent sales force.

According to Rogers, there are two basic reasons for the success of Mary Kay Cosmetics:

> *We filled a void in the marketplace when we began to teach skin care and glamour techniques, and we're still doing that today. Secondly, our marketing system, through which proficient beauty consultants achieve success by selling products at their retail prices at skin care classes and facials and by recruiting and building their own sales organizations, was a stroke of genius because the by-product has been management. In other words, we didn't buy a sales leadership team; they've been trained one by one.*

RAPID GROWTH

Mary Kay Cosmetics, Inc., rapidly evolved from a small regional cosmetics firm to a fully integrated manufacturer and distributor of personal care products. Since 1963, the growth of the company has been remarkable. In 1990, the sales force included nearly 200,000 women, and company revenues and consultant productivity hit record highs. Over one-third of Mary Kay's national sales directors achieved millionaire status by 1988, having earned from $1 million to $3 million in commissions during their entire Mary Kay careers.

The company began expanding geographically in 1970 when the first regional distribution center was opened in addition to the original one in Dallas. Centers are now located in Costa Mesa, California; Tucker, Georgia; Somerset, New Jersey; Bloomingdale, Illinois; and Dallas, Texas. In 1968 Mary Kay stock was offered over the counter, and in August 1976 it was listed on the New York Stock Exchange. In December 1985, the company was returned to private, family ownership through a repurchase of common stock.

The company formed its first international subsidiary in 1971 in Australia. Subsidiaries were also established in Canada in 1978, Argentina in 1980, West Germany in 1986, and Mexico in 1988. Future international expansion is under way in the Pacific Basin.

To achieve further growth in sales and in the size of the sales force, new basic skin care and glamour lines were introduced in the late 1980s. Since 1984, 95 percent of the product line has been improved and updated. Marketing strategies were developed to attract more career women to Mary Kay both as salespeople and as customers.

COMPETITION

The highly competitive cosmetic industry is considered a mature market by most industry analysts. Mary Kay's most direct competitor is Estee Lauder, whose Clinique skin care line is similarly priced and also attempts to project a "scientific" image. In a broad sense, Mary Kay competes against all other mass or prestige cosmetics companies. To see a comparison of prices against competitors', refer to Tables 9-1-3 and 9-1-4.

THE DISTRIBUTION PLAN

Its marketing and distribution plan has played an important role in the success of Mary Kay Cosmetics. The beauty consultant usually begins her association with Mary Kay as a customer. She is introduced to the products and learns about career possibilities at the skin care class. When she investigates the career opportunity, she finds that she will actually be in business for herself, but not by herself, as an independent beauty consultant. Only one "wholesale distributor" exists between the company and the consumer; each beauty consultant runs an individual business.

According to Bartlett, "Each Mary Kay consultant is an independent contractor. She is not an employee of the company. The consultant buys directly from the company on a wholesale basis and sells at retail. The difference between the two is her gross profit—anywhere from 40 to 50 percent of the retail price, sometimes as high as 60 percent during special promotions. Of course, she will have some expenses, but her net profit from retail sales will average over 40 percent. Profitability of the individual consultant selling at retail is one of the reasons for our continuing success and excellent market share in skin care and glamour." The Mary Kay career opportunity has become a serious career choice for thousands of women, from homemakers to new college graduates to seasoned businesswomen.

RECRUITING

Recruiting is an opportunity for the consultant to grow in her career and an opportunity for the recruit to begin a potentially rewarding Mary Kay career of her own. Consultants can earn commissions directly from the company of 4, 8, or 12 percent of each new recruit's production (dependent upon the number of active personal recruits). Just as teaching skin care classes is an important aspect of the business, so is recruiting for those interested in earning leadership positions and building a unit of independent retail salespeople.

TABLE 9-1-3   Mary Kay Glamour Product Price Comparison

Brand	Concealer	Powder Cheek Color	Pressed Powder	Loose Powder	Eye Color
Mary Kay	$7.50	$ 7.00 (refill) $15.00 (w/compact & brush)	$ 7.00 (refill) $15.00 (w/compact & brush)	$14.00	$ 8.00 (2 refills) $15.00 (w/compact & applicator)
Lancome	$11.50	$17.50	$18.00	$20.00	$18.00 (2 shades)
Estee Lauder	$11.00	$20.00	$15.00	$15.00	$20.00 (2 shades)
Elizabeth Arden	$10.00	$13.50	$13.50	$15.00	$15.00 (2 shades)
Clinque	$ 8.50	$11.50	$11.00	$14.50	$ 9.50 (1 shade)
Ultima II	—	$13.50	$13.00	$16.00	$10.00 (2 refills) $14.00 (w/compact & applicators)
Fashion Fair	—	$11.00	$11.00	$13.50	$11.00 (2 shades)

All Mary Kay prices are suggested retail, effective February 14, 1990.

Competitive prices based on first-quarter 1990 suggested retail prices.

Note that of all the brands listed above, only Mary Kay and Ultima II offer a refillable eye compact, and only Mary Kay offers refillable compacts for cheeks and powder.

RECOGNITION

As momentum builders, Mary Kay has structured a sales program that is filled with contests and rewards—in addition to regular income. Outstanding performance at every level in the independent sales force is always acknowledged. There are many forms of recognition, from having one's picture and performance highlighted in the monthly magazine, *Applause,* to incentive gifts, to major luxuries such as vacation trips, diamond jewelry, and cars—VIP cars, pink Buicks and Cadillacs.

The "Ladder of Success" is a recognition program that honors beauty consultants on the basis of quarterly sales achievements. Star consultants receive an attractive ladder pin set with a sapphire, ruby, or diamond. The higher the level of achievement, the more valuable the stone.

Quarterly contests are goal-setting tools. Every quarter, Mary Kay offers a different promotion with different prizes. Selecting a specific prize and achieving the corresponding sales and recruiting levels maintains consistency from quarter to quarter. The most well-known awards are luxury cars. Over

Eye Pencil	Eyebrow Pencil	Mascara	Lip Pencil	Lipstick	Lip Gloss	Complete Glamour Collection[a]
$ 6.50	$ 6.50	$ 7.50	$ 6.50	$ 8.00	$ 6.50	$ 93.00
$10.50	$12.50	$12.00	$11.50	$12.00	$11.00	$136.50
$10.00	$10.00	$12.00	$10.00	$11.00	$ 9.00	$128.00
$ 9.00	$11.00	$10.00	$ 8.50	$11.00	$10.00	$113.00
$ 8.50	$12.00	$11.00	$ 8.50	$ 9.50	$ 6.50	$109.50
$ 8.50	$12.50	$10.00	$ 8.00	$10.00	$ 9.50	$102.00[b]
$ 8.50	$ 7.50	$ 9.00	$ 7.00	$ 9.50	$ 9.00	$ 86.00[b]

[a]Includes concealer, cheek color with compact and brush, loose powder, two eye color refills with compact and applicator, eye defining pencil, eyebrow pencil, mascara, lip pencil, lipstick, lip gloss.
[b]Does not include concealer.

5,000 Mary Kay cars, including pink Cadillacs and Buicks, are on the road today.

SEMINAR

Mary Kay Cosmetics' annual seminar in Dallas is designed to be a tribute to the company and to the women who make it a success. Hosted by Mary Kay Ash and Richard Rogers, four consecutive three-day sessions welcome over 25,000 beauty consultants and sales directors from across the country. Throughout each seminar, Mary Kay Ash and Richard Rogers encourage women to "dream big"—to do as Mary Kay Ash did in 1963 when she founded the company. The seminar is also an opportunity for consultants to learn about new products, sales techniques, recruiting skills, and business management ideas. It is also an important arena for recognition, where those beauty consultants and sales directors with the highest sales and best recruiting performances during the past year receive prizes and applause.

TABLE 9-1-4   Mary Kay Basic Skin Care Price Comparison

	Cleansers			Cleansing Bars			Masks			Fresheners		
	$	Oz.	$/Oz.	$	Oz.	$/Oz.	$	Oz.	$/Oz.	$	Oz.	$/Oz.
Mary Kay[a]												
Formula 1	$ 9.00	4.0	$2.25	—	—	—	$11.00	4.0	$2.75	$10.00	6.5	$1.54
Formula 2	9.00	6.5	1.38	—	—	—	11.00	4.0	2.75	10.00	6.5	1.54
Formula 3	9.00	6.5	1.38	$11.00	4.2	$2.62	—	—	—	10.00	6.5[b]	1.54
Elizabeth Arden	14.00	8.5	1.65	11.00	5.5	2.00	13.00	3.5	3.71	11.00	8.5	1.29
Clinique	8.50	3.5	2.43	8.50	6.0	1.42	13.50	3.5	3.86	8.50	6.0	1.42
Lancome	16.50	6.8	2.43	16.50	5.0	3.30	17.50	1.9	9.21	14.50	8.4	1.73
Estee Lauder	12.50	4.0	3.13	13.50	5.0	2.70	16.00	2.0	8.00	11.00	6.75	1.63
Ultima II	15.00	4.0	3.75	—	—	—	—	—	—	15.00	6.0	2.50
Shiseido	18.50	4.2	4.40	9.00	2.6	3.46	25.00	2.8	8.93	25.00	5.0	5.00
Chanel	25.00	7.0	3.57	21.50	4.4	4.89	32.50	2.5	13.00	23.50	7.0	3.36
Fashion Fair	15.00	4.0	3.75	—	—	—	—	—	—	11.50	6.0	1.92

[a]All Mary Kay prices are suggested retail, effective July 19, 1989.
[b]Until new package is available, package actually contains 6.75 oz. ($1.48/oz.).

THE MISSION STATEMENT

In 1988, company president Dick Bartlett unveiled the company's mission statement:

> *To be preeminent in the manufacturing, distribution, and marketing of personal care products by providing personalized service, value, and convenience to Mary Kay customers through our independent sales force. To provide our sales force an unparalleled opportunity for financial independence, career achievement, and personal fulfillment. To achieve total customer satisfaction worldwide by focusing on quality, value, convenience, innovation, and personal service.*

Today, all corporate employees are guided by this statement's vision. Every division, every department, every employee at Mary Kay knows the company's objectives and how their contributions impact company performance and bring them closer to their ultimate goal of preeminence.

PREEMINENCE AT MARY KAY

Preeminence embodies Mary Kay Cosmetics' corporate, manufacturing, and distribution objectives. As defined by Webster's dictionary, preeminence is "outstanding; to have paramount rank, dignity, or importance." At Mary Kay, it

Moisturizers			Cream			Foundations Liquid			Oil-Free			5-Step Basic[c]
$	Oz.	$/Oz.	$	Oz.	$/Oz.	$	Oz.	$/Oz.	$S	Oz.	$/Oz.	$
16.00	4.0	$4.00	$10.00	0.5	$20.00	—	—	—	—	—	—	$56.00
16.00	4.0	4.00	—	—	—	$10.00	1.0	$10.00	—	—	—	
16.00	4.0	4.00	—	—	—	—	—	—	$10.00	1.0	$10.00	
18.50	4.2	4.40	17.50	0.8	21.88	25.00	1.35	18.52	14.00	1.0	14.00	81.50
16.00	4.0	4.00	13.50	.35	38.57	10.50	1.0	10.50	13.50	1.0	13.50	57.00
30.00	2.5	12.00	25.00	.32	78.13	24.00	1.2	20.00	22.50	1.0	22.50	102.50
20.00	1.75	11.43	25.00	1.0	25.00	15.00	1.0	15.00	17.50	1.25	14.00	74.50
26.00	3.0	8.67	35.00	1.38	25.36	18.50	1.25	14.80	—	—	—	74.50[d]
25.00	3.3	7.58	22.00	.45	48.89	25.00	1.1	22.73	—	—	—	118.50
40.00	1.7	23.53	50.00	1.0	50.00	42.50	1.0	42.50	35.00	1.0	35.00	163.50
15.00	4.0	3.75	13.00	1.5	8.67	10.50	1.0	10.50	—	—	—	52.00[d]

[c]Assumes cleanser (versus cleansing bar) and liquid foundation (versus cream or oil-free) foundation.
[d]Based on a 4-step program.

means producing the best products, offering the best career opportunity to women, and giving the sales force the best tools and training with which to offer consumers the best value, the most convenience, and the best possible personalized service.

A BETTER OPPORTUNITY FOR WOMEN

When Mary Kay Ash started the company in 1963, she did so with the fulfillment of a dream in mind. Today, the company is the outgrowth of Mary Kay's clear vision of a better economic opportunity for women. Currently there are almost 50 million working women in America. Not only can Mary Kay Cosmetics offer them a flexible, rewarding career opportunity as a beauty consultant, it can provide them with high-quality products, personalized service, and convenience. Market research indicates that the woman of the nineties demands things that work, buys brand names she knows, and wants value and quality. She prefers competent, personal service and convenient, enjoyable shopping.

In addition, research shows that the woman of the nineties is looking for financial security, increased time with her family, and feelings of "group membership" that help her gain a sense of identity. She wants to make her own choices. Mary Kay Cosmetics' personal sales structure and marketing plan have never been in a better position to succeed.

THE COMPANY PHILOSOPHY

From the beginning, the company has grown based upon the same philosophy: Every person associated with the company, from the chairman emeritus to the newest recruit, lives by the golden rule—"Do unto others as you would have them do unto you"—and by the priorities of God first, family second, and career third. Mary Kay has proven how successful these principles and priorities can be in the business world.

PRODUCT PROFILE

Mary Kay Cosmetics approaches beauty scientifically. Teams of experts in cosmetic chemistry, dermatology, physiology, biochemistry, toxicology, microbiology, analytical chemistry, process technology, and package engineering are continually testing and improving products.

A staff of trained skin care experts is available to answer questions and solve problems from consultants or customers regarding Mary Kay products. Their opinions and experience, combined with the company's continued emphasis on testing and improving existing products and developing new ones, help to ensure that all Mary Kay products are of the highest quality and packaged for the strongest market appeal.

The company maintains approximately 200 retail products, which not only helps keep the focus on upscale personal care products, but also allows the individual consultant to be competitive with a manageable number of items. Exhibit 9-1-1 presents a current list of products and prices.

THE SKIN CARE PROFILE

Consultants help each customer complete a skin care profile to determine which products are appropriate for her skin type. This step-by-step guide accurately and easily enables the consultant to recommend personalized formulas for each customer. (See Exhibit 9-1-2.)

BASIC SKIN CARE

Mary Kay's basic skin care program includes five steps: cleanse, retexture, freshen, moisture balance, and protect. For each step there is a specific formula developed to meet the needs of every customer's skin type (dry, normal, combination, oily, or blemish prone). All products, with the exception of Day Radiance cream foundation, are 100 percent fragrance free and clinically tested for skin irritancy, allergy, and comedogenicity. Most of the products are also safe for sensitive skin. Basic skin care products at Mary Kay account for about 30 percent of gross sales and are the most profitable product line for the company. Skin care products are what Mary Kay is known for. In fact, in a nationwide study among women who were regular facial skin care users, Mary Kay Cosmetics was most frequently mentioned as the best brand of skin care products by those who thought there was one best brand.

EXHIBIT 9-1-1 Current Product Lines and Prices for Mary Kay Cosmetics

To order, call your Beauty Consultant or use this form. ▮1 Check off your shade choices on the color chart at left and include with your order form. ▮2 Indicate products you wish to order by writing the price for each item in the box provided. If ordering more than one of any item, multiply the unit price by the quantity desired. ▮3 Total your order. Enclose form and shade chart (if applicable) in an envelope with a check or money order and mail to your Consultant. Or ask her about using MasterCard or Visa.

Personalized Collections	PRICE
Complete Collection (From $172.50)	
Basic Skin Care Plus Basic Glamour (From $122.50)	
Basic Skin Care (From $56.00)	

Basic Skin Care

CLEANSE	
Gentle Cleansing Cream 1, 4 oz.	9.00
Creamy Cleanser 2, 6.5 oz.	9.00
Deep Cleanser 3, 6.5 oz.	9.00
Purifying Bar, 4.2 oz.	11.00
Purifying Bar Refill, 4.2 oz.	9.00

RETEXTURE	
Moisture Rich Mask 1, 4 oz.	11.00
Revitalizing Mask 2, 4 oz.	11.00

FRESHEN	
Gentle Action Freshener 1, 6.5 oz.	10.00
Refining Freshener 2, 6.5 oz.	10.00
Blemish Control Toner 3, 6.5 oz.	10.00

MOISTURE BALANCE	
Enriched Moisturizer 1, 4 oz.	16.00
Balancing Moisturizer 2, 4 oz.	16.00
Oil Control Lotion 3, 4 oz.	16.00

PROTECT	
Day Radiance Cream Foundation, .5 oz.	10.00
Day Radiance Liquid Foundation, 1 oz.	10.00
IMPROVED! Oil-Free Foundation, 1 oz.	10.00
Cosmetic Sponges (pack of 2)	2.00

Refillable Compacts

Day Radiance Compact (empty)	6.00
Filled with Day Radiance Cream Foundation	16.00
Glamour Compact (empty)	6.00
Filled with two eye colors, retractable eye shadow brush and glamour blending brush	18.00
Filled with two eye colors, sponge tip applicator and glamour blending brush	17.00
Filled with two eye colors and sponge tip applicator	15.00
Filled with Powder Perfect cheek color or pressed powder and brush	15.00

Skin Supplements

Nighttime Recovery System, 2.8 oz.	25.00
IMPROVED! Daily Defense Complex SPF 4, 1 oz.	25.00
Extra Emollient Cleansing Cream, 4 oz.	9.00
Extra Emollient Night Cream, 2.5 oz.	11.00
Extra Emollient Moisturizer, 4 oz.	16.00
Moisture Renewal Treatment Cream, 2.5 oz.	18.00
Acne Treatment Gel, 1.25 oz.	6.00
Eye Cream Concentrate, .5 oz.	12.00
Eye Makeup Remover, 1.3 oz.	7.00

Glamour Collection

EYES		PRICE
Powder Perfect Eye Color*	Qty.____ ×	4.00
Sponge Tip Applicator	Qty.____ ×	1.00
Glamour Blending Brush	Qty.____ ×	2.00
Retractable Eye Shadow Brush	Qty.____ ×	2.00
NEW! Retractable Eyeliner Brush		2.00
Eye Defining Pencil	Qty.____ ×	6.50
Eyebrow Pencil ☐ Blonde ☐ Light Brown ☐ Brown ☐ Soft Black		6.50
Conditioning Mascara ☐ Black ☐ Brown		7.50
Waterproof Mascara ☐ Black ☐ Brown		7.50
Flawless Mascara ☐ Black		7.50

LIPS		
Lasting Color Lipstick	Qty.____ ×	8.00
Retractable Lip Brush	Qty.____ ×	2.00
Lip Liner Pencil	Qty.____ ×	6.50
Lip Gloss ☐ Natural ☐ Pearl		6.50

FACE		
Powder Perfect Cheek Color*	Qty.____ ×	7.00
Cheek Color/Pressed Powder Brush	Qty.____ ×	2.00
Creamy Cheek Color	Qty.____ ×	6.00
Blush Rouge		6.00
Powder Perfect Loose Powder ☐ Light ☐ Medium ☐ Dark		12.00
NEW! Retractable Loose Powder Brush		2.00
Powder Perfect Pressed Powder* ☐ Light ☐ Medium ☐ Dark		7.00
Facial Highlighter		7.50
Touch-On Concealer ☐ Light ☐ Medium ☐ Dark		7.50
Cream Concealer (Yellow)		7.50

Sun Essentials

Facial Sunblock SPF 15, 2.5 oz.	9.50
Oil-Free Facial Sunblock SPF 15, 2.5 oz.	9.50
Waterproof Sunscreen SPF 8, 4.5 oz.	9.50
Sensitive Skin Waterproof Sunblock SPF 15, 4.5 oz.	9.50
Super Sunblock SPF 30, 6 oz.	12.50
Lip Protector SPF 15, .14 oz.	10.00
Sunless Tanning Lotion, 4.5 oz.	10.00

Personalized Hair Care

Balancing Shampoo, 16 oz.	8.00
Balancing Conditioner, 16 oz.	8.00
Enriched Styling Gel, 5.5 oz.	5.00
Ultimate Styling Mousse, 5.25 oz.	7.00
Finishing Spray, 7.9 oz.	6.00

Fragrances

Tribute Fine Cologne, 1.9 oz.	23.00
Premonition Fine Cologne Spray, 1.75 oz.	25.00
Acapella Fine Cologne Spray, 1.9 oz.	25.00
Angelfire Spray Cologne, 1.75 oz.	16.00
Genji Fine Cologne Spray, 2 oz.	24.00
Intrigue Spray Cologne, 1.75 oz.	14.00

Body Care

	PRICE
Buffing Cream, 6 oz.	9.50
Cleansing Gel, 8 oz.	9.00
Moisturizing Lotion, 8 oz.	8.50
Exquisite Body Lotion, 8 oz.	8.50
Exquisite Dusting Powder, 3 oz.	15.00

Nail Care

Complete Nail Care Collection**	42.50
Basic Nail Care Collection (Steps 1–5)	25.00
Step 1: Treatment Oil, .45 fl. oz.	5.00
Step 2: Fortifier, .45 fl. oz.	5.00
Step 3: Binder, .45 fl. oz.	5.00
Step 4: Color Shield, .45 fl. oz. Qty.____ ×	5.00
Step 5: Protector, .45 fl. oz.	5.00
☐ Clear ☐ Satin Finish	
Quick Dry, .45 fl. oz.	5.00
Hand Cream SPF 4, 3 oz.	7.50
Advanced Nail Color Remover, 7.15 fl. oz.	6.50
Nail Care Thinner, .45 fl. oz.	3.50
Four-Way Nail Buffer	4.00
Emery Board	1.00

*Refills for compacts.
**Includes Steps 1–5 plus assorted products and tools for a complete manicure.

Products for Him

Quattro Cologne, 4 oz.	21.00
Tamerisk Cologne, 4 oz.	18.00
ReVeur After Shave Cologne, 3.75 oz.	14.00
Skin Management for Men Cleansing Bar, 4.2 oz.	9.50
Cleansing Bar Refill, 4.2 oz.	8.00
Toner, 5.5 oz.	8.50
Conditioner, 3 oz.	12.00
Oil Absorber, 3 oz.	12.00
Blemish Control Formula, 2 oz.	8.00
Shave Cream, 5.25 oz.	5.00

Total of Product(s) Ordered $ _____

Applicable Sales Tax $ _____

Total $ _____

NAME _____

ADDRESS _____

CITY, STATE, ZIP CODE _____

TELEPHONE _____

Check card used: ☐ VISA ☐ MasterCard

ACCOUNT NUMBER _____ EXPIRATION DATE _____

SIGNATURE _____

ALL PRICES ARE SUGGESTED RETAIL. ADD SALES TAX WHERE APPLICABLE. Mary Kay, Day Radiance, Acapella, Angelfire, Tribute, Genji, Intrigue, Premonition, Quattro, ReVeur, Tamerisk, Exquisite, Moisture Renewal, Skin Management and Sun Essentials are registered trademarks of Mary Kay Cosmetics, Inc.
© 1991 Mary Kay Cosmetics, Inc., Dallas, Texas 75247.   Printed in U.S.A.

Following is a description of the five-step Mary Kay basic skin care program:

- *Cleanse:* Cleansing cream, lotion cleanser, or cleansing bar cleans quickly and gently to remove makeup, surface oil, and impurities without stripping away natural moisture.

- *Retexture:* Facial mask/scrub improves the texture of skin, removes dead cells, and helps make pores appear smaller.
- *Freshen:* Skin freshener or toner completes the cleansing process as it conditions and tones facial skin, promoting a finer-textured appearance.
- *Moisture Balance:* Moisturizer or conditioner helps skin retain its optimum moisture balance, while improving hydration and smoothness.
- *Protect:* Day Radiance or Oil-Free Foundation provides protection as it covers minor imperfections to give skin a smooth, even-toned finish.

SKIN SUPPLEMENTS

To meet the special needs of a wide range of skin types and address specific skin care needs, Mary Kay created a line of skin supplements including Nighttime Recovery System, Moisture Renewal treatment cream, Daily Defense Complex, Extra Emollient Night Cream, Extra Emollient Moisturizer, Eye Cream Concentrate, Eye Makeup Remover, and Acne Treatment Gel. The skin care profile helps guide the consultant in recommending skin supplement products to her customers. Skin supplements make up roughly 10 percent of gross sales at Mary Kay.

EXHIBIT 9-1-2 Mary Kay Skin Care Profile Questionnaire

MARY KAY SKIN CARE PROFILE

Check the boxes that best describe your skin. Please be sure to answer all questions.

1. By noon, my facial skin usually feels . . .

☐ Tight, slightly dry or shows some flakiness ☐ Neither dry nor oily ☐ Slightly oily on the forehead, nose and chin (T-zone) ☐ Oily over most of my face

2. My pores can best be described as . . .

☐ Almost invisible ☐ Small ☐ Somewhat obvious in T-zone ☐ Very obvious

3. I experience problems with pimples, blackheads or whiteheads . . .

☐ Never or rarely ☐ Generally once a month ☐ Sometimes, most often in T-zone or along jawline ☐ Frequently

4. The general condition of my skin . . .

☐ Tends to be dry or tight ☐ Is neither excessively dry nor oily ☐ Is oily in some areas, dry in others ☐ Is generally oily

5. Considering appearance only, by noon my face generally looks . . .

☐ Dry with a matte or dull finish ☐ Fresh, neither shiny nor dull ☐ Slightly oily in T-zone ☐ Shiny and oily over most of my face

© 1982, 1983, 1989, 1990 MARY KAY COSMETICS, INC., DALLAS, TEXAS 75247 PRINTED IN USA 2690 L90

NAME ____________ (PLEASE PRINT)

DATE ____________ 19 ____

HOME PHONE ( ) ____________ BUS. PHONE ( ) ____________

STREET ADDRESS ____________

CITY ____________ STATE ____________ ZIP ____________

BIRTHDAY ____________ ANNIVERSARY ____________

OCCUPATION ____________

SPOUSE'S NAME ____________ SPOUSE'S BIRTHDAY ____________

HOSTESS' NAME/REFERRED BY ____________

6. Which of the following best describes your skin tone?

☐ Very fair to light ☐ Medium to dark olive ☐ Light bronze to ebony

7. Which of the following do you feel your skin needs most?

☐ Extra help to counteract signs of dryness and loss of elasticity? ☐ Protection from factors that accelerate the signs of aging?

☐ Help for the wrinkle and puffiness-prone eye area? ☐ A protective shield that minimizes moisture evaporation?

☐ Treatment for occasional or frequent blemishes? ☐ Non-oily moisturization to soothe stressed skin and minimize fine lines?

THE COLORLOGIC GLAMOUR SYSTEM

Mary Kay offers a complete line of lip colors, eye colors, cheek colors, and other products in a wide variety of shades. Each is created to harmonize with a woman's skin tone, hair color, individual wardrobe colors, and personal preference. There's a product and a shade for every mood and style, from dramatic to natural. The company's product and shade mix is carefully selected to ensure the line appeals to women of all ethnic backgrounds and age groups. Glamour products account for about 30 percent of gross sales.

PERSONALIZED BEAUTY ANALYSIS

With a combination of technology and glamour, this innovative, computerized beauty tool allows a woman to maximize the power of the ColorLogic Glamour System. The customer and the consultant answer a series of questions together. (See the questionnaire in Exhibit 9-1-3.) These questions include the customer's skin type, foundation shade, eye color, hair color, age, wardrobe preference, makeup preference, lip shape, eye shape, and face shape. After the questionnaire is filled out completely, the consultant mails it to the company. Within approximately two weeks, a personalized computer analysis is sent back to the consultant. The analysis recommends colors, products, and application techniques that will enhance the customer's features. The consultant then meets with her customer and reviews her beauty analysis. This tool helps the consultant recommend individualized colors and glamour techniques to bring out the best in each different customer. This is the only personalized analysis available today that recommends colors, plus tells the user how and where to apply them based on her facial features, personal coloring, wardrobe, and makeup preference.

MEN'S PRODUCTS

Mary Kay Cosmetics was one of the first cosmetic companies to focus on men's skin care needs. The Skin Management for Men system is scientifically formulated to meet the needs of a man's skin. The three-step regimen includes a cleansing bar, toner, and conditioner or oil absorber. Specialized products include shave cream and an acne medication. Mary Kay's men's products accounted for less than 5 percent of gross sales in 1990 but approximately 20 percent of the entire men's skin care market.

WOMEN'S FRAGRANCES

Following is a list of how the company describes its "scents for every mood, every occasion, every personal style":

- ACAPELLA: A spirited floral with "A style all your own."
- GENJI: A fragrant floral Oriental that "Makes the moment linger."

EXHIBIT 9-1-3 ColorLogic Personalized Beauty Analysis Questionnaire

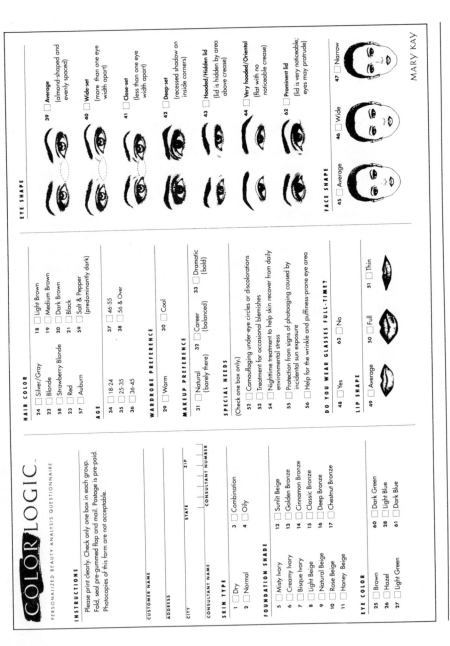

COLOR LOGIC

PERSONALIZED BEAUTY ANALYSIS QUESTIONNAIRE

INSTRUCTIONS

Please print clearly. Check only one box in each group. Fold, seal pre-gummed flap and mail. Postage is pre-paid. Photocopies of this form are not acceptable.

CUSTOMER NAME

ADDRESS

CITY _____ **STATE** _____ **ZIP** _____

CONSULTANT NAME _____ **CONSULTANT NUMBER** _____

SKIN TYPE

1 ☐ Dry
2 ☐ Normal
3 ☐ Combination
4 ☐ Oily

FOUNDATION SHADE

5 ☐ Misty Ivory
6 ☐ Creamy Ivory
7 ☐ Bisque Ivory
8 ☐ Light Beige
9 ☐ Natural Beige
10 ☐ Rose Beige
11 ☐ Honey Beige
12 ☐ Sunlit Beige
13 ☐ Golden Bronze
14 ☐ Cinnamon Bronze
15 ☐ Classic Bronze
16 ☐ Deep Bronze
17 ☐ Chestnut Bronze

EYE COLOR

25 ☐ Brown
26 ☐ Hazel
27 ☐ Light Green
60 ☐ Dark Green
28 ☐ Light Blue
61 ☐ Dark Blue

HAIR COLOR

24 ☐ Silver/Gray
22 ☐ Blonde
58 ☐ Strawberry Blonde
23 ☐ Red
57 ☐ Auburn
18 ☐ Light Brown
19 ☐ Medium Brown
20 ☐ Dark Brown
21 ☐ Black
59 ☐ Salt & Pepper (predominantly dark)

AGE

34 ☐ 18-24
35 ☐ 25-35
36 ☐ 36-45
37 ☐ 46-55
38 ☐ 56 & Over

WARDROBE PREFERENCE

29 ☐ Warm
30 ☐ Cool

MAKEUP PREFERENCE

31 ☐ Natural (barely there)
32 ☐ Career (balanced)
33 ☐ Dramatic (bold)

SPECIAL NEEDS

(Check one box only.)

52 ☐ Camouflaging under-eye circles or discolorations
53 ☐ Treatment for occasional blemishes
54 ☐ Nighttime treatment to help skin recover from daily environmental stress
55 ☐ Protection from signs of photoaging caused by incidental sun exposure
56 ☐ Help for the wrinkle and puffiness-prone eye area

DO YOU WEAR GLASSES FULL-TIME?

48 ☐ Yes
63 ☐ No

LIP SHAPE

49 ☐ Average
50 ☐ Full
51 ☐ Thin

EYE SHAPE

39 ☐ Average (almond-shaped and evenly spaced)
40 ☐ Wide-set (more than one eye width apart)
41 ☐ Close-set (less than one eye width apart)
42 ☐ Deep-set (recessed shadow on inside corners)
43 ☐ Hooded/Hidden lid (lid is hidden by area above crease)
44 ☐ Very hooded/Oriental (flat with no noticeable crease)
62 ☐ Prominent lid (lid is very noticeable; eyes may protrude)

FACE SHAPE

45 ☐ Average
46 ☐ Wide
47 ☐ Narrow

MARY KAY

352

- INTRIGUE: A unique Oriental scent that is "One of the most intriguing things about you."
- ANGELFIRE: A warm, floral/aldehydic scent "When you're ready for the next adventure."
- TRIBUTE: A light floral "In celebration of you."
- PREMONITION: A warm, rich Oriental that signals "The best is yet to come."

MEN'S FRAGRANCES

Mary Kay describes its men's fragrances as follows:
- QUATTRO: A subtle blend of spices and woods that is "A passion you share."
- TAMERISK: A scent of greens, spices, and woods. "It reinforces his style."
- TRIBUTE for MEN: A contemporary blend of fruits, musk, and sandalwood. "In celebration of you."

Mary Kay's men's and women's fragrances make up less than 15 percent of gross sales.

PERSONALIZED HAIR CARE

Mary Kay Cosmetics has also developed a line of hair care products to meet the needs of most customers. The line features shampoo, conditioner, and styling products to benefit every type and style of hair. These hair care products account for less than 5 percent of gross sales.

BODY CARE

Mary Kay's body care line is a natural extension of the five steps to beautiful skin: a scientifically formulated and uniquely balanced program to care for and beautify body skin. It includes three simple steps: buffing, cleansing, and moisturizing. Body care products account for less than 5 percent of gross sales.

SUN ESSENTIALS

Mary Kay Sun Essentials products include six items ranging in sun protection factors from 8 to 30, developed for all ages and all skin tones. These products are specifically formulated to give the most complete head-to-toe protection against the sun and its effects. They are completely compatible with the entire Mary Kay product line. All Sun Essentials sun protection products are safe for everyday use and clinically tested for skin irritancy and allergy by an independent laboratory under a leading dermatologist. They are all PABA free, fragrance free (except for Lip Protector, which has a small amount of fragrance), noncomedogenic, and protect the skin from damaging rays of the sun. Additionally, the Sun Essentials product lineup includes Sunless Tanning Lotion for a rich, natural-looking tan without the damage ultraviolet exposure can cause. Mary Kay's Sun Essentials make up less than 5 percent of gross sales.

NAIL CARE

Mary Kay Cosmetics has scientifically created a unique five-step approach to nail care. Laboratory tests have proven that with consistent use, these products are effective in helping maintain stronger, longer, more beautiful-looking nails. All products have been formulated to be used together. They provide nails with a perfect balance of flexibility and hardness for maximum wear and minimal chipping. The Mary Kay Advanced Nail Care System is compatible with sculptured nails, tips, wraps, and artificial nails. It includes products and instructions for preparation of the nails for the manicure, a five-step process, and recoating. Mary Kay's nail care products make up less than 10 percent of gross sales.

POINT OF SALES

Mary Kay consultants rely heavily on the women who hostess their skin care classes. A hostess for a consultant may be an acquaintance, a referral, or someone she just met through a cold call.

Most sales for a Mary Kay consultant begin with a skin care class. The main purpose of the class is to teach a personalized regimen of good skin care. It's a learning experience for millions of women, a social occasion, and the company's primary marketplace. It's where strong brand loyalty begins and long-term consumer buying relationships are established.

Classes are held in the home of a hostess who has invited no more than five friends to participate in a two-hour session. The consultant takes her guests through the Mary Kay skin care program, step by step. The *Beauty Book,* which provides a complete listing of products, available colors, and suggested retail prices, as well as instructions on how to use the basic skin care products, is the key literature piece used at the skin care class. The consultant offers personalized skin care and glamour techniques and demonstrates the proper application of all products. Mary Kay's specialty line of personal care products, including nail care and sun protection products, fragrances, and body care and men's skin care products, is also briefly presented. Because the Mary Kay consultant normally has merchandise on hand to fill orders taken during the class, her guests can return home and start their new skin care and glamour routines immediately.

In this intimate setting, the consumer receives more personal attention and instruction than is possible in a retail outlet. This in-home sales method also offers women the ability to try the products they like before they purchase them in a private, relaxed environment. Mary Kay feels that personalized attention is the most effective way to teach and sell skin care and glamour products. The consultant has a chance to get to know her customers on a personal basis, allowing her to provide a higher level of customer service.

The guests at the skin care classes are the lifeblood of the consultant's business. These guests provide the consultant with important networking possibilities, leading to new hostesses and customers.

THE IMPORTANCE OF CUSTOMER SERVICE

One of the most important aspects of a consultant's business is customer service. At Mary Kay it is believed that quality is total customer satisfaction. By providing each customer with personal attention and high-quality products, a consultant is able to build strong customer loyalty. Consultants have the unique opportunity to reintroduce personal contact and friendship into the marketplace. This consistent, individualized attention is something customers do not receive when shopping in a department store. Consultants do not forget about their customers after the initial purchase. At a selected point in time, the consultant will telephone the customer to see if she needs any additional products. These additional product sales are much easier than the initial sale. Mary Kay consultants also are able to offer an unconditional "satisfaction or your money back" guarantee on every product they sell. This is Mary Kay's way of helping the consultant and the company retain customer trust and goodwill.

CURRENT MARKETING TOOLS

Mary Kay consultants are supported by a variety of marketing tools. The company utilizes these tools to establish a positive image in the marketplace.

Direct Support

The Direct Support program incorporates the best features of direct mail and Mary Kay's direct-selling approach. Through the Direct Support program, the company supports the consultants by directly contacting their customers with a personalized letter and a beautiful four-color brochure featuring new product launches, limited-edition promotions, and gift-with-purchase offers. (See Exhibit 9-1-4 for an example.) There are typically four major programs per year, with each wave going to over three million customers. The consultant pays a small fee for each customer she enrolls in each program. There are four main advantages for the consultant who participates:

1. The consultant saves valuable time and money. By signing up preferred customers for the program, the consultant is liberated from time-consuming and costly mailings that would normally need to be done.

2. The consultant has more time to engage in personal contact activities such as skin care classes, facials, and ColorLogic Glamour System consultations, thereby giving the consultant a greater opportunity for increased sales and a larger customer base.

EXHIBIT 9-1-4 Mary Kay Cosmetics Direct Mail Brochure

The beauty of nature . . . a makeup collection inspired by the colors that surround us.

COUNTRYSIDE COLORS

MARY KAY

MARY KAY COMPACTS ARE REFILLABLE

Your Mary Kay glamour compact was designed to be used again and again. When you run out of your Day Radiance® cream foundation or Powder Perfect™ Eye or Cheek Color shade, don't throw the compact away. Just buy a refill and snap it into place. This not only saves you money, but also gives you one less item to recycle.

Our All-in-One Glamour Organizer (pictured far left) is a practical choice for the woman who travels or wants all her makeup shades in one convenient place. Just ask your Consultant how you can receive this item as a gift when you hostess a Mary Kay skin care class.

(fold in half to mail.)

PLACE STAMP HERE

MARY KAY
FACE-TO-FACE BEAUTY ADVICE

COUNTRYSIDE COLORS

©1991 Mary Kay Cosmetics, Inc. Dallas, TX 75247   Printed in U.S.A. 3164

356

3. The Direct Support program works directly alongside the consultant while she is actively working at her business. The consultant is reaching customers in an entirely new and professional way—with no additional demands upon busy schedules.

4. Direct Support is an efficient and effective means of advertising the consultant's products and services.

Exhibit 9-1-5 presents a promotion piece directed at consultants urging them to participate in a fall Direct Support program.

Although a powerful program in support of a personalized-service sales approach, the Direct Support program also addresses the question of customer retention, which is a major issue facing all forms of retailing in the nineties. In Mary Kay's case, customers tend to be lost when consultants leave the business, as well as for the more traditional reasons, such as moving. There have been over 12 million customers enrolled, and 4 million have been retained by assignment to another consultant. Since it costs five times as much

---

EXHIBIT 9-1-5   Direct Support Promotion to Mary Kay Beauty Consultants

to establish a customer as it does to retain her, this is a very important marketing edge for Mary Kay.

ADVERTISING AT MARY KAY

Mary Kay has advertised only lightly and sporadically for the last decade since the vast majority of promotional dollars is allocated to sales force incentives. In 1989 and 1990, an "advertorial" campaign ran in selected women's service books (see Exhibit 9-1-6). The advertising traditionally has attempted to link an interested customer back to a beauty consultant, since the products are only available through this specialized channel. Consultants often use these advertorials in personal presentations to help establish or gain credibility.

Mary Kay ran advertorials in the January 1990 issues of *Essence* and *New Woman* and received 561 inquiries from the former and 516 from the latter. Based on a survey of 294 of those who called, 92 percent obtained the name and number of a beauty consultant. Further, 67 percent contacted a consultant, 23 percent purchased product, and 16 percent became beauty consultants. Finally, it was estimated that every 100 calls generated approximately $1,500 in initial product sales.

MARKETING PUBLICITY

Marketing publicity seeks to keep the Mary Kay Cosmetics name and products on the minds of the beauty editors of the top beauty and fashion and women's service magazines in the nation. The editors, in turn, will sometimes include Mary Kay products within their features. The editors are updated on all new product launches through press releases and meetings with corporate staff. (Exhibit 9-1-7 presents a typical press release.) Additionally, when appropriate, the press is also briefed on the Mary Kay career opportunity or the company's policies and practices with respect to timely topics such as animal testing or environmental issues.

Mary Kay has also created Skin Wellness, a public service skin cancer awareness and prevention program, in response to the company's growing concern about skin cancer and the public's need for accurate information. This program has not only helped save lives but has also generated favorable publicity for the company among both the medical community and the general public.

1-800-MARYKAY

Mary Kay's toll-free telephone number, 1-800-MARYKAY, is printed on product packaging, advertisements, and consumer literature. Prospective customers call in to locate a beauty consultant in their area and/or learn more about the career opportunity. Additionally, existing customers who have lost their consultant can call 1-800-MARYKAY to locate another one. Leads are returned to proven performers within the sales force.

EXHIBIT 9-1-6   Mary Kay Magazine "Advertorial"

Looking Grrreat!!

Focal*point*

▼

A PERSONAL VIEW ON BEAUTY

LOOKING GRRREAT!! PROMOTIONAL SECTION

Holiday Sparkle. Give your holiday glamour look a festive flair with the **Mary Kay® limited edition collection of sparklers** for eyes, lips and nails. In three precious metal shades — silver, bronze and gold — these versatile products offer a range of exciting possibilities. Wear one sparkler alone for a subtle shimmer; combine with other glamour shades for extra special effects. To achieve the look shown: apply Gold eye sparkler on the brow and along upper and lower lashline; Bronze eye sparkler on the lid over Shimmering Rust eye shadow. On the lips: Gold lip sparkler over Ginger Pearl lipstick. □

Scents of Style. Celebrate the season with fragrance — a gift that's always appropriate, always appreciated. Mary Kay has an exclusive collection of scents just perfect for holiday giving — one certain to suit every style, every preference. Choose from an exquisite array of product forms — long-time favorites including cologne, soap, dusting powder, body lotion and bath and shower gel plus all-new body mousse, body gelee and scented bath beads. There's no better way to add to the love and the laughter — the magic and the memories — that make the holiday season special. Pictured, selected gifts of **Genji®** fragrance: Perfumed Body Mousse, Fragrant Body Gelee and Fine Cologne Spray. □

For the special men in your life — a gift of fragrance that lets you speak without saying a word. The Mary Kay holiday collection includes an assortment of distinctive scents and fragrance forms including cologne, soap, shower gel and liquid talc, a light lotion that drys to a fragrant, powdery finish. Shown here, Tamerisk® Liquid Talc.

▶

Discover your personal beauty resource. A professional Mary Kay Beauty Consultant can help you define your own unique beauty style. She'll personalize a skin care and beauty routine just for you, show you the latest products and explain how to simplify your holiday shopping with elegant gifts and convenient service. For information on the products featured here, call your Mary Kay Beauty Consultant, or call **1-800-MARY KAY** to locate a Consultant in your area. □

EXHIBIT 9-1-7 Mary Kay Cosmetics Press Release

MARY KAY
FACE-TO-FACE BEAUTY ADVICE

FOR IMMEDIATE RELEASE
May 13, 1991

CONTACT: Marcia Shivers or Terrie Hoffman
Marketing Publicity
(214) 905—5331 or (214) 905—5332 Kim Cravetz (212) 697—5600
Hill & Knowlton Inc.

THE TAPESTRIES COLLECTION BY MARY KAY ANTICIPATES FALL'S RETURN TO COLOR

DALLAS...Rich, striking colors will be the new spin on the color wheel for fall fashion and glamour. Anticipating the fall forecast for an explosion of color, Mary Kay Cosmetics introduces TAPESTRIES, a limited edition glamour collection of eye colors, cheek colors, and lip and nail color sets.

TAPESTRIES Powder Perfect eye colors range from earthy tones of Sage and Topaz to more neutral shades of Cameo and Platinum, to bluer tones of Lapis and Lavender. With shades perfect for every skin tone, the eye colors may be applied dry or wet depending on the desired look.

Green will be prominent on the color palette for fall fashion. Reflecting this influence, TAPESTRIES weaves a green undertone through many of its eye colors. The shades are so versatile that they can go from a colorful, dramatic look to a softer, more natural look just by varying the amount applied.

The collection features both warm and cool Powder Perfect cheek colors. On the warmer side, Ginger is a medium peach with brown undertones. And for skin tones that appreciate cooler colors, there's Orchid, a versatile blue—pink shade.

And for the final touch, TAPESTRIES includes four lip and nail sets. There are two pearlized warm colors of Peach Pearl and Copper. Cool colors are a pearlized Rose Mauve and a matte—finish Magenta.

—more—

ADD ONE
TAPESTRIES

Lasting Color Lipstick is a long—wearing formula which provides rich, radiant color as it conditions lips. And Nail Color Shield offers maximum protection, long wear and super shine.

TAPESTRIES Powder Perfect eye colors and cheek colors are a silky—smooth formula that conditions skin as it provides long—lasting color. All items in the collection are dermatologist—tested and safe for sensitive skin.

TAPESTRIES are packaged in richly colored cartons of blues, greens and mauves woven into a floral tapestry design. The eye colors and cheek colors feature a special floral emboss.

Limited edition TAPESTRIES for fall 1991 will be available through independent Mary Kay beauty consultants from July through September. Consumers may locate a consultant in the Yellow Pages under "Cosmetics/Retail" or by calling 1—800—MARY KAY.

Mary Kay Cosmetics Inc. manufactures and distributes more than 200 premium skin care, glamour, hair care, body care, nail care, sun protection and fragrance products through a worldwide sales force of more than 200,000 independent beauty consultants.

—30—

Mary Kay Cosmetics Inc.   8787 Stemmons Freeway   Dallas, Texas 75247-3794
(214) 630-8787   FAX (214) 905-5908

WORD-OF-MOUTH ADVERTISING

Word-of-mouth advertising has been a major tool in building Mary Kay's 98 percent aided awareness in the marketplace. Most consultants start as loyal users and are delighted to share with friends, family, and acquaintances the positive experiences they have had with Mary Kay products and services.

CONSUMER BROCHURES

In addition to the consumer brochures distributed through Direct Support, the sales force can purchase a selection of brochures that feature different product lines from the company. These brochures, typically including color photography, are then distributed by the consultant to her customers to help reinforce her professional image and educate her customers about Mary Kay products, proper skin care, glamour techniques, and other related topics.

CUSTOMER AND SALES FORCE PROFILES

Profiles of Mary Kay's beauty consultants and customers are presented in Table 9-1-5. (Figures have been altered to protect confidential information.)

THE FUTURE ROLE OF ADVERTISING

The company has discovered through extensive customer research that many women who have no direct contact with the company have an outdated or negative view of its products and its sales force. Actual customers, however, exhibit great loyalty to the products and to their beauty consultant.

Curran Dandurand, senior vice-president of the marketing group, has wondered about the possibility of developing an advertising program that will not only have immediate impact but also demonstrate that the company's dollars can be profitably allocated to consumer-oriented programs, in addition to the extensive sales force incentives already in place.

She has a budget of $3 million for next year, and, if upper management is convinced of the program's likelihood of success, could look forward to twice that much in the following year. The budget covers production costs and media expenses. Hence, Dandurand has asked her group to recommend how to make the best use of a limited budget relative to that of Mary Kay's competitors in the cosmetics industry. What sort of program should they create? How should the dollars be allocated? Should they recommend mass media and, if so, which specific vehicles? What should be their message to consumers? To what degree, if any, should they address recruiting issues? How will they measure results to convince upper management of the program's success?

TABLE 9-1-5   Mary Kay Beauty Consultant and Customer Profiles

Beauty Consultant Demographics		Customer Demographics	
Marital Status		*Average Age*	
Married	78%	42	
Single	12		
Divorced	8	*Ethnicity*	
Widowed	2	White	88%
		Black	8
Age		Hispanic	4
18–24	10%		
25–34	30	*Employment Status*	
35–44	32	Full time	50%
45–54	20	Part time	25
55 and over	8	Not employed	25
(Average age: 36)			
		Average Household Income	
Education		$41,000	
College or more	75%		
		Average Longevity as a	
Ethnicity		*Mary Kay Customer*	
White	85%	6 years	
Black	9		
Hispanic	6	*Education*	
		College or more:	68%
Area Worked			
Urban/Suburban	75%		
Rural	25		
Average Household Income			
$42,000			
Have Other Employment			
70%			
Tenure with Mary Kay			
Less than 1 year	35%		
1 to 3 years	27		
3 to 5 years	13		
5 to 10 years	20		
Over 10 years	5		
(Median years: 2.0)			

Questions for Discussion and Review

1. Should advertising efforts be targeted primarily toward recruiting consultants, stimulating demand among present users, encouraging present nonusers to try Mary Kay, or focusing on some other audience? What are the advantages and disadvantages of targeting each of these groups? How viable would it be to target a combination of these or other groups? Why?

2. How are Mary Kay's distribution, pricing, and product mix related to possible advertising strategy recommendations? Which of the other marketing mix elements— product, price, place—is most important in developing an advertising strategy for Mary Kay? Why?

3. How could a new advertising campaign be most effectively

integrated into Mary Kay's well-established marketing strategies? More specifically, how might the sales efforts of the consultants be most effectively supported by advertising? Should some sort of responsibilities for advertising be structured around the consultants?

4. Given the $3 million appropriation, would a national or a regional test of advertising's ability to contribute to Mary Kay's marketing success be most appropriate? Why?

C A S E   **9 - 2**

Allen Specialty Company

Allen Specialty Company, located in Detroit, Michigan, manufactured a line of ballpoint pens and mechanical pencils and, in the past five years, had added a line of stationery. Allen products were sold to stationery and office supply wholesalers and retailers, as well as to department stores, discount houses, drugstores, variety stores, and supermarkets. A field sales force of 82 persons operated out of six district sales offices. Allen management believed that a critical factor in the company's sales success was the coordination of its national advertising with the activities of Allen salespeople and dealers.

The sales promotion program was the responsibility of the sales promotion manager, Jack Biggerstaff, and his staff, in conjunction with the sales planning committee at Allen headquarters in Detroit. The sales planning committee consisted of the managers of merchandising, advertising, and marketing research. The sales promotion plan for both new and existing products described objectives and roles of salespersons and dealers; anticipated sales; national, local, and trade advertising; and point-of-purchase displays, deals, premiums, and contest offers.

With the approval of the sales promotion plan by the sales planning committee and Biggerstaff, the sales promotion department prepared sales promotion kits for the Allen sales staff. The kit included advertising proofs, product samples, illustrations of the point-of-purchase displays, samples of premiums offered, and a description of the special deal or contest featured in the promotion.

The sales promotion department prepared a timetable for each promotion plan, showing the date when each advertisement would appear in various media. The timetable was distributed to the sales force and to dealers to enable them to time their sales and advertising to coincide with the national advertising and thereby achieve full impact from the advertising.

When the sales promotion plan was approved by headquarters, it was presented to Allen sales personnel at meetings in each of the six district sales offices. The sales promotion manager and the field sales promotion manager,

---

This case appears in *Sales Management 5/E* by Edward Cundiff, Richard Still, and Norman Govoni. Englewood Cliffs, N.J.: Prentice-Hall, 1988, pp. 261–263. It is intended to be used as the basis for classroom discussion, and not to illustrate either the effective or ineffective handling of an administrative situation. Used by permission of Prentice-Hall.

who reported to the former and whose job was to work with Allen salespeople and dealers on sales promotion projects, made the presentation. Following the meetings, the field sales promotion manager trained the salespeople to properly present the promotion and called on key dealers to enlist their support.

The sales promotion program used with a recent new product introduction was typical of Allen's efforts. In addition to the objectives and timetables, the sales promotion program included (1) selling tools for Allen salespeople—circular letters describing the promotion, a visual presentation portfolio for making promotion presentations, product samples, and reprints of consumer advertisements; (2) selling tools for Allen dealers—presentation kits for selling the new product to consumers, mail circulars to send to consumers, mailing folders for use by dealers, sample folders, and a considerable amount of prize money for dealers' sales personnel; and (3) advertising support for Allen dealers—advertising in national media and sample folders to be sent to consumers who responded to a coupon offer.

One sales promotion program was presented each week in the district offices in late November and December. When the schedule was announced, Mike Halloran, assistant sales manager in charge of the Pacific Northwest district, called Jack Biggerstaff to complain that the sales promotion orientation session in his district had been scheduled for December 27—a quiet week when many of his salespeople had found extra time to spend with their families and when several had customarily taken short skiing vacations. Biggerstaff explained that the promotion plan would not be completed until mid-November, and since these sales promotion meetings were conducted by home office personnel in the six sales regions, it was not possible to schedule more than one a week. It was tough, but Halloran's district had drawn the bad week this year.

Halloran responded that he thought the sales promotion sessions were a waste of time anyway. His salespeople lost two productive days in these sessions, and, in his opinion, knowledge of details of the Allen Company's advertising and promotion plans didn't make the sales rep's job of selling to wholesalers and retailers any easier. Anyway, it was the responsibility of the field sales promotion manager to work with the individual salespeople and call on key dealers. He also complained that when these sessions were scheduled in mid-November, they interfered with sales productivity in the busiest season of the year.

Questions for Discussion and Review

1. Evaluate the Allen Specialty Company's organization and plan for coordinating sales and advertising.

2. How should Biggerstaff answer Halloran's complaint?

CASE 9 - 3

Owens-Illinois, Inc., Forest Products Division

As Roy LaFontaine, director of marketing for the Box Operations of Owens-Illinois' Forest Products Division, hurried down the hall for a meeting with the general manager, he reflected on the recommendation he was about to make concerning the marketing budget. There had been strong pressure from the managers of the box plants to increase the field sales force. The number of new sales personnel being considered was 21, involving a salary, travel, and training expenditure of nearly $900,000. This decision would have been fairly straightforward under ordinary circumstances. However, the imposition of a strict corporate limit on budget increases of 6 percent made the decision more difficult. These circumstances were forcing a trade-off between either adding the sales personnel but reducing the advertising budget by $300,000 or holding the line on the advertising budget but not increasing the field force quite as much. Some middle-ground alternatives were also possible.

COMPANY BACKGROUND

Owens-Illinois, Inc. (O-I), was one of the world's leading and most diversified manufacturers of packaging products. Within its two major operating units, the domestic and international operations, the company manufactured and sold a broad range of products. These included glass containers, containerboard, corrugated and solid fiber shipping containers, composite cans, multiwall paper and plastic shipping sacks, plastic shrink and stretch film, plywood and dimensional lumber, semirigid plastic containers, metal and plastic closures, metal containers, and disposable paper and plastic cups, tubs, lids, and plates. Another important part of O-I's business consisted of specialized glass products, such as television bulbs for color and black-and-white picture tubes, scientific and laboratory glassware, and tumblers, stemware, and decorative items for household and institutional use. In addition, some overseas affiliates manufactured flat glass and related products.

In 1976, O-I operated more than one hundred manufacturing and related facilities in twenty-seven states and employed more than 50,000 persons in the

This case was written by Morton Galper, and appears in *Sales Management 5/E* by Edward Cundiff, Richard Still, and Norman Govoni. Englewood Cliffs, N.J.: Prentice-Hall, 1988, pp. 264–277. It is intended to be used as the basis for classroom discussion, and not to illustrate either the effective or ineffective handling of an administrative situation. Used by permission of Prentice-Hall.

United States. In addition, foreign affiliates in which O-I had a 50 percent or more equity interest employed about 32,000 persons in twenty-one countries outside the United States. These affiliates operated eighty-three plants and other facilities in Europe, Latin America, Canada, the Far East, the Caribbean, and Australia.

Owens-Illinois was organized into three lines of business: Packaging, Consumer and Technical, and International. Packaging included the Glass Container Division, Forest Products Division, Plastic Products Division, and Closure and Metal Container Division. Consumer and Technical included the Lily Division, Television Products Division, Kimble Division, and Libbey Glass Division. International was responsible for substantially all of Owens-Illinois' international operations and was organized principally on geographic lines— the European Division, Western Hemisphere Division, Far East/Pacific Operations, and Overseas Forest Products Operations. Owens-Illinois considered each major business segment to be a separate line of business.

TABLE 9-3-1 **Owens-Illinois, Inc., Corporate Income Statements for the Five Years Ended December 31, 1976 (millions of dollars)**

	1976	1975	1974	1973	1972
Revenues:					
Net sales	$2,571.77	$2,273.2	$2,116.4	$1,856.9	$1,636.3
Other	54.1	56.8	47.7	44.6	32.8
	$2,625.8	$2,330.0	$2,164.1	$1,901.5	$1,669.1
Costs and expenses:					
Manufacturing, shipping, and delivery	$2,123.3	$1,895.9	$1,741.3	$1,525.9	$1,332.0
Research, engineering, selling, administrative, and other	285.9	248.5	238.3	216.5	198.2
Interest	42.6	43.7	38.0	31.6	26.7
	$2,451.8	$2,188.1	$2,017.6	$1,774.0	$1,556.9
Operating profit:	$174.0	$141.9	$146.5	$127.5	$112.2
Provision for income taxes	63.1	51.0	58.6	50.2	45.0
Minority shareholders' interests in earnings	4.2	3.6	4.4	2.8	2.6
Earnings before extraordinary items	$106.7	$87.3	$83.5	$74.5	$64.6
Extraordinary items	71.6	—	—	56.4	4.4
Net earnings	$178.3	$87.3	$83.5	$130.9	$69.0
Preferred and preference dividends	3.7	3.7	3.8	3.8	3.8
Net earnings applicable to common shares	$174.6	$83.6	$79.7	$127.1	$65.2

TABLE 9-3-2   Owens-Illinois, Inc., Corporate Balance Sheets for the Five Years Ended December 31, 1976 (millions of dollars)

	1976	1975	1974	1973	1972
Assets:					
Current assets	$ 801.1	$ 635.0	$ 648.0	$ 581.9	$ 507.1
Investments and other assets	248.3	249.0	238.9	189.9	174.5
Property, plant, and equipment, net	1,145.8	1,063.9	958.4	870.7	816.3
	$2,195.2	$1,947.9	$1,845.3	$1,642.5	$1,497.9
Liabilities:					
Current liabilities	$ 391.2	$ 324.6	$ 312.6	$ 325.7	$ 238.9
Long-term debt	551.8	571.9	553.3	417.4	420.8
Reserves and other credits	206.2	168.1	161.1	141.2	126.2
Minority shareholders' interests	38.5	35.3	28.4	25.7	25.0
	$1,187.7	$1,099.9	$1,055.4	$ 910.0	$ 810.9
Shareholders' equity:					
Capital	$ 214.2	$ 142.5	$ 144.1	$ 144.6	$ 149.3
Retained earnings	793.3	705.5	645.8	587.9	537.7
	$1,007.5	$ 848.0	$ 789.9	$ 732.5	$ 687.0
Equity and liabilities	$2,195.2	$1,947.9	$1,845.3	$1,642.5	$1,497.9

The company had grown steadily in assets, sales, and profitability between 1972 and 1976. Net sales in 1976 were $2,572 million with $106 million in after-tax profits. The sales increase since 1972 had been just over 57 percent, and after-tax earnings had grown somewhat faster, rising by 65 percent over this same period. (See Tables 9-3-1 and 9-3-2 for income statements and balance sheets.)

CORPORATE MANAGEMENT

The philosophy of O-I's senior management was oriented toward a decentralized operation with a high degree of autonomy at the division level. The corporate organization included staff specialists in key functional areas, who interacted with the divisions on a policy and guidance level. Four corporate staff departments had a direct or indirect influence on the marketing decisions of the various divisions:

1.   Department of Economic Research (ER), headed by Elmer Lotshaw
2.   Department of Corporate Marketing (CM), led by Benjamin Colosky
3.   Department of Business Analysis (BA), under Richard Beck
4.   Advertising and Communications Department (AC), directed by Thomas Weiss.

The first three of these functions were grouped together within the Department of Planning, reporting to the director of planning (who was vice-president of the corporate staff).

Department of Economic Research (ER)

This department was responsible for developing and maintaining industry statistics (shipments, capacity, price levels) as well as product line market share data on the major market areas served by O-I. ER also prepared and distributed three-month moving forecasts as well as long-range forecasts of these markets. This was accomplished both through use of corporate forecasting models and ongoing participation in the data-gathering activities of the various industry trade associations.

Department of Corporate Marketing (CM)

This department was responsible for consulting with the operating divisions on the development and implementation of their marketing strategies and plans. The director of CM was also a member of the Corporate Marketing Committee, which sought to increase the effective utilization of the corporation's marketing resources. A vital role performed by CM in its consulting role was to reconcile conflicting industry forecasts among operating divisions that served the same market segments with competitive products (for example, Glass Container, Plastic Products, and Closure and Metal Container divisions).

Department of Business Analysis (BA)

This group was the guardian and coordinator of the planning process within O-I. The latter was a "bottom-up" process—from the product groups within the divisions to the division manager to the president—with the resulting plan ultimately presented for approval or modification to the Executive Policy Committee, which consisted of the chairman and CEO, three senior vice-presidents, and the presidents of Domestic Operations and International Operations. This annual effort was divided into three separate but interrelated stages.

The first stage was the strategic plan. It was prepared in June of each year and generally focused on the following questions: What is or will be happening in the product markets served by the division? How will these occurrences affect O-I and its competitors? What strategic responses are expected by competitors? And finally, what strategic responses does the division plan to make? This was not intended to be a financial plan, but a description of the anticipated environment and responses to it.

The second stage was to convert these descriptions into financial plans. The latter were intended to spell out the financial implications of the environment and the strategies identified earlier.

The final stage, the annual plan, was prepared in the fall and laid out in detail the operating plans and programs for the coming year for each product line and division. These were developed in the context of corporate guidelines for profitability and expenditure levels established by the Policy Committee after evaluation of the strategic plans and their financial implications. It was at this stage that the detailed decisions about sales manpower and advertising expenditures were made. Divisional management was generally considered to have wide latitude in making these decisions, provided the corporate guidelines were fulfilled. These plans were formally reviewed by the operating personnel at the six-month point to make any adjustments in light of changing circumstances.

BA analyzed the plans prepared by the divisions and made recommendations to the Policy Committee as well as suggested changes to divisional management. BA's role was particularly significant in areas related to capital investment decisions and new product programs.

Corporate Advertising and Communications Department (AC)

In 1972, this department became the locus of the advertising, print and audiovisual creative services, and trade show activities for a number of divisions and product groups (Packaging and International businesses, Kimble and Television Product divisions, as well as the Electronic Materials and Venture Marketing activities). AC provided assistance to these units in overall marketing communications planning as well as supplied creative resources both internally and from outside suppliers. AC also implemented two major corporate communications projects: a corporate advertising program in print media and a corporate identity program, which emphasized appropriate and consistent graphics on all O-I property and communications.

Together this represented a budget in excess of $7 million for advertising and related communications in 1976. The budget was broken down approximately as follows:

Activity	Budget (in millions of dollars)
Corporate advertising and communications	$1.8
Divisional advertising and promotion	5.2
Total	$7.0

The director of AC identified the following decision elements that he thought reflected the key dimensions used in setting the advertising budget at both the corporate and divisional level:

1. Historical expenditure level (as a frame of reference)
2. General satisfaction with results of prior expenditures
3. Conformance with corporate expenditure and profit and loss guidelines
4. New product introductions
5. Promotable advantage(s) in the product

6. Number of market segments pursued

7. Sales potential of typical customer sought.

The director of AC stated that no formal guidelines were used by his office in assisting the various divisions in establishing their advertising budgets. He did comment that the department had an important educational role in getting the divisions to consider the communications program (advertising, publicity, etc.).

In pursuing this broad objective, the AC undertook a number of specific activities:

1. Established a checklist of tasks that advertising could perform for the divisions and the corporation as part of the annual communications presentation.

2. Conducted readership and message recall studies to indicate the cost effectiveness of the advertising programs.

3. Conducted several image studies among the financial and business community to determine their attitudes toward and opinions of O-I.

4. Continually analyzed Starch readership reports to monitor and compare effectiveness of competitive advertising.

O-I FOREST PRODUCTS DIVISION

The Forest Products Division (FPD) was one of the country's largest fully integrated manufacturers of containerboard and corrugated boxes. Its integrated operations consisted of 1,300,000 acres of woodlands, three plywood and lumber mills, four containerboard mills, and twenty corrugated box plants. These activities were divided into three separate operating units within the division. Primary Operations, which was responsible for all forestry and papermaking activities through the production of containerboard, and Box Operations, which was responsible for the manufacture and marketing of corrugated boxes, were the principal volume-producing arms. The third group, Special Products Operations, manufactured and marketed two other classes of packaging materials.

Composite Cans

Composite cans are spirally wound containers that consist of layers of paper in various combinations with foil and plastic. These cans were generally less expensive than metal containers, permitted better graphics, and had certain technical advantages over metal in competitive applications. Areas of application were snack foods, motor oil, and frozen citrus concentrate.

Bag and Film Products

This product area included multiwall paper bags, plastic shipping sacks, and polyethylene packaging films.

TABLE 9-3-3   Forest Products Division Sales (in millions of dollars)

	1976	1975	1974	1973	1972	1971
Forest Products Division sales	$385	$318	$380	$316	245	$211

FPD's 1976 sales in total were approximately $450 million. These were roughly divided as follows:

Primary operations (including lumber operations)	$200 million
Box operations	175 million
Special products	75 million
Total	$450 million

The sales figures reported externally were lower (see Table 9-3-3 for the FPD's five-year sales history), since a significant portion of the division's sales were internal (to itself or to the glass container division).

BOX OPERATIONS (BO)

Box Operations, which supplied corrugated shipping containers to over 4,000 customers, consisted of twenty corrugated box plants organized into three regional groups (southern, northern, and western).

Each plant served a highly localized geographic market generally encompassing customers within a 150-mile radius of the facility. The high weight-to-value ratio of the product created a competitive disadvantage due to shipping costs when the plant solicited business outside of the 150-mile range. The individual plants were organized to operate on a semiautonomous, decentralized basis, creating, as one manager put it, "twenty 'independent' medium-sized businesses." The general managers of the box plants, who were evaluated on their contribution to divisional/corporate profits, had wide-ranging decision-making authority, as described below.

1. Plant management was responsible for pricing (within broad guidelines established by the general manager of Box Operations), customer service levels, product lines offered, types of customers served, etc.

2. Each plant had its own sales organization, including a sales manager and a sales force of four to ten people. Plant managers determined the number of salespeople, their deployment, and their compensation levels.

3. Each plant purchased its paper at an established transfer price from the paperboard mills of the primary operations.

By contrast, plant management had very limited involvement in other significant marketing decisions. Among the latter were determining marketing strategy, developing marketing programs, organizing and providing sales training, establishing the nature of and expenditure level for advertising and sales promotion programs, coordinating national account strategies, and providing customer services and technical support in package design as well as packaging systems.

These functions were the responsibility of the director of marketing in Box Operations.

MARKETING ACTIVITIES

As noted, the marketing functions in BO were sharply divided. The individual plants controlled product, pricing, market selection, and personal-selling activities. The director of marketing, with assistance from the corporate advertising department, was essentially responsible for the strategy, communications, service, and support functions.

The personal-selling function was conducted by twenty separate sales organizations, each serving a limited geographic area and each headed by a sales manager, who reported to a specific plant manager. In total, 105 sales personnel (as of 1976) were in the field, representing an expenditure of $10.5 million, or approximately 6 percent of BO's sales.

Advertising and sales promotion expenditures totaled $370,000 in 1976. These included $110,000 for literature and special presentations and $260,000 for advertising in trade media.

The trade media used in the advertising campaign encompassed both two horizontal packaging journals and two selected general business publications that covered the most significant user markets served by O-I. See Table 9-3-4 for a list of publications and the insertion schedule used in each.

In discussing the marketing communications effort by BO, Roy LaFontaine observed:

> *Packaging is a custom product, and the role of the salesman in getting business is extremely important. He interprets the customer's needs and translates them into a specific design. Of course, he has help from specialists, but he's the one the customer looks to.*
>
> *Advertising in trade media reminds customers that we exist and also tries to present a unified image. You know, when you have twenty independent businesses and you're trying to implement an overall strategy, these things are certainly needed. Also, we tend to emphasize in advertising our design, consulting, and support services, because those represent our competitive edge— particularly in relation to the smaller competitors. We also put a good deal of money into product literature and special presentations in support of the sales force. As I mentioned earlier, they are the vital link to the marketplace in this business.*

TABLE 9-3-4   Trade Media Employed by Box Operations
and Their Insertion Schedules

Media	Number of Insertions	Insertion Schedule				
		January	February	March	April	May
Packaging Digest	6	X		X		X
Modern Packaging	6		X		X	
Purchasing	7	X	X			X
Buiness Week (Industrial)	8	X		X(2)	X	

The plan for 1977 called for an increase in sales from $175 million to $200 million. This 15 percent increase was expected to be achieved by a 7 percent expansion of physical volume (square feet of corrugated board) and an 8 percent general price increase, which had recently been put into effect.

The marketing program to accomplish this goal primarily involved a planned 20 percent increase in the field force, which had been projected to expand to 126 sales personnel over the year. To accommodate this growth while remaining within the corporate guideline of a 6 percent overall expenditure increase from 1976, the planned advertising budget had been reduced to $80,000 for the year.

The director of marketing indicated that this initial plan grew from a conscious trade-off discussion in a meeting among himself, the general manager of the FPD, and the general manager of BO. The original impetus for a sales force expansion came from the individual plant managers, as part of the 1977 planning process. In arriving at their judgments concerning plant volume projections and sales force needs, the individual plant managers had available corporate expenditure guidelines and industry economic trends (volume, price levels, user segments affected) supplied by the BO marketing department, as well as detailed data on business mix, growth potential, and penetration within their own geographic service area.

In discussing these allocation decisions further, the director of marketing cited the following considerations, which he believed to be primary factors:

1. Box Operations had not added any sales personnel since the early 1970s as a result of a series of head-count reduction programs.

2. BO had been losing market share.

3. There was insufficient sales coverage in two growing market areas: Texas and Wisconsin.

4. The division needed to improve the quality of its sales personnel. The addition of new people would provide greater opportunities to weed out marginal performers.

5. There appeared to be a need for more promotable sales managers.

6. A significant mill expansion was under way, with an additional investment

Insertion Schedule

June	July	August	September	October	November	December
X			X		X	
X		X		X		X
X	X		X		X	
X		X		X		X

of $100 million expected to produce increased capacity in 1977 and in 1979–1980.

7. BO's growth objective in its 1977 strategic plan was to expand sales at a rate 1 percent faster than the industry's current growth.

8. The discussion of the number of additional sales personnel was based on an annual sales volume guideline per new salesperson of $500,000. This represented $10.5 million of the $25 million sales growth for the operation as a whole. (The sales volume produced by the operation's present sales force averaged $1.7 million per field salesperson.)

In addition to these factors, the basic framework of BO's marketing strategy also seemed to be reflected in these planned allocation decisions. According to the director of marketing, BO had been seeking to position itself as a high-volume, low-cost producer with the aim of supplying customers whose volume of corrugated purchases was at least $50,000 per year. Further, BO preferred customers for whom the cost of corrugated packaging was a significant part of the product's value and characteristics. The management saw a competitive advantage stemming from its design, consulting, and support services, which had been directed toward the customer's production engineering and packaging specialists.

The operation served 4,000 customers nationwide on a direct basis, representing an average of 200 customers per plant location. The management estimated that some 20,000 to 30,000 potential customers, covering the spectrum of SIC categories, met its criteria for a prime customer target.

The process involved in these budgets was a "bottom-up" approach as detailed in the O-I corporate description. The budget was reviewed in progressively broader degrees of aggregation at each management level from the plant manager up to the Executive Policy Committee. The key marketing decisions for a product market area were generally made at the operations level within this division. The communications choices generally had been made not as formal trade-off decisions, but as individual judgments of responsible managers. These judgments were made with differing frames of reference and perspectives. The decisions made during the 1977 budgetary process reflected a conscious trade-off process, while at the same time they demonstrated the dominance of personal selling in the communications mix.

TABLE 9-3-5   Corrugated Container Industry Shipments (in dollars)

Year	Total	Corrugated	Solid Fiber
1960	$1,791,171,100	$1,746,525,600	$44,645,500
1961	1,820,090,000	1,777,068,100	43,021,900
1962	2,000,415,600	1,956,573,300	43,842,300
1963	2,067,429,400	2,027,179,900	40,249,500
1964	2,213,855,300	2,175,406,500	38,448,800
1965	2,406,758,600	2,367,541,000	39,216,700
1966	2,730,785,600	2,673,737,100	57,048,500
1967	2,814,803,600	2,761,635,200	53,168,400
1968	3,043,600,900	2,990,444,200	53,156,700
1969	3,320,521,800	3,268,934,500	61,687,300
1970	3,311,044,100	3,296,369,600	42,679,500
1971	3,463,680,200	3,422,262,100	41,118,100
1972	3,959,924,500	3,919,862,500	40,061,600
1973	4,862,065,300	4,815,186,600	46,569,700
1974	5,792,984,900	5,742,302,300	50,683,600
1975	5,623,765,200	5,578,612,500	45,152,700

EXHIBIT 9-3-1   1975 Corrugated Shipments by Industry Segments

Segment	Percentage
Food & Beverage	36%
Paper & Printed Material	12%
Glass & Ceramic	11%
Chemicals, Drugs, Cosmetics	7%
Metal & Machinery	6%
Appliances & Electrical	5%
Clothing, Textiles, Leather	5%
Rubber & Plastic	5%
Furniture & Wood	4%
Transportation Equipment	2%
All Other	7%

CORRUGATED BOX INDUSTRY

The corrugated box industry was a large, mature, slow-growth, capital-intensive business involving a commodity product. In 1975, total sales were $5.6 billion, representing 194.3 billion square feet of corrugated containers. This was the equivalent of 18 percent of the dollar value of all packaging materials sold in that year. The compounded annual growth in unit volume of products sold from 1960 to 1975 had been 3.9 percent, and the growth rate in dollar volume over this period had been 7.9 percent. The latter figure reflected the effects of inflation over the past several years. (See Table 9-3-5 for dollar shipments of the industry since 1960.)

The users of corrugated boxes covered the full spectrum of U.S. industry. The food and beverage segments dominated, totaling 36 percent of the corrugated volume in 1975. The next largest segment, paper and printed material, only accounted for 12 percent of shipments. (See Exhibit 9-3-1 for

---

EXHIBIT 9-3-2   Corrugated Shipments by Region in 1975

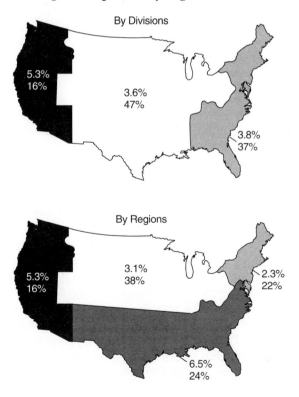

Note: Top numbers indicate average annual growth rate from 1960 to 1975. Bottom numbers indicate share of national total in 1975.

Source: Fibre Box Association

details concerning the remaining customer segments.) Industry shipments very closely paralleled the level of overall economic activity both on a national and a regional basis. (Exhibit 9-3-2 shows the breakdown of shipments by region in 1975 as well as the corresponding growth rates in each region since 1960.)

COMPETITION

The industry was made up of 759 companies, operating 1,385 plants. The largest company in the industry, Container Corporation of America, had only a 7 percent market share. O-I, the number six company in the trade market (external sales), had a 3.8 percent market share. The other major firms which fell in between included International Paper, Weyerhauser Corporation, Inland Container, and Horner Waldorf.

In spite of the large number of firms in the industry and the relatively small shares enjoyed by the major producers, the ten largest companies had a total market share of 43.9 percent in 1975. The next ten companies shared 21.2 percent of the market.

Another facet of the competitive structure related to the degree of vertical integration within the industry. In 1975, 78 percent of the industry's output was produced by firms supplying at least 50 percent of their own container-board. In 1960, 67 percent of the output was from integrated firms, and in 1950, only 53 percent came from these sources.

DECISION

Roy LaFontaine opened his presentation to the general manager with a restatement of the alternatives he had been considering:

> Bill, I have been evaluating the alternatives with respect to next year's marketing budget. I believe there are three worth considering.
>
> We can keep the mix the same as last year with 105 salesmen and about a $400,000 ad budget, for a total of $10.9 million.
>
> Or we can increase our field force by 21 people and cut our advertising and promotion expenditures by $300,000 to about $80,000 and increase the total budget to $11.4 million.
>
> Or possibly a third alternative would be to increase the sales force by 10 and keep the advertising and promotion budget at about $400,000. This would produce a total budget of about $11.3 million. After careful analysis and evaluation, here's what I think we should do. . . .

Questions for Discussion and Review

1. How do the data presented in the case on past industry and O-I sales, etc., influence planning the FPD communication mix for 1977?

2. Evaluate the three alternatives LaFontaine believes are open to O-I's Forest Products Division. Which course of action is most appealing? Why?

3. What additional alternative communication mixes should the FPD consider?

4. Overall, which course of action would be most appropriate? Why?

10

Sales Promotion

A new brand manager comes in and says, "What can I do to make a mark?" He can't fool around with advertising too much because of bureaucracy and because the system is already in place. But he knows if he puts a consumer promotion together, all of a sudden market share will move.[1]

Lou Houk
FRANKEL & CO. (sales promotion agency)

Over the past 15 years, many marketers have made significant shifts in their marketing communication investments, reducing traditional media advertising and expanding sales promotion activities. Partially as a result of these shifts, while both advertising and sales promotional investments have grown, sales promotion has grown at a faster pace. Evidence of this trend is provided by examining changes in the proportion of total advertising and sales promotional appropriations invested in each of these two forms of promotion. For example, in 1980, 43 percent of the total was invested in advertising and 57 percent in sales promotion. In 1988, however, advertising had dropped to 31 percent of total expenditures and sales promotion had expanded to 69 percent.[2]

Numerous complex factors underlie this fundamental shift towards sales promotion. These factors include the following:

1. The growing market power and sophistication of retailers have led them to demand marketing dollars from manufacturers.

---

[1]Aimée Stern, "The Promo Wars," *Business Month* 130, no. 1 (July 1987): 44–46.

[2]Russ Bowman, "Dollars Up but Cooling Down," *Marketing and Media Decisions* (July 1989): 123–126.

2. Checkout scanner data has enabled accurate, on-line sales tracking data to be placed in the hands of retailers.

3. Sales promotion can have a more immediate impact on sales than can advertising.

4. A short-term orientation by marketing managers has created a dependence on sales promotion to achieve monthly or quarterly sales quotas.

5. Sales promotion is more directly accountable than advertising.

6. The fragmentation of traditional mass media advertising vehicles has sapped their power.

The increasing reliance on sales promotion makes it crucial that marketing communication managers understand this important tool and how to blend it most effectively into the firm's communication mix. In this chapter, sales promotion and its partnership with advertising will be examined.

THE NATURE OF SALES PROMOTION

Consumer sales promotions are marketing offers that provide an additional incentive—beyond inherent product benefits—to purchase a brand by temporarily changing its price/value vis-à-vis the competition's. Trade and sales force promotions, while similar to consumer promotions, are used to stimulate channel member and/or sales force effectiveness. Exhibit 10-1 presents a brief description of ten of the more common sales promotion techniques used by marketers following a pull strategy of stimulating consumer demand for their brand. In addition, Exhibit 10-1 presents a description of five common sales promotion techniques directed at increasing the push supporting brands provided by channel members and the sales force. Note that there are many variations and combinations of these categories of sales promotion.

Exhibit 10-2 outlines some of the major characteristics of sales promotion. As indicated in this exhibit, both benefits and hazards are associated with these promotional activities. In planning the firm's possible use of sales promotion, the marketing communication manager should carefully weigh these pros and cons.

When identifying both the general type of sales promotion to be employed and its specifics, management should consider the characteristics of an ideal promotion. Ideally, a sales promotion program should be all of the following:

- *Appealing from the target audience's perspective* (the KEY)
- Easily integrated into all other areas of the firm's marketing communication mix in a way that provides synergies
- Able to meet all legal restrictions and free of liability concerns
- Inexpensive for the firm
- Easy to understand and administer
- Unique and insulated from competitive response
- Consistent with the brand's image and past marketing activities.

EXHIBIT 10-1   Common Sales Promotion Activities

Consumer Promotions: Pull Strategy

- *Sampling*—provision of the product at no or a small charge for purposes of trial use, as when a four-ounce box of ready-to-eat cereal is delivered to all houses in targeted ZIP codes.

- *Coupons*—certificates offering a price reduction, such as 25¢ off suggested retail price.

- *Contests*—the awarding of prizes based on some skill or ability, as when consumers submit a statement of 25 words or less indicating why they use Brand X.

- *Sweepstakes*—the offering of prizes to consumers who submit their names to enter a drawing or chance selection process.

- *Rebates*—offers to return a portion of the purchase price after purchase; for example, $2,000 cash back from the manufacturer on the purchase of a new automobile.

- *Price-off packages*—price reductions that are indicated on the package, such as "50¢ off."

- *Value packs*—price reductions achieved by including more product at the regular retail price, as when a 12-ounce size is expanded to 16 ounces and sold for the regular 12-ounce price.

- *Premiums*—rewards offered for purchasing a brand, such as a toy in a box of cereal.

- *Cross-promotions*—two or more marketers' jointly featuring a special offer; for example, an airline and a camera company offering a free camera as a premium for ticket purchases.

- *Price deals*—temporary price reductions, such as 50 percent off during a closeout sale.

Trade and Sales Force Promotions: Push Strategy

- *Price deals*—limited-time special discounts or price reductions; for example, "for every two cases purchased prior to June 1, receive a third case at half price."

- *Contests*—the awarding of prizes for achieving a certain level of sales or for outstanding performance, such as a trip for two to Hawaii for all salespersons and retailers who exceed their yearly quotas.

- *Push money*—money paid to salespersons to promote specific brands or items.

- *Cooperative advertising*—reimbursement of retailers by manufacturers for advertising their brand, such as 50 percent reimbursement from a co-op fund, based on sales.

- *Slotting allowances*—money paid to obtain or retain distribution at the retail level.

EXHIBIT 10-2   Characteristics of Sales Promotion

Benefits

- Sales promotions can stimulate sales that would not have occurred in their absence.

- Sales promotions are useful in stimulating an immediate consumer response.

- Sales promotions enable marketers to cut price on a short-term basis.

- Sales promotions typically provide easily measurable results.

- Sales promotions can create new users or encourage current users to trade up or remain loyal; they can also encourage trial, loading (purchasing an abnormally large quantity to take advantage of temporarily favorable terms), and continuity and reinforce advertising.[a]

Hazards

- Sales promotions do little to build consumer loyalty or provide real or lasting differentiation from the competition.

- Consumers may come to regard the deal price as the expected price.

- Marketers can become addicted to sales promotions in order to increase sales in the short term, fueling a promotion war that can saddle all firms with increased costs for dubious benefits.

- Price promotions run the risk of turning brand categories into commodities in which competition is based predominantly on price.

- Sales promotions are often subject to abuses by channel members; for example, no pass-through (the retailer simply pockets a discount intended for consumers); forward buying (stocking up of purchases at deal prices for sales in future periods); diversion (reduced-price products are sold by retailers to other retailers); and coupon misredemption.

- Sales promotions may not stimulate repeat purchases after the promotion has ended.

---

[a]Don Schultz, *Strategic Advertising Campaigns* (Lincolnwood, Ill.: NTC Business Books, 1990), 472.

The Impact of UPC Profitability Analysis on Sales Promotion

Beginning in the mid-1970s, checkout scanner data generated off Universal Product Codes, coupled with sophisticated data analysis techniques, revolutionized how retailers evaluate the allocation of shelf space and sales promotions.[3] Using complex computer-based tools, retailers are able to

---

[3]Don Schultz, *Strategic Advertising Campaigns* (Lincolnwood, Ill.: NTC Business Books, 1990), 454–455.

examine the profitability of all brands carried in deciding which items to stock, which to drop, and which to promote. To convince retailers to carry and promote their brand(s), manufacturers must be able to provide sophisticated UPC profitability data that support their products. Without such data to back up their recommendations, the chances of a manufacturer convincing a knowledgeable retailer to participate in a promotion are limited.

Further, as Schultz notes, "Advertising planners must understand that planning sales promotion today is a very complex and sophisticated process, one which goes far beyond just preparing a coupon drop or inserting a premium in the carton."[4]

Marketing Reservations about Sales Promotion

Although when compared to traditional media advertising, sales promotions often offer the marketer significant benefits, their use is not without its limitations and potentially negative side effects. In addition to the reservations expressed in Exhibit 10-2, several general reservations regarding sales promotion will be discussed next.

First, there is concern that a heavy reliance on sales promotion undermines brand loyalty. Phillips (CEO of Ogilvy & Mather advertising agency) suggests that "brand rape" occurs when marketing management takes investment dollars away from advertising and other nonprice marketing communication to run short-term price promotions.[5] Phillips maintains that marketers have been teaching consumers to respond to price for years and that this is undermining brand equities. To remedy this situation, he suggests that marketers should replace coupons and freestanding inserts with promotions that revolve around the brand's positioning and key consumer benefit.

Note also that strong brands with loyal consumers are in a much stronger position to resist channel member demands for concessions on slotting allowances and other forms of reseller support. A relatively undifferentiated brand that has not been established in the market through advertising is in a much weaker position in dealing with powerful retailers.

Second, consumers can become insensitive to promotions and take them for granted, refusing to purchase a brand that does not offer a rebate or discount. When all competitors offer a rebate, its marketing leverage is lost, and all competitors are saddled with higher costs.

Third, Artzt (chairman of Procter & Gamble) cautions that too few marketing people understand the value of advertising in creating "quality brand trial" and building the long-term franchise of a brand.[6] P&G's

---

[4]*Ibid.,* 455.

[5]"O&M's Phillips Decries 'Brand Rape,'" *Advertising Age,* May 14, 1991, 52.

[6]Edwin Artzt, "Grooming the Next Generation of Management," *The Advertiser* (Spring 1992): 66–70.

experience with advertising versus price promotions has indicated that customers who try a brand because of price promotion will be far less profitable over the long haul than customers whose trial was stimulated by advertising.

Integrating Advertising and Sales Promotion

Advertising and sales promotion frequently play directly coordinated and complementary roles in the marketing communication mix. For example, advertising can be used to create awareness of plus favorable attitudes toward the brand, and sales promotion can be used to supplement these effects by inducing trial. Even more obvious is the situation in which advertising is used to announce and promote a contest, sweepstakes, or cents-off coupon offer. The advertising may even be used to deliver the coupon to the consumer as a component part of a full-page newspaper ad in the food section.

As advocated in earlier sections of this text, the key to successful marketing communication is integration. Powerful synergies are possible when advertising and sales promotion are carefully coordinated. On the other hand, uncoordinated and inappropriate sales promotions run the risk of damaging the long-term image of a brand—an image established through advertising and other means, at great expense, over a period of many years.

For example, a complicated and boring contest with inappropriate prizes can undermine a brand's high-quality image, cultivated by years of effective advertising. On the other hand, careful timing of and coordination between a flight of media advertisements touting a brand's benefits and a 50¢ off coupon drop may drastically increase response. Or, if a coupon print advertisement is used to distribute the sales promotion offer, the impact of the ad *and* the promotion may be multiplied by coordinating it with the brand's television commercials. The selection of a premium offer is another sales promotion decision that should be made in light of the target audience of the marketing program, benefits stressed in advertising, personality or image established for the brand, and so on. If the planner fails to intelligently mold a promotion that fits these other components of the mix, disaster is possible.

The same principles apply to trade and sales force promotions. For example, by applying the same unifying campaign theme or trade characters across all forms of marketing communication, a marketer magnifies the impact of all components of the program. Consistency of voice is important in all of the firm's communication.

To capitalize on possible synergies, the marketing communication planner must clearly focus on the fact that important interactions occur between all elements in the mix. In contemplating possible synergies, the planner should carefully evaluate the mix in a holistic manner from the prospective customer's perspective. This perspective is most relevant to winning the consumer's patronage and planning the firm's communication program.

Suggested Readings

Blattberg, Robert, and Scott Neslin. *Sales Promotion: Concepts, Methods and Strategies.* Englewood Cliffs, N.J.: Prentice-Hall, 1990.

Quelch, John. *Sales Promotion Management.* Englewood Cliffs, N.J.: Prentice-Hall, 1989.

Schultz, Don. "Sales Promotion." Chap. 13 in *Strategic Advertising Campaigns.* Lincolnwood, Ill.: NTC Business Books, 1990.

Schultz, Don, and William Robinson. *Sales Promotion Management.* Lincolnwood, Ill.: NTC Business Books, 1986.

Totten, John, and Martin Block. *Analyzing Sales Promotion: Text and Cases.* Chicago: Commerce Communications, 1987.

Exercises

1.   School Properties USA is a company that develops grass-roots sponsorship opportunities for firms wanting to cater primarily to teenagers. The firm has already set up sponsorships, as well as conducted event merchandising, sales promotions, and other promotional activities, in 16 states. It expects to promote events reaching 75 percent of all U.S. high school students in five years.

The owner of School Properties feels that the company allows sponsors to reach the families of the high school students just as effectively. He points out that high school football and basketball games attract more than 400 million paying spectators every year. The potential audience of this type of sponsorship is very capable of justifying the economic investment in marketing: teenagers spend over $60 billion annually and their parents, about $250 billion.

Assume you are trying to assemble a list of corporations and products that would benefit from sponsoring promotional campaigns through School Properties USA. What corporations and/ or products would you list as the top 20 candidates for this project? Do you feel sponsorships would be as effective as, say, free products such as soft drinks or hamburgers? Why? Why not?

Discuss the possibilities offered by this type of promotional activity. Compare it to advertising. What are the advantages and disadvantages a marketer should consider when making a decision in this area?

Source: Scott Hume, "Marketers Rally Around School Sponsorships," *Advertising Age,* June 1, 1992, 32.

2.   The spiraling costs of marketing and releasing movies have prompted Hollywood executives to use cross-promotions to appeal to the target audiences for their product. As an example, consider the 1991 Disney release *The Rocketeer,* based on an obscure comic book hero. Walt Disney Company wanted to appeal to a primary audience of children aged seven to twelve and a secondary audience of teenagers. The company was considering offering *Rocketeer* toys at McDonald's outlets to all buyers of Happy Meals. Another possibility was to give free glider toys and Kid's Personal Pan Pizzas to Pizza Hut customers. Other proposals included scratch-and-win theater tickets valid for free Cokes or popcorn and a sweepstakes contest that would allow the winner to spend a long weekend at Disney World with his or her family.

Which of the promotions considered do you feel would be most effective in spurring attendance to The *Rocketeer?* Is the quality of the movie a factor to be considered when choosing specific promotions? Why?

Source: Thomas R. King, "See the Movie! Eat the Lunch Special!" *The Wall Street Journal,* June 4, 1991, B1 and B6.

3. A major manufacturer of breakfast cereals was considering an introductory promotion for a new fat-free granola-type cereal. The marketing vice-president had decided to use coupons as one of the major promotional tools. Fifty-cent-off coupons could be placed in either Sunday newspaper supplements or selected magazines, such as *Family Circle* or *Good Housekeeping.*

The total paid circulation of the Sunday newspaper magazine network was 16,353,000, and the cost of a four-color page was about $250,000. The joint circulation of *Family Circle* and *Good Housekeeping* was about 10,250,000, and the cost of a four-color page in both magazines was about $190,000. The rate of coupon redemption for the two media was different, however. It was 2.1 percent for the Sunday newspaper magazine network and 5.6 percent for the two magazines.

Which of the two proposed media vehicles would you choose to carry your coupon? Why?

4. The Marlboro Grand Prix of New York was scheduled to begin in 1993, and the event organizer was busy trying to line up corporate partners so that the race would be a very profitable venture. The event cost between $12 million and $15 million a year, and the organizer wanted as few sponsors or partners as possible to avoid clutter.

In addition to Philip Morris Co.'s Marlboro, title sponsor of the event, eight other sponsors were sought. These would pay $1.54 million each in 1993, $1.7 million in 1994, and $1.86 million in 1995. In return, their names would be attached to the title of the event and incorporated in all advertising and promotion, including that done by the broadcasting network. Other promotional opportunities would be available at additional cost.

The organizer was concerned that antismoking feeling would hurt his chances of securing major sponsors to share the stage with Marlboro. He felt that food and soft drink companies would be reluctant to be allied with a cigarette manufacturer. Do you think this is a problem? Do you think being tied to a cigarette name would hurt the image of a company or a product? Discuss.

Source: Scott Hume, "Marlboro Grand Prix Races for Sponsors," *Advertising Age,* July 20, 1992, 25.

New Chase Condominiums

BACKGROUND

In partnership with the Dutch company Wilma, the Shawntana Development Corporation built a 164-unit condominium project. The project, named New Chase, occupied a 6.8-acre site in Fountain Valley, California. New Chase was located near many commercial and retail businesses. Further, the project was close to several amenities in the area. For example, New Chase was located 5 miles from the Pacific Ocean, 3 miles from a major shopping center, 1 ½ miles from an airport, and 1 ½ miles from a golf course in a prestigious community.

The project was made up of three basic units (see Exhibit 10-1-1 for the three floor plans). Each plan's number of units, size, and average selling price are indicated in the following table:

Plan	Number of Units	Square Footage	Bed/Baths	Average Selling Price
Atherton	56	724	1/1	$75,000
Brighton	52	910	2/1	$85,000
Sylvan	56	1,106	2/2	$94,000

In addition, the project included a swimming pool, pool building, and spa. Exhibit 10-1-2 lists some of the features of New Chase.

New Chase was classified as "affordable housing." This meant that Shawntana was required to sell 25 percent of its units to households earning no more than 120 percent of the median income in Orange County.

At the time of the initial offering, the median income in Orange County was $33,425. Therefore, 25 percent of the New Chase units had to be sold to households with incomes no greater than $40,110 per year ($33,425 × 1.20). The remaining 75 percent could be sold as either "affordable" or "conventional" housing.

As part of Shawntana's arrangement with the local governments and planning boards that had approved the project, Shawntana was to provide financing for the "affordable" buyers in the form of 20-year loans with fixed interest rates of approximately 10 percent.

Given the size, price range, and financing of the project, management felt that the target market was primarily first-time homebuyers. Management

---

This case was written by John H. Murphy, The University of Texas at Austin. The case is intended for use in generating class discussion and not to illustrate either the effective or ineffective handling of an administrative situation. Used by permission of Shawntana Development Corp.

EXHIBIT 10-1-1 **New Chase Condominiums: Floor Plans of the Three Basic Units**

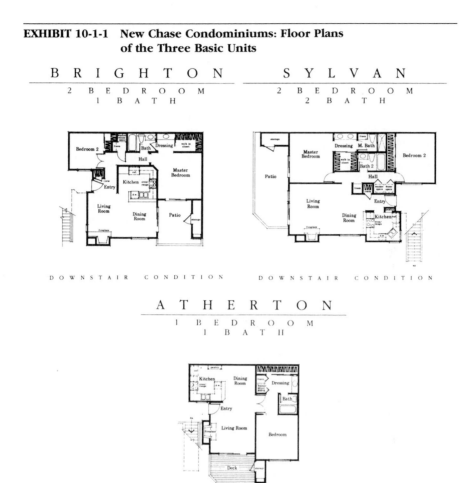

estimated that probably 80 percent to 90 percent of eventual buyers lived within a five-mile radius of the site, with the balance coming from the Orange County/Los Angeles area at large. Further, management believed that the best prospects were young professionals, young couples who both worked, and singles who shared expenses.

THE MARKETING PLAN

Shawntana's sales objective was to maintain an average sales rate of three units per week throughout a two-phase selling period spanning 13 months. Phase I began August 1 and ran through February 15 of the next year. Phase II began February 16 and ran through August 31.

EXHIBIT 10-1-2   Features of New Chase Condominiums

Distinctive Exteriors

- Private balcony or patio
- Fire-protective asphalt shingle roofs
- Individually assigned covered parking
- Combination stucco and wood siding
- Handsome architectural detailing
- New West color schemes
- Underground utilities
- Dramatic oversized 8' sliding glass doors

Inside Every Home

- Central air conditioning
- Energy-saving, heat-circulating, wood-burning fireplace with ceramic tile face and crown mold mantel
- Individual laundry appliance hookup
- Custom draperies
- Mirrored wardrobe doors in master dressing area
- Walk-in closets (Brighton & Sylvan)
- Oversized 9' ceilings in ground-level units
- Dramatic vaulted ceilings in upper-level units
- Excellent carpeting selections (100% ANSO nylon)
- Extensive variety of versatile space arrangements
- Private storage rooms
- Polished brass Schlage hardware
- Hand-carved, solid wood entry door with sunburst window

- Choice of decorator-selected, cushioned vinyl flooring in kitchen, bath, and laundry area
- Prewired for cable television or standard antenna and telephones
- Lifesaver smoke detectors

Deluxe Kitchens

- Custom-designed easy-care European-style cabinetry
- Ceramic tile countertops with solid oak edging
- Magic Chef built-in appliances including continuous cleaning range, hood, dishwasher, and disposal
- Storage pantry
- Designer-selected track lighting
- Double-compartment sink with MOEN single-lever fixture
- Prep for ice maker hookup

Beautiful Baths

- Compartmentalized dressing and tub areas
- Decorative MOEN wide-spread fixtures in master bath
- Easy-care, tile-patterned tub and shower enclosures
- Cultured marble pullman
- Oversized plate glass mirrors

Energy-saving Features

- Energy-efficient furnace, water heater, and air conditioning systems

- Fully insulated, double-framed party wall-separation
- Extra-thick sound and energy insulation in walls and ceilings
- Sound-deadening, lightweight concrete between party floors

Community Recreation

- Lush, parklike landscaping and waterscape
- Heated swimming pool
- Two whirlpool spas
- Two sun deck areas
- Direct access to biking, jogging, and equestrian trails

Locational Advantages

- Centrally located to employment
- Within minutes of Mile Square Park, Newport Beach, South Coast Plaza, and Westminster Mall
- Ideally situated between San Diego Freeway (405) and Garden Grove Freeway (22) for easy access to San Diego, Riverside, and Los Angeles counties

Membership in Homeowner's Association Includes:

- Hot and cold water
- Gas
- Recreation facilities
- Trash collection
- Exterior building and landscape maintenance
- Fire and liability insurance

Due to ongoing research, Shawntana Development Corporation reserves the right to change plans, specifications, pricing, or terms without prior notice or obligation.

Shawntana planned to use an advertising agency that specialized in real estate advertising and collateral materials, plus a separate public relations firm. Both of these firms would be paid a negotiated straight fee for their services.

In addition, a firm specializing in real estate sales would be retained to serve as the exclusive sales agent for the development. This firm would be compensated on a straight 1 percent of gross selling price commission basis. Two salespersons would work as on-site sales representatives between 9:00 A.M. and 6:00 P.M. on weekends, and one person would work during the week. As part of the agreement, Shawntana was responsible for supplying all sales support tools (such as brochures, business cards, and stationery) plus an office (condo unit) equipped with desks, furnishings, telephones, and refreshments.

Media advertising was to be concentrated exclusively in newspapers. Shawntana's advertising agency planned to place ads in the *Los Angeles Times* Orange County edition's Saturday "At Home" section and Sunday "Real Estate" section. In addition, ads were to be placed in the *Orange County Register/ Bulletin.*

Exhibit 10-1-3 presents representative quarter- and full-page newspaper ads to be used in promoting the development. Based on recent ABC Publisher's Statements for Orange County only, the *Register/Bulletin*'s Sunday circulation was 360,400 and Saturday circulation was 307,100. The *Times* had an Orange County circulation of 210,000 on Sunday and 158,200 on Saturday. The *Register/Bulletin*'s combined Saturday or Sunday per-column-inch rate for real estate was $61.84, with a pickup rate of $37.79. Color premiums were black plus one color for $775, two colors for $1,065, and three colors for $1,305. The rate of the Orange County edition of the *Times* was $25 for daily and $31 for Sunday coverage for a 1,500-inch contract.

To help achieve Shawntana's sales objectives, $139,000 was set aside to pay the sales agent and $187,500 earmarked as an appropriation for advertising and all other promotional expenses. Roughly 60 percent was to be allocated to Phase I and 40 percent to Phase II. The $187,500 appropriation was to cover all advertising media expenses, brochures and pamphlets, flags/banners/on-site signs, personal selling support expenses, public relations activities, move-in kits, consultant's fee, and marketing research.

The total $326,500 appropriation for promotional communication had been included in the marketing plan section of the financial prospectus used to secure backing for the project. This sum seemed adequate enough to help assure financial partners that the project would be able to meet its proposed cash flow projections.

THE MARKETING COMMUNICATION BUDGET

In planning the overall marketing of the project, management needed to budget the total $187,500 appropriation by expense categories—that is, to determine how much to budget for media advertising, ad production, personal selling support materials/supplies/expenses, sales promotional expenses, pub-

EXHIBIT 10-1-3   Representative Newspaper Advertisements for New Chase Condominiums

lic relations and publicity activities, on-premise signs, banners, brochures, any catering for the "Grand Opening" event, and so on. In addition, part of the budget would have to be earmarked for compensating the advertising agency and public relations specialist.

Further, the issue of the timing and coordination of media advertising and any special events needed to be decided. All newspaper advertising and other activities needed to be tentatively scheduled for the entire planned 13-month marketing effort. In addition, contingency plans for reduced and expanded promotional activities needed to be addressed and decision dates determined.

A number of important considerations had to be weighed in determining the balance among media advertising, personal selling, and other elements in New Chase's communication program. These included such factors as the nature of the project, target audience, likely effectiveness of various promotional pieces, and any seasonal considerations.

Questions for Discussion and Review

1. Is the total promotional appropriation adequate to accomplish the sales objective of an average of three units per week?

2. How does the interrelationship between advertising and other promotional tools affect the budgeting decision? Which tool is most important? How important an issue is the coordination of these tools?

3. What external factors would have an important influence on the success of New Chase's promotional communications efforts?

4. How common is the practice of establishing an overall appropriation prior to developing a specific budget?

5. What areas of the budget would be adjusted first if unit sales were more rapid than planned? If sales lagged behind the forecasted three units per week, what appropriation or budget changes would be in order?

6. How does the attractiveness of New Chase's pricing and financing package influence the role of promotional communication in marketing the complex?

C A S E   **10 - 2**

Al's Formal Wear

BACKGROUND

Al's Formal Wear of Fort Worth, Inc., operated over 60 stores in five states. The firm's corporate office was located in Euless, Texas, and the majority of the firm's stores were in Texas. The firm's operations in Austin, Texas, which are described in this case, were similar to those in its many other markets.

This case was written by John H. Murphy, The University of Texas at Austin, to generate class discussion and not to illustrate either the effective or ineffective handling of an administrative situation. Used by permission of Al's Formal Wear.

Al's business was the rental and sales of tuxedos. Although the foundation of Al's business was weddings, high school proms and other social events were very important. Al's had four stores in Austin—two stores in shopping malls on the near north side (Northcross and Highland malls), a central store located on "The Drag" (Main Street) in the student area near The University of Texas, and a store in the south-central area of the city.

Sales

Roughly 70 percent of Al's total revenue in Austin came from rentals and 30 percent from retail sales. Over the past few years, sales had become an increasingly larger proportion of total revenue. The average rental fee for a tux jacket and pants was $45 to $48, and shoes rented for $6 and accessories for a nominal charge. Al's sold both new and used tuxedos, with new tuxes priced from $185 to $375. A used basic black satin peak tux sold for $95 to $175.

Al's carried lines from Pierre Cardin, Dynasty, Robert Wagner, YSL, Lord West, Bill Blass, and After Six. Total revenue for Al's Austin stores was about $800,000 last year. The Northcross Mall store accounted for roughly 40 percent of revenue; the central store, 28 percent; south store, 22 percent; and Highland Mall store, 10 percent.

Typically, about 40 percent of Al's volume came in the March through May high school prom season. Weddings tended to cluster in June, July, and August. Retail sales, on the other hand, concentrated in the fall months of September through December.

Customers

Each of the four Austin stores had a very different clientele. The university area store did a large rental business with fraternity members, and roughly 75 percent of its customers were under 35. Besides college men, the store did business with a fair number of young professionals. Much of the business of the store located at Northcross Mall came from first and second marriages of men between the ages of 25 and 40. This store was located near high-income areas and had a strong sales business.

The Highland Mall store drew on a mix of both higher and lower income men of all ages. The south store did very well among Mexican-Americans, who were frequent users of tuxes for special social occasions. The "Quinceanera," a coming-out party given in honor of a girl's fifteenth birthday, was a customary social event that generated significant volume for Al's south store. Since birthdays occurred throughout the year, the Quinceaneras, or "sweet fifteen" parties, were distributed year round.

Competition

Al's presently had approximately a 60 percent share of the Austin market for tuxedo rentals. Al's primary competitors in Austin were Q's Formal Wear, Ascot Tuxedos, Horace's, Royal Tux, and Gingiss. Q's concentrated on the fraternity business and used the past friendship ties of the owner to encourage this business. Horace's was an old, established firm that also did a strong fraternity business. Royal Tux had two stores in Austin—one close to Al's south store and the other located near Al's store at Northcross Mall. Gingiss also had two stores in Austin and was a franchise operation based in Atlanta, Georgia.

Al's key benefit was selection and readily available merchandise. All of its competitors occasionally overextended themselves by booking large wedding parties and then having difficulty filling all the orders. Al's emphasized repeat customers and customer satisfaction by maintaining a customer file and encouraging telephone reservations by repeat customers.

Advertising

Al's typically allocated 6 percent of sales to advertising. In the past, Al's had used high school newspapers, the Yellow Pages, the *Austin American-Statesman* (the major newspaper in Austin), the *Daily Texan* (The University of Texas student newspaper), and several local radio stations to promote its rental and sales business. Exhibit 10-2-1 presents a Yellow Pages ad and a small newspaper ad.

MAJOR SALES PROMOTIONS

Sales promotional activities played a prominent role in Al's overall marketing efforts, and, hence, deserve special attention. These activities had to be carefully coordinated with Al's advertising, personal selling, and publicity. Two sales promotional programs were most important—bridal shows and an annual sales promotion targeted to the high school prom market. Both of these promotions will be described next.

Bridal Shows

Al's largest promotional events of the year were its bridal shows. Last year two shows were held. During the last week in January, the show was housed in the main ballroom of a major hotel in north-central Austin, and about 650 people attended. The third week in September a similar show was held in the ballroom of another major hotel located in the downtown area, and about 400 people attended.

The hotels donated the ballrooms and a champagne reception to support the show. Al's cosponsored the shows with 12 other firms whose businesses were related to weddings, including American Airlines, a bakery, a travel agency, and a florist. The secondary sponsors each paid $450 to participate, and each set up a booth and contributed a door prize.

The bridal shows were promoted primarily through newspaper ads and radio spots. Letters promoting the shows were also mailed to all brides-to-be whose engagement announcements appeared in local newspapers. A free honeymoon to Cancun, Mexico, was given away to encourage attendance. Admission to the show cost $2.50. Of those who attended, about half were brides-to-be.

EXHIBIT 10-2-1   Yellow Pages Ad and Newspaper Ad for Al's Formal Wear

All brides-to-be who attended received a follow-up mailing, and more than half later booked their wedding parties through Al's. Hence, the shows were considered to be very successful.

High School Prom Promotions

Al's attempts to encourage business from high school students during the prom season centered around a different promotion each year. The special rental promotion was advertised and supported by four or five seniors recruited to be

Al's representatives at each school. All high schools in a large five-county area were included in Al's definition of its target market.

The prom promotions had three major objectives:

1. To increase unit rentals to area high school students who would attend junior or senior proms
2. To increase the rental dollar volume by encouraging high school students to trade up to higher quality tuxes and accessories
3. To encourage high school students to come in and make the rental arrangements early (at least three weeks prior to their prom).

One of Al's most successful prom promotions was an offer of a free T-shirt. The T-shirt had a tux tie, studs, and lapels printed on the front along with an Al's logo. One year a Chinese fortune cookie promotion was used. Students were encouraged to come in to an Al's location and choose a fortune cookie, which contained a slip of paper indicating how much of a discount they would receive.

Another year, a Donkey Kong arcade game was installed in each of Al's stores, and the discount on tux rental was determined by the student's score after playing one free game. This promotion was considered less successful than the fortune cookie promotion and much less successful than the T-shirt promotion.

Exhibit 10-2-2 presents a newspaper ad featuring a free top hat and cane offer. This prom promotion was a failure. Two factors contributed to its failure. First, only about one-third of all rentals were tuxes with tails, which logically lent themselves to the featured accessories. Second, the top hats were made of plastic and looked cheap, which detracted from the sophisticated look of Al's attractive tuxes.

One of the most successful prom promotions was an offer of a free pair of "Miami Vice" sunglasses for early rentals. (The sunglasses cost Al's about $2 each.) This offer was advertised in newspapers and through a postcard mailing to all junior and senior high school boys in the five-county market area. Exhibit 10-2-3 presents this postcard mailer.

This promotion tied in with a new line of "Miami Vice" tuxes from After Six. These tuxes came in three colors—Fiesta Blue, Flamingo Pink, and White Heat—and rented for $64.95 versus $45 or so for the tuxes rented by the vast majority of high school students in other years. The tie-in and popularity of the "Miami Vice" tuxes enabled Al's to substantially increase its dollar volume on rentals to high school students.

THE NEXT HIGH SCHOOL PROM PROMOTION?

As he began to develop his marketing plans for next year, Ron Brumble, the Austin area supervisor, was most concerned about developing a new concept for a high school prom promotion that would work as well as the "Miami Vice" sunglasses tie-in.

EXHIBIT 10-2-2   Newspaper Ad Describing Al's Free Top Hat and Cane Offer

Although he felt he could devote as much as $12,000 to the cost of the promotion and attendant advertising, he realized that the ideal prom promotion would be much less expensive. He wanted a promotion that was clever and attractive to the target audience, as well as inexpensive, easy to understand, and easy to administer. In short, he wanted a promotion that would efficiently accomplish the predetermined objectives.

EXHIBIT 10-2-3   Postcard Mailer for Al's "Miami Vice" Sunglasses Prom Promotion

Prom '86 at Al's

Reserve your tuxedo early and beat the rush.
FREE GIFT. Free sunglasses*, a $10.00 value, when you rent your tuxedo at least 3 weeks before your Prom.**

STUDENT DISCOUNTS.
DESIGNERS. We offer: MIAMI VICE • BILL BLASS • DYNASTY • YSL • PIERRE CARDIN • ROBERT WAGNER •
LORD WEST • AFTER SIX

OPEN LATE. All locations will be open until 8 p.m. MONDAY THROUGH THURSDAY for your convenience during March, April and May.

Monday-Thursday 9:30-8:00
Friday 9:30-6:00, Saturday 9:30-5:30

Al's FORMAL WEAR

2828 Guadalupe, 472-1697   1818 W. Ben White, 443-6980
Northcross Mall, 451-0281   Highland Mall (Opens March '86)

*While supplies last. **Valid through June 1, 1986. No other discounts apply.*

TEXAS
Amarillo
Arlington
Austin
Carrollton
Corpus Christi
Dallas
Denton
El Paso (Timely Formal Wear)
Fort Worth
Garland
Harlingen
Houston (Tux 'n Tails)
Hurst
Irving
Lewisville
Longview
Lubbock
McAllen
Plano
Richardson
San Antonio
Temple
Tyler
Victoria
Waco
Wichita Falls
OKLAHOMA
Oklahoma City
Tulsa
LOUISIANA
New Orleans / Metairie
Gretna
Shreveport
FLORIDA
Miami
Hollywood
Lauderdale Lakes
CALIFORNIA (Pacific)
San Jose / Santa Clara

Corporate Office:
2021 Airport Freeway
Euless, Texas 76039
817-571-0283

Questions for Discussion and Review

1. What conclusions can be drawn from the information provided on Al's past high school promotions?

2. How important are the campus representatives likely to be in facilitating the success of a prom

promotion and rentals in general? How might they be most effectively utilized?

3. What kinds of special problems does the target audience of male high school juniors and seniors pose for Al's in developing a prom promotion? What are examples of inappropriate promotions that might lead to administrative, legal, or other problems?

4. What key considerations should be used in evaluating the viability of potential prom promotions?

5. In general, to stimulate prom rentals, would advertising or a sales promotional offer tend to be more important? Why?

6. Are there current fads or trends among high school males that might be tied into an Al's prom promotion? What risks are associated with such trends?

C A S E   **10 - 3**

Barton Creek Square Shopping Center

Barton Creek Square shopping center (BCS) was a 1.4 million-square-foot regional shopping mall located in the southwestern area of Austin, Texas. The mall featured six major department stores—Dillards, Foley's, J C Penney, Montgomery Ward, Scarbroughs, and Sears. In addition to these six major tenants, the mall contained a diverse range of more than 160 smaller retail stores (see Exhibit 10-3-1).

BCS was developed and managed by Melvin Simon & Associates of Indianapolis, Indiana. The mall was unofficially opened in October 1981, and the grand opening took place in March 1982. Tenant sales per square foot were excellent, and the percentage of available space leased was running over 90 percent. Percentage sales increases over last year for the first six months of the present year were as follows: January (+18.8 percent), February (14.2 percent), March (+15.5 percent), April (+20.4 percent), May (+21.5 percent), and June (+18.7 percent). When analyzed by categories, tenant sales increases were particularly strong in the clothing and jewelry stores categories.

This case was prepared by John H. Murphy, The University of Texas at Austin. The case was prepared to serve as the basis for class discussion rather than to illustrate the effective or ineffective handling of an administrative situation. Used by permission of Melvin Simon & Associates, Inc.

EXHIBIT 10-3-1 Barton Creek Square Tenants

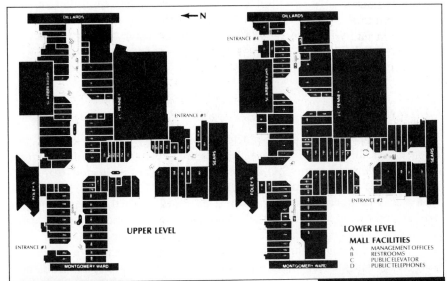

BARTON CREEK SQUARE

GENERAL MERCHANDISE
232	UNITED JEWELERS & DISTRIBUTORS
265	WALGREENS

FOOD
106	ORANGE JULIUS
112	OLGA'S KITCHEN
126	WILLIE'S PIES OF TEXAS
133	WYATT'S CAFETERIA
158	LUCA PIZZA
167	ALL AMERICAN HERO
201	CHELSEA STREET PUB
209	HSIN YUAN FORTUNE COOKIE
233	THE GREAT HOT DOG EXPERIENCE
261	BARKER'S JUBILATION
262	POTATOES, ETC.
273	FAMOUS CORNDOGS
287	CHICK-FIL-A

FOOD SPECIALTY
131	GENERAL NUTRITION CENTER
142	MORROW'S NUT HOUSE
147A	SWENSEN'S ICE CREAM
172	KARMELKORN
180	LAMMES CANDY
182	THE ORIGINAL GREAT AMERICAN CHOCOLATE CHIP COOKIE COMPANY
211	MEAN BEAN MACHINE
214	VITA-FOODS
252	SEE'S CANDY
275	HICKORY FARMS
279	THE FAMOUS ICE CREAM BAR SHOP

MEN'S/WOMEN'S APPAREL
110	ON THE MOVE
116	COUNTY SEAT
165	BEALLS
169	THE BELT BUCKLE
207	THE GAP
216	MERRITT, SCHAEFER & BROWN
219	JUDY'S
228a	BENETTON
251	JEANS WEST
255	PAT MAGEE'S
260	CAMPUS LIFESTYLES
270	MILLER'S OUTPOST
281	BENJAMIN'S

MEN'S APPAREL
107	K-G MEN'S STORE
146	RICHMAN BROTHERS
151	CHESS KING
159	J. RIGGINGS
161	THE TOGGERY
175	OAK TREE
205	J. DAVID'S
225	ELLIOTT'S BOY'S AND YOUNG MEN'S WEAR
263	GINGISS FORMAL WEAR CENTER

WOMEN'S APPAREL
104	LANE BRYANT
114	STUARTS
117	CASUAL CORNER
138	YARING'S
140	LERNER
147	JEAN NICOLE
149	MOTHERCARE
150	FOXMOOR
156	PARKLANE HOSIERY
176	FASHION CONSPIRACY
179	WOMAN'S WORLD SHOPS
217	THE LIMITED
218	THE COLONY SHOP
220	ACCESSORY LADY
228	HIT OR MISS
229	PECK & PECK
230	UPS-N-DOWNS
231	CATHERINE'S STOUT SHOP
242	LOVERS
244	J. HARRIS
245	BROOKS
258	MOTHERHOOD MATERNITY SHOP
259	FREDERICK'S OF HOLLYWOOD
280	PAUL HARRIS
282	LIMITED EXPRESS
283	CONTEMPO CASUALS

CHILDREN'S APPAREL
237	CHILDREN'S OUTLET
254	CAROLYN'S CHILDREN'S CORNER

SHOES
115	BAKER'S SHOES
123	FOOT SCENE
135	THOM McAN SHOES
152	BUTLERS SHOES
173	HANOVER SHOES
174	FOOTPRINTS
177	FOOT LOCKER
181	HARDY SHOES
184	KINNEY SHOES
210	FLORSHEIM SHOE SHOP
221	FOOT ACTION
222	9 WEST
239	SHOE BOX
243	JARMAN SHOE STORE
246	HEROLD'S SHOES
247	THE WILD PAIR
250	BURT'S SHOES
253	STRIDE RITE
274	ENDICOTT JOHNSON SHOES
276	NATURALIZER
278	REVELATIONS

JEWELRY
111	ZALES JEWELERS
120	JAMES AVERY CRAFTSMAN
121	J. B. ROBINSON JEWELERS
127	MISSION JEWELERS
136	PIERCING PAGODA
137	J. A. KEEPSAKE DIAMOND CENTER
148	GORDON'S JEWELERS
154	THE PASSPORT-JEWELERY AND GIFTS
171	KRUGER'S JEWELERS
215	CORRIGANS JEWELERS
223	JOE KOEN & SONS JEWELERS
249	STELFOX JEWELERS
256	CLAIRE'S BOUTIQUE
277	HELZBERG DIAMONDS

HOME FURNISHINGS/SPECIALTY
113	LOWERY ORGAN
119	DECK THE WALLS
134	PACK IT IN
141	BACK HOME FURNITURE
189	THE HOME FRONT
206	THE GRATE FIREPLACE SHOPPE
212	CARGO FURNITURE
235	BARTON CREEK GALLERY
240	BUTTERFIELDS ETC.
264	WORLD BAZAAR
267	VIDEO CONCEPTS
272	PAUL'S INTERIORS
288	GOLDEN DOLPHIN BATH & GIFTS BOUTIQUE

CARDS/BOOKS/GIFTS
109	B. DALTON BOOKSELLER
111A	AUSTIN BOOK SELLERS
118	THE CROWN SHOP
144	AUSTIN PEWTER COMPANY
145	WICKS 'N' STICKS
157	FIFTH AVENUE FLORAL & GIFT
178	SPENCER GIFTS
188	COACH HOUSE GIFTS
208	ZONDERVAN'S FAMILY BOOKSTORE
227	SUMMIT STATIONERS
268	WALDEN BOOKS
271	CARD & QUILL HALLMARK

PERSONAL/PROFESSIONAL SERVICES
125	TEXAS STATE OPTICAL
128	GREAT EXPECTATIONS-PRECISION HAIRCUTTERS
129	WALKER RESEARCH
132	REPUBLIC BANK
162	VIEWPOINT-CENTURY OPTICAL
187	R & S ENGRAVING & KEY SHOP
203	FIRST FEDERAL SAVINGS
213	REGIS HAIRSTYLIST
234	KINDERFOTO
266	ROYAL OPTICAL
289	SUNGLASSES ETC.

HOBBY/SPECIAL INTEREST
148A	IT'S A SMALL WORLD
168	TOYS BY ROY
170	OSHMAN'S SPORTING GOODS
183	PHIDIPPIDES SPORTS
285	KAY-BEE TOY AND HOBBY

ENTERTAINMENT/ELECTRONICS
103	HASTINGS RECORDS AND TAPES
130	ALADDIN'S CASTLE
185	RADIO SHACK
284	CAMELOT MUSIC

SPECIALTY SHOPS
101	DOCKTOR PET CENTER
122	PIPE PUB
124	CUTTING EDGE CUTLERY
153	HOUSTON TRUNK FACTORY
155	T-SHIRTS +
186	SO-FRO FABRICS/SINGER
202	FOX ONE HOUR PHOTO
224	HOFFRITZ CUTLERY
236	JO ANN FABRICS
248	MERLE NORMAN

COMPETITION

The major competition for BCS was Highland Mall, the only other regional shopping center in Austin. Highland Mall was located in near-north-central Austin (see Exhibit 10-3-2). Several other smaller malls and strip centers located within a mile of BCS—Lake Hills, Westgate, Southwood, and Westwood—were not strong competitors.

CUSTOMERS

Research revealed that geographically, the primary market area for BCS consisted of all of Austin south of West 38th Street and west of IH 35 (see Exhibit 10-3-2). In terms of ZIP codes, past studies indicated that BCS's primary trade area consisted of 78703, 04, 35, 36, 37, 45, 46, 48, and 49. The typical BCS shopper tended to be white, be a little older than average for the market, and live in a household with above-average income. BCS was located near many of the newer and most affluent residential areas of the city.

Access primarily by automobile, the lack of movie theaters or an ice rink to serve as a magnet, and tight security had helped BCS avoid the problem of becoming a hangout for junior and senior high school students. Mall management was concerned with maintaining a pleasant, inviting shopping environment for people of all ages.

MARKETING PROGRAMS

Simon's BCS mall management was responsible for developing and implementing a coordinated marketing program for the mall. Individual stores were required to participate under the terms of their lease agreement. Individual store owners did not have veto power over the overall marketing program, as was often the case in malls where tenant associations were responsible for advertising and promotions.

The vast majority of BCS's tenants contributed to a promotional fund based on square footage leased. For the average tenant, this contribution was approximately 50¢ per square foot per year. However, the six major department stores did not contribute to this fund. These stores owned their own buildings rather than leasing from Simon.

The nature of Simon's lease agreement built in a strong incentive for mall management to develop an effective promotional program that would benefit all tenants. Most tenants were on a 6- to 15-year lease agreement which specified that they pay rent plus a percentage on sales volume over a specified level. Hence, mall management had a vested interest in helping individual stores increase their sales volume through an effective marketing program.

Simon's BCS marketing program involved four major components: advertising, merchandising promotion, tenant support, and community involvement. Examples of tenant support activities were sales force motivation and

EXHIBIT 10-3-2 ZIP Code Map of the Austin Area

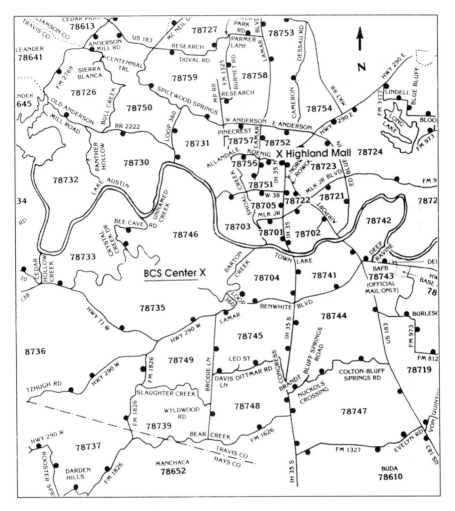

merchandise display programs developed by Simon to help tenant retailers market their wares more effectively. Community involvement efforts were often joint projects planned with the YMCA, Girl Scouts, Austin Women's Center, and other local clubs and civic organizations. Exhibit 10-3-3 presents an ad promoting a community involvement program cosponsored by the mall and Seton Medical Center.

In developing the image of BCS, management had attempted to carefully position the mall vis-à-vis the competition. All marketing activities had to be tailored to be consistent with the following positioning statement: "BCS is Austin's most convenient place to shop, with the city's greatest selection of quality merchandise in a pleasant and attractive setting."

EXHIBIT 10-3-3   Ad for a Community Involvement Program Cosponsored by the Mall

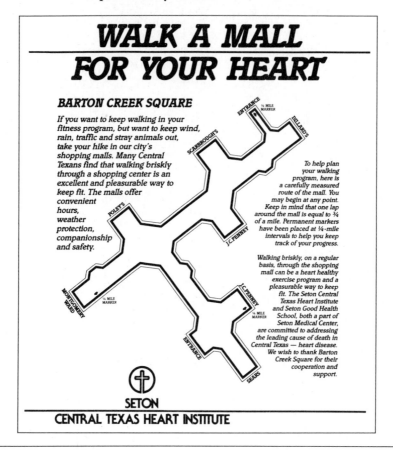

This positioning statement was significant both for what it covered and what it did not cover. For example, price was not mentioned as part of the appeal of the shopping center.

In the past, BCS had developed separate advertising efforts for seven seasons: January (Winter Clearance), March/April (Spring), May/June (Summer), July (Summer Clearance), August/September (Back-to-School), October (Fall), and November/December (Christmas). These efforts were advertised primarily through insert sections in the local newspaper, the *Austin American-Statesman,* and through radio and television commercials. In addition, BCS utilized event marketing such as the "All-American Sidewalk Sale" and a spring fashion show.

BCS's total advertising and promotional appropriation for the current year was approximately $220,000. Roughly 75 percent of this amount was for advertising (media and production) and 25 percent was for promotional expenses. In the past, BCS had used six newspaper tab sections, one each in January, March, July, August, November, and December. A budget breakdown by seasons had been roughly as follows: Winter Clearance (10 to 12 percent), Spring (13 to 17 percent), Summer (14 to 17 percent), Summer Clearance (7 to 9 percent), Fall (14 to 17 percent), Fall Clearance (9 to 10 percent), and Christmas (21 to 26 percent).

In the past, television commercials had been used in January, for three to four weeks in the spring, for one week in July, for three to four weeks in August, and for five weeks in November/December. TV buys had concentrated on local network affiliates. Radio had also been used heavily as a support medium, with approximately an equal amount invested in television and radio.

BCS management used Simon's in-house ad agency (Creative Marketing Services) to develop and place all advertising. The agency was located in Indianapolis, and distance plus the lack of familiarity with the local Austin market occasionally caused problems. The in-house agency sold its services to BCS. For example, a television commercial cost roughly $800, and radio commercials were roughly $200 each. Local management selected commercials from a catalogue and was given some control over copy.

In developing her marketing plan for the coming year, Helen Hoff, BCS's marketing director, was concerned about two special promotional programs. One of the programs was to be a promotional event jointly sponsored by the mall and the mall's 26 tenants who sold jewelry. The other special thrust was to be an attention-getting program to stimulate new residents in BCS's primary trade area to shop at the mall.

Hoff felt that these two special efforts were crucial to effectively marketing the mall during the coming year. Both programs would have to be described in detail and include a set of objectives, a budget, a complete time schedule, and a reasonable means for evaluating their success or failure.

JEWELRY MERCHANDISING EVENT

This promotion posed a particularly difficult challenge because, to be most successful, all 26 jewelry retailers would have to participate. The 13 jewelry stores and 13 other retailers who carried jewelry were direct competitors, and their images ranged from discount to high fashion. Hence, suggesting a generic event in which all would participate was a difficult assignment.

It was important that a merchandising event generate customers and not just traffic. Therefore, in addition to developing a clever idea, Hoff had to have a carefully thought-out plan for selling it to the jewelry retailers to ensure their participation.

NEW RESIDENT PROGRAM

Since the Austin market was attracting new residents at a rapid pace, Hoff believed that some sort of newcomer contact program was essential. The program's goal was to reach all new residents in BCS's primary trade area with a memorable incentive to shop at the mall. The first step would be to determine how to identify the new residents to be contacted. Designing a program to motivate new residents to shop at the mall that would be fair to all tenants was not an easy task.

Questions for Discussion and Review

1. What are some of the unique challenges faced by mall management in developing a marketing program for a diverse range of retailers?

2. Which of the two special projects—the jewelry merchandising event or the new resident program—poses the most difficult problem? Why?

3. Which areas of the mall's marketing communications program are most important? Why?

Public Relations

*Increased access to the marketplace carries with it the
obligation to use such access in a responsible manner.
Business has most to lose from public misinformation
and, therefore, should take every possible step to
improve the quality of public information and debate.*[1]

S. Prakash Sethi

Public relations is the vehicle through which an organization shows its public
responsibility, its sensitivity to social problems, and its concern for the various
publics with whom it interacts. Public relations is a function often misunderstood. It has often been confused with marketing and advertising because it is
similar in some respects; however, the primary objective of marketing is that
of selling products or services, while public relations attempts to "sell" the
whole organization. Also, while advertising is paid communication, public
relations often operates through nonpaid media.

This chapter describes how public relations complements the other
communication functions of a firm. Because public relations establishes the
mutual understanding between a corporation and its publics, it will indirectly
affect the results of advertising campaigns and the overall marketing strategy of
the firm. It is important, therefore, that we understand how public relations
works.

---

[1]S. Prakash Sethi, "Battling Antibusiness Bias: Is There a Chance of Overkill?" *Public Relations
Journal* (November 1981): 64.

THE MANY PUBLICS OF A FIRM

Corporations are entities that must deal with a large range of constituencies. While the old-time peddler could concern himself primarily with his customers, today's firms do not have that luxury. Customers and potential customers are still very important; however, they are only one of several important groups with whom a company deals on a daily basis.

Several definitions and classifications of these publics can be found in the literature. A general categorization is to separate them into internal publics, or those who are inside the organization, and external publics, or those not directly connected with the organization.

Internal publics are, for example, the employees of the firm, its stockholders, and its board of directors. Agents, dealers, and company representatives could also be considered internal publics in that they represent the company to the outside world, even though they are not directly employed by it. These publics are very important because they represent the firm's human resources. Without their support, the firm would be unable to operate. The company must communicate regularly with its internal publics to maintain their support and to provide them with the necessary information for meaningful interaction with external publics. The public relations function in this case can be carried out through internal memos, company events, and company magazines, among other means.

The external publics of the firm are indirectly connected with it. Among these publics are the company's customers, its suppliers, the government, the press, consumer advocates, and financial institutions. These groups exert a number of influences on the firm, some of which are more easily quantifiable than others. For example, customers may choose to purchase or not to purchase the products and services offered by the firm, and its suppliers' interaction with the company is usually straightforward as well. The effect of government on the firm, however, may be very diverse. It may range from direct regulation to legal constraints on specific forms of advertising or media channels.

It is important for the firm to understand the influence of its external publics on its long-term success. To ignore the role of government, potential investors, or consumer advocates is not only shortsighted, but potentially very risky. The firm must communicate with its external publics and use every possible channel to maintain a positive image and to provide the needed support to all of its other functions.

THE MANAGEMENT OF PUBLIC RELATIONS

In recent years, public relations has become a management function. As such, it has achieved a higher organizational stature and has assumed many of the characteristics of other management functions.

In some companies, public relations still plays a minor role, and the public relations officer reports to a middle-management level. In these cases, public relations deals only with rudimentary communications with the firm's employers or its customers. More frequently, however, public relations has a more prominent role in the overall management of the company. Often, the public relations officer reports directly to top management. In such cases, the public relations function is designed to handle most communications with the firm's internal and external publics. It becomes the voice of the firm and its management's official interpreter.

Among the many functions of public relations are reaching the firm's employees, coordinating interaction with legislators and with the community, and conducting public opinion research. Public relations, therefore, should be planned, organized, and evaluated as thoroughly as any other management function. This section briefly examines each of these steps.

Planning Public Relations

Before organizing for public relations work, objectives and strategies must be established. To approach public relations as solely a process to correct problems or diffuse negative perceptions is a major mistake. Images and reputations are built over a long period of time; therefore, the firm's public relations goal and objectives and the structuring of the public relations strategy are essential to the firm's success.

Organizing the Public Relations Function

The organization of the public relations function will determine its role within the firm. Such organization must include the reporting hierarchy of this function, its interface with other communication functions, and the structuring of its budget.

Public relations departments could include a legal staff, depending on how complex the firm's relationships with government or special interest groups are. In addition, specific technical functions such as publishing could report to the public relations manager.

Public relations departments range from one-person operations to large staff divisions. Some firms use very centralized management for public relations, while others may contract out the entire public relations task.

Evaluating Public Relations

The firm exists in a dynamic, competitive environment. Changes in such an environment will affect the overall public image of the firm and its perception by both internal and external publics. It is important, therefore, to take the pulse of the public relations activities of a company. Any evaluation of the results of public relations activities must take into consideration the short-term and long-term objectives of the public relations campaign. Research and other types of evaluation must be used to assess such results. The firm must be able to adapt its strategy to the ever-changing conditions of the market. Without such an evaluation, it would be impossible to do so.

PUBLIC RELATIONS AND ADVERTISING

Traditionally, advertising has been used for the ultimate purpose of selling products or services. Whether advertising informs or attracts attention to the product, it is engaged in one of the many steps necessary to accomplish a sale. A different type of advertising emerged when public institutions, and especially government, sought to employ this form of mass communication to build support for particular programs. Corporations joined in and stressed values and objectives that were not immediately related to sales of products and services.

This was the case with the 1936 Warner & Swasey campaign stressing the power of America as a nation and the importance of business for its future.[2] In addition, the campaigns undertaken by the government of Franklin Delano Roosevelt to sell its economic and educational programs were another example of the use of advertising for nontraditional purposes.

Recent examples of this type of advertising are more plentiful. Researchers have tried to classify and isolate the types of advertising that could be considered public service. The following discussion examines some of them.

Counteradvertising

After the 1960s, the regulation of advertising was advocated by several consumer groups. This movement was fueled by both consumerists and governmental regulatory bodies during the 1970s.

One of the weapons consumer interest groups used to get public attention for their cause was a form of advertising that came to be known as *counteradvertising.* These were messages intended to question or counter the claims of large corporate advertisers. Examples of this type of public communication were the ads protesting nuclear power plants.

This type of advertising was sponsored by groups such as Public Media Center (PMC) of San Francisco. Such groups raised their own funds and purchased media like any other advertisers. Some counteradvertising also ran free of charge, calling on the fairness doctrine principle that allows equal time for opposing viewpoints on controversial issues.

Corrective Advertising

One of the remedies the Federal Trade Commission enacted to counter the effects of what it deemed deceptive or unfair advertising was so-called corrective advertising. The philosophy of *corrective advertising* was to use the same media channel and a corresponding budgetary allocation to send a message to the public that *corrected* the information or impression created by the deceptive or misleading ad. An example of this occurred when the Ocean Spray Cranberry Juice Cocktail was advertised as containing more "food

---

[2]Fraser P. Seitel, *The Practice of Public Relations,* 2d ed. (Columbus, Ohio: Charles E. Merrill Publishing Co., 1984), 239.

energy" than any other breakfast drinks. "Food energy" was defined by the FDA as calories, but the Federal Trade Commission ruled that the impression caused by the ad was that of greater nutritional value. The FTC required Ocean Spray to run corrective ads explaining what "food energy" meant on the same media channels that had been used for the original advertising campaign.

Corrective advertising is still a remedy that can be required by regulatory order. In recent years, however, it has not been employed a great deal.

Image Advertising

A more general form of advertising that does not directly promote products or services is the kind of message used by a company to publicize those of its programs designed to serve the public interest. The purpose of this type of mass communication is to establish the firm as a "good citizen" of the community, dedicated to doing its share for society.

Image advertising tries to distract public attention from controversial issues while focusing it on some of the positive characteristics of the firm. This type of advertising was very popular among oil companies during the oil embargo. Firms dealing with sensitive environmental or social issues such as companies engaged in mineral exploration or the production of controversial prescription drugs are more likely to engage in image advertising.

Issue Advertising

Issue or advocacy advertising is a more recent phenomenon. During the 1980s, corporations became more and more concerned with taking a public stand on issues such as AIDS, the environment, and government intervention. Networks and other media began to allow and accept the more controversial advocacy advertising. A survey by the Association of National Advertisers, Inc., revealed that 200 U.S. corporations collectively spent close to $675 million annually for what could be classified as public relations advertising during the period from 1977 to 1981.[3] This effort has increased since then, and issue advertising is more common than ever today.

THE FUTURE OF ADVERTISING AND PUBLIC RELATIONS

As companies begin trading more and more in global markets, and as social issues become increasingly more popular, public relations advertising will continue to prosper and grow. The effectiveness of this type of advertising has not yet been assessed, however. Some critics have stated that it could have negative repercussions and "turn off" potential customers. Others have

---

[3]Peg Dardenne, "The Cost of Corporate Advertising," *Public Relations Journal* (November 1981): 30.

concentrated on evaluating public service advertisements on the basis of the strength of their message and creative execution.

Future advertisers will have to assess the value and importance of tackling social issues with their advertising campaigns. In addition, they should explore alternative ways of communicating a positive image of their company and its products. Perhaps a combination of product and different institutional messages may prove to be the most effective way to communicate with the many audiences of a firm. It is essential, however, to explore all options in order to remain competitive in our changing world.

Suggested Readings

Garbett, Thomas F. *Corporate Advertising: The What, The Why, and the How.* New York: McGraw-Hill, 1981.

Greyser, Stephen A. "Changing Roles for Public Relations." *Public Relations Journal* (January 1981): 18–25.

Jefkins, F. W. *Marketing and PR Media Planning.* New York: Pergamon, 1974.

Lloyd, Herbert. *Public Relations.* New York: International Publishing Service, 1974.

Sacks, William S. "Corporate Advertising: Ends, Means, Problems." *Public Relations Journal* (November 1981): 16–17.

Stevens, Art. "What Is New in Product Publicity?" *Public Relations Journal* (December 1981): 16–17.

Welty, Ward. "Is Issue Advertising Working?" *Public Relations Journal* (November 1981): 29.

Exercises

1. A major computer manufacturer is facing decreasing sales and tougher competition. In order to meet its financial demands and to plan future competitive action, top management has decided to lay off 10 percent of its work force across the board. The vice-president for public relations sent a memo to the company CEO suggesting that the firm engage in a major public relations campaign announcing the layoffs and explaining that this action would increase the overall efficiency of the firm. The vice-president of marketing objected to the suggestion, arguing that such a campaign would damage the firm's reputation and affect sales. What do you think the company should do?

Do you agree with the vice-president of public relations? Explain.

2. The social concern for the environment has spread to all segments of society in recent years. Fast-food firms have engaged in campaigns advertising the changes in their packaging as a response to environmental concerns. Do you feel this type of advertising would benefit the manufacturers of most consumer products? Why? What type of company is most likely to benefit from this approach? Explain.

3. Do you think corrective advertising is an appropriate remedy for deceptive or misleading advertising? Discuss.

Shawntana Development Corporation

Mark Conzelman and Bart Hansen, the co-owners of Shawntana Development, were surprised by the objections they had received in response to a newspaper advertisement for New Chase, their company's first project (see Case 10-1). Several months into Phase I of the project, the ad presented in Exhibit 11-1-1 appeared in the real estate sections of both the *Orange County Register* and the *Los Angeles Times,* Orange County edition. Residents of nearby Pomona, California, objected to negative references to their city in the ad and demanded that the ad be dropped.

Pomona had an image problem associated with the industrial nature of its employment base, the activities of local motorcycle gangs, and a high concentration of relatively low-income households. However, before approving the ad suggested by their advertising agency, Conzelman and Hansen had briefly discussed the possibility that some people might object to the copy. In their judgment, the reference to Pomona was nothing to worry about.

After the ad's initial appearance, Shawntana had received several telephone calls from individuals objecting to the derogatory reference to Pomona and requesting that the ad be dropped. When the ad ran again, more calls were received. In addition, Hansen had received a call from the Pomona city attorney, who reported that the ad had been the subject of a heated discussion at the city council meeting. As a result, the council had instructed the city attorney to contact Shawntana and request that the ad be dropped and to mention the possibility of a lawsuit if the ad appeared again.

This left Conzelman and Hansen in a dilemma. Their first reaction was to simply drop the ad. On the other hand, they felt that the copy referred to something everyone in Orange County was well aware of and, hence, was not out of line. They reasoned that under the First Amendment right of free speech, Shawntana could make such references. Why should they buckle under to the complaints of a few overly sensitive people?

Since the ad was scheduled to appear again the next weekend, they needed to make a decision before the cancellation deadline the next day at 4:00 P.M. Before making a decision, they agreed to contact their public relations and advertising agencies and their attorney for advice.

This case was written by John H. Murphy, The University of Texas at Austin. The case is intended for use in generating class discussion and not to illustrate either the effective or ineffective handling of an administrative situation. Used by permission of the Shawntana Development Corp. Parts of the Pomona advertising scenario are fictitious.

EXHIBIT 11-1-1 New Chase Newspaper Advertisement

Questions for Discussion and Review

1. What ethical and public relations considerations are raised by the offensive ad and the response of concerned citizens and public officials?

2. If the ad appears again, how likely is the city of Pomona to file the threatened lawsuit?

3. What are Shawntana's options in responding to the request that the ad be dropped?

4. What additional information should Shawntana executives obtain before making a decision about how to respond to the request that they drop the ad?

C A S E **11 - 2**

Central Hospital

Central Hospital in Bloomington, Illinois, is a 400-bed, multispecialty community hospital providing ambulatory care, acute care, and psychiatric care services to residents living within a 30-mile radius of the twin cities of Bloomington-Normal. The nonprofit hospital is located close to a large state university. Central Hospital is also located close to what is recognized as the poorest neighborhood in the twin cities, an area of run-down homes with a population that is 90 percent black, 5 percent white, and 5 percent "other."

Three years ago, the board of directors of Central Hospital approved a plan to seek approval to build a new ambulatory care facility to replace its inadequate facilities located within the existing hospital structure. Last year, the hospital was awarded a certificate of need by the Illinois Health Facilities Planning Board to construct a new 40,000-square-foot ambulatory care building.

The hospital's chief executive officer, health planner, and vice-president of operations worked exclusively with the architect to plan the new facility, taking the plan to the hospital's board of directors for ultimate approval.

The plan they took to the board proposed a two-story ambulatory care facility with an attached parking garage, extending from the west end of the existing hospital structure, which housed the current outpatient area. The only drawback of the plan was that the new facility would extend across a section of Moon Street. It was determined by the architect that the facility could not

This case was prepared by Debra Low, Arizona State University, and Charles H. Patti, University of Hartford, and is intended for generating classroom discussion, not to illustrate the effective or ineffective handling of an administrative situation. The identity of the hospital has been disguised. Used by permission.

be built over the street and that a portion of Moon Street would therefore have to be purchased from the city of Bloomington to accommodate the new facility.

Twelve of the thirteen board members heartily endorsed the plan, provided that the street could be purchased for less than $50,000 from the city. The thirteenth board member, Bill Smith, the board's only black, noted that the proposed street was the only major artery to the poor neighborhood located just south of the hospital. He noted that the local residents would have to drive three blocks around the proposed facility to get to and from the closest boulevard under the proposed plan. Moon Street was currently the most convenient access street.

Paul Jones, the hospital's chief executive officer, noted that the proposed plan was the most efficient and cost-effective plan possible. He further noted that he was certain the neighborhood would support any project that Central Hospital sponsored. "What's more important," he argued, "a health care facility or a three-block detour?"

The board of directors voted. Ten approved the project, two voted against the project, and one abstained. The project was passed.

The day before the public hearing, Florence Cummings, an outspoken black who was highly respected in the area, charged that Central Hospital had "ignored the needs of the area residents by proposing to close down our street." She further stated, "Central Hospital is insensitive to our needs. We were never informed of their plans until after the fact. Nobody ever asked us how we felt — or what services we'd like to get from Central Hospital."

Paul Jones's response to the press was: "Central Hospital is providing area residents with the highest quality health care. Our health care professionals have developed this excellent facility for the people we serve. We care."

Florence Cummings and a cadre of 60 local residents picketed the hospital on the day of the public hearing. They also testified against the plan at the public hearing. Despite the protest, the health systems agency voted in favor of the project, and the state ultimately awarded the certificate of need.

On the day of the ground breaking, hospital administrator Paul Jones was quoted by the press as saying, "It is obvious that Central Hospital is sensitive to the needs of our health care consumers." Florence Cummings and a number of persons picketed the ground-breaking ceremonies.

Questions for Discussion and Review

1. What immediate action should Central Hospital take to deal with Florence Cummings and the irritated local residents?

2. What actions would be appropriate for the hospital to take within the next two months?

3. If you had been the director of communications for Central Hospital three years ago, what actions would you have recommended to Paul Jones?

Freeport-McMoRan

The 1990s witnessed a growth of environmental movements across the world. The concern for the environment was particularly strong in the United States, where several environmental movements and associations existed. Some such groups became a vocal and at times aggressive force in our society, taking stands and adopting causes with zeal. One example was Greenpeace, blamed at times for violent demonstrations and attacks on physical property of some corporations. Greenpeace activists took it upon themselves to show their disapproval of "antienvironmental business practices" in radical and some-times destructive ways.

The public interest in "green issues" motivated several companies in-volved in mineral exploration, medical testing, and oil refining, to name a few, to communicate their own story to the public. Several firms developed public service announcements that were broadcast on national television. Such PSAs concentrated on selling the public the "other side" of the story.

Another reaction to environmentalists' attacks was the development of "green marketing" appeals. Emphasis was given to creating environmentally conscious packaging, nonaerosol products, and the like. While no clear strategy seemed to exist for reacting to the attacks of environmentalist interest groups, companies were willing to try new approaches to deflect their criticisms.

THE PROBLEM

Freeport-McMoRan was one of the Fortune 500 companies. Its business was mainly the extraction of natural resources, and it primarily produced sulfur, oil, gas, copper, and agricultural fertilizers. Most of the company's explorations were in the United States and Indonesia, where Freeport operated one of the world's largest open-pit copper mines.

Freeport had always been concerned with environmental issues. It had taken care in rebuilding and relandscaping areas that had been stripped by mineral mining. It had also been very responsive to community needs and issues. The company had contributed money to schools and city projects throughout the years.

This case was written by Isabella C. M. Cunningham, The University of Texas at Austin. The case is intended for use in generating class discussion and not to illustrate either the effective or ineffective handling of an administrative situation. Used by permission of Freeport-McMoRan Inc.

Recently, because of the company's investments in specific tracts of land in central Texas for the purpose of development, it had drawn the attention of environmentalists. Groups opposed to the development of the land had accused the company of being environmentally irresponsible and had criticized Freeport's Indonesia operation. The criticism had hurt Freeport's public image. While the company did not produce any consumer products, it felt that public opinion of the company was important in its dealings with politicians, investors, the media, and future potential employees. It was important, therefore, that the company develop a program to communicate to these various audiences its social contributions, concern with the environment, and economic impact on the communities in which it operated.

Freeport had been involved in several environmentally and socially beneficial projects, but two appeared to have had a substantial and lasting impact. One such project was its contribution to the city of New Orleans to revitalize, rebuild, and maintain city playgrounds in low-income areas. The company's chief executive officer, Jim Bob Moffett, believed that companies should contribute to the well-being of the communities in which they operated. "Giving back" became the Freeport motto for its projects in New Orleans. The city playgrounds were important to the children who otherwise would not have had a place to congregate and engage in healthy pastimes. Early in 1991, Freeport adopted the Stallings playground, then dilapidated, with an old refrigerator thrown in the no longer operational swimming pool. Later that year, Stallings reopened with a spanking new face, an operating pool, and several outdoor basketball courts. The residents of the area were so proud of the new facility that they took it upon themselves to make sure it was not misused or vandalized. Freeport went on to "adopt" or stimulate the adoption of another eight such playgrounds in the following months. The playgrounds were a wonderful addition to the city's facilities.

Another project of which Freeport was extremely proud was the development of Morrow Swamp in Florida. Agrico, a subsidiary of Freeport-McMoRan, was engaged in the mining of mineral fertilizers in Florida. The law in that state required firms that did strip mining to reclaim the land. Freeport, however, was already reclaiming the land before the law required it. Also, it spent a lot more on the Morrow Swamp project than was required by law. It developed a wildlife refuge for indigenous animals and invested lavishly in a landscape project that would last for many generations.

In addition, Freeport had created jobs and economic opportunities for many Louisiana communities, as well as for several communities in other areas in which it operated.

THE COMMUNICATIONS PROGRAM

James Robinette, Freeport's vice-president for communications, felt that the best way for the company to reach all the audiences to whom it wanted to take its message was to develop a series of public service commercials that would be broadcast through spot TV buys. The PSAs would emphasize Freeport's economic, environmental, and social contributions so as to promote the firm's image in a positive manner.

The public relations agency hired by Freeport disagreed with Robinette. It felt that it was more important to develop a public presence for the company's CEO and follow his speeches and public appearances with press releases.

"Jim Bob has the charisma of a Lee Iacocca," the president of the public relations agency stated. "His physical appearance and his forceful personality will be a lot more memorable than any PSA. Just book him for some key appearances and press conferences on the road, and then let's build a number of press releases on that."

There were some serious questions to be dealt with when analyzing each strategy. One dealt with the desirability of having a corporate image tied permanently to the personality of its CEO. What would the company do if the CEO decided to change jobs? Yet some people felt that PSAs were not a very effective form of communication. Perhaps the company should instead deal with the environmentalists' attacks head on, through public debates, press stories, talk shows, and the like.

Questions for Discussion and Review

1. What is the best way for Freeport McMoRan to reach its intended audiences with messages that communicate all the environmentally and socially responsible projects it has financed and supported?

2. Do you agree with the public relations agency's position?

3. Do you agree with Robinette? What types of PSAs should the company develop in this case? Explain your position.

12

Direct Marketing

. . . a marketing data base becomes the G-2, the intelligence-gathering apparatus that allows marketers to implement their marketing strategies most efficiently . . . allowing the company to precisely target and communicate with its audience while the competition serenely sips champagne and nibbles foie gras, *oblivious that a major attack has taken place.*[1]

Jock Bickert

Over the past decade, direct marketing has become an increasingly sophisticated and important means of communicating with customers and prospective customers for all types of businesses. Further, experience has demonstrated that when integrated with other communication mix elements, direct marketing not only creates plus business in its own right, but plus business for the sales force and dealers.[2] This chapter briefly covers some of the basics involved in this growing area of marketing communication. The chapter begins with an overview of what is involved in managing a direct marketing program and then focuses on the crucial topic of data base marketing.

In an era of expanding technology, products, and competitors, the key underlying assumption of direct marketing is that effective marketing strategies require precise knowledge of increasingly segmented target audiences. At its heart, direct marketing focuses on intelligently applying information about customers and prospects to forge attractive marketing

---

[1]Jock Bickert, *Adventures in Relevance Marketing* (Denver: Briefcase Books, 1991), 3.

[2]Bob Stone, "The Principles and Techniques of Interchannel Marketing," *The Direct Marketing Manual* (New York: Direct Marketing Association, 1989), Resource Report 605.01, 1–3.

EXHIBIT 12-1   Ten Major Areas of Responsibility in Direct Marketing[a]

1. *Product selection and development*—evaluating market potential, the competition, potential profit margins, and fit with other marketing communication activities.

2. *Strategic planning*—establishing objectives, developing planning models, conducting business analyses, and developing strategies.

3. *Market and media selection/scheduling*—selecting and/or developing appropriate mailing lists or data bases and identifying the most efficient media to deliver the message.

4. *Creative development*—presenting the offer in a memorable and appropriate manner through the development of creative strategy and executions.

5. *Research*—applying a variety of research techniques to gather background information for decision making in other steps. Examples include exploratory research using survey questionnaires and focus groups.

6. *Testing procedures*—measuring response to the offer. This area is the heart of the accountability of direct marketing. Such factors as the offer itself, price, and variations by geographic region, by demographics, and by media are evaluated by comparing response rates.

7. *Fulfillment*—deciding which shipping facilities, returned goods procedures, carriers, and so on to use.

8. *Budgeting and accounting*—determining appropriate financing costs, cash flow procedures, accounting systems, and credit card affiliations and monitoring program performance.

9. *Customer service*—handling sales correspondence, adjustments, and complaints, plus activation and reactivation.

10. *Personal and supplier relations*—fostering productive relationships with suppliers, list brokers, printers, artists, envelope houses, fulfillment firms, space reps, and other marketing specialists within the firm.

---

[a]Bob Stone, *Successful Direct Marketing Methods,* 4th ed. (Lincolnwood, Ill.: NTC Business Books, 1988), 23–24.

---

programs—marketing programs aimed at developing an interactive, long-term relationship between the marketer and the customers whose needs it seeks to serve.

Hodgson points out that direct marketing involves three crucial characteristics. First, during the marketing process a response takes place "sight unseen." That is, something occurs without any personal contact between the marketer and the prospect (that is, without the intervention of a retailer). Second, the audience for the firm's offer is selected using information contained in a data base. Third, the success of the process is measurable.[3]

Astute marketers realize that direct marketing offers many firms important opportunities to expand their sales and that capitalizing on this potential requires a special expertise distinct from that required by traditional media advertising and other forms of marketing communication. Exhibit 12-1 presents ten major areas of responsibility that must be addressed to effectively operate a direct marketing program. Stone suggests that in order to handle these areas effectively and be successful direct marketers, firms need to hire

---

[3]Richard Hodgson, *An Introduction to Direct Marketing* (New York: The Direct Marketing Educational Foundation, 1990), monograph, 2–6.

direct marketing experts. Hence, it is not surprising that firms are increasingly establishing separate direct marketing units to supplement other marketing and advertising functions.[4]

Three broad categories of direct marketing can enter a firm's marketing communication mix: (1) *direct response*—a system in which the marketer's message, regardless of the medium used, seeks to stimulate a direct, measurable response from the target audience; (2) *direct mail advertising*— use of the United States Postal Service to make direct contact with prospective customers; and (3) *data base marketing*—an integrated system structured around information on customers and prospects and their purchasing preferences and history.[5] Note that the increased use of both category one (direct response) and category two (direct mail) has been and will continue to be driven by the expansion of category three (data base marketing).

Underlying the growth in the application of data base marketing are the increasingly sophisticated capabilities of computers to handle and manipulate large data files, advanced statistical techniques, and the measurability of direct marketing, as well as the growing acceptance of toll-free telephone numbers to conduct business and use of credit cards to make purchases.[6] Given the past growth of data base marketing and the fact that it is forecasted to become an increasingly important means of selling products, the remainder of this chapter focuses on the basics of data base marketing.

DATA BASE MARKETING

The general strategy of data base marketers is to begin by purchasing or developing a computer file of customers and prospects. This file includes information such as name, address, telephone number, past purchases, life-style activities, and interests. Using this information, the marketer formulates and then conveys specialized offers to segments of the data base based on known correlations between likely demand for specific offers and the other variables included in the data base. American Express, American Airlines, and Spiegel are examples of companies that have for a number of years successfully applied their knowledge of their customers to determining which groups receive specialized product offers. The goal of these companies is to build a relationship with their customers over time based on a two-way stream of communication and information.[7]

---

[4]Bob Stone, *Successful Direct Marketing Methods,* 4th ed. (Lincolnwood, Ill.: NTC Business Books, 1988), 23.

[5]Don Schultz, *Strategic Advertising Campaigns,* 3d ed. (Lincolnwood, Ill.: NTC Business Books, 1990), 498–504.

[6]*Ibid.,* 495–496.

[7]Don Schultz, "Maybe the Difficulty in the Definition Is the Difference," *Journal of Direct Marketing* 5, no. 1 (Winter 1991): 4–6.

Developing the Data Base

The most important element in successful direct marketing is the development and maintenance of a computer data base containing information on individual customers and prospects. The data base includes each individual's name, address, purchase history, and other information pertinent to effectively marketing the firm's products/services through a targeted program. It may initially be created through available sales transaction files and supplemented by harvesting (adding to the firm's own data base) individuals who respond to offers from rented lists of prospects.

A myriad of lists are made available for rent (or purchase, but this is rare) by specialized firms and list brokers. For example, Donnelly Marketing uses census data on income, age of the household head, etc., to identify prospects who live in selected areas, such as certain ZIP codes, who meet specified criteria. The Lifestyle Selector, developed by National Demographics & Lifestyles, is another example of a widely used external data base. It contains 28 million names, along with demographic and life-style information. Standard Rate & Data Service, Inc., publishes the most comprehensive directory of information on mailing lists and data bases. This directory, *Direct Mail Lists, Rates & Data,* is updated regularly and includes costs, formats, restrictions, and other details. In addition, list brokers have the ability to sort, merge, and purge several lists to custom design a specific prospect profile. By creating a list of prospects who meet criteria related to interest in and purchase of items in a product category, the marketer is practicing market segmentation and increasing the probability that its offer will be appealing to those contacted.

Manipulating the Data Base

Once data on each individual customer or account are captured, it is possible to track the profitability of each and to structure an appropriate program of customer contact. Stone describes two systems for evaluating customers using data on past purchases. These systems (R-F-M and FRAT) assign points to customers based on the most commonly captured and useful transactional data: recency, frequency, monetary amount, and type of merchandise purchased. For example, in rating customers' purchases over the past twelve months, 20 points might be assigned if a purchase had been made in the past three months, 15 for a purchase made in the past six months, and so on. The other three variables are assigned points in a similar fashion.[8]

By weighting these variables and summing the points a customer receives on each, a marketer is able to accurately forecast which customers are most likely to respond to an offer (the higher the points total, the more likely the customer is to buy again). Hence, contact is made only with customers who have a points total above some minimum level. The system is constantly updated and evaluated to determine if it is working effectively.

---

[8]Stone, *Successful Direct Marketing Methods,* 30–32.

In addition, such a data base provides the marketer with a wide range of target marketing and cross-selling opportunities to apply past purchase information to determining what sort of offer to convey to which customers. For example, a computer company can send a follow-up mailing featuring appropriate new software only to those customers who have purchased high-performance Macintoshs in the past year. Or a garden supply center could identify customers who purchased flower bulbs last fall to receive a promotional piece featuring fall gardening tools that will be mailed in September.

In addition, several mathematical techniques can be applied to data bases to develop improved marketing programs. These techniques (for example, multiple regression, Automatic Interaction Detector, and cluster analysis) are complex and typically involve the counsel of a statistician. The advantages of such techniques depend on the value of the output or information generated and how useful it is to making marketing decisions.[9]

Maintaining the Data Base

Data bases require constant maintenance. Sales orders must be processed through the data base, regular management control reports on data base activity must be supplied, and so on. The value of the information contained in a data base is a direct function of its accuracy and relevance. To ensure the integrity of the data base, a firm may assign a staff person or contract with a specialist in data base management to handle these tasks.

Other Steps in Direct Marketing Using the Data Base

In addition to developing and maintaining the data base, several other steps must be carefully planned and implemented to conduct a successful direct marketing operation. These steps include establishing clear-cut objectives for each program, selecting an appropriate offer, testing the offer, selecting the most appropriate medium to convey the offer to prospects, and fulfilling the offer. These steps are followed by an evaluation of the program's operation and success and planning for future offers (refer again to Exhibit 12-1).

Suggested Readings

Bickert, Jock. *Adventures in Relevance Marketing.* Denver: Briefcase Books, 1991.

Rapp, Stan, and Tom Collins. *The Great Marketing Turnaround.* Englewood Cliffs, N.J.: Prentice-Hall, 1990.

Schultz, Don. "Direct Marketing." Chap. 14 in *Strategic Advertising Campaigns.* 3d ed. Lincolnwood, Ill.: NTC Business Books, 1990.

Stone, Bob. *Successful Direct Marketing Methods.* 4th ed. Lincolnwood, Ill.: NTC Business Books, 1988.

The Direct Marketing Manual (New York: Direct Marketing Association, 1989).

The Retail Revolution: Direct Marketing. Vol. 7. New York: Direct Marketing Association, 1989.

[9]C. Rose Harper, "Lists and Databases," *The Direct Marketing Manual* (New York: Direct Marketing Association, 1989), Resource Report 301.01, 1–6.

Exercises

1. During 1992, advertising expenditures on direct response tools were higher than ever before. Even catalogs—the great-grandaddy of direct marketing tools—reported a 36 percent increase in revenues. Most catalog proponents felt that their profits would continue to grow because of the increase in working women who had less time to shop.

One other direct response tool that showed considerable growth was direct-sell television. Direct-sell television had been growing at an average of over 30 percent per year in revenues, and this trend was expected to continue for a few years. Proponents of this medium felt it was a better way for first-time direct response marketers to enter the highly competitive field. Others felt it was a better tool to measure advertising response than general awareness advertising.

What is your position on this controversy? Do you feel catalogs will continue to grow? What is the potential for direct-sell television in your opinion?

2. TV Answer, the national owner of an interactive TV channel, signed an exclusive agreement with Hewlett-Packard Co. (H-P) to provide and sell to viewers the computerized equipment to be attached to each viewer's television so he or she could buy the products advertised on TV Answer. The system was a wireless interactive TV system scheduled to go on the air by April 1993.

Viewers with the H-P equipment would be able to perform bank transactions, pay bills, and respond to traditionally broadcast commercials by requesting information. They could also buy products through TV Answer's shopping service.

TV answer was marketing the system to advertising agencies to sign more advertisers. Advertisers would pay an average of $2 per consumer inquiry. The fees for each shopping or service contract were negotiable. Viewers would be able to direct order custom-designed products, as in the example for a pizza marketer shown in Exhibit 12-2. H-P expected to sell over 1.5 million devices for TV Answer in the first year.

One major competitor of TV Answer was Prodigy Service, an interactive computer system owned jointly by IBM and Sears, which had over 1.4 million subscribers. Personal computer owners who subscribed to Prodigy could do everything TV Answer subscribers could do but had control over the time at which they decided to shop for products. While they could also interact with commercials shown on Prodigy by asking questions, they were limited to those firms that advertised on the system. The graphics of Prodigy were not as sophisticated as TV Answer graphics, and the waiting time involved was greater because the system worked through telephone modems.

Consider having to make a choice between TV Answer and the Prodigy system. Which of the two would you choose if you were a travel agent? Why? If you were the marketing vice-president of a chain of specialty food stores? Why?

Source: Christy Fisher, "Marketers Answer Interactive TV Call," *Advertising Age,* March 30, 1992, 36.

3. During the early 1990s, it was believed that brand loyalty for consumer package goods in the United States was eroding rapidly. Recessionary pressures and an increased shift of advertising dollars to special promotions were blamed for the decrease in brand loyalty for many products.

A study conducted by the NPD Group, which tracked the brand equity of 50 major package goods brands from 1975 to 1992, revealed that the average market position of 45 of the 50 brands had declined only 8 percent in those 17 years.

A caveat accompanying that information was the fact that the sample of brands used in the study only included brands that were number 1, 2, or 3 in their categories. Also, instead of measuring repurchasing patterns, NPD measured each brand's "share of requirements satisfied" to assess brand loyalty. The "share of requirements satisfied" was obtained by dividing purchases of a specific-category brand by total category purchases.

Some marketers believed that brand loyalty was eroding in the United States because as consumers become more affluent and more educated, they shop with better information and are less vulnerable to image advertising. These marketers felt that the right combination of image advertising and direct response promotions and advertising was essential to the product's success.

NPD's research results suggested that there was merit in continuing to invest large amounts on image advertising. NPD's CEO stated that "where manufacturers have not maintained share of advertising voice, brand equity has declined."

Do you believe image advertising is important to maintaining brand loyalty? Do you feel direct response promotions are harmful to brand loyalty? Explain your position.

Source: Scott Hume, "Brand Loyalty Steady," *Advertising Age,* March 2, 1992, 19.

4.   In 1990, the average American spent over $51 on pretzels, popcorn, and other salty snack products. That represented a 7 percent increase over 1989 sales.

Potato chips were the most popular salty snack, as they were bought by 80 percent of the total households. The major competitor of potato chips was tortilla chips. These were bought by 58 percent of all households, but their penetration was increasing at a very fast rate.

The manufacturer of a fast-growing tortilla chip snack product marketed at a regional level wanted to take advantage of this market trend to increase its market share. Because of the size of the company, direct response advertising and promotions was believed to be the most effective and economical way to reach potential customers. It wanted to consider the use of in-store coupons, tie-ins with hot sauce manufacturers, and taste stands in supermarkets, among other direct response tools.

Prepare a direct response plan for the tortilla chip manufacturer. What do you think would be the best direct response tool to spur sales of tortilla chips? How do you suggest the manufacturer should use direct response promotions? Explain.

Source: Richard Gibson, "Tortilla Chips Gain on Other Salty Snacks," *The Wall Street Journal,* February 14, 1992.

EXHIBIT 12-2   Direct Order System for a Pizza Marketer

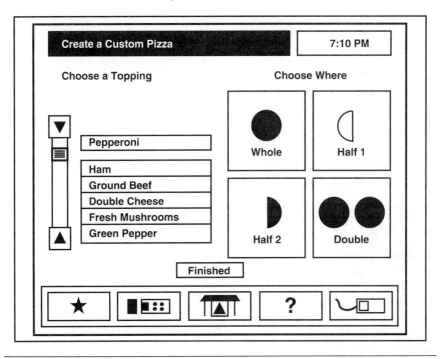

Source: Christy Fisher, "Marketers Answer Interactive TV Call," *Advertising Age,* March 30, 1992, 36.

Rooster Andrews Sporting Goods, Inc. (B)

In planning the Rooster Andrews Sporting Goods (RASG) marketing program for the coming year, Ron Habitzreiter was particularly excited about the potential of a direct marketing program of some sort for expanding sales. (See Case 3-2.) As he contemplated how RASG might use direct marketing, Habitzreiter was interested in exploring three types of direct marketing activities—direct response media advertising, data base marketing, and direct mail. Of these three, data base marketing, designed around a customer and prospect computer data file, seemed to hold the most immediate potential. However, he felt that he needed to carefully consider how RASG might use any or all of these forms of direct marketing and how to implement any recommended program(s).

Over the past several years, RASG had implemented a direct marketing program that had met with mixed success. A computer data base had been developed that included roughly 6,000 names. The data base included approximately 3,000 names and addresses of all men and women who had earned a varsity sports letter at The University of Texas (UT) since 1942 and approximately 3,000 names and addresses of individuals who had ordered merchandise from RASG through the mail in the past. No purchase or other information was included in the data base.

Approximately once a year a direct mail piece featuring merchandise with "Texas" or "Longhorns" printed on it had been mailed to this list. See Exhibit 12-1-1 for a recent example. Habitzreiter believed that the response to RASG's direct mail piece featuring Longhorn paraphernalia was strongly influenced by the fortunes of the Texas football team. Coming off a conference football championship season, orders were strong, but when the football team had a poor season, interest in the items offered in the RASG mailer dropped substantially.

Another data base of names and addresses of individuals who had had their tennis racquets strung by RASG had been compiled. Although approximately 4,000 names were included on the list, Habitzreiter had not contacted these tennis players because the low profit margins on tennis racquets, balls, and other merchandise made sales of these items relatively unattractive.

This case was written by John H. Murphy, The University of Texas at Austin, and is intended as a basis for classroom discussion, not to illustrate the effective or ineffective handling of an administrative situation. Used by permission of Rooster Andrews Sporting Goods, Inc.

EXHIBIT 12-1-1   Rooster Andrews Sporting Goods Mailer

MAIL ORDERS: **ROOSTER ANDREWS SPORTING GOODS   PO BOX 2163   AUSTIN, TEXAS 78768**

ITEM #	QUANTITY	SIZE	YOUTH	ADULT	COLOR

VISA/MC# _____   EXP DATE _____

Orders must be received by December 2 to insure delivery for Christmas. Prices will be valid until August 1, 1990.

Name _____

Address _____

City _____ State _____ Zip _____

ENCLOSED IS MY CHECK OR MONEY ORDER FOR $ _____
VISA & MC ACCEPTED.

Order your Longhorn Football items from Rooster Andrews and receive immediate shipment of your purchase. Rooster Andrews will include the cost of shipment and tax in the price paid so you need only send the exact amount indicated. PLEASE BE CERTAIN TO INCLUDE THE CORRECT SIZE AND COLOR WHERE APPROPRIATE.

17
RUSSELL 69809 CREW SWEATSHIRT #80047079
RUSSELL 69609 SWEATPANTS #80047061
Sweatsuits—Adult suits in Texas Orange or White; matching fleece sets of cotton and polyester blend. Shirts have crew neck with knit sleeves and bottom. Pants feature drawstring elastic waiste and elastic cuffs. Texas logo printed on front of shirt and left pants leg. Available in adult S, M, L, XL. Specify size and color and Suit or Shirt.
Suit **$33.00**
Shirt Only **$18.00**

RUSSELL 99809 YOUTH CREW SWEATSHIRT #80047194
RUSSELL 99609 YOUTH SWEATPANTS #80047160
Sweatsuits—Youth suits in White only with Texas Orange print. Matching fleece sets of cotton and polyester blend. Shirts have crew neck with knit sleeves and bottom. Pants feature drawstring elastic waists and elastic cuffs. Texas logo printed on front of shirt and left pants leg. Available in Youth, S, M, L. Specify size and Suit or Shirt.
Suit **$33.00**
Shirt Only **$18.00**

RABBIT SKINS SWEATSHIRTS #76871029
RABBIT SKINS SWEATPANTS #76871045
Sweatsuits—Juvenile, Infant and Toddler Suits in White only with Texas Orange print. Matching fleece sets of cotton and polyester blend. Shirts have crew neck with knit sleeves and bottom. Pants feature drawstring elastic waists and elastic cuffs. Texas logo printed on front of shirt and left pants leg. Available in juvenile 2, 4, 6 and infant/toddler 6 mos., 12 mos., 18 mos. Specify size and Suit or Shirt.
Suit—**$23.00**
Shirt only—**$12.00**

4
R.C. SPORTS "TEXAS" SPORT SHIRT #77078053
Horizontal stripe jersey knit 50/50 sport shirt with open sleeve and fashion collar. Embroidered with contrasting Texas logo on left chest. Available in Texas Orange with White trim or White with Texas Orange trim. Sizes S, M, L, XL. Specify body color and size. **$30.00**

18
SIPES 26KX KASHA TEXAS JACKET #824260821
Nylon "Texas" Jacket—water repellant oxford nylon jacket in Texas Orange with White sewn on full block letters "Texas" on back. Soft kasha lining and draw string bottom, button closures. Available in adult S, M, L, XL. The classic fan jacket. Specify size.
$40.00

19
SWINGSTER #90478033
Satin "Texas" Jacket—high luster satin jacket with Texas Orange and White knit sleeve, neck and wrist trim. Full block "Texas" sewn on back. Available in adult S, M, L, XL. Fashionable and new. Specify size.
$50.00

In planning any direct marketing program(s), Habitzreiter realized he needed to develop a comprehensive proposal with detailed cost and revenue estimates. For example, in proposing a data base marketing plan, he felt he would need to clearly outline objectives, how the data base would be created and maintained, the nature of offers made to prospects, how the program would be evaluated and adjusted, and so on.

Questions for Discussion and Review

1. What implications do RASG's past advertising and marketing activities suggest for any proposed direct marketing efforts?

2. What major considerations would play a role in evaluating the viability of direct marketing for RASG? Why is each of these considerations important?

3. How good a measure of potential success are RASG's past direct marketing programs? Why?

C A S E   **12 - 2**

SpaceSmart

In the spring of 1988, key personnel at *The Chef's Catalog* met to evaluate the company's latest venture, a catalog featuring space-saving furniture, appliances, and accessories. Named *SpaceSmart,* the catalog was launched to supplement *The Chef's Catalog*'s sales and to target an audience with a specific life-style. (See Appendix 12-2 for a sample of a portion of the catalog.) President/CEO Marshall Marcovitz, buyer Arlene Harris, marketing manager Karen Rutkiewicz, and creative director Marcia Horwich had examined the results of the first mailing and were hopeful that during their meeting they would generate ideas that would help to improve the catalog.

ABOUT THE COMPANY

SpaceSmart, tag lined "Neat new ideas for a well organized home," represented the first time *The Chef's Catalog* had sold merchandise other than kitchenware and household accessories. Since its incorporation in 1979, *The Chef's Catalog,* based in Northbrook, Illinois, had tapped the upscale gourmet

---

This case was prepared by Mark Desky under the direction of Associate Professor Ted Spiegel and Professor Paul Wang, Northwestern University, as a basis for class discussion rather than to illustrate either effective or ineffective handling of an administrative situation. Copyright 1989 Northwestern University. Used by permission.

cooking and appliance market. With a $150,000 investment, president/CEO Marshall Marcovitz created his first catalog, a slim production in black and white. The issue mailed to about 100,000 potential customers and featured about 1,000 products. In 1989, *The Chef's Catalog* boasted eleven editions throughout the year (three basic catalogs and a variety of remails and cover signature changes) and 400,000 customers. Sales approached the $12 million mark.

The company made the decision to open a pilot retail store in late 1986. It was felt there was a synergy between the catalog and a store, since that would be a vehicle to capture the non-mail-order kitchenware customer. The store was also a vehicle to liquidate overstocked items and conduct direct consumer research. The company now has two retail stores, one in Naperville, Illinois, and one in Highland Park, Illinois. Cooking classes and demonstrations are offered in a fully equipped kitchen to position the stores as having everything for the serious cook. All sales personnel at the stores boast several years of cooking experience.

ABOUT THE CEO/PRESIDENT

Certainly Marcovitz, president/CEO of the company, is no stranger to the food industry. In 1956, with degrees in marketing and English and a stint as a travel and food writer in Europe behind him, Marcovitz landed a job with Edward Don, Inc., the world's leading distributor of food service equipment, located in North Riverside, Illinois. He was vice-president and chief marketing executive of Edward Don, Inc., with major responsibility for the development of the direct marketing division. He created a national business-to-business program that expanded the company's sales considerably. In 1977, he left the company and subsequently created *The Chef's Catalog.*

Without hesitation, Marcovitz says the greatest strength he brings to *The Chef's Catalog* is merchandising know-how. And Marcovitz hoped this merchandising savvy—so useful in countering competition from rivals *Williams-Sonoma, Colonial Garden Kitchens,* and *The Wooden Spoon*—would be helpful in launching a new "life-style publication" in 1988. Instead of cookware and appliances, Marcovitz and buyer Arlene Harris focused on furniture, appliances, and accessories for the home. "It seemed like there were a lot of consumer indicators pointing to a need for *SpaceSmart* products. New homes and apartments generally had less space, and there was generally more interest in getting organized," Marcovitz said. "With the advent of video recorders and cable television, more and more people are staying at home. And they are trying to make the most of the space around them."

A National Housewares conference in 1987 confirmed what Marcovitz had suspected. There was a profusion of new products being introduced that would help people get organized and maximize their space. Sales of space-saving items for the home were experiencing tremendous growth in relation to other merchandise categories.

ABOUT THE COMPETITION

Many catalogs featured space-saving furniture in their publications, but few committed entire issues to it. Williams-Sonoma, which created a catalog that competed with *The Chef's Catalog*, published *Hold Everything*. This publication featured furniture for the home. Other competitors included *Place Wares, Container Solutions,* and *Space Options.* Marcovitz saw a niche in targeting upscale customers who were looking to make the most of the dwindling space in their homes. "None of the catalogs out there answered the question on how to be smart about space," he said. "We hoped to take a more functional, deeper approach."

ABOUT THE CATALOG

When the 32-page catalog was mailed in February 1988 to 226,000 potential customers, executives at *The Chef's Catalog* were optimistic about its success. Based on the company's previous experiences with *The Chef's Catalog*, personnel projected that *SpaceSmart* would generate 4,769 orders with sales of $238,430 and a response rate of 2.1 percent. Within weeks, *The Chef's Catalog* executives knew *SpaceSmart* would have to be reviewed. By July—nearly six months after the mailing—3,026 orders accounted for $155,054 in sales and a 1.34 percent response rate. See Exhibit 12-2-1.

Postage and production costs for *SpaceSmart* were estimated at about $134,000. See Exhibit 12-2-2. The four-color catalog carried a wide range of products—211 in all. Double-page spreads were labeled with appropriate headings: "ClosetSmart" for closet accessories; "KitchenSmart" for wire baskets, appliances, and cookery; "EntertainSmart" for kitchen tables and wine racks; "OfficeSmart" for desks and pencil sharpeners; "BathSmart" for electric massagers and electronic scales; "LaundrySmart" for ironing boards and rubber hangers; and "OutdoorSmart" for portable gas grills and garden tote tools. The catalog included both a 1-800 number and order form with self-addressed envelope for ordering. About 53 percent of customers ordered by mail compared to 43 percent by phone.

Table 12-2-1 shows a breakdown of sales by spread and Table 12-2-2 shows a breakdown by product category.

MAILING LISTS

Neither Marcovitz nor marketing manager Karen Rutkiewicz perceived the *SpaceSmart* customer to be any different than *The Chef's Catalog* customer—an upscale professional who was interested in high-quality merchandise. To target this audience, *SpaceSmart* relied on a mix of rented and in-house lists. Table 12-2-3 shows a breakdown of rented lists and their raw responses.

SpaceSmart relied on new lists as well as on lists that had proven successful for *The Chef's Catalog. Boston Proper* gifts catalog, which features

EXHIBIT 12-2-1   7/12/88 Final Report: *SpaceSmart* Actual By-Week Orders and Sales Distribution: Marshall, Julius, Marcia, Mark

Circulation: 226,000
Planned Orders: 4,769
Planned Sales: $238,438
Drop Date 2/15/88

Workweek Ending	Actual Orders				Actual Sales				Cumulative Average Order	Cumulative Response
	Weekly Orders	Weekly % Done	Cumulative Orders	Cumulative % Done	Weekly Sales	Weekly % Done	Cumulative Sales	Cumulative % Done		
1 2/26	179	5.92%	179	5.92%	10,316	6.65%	$10,318	6.65%	57.64	0.06%
2 3/4	724	23.93	903	29.84	36,874	23.78	$47,192	30.44	52.26	0.40
3 3/11	543	17.94	1,446	47.79	26,118	16.84	$73,310	47.26	50.70	0.64
4 3/18	384	11.85	1,830	57.83	15,016	9.68	$88,326	56.96	50.47	0.77
5 3/25	190	6.28	2,020	64.11	8,335	5.38	$96,661	62.34	49.83	0.86
6 4/1	266	8.79	2,286	72.90	12,777	8.24	$109,438	70.59	49.61	0.98
7 4/8	107	3.54	2,393	76.44	5,015	3.23	$114,453	73.81	49.48	1.02
8 4/15	130	4.30	2,523	80.73	8,152	5.26	$122,605	79.07	50.19	1.08
9 4/22	80	2.64	2,603	83.38	2,704	1.74	$125,309	80.62	49.67	1.12
10 4/29	104	3.44	2,707	86.81	5,991	3.86	$131,300	84.68	49.98	1.16
11 5/6	50	1.65	2,757	88.47	2,000	1.29	$133,300	85.97	49.79	1.18
12 5/13	76	7.51	2,833	90.98	5,304	3.42	$138,604	89.39	50.35	1.22
13 5/20	59	1.95	2,892	92.93	3,950	2.55	$142,554	91.94	50.69	1.24
14 5/27	44	1.45	2,936	94.38	2,264	1.46	$144,818	93.40	50.71	1.26
15 6/3	28	1.93	2,964	95.31	1,590	1.03	$146,408	94.42	50.77	1.28
16 6/10	34	1.12	2,998	96.43	2,384	1.54	$148,792	95.96	50.99	1.29
17 6/17	28	1.93	3,026	97.36	1,340	0.86	$150,132	96.83	50.96	1.30
18 6/24	38	1.99	3,064	98.35	1,466	0.95	$151,598	97.77	50.94	1.32
19 7/1	21	1.69	3,045	99.04	1,730	1.12	$153,328	98.89	51.16	1.33
20 7/8	29	1.96	3,114	100.00	1,726	1.11	$155,054	100.00	51.24	1.34
Projection:			4,769 Orders				$238,430 Sales			2.1% Response Rate

433

EXHIBIT 12-2-2   Postage and Production Costs for *SpaceSmart*

	Innerspace Plan		200,000	Innerspace Actual Costs		200,000
	Quantity	Cost	Cost per	Quantity	Cost	Cost per
Creative						
Photography		$ 5,000		34	$ 5,531.20	$162.68
Dupes/Stripping	0	$ 0	$ 0.00	34	$ 325.50	$ 9.57
Type	32	$ 1,600	$ 50.00	34	$ 2,226.00	$ 65.47
Stats		$ 1,000		34	$ 609.55	$ 17.93
Copy		$ 500				
Illus of house/ aug art				1	$ 337.00	
Subtotal	32	$ 8,100	$253.13	34	$ 9,029.25	$265.57
Production						
Separations						
Body	32	$ 16,800	$525.00	32	$ 24,915.00	$778.59
Order form		$ 0				
Subtotal	32	$ 16,800	$525.00	32	$ 24,915.00	$778.59
Printing/Mailing						
Body	200,000	$ 37,000	$ 0.185	236,528	$ 49,225.66	$ 0.208
Order form (BACK ON PRESS FOR 45%)	210,000	$ 8,400	$ 0.040	251,000	$ 7,296.67	$ 0.029
Subtotal	200,000	$ 45,400	$ 0.227	236,528	$ 56,522.33	$ 0.239
Merge/purge	200,000	$ 600	$ 0.003	226,046	$ 800.59	$ 0.004
Lists						
Rental	150,000	$ 11,250	$ 0.075	155,184	$ 16,803.00	$ 0.108
Exchange	0	$ 0	$ 0.000	22,080	$ 136.00	$ 0.006
Subtotal	150,000	$ 11,250	$ 0.075	177,184	$ 16,939.00	$ 0.096
Misc. Mailings						
SVB 2/19/88				2,246	$ 100.00	$ 0.045
SVB 3/29/88				1,772	$ 100.00	$ 0.056
SVB 4/20/88				1,361	$ 100.00	$ 0.073
Subtotal				5,379	$ 300.00	$ 0.056
Postage						
Drop #1	190,000	$ 23,750	$ 0.125	226,128	$ 25,780.37	$ 0.114
Drop #2 SVB 2/19/88				2,246	$ 280.75	$ 0.125
Drop #3 SVB 3/29/88				1,772	$ 221.50	$ 0.125
Drop #4 SVB 4/28/88				1,361	$ 227.23	$ 0.167
Subtotal				231,507	$ 26,509.90	$ 0.115
Grand Total	190,000	$105,900	$ 0.557	$231,507	$133,986.54	$ 0.579

TABLE 12-2-1 SpaceSmart Sales by Spread as of May 25, 1988

Spread	Description	Number of Items	Gross Sales	Spread % of Sales	Average Sales/Item
22–23	Office	20	$11,593	8.88%	$579.65
6–7	Closet	23	11,586	8.88	503.74
30–31	Outdoor	12	11,257	8.62	983.08
26–27	Laundry	15	9,668	7.41	644.53
10–11	Kitchen	14	9,290	7.12	663.57
16–17	Entertain/Kids	18	8,319	6.37	462.17
2–3	Miscellaneous	11	8,038	6.16	730.73
28–29	Travel/Work	19	7,716	5.91	406.11
24–25	Bath	14	7,638	5.85	545.57
8–9	Closet	15	7,588	5.81	505.87
4–5	Closet	19	7,186	5.51	378.21
14–15	Kitchen	13	7,101	5.44	546.23
20–21	Office	17	6,751	5.17	397.12
12–13	Kitchen	12	5,457	4.18	454.75
18–19	Kids	16	5,152	3.95	322.00
Back Cover	Miscellaneous	7	5,021	3.85	717.29
Order Form	Miscellaneous	9	1,162	0.89	129.11
Totals		254	$130,523	100.00%	$513.87

housewares and women's apparel, pulled the best for *SpaceSmart* with a raw response rate of 2.01 percent. Another notable rented list was *Solutions* (raw response rate of 1.71 percent), which promises to "solve the problems of everyday life" with health, household, garden, security, travel, and automotive products and services. In-house lists of *The Chef's Catalog* customers pulled no better than rented lists, with response rates ranging from .99 percent to 1.62 percent. See Exhibit 12-2-3 for more information.

TABLE 12-2-2 *SpaceSmart* Sales by Product Category as of May 25, 1988

Description	Number of Items	Gross Sales	Spread % of Sales	Average Sales/Item
Closet	57	$26,360	20.20%	$462.46
Office	37	18,344	14.05	495.78
Kitchen	39	21,848	16.74	560.21
Kids	25	9,312	7.13	372.46
Entertainment	9	4,160	3.19	462.17
Outdoor	12	11,257	8.62	938.08
Laundry/Bath	29	17,306	13.26	596.76
Travel	19	7,716	5.91	406.11
Miscellaneous	27	14,221	10.90	526.70
Totals	254	$130,523	100.00%	$513.87

TABLE 12-2-3   Breakdown of Rented Mailing Lists

Mailing List	Raw Response
Bloomingdale's by Mail	1.41%
Boston Proper	2.01
Colonial Garden	1.03
David Kay Gifts	1.16
Giggletree	1.10
Hollfritz for Cutlery	1.37
Horchow Collection	1.09
Nature Company	0.79
Norm Thompson	1.05
Paragon	1.33
Petals	1.02
World's Fare	1.64
Casual Living	1.25
Conran's	1.43
Domestications	0.98
Lillian Vernon Buyers	0.80
Plow & Hearth	1.46
Potpourri	1.00
SGF Mail Order Buyers	1.15
Solutions	1.65
Spiegel Houseware	0.89
Stitchery	0.71
Touch of Class	1.47
Thomas Oak & Sons	0.40
Changing Homes	0.58
Chefs Seg 1[a]	1.32
Chefs Seg 2	1.15
Chefs Seg 3	1.09
Chefs Seg 4	1.15
Chefs Seg 5	1.09
Chefs 87 Pd Reqs[b]	0.99
Chefs W88 3× Multis[c]	1.62

[a]Chefs Seg 1 through Chefs Seg 5 represent *The Chef Catalog*'s best customers based on recency, frequency, and amount of purchase.

[b]Chefs 87 Pd Reqs represents *The Chef's Catalog*'s customers who requested a *Chef's* catalog via a space ad in the magazines.

[c]Chefs W88 3× Multis represents names that appeared on three or more lists rented by *Chef's* for its Winter '88 catalog program.

ADVERTISING

About 6,800 customers requested the catalog via a space advertisement that ran in national publications such as *Creative Ideas for Living* and *House Beautiful.* Respondents to the advertisement paid one dollar in exchange for a *SpaceSmart* catalog. A breakdown of the magazines, the cost per thousand, responses, and revenue is available in Exhibit 12-2-4. Customers who responded to the ads accounted for $6,500 in sales.

REACTION TO THE CATALOG

Each of the departments at *The Chef's Catalog* was quick to blame itself for *SpaceSmart*'s failure. "There were no promotions, no excitement," said marketing manager Karen Rutkiewicz. "And we conducted only preliminary, loose research."

Product manager Arlene Harris, who began her career at the company as a salesperson at one of the retail stores, cited different problems. On merchandising:

- "We have to decide what categories we want to be in and stick with them. We can't be all things to all people."
- "We have to find great products that aren't carried by the mass merchants."
- "*SpaceSmart* has to be involved in more furniture items. How else can you define space and be smart about it?"

On display:

- "We need to make the catalog more instructional and visual. We need to show the products functioning."

On testing:

- "Is 200,000 really a fair test? For the first venture, this was a good catalog."
- "When I first started this I wasn't experienced in seeking out organizational merchandise. Now I know a lot more."

THE MEETING AND FUTURE CONSIDERATIONS

Marcovitz, Rutkiewicz, Horwich, and Harris arrived at the April meeting armed with suggestions on how to improve *SpaceSmart*. Their ideas included the following:

- Switching to a digest format (roughly 5½ inches by 8¼ inches) because of a 33 percent postal rate increase that took effect in April 1988. About $134,000 was spent to produce 236,000 copies of the premier catalog. See Exhibit 12-2-5 for more information.
- Avoiding "smaller items," such as padlocks and paperweights, and products available in mass merchandising outlets. Including "more substantial" items, such as closet organization kits, to increase the dollar order size.
- Showing more products per page.
- In future mailings, stressing categories that sold well in the premier issue.
- Offering promotional deals, such as a gift with a purchase and a two-for-one special.

The four executives were faced with three options: (1) retest the catalog, (2) discontinue the catalog, and (3) keep the catalog alive in a different form, such as several pages bound into particular editions of *The Chef's Catalog*.

EXHIBIT 12-2-3 SpaceSmart Breakdown of Rented Mailing Lists

Source Code	List Name	Drop Date	Mail Quantity	Raw Orders	Adj Orders	Raw % Response	Adj % Response	Raw Sales	Adj Sales
1021	BLOOM 6 MO $50+	2/15/88	7,170	101	105	1.41%	1.46%	$4,672	$4,869
1022	BOSTON PROPER 6 MO	2/15/88	6,666	134	139	2.81%	2.08%	$6,568	$6,845
1024	COL GARDEN 3 MO	2/15/88	7,412	76	79	1.83%	1.86%	$4,030	$4,200
1026	DAVID KAY 6 MO	2/15/88	6,962	81	84	1.16%	1.28%	$3,391	$3,534
1027	GIGGLETREE 6 MO $25+	2/15/88	6,824	75	78	1.18%	1.14%	$4,872	$4,243
1028	HOFFRITZ 6 MO FEM	2/15/88	6,924	95	98	1.37%	1.42%	$6,326	$6,592
1029	HORCHOW HOUSEWARE 6 MO $50+	2/15/88	6,984	76	79	1.89%	1.13%	$2,827	$2,946
1010	NATURE CO 6 MO $46+ FEM	2/15/88	7,894	56	58	0.79%	0.82%	$3,347	$3,488
1011	NORM THOMPSON 6 MO FEM	2/15/88	7,158	75	78	1.85%	1.88%	$3,104	$3,235
1012	PARAGON 6 MO $50+	2/15/88	7,009	93	96	1.33%	1.37%	$4,003	$4,172
1013	PETALS 6 MO	2/15/88	7,091	72	75	1.82%	1.05%	$2,931	$3,054
1014	WORLDS FARE 6 MO	2/15/88	7,088	116	128	1.64%	1.78%	$4,365	$4,549
1015	CASUAL LIVING 12 MO $40+	2/15/88	7,832	88	91	1.25%	1.30%	$4,601	$4,795
1016	CONRAN 6 MO FEM	2/15/88	6,988	99	102	1.43%	1.48%	$4,385	$4,570
1017	DOMES 6 MO $25+	2/15/88	7,583	74	77	0.98%	1.01%	$2,929	$3,052
1018	LIL VERNON 3 MO $48+ HOUSEWARE	2/15/88	7,344	59	61	0.88%	0.83%	$2,974	$3,099
1019	PLOW/HEARTH 6 MO $50+ FEM	2/15/88	6,984	181	185	1.46%	1.51%	$5,824	$6,069
1020	POTPOURRI 3 MO $30+	2/15/88	7,238	72	75	1.00%	1.03%	$3,419	$3,563
1021	SGF 6 MO $50+	2/15/88	6,972	80	83	1.15%	1.19%	$3,284	$3,422
1022	SOLUTIONS 6 MO $48+	2/15/88	7,133	118	122	1.65%	1.71%	$7,465	$7,779
1023	SPIEGEL $50+ FEM HOUSEWARE	2/15/88	7,483	66	68	0.89%	0.92%	$3,262	$3,399
1024	STITCHERY 6 MO $30+	2/15/88	7,586	53	55	0.71%	0.73%	$1,681	$1,752
1025	TOUCH OF CLASS 6 MO $40+	2/15/88	7,878	104	108	1.47%	1.52%	$4,194	$4,371
1026	THOMAS OAK	2/15/88	6,255	25	26	0.48%	0.41%	$923	$962
1027	CHANGING HOMES SUBS	2/15/88	7,462	43	44	0.58%	0.60%	$1,528	$1,584
1030	CHEFS SEG 1	2/15/88	6,979	92	95	1.32%	1.36%	$5,286	$5,509
1031	CHEFS SEG 2	2/15/88	6,979	84	87	1.28%	1.25%	$4,647	$4,843
1032	CHEFS SEG 3	2/15/88	6,980	92	95	1.32%	1.36%	$4,143	$4,317

Raw Average Order	Adj Average Order	Adj Sales/ Book	Adj Cost of Goods	Adv Costs	List Cost	Total Profit	Profit/ Book	Profit/ Order
$46.26	$46.58	$0.68	$2,678	$3,657	$998	($2,456)	($0.34)	($23.55)
$49.81	$49.36	$1.03	$3,764	$3,400	$761	($1,081)	($0.16)	($7.79)
$53.83	$53.48	$0.57	$2,310	$3,780	$593	($2,483)	($0.33)	($31.57)
$41.86	$42.16	$0.51	$1,944	$3,551	$683	($2,643)	($0.38)	($31.54)
$54.29	$54.67	$0.62	$2,334	$3,480	$642	($2,213)	($0.32)	($28.51)
$66.59	$67.86	$0.95	$3,626	$3,531	$656	($1,221)	($0.18)	($12.42)
$37.28	$37.46	$0.42	$1,628	$3,562	$947	($3,183)	($0.46)	($48.47)
$59.77	$60.19	$0.49	$1,918	$3,618	$835	($2,883)	($0.41)	($49.76)
$41.39	$41.68	$0.45	$1,779	$3,651	$864	($3,059)	($0.43)	($39.41)
$43.84	$43.35	$0.60	$2,294	$3,575	$877	($2,574)	($0.37)	($26.75)
$48.71	$48.99	$0.43	$1,680	$3,616	$844	($3,086)	($0.44)	($41.42)
$37.63	$37.89	$0.64	$2,502	$3,611	$618	($2,174)	($0.31)	($18.11)
$52.28	$52.65	$0.68	$2,637	$3,586	$685	($2,034)	($0.29)	($22.33)
$44.29	$44.60	$0.66	$2,513	$3,523	$699	($2,166)	($0.31)	($21.14)
$39.58	$39.86	$0.40	$1,679	$3,867	$752	($3,246)	($0.43)	($42.39)
$50.41	$50.76	$0.42	$1,705	$3,745	$45	($2,396)	($0.33)	($39.24)
$57.66	$56.07	$0.88	$3,338	$3,521	$700	($1,490)	($0.22)	($14.25)
$47.49	$47.62	$0.49	$1,968	$3,687	$45	($2,129)	($0.29)	($28.57)
$41.85	$41.34	$0.49	$1,882	$3,556	$931	($2,947)	($0.42)	($35.59)
$63.26	$63.71	$1.89	$4,279	$3,638	$854	($991)	($0.14)	($8.12)
$49.42	$49.77	$0.46	$1,878	$3,776	$851	($3,097)	($0.42)	($45.34)
$31.72	$31.94	$0.23	$963	$3,828	$46	$3,086	($0.41)	($56.26)
$40.33	$40.61	$0.62	$2,424	$3,618	$851	($2,494)	($0.35)	($23.17)
$36.92	$37.18	$0.15	$529	$3,198	$559	($3,316)	($0.53)	($128.18)
$35.35	$35.68	$0.21	$871	$3,886	$579	($3,672)	($0.49)	($82.52)
$57.46	$57.86	$0.79	$3,030	$3,559		($1,088)	($0.15)	($11.35)
$55.32	$55.71	$0.69	$2,663	$3,559		($1,380)	($0.28)	($15.00)
$45.83	$45.35	$0.62	$2,375	$3,568		($1,617)	($0.23)	($16.98)

(continued)

EXHIBIT 12-2-3 *(continued)*

Source Code	List Name	Drop Date	Mail Quantity	Raw Orders	Adj Orders	Raw % Response	Adj % Response	Raw Sales	Adj Sales
1033	CHEFS SEG 4	2/15/88	6,976	80	83	1.15%	1.19%	$4,264	$4,444
1034	CHEFS SEG 5	2/15/88	6,980	76	79	1.89%	1.13%	$3,101	$3,315
1035	CHEFS 87 PD REQS	2/15/88	6,977	69	71	0.99%	1.02%	$3,133	$3,265
1036	CHEFS W88 3× MULTIS	2/15/88	6,977	113	117	1.62%	1.68%	$6,445	$6,716
	SUBTOTAL		226,332	2,638	2,738	1.17%	1.21%	$127,196	$132,551
1028	BULK CAT REQS		7,393	127	131	1.72%	1.78%	$5,586	$5,821
1041	BOUNCEBACK			18	19			$1,044	$1,800
	TOTAL		233,425	2,783	2,888	1.19%	1.23%	$133,826	$139,468
	1037 MISC MAIL			30				$1,754	
	1038 MISC RING RESPONSE			67				$3,898	
	TOTAL UNKNOWNS			97				$5,644	
	TOTAL ALL ORDERS (HOUSE AND OUTSIDE)			2,882				$139,696	

Note: Added to misc ring response and total of all: 52 orders, $2,986. These are phone orders processed as Chef's because misc codes were not set up.

EXHIBIT 12-2-4 *SpaceSmart* Spring 1988 Media Summary Premier Edition

Publication	Circulation	Gross Cost	Net Cost	Cost Per Thousand Gross	Response	Revenue
Home	900,000	$2,465	$2,095	$2.74	1,540	960.50
Metropolitan Home	700,000	2,500	2,125	3.57	2,409	1,920.60
Creative Ideas	775,000	1,765	1,496	2.27	437	437.00
Family Circle	5,400,000	3,350	3,250	0.62	413	805.91
1,001 Home Ideas	1,500,000	1,050	1,018	0.70	283	565.51
House Beautiful	800,000	2,910	2,474	3.64	1,442	1,297.00
Total	10,075,000		$12,458			
Woman's Day	5,200,000[a]				397	397.00
Chef's Newsletter	192,000[b]				155	155.00
Nationwide Shopper[c]					7	10.50
					7,083	6,549.02

[a]Free ad because of Chef's ad.
[b]No charge.
[c]Coffeetable book, no charge for ad.

Raw Average Order	Adj Average Order	Adj Sales/ Book	Adj Cost of Goods	Adv Costs	List Cost	Total Profit	Profit/ Book	Profit/ Order
$53.38	$53.67	$0.64	$2,444	$3,558		($1,558)	($0.22)	($18.82)
$41.86	$42.15	$0.47	$1,823	$3,568		($2,868)	($0.30)	($26.30)
$45.41	$45.72	$0.47	$1,796	$3,558	$55	($2,144)	($0.31)	($38.83)
$57.84	$57.44	$0.96	$3,694	$3,558	$65	($681)	($0.09)	($5.14)
$48.22	$48.56	$0.59	$72,983	$115,276	$16,939	($72,567)	($0.32)	($26.58)
$43.98	$44.29	$0.79	$3,282	$3,778	0	($1,151)	($0.16)	($8.76)
$58.00	$58.41		$598	$0	0	$498		$26.28
$48.89	$48.42	$0.68	$76,703	$119,847	$16,939	($73,228)	($0.31)	($25.43)
$58.47								
$58.86								
$58.19								
$48.47								

EXHIBIT 12-2-5   5/16/88 Cost per Book, *SpaceSmart* Retest

	32 Pages 5 3/8 8 1/4 1,496 Square Inches	48 Pages 5 3/8 9 1/4 2,244 Square Inches	32 Pages 8 1/4 10 3/4 2,838 Square Inches
100,000			
CREATIVE $260/PG	$8,320	$12,460	$8,320
DUPE/STRIP $150/PG	$4,600	$7,200	$4,800
SEPARATIONS $400/PG	$12,800	$19,200	$12,800
O/F PRINT $32/M	$3,200	$3,200	$3,200
MERGE/PURGE $4/M	$400	$400	$400
LISTS BOX $90/M	$7,200	$7,200	$7,200
POSTAGE $160/M	$16,000	$16,000	$16,000
Subtotal	$52,720	$65,680	$52,720
PRINT 45# NORTHCOTE	$11,600	$18,400	$19,200
Total	$64,520	$84,090	$71,920
COST PER BOOK	$0.645	$0.641	$0.719
PRINT 45# CAROLINA	$11,000	$17,200	$17,900
Total	$63,720	$82,850	$70,620
COST PER BOOK	$0.637	$0.829	$0.706

(continued)

EXHIBIT 12-2-5 *(continued)*

	32 Pages 5 3/8 8 1/4 1,496 Square Inches	48 Pages 5 3/8 8 1/4 2,244 Square Inches	32 Pages 8 1/4 10 3/4 2,838 Square Inches
400,000			
CREATIVE $260/PG	$8,320	$12,400	$8,320
DUPE/STRIP $150/PG	$4,800	$7,200	$4,800
SEPARATIONS $400/PG	$12,800	$19,200	$12,800
O/F PRINT $28/M	$11,200	$11,200	$11,200
MERGE/PURGE $4/M	$1,600	$1,600	$1,600
LISTS 80% $90/M	$28,800	$28,800	$28,800
POSTAGE $150/M	$60,000	$60,000	$60,000
Subtotal	$127,520	$140,480	$127,520
PRINT 45# NORTHCOTE	$28,900	$44,300	$57,800
Total	$156,420	$184,780	$185,320
COST PER BOOK	$0.391	$0.462	$0.463
PRINT 45# CAROLINA	$26,400	$40,400	$52,800
Total	$153,920	$180,880	$180,320
COST PER BOOK	$0.385	$0.452	$0.451
750,000			
CREATIVE $260/PG	$8,320	$12,460	$8,320
DUPE/STRIP $150/PG	$4,800	$7,200	$4,800
SEPARATIONS $400/PG	$12,800	$19,200	$12,800
O/F PRINT $25/M	$18,750	$18,750	$18,750
MERGE/PURGE $4/M	$3,000	$3,000	$3,000
LISTS 80% $90/M	$54,000	$54,000	$54,000
POSTAGE $138/M	$101,250	$101,250	$101,250
Subtotal	$202,920	$215,880	$202,920
PRINT 45# NORTHCOTE	$49,300	$75,000	$103,600
Total	$252,220	$290,880	$306,520
COST PER BOOK	$0.336	$0.388	$0.409
PRINT 45# CAROLINA	$44,600	$67,900	$94,400
Total	$247,520	$283,760	$297,320
COST PER BOOK	$0.330	$0.378	$0.396

Opinions at the meeting were mixed. Everyone noted that consumer interest in the home-organization category was high and recognized that *The Chef's Catalog* was prepared to handle the additional volume. In addition, *SpaceSmart* had accumulated a customer base of 3,000; about 7,000 people had requested catalogs via *The Chef's Catalog* or the space ad that ran in national publications.

The risks of continuing the project were apparent enough. Furthermore, a triple cost increase had recently boosted the prices of postage, paper, and ink. "Under these conditions, we can't afford to throw catalogs out," Marcovitz said. "The concept of *SpaceSmart* is valid, but the interest level here is definitely not what it used to be."

Questions for Discussion and Review

1. As described in the case, does the basic concept of the *SpaceSmart* catalog have merit? Why or why not? Is this concept effectively communicated through the information presented in the appendix? Why or why not?

2. What are the major assumptions underlying management's projected success of the *SpaceSmart* concept?

3. What conclusions can be drawn from an analysis of the responses received from each of the mailing lists?

4. Were the magazine advertisements encouraging consumers to request a *SpaceSmart* catalog effective? Why or why not?

5. What are the most plausible explanations for the disappointing consumer response to the *SpaceSmart* catalog?

6. Which of the three options (retest the catalog, discontinue it, or keep it alive in a different form) is most appropriate at this point? Why? Are there other options which management should explore? If so, what are the most attractive other options? Why are they attractive?

Appendix 12-2
Portion of Premier *SpaceSmart* Catalog

C A S E   **12 - 3**

Yeck Brothers: Federal Express Saturday Pickup

Yeck Brothers Company, founded in 1938, is a direct mail agency located in Dayton, Ohio. With approximately 70 employees, it services clients from coast to coast and is particularly well-known for its work in the field of business-to-business and financial direct mail.

Yeck Brothers guides projects "from problem to post office," serving as a single source for its customers, doing the necessary research, planning, copywriting, design, and production for and mailing of the packages. Typical business-to-business problems include getting leads, image building, sales force motivation, research, and surveys by mail, as well as pure advertising to market segments and direct sales, plus the development of sales through third parties or at retail locations.

In 1983, one of Yeck Brothers' premier accounts was Federal Express Corporation. The award-winning work of Ally & Gargano, Inc., general advertising agency, made the job of direct marketing not only easier but more cost/objective efficient. Federal Express had over a billion dollars in sales, 18,000 employees, and an advertising budget of $30 million.

The budget was typically allocated as follows:

Television	$10,000,000
Consumer magazines	4,000,000
Spot TV	7,000,000
Spot radio	3,000,000
Premiums	1,000,000
Direct mail	2,000,000
Trade shows	1,000,000
Point of purchase	1,000,000
Miscellaneous	1,000,000

Federal Express wanted to expand its five-day-per-week pickups to include all-day pickup on Saturday for Monday morning delivery. Saturday deliveries were nothing new to Federal Express, but it had never picked up packages on Saturday.

The company saw three hypothetical customer problems that would be solved by the service. The first customer problem was the actual generation of packages on Saturday that currently either waited until Monday for pickup or required Sunday or Monday delivery via more expensive and less convenient means, such as taxicabs and counter-to-counter airline services. The second involved packages expected to be shipped Friday night for Monday morning delivery but that just couldn't be readied in time. The third problem involved people who would like Friday-to-Monday turnaround for complete communication. A Saturday pickup would allow them to send packages or documents Friday night for delivery on Saturday, with a response picked up Saturday for receipt on Monday.

Management felt a Saturday market existed, but it didn't know how fast it could achieve a profitable share. What's more, the prospect of launching a Saturday service was not one to be taken lightly. Flying a fleet of airplanes to and from Memphis and key cities across the country overnight and loading thousands upon thousands of packages into trucks for delivery in more than 20,000 ZIP codes before 10:30 the next morning runs up a tidy bill for fixed costs every day. To add another day to the current Monday through Friday service was a major step. And once begun, it would be difficult to stop.

Federal Express conducted extensive market research to determine where, why, and how many "rush" packages or priority letters were currently being generated on Saturday for delivery Monday morning by other means and what the size of the ultimate market for such a Saturday-Monday service might be.

Federal Express had extensively researched Saturday pickup service prior to approaching Yeck Brothers. Federal Express market forecasts predicted that 4,000 packages would be shipped on the first weekend the service was offered and the volume of shipping would increase steadily over the following 18 months to a profitable level of 19,000 packages per weekend.

Focus group interviews revealed that the regular shipper (those already shipping on Saturdays) and occasional shippers (those irregularly shipping on Saturdays) wholeheartedly approved of a Saturday Federal Express pickup. Nonshippers (those who didn't envision a need for Saturday shipping) were not only neutral about Saturday delivery but expressed concern that Saturday shipping might lead to an additional workday—a big turnoff.

Respondents said the Federal Express reputation for dependable service increased the appeal of Saturday delivery. The $10 surcharge was not seen as a barrier to use, as cost was secondary to reliability when it came to important Saturday deliveries.

John Harkins, group vice-president at Yeck Brothers Company, Federal Express's direct marketing agency, was called in to discuss the promotion. He was given three objectives by Carole Presley, vice-president of corporate marketing for Federal Express:

1. To announce the new service to customers
2. To interpret the benefits of it in a dramatic and memorable way
3. To generate trial usage of the new service as promptly and extensively as possible.

(See Appendix 12-3A, which describes Yeck's assignment, and Appendix 12-3B, which describes the Federal Express Saturday service marketing plan.)

Harkins knew the Saturday service introduction was of major importance to Federal Express, and Federal Express was of major importance to Yeck Brothers. A successful initial campaign could pay for itself many times over in pushing forward cash flows. Harkins decided to have three creative teams compete to develop the strategy and creativity needed to meet the outlined objectives.

Yeck Brothers had been given half of the $1.5 million allocated to promotion as its budget for direct marketing. Federal Express had a customer list of 237,000 past customers sorted into several categories by annual usage:

Group	Yearly Usage	Number of Names
A	100,000+	5,000
B	5,000–99,999	10,000
C	1,000–4,999	20,000
D	500–999	40,000
E	50–499	62,000
F	< 50	100,000

PROPOSAL FROM TEAM ONE: BLITZ

Team One proposed a teaser campaign; that is, a series of mailings that initially obscured the purpose of the campaign while only announcing the date October 1 as starting "A New Morning," then through a succession of mailings revealed increasing information asking for potential clients to call an 800 number to sign up for their initial October 1 shipments. Class A would receive a total of twenty mailings over 15 weeks; class B, fifteen; class C, ten; class D, five; class E, three; and class F, one. The mailings were projected to cost about $985,000.

PROPOSAL FROM TEAM TWO: COFFEE CAKE

The second strategy/creative team suggested a concentration of effort on heavy users. A team member's uncle was involved with a bakery that was significantly under production capacity and that had an 8-inch round coffee cake that he believed to be an outstanding taste delight. It was suggested that these coffee cakes be sent to lists A through D via Federal Express. Federal Express could be asked to deliver these coffee cakes on days prior to October 1 that ran under capacity. The recipients would most likely be receiving packages anyway. Estimated cost per unit was about $13.

PROPOSAL FROM TEAM THREE: FREQUENT FLYER

The last team suggested sending out a catalog of gifts from a sales contest company. Points would be awarded to the individual responsible for each Saturday pickup. Federal Express computers could easily keep track of these points, which could be earned over the next 18 months, and redeemed upon request. Team Three felt that the increase in business would cover the cost of the goods given away. Catalogs would be supplied from the sales promotion company, and hence the entire list could be mailed at $925,000.

In reviewing the data supplied by Federal Express, Harkins wondered if Federal Express management looked at his direct marketing budget as an expense or a budget. In reviewing the package profitability of the Federal Express product mix, Harkins estimated that if his $750,000 budget could gain the full 19,000 packages expected 18 months down the line in the very first week, the $750,000 investment would pay for itself in profit 13 times over.

Questions for Discussion and Review

1. Which, if any, of the three strategies should Harkins pursue? Why?

2. What other direct marketing strategies might be appropriate? Why?

Appendix 12-3A
Agency Discussion Brief

On Saturday, October 1, 1983, Federal Express will extend its service offering to include a Saturday pickup/drop-off service for Monday delivery. While this service is available only to those in AA/AM areas in the 48 contiguous states, it does, in effect, mean a six-day shipping capability for 85 percent of consumers in our directly served area. (Fifteen percent are in PM areas, which will not have pickup or drop-off capability.)

This service offering is made possible through utilization of seven or eight FEC aircraft, extensive trucking, and a Sunday midday hub sort. It is also likely that commercial airlines will be used to expedite isolated packages that cannot justify the cost of trucking and/or our own airlift.

Attached is a draft of the marketing plan, which outlines key objectives, program opportunities, detailed features of service, and volume projections.

It is the purpose of this brief to solicit your proposals in the areas of advertising, promotion, and direct mail to support the launch of Saturday service. Therefore, it is appropriate to discuss what we know—and don't know—regarding this market. Some of the latter concerns will be addressed in focus groups in the next two weeks.

WHAT WE KNOW

Even though research efforts have been somewhat limited due to time constraints, we have learned that a greater propensity to use Federal's Saturday service exists among our own customers than among non-FEC users. While 40 percent of our discounted customers and 28 percent of our list customers definitely or probably would use the new service, that figure is only 7 percent among non-FEC users. Further, research indicates at least 60 percent initial conversion from customers presently sending packages/documents on Friday or Monday for next business day delivery via Federal. (The vast majority—80 percent—are sending them Friday for Monday delivery.) *Clearly the challenge is to build incremental volume among our customer base and to convert packages from actual and potential users of competitors.*

Heavier shippers appear to perceive greater use of the Saturday service than do light shippers. Yet the major portion of the volume will accrue from the large group of low-revenue shippers. They also appear to be more sensitive to the surcharge and are less committed to Federal on an ongoing, high-volume basis. *Hence, the challenge is to demonstrate to this group the benefits of Federal service and to exploit any latent demand that exists.*

In general, there was little evidence of any barriers to a Saturday service other than perceived need for it. There appears to be high acceptance of the concept yet low actual usage. In fact, 60 percent of Federal's customers believe we now offer a Saturday pickup service. Research also shows that even a $10 surcharge is considered to be a reasonable rate per package.

Customers and nonusers of FEC alike told us that they especially like the added convenience in the form of a new service option, the Monday delivery aspect, and the pickup feature. In fact, two-thirds of the FEC customers prefer to call for pickup as needed over the option of dropping the package off.

The fact that the Saturday service concept is so well accepted, combined with the weaknesses in competitive offerings (see Exhibit 12-3-1), indicates

EXHIBIT 12-3   Saturday Service Competitive Profile

Competitor	Estimated Volume	Surcharge	Pickup/Delivery	
Airborne	400–500	No	$ 6.00	
BNAF	400–500	$ 9.00	9.00	No charge before 12 noon for pickup
Emery	150–300	15.00	15.00	$25 for shipments over 100 lbs.
Express Mail	No estimate	5.60	5.60	
DHL	No estimate	10.00	No	
Purolator	No estimate	No	10.00	Regional Saturday delivery only via trucking; no Saturday pickup
Airlines	No estimate	Yes	Yes	

there truly is an opportunity for Federal to introduce a Saturday service based on three major strengths:

1. An added convenience
2. Reasonable and competitive pricing
3. Reliable Monday morning delivery.

It is the role of advertising and promotion to enable us to tap that market by generating high awareness and usage quickly.

WHAT WE DON'T KNOW

However, there are still many unanswered questions surrounding a Saturday service offering. In an attempt to answer some of them—especially from a communications aspect—several focus groups have been set up in the next couple of weeks. The groups will consist of respondents in five main groups: (1) professional/managerial ("generator") users, (2) Saturday shippers, (3) recipients of Saturday packages, (4) UPS users, (5) Friday "turndowns" who call Federal for a pickup too late.

These groups will attempt to answer as many of the following questions as possible:

1. Why is weekend service needed? By whom? For what specific situations will the service be used?
2. How much demand is created by those who missed cutoff times on Friday? How much by those working normal Saturday hours? How much by emergency needs?
3. How much demand is created by professionals/managerials vis-à-vis shipping or mailroom implementers?
4. Are there any market segments who tend to use/need weekend service more than others? Can they be classified by job function? By industry? By geography?
5. How do current weekend shippers determine what company to use for Saturday shipping?
6. Is there an opportunity to sweep the dock of UPS packages sitting there from Friday to Monday?
7. To what extent does the consignee affect Saturday shipping patterns?
8. Is there a dominant competitor?
9. Is there seasonality in demand for Saturday service? Are there routine versus sporadic patterns?
10. What are the dynamics of Friday/Monday conversion? Is the 60 percent figure real?
11. Can we more efficiently predict the Saturday product mix?

The fact remains, however, that whether or not the groups provide insight into these issues, Saturday service promotion and advertising will have to be developed on what we know (and can learn) and what our best judgments are concerning the unanswered issues.

COMMUNICATIONS AUDIENCE

Research has provided very little insight as to who the potential users of Saturday service will be. There are currently about 28,000 to 30,000 packages sent each Friday for Saturday delivery, but little is known regarding the dynamics of that shipping pattern. Nor has information to date uncovered any particular market segment either by function or industry type to whom messages can be targeted. However, it is possible to identify several groups who are potential candidates for a Saturday pickup service. Perhaps the upcoming focus groups will confirm or eliminate some of the following presumed types:

1. Those for whom emergency needs arise
2. Those working on Saturday who want/need to clean off their desk/dock before Monday
3. Those who missed normal cutoff times on Friday
4. Those who would rather work on Saturday than stay late on Friday night
5. Those who may need or use such a service to speed their way of doing business but for whom the benefits of Saturday service are not obvious
6. Those currently using the postal service who are inconvenienced by having to get to a post office by noon or by driving to an airport
7. Those businesses which generate UPS packages on weekends and would rather sweep the dock than wait for their regular UPS Monday pickup.

For some of the groups above, merely announcing the availability of Federal's Saturday service will be enough to generate usage. However, for most of them the message will have to explain business applications, benefits, and productivity issues in order to tap latent demand.

GOALS AND EXECUTION

From the above discussion, two objectives emerge:

1. To announce the availability of Federal's Saturday service inherent in which are the features of service closely associated with our reputation and
2. To exploit latent demand by demonstrating the key benefits and application of Saturday service.

Two issues are important in executing those objectives:

1. *Timing of the message:* Given the constraints of very limited budgets and limited knowledge of the marketplace, every effort must be taken to reach the audience with communications as close to the point of sale as possible.

I trust a great deal of creative thought will be exercised as to how we can reach these groups most efficiently.

2. *Continuity of the message:* To the extent possible it is also necessary to reinforce the message to sustain high levels of awareness. This will also require some creativity given the same budget constraints. However, Federal does have an enthusiastic work force in the field that can help in this area.

I can't stress enough the importance of generating volume quickly and maintaining its momentum throughout FY 84—particularly incremental volume rather than Friday/Monday converted volume.

Essentially Saturday service translates to another day of the week during which to transact business. And that service carries with it virtually all of the features of Federal's weekday service. It provides another opportunity to handle crisis situations and/or increase productivity.

One area of concern arises, however, if the Saturday service is positioned in such a way that potential users come to regard the service as just another shipping day for Federal Express. They could reason that if Saturday is just like any other shipping day, why then is Federal Express charging an additional $10 for every package? The copy should strive to position Saturday service as an opportunity to extend their workweek, and now they have at their disposal the most reliable and consistent service in the industry to solve their shipping needs.

CALL TO ACTION

I have given you all the information on Saturday service to date, but I expect the focus groups to provide additional insights that will help us from a communication standpoint. Therefore, I urge that you send the person who will be most closely associated with the project to as many of the groups as is feasible.

Ally & Gargano has already been advised of the advertising budget, to include television, print, and production. However, I would like to discuss with Yeck and Matthew-Lawrence the dollars allocated for promotion/direct mail. Upon reading this document, I ask that you contact me to finalize your respective budgets.

As with many of our projects, we are down to the wire before actual implementation, and some key decisions have not been made. I'll keep you informed of any changes that may occur, but I'd like you to develop your respective programs assuming the information contained in this brief. (I don't anticipate any major ones that will impede your progress.) I'd like to see a comprehensive plan as well as recommended concepts no later than Tuesday, August 11. I will be available for questions, additional information, etc., until Friday, July 29, at noon, after which I plan to take a week of much-needed vacation!

Thank you for your ongoing support and cooperation.

Appendix 12-3B
Federal Express Saturday Service Marketing Plan

Effective Saturday, October 1, 1983, Federal Express will extend its current Saturday delivery service to include a Saturday pickup/drop-off service for Monday delivery. (Standard Air Service will be delivered by Tuesday.)

KEY OBJECTIVES

- To expand Federal's current volume base and enhance growth potential through incremental volume and new customers.

- To further strengthen our ability to satisfy customer needs vis-à-vis the competition in an area that is devoid of a dominant leader.

- To generate incremental revenue and to achieve profitability sooner than forecast.

PROGRAM OPPORTUNITIES

1. *Saturday service has a volume potential of at least 19,800 pieces per Saturday.* (See Weekend Service table that follows)
   a. While half of this business ultimately comes from conversion from our Friday or Monday business, the other half represents new business.

Weekend Service: Saturday Pickup/Monday Delivery

Month	Best Estimate of Saturday Volume[a]	Source of Packages[b]	
		Conversion	New Business
1	4.0	2.4	1.6
2	4.8	2.9	1.9
3	5.8	3.4	2.4
4	6.7	3.9	2.8
5	7.7	4.4	3.3
6	8.6	4.9	3.7
7	9.6	5.4	4.2
8	10.5	5.9	4.6
9	11.4	6.3	5.1
10	12.3	6.7	5.6
11	13.3	7.2	6.1
12	14.2	7.6	6.6
13	15.2	8.0	7.2
14	16.1	8.4	7.7
15	17.0	8.8	8.2
16	17.9	9.1	8.8
17	18.9	9.5	9.4
18	19.8	9.9	9.9

[a]All volume data is reported in thousands of packages. Volume data indicates volume level per Saturday of designated month.

[b]The following product mix is assumed: P1 (41%), CP (35%), P2 (9%), OL (15%).

b. Saturday service not only provides new business on the weekend but also has the potential to enhance volume conversion from competitors during the week.

c. The volume potential represents a minimum level of opportunity. Although not possible to quantify, we believe there is latent demand for Saturday pickup due to the high acceptance of the concept among customers surveyed.

2. *The service can generate $5.6 million in additional revenue.*
   a. Research indicated—particularly among heavier shippers—that a $10 per piece surcharge is not considered prohibitive for Saturday shipping needs.
   b. Given reasonably strong acceptance of this surcharge level, revenue-generating potential is approximately $5.6 million in FY 84 from new business.
   c. Incremental costs will be the result of extended utilization of existing resources, as no additional capital or facilities will be required.
   d. Because both Gemini and International Service will require weekend operations, volumes/revenue generated by Saturday service will enhance productivity.
   e. Through additional research, service features will be refined to further meet customer needs, with the goal of generating a profitable service sooner than forecast.

3. *Saturday service provides Federal Express with a presence in this market.*
   a. Investigation of the competitive environment indicates that Federal is among the minority of carriers who do not offer Saturday pickup service. Of the major ones only Purolator and UPS do not offer some type of Saturday service.
   b. Failure to participate in this market provides our competitors with an opportunity to identify one area of service advantage versus Federal Express. It also forces a large number of our customers to use the competition because we provide no alternative.
   c. The lack of information available seems indicative of our competitors' reluctance to devote the necessary time and money to create a successful weekend service.
   d. Major express carriers offering weekend service all use commercial airlines. Therefore, their dependence on the airlines makes it nearly impossible for the individual carrier to control and/or maintain an acceptable service level.
   e. Union agreements require full staffing despite insufficient weekend volume opportunities.
   f. Purolator does not offer cross-country weekend service but will truck packages regionally on the weekend.
   g. Except in the case of Express Mail, only major city volume is delivered on Monday and smaller points on Tuesday. Express Mail offers overnight delivery seven days a week.
   h. None of the express carriers actively promotes its Saturday service.

4. *Federal Express can provide a competitively superior Saturday service and thus strengthen our overall superiority in the air express market.*
    a. It appears that competitors do not view the weekend market as a volume opportunity and have therefore not promoted it.
    b. Analysis indicates three key weaknesses in competitive offerings of a Saturday pickup service.
        I.   Lack of a firm Monday delivery commitment
        II.   Confusing shipping arrangements and pricing structures
        III. Very often, high surcharge levels.
    c. By offering an easily understood, reliable, and reasonably priced service, Federal can further support its positioning as the premier air express.

5. *Saturday pickup service complements our Saturday delivery service, thus reducing customer confusion and thus meeting customer expectations.*
    a. Currently 10 percent of weekend calls to the Memphis call center represent requests for Saturday pickup (approximately 4,300 calls during the month). Some of these stem from the assumption that it is available since we deliver packages on Saturday.
    b. Sixty percent of our customers currently believe that we now offer Saturday pickup.
    c. By indicating the service is not available, we divert customers to trial usage of our competitors.

FEATURES OF SERVICE

Federal's weekend offering will provide customers with the option of having packages picked up or dropping packages off as late as 5:00 P.M. on Saturday with a Monday delivery commitment, as outlined in our Service Guide. In most cases there will be a $10 surcharge per package for this service.

SERVICE AREA DEFINITION

Saturday pickup and drop off will be available to customers in AA (10:30) and AM (noon) areas. Monday delivery will be made in accordance with current delivery commitments (AA, AM, PM). Out-of-delivery areas will also receive packages as defined by current commitments in the Service Guide. Neither pickup on Saturday nor delivery on Monday is available to Puerto Rico with normal delivery commitments.

SERVICES OFFERED

All services currently offered during weekdays will be available, assuming that only FEC aircraft and trucks are used. This includes P-1, SAS, OL, CP, perishables, restricted articles, and Signature Security Service. (The last two will not be available if commercial airlines are used at all.) All weights up to 125 pounds will be accepted.

ACCESSIBILITY

Customers will have the option of on-call pickups, regular pickups, or dropping packages off at most stations or convenience centers until 5:00 P.M. Dropboxes will not be picked up on Saturday, and a sign affixed to each dropbox will alert the customer to Saturday nonavailability.

PRICING

The $10 surcharge will continue to be applied for all Saturday delivery packages. There is also a $10 surcharge for each package tendered to Federal Express on Saturday, whether picked up or dropped off.

The current surcharges for SSS, restricted articles, address correction, and prepaid nonaccount billing will also apply for Saturday service.

DISCOUNTS

Qualified customers as identified by sales representatives may receive a surcharge waiver as outlined in the approved guidelines. Surcharges for Saturday service do apply toward determining a customer's gross revenue; its discount will be calculated by dividing its total revenue including Saturday packages by five days per week.

LIMITATION OF LIABILITY

The liability of FEC is limited to the sum of $100 unless a higher value is declared and a charge of 30¢ per $100 additional is paid. Maximum declared value is limited to $25,000. (This policy is the same for weekday service.)

BILLING

No changes to the airbill or Express Manifest are necessary. The Saturday surcharge and waiver option will be driven by the ship date written in by the pickup courier and by drop-off marks should the package be dropped off.

HOLIDAYS

Saturday delivery, pickup, and drop off will be available on long holiday weekends. Packages normally scheduled for delivery on Monday will be delivered on Tuesday and Standard Air packages on Wednesday.

VOLUME PROJECTIONS

Volume is projected to reach 19,800 packages/weekend within 18 months, including Standard Air. Sixty percent of the packages are expected to come from current FEC Friday/Monday business. Conversion is expected to drop to 50 percent after 18 months.

Projections are based on a $10/package surcharge and the availability of normal FEC pickup and drop-off options as late as 5:00 P.M. The monthly projections include the source of packages (conversion of current FEC business or new business). After 18 months, half of the packages are expected to be new business.

ADDITIONAL CONSIDERATIONS AFFECTING ADVERTISING AND MARKETING COMMUNICATION DECISIONS

*T*he two chapters in this final section of the book briefly examine some of the crucial issues related to (1) the business partnership between a marketer and an advertising agency, and (2) the difficult issues centered around ethical dilemmas that often challenge marketing communication managers. Chapter 13 presents a discussion of several major components which affect the working relationship between a marketer and outside suppliers of marketing communication advice—advertising agencies. These issues include the decision to employ a full-service agency versus an in-house department versus the use of *a la carte* services; agency selection and compensation; client approval of the agency's creative recommendations; agency performance reviews; and guidelines for fostering the most productive client/agency relationship.

In Chapter 14 some of the most common ethical issues facing advertising and marketing communication management are identified and briefly discussed. These issues include the ethics of creativity; advertising controversial products; advertising directed to children; intrusive or annoying advertising; and ethical issues in client/agency relations. Critical observers of advertising might suggest that ethical advertising is an oxymoron. Fortunately, this is not the case. Marketing communication management realizes that it must be ethical in all decision making. Therefore, it is appropriate to conclude our examination of marketing communication management with a review of representative ethical issues.✤

Client/Agency Relations

*I have learned that you can't have good advertising
without a good client, that you can't keep a good client
without good advertising, and no client will ever buy
better advertising than he understands or has an
appetite for.*[1]

Leo Burnett

THE NATURE AND IMPORTANCE OF CLIENT/AGENCY RELATIONSHIPS

Business firms hire advertising agencies to add efficiency and impact to their marketing activities. Agencies offer their clients a number of advantages, including creative talent, business and marketing expertise, cost savings, and outside objectivity. Agency personnel are communication specialists who are retained by their clients to provide marketing counsel covering an increasingly wide range of activities.

As marketers' needs for greater coordination and leverage of all their communication efforts have intensified, traditional advertising agencies, which in the past had concentrated heavily on mass media advertising, have broadened their menu of services. Many advertising agencies have restructured their organizations, added personnel, and positioned themselves to offer their clients *integrated marketing communication programs* that include direct marketing, sales promotions, public relations, and other services in addition to advertising.[2]

---

[1]Leo Burnett, *100 Leo's* booklet (Chicago: Leo Burnett Company, 1991), 57.
[2]David Kalish, "The New Advertising," *Agency,* Fall 1990, 28–33.

The relative contributions of agency personnel and client personnel to the development of promotional campaigns vary considerably across relationships and situations. In some instances, the client develops only a general statement of the direction the advertising should take, and with scant guidance the agency develops the entire campaign. The firm's advertising department may only cursorily review and then approve the plans suggested by the agency.[3]

In other situations, the firm's advertising or marketing department may specify the advertising strategy and tactics in considerable detail, and the agency merely executes the orders. In between these extremes lie the teamwork situations and give-and-take relationships typical of most client/agency relationships.[4]

The importance of advertising agencies is reflected in the volume of billings placed by agencies for their clients. In 1989, the *Ad Age* 500 largest agencies in the United States placed $36.6 million in U.S. media.[5] This represents roughly 30 percent of total domestic media spending, estimated at $124 million.[6] In addition, thousands of smaller agencies placed a significant portion of the remaining media dollars. There is no question that advertising agencies dominate the mass media advertising business, particularly among firms advertising on a national and international basis. Further, advertising agencies are attempting to carve out an expanded role for themselves across the complete range of integrated marketing communication activities. How well these communication specialists satisfy their clients' evolving needs will determine their role in the broader marketing communication environment.

ISSUES IN THE CLIENT/AGENCY RELATIONSHIP

A number of crucial marketing communication management decisions revolve around the client/agency relationship. The most fundamental decision is whether the firm should handle advertising and other marketing communication tasks in-house or employ a full-service agency or a confederation of *a la carte* providers of special services (for example, media buying firms and promotions specialists).

If the decision is to employ an agency, management faces the task of selecting an agency. Then, once an agency has been selected, management faces supervision, evaluation, and compensation decisions in addition to ongoing decisions regarding approval of the agency's creative, media, and other recommendations. Each of these major areas is briefly discussed in this chapter. In the concluding section of this chapter, the general subject of fostering a productive client/agency relationship is explored.

---

[3]Leo Bogart, *Strategy in Advertising* (Lincolnwood, Ill.: NTC Business Books, 1986) 67–68.

[4]*Ibid.*

[5]R. Craig Endicott, "*Ad Age* 500 Grows 9.7%; Billings Top $85 Billion," *Advertising Age,* March 26, 1990, S1–2.

[6]Gary Levin and Jon Lafayette, "Ad Spending Hikes May Lag Inflation," *Advertising Age,* December 17, 1990.

In-house Department, Full-Service Agency, or a la Carte *Services?*

The basic decision of whether the marketer would be better served by handling its advertising in-house or employing the services of outside specialist firms is influenced by a number of considerations. Perhaps the five most important considerations are *control, cost, volume of advertising, objectivity,* and *effectiveness.* Clearly, an advantage of an in-house approach is control in directing the activities of the firm's employees who are responsible for developing advertising. In addition, management can be more confident that it will have direct access to and the thoughtful attention of an in-house staff.

A second major advantage of an in-house approach can be cost. In a situation where large media expenditures are involved, the firm receives the entire 15 percent commission as a rebate from a house agency. Note that departments can proclaim themselves to be agencies and encounter little difficulty in being recognized by the media as eligible for the agency discount. Depending on the firm's advertising requirements, there may be other cost savings advantages to an in-house department or agency.

An obvious consideration in evaluating the feasibility of establishing an in-house advertising organization is whether the firm generates enough work to employ a full-time staff. Also, firms with highly cyclical advertising efforts are *not* well suited to using an in-house staff approach.

Objectivity is a major benefit of using outside people. Agencies typically provide a valuable cross section of experience gained in advertising a range of products and services. Since agency personnel are independent from the client organization, they are freer to contradict conventional wisdom and upper management's opinions. Further, since agency personnel often work on several accounts at the same time, they can be more objective about each advertiser's situation.

Effectiveness should perhaps be the most important consideration in choosing between an inside staff and outside specialists. Can an agency's expertise and skills in developing strategy, concepts, and creative executions, and in media planning and other areas be equaled by an in-house operation? Agencies seem to be particularly attractive to creative people who like the independence and entrepreneurial environment not available in an in-house advertising department. Hence, agencies offer a strong pool of creative talent not always available to advertising departments or in-house agencies.

Gardner argues against house agencies by pointing out that they suffer from a narrowed focus, which handicaps their effectiveness. They lose the stimulus of cross-fertilization of ideas and run a greater risk of going stale than an outside agency. Also, the advertiser loses flexibility in firing nonperformers—it is relatively easy to change agencies, more difficult to make sweeping personnel changes with an in-house staff.[7]

---

[7]Herbert S. Gardner, *The Advertising Agency Business* (Lincolnwood, Ill.: NTC Business Books, 1989), 101–103.

An evaluation of whether to employ a full-service agency or subcontract portions of the job and retain some in-house is complex. This decision turns on the availability of such specialists, their expertise, what can be negotiated at what cost, and potential problems with coordination of the firm's marketing communication efforts. The two most widely available *a la carte* services are media buying and creative services. Both advertisers and agencies are increasingly using media buying services. An advantage of independent services is flexibility, since they typically can be used on a trial basis and evaluated based on experience.

Agency Selection

The selection of an advertising agency is a difficult and important task—a task that, if sloppily done, will most likely have to be repeated soon. Also, if a poor choice is made, it is likely that considerable time and money will have been wasted. Therefore, an advertiser should view the development of a careful selection procedure as an investment that can potentially pay huge dividends.

The Association of National Advertisers (ANA) recommends that an advertiser should begin the process of selecting an agency by defining its own service requirements and establishing selection criteria. This guides the advertiser in gathering information about prospective agencies. The ANA suggests a sequence of six broad steps be followed in the process of selecting an agency. These steps, along with examples of the types of questions that must be addressed at each step, are presented below.[8]

1. *Establish selection criteria.*

2. *Devise a plan of operation.* Who is to be responsible for planning and conducting the search? Will consultants who specialize in agency relations be involved? Will a selection committee be formed? Should the search be made public? What information should the advertiser provide to prospects?

3. *Develop a list of agencies for consideration.* How many agencies should be considered? What type of initial contact should be made to determine if agencies are interested in the advertiser's account? Should a screening questionnaire be used? If yes, what specific information should be requested?

4. *Narrow the list to a manageable number.* Should personal visits be made to the most promising agencies? What should be discussed in informal, preliminary meetings?

5. *Request agency presentations.* How many agencies should make presentations? What about the location, timing, and requested content? Should the agencies be compensated? Should the agencies be asked to prepare speculative presentations that include a complete campaign or actual creative work? How will the presentations be formally evaluated?

---

[8]"Selecting an Advertising Agency" (New York: Association of National Advertisers, 1977).

6. *Make the final decision.* Patti and Frazer suggest that in making an agency selection decision, chemistry—or the human factor of how well the key contacts in a potential relationship get along—is crucial. These authors also suggest the use of four criteria in evaluating potential matches between the advertiser and agencies: the agency's range of services, experience, stability, and philosophy.[9]

Ogilvy recommends a simpler procedure. He suggests simply identifying those agencies which have produced current print ads and commercials that you admire. Next, meet with the head and creative director of each of these agencies that is available to make sure the interpersonal chemistry is good. Ask to see each of the finalists' six best print ads and six best television commercials. Pick the agency whose campaigns interest you the most.[10]

Compensation

In recent years a growing number of advertisers have examined their compensation arrangements with their advertising agencies, particularly in situations where the agency received a standard 15 percent media commission. The purpose of such examinations has been to explore the possibility of (1) achieving advertising cost reductions, (2) developing a more equitable arrangement for both parties, and (3) encouraging and rewarding outstanding work.

Several factors have motivated such examinations, including the following:

- Slow growth of the economy and of markets plus increased competition resulted in short-term pressures on publicly held companies to aggressively search for ways to reduce operating and marketing costs.

- The prices paid for agencies in mergers and acquisitions have created the perception that agencies make excessive profits.

- There is a trend toward using narrow specialists, who are compensated on a fee or retainer basis, to handle parts of firms' marketing programs (such as media buying or trade show promotions).

- Increasing media costs have fueled historical suspicions about an agency's media recommendations when compensation is tied to media commissions.

- Alternative compensation schemes have received considerable publicity in the trade press and at trade association meetings.

The net product of these examinations has been the erosion of the traditional 15 percent media commission as a means of determining agency compensation. ANA studies over the past several years have documented this trend. In 1983, 52 percent of all responding advertisers indicated that they

---

[9]Charles H. Patti and Charles F. Frazer, *Advertising: A Decision-Making Approach* (Hinsdale, Ill.: The Dryden Press, 1988), 48–49.

[10]David Ogilvy, *Ogilvy on Advertising* (New York: Crown Publishers, 1983), 66.

compensated their agencies using a 15 percent commission. In the 1989 ANA study, this percentage had fallen to 35 percent.[11]

In developing a compensation procedure, the advertiser and agency strive for an equitable arrangement in light of the services provided that, ideally, provides some incentive for the agency to produce outstanding work. In designing a compensation system, the ANA recommends the parties consider four areas: equitability, adaptability, administrative simplicity, and incentives.[12]

Intelligent marketers recognize that their business must be profitable to their agencies and other suppliers. As Howard Liszt, president of Campbell-Mithun-Esty Minneapolis, notes, "There's broad acceptance among clients that it's in their best interests that their account be profitable for their agency. The smarter clients understand that's what gets it the best people on their account. That's what gets it the best service."[13]

Although a myriad of compensation arrangements have been developed, three basic alternatives to the standard 15 percent will be discussed next: (1) the labor-based fee or retainer; (2) some fixed percentage less than 15 percent; or (3) an incentive-based sliding scale that bases the percentage paid on the performance of the agency.

Fee or Retainer. Ogilvy recommends and stresses the advantages of a fee-based system in which a client pays only for services used.[14] Under this approach, each person who works on the account keeps track of his or her time and bills the client at an hourly rate that includes an allowance for direct salary, agency overhead, and profit. The agency also bills the client for other nonsalary expenses incurred in servicing the account.

For example, to determine the billed rate for an employee who earns $40,000 per year, the agency begins by dividing this salary by a standard year of 1,600 hours. Then an overhead charge is added to direct salary (Gardner states that for every $1 in direct salary the average agency person has to carry $1.174 in overhead).[15] Finally, the agency adds a profit target of 20 percent of gross, which requires a markup of 25 percent. Hence, in this example the $40,000-per-year agency person's billed rate is $67.94, or $68.00 per hour.

$$\$40,000/1,600 = \$25$$
$$\$25 + (\$25 \times 1.174) = \$54.35$$
$$\$54.35 + (\$54.35 \times .25) = \$68.$$

Two alternatives to billing clients hourly fees are a job fee or a retainer. In some cases it may make sense for the agency to simply estimate the costs of

[11]William M. Weilbacher, *Current Advertiser Practices in Compensating Their Advertising Agencies* (New York: Association of National Advertisers, 1989), 5–6.

[12]*Agency Compensation: A Guidebook* (New York: Association of National Advertisers, 1989), 19.

[13]Terence Poltrack, "Pay Dirt!" *Agency,* July/August 1991, 20–25.

[14]Ogilvy, *Ogilvy on Advertising,* 55.

[15]Gardner, *The Advertising Agency Business,* 54.

completing a project and submit a proposal indicating what will be accomplished for a total job fee. In other situations, it may be appropriate for the agency to estimate all expenses involved in handling an advertiser's account, add overhead plus profit, and suggest a retainer fee to be billed monthly. In each case, provision should be made for periodic review and possible adjustment of fees and retainers.

Fixed Percentage Less than 15 Percent.   In many situations, after a thorough discussion of the level of service expected by an advertiser and the volume of media expenditures, agencies have agreed to rebate a portion of the 15 percent media commission to the advertiser. This is logical in situations where the advertiser's expectations of agency service (research, merchandising, media planning and buying, creative services, and so on) are minimal, and a large volume of media investment is planned. In such situations, Achenbaum argues that advertisers should pay considerably less than 15 percent, perhaps as low as 7 percent.[16] Note that media buying firms often operate on a 2½ to 3 percent commission on the media they place.

Incentive Plans.   The ideal compensation plan would contain incentives to stimulate agencies to deliver a superior performance and would reward them with participation in the brand's success. The incentive compensation plans developed by two advertisers—Campbell Soup and Carnation—will be briefly described next.

The incentive plan developed by Campbell Soup is based on first establishing a base rate of compensation between 13 percent and 15 percent for each brand. Next, a reasonable sales volume increase for the year is targeted for the brand. If the brand's sales exceed the targeted volume, the agency's base rate is increased. For example, if sales exceed the targeted increase of 5 percent for Swanson frozen pot pies, the agency's base rate is increased from 13.25 percent to 14.5 percent. If volume rises by 10 percent, the rate would go to 15 percent.[17]

Carnation's incentive agency compensation plan is based on advertising research results. Carnation stresses that the incentive is strictly a bonus with no change in the firm's basic fixed commission (reported to be below 12 percent in many cases). Carnation negotiates with its agency to set target test scores that determine how large a flat-fee bonus the agency earns. The research upon which the system is based is conducted using the Advertising Research System.[18]

Other Expenses.   In addition, the advertiser and its agency need to reach clear agreement on what conventions will be followed in billing the advertiser

---

[16]Cleveland Horton, "Achenbaum Puts His Cards on the Table," *Advertising Age,* May 9, 1988, 1+.

[17]Judann Dagnoli, "Campbell 'Incentive' Pares Agency Pay," *Advertising Age,* April 30, 1990, 53.

[18]Marcy Magiera, "Carnation Links Pay, Research," *Advertising Age,* March 6, 1989, 1+; and Bradley Johnson, "Pay Plan Works: Carnation," *Advertising Age,* January 8, 1990, 8.

for expenses related to the development and placement of its advertising. For example, will the standard 17.65 percent markup[19] be applied to production charges incurred for the development of broadcast commercials, equipment purchased on behalf of the client, travel, telephone expenses, and so on? Further, clients typically agree to partial, inventory, or progressive billing for items that require out-of-pocket costs as a job is developed.[20] All such issues need to be clearly agreed upon and explicitly covered in the client/agency contract.

Approval of Creative Work

It is a cliché in the advertising agency business that the trick is not just developing great advertising, it's also getting that advertising approved by the client. Clients can be difficult when it comes to approval of creative work. On the one hand, they want great advertising, but on the other hand, they tend to be conservative and cautious. Creativity in advertising often requires risks and innovation, which are often unsettling to client management.

Further, client management personnel realize the importance of creative executions to the success of the firm's advertising and have opinions about what they believe is good or bad, appropriate or inappropriate advertising for their product or service. But they lack objectivity and expertise. This often leads to conflicts with their agency on the issue of client approval of creative work.

Too often clients forget why they hired their agency—agency personnel are experts in making efficient and effective use of communication tools. *In terms of creative services, the agency's job is often to stretch its client's thinking about how to communicate with its target audience in a fresh, memorable way that sells the product.* This is particularly true in a marketplace crowded with similar brands and similar advertising selling those brands. It is hard to convince the management of a company that has experienced a 10 percent sales increase in the last year that it is forfeiting opportunity costs by sticking with a weak advertising campaign. The client's response—"We must be doing something right!"—may be glossing over a multitude of advertising and marketing blunders.

At the same time, in the interest of avoiding conflict with their client in the short run, agency personnel are tempted to present "safe" creative ideas they believe the client will approve. This trap undermines the client/agency relationship. The mission of the agency should be to present objective creative recommendations about how to use advertising to its full potential, *not* to present safe creative work the client is sure to approve. As Leo Burnett noted,

---

[19]Note that the rationale for 17.65 percent is that a charge or bill must be marked up this amount so that the markup will represent 15 percent of the total cost presented to the client. For example, if an agency supervises the development and production of a brochure and the printer's bill is $12,500, the agency marks up the bill 17.65 percent, or $2,206.25. The client is billed $14,706.25. The agency's markup is 15 percent of the client's total bill ($2,206.25 divided by $14,706.25).

[20]Gardner, *The Advertising Agency Business,* 76–77.

"I have learned that trying to guess what the boss or client wants is the most debilitating of all influences in the creation of good advertising."[21]

Gardner points out this danger. He notes that the objective of too many shortsighted agencies is to *please* their clients rather than *serve* their best interests. He suggests that "such agencies are unwittingly proceeding on the assumption that the client knows more about advertising than they do."[22]

Viewed in this light, some initial client/agency disagreement over approval of creative work may be the sign of a healthy and natural relationship. The client has an obligation to question the agency's creative ideas, and the agency has a similar obligation to back up its recommendations with a persuasive, logical rationale. It is the agency personnel's responsibility to sell their ideas in the face of client hesitation. The ability to sell sound, daring, and appropriate creative ideas in the face of client opposition is one of the hallmarks of an outstanding agency.

As discussed in an earlier chapter, a key benefit of developing a statement of creative strategy through teamwork is that it helps all parties involved reach a clear consensus about the direction of the advertising. After the strategy statement has been approved, it becomes a road map for creative personnel to follow in their work and the standard against which management evaluates proposed creative executions. "Is the execution on strategy?" should be client management's primary focus in reviewing creative work.

Finally, the discussion in this section is not intended to suggest that a nervous client is always wrong in hesitating to approve a solid agency's creative recommendations. In fact, the client may be correct in rejecting the proposed creative ideas. On the other hand, too much advertising is killed or severely maimed by overzealous client management. Therefore, the purpose of the foregoing discussion is to suggest that client management should place more trust in its agency's creative judgment than is typically the case. If the agency is a good one, its creative personnel are talented professionals who understand their client's product/market situation and have thoughtfully addressed their client's communication needs. After all, that's why the agency was hired. As Ogilvy notes, "Clients get the advertising they deserve. Don't keep a dog and bark yourself. Any fool can write a bad advertisement, but it takes a genius to keep his hands off a good one."[23]

Performance Reviews

All advertisers constantly review the performance of their advertising agency on an informal basis. Unfortunately, too few advertisers go beyond an informal, impressionistic review of their client/agency relationship. This is a mistake because a review often reveals a minor problem before it develops into a major one that can reduce the effectiveness of the firm's advertising and threaten the relationship.

---

[21]Burnett, *100 Leo's,* 37.

[22]Gardner, *The Advertising Agency Business,* 6.

[23]Ogilvy, *Ogilvy on Advertising,* 67.

Though typically identified as an agency performance review, such reviews should be viewed as an evaluation of the health of the client/agency relationship. The objective of a review is to help ensure that the agency best serves its client's needs and to foster preventive maintenance of the relationship. The underlying assumption is that both parties have a shared responsibility to jointly ensure that the business relationship is mutually profitable and productive. Both have a vested interest in seeing their relationship succeed. Conducting a review of that relationship annually, or at more frequent intervals, is simply an investment in ensuring the long-run success of the partnership. Agencies should view the review as an opportunity to explore areas in which they can improve their level of service to their clients.

The review should be formal and should gather information from across a wide range of topics from the perspective of individuals in a variety of positions in both organizations. Both rating scales and qualitative measures should be part of the evaluation.

Zeltner studied the performance reviews of 36 companies for the Association of National Advertisers. He noted that while there was considerable variation in terms of structure, grading techniques, and so on, seven broad goals for conducting the reviews emerged. These seven were (1) to determine if specific, measurable advertising and/or marketing objectives were achieved; (2) to evaluate the caliber, scope, and adequacy of staffing; (3) to assess the amount and quality of strategic contribution; (4) to evaluate tactical performance; (5) to clarify satisfaction or dissatisfaction with the relationship; (6) to establish a benchmark against which to measure progress; and (7) to establish a constructive dialogue on corrective actions.[24]

Zeltner notes what should be a logical link between agency performance reviews and agency compensation. Advertisers using such a link reward their agency for superior performance (typically, for increasing market share above previously established objectives) and reduce compensation for subpar performance. Zeltner points out that the trend toward tying evaluation and compensation should expand in the future: "American business management is increasingly insistent on tying supplier income to business conditions and marketplace results and in an advertising context, agency evaluations look like a handy and justifiable tool to accomplish just that."[25]

Brown-Forman's evaluation procedure provides an excellent example of an assessment. Its assessment is divided into two major segments: (1) a section in which the client evaluates its agency's performance and (2) a section in which the agency evaluates its client's performance. In the first segment, the client evaluates the agency's performance in the following areas: creative (strategy, execution, and administration); account service; media (planning and buying); research; senior management; and meeting assigned objectives.[26]

---

[24]Herbert Zeltner, *Evaluating Agency Performance* (New York: Association of National Advertisers, 1991), 7–9.

[25]*Ibid.,* 31.

[26]*Ibid.,* Appendix B.

TABLE 13-1   Areas of Client Performance Evaluated by Brown-Forman Beverage Company's Agencies

1. Articulates marketing objectives and strategies effectively—allows give and take.
2. Gets strategy buy-in and direction early enough from senior management.
3. Provides clear and constructive feedback to agency on its work—to the right people, early enough.
4. Sets clear priorities for projects and tasks and sticks to them.
5. Sets reasonable deadlines; streamlines the advertising approval process as much as possible.
6. Has broad perspective and vision—keeps the BIG PICTURE in mind.
7. Sets high standards and demands excellence.
8. Fosters relationships based on true partnership and mutual trust.
9. Rewards superior performance—financially or with recognition.
10. Is accessible and makes advertising a reasonable priority.
11. Is willing to take considered risks.
12. Encourages agency initiative and creativity.
13. Encourages agency participation on brands beyond media advertising.
14. Is an account that agency people want to work on.

Note: In each area, the client is given a quantitative score (1 to 10), with 10 = "outstanding, one of the best"; 9, 8, 7 = "above average, better than most"; 6, 5 = "average, acceptable"; 4, 3, 2 = "below average, possible weakness"; and 1 = "poor, clearly inferior." In addition, the evaluation form includes room for comments on each area and encourages the agency to cite specific examples wherever possible.

Source: Herbert Zeltner, *Evaluating Agency Performance* (New York: Association of National Advertisers, 1991), Appendix B.

The areas of *client performance* used by Brown-Forman's agencies provide some excellent insights into how a client should contribute to the process of developing outstanding advertising. These areas are presented in Table 13-1. The issues raised in Table 13-1 serve as an excellent reminder that clients play a determining role in the effectiveness of communication programs recommended by their agency.

Finally, the performance review should be a serious but open and positive exercise designed to foster better communication. The advertiser should work to communicate to its agency that the process is designed to be constructive, not destructive. Once a problem area has been identified, the two should adopt a team problem-solving approach to correcting the deficiency.

FOSTERING A PRODUCTIVE CLIENT/AGENCY RELATIONSHIP

A sound, productive working relationship between an advertiser and its agency does not happen by accident. Such a relationship requires the constant attention of both parties. The benefit of a sound advertiser/agency relationship is more effective advertising developed through an efficient process that rewards both parties.

Before examining several steps advertiser and agency personnel can take to help foster a smoother and more productive relationship, we will identify common reasons for unhappy relationships. Berkman and Gilson suggest three common reasons why even agencies that produce solid advertising for their clients are fired: (1) poor communication, (2) the fact that advertising is subjective, and (3) changes in the client's management or market position.[27]

Of these three, the one the advertiser and agency can do the most about is poor communication. In fact, miscommunication or the lack of clear communication appears to be the most commonly cited problem that clouds such relationships. Miscommunication undermines the relationship in many ways, but fortunately the following steps can be taken to avoid these problems:

1. *Both parties must be committed to open communication.* Waring stresses the need for an agency to build a candid, personal relationship with clients. She recommends that the agency work to form an interlocking communication network that encourages contact at every level as a means of reducing the chance of a communication breakdown.[28]

2. *Agency personnel must show initiative in ensuring open communication and following up on client contact, etc.* For example, agency personnel must document all client contact and decisions through call reports, which are distributed to personnel on both sides of the relationship.

3. *The client should conduct a periodic (at least yearly) performance review of its agency.* This often offers the two parties an opportunity to deal with problems before they reach a crisis stage.

4. *The issues of advertiser and agency expectations of what work will be performed, how the agency will be compensated, and so on, should be clearly covered in the contract.* A clear, thorough contract can guide the parties past a number of communication trouble spots. Importantly, the contract sets the tone for the entire relationship.

In addition, Engel, Warshaw, and Kinnear suggest that advertisers maintain a top-level liaison; evaluate promotion in a marketing context (when sales drop, don't automatically blame advertising without investigating other probable causes); do not abandon a campaign prematurely; do not be carried away by creative execution at the expense of a clearly communicated consumer benefit; emancipate the agency from fear (Ogilvy suggests a new agency should be given a five-year contract!); simplify approval (don't require advertising to be strained through too many levels); and permit the agency to make a profit.[29]

---

[27]Harold W. Berkman and Christopher Gilson, *Advertising: Concepts and Strategy* (New York: Random House, 1987), 254–255.

[28]Cathy Taylor, "Waring Wins Back Agency and Clients," *Adweek,* May 28, 1990, 22.

[29]James F. Engel, Martin R. Warshaw, and Thomas C. Kinnear, *Promotion Strategy—Managing the Marketing Communication Process* (Homewood, Ill.: Irwin, 1987), 254–256.

Richie suggests three telltale signs of a healthy relationship from the agency's perspective:

1. The client seeks the agency's views on marketing matters outside its present assignments.

2. The client includes agency personnel in internal "closed meetings."

3. The client calls the agency with "scoop" information about a breaking development.[30]

Each of these signs indicates that the client trusts the agency and believes that agency personnel are smart and understand their business. Further, such contact indicates that the client values its agency's judgment.

Suggested Readings

Agency Compensation: A Guidebook.
New York: Association of National
Advertisers, 1989.

Fulton, Sue, and Ed Buxton. *Advertising Freelancers.* New York: Executive
Communications, 1985.

Gardner, Herbert S. *The Advertising Agency Business.* Lincolnwood, Ill.:
NTC Business Books, 1989.

Lyons, John. *Guts.* New York: Amacon,
1987.

McNamara, Jay. *Advertising Agency Management.* Homewood, Ill.: Dow-
Jones Irwin, 1990.

Mayer, Martin. *Whatever Happened to Madison Avenue?* New York: Little,
Brown, 1991.

Ogilvy, David. *Ogilvy on Advertising.*

New York: Crown Publishers, 1983:
Chapters 4, 5, and 6.

Perrin, Wes. *Advertising Realities.*
Mountain View, Calif.: Mayfield
Publishing, 1992.

Poppe, Fred C. *50 Rules to Keep a Client Happy.* New York: Harper &
Row, 1987.

"Selecting an Advertising Agency," New
York: Association of National
Advertisers, 1977.

Weilbacher, William M. *Choosing an Advertising Agency.* Chicago: Crain
Books, 1983.

Zeltner, Herbert. *Evaluating Agency Performance.* New York: Association
of National Advertisers, 1991.

Exercises

1. The advertising agency business went through some economic difficulties during the late 1980s and early 1990s. In an effort to increase their revenues, some agencies developed subsidiaries that provided management consulting services to their clients. These new units addressed client needs traditionally handled by outsiders. As an example, one such consulting job involved assessing the relationship between a client's new business and existing business and determining how to meld the two.

Another innovative way agencies tried to increase their business was by establishing media consulting units. Lowe & Partners established the Lowe Cable Group, whose purpose was to

---

[30]Laurel J. Richie, "Telltale Signs of a Healthy Client Relationship," *Viewpoint,* September/October 1990, 17–18.

provide information about the cable TV industry and keep the agency aware of changes in cable that might have significance for noncable clients.

Some critics said this type of "vertical marketing" expansion was not ethical. Agencies, they claimed, were encroaching on a business in which they had no expertise. In addition, they were using advertising as bait to attract clients who would otherwise use other types of firms for gathering important information.

Do you feel the development of such agency subsidiaries helps or harms the client/agency relationship? Why?

Are there any specific services an agency should never provide to a client? Explain.

Source: Pat Sloan, "Agencies Branch into Consulting," *Advertising Age,* June 22, 1992, 16.

2. The Green and Witt advertising agency had just obtained a new client— Bank Two, a large financial corporation headquartered in Florida. Ed Alvey, the agency's creative art director, was delighted with the new account because it would give him the opportunity to develop an idea with which he had been toying for a long time. He had developed a series of advertisements around endangered animal species that should earn him a Clio nomination, no matter what product they were used for.

The marketing vice-president for Bank Two had given the agency the account because he wanted to increase awareness of his financial institution. Such an increase in awareness was necessary for the next step: selling specific financial services. He had little knowledge of advertising and had complete confidence in the agency because of its reputation for reliability.

The agency account executive for Bank Two was Karen Little, a very dynamic marketing major from Stanford University. While Little felt Alvey usually had great ideas, she was very concerned that the image projected for Bank Two by advertising be consistent with the financial institution's perceived mission and services. She was not completely confident that endangered species ads were the proper way to communicate such an image.

After the initial meeting with the client, Alvey and Little had an argument. Alvey told Little that he wanted to pursue his idea because it would bring notoriety to both the agency and its client and would also allow him to compete in the Clios. Little disagreed, saying that she wanted ads for her client that would imply seriousness, reliability, and a high level of services so that the client could capitalize on the ads and then also use them for future promotions.

The argument was not settled. If you were Little, would you make known to the client your reservations regarding the creative idea developed by Alvey? What should the agency do with regard to the Bank Two account? Should the creative ambition of the art director give way to the client's best interests?

Source: "The Party's Over," *The Economist,* February 1, 1992, 69–76.

3. Publicidad, a small advertising agency located in San Antonio, Texas, had been handling all the advertising for El Manuelito Mexican food manufacturers for six years. This was not a large account, but it was one of the first accounts ever obtained by the agency. The client was always punctual in paying the agency, and they had a good working relationship.

Last week, the CEO of La Casa Mexican food manufacturers called the senior partner of the agency. He was unhappy with his present agency and wanted to explore the possibility of taking his account to Publicidad. It was an extremely large account and would double Publicidad's revenues. The problem, however, was that La Casa did not want Publicidad to handle any other Mexican food manufacturer.

Should Publicidad drop El Manuelito so that it can work for La Casa? What should the senior partner of Publicidad do?

4.   Current trends indicate that advertising in the future may change in strategy and scope and interact increasingly with all the other marketing functions. As such, it could be argued that the advertiser should retain more

control of the advertising function, as a strategic practice. This would help ensure protection from competitive inroads.

If such a rationale were to be taken to an extreme, one could argue that advertising agencies should be replaced completely by in-house advertising departments.

Do you feel this forecast is accurate? How do you feel the agency of the year 2000 will be constituted? Should clients maintain strict and complete control of their accounts? Why or why not?

C A S E   **13 - 1**

Columbia Savings (B)

Shortly after being named president of Columbia Savings (CS), David Woburne had hired a full-service advertising agency (Boyton & Dodds) to help revitalize the firm's downtrodden image. Woburne had worked with the agency before and had considerable confidence in its abilities. In addition, he was good friends with both the principals of the agency. (See Case 6-3.)

After four years of working with the agency, David Carlyle, vice-president of marketing at CS, believed that while some of its early work had been strong and effective, lately it was pretty dull. Further, he believed that the solid growth CS had experienced was due more to its attractive rates than its advertising campaigns. In addition, during this period the market had experienced steady growth, and Carlyle believed in the maxim, "All boats rise with the tide." In hinting at his lack of enthusiasm for the agency's creative efforts, Carlyle had generated comments from Woburne such as, "But like the boys at B&D said, it's fundamentally sound and fits our personality."

In the past two years, several banks and S&Ls had developed what Carlyle felt were aggressive advertising and promotional programs. The competitive advertising he believed was the most clever and memorable had received considerable recognition in local and regional advertising awards competitions. The ideas and executions behind this campaign had been developed by a two-person team who operated a local creative boutique—Navajo Inspiration.

The apparent success of these relatively new campaigns, coupled with the emergence of other local *a la carte* advertising and marketing services such as media buying, research, and graphics services, opened up some interesting possibilities in Carlyle's judgment. In addition, he was concerned with stretching CS's advertising dollars as far as possible. Boutiques, which operated on a fee basis, were touted in the trade press as being less expensive than a full-service shop.

In considering the use of a creative specialist, Carlyle wondered about his own small marketing department staff's ability to handle all its current responsibilities. The bank's current agency did help with planning and some special events. His department was responsible for new business development in addition to all marketing communications—advertising, promotion, publicity, internal newsletters, and more. CS's marketing budget exceeded

This case was written by John H. Murphy, The University of Texas at Austin. It is intended to be used to generate class discussion and not to illustrate either the effective or ineffective handling of an administrative situation. The identities of the firms involved have been disguised.

$650,000 not including salaries and some other indirect costs. The bulk of this budget went into advertising, split roughly 60/40 between broadcast and print.

Carlyle felt the time had come to broach the issue with Woburne. He was comfortable in suggesting they discuss the matter because Woburne enjoyed challenging the status quo and took pride in his own openness to seriously considering "any suggestion from any source," as he put it.

In initially considering the idea of some sort of change in CS's present agency relationship, Woburne sensed Carlyle's enthusiasm for such a change but raised several questions. First, would there really be a cost savings? Second, had Carlyle pushed the present agency for a different tack in their creative work? Third, for a financial institution, how much creativity was appropriate? (Woburne discounted the award-winning campaign as too zany for the serious older saver. "My nephew loves that stuff, but he's only ten years old!") Finally, he pointed out the wealth of marketing experience the principals of their present agency possessed. In concluding their discussion, Woburne suggested that Carlyle think through all alternatives, including the possibility of adding staff and taking the account in-house, before making a formal written recommendation for consideration by the executive committee.

Questions for Discussion and Review

1. How do general considerations applying to the full-service agency versus boutique question fit CS's situation?

2. What are some additional alternatives for handling CS's advertising?

3. How might Woburne's past experiences with the present agency influence his reaction to Carlyle's suggestions? How typical is this?

C A S E   **13 - 2**

Capital National Bank

Responding to a directive from top management, Gene Kincaid, marketing director of Capital National Bank (CNB), had quickly initiated an advertising agency review. In the review, the bank's incumbent agency and another agency were scheduled to compete for CNB's account.

This case was written by Gene Kincaid, Hyundai Electronics, San Jose, California, and John H. Murphy, The University of Texas at Austin. It is intended to be used to generate classroom discussion and not to illustrate either the effective or ineffective handling of an administrative situation. Used by permission of Texas Commerce Bank-Austin.

As Kincaid reflected on the very close and positive working relationship he had had with the incumbent agency, he wondered if he could be completely objective in evaluating the two firms. Further, he was concerned that perhaps the review procedures were not fair to the two agencies or would not provide the most appropriate evaluation of which agency was best suited to handle the CNB account.

The whole situation had unfolded quickly, and the entire process—from the decision to initiate a review to the awarding of the account—was scheduled to occur in less than a month. At this point in the process (Tuesday, August 11), Kincaid felt he needed to go over the agency assignment and the ground rules of the review one more time prior to distributing the assignment to the two agencies, who were anxious to get started.

BACKGROUND

CNB, located in Austin, was among the larger banks in Texas, with approximately 600 employees and total assets of over $800 million. CNB was a member bank of a large holding company—Texas Commerce Bancshares, Inc. However, under Texas banking law and the holding company organizational structure, each member bank's management operated autonomously within its geographic market and contributed to holding company profitability on a consolidated basis.

The bank's advertising agency of record for the previous five years had been Ketchum–Houston, a division of Ketchum, MacLeod & Grove Inc., a major national advertising agency headquartered in Pittsburgh. The agency of record for the parent holding company and the holding company's flagship bank, Texas Commerce–Houston, was Benton & Bowles–Houston.

Ketchum's track record with CNB over the previous five years had been excellent. CNB's advertising was locally acknowledged as some of the highest quality advertising in the Austin market. In addition, CNB's advertising was nationally recognized, having earned industry awards for excellence presented by the Bank Marketing Association. However, it came as no surprise to Ketchum when Kincaid informed it on Friday, August 7, that the account had been opened for review.

THE DECISION TO REVIEW

The decision to review CNB's agency relationship with Ketchum–Houston was made for business reasons unrelated to Ketchum's creative, media, or account service performance. Rather, the decision was based on corporate considerations related to CNB's affiliation with its parent bank holding company and events that had occurred within the holding company. In December of the preceding year, Texas Commerce Bancshares conducted an agency review and switched from its incumbent, Ketchum–Houston, to Benton & Bowles–Houston. Since the parent holding company's switch, 41 of the 42 member banks had moved their account from Ketchum to Benton & Bowles. Only Capital remained with Ketchum.

After the holding company's change, Benton & Bowles aggressively solicited CNB's business throughout much of the first seven months of the present year. The early August decision to review CNB's agency relationship was initiated by the bank's senior management and supported by the parent holding company's senior management. This decision was communicated by Frank Phillips, CNB's president, to Kincaid, who was given primary responsibility for organizing and implementing the review.

THE REVIEW PROCESS

As a first step, Phillips and Kincaid agreed that an agency screening phase to identify viable firms to be invited to compete for CNB's account was unnecessary. Only Ketchum and Benton & Bowles were invited to participate.

After Ketchum and Benton & Bowles, in that order, were notified of the review and the information became public knowledge, several other agencies expressed an interest in competing for the business. These requests to participate were declined. Kincaid thanked the inquiring agencies for their interest but explained that the initial screening had already occurred and that no additional agencies would be considered.

Next, Phillips and Kincaid identified members of CNB's upper management who would serve on a review committee and agreed on a rough outline of the agency assignment to be used as a basis for evaluating the two shops. Five review committee members were picked to form a committee of seven, including Phillips and Kincaid.

The committee members were selected to include the managers of the organizational areas most directly impacted by CNB's advertising. Kincaid felt the size of the committee was large enough to encourage a wide variety of opinions, yet small enough for meaningful interaction and participation by all members. After the two agencies had presented their recommended solutions to the agency assignment, each committee member would have one vote in selecting the winning agency. The total number of committee members was odd to avoid a tie. The members of the review committee were identified as Bob Present, chairman of the board and chief executive officer; Frank Phillips, president and chief operating officer; Jim Saxon, senior executive vice-president of finance and administration; Mike Doyle, executive vice-president of general banking services; Milam Johnson, executive vice-president of investment management; Charles Miller, senior vice-president of personal banking services; and Gene Kincaid, managing officer of marketing and public relations.

The review committee was convened formally in a planning session, and five broad areas were discussed. First, the committee was briefed on the agency review process and what was expected of each member. Second, Kincaid reviewed his initial meetings with the agencies after each had been told the CNB account was under review. Third, Kincaid previewed the upcoming sequence of events with emphasis on the 30-minute individual meetings between the review committee members and the agency presentation teams. Fourth, the group discussed the proposed agency assignment. Finally, a recommendation by Kincaid to compensate each agency up to $5,000 for presentation expenses was rejected.

THE AGENCY ASSIGNMENT

The proposed agency presentation assignment package is presented in Exhibit 13-2-1. The proposed assignment package contained a brief description of the advertising assignment, a presentation schedule, a review committee roster, and two project input sheets. This package was to be distributed to the agencies on Friday, August 14. Following the distribution of the assignment, 30-minute meetings between each review committee member and the agency presentation teams were to be arranged. Further, Kincaid would be available to the agencies to respond to requests for additional information.

EXHIBIT 13-2-1 Agency Presentation Assignment Package

Presentation Assignment

1. Present creative concepts for a three-week campaign to change the name of the bank from Capital National Bank to Texas Commerce Bank–Austin.
    Campaign elements: a. one 30-second television spot
    b. one 60-second radio spot
    c. one full-page newspaper ad
    d. one outdoor painted board design
    e. one point-of-purchase display for lobby and office use
    f. one statement stuffer

2. Present a creative concept for one institutional TV spot for Texas Commerce Bank–Austin.

3. Present a creative concept for one newspaper advertisement for a new product to be promoted immediately, "the All Savers Certificate of Deposit."

4. Present a recommended media plan and budget for the next fiscal year.

5. Present the day-to-day account service structure for Capital, including:
    a. creative personnel
    b. media personnel
    c. account management.

Considerations

Assignment #1: estimated production budget—$36,000 total
Assignment #2: comparable budget to existing institutional TV
Assignment #3: page dominant ad

Agency Review Presentation Schedule

August 31, Benton & Bowles
2:30 P.M.–3:30 P.M.
Boardroom—Capital National Bank
September 1, Ketchum–Houston
10:00 A.M.–11:00 A.M.
Boardroom—Capital National Bank

(continued)

EXHIBIT 13-2-1   *(continued)*

Capital National Bank Agency Review Committee

Bob Present—Chairman of the Board and Chief Executive Officer
Frank Phillips—President and Chief Operating Officer
Jim Saxton—Senior Executive Vice-President—Finance & Administration
Mike Doyle—Executive Vice-President—General Banking Service
Milam Johnson—Executive Vice-President—Investment Management
Charles Miller—Senior Vice-President—Personal Banking Services
Gene Kincaid—Managing Officer—Marketing and Public Relations

1. KEY MARKETING FACTS
   a. With the name change, TCB—Austin will lose all previous TV spots. This presents an opportunity to modify or change the format somewhat to be a little more intrusive and yet still retain the flavor and tone of past campaigns.
   b. All other downtown banks are currently dedicating significant portions of their marketing efforts to promoting their ATM networks. Opportunity exists to solidify our movement toward a commercial position by promoting a clear, consistent image to our target market.

2. COMPETITIVE EVALUATION (institutional TV or most recent campaign)
   ANB—Most recent emphasis on ATM system—"Anytime" and "The Three-Bank Family of the Biggest Bank in Austin." Good positioning as largest, strongest, oldest bank, with three locations: northwest, south, and downtown.
   City— Most recent emphasis on ATM system—"Teller 2" and crystal glassware premium campaign to attract deposits.
   American—Promotion of MPACT ATM most recently—"We're your financial resource" theme not dominant now.

3. PROBLEM ADVERTISING MUST SOLVE
   New institutional TV must build upon the successful format used in the past four years; must be similar enough to be compatible but with a creative twist to differentiate from old. Expect spot to run for two to five years.

4. ADVERTISING
   In a believable way, create positive awareness for TCB—Austin and foster the position that we:
   a. seek creative and innovative ways to solve financial problems.
   b. take the time to get to know companies that we work with and therefore have special expertise and drive.
   c. have a professional staff that is highly qualified and genuinely wants to provide quality service in a friendly way.

5. COPY STRATEGY
   a. Prospect definition: Target market—35 years or older; $30,000 or more in income; executives, professionals, managers, and entrepreneurs; influence over business banking decisions.
   b. Promise
   c. Reason why

6. MEDIA OBJECTIVES
   a. Demography—Target market skewed to the high end in age and income.
   b. Geographic coverage—Austin SMSA and trade area.
   c. Seasonality—Not applicable.
   d. Reach and frequency.

7. MEDIA PROGRAM
   Television with print support (newspaper and magazine)

8. MANDATORIES AND LIMITATIONS

Addendum

CNB name since 1934 chartered . . . variety of logos.

TCB logo since 1977, when we changed logos; continual use of logo and emphasis of logo in all ads for four years.

EXHIBIT 13-2-1 *(continued)*

Some local institutions took "locally owned—independent" position for a while (one S&L still does—Franklin Savings).

Banks:

1. Austin National Bank—$665 million—a three-bank local holding company—"the three-bank family of the biggest bank in town."
2. Capital National Bank—$603 million—member TCB—"All you need is Capital."
3. City National Bank—$445 million—member First City Banc—"More bank."
4. American National Bank—$338 million—member Mercantile Banc—"Your financial re-source."

Some resistance inside the bank.

Among our target market, the name change is probably not a factor; they are sophisticated enough to know that "hometown" ownership doesn't mean anything, money is money, decisions for business are done here and not in Houston, "member of holding company" simply means more money available.

We may be the first local major bank to change its name to the holding company umbrella (one or two suburban banks have begun to change).

Austin National is open to holding company acquisition.

Name will be Texas Commerce Bank–Austin.

Name change to occur November 15th—strategy is to spend three to four weeks telling about the change, then back to business as usual.

Audiences: officers, staff, customers, target market, Austin community.

Key is a positive position statement—Taking our place in the best holding company in the state; Put Austin in Commerce—Bring Commerce to Austin—Bring Texas Commerce to Austin.

Customers will fall into two broad groups: a very small, vocal minority (a generally older group) that will express dismay and threaten to change banks, very few doing so, or (the vast majority of our customers) an informed group who know the change will not affect their relationship or are apathetic toward the bank in any event.

Expect neutral to mildly negative press coverage, but not a skipped-over-lightly attitude; major feature in business section for a day or two.

Position: Positive change for the better, outward show of strength with the same people running the bank. Somehow maybe important to preempt the anti-holding-company propaganda that is sure to come.

Do not forget TCB—Barton Creek, our new suburban bank; possibly use it to introduce the name change, growing and changing to meet Austin's needs. Note: Now we can start using Austin in our work and maybe overpower Austin National Bank with our logo—sort of the best of all worlds—Austin in our name (the biggest bank in town) and our logo for recognition. We will lead the downtown banks in changing names to meet the changing needs of Austin commerce.

Questions for Discussion and Review

1. Are speculative advertising agency presentations appropriate? Or are they wasteful and unethical, as some individuals contend?

2. Realistically, should an advertiser be able to select the most appropriate agency after thorough study of the agencies' past work, their character, capabilities, motivation, and mutual compatibility, without speculative presentations? Does this vary with each situation?

3. Does the agency selection procedure established by Capital National Bank provide the basis for a complete and fair evaluation of the two agencies involved? What are the strengths and weaknesses of the procedures established? What changes in the evaluation procedures would be appropriate? Why?

C A S E   **13 - 3**

The Dallas Morning News

MEMORANDUM

TO: Barbara van Pelt, Promotion Manager
FROM: Harold Gaar, Marketing Director
DATE: March 1, 19XX
RE: Development of a Procedure to Follow in Selecting an Advertising Agency

The purpose of this memorandum is to briefly describe a project that needs our immediate attention. The project is to outline a procedure to follow in selecting a new agency to handle our advertising and assist us with other marketing activities.

As you know, this project is necessary because our present agency, Cunningham & Walsh, is closing its Dallas office. This is regrettable in that we have been pleased with its work and we have had a productive relationship.

The procedure should cover all aspects of the process including: (1) soliciting prospective agencies, (2) gathering initial information on each, (3) reducing the number for serious consideration, (4) interviewing the serious contenders, (5) reviewing their past work for their clients, (6) perhaps developing an assignment for the finalists to tackle and present to us, and (7) making the final decision. There are also some other considerations. For example, should we pay the finalists if we ask for presentations that involve the development of example ads? What should be the time frame of the process? Who should be involved in the selection process at *The News*?

This case was written by John H. Murphy, The University of Texas at Austin. It is intended to be used to generate class discussion and not to illustrate either the effective or ineffective handling of an administrative situation. Used by permission of *The Dallas Morning News*.

These are just my initial thoughts. Undoubtedly there are other issues beyond those briefly described above which we need to include in our procedure. I'm counting on you to do some research and bring these issues to my attention.

Since we work with and depend on the goodwill of all the agencies that will be involved, we are in a somewhat unique situation. We must take great care not to offend any of the agencies that might become involved at any point in the process.

In completing this project you should develop several alternative suggestions under each of the major issues identified above plus any major issues you identify. Your report (in the form of a memo) should clearly describe each of your alternatives and provide a balanced discussion of its pros and cons.

Obviously, this is an extremely important assignment. The selection of the most appropriate agency will have a significant effect on the success of all our marketing efforts in the future.

We'll use your report as the basis for developing our recommendation to top management as to how we should proceed. We'll only present one recommendation to top management, but we need to carefully consider other approaches at each step in the process.

Communications Center, Dallas, Texas 75265, Telephone (214) 977–8222

Questions for Discussion and Review

1. What factors or considerations determine how attractive a potential client is to an agency? How attractive a potential client would the *News* be to Dallas advertising agencies?

2. Would it be appropriate for the *News* to ask Cunningham & Walsh to be involved in the process? Why or why not? If yes, to what extent and in which phases of the selection process might the *News* appropriately seek Cunningham & Walsh's assistance? Why?

3. What procedures should be followed in each of the seven steps in the selection process identified by Gaar? Which of these steps is most important in ensuring that the most appropriate agency is selected? Why?

4. What additional suggestions or issues should van Pelt include in her report?

C A S E **13 - 4**
Wensley Industries

The Williams advertising agency had devoted over six months of effort to the development of a new advertising campaign for its biggest client, Wensley Industries. The campaign was for a new product that was scheduled to be introduced in September. Bill James, the agency's management supervisor, had informed Wensley's advertising manager, Alfie Thomas, of the progress on the campaign at various stages of development but had not revealed the creative strategy. He had explained: "Alfie, we think we have a great idea, but we don't want to expose it to you until it has had some preliminary pretesting. It wouldn't be fair to ask your approval at this stage."

Alfie was fully informed on details of media recommendations and budgets and had given Bill James authority to make certain television buys for the introduction of the new campaign in about four months. He was, however, impatient to see the creative recommendation and was irritated somewhat that he had not been involved in its development. Secretly he believed he was very creative and could make substantial contributions. Bruce Jenkins, the agency's creative director, who headed the team working on the campaign, had insisted that the creative work should not be revealed until the agency was ready to recommend it. He said, "Alfie is a good guy, but he's not very creative. If he gets into it, he'll foul it up."

In late April, Bill called Alfie and said the creative plan was ready. Further, Bill asked Alfie to come to the agency's New York headquarters for a Wednesday afternoon meeting to discuss it. He also asked Alfie to schedule a meeting the following week with Ted Alford, Wensley's general manager, and other top executives. Bill said, "If you approve of the idea, Alfie, and okay the budget for further pretesting, we should try to get tentative approval from top management." Alfie realized that if further testing were required, the time schedule to prepare the campaign for fall release would be very tight, but he reluctantly agreed to arrange the meeting with Ted Alford.

Alfie flew to New York for the Wednesday afternoon meeting. John Williams, chairman of the agency, presented the campaign to Alfie and gave the rationale behind it. It was a very daring campaign, which was sure to attract

This case was written by Robert E. Anderson, The University of Texas at Austin. It is intended to be used to generate classroom discussion, and not to illustrate either the effective or ineffective handling of an administrative situation. The identities of the firms have been disguised.

public attention but might invite substantial criticism. Williams described the preliminary research that the agency conducted at its own expense and noted that several focus groups' reactions to the campaign were favorable. Now he wanted to have an animated storyboard prepared and pretested at an estimated cost of $13,500, to be paid by the client.

Alfie responded enthusiastically. He recognized the creative excellence of the campaign and knew that it would be unique in the industry. He telephoned Ted Alford and confirmed the meeting with top management for the following Wednesday morning. He caught an evening flight back to the client's midwestern headquarter city.

The next day Alfie called Bill James, and the following discussion ensued:

Alfie: "That was a great meeting, Bill, and an exciting creative approach. I think we have a winner. I'm sure Ted will go along, so why don't you get the animated storyboard started right away?"

Bill: "Okay. It will cost about twenty-five hundred bucks to make it, but if we get with it, maybe we'll have it ready to show Ted next Wednesday."

Alfie: "The budget of $2,500 is okay. Try to have it ready. Now, do you have any plans for an alternative campaign? If Ted shoots this down, we should be ready to show him something else. Otherwise, we'll never make those fall schedules."

Bill: "We weren't planning on getting this campaign turned down. We really don't have an alternate. Let's just give this our best shot, and if Ted won't buy it, we'll just have to start over again."

Alfie: "But Bill, we just don't have time. We have to get some kind of tentative approval Wednesday. I'm all for this campaign, but I don't want to be left hanging if Ted thinks it's too dangerous. I'd look foolish."

Bill: "We'll all look foolish if we come in with a shoddy campaign thrown together over the weekend. And besides, Bruce wouldn't have his heart in it long as he thinks his big idea has a chance."

Alfie: "The heck with Bruce. If this idea bombs it's my hide, not his. Get another creative director to develop the alternate."

Bill: "That won't work. He wouldn't have the background for the campaign. Let me talk this over with John Williams and get back to you."

Alfie: "Okay, but be sure you understand. I want an alternative campaign, and until you get one there's not going to be a meeting with Ted Alford."

Questions for Discussion and Review

1. Given the facts of the situation, what is your assessment of Alfie's position?

2. How should Bill James handle the situation?

3. Could an irate Alfie actually fire the agency in this situation? Knowing that Wensley is the agency's biggest account, how should John Williams react to the situation? What are his risks?

CASE　　13 - 5

Gordon, Wolfberg, Miller & Friends

Jane Gordon and Mary Wolfberg had formed their advertising agency, Gordon & Wolfberg (G&W), on the basis of a mutual respect for each other and their complementary talents. The two principals in the agency had been friends since their high school days in Evanston, Illinois, and both had studied advertising at the University of Illinois. After graduation, the two friends had gone their separate ways. Gordon had taken a media buying job in the Dallas office of a large Chicago-based agency and after two years had moved to an account executive position working with a large package-goods client. Wolfberg had initially taken a job as copywriter/artist with a struggling agency, but after nine months the agency lost its principal account and folded. Next, Wolfberg's artistic talents landed her a position as a creative artist with Hallmark Cards in Kansas City.

As a result of professional contacts established through the local ad club, Gordon had received an offer to become the advertising manager of a large manufacturing firm with offices in Dallas. At that time, the firm had media billings of roughly $1.2 million. Although the offer was attractive, she viewed the situation as an opportunity to establish her own agency. Gordon suggested that the firm's present vice-president of marketing could handle the job in a "partnership" with her new agency. After considerable discussions, the owner of the manufacturing firm, who was extremely unhappy with the results of the firm's advertising efforts, bought Gordon's idea and agreed to fire the present agency as soon as Gordon could assume responsibility for the firm's advertising. Wolfberg instantly accepted Gordon's proposal that they jointly form an agency to handle the manufacturer's account.

Ownership of the agency was divided 60/40 between Gordon and Wolfberg. Both of the principals began their new enterprise with considerable enthusiasm and dreams of quickly adding significant new accounts. During the first two years of the agency's operation, several small clients were picked up by G&W. However, both the principals were dissatisfied with their efforts to add at least one major account.

In an attempt to correct this perceived shortcoming, Jack Miller, a seasoned and highly successful account executive from a major Dallas agency, was hired to concentrate on pitching prospective new clients. Gordon and Wolfberg each gave Miller 10 percent ownership in the agency, which became Gordon, Wolfberg, Miller & Friends (GWMF).

This case was written by John H. Murphy, The University of Texas at Austin. It is intended to be used to generate classroom discussion, and not to illustrate either the effective or ineffective handling of an administrative situation. The identities of the firms have been disguised.

Since GWMF's formation, the agency had grown to about 25 accounts and handled media billings of about $27.5 million. The agency employed about 40 individuals and hired outside free-lance talent such as photographers or copywriters when the work load justified additional help.

As fate would have it, on a Monday morning developments with three different clients reached the point where a decision was sorely needed regarding what action to take. These developments required the immediate attention of Gordon, Wolfberg, and Miller. To handle these problems adequately, the three principals would have to agree upon a course of action to resolve each by the next morning.

SURE FINE DAIRIES

The first of the problem areas involved an important client, the Sure Fine Dairies. Sure Fine Dairies executives had approved GWMF's recommendation to place $125,000 in outdoor showings and a spot radio schedule costing $57,000 to support the 12-week introduction of a new line of natural yogurt flavors. Further, it was understood that an additional 12-week campaign to reinforce the initial efforts would probably be approved.

At the same time, Sure Fine wanted GWMF to develop six multimedia displays that would present the history of Sure Fine and show the procedures used to process dairy products. The displays were to be used for special events or programs (for example, the state fair), and three would be housed permanently at Sure Fine Dairies.

In order to produce the type and quality of displays Sure Fine wanted, GWMF would require special film work, sophisticated audiovisual equipment, and the hiring of a photographer and talent for the voice-over. An estimate on the expenses involved in producing the displays was as follows:

Audiovisual equipment (cost to agency)	$17,621
Materials (cost to agency)	2,567
Talent, sound, production (cost to agency)	4,000
A/E supervision time = 50 hours, @ $65/hour	3,250
Total	$27,438

In figuring its cost estimates to develop the six displays for Sure Fine, GWMF followed the accepted agency practice of marking up all work contracted outside by 17.65 percent. Thus, the estimate presented to Sure Fine for its approval was $31,707.

When the account executive from GWMF presented the estimated costs and requested Sure Fine's approval, the Sure Fine marketing manager balked at the additional charges for agency markup on "outside services" ($4,269). The marketing manager said that he did not mind paying a commission to the agency on the media advertising, but he objected to a fee being charged on other services. Further, he suggested that perhaps GWMF did not appreciate Sure Fine's business and that he wanted a special deal if the markup was a standard practice. The account executive told the marketing manager that he would check with the principals of GWMF and come by on Tuesday to discuss the situation further.

WOODY'S

The second problem involved Woody's, a regional chain of fast-food restaurants. The chain had multiple locations in Dallas, Fort Worth, Houston, San Antonio, Amarillo, Beaumont, Tyler, and Lubbock. Periodically, Woody's ran a burst of advertising promoting a "Buy-One-Get-One-Free" weekend sale. These weekend promotions had been extremely successful in the past. Woody's management had always been extremely pleased with consumer sales during these promotions and felt such sales contributed heavily to business in slow periods. Woody's executives gave most of the credit for the success of the promotion to GWMF's high-quality creative advertising strategy and executions.

Through an unexplainable error, most likely on the part of GWMF's new assistant traffic manager, fifteen 30-second and eighteen 10-second television spots promoting the "Buy-One-Get-One-Free" sale had not appeared as originally planned on the Friday evening prior to the sale. To make matters worse, sales during the promotion were about half of their usual level for an average weekend during such a sale.

Woody Burkehart, owner of Woody's, was extremely upset after watching the 10 P.M. news only to discover that his ads did not appear. Burkehart attributed the dismal sales performance to the scheduling error. "The promo never had a chance after we missed those front-end spots. This error robbed the spots and newspaper ads that did run of their impact. If there had been time, I'd have canned the whole promotion after the foul-up on the opening spots."

The account person who handled Woody's apologized for the scheduling problem and pointed out that two other factors contributed to the poor sales performance: (1) light snow and sleet made travel by car dangerous during much of the weekend in most of the markets served by Woody's, and (2) competitive advertising and price promotion by other fast-food restaurants was unusually heavy over the weekend of Woody's "Buy-One-Get-One-Free" promotion.

Burkehart rejected these explanations. Further, he literally demanded that Gordon and Miller be in his office the next morning to discuss some sort of arrangement to "make good" on the botched promotion, the likelihood of such a situation's occurring again, and the future of the relationship between GWMF and Woody's.

HOMEWOOD SAVINGS & LOAN

The third client that would require attention the next day was Homewood Savings & Loan. Homewood had been a solid client of GWMF's for five years but recently had become unhappy with the quality of the agency's creative efforts.

In the 15 years since its founding, Homewood had grown from a single location in Dallas to eight branches plus a downtown headquarters, and it presently had deposits of over $900 million. However, in the last six months, new accounts had slowed to a trickle despite the fact that the service areas of the branch locations had experienced strong growth.

When the marketing manager at Homewood, who was under pressure to correct the meager new accounts problem, complained to GWMF's account executive about the "stale" creative efforts, the A/E responded that the campaign represented the creative people's best efforts. Further, the A/E explained that the present efforts built logically on past Homewood promotions and advertising. Finally, the A/E suggested that Homewood's media budget of only $750,000 was a stumbling block to the development of the sort of impact that was necessary in the highly competitive Dallas financial market. (As a result of fee work and preparation of collateral materials, GWMF considered Homewood an excellent client.)

Homewood's advertising manager questioned whether GWMF's creative group really devoted much time or energy to his account. The advertising manager went on to say: "Don't tell me you're not capable of a stronger creative execution of our ads. It sure seems strange that Jack Miller is going around town touting your shop's expertise in creativity and showing award-winning commercials for almost all your clients except us!"

The A/E's conversation with the ad manager ended on a very sour note. In so many words, the ad manager threatened to fire GWMF and look for some new creative blood. The advertising manager ended the discussion with the following request: "The executive board of Homewood is meeting for dinner and a working session to review our marketing efforts tomorrow evening at the Petroleum Club. Please ask Jack Miller to join us around seven o'clock. Better still, ask Jack to meet me here at the office about five so we can talk prior to meeting with the board."

Questions for Discussion and Review

1. How should GWMF respond to each of the situations involving its clients? What are the likely implications of GWMF's responses?

2. Are the immediate problems related in any way? How?

3. What general principles of client/agency relationships are involved in the three situations?

4. How might each of these problems have been avoided?

14

Ethical Considerations

The advertising person's role on any side of the
business is to help a company understand its customers
and their needs better; to help a company respond to
and speak to those needs, efficiently and effectively.
Advertising is an honest business, a noble business, the
engine of the American economy.[1]

Bob Lauterborn

Advertising professionals have often been criticized for using the persuasive power of words and images in an unethical fashion. Advertising is very visible in our society; therefore, it is almost inevitable that it would be the target of criticism. Some such criticisms may well be justified. In fact, one can easily find fault with the manner in which early patent medicine ads were written. The boisterous manner in which advertisers touted that certain tonics could cure anything from sore throats to cancer was bound to offend many.

On the other hand, advertising professionals have engaged in self-policing practices designed to prevent such offensive practices by the less ethical members of the profession. The National Advertising Review Board (NARB), the National Association of Broadcasters (NAB) code, and the network clearance departments are only a few examples of the dedication to upholding ethical standards shown by most members of the advertising community.

Some advertising giants have spoken out against unethical practices. Both David Ogilvy and John O'Toole have published their thoughts on this subject and have suggested that much could still be done to create a better order in advertising's ethical house. This chapter is concerned with posing some ethical

---

[1]Bob Lauterborn, "Ethics: Whose Responsibility?" *Advertising Age,* May 23, 1988, 16.

questions for consideration by advertising students. Many more are not addressed here. This chapter highlights only a few of the most common, and perhaps debated, questions. It is hoped that they will remind our future professionals that their responsibility is multifaceted. The tools available to advertisers are very powerful; they must be used for the purposes for which they were intended, or as Bob Lauterborn eloquently stated in the quote that began this chapter, "to help marketers to respond to consumers' needs efficiently and effectively."

SPECIFIC ISSUES IN ADVERTISING ETHICS

Advertising communication is designed to attract attention and to persuade. The function of persuasion itself has drawn the attention of ethical scholars throughout centuries. The fact that advertisers and others can use verbal or visual images to induce behavior has in itself a somewhat negative connotation. Philosophers have always advocated that those who utilize persuasion must bear the burden of proof that such activity is not harmful in any way to the audience for which it is intended.[2]

Advertising ethics, therefore, is concerned not only with the economic consequences of advertising actions, but also with the direct and indirect social and moral consequences they may have on the public in general. Critics argue that the act of advertising certain products may profoundly affect social values. An example of this argument is the recent debate on the appropriateness of advertising alcoholic beverages.

An examination of what has been written by advertising critics reveals several distinct areas of concern. This chapter will describe some of them.

The Ethics of Creativity

The development of advertising appeals and persuasive messages is aided by the creative ability, imagination, artistry, and wit of professionals. It is no mere accident that advertising has been compared numerous times to show business. Pictures and words, images and double entendres, appeals to emotions and fears have all been generously utilized to secure the attention and the favor of consumers.

The creative aspect of advertising is therefore one of the most vulnerable areas of advertising ethics concern. The responsibility of those who create advertising messages is not merely to ensure that they employ only truthful statements; it goes farther than that. If the overall impression created by the advertising message is misleading to the public, the advertiser could be found in violation of federal regulations. However, an even stricter code could be applied by the review process used by major networks, other media agencies, and the NAB.

---

[2]Donald W. Jugenheimer, "Ethical Rights and the Advertising Audience," in *Papers on Advertising and Ethics*, Advertising Working Papers 12 (Urbana, Ill.: University of Illinois, May 1982), 11.

In addition, some statements and images, even if truthful or not misleading, should be avoided because they are socially offensive. Examples are advertisements that portray women or minorities in a disparaging or socially unacceptable fashion. Cartoon figures such as the Frito-Lay "Frito Bandito" are not immune to such scrutiny.

Explicit words and images are also to be used with discretion and caution. Until recently, any type of nudity was considered socially unacceptable. Now a more common sight in commercials, nudity is not as offensive to most as profanity. While the specific determination of what is socially acceptable varies with time and place, it is important to note that the creative element of advertising should always respect the social standards of morality and good taste.

To be considered ethically acceptable, therefore, advertising messages should be truthful, should not mislead, and should not offend social standards of morality and good taste. It is unfortunate that this rule is often violated by advertisers. Recent examples of commercial messages that have been targets of criticism are the Boston Prepatory Company ad shown in Exhibit 14-1 and the sexually explicit advertising campaign for Calvin Klein products in the early 1990s.

Advertising Controversial Products

Another ethical problem confronting advertisers has to do with the nature of some of the products they promote. Among such products are cigarettes and alcoholic beverages.

Society does not prohibit the manufacture or sale of cigarettes. The advertising and promotion of cigarettes, however, is both regulated and opposed by some groups as an undesirable practice. Cigarettes have been proven harmful to health, and the promotion of a product that may cause cancer is considered unethical because it involves the use of persuasion. Some advertisers have spoken out against this practice and have refused to handle cigarette accounts. David Ogilvy made public his stand on the issue several years ago. Other advertisers have joined in in recent years.

Sam Blum in a 1966 article mentions that there is a code of ethics observed by the cigarette industry. This code insists that advertising neither appeal directly to teenagers nor be based on health claims.[3] This is not enough, however, for those who feel that cigarettes should not be advertised at all. Advertising professionals, therefore, are called upon in this case to establish and observe ethical rules that go beyond legal responsibilities and acceptable industry standards.

A similar problem is the advertising of alcoholic beverages. While it would be difficult to find a large constituency proposing or supporting a ban on the sale and consumption of alcoholic beverages, many support strong restrictions

---

[3]Sam Blum, "An Ode to the Cigarette Code," *Harper's,* March 1966, 60–63.

EXHIBIT 14-1   Boston Prepatory Company Ad

THE REAL AMERICAN DESIGNER.

Source: Courtesy of the Boston Prepatory Company, New York, N.Y.

on advertising for such products. The rationale in the case of alcoholic beverages is very similar to that for cigarettes.

Is it fair to expect advertisers to refrain voluntarily from promoting such products? Should they be empowered to police social behavior and limit the ability of cigarette and alcoholic beverage manufacturers to use mass communications? The question has not been clearly answered and will be debated for years to come, or until regulatory agencies intervene and claim such responsibility.

The Ethics of Using Media

Several ethical issues are directly derived from the use of media by advertising professionals. Among those most debated are advertising during programs directed strictly at children, advertising that is intrusive or annoying because of its frequency, advertising within programs or media vehicles with objectionable content, and using the persuasive powers of the media to promote products that are not socially or economically desirable. One example would be products that are not environmentally sound, such as cleaning products that pollute the water supply. Another example is the advertising of premiums in cereal boxes to promote sales of overpriced items and encourage brand loyalty. This practice has been criticized for leading economically disadvantaged consumers to buy branded food products at a higher cost, when they could achieve the same nutrition goals by purchasing generic or store brands of equal quality. This economically undesirable behavior has been attributed to the promotion and advertising of major national brands. We will briefly discuss each of these.

Advertising Directed to Children.   This topic has had wide public debate. Children are considered more vulnerable and impressionable than average consumers, and advertising directed to them is objectionable on that basis alone. In addition, when advertising messages can be confused with programs, or when they promote products that could be misused or are seen as objectionable (such as drugs or candy), the issue of ethics becomes even more urgent.

Several ethical codes for advertising directed to children have been proposed by advocacy groups, networks, and even advertising practitioners. The debate is still very much alive and will continue for years to come.

Intrusive or Annoying Advertising.   Intrusive or annoying adver-tising—advertising in which the public is repeatedly exposed to the same message—is also a target of debate. However, the controversy in this case is not as heated as that surrounding some of the other issues discussed in this chapter. Intrusive advertising is objectionable to those people who believe it constitutes an invasion of privacy. Advertisers argue that in order to get consumers' attention, they should be allowed to place advertisements within programs and as frequently as they deem necessary.

Advertising Placed in Media Vehicles of Objectionable Content.   Examples of media vehicles which are considered by some as objectionable because of their content are the Playboy channel; MTV; and some periodicals such as *The National Enquirer, Playboy* magazine, or tabloids and magazines with explicit sexual or extremely violent content. This advertising is opposed because it indirectly supports such vehicles economi-cally. It is argued that the objectionable media would not exist if it were not for the income derived from advertising. While there is no clear evidence that this is so, it is important to underscore that when advertising is viewed as supporting media considered immoral or socially undesirable, it becomes an ethical issue.

The Persuasive Powers of the Media. Finally, as media vehicles become more powerful channels of persuasion and entertainment, their usage for the purpose of selling products will be more closely scrutinized by society. In addition, the use of powerful persuasive techniques to promote products such as expensive and faddish toys will be the subject of discussion. Is it ethical to promote gambling even though the practice itself is legal? This topic as well is left to the discretion and judgment of advertising professionals.

These are among the most common ethical issues deriving from the practice of advertising itself. The list is not comprehensive, but it is designed to point out that the content, mechanics, and intended audience of advertising are all important factors when deciding its ethical parameters. Just as lawyers and accountants do, advertisers must consider all these issues when developing a code of ethics for themselves.

Although there is no evidence that subliminal advertising works, advertisers must regularly address a skeptical public's concern about this issue. Failure to deal openly and frankly with the issue of subliminal advertising will only serve to increase public skepticism.

ETHICAL ISSUES INVOLVING CLIENT/AGENCY RELATIONSHIPS

Advertisers aggressively pursue their clients. The same is not true of other professional groups. We do not see accounting firms or law firms making cold calls on prospective clients who are using the services of a competitor. Advertising agencies, however, frequently approach accounts of competitors and try to attract their business through what are commonly known as "speculative presentations."

Other advertising practices might also be viewed as less than desirable if used by other professional groups. For example, the commission given by media to advertisers could be considered a "kickback" as opposed to fair compensation for services.

Criticisms have highlighted those practices and others, such as the misuse of research data and the "industrial espionage," called by some "marketing intelligence," which is often utilized to attract clients to an agency.

The issue of whether advertising professionals have a more lax code of ethics than other professionals has surfaced so often that periodicals such as *Advertising Age* have conducted occasional surveys to assess standards of behavior. An example of such a survey can be seen in Exhibit 14-2.

The discussion is viewed by many as a nonissue. Ethical behavior should be the same for all professionals, regardless of whether they practice advertising or accounting.

EXHIBIT 14-2   How Do Your Ethics Compare with N.Y.?

Do the ethical standards of advertising people in the Big Apple differ from those of their fellow professionals elsewhere in the U.S.?

If you'll answer this questionnaire, we'll find out.

Members of the Advertising Club of New York are completing a similar questionnaire, and *Advertising Age* wants to compare their answers with a national sample.

Ad Age also will supply regional breakouts of the responses so that the ad industry will be able to point to parts of the country in which ethical standards seemingly are highest, lowest or merely borderline.

The questionnaire was created for an ethics seminar being hosted by the Center for Communications on March 16.

Circle your response to each ethical situation.

Deadline is March 19.

Send completed questionnaires to: Ethics Survey, *Advertising Age,* 220 E. 42nd St., Suite 930, New York 10017.

1.   You are competing with three other agencies for the Magnasonic consumer electronics business. Its chief competitor is Rolavision, handled by XYZ Advertising. XYZ's account supervisor on Rolavision has interviewed with you recently for a job. You hire him, specifically to help with the Magnasonic pitch.

1. Ethical   Unethical

2.   A good friend of yours calls and says an associate of his is looking for a new advertising agency. His associate knows little about advertising and has asked for his advice. He offers to recommend your company provided he will be paid a finder's fee of $20,000 if you land the business. You agree.

2. Ethical   Unethical

3.   Same as Question 2, but your friend is in the business of consulting for clients looking for new advertising agencies, and he is being paid a fee by his client.

3. Ethical   Unethical

4.   Your agency is one of four semifinalists asked to participate in a competition for a new product assignment from a major toy marketer. While the agency has had experience in marketing to children, this assignment would be your agency's first in the toy category—and with a leading manufacturer. During a final briefing your prospective client discloses that the "new product" is a compatible set of war toys complete with pseudo-ammunition, guns, etc. Your agency decides that it will accept this assignment if it is awarded to them.

4. Ethical   Unethical

5.   You and two other agencies are in the final stages of a competition. Part of your pitch has to do with recommending and supporting a new marketing strategy. Late one evening, a few days before the scheduled presentation, you are proofing your slides at a slide supply house. By accident, you are handed a fairly complete set of slides put together for one of your competitors. You have enough time to examine and get the gist of it before returning the set to the supplier, who is embarrassed at his mistake. When you return to the office, you make significant changes in the way your agency presents itself so as to attack your competitor's recommended strategy in a direct and forceful manner without, of course, revealing to anyone that you have information on your competitor's actual recommendations.

5. Ethical   Unethical

EXHIBIT 14-2 Continued

6. Same as Question 5, except your competitor's slides are in a file folder on the worktable next to you. You have to wait for the supplier to leave the room before you peek at them.

6. Ethical   Unethical

7. You've been invited to compete for the business of a retail chain that has headquarters in the Southeast. The chain is run autocratically by its 75-year-old founder. Every member of his senior management team is white, male and more than 40 years old. In past discussions, you've come away with a clear impression that they are narrow-minded, too. As it happens, a few months ago your agency lost the business of a large New York retail chain. You did excellent work for the chain, and the account supervisor who knows all about the business still works for you but has been without an assignment for more than three months. The problem is, the account supervisor is a 35-year-old woman. You decide not to use her in your presentation.

7. Ethical   Unethical

8. Same as Question 7 except that your account supervisor is male, 45 years old and black. You decide not to include him in the presentation.

8. Ethical   Unethical

9. Your agency is looking to hire a senior account management person. You interview a management supervisor who promises to bring with him one of the accounts he is responsible for at his current agency if you hire him at the salary he is asking. You hire him, and the account comes to you.

9. Ethical   Unethical

10. You and three other agencies are in a competition for a major airline account. As luck would have it, a good friend of yours is sleeping with the secretary for the airline's marketing VP. She's very indiscreet and tells your friend all about the exciting things going back and forth at her company during the review, including the individual views of the members of the airline's agency selection committee. Your friend gives you feedback on all your meetings and on your competitors' meetings with the airline.

10. Ethical   Unethical

11. Same as Question 10, except your friend asks for a consulting fee, with a bonus if you get the business.

11. Ethical   Unethical

12. Your agency is being considered by a group of restaurants that offers "good tasting" food at low prices. They ask your company to develop a better "price" story since they will soon be cutting their prices even further. When the agency delves into the reasons why the company can continue to serve the same "good tasting" food at even lower prices, it learns that the group has found a supplier of slightly "off" food. While the food is not yet spoiled, it is close to that stage and requires significant additional seasonings and preservatives. Your agency accepts the assignment.

12. Ethical   Unethical

Check one:

☐ Advertiser   ☐ Agency   ☐ Media   ☐ Other

Company location: _____

A PROPOSED SOLUTION TO THE QUESTION OF ADVERTISING ETHICS

According to Donald W. Jugenheimer, a code of ethical standards can be designed to provide a foundation for the measurement of the practice of advertising.[4] He bases his proposed code on three principles espoused by LaCroix.[5]

Four major kinds of rights established by ethical scholars would compose this code: contract rights, merit rights, positive rights, and dignity rights. *Contract rights* are related to any sort of agreement on the part of those establishing a business or private relationship. *Merit rights* are those that accrue to people who have performed actions deserving of reward. The rewards are determined by the specific standards existing for the practice in question, ranging from sports practices to religious practices, for example. *Positive rights* are those derived from legislative or judicial action. Finally, *dignity rights* are those belonging to persons simply because they are persons within a specific social environment.

This system awards rights to parties independent from the specific professional environment under discussion. Therefore, ethical behavior could be assessed on the merits of the behavior itself and not because of its ties to the practice of advertising.

CONCLUSION

E. B. Weiss stated, "In advertising, the too common tendency is to ask 'Is it legal?' If the answer is yes, then presumably advertising has demonstrated its responsibility to society. But what modern society is demanding is that advertising hew more closely to an ethical line, not merely to legal guideposts."[6] This position is shared and supported by many professionals and academicians in advertising. The development of a code of ethics is not an easy task. By definition, ethical behavior is determined by social values, and those are subject to individual interpretation. It is possible, however, to agree on some basic principles of behavior that are acceptable by the vast majority in the profession.

The importance of ethical behavior cannot be belittled or ignored. The survival of professional standards is inherent to the survival of the profession itself. If advertisers are to achieve the respect and stability they desire, they cannot wait for regulation to determine what is acceptable behavior in advertising. They must be proactive and mature, enforcing the type of standards demanded by social interests, human decency, and moral imperatives.

---

[4]*Ibid.,* 12.

[5]W. L. LaCroix, *Principles for Ethics in Business,* rev. ed. (Washington, D.C.: University Press of America, 1979).

[6]E. W. Weiss, "Needed Soon: Mature Advertising for a Mature Society," *Advertising Age,* March 1, 1971, 33.

Suggested Readings

Baker, Sam S. *The Permissible Lie.* Boston: Beacon Press, 1968.

Bayles, Michael D. *Professional Ethics.* Belmont, Calif.: Wadsworth Publishing Company, 1981.

Capitman, William G. "Morality in Advertising: A Public Emperative." *MSU Business Topics* (Spring 1971): 21–26.

"Ethics and Marketing." In Lectures from a Symposium Sponsored by the Merrill Cohen Memorial Fund and the Graduate School of Business Administration of the University of Minnesota, April 1966, edited by J. Russell Nelson and Aubrey Strickland.

Kottman, E. John. "Truth and the Image of Advertising." *Journal of Marketing* 33 (October 1969): 64–66.

Levitt, Theodore. "The Morality(?) of Advertising." *Harvard Business Review* (July–August 1970): 84–92.

Stevens, Edward. *Business Ethics.* New York: Paulist Press, 1979.

Exercises

1. In 1991, Phone Programs USA broadcast an advertisement directed to children for the Phone Program's RoboCop Phone 900 number. The RoboCop character in the commercial urged viewers to help him fight the drug lords, stating, "Your telephone is linked to my weapon system. Call now to activate." The NAD Children's Advertising Review Unit (CARU) questioned the spot because it said it could raise unrealistic expectations among children. Do you agree with CARU's objection? What do you feel Phone Programs USA should do?

Source: Janice Kelly, "NARB to hear Alpo, Gillette Cases," *Advertising Age,* June 24, 1991, 54.

2. After the sales success of some products featured in films, many advertisers are pursuing product placement as an alternative to media purchases. There is growing resistance among consumer advocates, however, to the practice of product placement. It is argued that product placement is another form of subliminal advertising and does not convey any relevant information to consumers. Product placement, they say, uses emotional tools to persuade people to consume products they do not need. What is your position on this subject? Are the consumer advocates' arguments legitimate?

3. A New York organization called the Council on Economic Priorities has sold 200,000 copies of a guide called *Shopping for a Better World.* This 132-page pamphlet lists 1,300 products in alphabetical order and indicates through a special code whether the manufacturer of the product is engaged in practices some may deem unethical or objectionable. Such practices include trading with South Africa, failing to protect the environment, and catching dolphins in fishing nets. Not many products commonly sold by supermarkets are immune to the pamphlet's scrutiny. Do you feel consumers should be informed about corporate practices that may be morally or socially objectionable? Should advertising professionals decline to handle certain accounts because of such corporate practices? Comment.

Source: Joe Queenan, "Ethical Shopping," *Forbes,* April 17, 1989, 80–81.

C A S E   **14 - 1**

The Maryland State Planning Council on Developmental Disabilities

Cathy Raggio, director of the Maryland State Planning Council on Developmental Disabilities (MD), and Barry Smith, president of Smith Burke & Azzam Advertising (SB&A), had reached an impasse in their meeting to discuss the approval of two television commercials. SB&A, a large, full-service agency based in Baltimore, had recently agreed to handle the council as a public service account for no compensation. Since the relationship had been warm up to that point, the impasse came as an embarrassing surprise to everyone involved.

MD had contacted SB&A for assistance with a marketing problem through the Advertising Association of Baltimore (a local trade organization made up of agencies and media and production suppliers). MD was seeking state legislative approval of a bill that would provide funding for services for disabled persons above the age of 21. (The existing law did *not* allow funding of these services.) Although the bill had been introduced in the Maryland legislature on several occasions, it had always been defeated.

In seeking to affect the outcome of the legislative process, SB&A's proposed strategy was direct: *Create vocal public support for passage of the bill, creating pressure on the state legislature.* The agency recommended exclusive reliance on television to deliver emotional messages. Two commercials were recommended:

1. Beginning six weeks before the bill was to be up for a vote, a single 30-second public service announcement (PSA) would be aired for three weeks. The purpose of the spot ("Debbie") was to illustrate that disabled people were not necessarily disabled in terms of their value to society and to personalize the situation faced by disabled adults. (See Exhibit 14-1-1.)

2. Beginning three weeks before the bill was to be up for a vote, a second PSA would begin airing in place of "Debbie." The sole purpose of this spot was to create and document a public outcry for passage of the bill. The recommended TV spot ("John") is presented in Exhibit 14-1-2.

This case was written by Barry L. Smith, Smith Burke & Azzam, and John H. Murphy, The University of Texas at Austin. The case is intended for use in generating class discussion and not to illustrate either the effective or ineffective handling of an administrative situation. Used by permission of Smith Burke & Azzam, Inc.

EXHIBIT 14-1-1 Storyboard of the Proposed "Debbie" Commercial

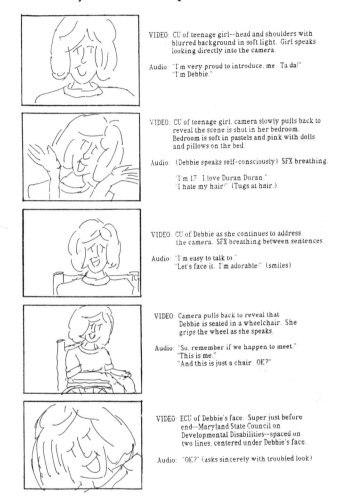

VIDEO: CU of teenage girl--head and shoulders with blurred background in soft light. Girl speaks looking directly into the camera.

Audio: "I'm very proud to introduce, me. Ta da!"
"I'm Debbie."

VIDEO: CU of teenage girl, camera slowly pulls back to reveal the scene is shot in her bedroom. Bedroom is soft in pastels and pink with dolls and pillows on the bed.

Audio: (Debbie speaks self-consciously) SFX breathing.

"I'm 17. I love Duran Duran."
"I hate my hair!" (Tugs at hair.)

VIDEO: CU of Debbie as she continues to address the camera. SFX breathing between sentences.

Audio: "I'm easy to talk to."
"Let's face it. I'm adorable." (smiles)

VIDEO: Camera pulls back to reveal that Debbie is seated in a wheelchair. She grips the wheel as she speaks.

Audio: "So, remember if we happen to meet."
"This is me."
"And this is just a chair. OK?"

VIDEO: ECU of Debbie's face. Super just before end--Maryland State Council on Developmental Disabilities--spaced on two lines, centered under Debbie's face.

Audio: "OK?" (asks sincerely with troubled look)

At the beginning of the meeting to review the agency's recommendations, Raggio and her staff had all responded enthusiastically to the proposed plans. Raggio's immediate response to Smith's description of the commercials was, "Barry, as you describe the action, these should be truly moving commercials that hit people head on. They're just great! Thank you so much for this. When can we start production?"

Smith had indicated that the agency would begin the search immediately for a disabled adult to play the role of "John" and a young woman to play "Debbie." Smith asked for Raggio's assistance in locating an appropriate disabled individual to appear as "John."

Smith stated that the agency would also begin the search for "Debbie" by contacting appropriate actresses on file at the agency plus a number of model

EXHIBIT 14-1-2   Storyboard of the Proposed "John" Commercial

VIDEO: Family seated around dinner table. Father, mother, daughter and son. Light over table dinner dishes are cleared by mother and daughter. Birthday cake is brought in and placed on the table.

Audio: ANN: "Birthdays for John weren't always happy." He was born severely retarded. But though his early years were hard for everyone, there was always hope. Hope through special education provided by the state."

VIDEO: CU of father. Father speaks with love and understanding.

Audio: FATHER: "Happy Birthday, son."

VIDEO: CU of retarded son. Cut to CU of family members singing "Happy Birthday" in the background.

Audio: ANN: "Today John is 21. He got a long way to go. But he can speak. He's learning to read. He thinks it's a happy birthday. He's **wrong**." SFX: Family singing in background ANN VO.

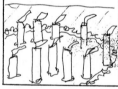

VIDEO: ECU of birthday cake and candles flickering. John takes careful breath and blows out candles.

Audio: ANN: "At 21 the special education program ends. People like John are put on a waiting list for adult programs. Two out of 100 get in. For the rest, the work stops. The learning stops. The hope is gone. (Family continues to sing Happy Birthday in background but it becomes distorted and ends.)

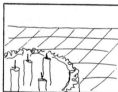

VIDEO: Dissolve from blown out candles to black. Then super of "I've heard about John and I think it's wrong." Then add super at the bottom of first super--Maryland Association of Retarded Citizens. P.O. Box 1957 Baltimore, Maryland 21203.

Audio: ANN: "Please help us change this system. Just write a card or letter that says (add Super) I've heard about John and I think it's wrong. Send it to the (add second Super) Maryland Association for Retarded Citizens. Post Office Box 1957: Baltimore, Maryland.

and talent agencies. At that point in the discussion a puzzled look came over Raggio's face. She strongly objected to the use of anyone other than a disabled person served by the MD. Raggio explained, "One of our missions is to serve disabled persons by helping other people in the general population understand what it's like to be disabled. Who could better communicate this than an actual disabled person? Why, if we were to use an actress and just put her in a wheelchair and the public found out, the Association would look very foolish. I'm sorry, but we *cannot* approve anyone appearing as Debbie except a real handicapped person."

Smith responded by pointing out that the agency wanted the best actress—disabled or not. He stressed that he could help disabled people more by creating a great commercial than by hiring one disabled person for a single

PSA spot with a talent fee of $200. Further, he explained that his agency had built its reputation on outstanding creative work. To produce such work required that clients trust the agency's judgment in the creative area. Finally, he stated that the agency would refuse to do the spots unless it was unrestricted in the selection of talent.

Raggio shook her head and said there was nothing more to discuss.

Smith concluded the meeting by stating, "Well, I trust you people understand where we're coming from on this and why. I hope you will change your minds after you have had time to think it over. Our agency sincerely wants to produce what would be most effective and, hence, best for Maryland Disabilities and the people you serve. Let's discuss this again tomorrow after we've both had a chance to mull it over some."

Questions for Discussion and Review

1. Would the use of an actress to play the part of a handicapped person in the commercial constitute deceptive advertising?

2. How does the fact that the MD is a nonprofit organization and a public service account for the agency enter into an evaluation of the situation?

3. Should the client meet its agency's demand and agree to give the agency creative control over casting?

4. Is there some sort of compromise that might be agreeable to both parties?

5. How important is creative control by an advertising agency in developing outstanding advertising? Are there situations where it is more important than others?

6. How often do similar situations surface in client/agency relationships?

C A S E **14 - 2**

Healthmax

Six months ago, Mediacom, an advertising agency located in the Southeastern United States, won the Healthmax account. At the time, agency management was elated to win this account, even though its current billings of $5 million a year made it one of the smallest in the shop.

This case was written by Linda M. Scott, University of Illinois at Urbana–Champaign. This case is not intended to represent the personalities or policies of any actual persons or corporations. The case itself was designed to serve as the basis for classroom discussion and not to illustrate the effective or ineffective handling of an administrative situation. Used by permission.

Healthmax was a fast-growing health maintenance organization (HMO). With facilities in 15 states and some of the country's largest corporations as members, it was one of the biggest HMOs in the United States—and sure to get bigger. Mediacom expected that Healthmax's advertising campaigns, which were presently conducted on a market-by-market basis, would "go national" within 18 months and that billings would exceed $25 million within two years.

In the mid-1980s, health maintenance organizations had become a popular answer to the rising costs of employer-subsidized health insurance. The price of medical care had increased substantially over the previous decade, causing the cost of maintaining traditional policies to become burdensome to the employers that offered them. Most companies offered policies that allowed their employees to visit the doctor or hospital of their choice in the event of illness. The insurance company would pay 80 percent of expenses, after annual deductibles had been paid. Usually, no preventative treatments or programs were covered—not even immunizations for small children, which could be very expensive for the parents. Under this system, none of the parties directly responsible for the health care transaction—doctors, hospitals, or patients— had any real incentive to keep the cost of illness down. On the contrary, the fear of malpractice suits on the part of the medical establishment, coupled with increasing "consumerism" among patients, resulted in more second opinions, tests, and other expensive safeguards. As a result, the premiums for these policies were soaring.

Health maintenance organizations offered an alternative. Under this kind of system, employees and their families became members of a health care organization that usually included private doctors of all specialties, as well as a hospital run by the HMO. Employers and employees paid a set amount every month for membership, regardless of the employees' present health condition. Then, when a member became ill, he or she received whatever care was needed at no additional cost. This frequently even included prescriptions. There was no deductible. Preventative care programs, including immuniza- tions for children, were not only covered, but encouraged, in order to control illness and thus keep costs down.

Keeping the costs down, in fact, was the name of the game for HMOs. With a fixed income coming in from corporations, the organization's mission became managing the cost of delivering the necessary services. Therefore, "unnecessary" tests were eliminated. Shorter hospital stays were mandated. Second opinions, however, were encouraged, since the time of a second doctor was cheaper than most major procedures. In many organizations like Healthmax, both doctors' offices and hospital units were evaluated periodically as profit centers, so physicians and nurses were held responsible for maintaining margins by controlling the cost of procedures performed. It is important to note that all patient members were required to seek treatment from the HMO's doctors or hospitals for any condition. The only exception was a certifiable emergency that occurred in a town in which there was no organization-owned facility.

It seemed to be a scheme in which everyone won. Employees had ongoing health care at minimal costs, the corporation could control its premium, and the HMO had to take responsibility for its own cost structure. Healthmax had grown rapidly in the first flush of enthusiasm for the concept. Mediacom saw this account as a terrific entrée into the future of services and the burgeoning health care industry.

Healthmax, like most HMOs but unlike most hospitals, was run by management professionals instead of by doctors. Although it had been founded by a physician and had physician board members in each of its local facilities, the doctors had little actual influence. Instead, there were MBAs at every level. The top management included the founder and his daughter, he a doctor and she an MBA, and the daughter's husband, a former accountant, who was now in charge of marketing.

It was the marketing manager, Jason Edwards, who was Mediacom's contact person. Under his guidance, the agency was to develop advertising with a complex mission. A consumer-oriented campaign was to act as a pull-through mechanism by getting employees to ask their employer to provide the option of choosing an HMO; once an employer adopted Healthmax, the campaign would presumably help encourage more employees to enroll in that program, rather than choose the traditional health insurance option. Few companies offered only an HMO.

Despite the agency's initial optimism, management of the account had proven problematic. After six months, no advertisements had been produced. Agency and client had been unable to agree on a creative strategy or a target audience. The client, who was unfamiliar with marketing practices, apparently saw no need for clear strategic agreements yet was angry when creative ideas presented did not fit his ill-defined personal expectations. The continued disagreement and inertia had strained relations between agency and client— Edwards would no longer speak to anyone at the agency except the general manager, Steve Shea.

Therefore, when the Philadelphia office of the agency called asking to transfer one of its account supervisors whose husband was relocating, Shea was delighted for the opportunity to change account managers. The new supervisor, Emily Stanton, was an MBA with "packaged goods" experience and had a string of award-winning campaigns to her credit. Shea felt her credentials would impress Edwards, who was beginning to complain that the present managers were "unprofessional." And, in fact, when Shea called Edwards with the news, the client was very pleased, remarking that he "would be glad to be working with someone who knew something about business for a change."

Stanton arrived within a month, grateful to the agency for accommodating her need to move and determined to turn the account around. But she found her account team discouraged, demoralized, and untrusting. She called the first client meeting to explore the issue of target audience. She had studied what demographics were available; however, since 80 percent of American citizens were covered by health insurance of some kind, the campaign's demographics were identical to those of the population. The target audience, therefore, would have to be defined according to the likelihood that a given group would respond to the benefits offered by Healthmax. That meant that the benefit and the target would be defined simultaneously.

Stanton felt that the benefits offered to families with children, such as preventative health care, maternity benefits, and "well-baby care," were the most impressive and would appeal to the largest audience. The enormous expense of "uncovered" health care for a small child was fresh in her mind, as her own baby was only eight months old. However, she wanted to hear Edwards' thoughts on the subject, see any information the company might have on its members, and generally give a strong appearance of wanting to work as a team with the client to make this decision.

Edwards joined the agency team in the meeting room promptly. Stanton tried to appear cheerful, though her colleagues at the table were unanimously sullen. She opened, "Jason, we're here today to talk about the target audience for the new Healthmax campaign. We have done our homework and have a few ideas, but I'd like for this meeting to be an exploratory session in which we share thoughts and information and work toward a consensus about the target." Edwards smiled and nodded, indicating that he was pleased with her attitude. She continued, "What can you tell us about the present members' demographic profile?"

"Well, Emily, it's just what you would expect. Families are drawn to Healthmax because of the benefits of immunization and ongoing care for generally healthy children. But what we need to do is concentrate not on the kind of people we have now, but on those we wish to attract. And that is a function of the profitability of procedures that people in different demographic groups are most likely to have. For example, I can tell you that one thing we have too many of right now is married women. We lose money on maternity care and childbirth. While we make a moderate margin on the care of children, the big profits are in other kinds of procedures."

"For example?"

"Well, our biggest money-maker in terms of both margin and volume is 'therapeutic abortions.' Technically, those are abortions given to protect the mother's health. It's a bit of a euphemism, however, since a health reason can almost always be found, even if it's 'emotional' health. Now, major surgeries and diseases can also be profitable, especially among the elderly, because of special arrangements with Medicare. But to be perfectly honest, the fact that patients can't choose another doctor or hospital becomes a touchy subject when major illnesses occur. So, I'd really like to see us concentrate on selling abortions. Since you're a real businessperson yourself, I'm sure you can see why."

"Maybe so, but I can't see us doing a campaign that encourages abortions—surely the public and member relations fallout from such a campaign would be too damaging," replied Stanton, trying to find an acceptable weakness in this approach, which she found distasteful.

"Hey, you're the ad folks!" He elbowed her conspiratorially, winking. "You guys can say these things without really saying it, can't you?"

Stanton laughed nervously, and answered, "That's the public perception of advertising, Jason, but the truth is that a clear statement of an advertiser's message has enough trouble cutting through the clutter. A veiled message would be a poor use of media dollars."

Jason pulled back in mock amazement. "Are you telling me you can't do it? Maybe I had better find an agency that's a little more creative!"

Deciding to salvage whatever positive step she could from the meeting, Stanton offered, "Jason, let's agree to target single adult females. That would be an important accomplishment for today. I'd like to talk to my creative people about how to handle such a delicate topic before committing to you to do this kind of campaign. I'll get back to you next week—would that meet with your timetable?"

"Hey," answered Edwards, smiling tensely, "I've already waited six months! We thought Mediacom was a real hot, 'can-do' agency when we hired you. Let's see some of that now. Let's agree to have rough storyboards next week, targeted to single women. Make it soft, make it palatable. But make sure that the promise of safe, confidential, judgment-free abortions comes through."

Back at the agency, Stanton went directly to Shea's office. She closed the door and told him what had happened. He was shocked and dismayed but reminded her, "The Healthmax business is important to this agency, Emily. Let's not blow it. Surely there's some way around this. Some way to give him what he wants without compromising ourselves. Work with him."

"Can't we go around him? Are we sure that his bosses know what's going on here?"

"Are you kidding? The next level up is the man's own wife. After that, it's his father-in-law, who doesn't want to be bothered to do anything but make the press conferences. Forget it. We work with Edwards."

"Steve, what are we going to say in this copy? How can we live with ourselves knowing we may be pushing women into getting abortions when the real purpose is to save Healthmax money?"

Steve was silent for a moment and then said quietly, "Listen, Emily, we're not going to make anybody get an abortion. Abortion is a private, personal decision that a woman has to make for herself. If we're informing her of a safe alternative that keeps her from having to shop abortion clinics and getting into God knows what kind of terrible situation, what's wrong with that?"

Emily exploded. "I'll tell you what's wrong with it! In this case, her regular physician is operating out of a 'profit center,' not a doctor's office. That means that the person she'll turn to for advice and support has a vested interest in encouraging her to choose abortion. And she doesn't have any choice about where she seeks her advice—she's stuck getting any health service she needs from Healthmax."

"Emily, I really think that's unfair. The Healthmax doctors are still doctors. And I think you're underestimating the target's ability to make her own decisions. I also think you're overreacting to what's been asked of us. Go get your creative guys together. Work up some nice little campaign like . . . I don't know . . . 'It's your right to choose.' That will be ambiguous under the circumstances. Maybe the key visual is some healthy-looking girl in a jogging suit. Bury the abortion bit in the body copy . . . something like that."

"And if he wants it clearer than that? Like really heavy-handed?"

"We'll think about resigning the account."

The words felt like blows. They were both quiet for a minute.

"The guy's a jerk anyway. It's not worth all of this."

"Emily! This is an important account—and I expect you to treat it that way."

"Sorry. I'll call a meeting of the creative team for tomorrow morning."

As she left Shea's office, Stanton wondered if she was overreacting. She had to admit to herself that she still wanted to turn the account around—it would ruin her track record to fail. She still felt warm gratitude toward the agency for helping her to relocate when her husband was transferred and she herself barely back from maternity leave. This was the least she could do in return. By six o'clock, Stanton had convinced herself she could handle it. But later that night, as she put her own child to bed, she had to recognize a little twinge of conscience.

Questions for Discussion and Review

1. What is the agency's responsibility for this client's communication strategy?

2. Is there any way to compromise on this issue? Any way to "say it without saying it"?

3. What about Steve Shea's argument that the advertising is just providing information to a consumer who will make her own decisions? Is that valid?

4. Is Emily Stanton overreacting? What should she do?

5. Should the agency consider resigning this account? If so, why, and at what point should it resign?

6. What role should an individual's personal values play in such situations? Would the quality of the agency's efforts be likely to be affected by the misgivings of a member of the account team?

CASE **14 - 3**

Abel, Atwater and Combs Advertising and Public Relations

Robert Abel, a principal of Abel, Atwater and Combs (AAC), was delighted when an intermediate-sized Santa Clara Valley vintner invited AAC to compete with three other agencies for its account. While the vintner's ad budget of $200,000 was not impressive, Abel believed the prospective client held

---

This case was written by John H. Murphy, The University of Texas at Austin. The case is designed to serve as the basis for classroom discussion and not to illustrate either the effective or ineffective handling of an administrative situation. The identities of the firms involved have been disguised.

considerable potential for growth and the account would add prestige to the agency. Also, as a wine connoisseur, he relished the thought of working with this vintner due to its excellent reputation.

AAC was a well-established San Francisco advertising and public relations agency with media billings of just over $23 million the previous year. The agency had 58 employees and served 37 clients. The agency's clients had traditionally been weighted toward business-to-business and industrial accounts. Its largest account was a manufacturer of commercial transportation and industrial vehicles. In addition, AAC handled a wide range of smaller consumer and retail accounts. These accounts included a regional supermarket chain and two noncompetitive automobile dealerships.

Abel was somewhat surprised to discover that his partner, Judith Atwater, did *not* share his enthusiasm for pitching the wine account. Atwater quoted statistics from MADD (Mothers Against Drunk Driving) in expressing her concerns about pitching any alcoholic beverage.

Atwater: "Alcohol-related automobile accidents killed 24,000 people and injured 670,000 others last year. I don't know how much of that was due to wine advertising, but I'm not sure I want any part of promoting alcoholic beverages, even if we could use the business. Two of my son's best friends at Palo Alto High School were seriously injured last summer after a drinking party. I shudder everytime I think about it."

Abel: "Judy, we're not talking about getting people drunk and encouraging them to drive cars. Nor would we be suggesting consumption by teenagers. Further, there is a real question about the effects of booze advertising. I believe those who point out that it just causes brand switching and does not increase consumption. Besides, we need this account, and if we don't pitch for it, someone else will be happy to take the account."

Atwater: "Bob, those are simply rationalizations. I don't think anyone could deny that alcoholic beverage advertising glamorizes drinking and portrays it as an important part of today's life-styles. Teenagers seem particularly susceptible to influence by such advertising. Given all the negative consequences associated with drinking, this is troubling. I'm not at all certain that going after this account would be the right course for us to follow. Over the past several months I've been asking myself some questions about the ethics of advertising any alcoholic beverage."

Abel: "Although we do not have much time to decide if we are going to pitch the account, I can tell this is an important issue for you. I respect that. Why don't we put together a position paper laying out the pros and cons of having an alcoholic beverage client? It seems to me that this paper should address both the issues of the ethics of helping to promote alcohol consumption and the effects of such advertising. This would help focus our thinking in deciding whether or not we want to go after this account."

Questions for Discussion and Review

1. Are Atwater's misgivings about working on an alcoholic beverage account reasonable? Is it appropriate for an advertising person to express such concerns? Why or why not?

2. What key ethical, business, and practical issues or considerations should be considered by Abel and Atwater in reaching a decision about whether to pitch the wine account? Which of these issues or considerations are most important? Why?

3. Should the agency pitch the wine account? What rationale supports your recommendation?

4. What other product or service categories logically could pose the same or similar types of dilemmas for advertising and marketing people?

C A S E   **14 - 4**

Decker, Villani & Bishop

Decker, Villani & Bishop (DV&B) was a relatively large regional advertising agency based in Charlotte, North Carolina. The agency had a growing stable of accounts with annual billings approaching $59.4 million. With only 87 employees, DV&B was unusually profitable for an agency its size. DV&B was not well known outside North Carolina, but the advertising community in the state regarded the agency as a progressive, reliable, marketing-driven shop.

MAJOR CLIENT: THE OLD NORTH STATE BANK

DV&B's largest single account (accounting for 21 percent of income and 26 percent of profits) was the Old North State Bank, or ONS. Branch banking was common in North Carolina, and the largest banks had over 100 branches, with commensurate assets and advertising budgets. ONS was one of the larger banking operations in the state, though far smaller than such regional banking powers as NationsBank and Wachovia. ONS was also one of the more aggressive operations, openly boasting of its intentions to become the largest bank in the state within five years. To achieve this goal, ONS relied on strong customer relations and innovative financial services to retain present customers and attract new ones. ONS was also a believer in advertising, making heavy use of newspaper, radio, and outdoor media.

Six years earlier, DV&B had been the surprise winner when ONS had invited five agencies to participate in an intensive competitive review. DV&B

This case was written by George R. Franke, Virginia Polytechnic Institute and State University, and John H. Murphy, The University of Texas at Austin, to serve as the basis for classroom discussion, and not to illustrate either the effective or ineffective handling of an administrative situation. The individuals and the situations described in the case have been disguised.

had been the smallest agency competing for the account, but a dynamic presentation, a solid creative record, and good chemistry between the agency principals and the bank officials had overcome the efforts of the larger and better-known agencies. Since landing the account, DV&B had assigned its most talented employees to work on ONS's advertising and had grown along with the bank.

Rick Villani, a founder of DV&B, had the ultimate responsibility for servicing the ONS account. Mary Burnett was the ONS account manager and was in charge of day-to-day activities on the account. Working for her were two assistant account executives and a management trainee. Janet Decker supervised the creative teams working on ONS advertising.

Villani commented on the ONS account:

Many people in the agency business feel that when we landed the Old North State account we came of age. I happen to disagree — we'd been doing top-flight work for our clients since the agency started—but getting ONS did put us on the map as a regional advertising agency.

We've been fortunate enough to earn several creative and marketing awards for our work for ONS. We've been able to use the high visibility of ONS to land other clients and attract new talent to the agency. The credit for this is due to a great working relationship between the bank's management and our own. Our talents combine with theirs to produce a payoff at the bottom line for everyone involved.

DV&B'S ACCOUNT MANAGEMENT TRAINING PROGRAM

One year before, DV&B had instituted an account management training program. The purpose of the program was to provide new assistant account executives with exposure to all aspects of the agency's operation, and to groom them for rapid movement into positions of account responsibility. The program required a year to complete and involved assignment to the various functional departments of the agency for a period of several months each. In addition, the program involved seminars and assignments made by top management of the agency.

After a year's experience with the program, DV&B's management was largely satisfied with the results, but there was general concern over the drain on agency resources. Not only were the trainees relatively unproductive for much of the year, they required time to teach and supervise. Changes were planned for the second year of the program to give the trainees meaningful assignments and real responsibilities more quickly than before.

To fill the two available positions for the second year of the training program, DV&B interviewed undergraduate and MBA students at several universities in North and South Carolina. After an initial campus interview, the most promising candidates were invited to spend a day at the agency. During the day the interviewees met with all of DV&B's top account, creative, media, and other administrative executives. After considerable discussion among DV&B's executives, a consensus was reached regarding which individuals should receive an offer.

Karen Watkins, a recent graduate with a concentration in advertising and marketing, was one of two individuals hired to enter the second year of the program. "One of my strengths is that I can see what needs to be done and then do it," she had said in an interview. "I work well with other people, but I don't need a team backing me up or anyone holding my hand." Although several individuals involved in the selection process were impressed with Watkins and thought she was the kind of aggressive self-starter DV&B wanted, several others had reservations about her maturity and motivation. As a result of the divided opinions, she had not been contacted during the first round of offers but was offered a position after two other candidates had turned the job down.

Watkins had entered the management training program with high expectations about her future at DV&B. Overall, during her first six weeks at the agency she had done a solid job of handling her responsibilities and showing initiative. Her mandatory review after one month was positive with two exceptions: (1) Her attitude toward tasks she regarded as menial was poor—for example, she did not feel she should be asked to do store checks for a package-goods client, and her performance on the task was sloppy; and (2) she seemed to resent having to work late and on weekends, especially when the other trainee, working on different accounts, was able to leave.

On the positive side, she was a very hard worker on projects that interested her. On her own initiative, she had written a lengthy memo about several small businesses in the Charlotte area that she believed had substantial growth potential with the right kind of advertising. She also impressed her supervisors with her intelligence, her knowledge of the basics of the advertising business, and her intuitive feeling for what would work and what wouldn't. In addition, she got along extremely well with other people and clearly possessed the interpersonal skills necessary for account work.

A MAJOR FOUL-UP ON THE ONS ACCOUNT

Early on a Sunday morning Villani received a telephone call from Mary Burnett, who had just been stunned by a phone call from her good friend, the marketing vice-president at ONS. The vice-president was extremely upset about an error he had just found in the ONS ad in the "Homes" section of the Sunday paper. Instead of offering fixed-rate home mortgages at a competitive 9 percent, the rate shown in the ad was an unbelievable 5 percent—the first-year rate for an adjustable mortgage. The ad stated that the rate offer was good for one week but did not include any qualifications concerning the availability of funds or "first come, first served." Ironically, the ad's headline read, "Old North State challenges *anyone* to offer a better mortgage deal." At 5 percent, ONS could be sure that no one would.

The ad had been placed through the Newspaper Association of America's Newsplan in every major Sunday newspaper in North Carolina and several minor ones, covering such cities as Charlotte, Wilmington, Raleigh, and Durham. This meant that the ad had been received in over 1,000,000 homes. Even though the largest papers were distributed over a wide area, DV&B felt it was important to give ONS a "hometown" image by placing ads in local papers. Thus, some readers of the Greenville *Daily Reflector* might also have seen the ad in the Raleigh *News & Observer,* for example. The cost to ONS for running the quarter-page, black-and-white ad was over $10,000.

The vice-president had posed several questions to Burnett, which she needed Villani's help in answering: What steps needed to be taken to prepare for the onslaught of delighted home buyers that ONS could expect on Monday morning and during the week? How did the mistake happen? And if it were DV&B's fault, what did the agency intend to do about it?

Villani suggested to Burnett that they and the creative team handling the ONS assignment should meet at the DV&B office shortly after lunch that day. If necessary, others working on the ONS account could be involved later in the day. She agreed and promised that she would find out who was responsible for the mistaken figure in the ad by that time. Villani said he would make the necessary phone calls and hung up.

Burnett knew that it was her job to prevent such foul-ups from happening, so the responsibility for the situation was hers. However, she knew that she was not directly to blame, and she had a good idea who was. She immediately drove to the office and confirmed her suspicion. The original copy for the ad was correct, but unfortunately, the error had occurred during production within the agency. The mechanical artwork with the 5 percent figure had been approved by Karen Watkins. Burnett had assigned Watkins the task of proofing the ONS ad, stressing to her the importance of the task and the necessity of asking for help if she needed it. Clients typically sign off on creative work before it is given to the media, but ONS maintained that proofreading was DV&B's job, not the bank's. Until Watkins' failure to catch the error made in setting up the ad, ONS had never had a reason to regret this policy. Wondering how Watkins could have made such an unfortunate mistake, Burnett started to prepare for the upcoming meeting.

On Monday morning, Watkins found a note on her desk asking her to meet with the account manager and Villani as soon as she arrived. Hurrying to Villani's office and totally unaware of the foul-up, she thought that this was an exciting way to start her seventh week at DV&B.

Questions for Discussion and Review

1. How serious was the foul-up? Must ONS honor the offer? If not, what can it tell its customers on Monday?

2. What is DV&B's best course of action? The bank's? Is there some way to turn this situation into an advertising/promotional/public relations *opportunity?*

3. What action should DV&B take regarding Karen Watkins? If you were Villani, what questions would you ask Watkins and the account manager before making a decision?

4. How might such a problem have been avoided?

C A S E   **14 - 5**

Barrymore Brothers Supermarkets, Inc.

Barrymore Brothers (BB) was a large regional supermarket chain with stores in three southwestern states. Throughout the region, the chain had an excellent reputation in terms of the quality of its produce and meats, its prices, its service, and number of convenient locations. In addition, the chain was among the largest retail advertisers in both print and broadcast media in all of the markets it served.

In Central City, where BB held well over a 50 percent market share, the local newspaper, *The Banner-Tribune (B-T)*, had come to rely on BB for a major advertising schedule that included full-page ads and spreads not only on food day (Thursday) but also on other days during the week. The *B-T* was the only major newspaper in Central City and enjoyed a household penetration of 63 percent daily and 74 percent on Sunday. BB's advertising provided an important source of linage and revenue for the *B-T*. At the same time, Andrea James, BB's executive vice-president in charge of marketing, attributed a significant portion of the firm's success in Central City to a consistent advertising schedule in the *B-T*.

James believed that it was important to keep BB's advertising fresh and in tune with grocery shoppers' concerns—to deal with, as she put it, "more than just price specials. To respond to our customers' needs. To illustrate that Barrymore is a concerned member of the local communities we serve. . . ."

So, for example, BB had addressed nutritional labeling, tamper-resistant packaging, and unit pricing in past advertising. Present shopper concerns focused on the effect on grocery prices of a devastating drought that had hit farmers throughout the United States. The drought had received extensive news coverage during the spring and early summer as its effects became more severe. To respond to these concerns, BB announced in its advertising and in-store promotion beginning the last week in June that BB would freeze all prices at their present levels until October 1. BB's message was that this policy made BB "your insurance against the rising costs of the drought."

In the Monday, August 15, *B-T*, an editorial column questioning BB's real motives in announcing the price freeze appeared under the byline of an editorial writer. Under the headline "Barrymore's Price Freeze a Sham?" the author questioned whether the chain would experience any major price

---

This case was written by John H. Murphy, The University of Texas at Austin. The case is designed to serve as the basis of classroom discussion and not to illustrate either the effective or ineffective handling of an administrative situation. The identities of the firms have been disguised.

increases related to the drought until after October 1 anyway. If not, the author suggested that the freeze might not be hurting BB or protecting shoppers. The editorial also pointed out that the real purpose of the freeze might be to prepare shoppers so they would not complain about major price jumps after October 1. While not directly referring to BB, the author concluded her editorial by discussing other questionable "price special" marketing practices used by supermarkets. The editorial was accompanied by a cartoon that portrayed a BB board of directors meeting in which the directors were applauding the presentation of a cartoon plan showing consumers distracted by the words "price freeze" while a giant screw moved toward them from behind (see Exhibit 14-5-1).

On Tuesday morning, August 16, James met with Clarke Barrymore, president of BB, to discuss the editorial and what action they might take in response. Barrymore was upset by the editorial and stated that he favored suspending all advertising in the *B-T* for at least the next month. Barrymore stressed that the fact of the matter was that substantial price increases had already occurred and were anticipated to escalate prior to October 1. To support his point, Barrymore cited a Washington source who indicated that the Department of Commerce would report later in the week that "grocery prices jumped 1.4 percent in July, the biggest monthly increase in over four years, as the drought's effects reached supermarket checkout counters."

Barrymore stated that he was shocked that management at the *B-T* would run such an editorial without checking the facts with BB first. He noted that BB

EXHIBIT 14-5-1   Cartoon That Accompanied the *Banner-Tribune* Editorial

Source: Art Courtesy of Randy Tatum.

had been one of the *B-T*'s largest advertisers for over 20 years, and this was the thanks they received.

Barrymore concluded their meeting by asking James to prepare a recommendation as to what actions BB should take in response to the editorial. James was asked to report her recommendation to the executive committee at a special breakfast meeting the next morning. Finally, Barrymore instructed James to arrange a meeting to discuss the matter with the *B-T* publisher, Gary Sullivan, and ad director, Karen Carter, for the next afternoon at 2:00 P.M.

Questions for Discussion and Review

1. What impact is the editorial likely to have on consumer attitudes toward BB? What considerations influence your response to this question?

2. Did the *B-T* act responsibly in running the editorial?

3. What course of action should James recommend?

4. What should be the relationship between the editorial side and the advertising side of the media? How often do such conflicts arise?

C A S E　　14 - 6

ComputerCraft

In December, KTRH-AM and KLOL-FM, sister stations in Houston, Texas, owned by the Rusk Corporation, released the details of their annual "client promotional trip." Previous trip destinations had included the South of France, the Caribbean, and many others over the years, and the announcements were always eagerly anticipated by the stations' sales reps (who could qualify for trips) and their advertisers. The stations did a magnificent job of finding an exotic locale and working with travel specialists to put together an all-expenses-paid gift to their clients and incentive reward for their sales force. As with many other media companies, the objective of this package was to thank good clients, reward performance by the sales staff, build relationships, and most importantly, generate incremental business for the station.

This case was written by Bill Penczak, vice-president and group account supervisor of Fogarty & Klein/Winius Brandon. The case is intended for use in generating class discussion and not to illustrate either the effective or ineffective handling of an administrative situation. Used by permission.

KTRH-AM had an all-news format. As with most such formats, listeners tended to be upper income, male, and within the 35–54 age group. The station had an excellent qualitative audience profile, and even though it was an AM format, consistently ranked among the top five or six stations in the Houston Arbitron ratings. Advertisers selling business products, such as banking or computers, or high-ticket items, such as luxury automobiles, usually included the station in their radio buys. Because of its high average quarter-hour ratings, especially during morning drive time, and the excellent qualitative audience, KTRH commanded some of the highest unit-cost spots in the Houston radio market.

The ComputerCraft division of Businessland, Inc., had recently become an extensive user of radio. When Fogarty & Klein (F&K) had won the ComputerCraft account in an agency review six months ago, one of the agency's recommendations was to limit the use of newspaper and include radio as a larger part of ComputerCraft's media mix. While radio was traditionally a mass-audience vehicle, the agency suggested that the addition of the right radio stations—those with formats that attracted the target audience of upscale, male business decision makers—would, in some cases, double the frequency of exposure and increase media reach by one-third over a four-week period.

In early January, the KTRH rep made a presentation to the media planner and the account team at F&K who worked on the ComputerCraft account. The agency had already placed a significant schedule with the station, especially in the fourth quarter, when year-end decisions and manufacturer rebates spiked personal computer sales. The gist of the presentation was that the stations were putting together their annual promotional trip and that ComputerCraft would qualify for a trip for two to Istanbul, Turkey, by spending $12,000 more with KTRH-AM before the deadline of March 31.

The problem was that although the agency had planned a radio flight in late March and April, it had not planned to spend that dollar level on KTRH. The flight, which had already been budgeted and approved by ComputerCraft, had allocated approximately $6,000 to KTRH, and about half that was scheduled after the deadline. The scheduling was based on historical sales during the period, and the flight included some other stations that delivered the target effectively.

Questions for Discussion and Review

1. What about the option of moving dollars from secondary stations already scheduled? What other options might the agency suggest? What should the role of the account manager be in this situation?

2. What should F&K recommend to its client, who had expressed some interest in the trip?

3. Providing perquisites such as tickets and lunches is a common business practice. Do they impact the decisions of a media planner of integrity? What policies should be established to prevent problems in this area?

Media Costs Data[a]

ELECTRONIC MEDIA

Network Television (1990 to 1991)
Prime Time (ABC, CBS, NBC)
Unit Costs and Efficiencies

		Avg. 30-Second Commercial		
			CPM	
	Unit Cost	Homes	Women 25–54	Adults 25–54
Fall 1991	$ 92,600–126,000	$7.70–13.50	$18.00–22.00	$10.40–17.30
Winter 1992	104,700–119,500	7.50–16.00	17.50–21.00	10.00–15.20
Spring 1992	98,300–132,600	9.10–17.20	23.50–27.50	13.00–20.70
Summer 1992	70,100– 94,600	8.20–14.10	19.00–26.00	12.50–22.70

NOTE: Cost-per-thousand (CPM) range reflects long-term network guarantees.

Spot Television (1991)
Costs Cumed by Market Groups

		Cost/HH Rtg. Point			
Markets	% U.S. TV HH	Prime Time	Daytime	Early Evening	Late Evening
Top 10	31	$ 5,234	$1,521	$1,722	$2,253
Top 20	45	7,280	2,148	2,479	3,294
Top 30	54	8,832	2,657	3,100	4,133
Top 40	61	9,686	2,959	3,461	4,644
Top 50	67	10,472	3,229	3,815	5,101
Top 60	72	11,070	3,434	4,072	5,442
Top 70	76	11,539	3,597	4,291	5,729
Top 80	80	11,971	3,752	4,482	5,977
Top 90	83	12,344	3,892	4,652	6,193
Top 100	86	12,709	4,027	4,813	6,410

Source: *Media Market Guide*, 4th Quarter projections. *(continued)*

[a]The information presented in this appendix is taken from the *1992 Leo Burnett Media Costs & Coverage* guide and is reproduced by permission. This widely used and accepted guide is prepared annually by the Leo Burnett agency. For more information, write to the Media Research Department; Leo Burnett U.S.A.; 35 West Wacker Drive; Chicago, Illinois 60601.

ELECTRONIC MEDIA *continued*

	Spot Radio (1991) Cost per Metro Area Rating Point Summary				
Markets	**Men 18–34**	**Men 25–54**	**Women 18–34**	**Women 25–54**	**Teens 12–17**
Top 10	$1,190	$1,600	$1,168	$1,537	$ 767
Top 20	1,665	2,231	1,635	2,150	1,090
Top 30	2,045	2,771	2,004	2,676	1,377
Top 40	2,319	3,180	2,273	3,065	1,570
Top 50	2,547	3,537	2,499	3,412	1,753
Top 60	2,741	3,808	2,685	3,668	1,890
Top 70	2,880	4,011	2,823	3,861	2,003
Top 80	2,999	4,205	2,932	4,041	2,094
Top 90	3,110	4,380	3,033	4,201	2,175
Top 100	3,204	4,526	3,124	4,331	2,245

Source: *Media Market Guide,* 4th Quarter 1991.

OUT-OF-HOME MEDIA

	Outdoor (1991)					
Data for Top 100 Core Markets						
	100 GRPs			**50 GRPs**		
Markets	**No. of Reg. Panels**	**No. of Ill. Panels**	**Monthly Cost**	**No. of Reg. Panels**	**No. of Ill. Panels**	**Monthly Cost**
Top 10	717	2,226	$1,591,447	393	1,162	$ 858,143
Top 20	1,199	3,114	2,223,772	664	1,610	1,186,056
Top 30	1,638	4,599	3,240,169	888	2,366	1,710,401
Top 40	1,878	5,094	3,558,072	1,017	2,620	1,878,496
Top 50	2,301	5,673	3,982,851	1,250	2,913	2,110,538
Top 100	3,748	7,223	5,156,465	2,046	3,710	2,740,123

Note: In addition to standard posting, painted display bulletins may be purchased in most major markets. These are known as "rotaries" because they usually are moved from site to site on a 60-day cycle. Painted bulletins typically measure 14′ x 48′ as compared with 12′ x 25′ for standard posters.

Source: Institute of Outdoor Advertising.

PRINT MEDIA

Newspapers (1991)
**Cost and Coverage Cumed
By Top Market Groups**

Daily newspapers in each market are included on the basis of circulation rank, until the combined circulations exceed 50% coverage of the market.

Market	No. of Papers	No. of Homes (000)	Total Circ. (000)	Daily Inch Rate-B/W	Cost per Page B/W
Top 10	136	28,099	19,301	$ 8,419	$ 969,065
Top 20	254	40,629	26,995	12,130	1,437,792
Top 30	353	49,349	32,397	14,929	1,785,863
Top 40	455	55,917	36,096	16,871	2,033,759
Top 50	552	61,472	39,489	18,639	2,269,885
Top 60	642	66,112	42,396	20,250	2,481,480
Top 70	732	70,079	44,816	21,764	2,677,250
Top 80	807	73,486	46,812	22,985	2,831,142
Top 90	872	70,447	48,713	24,014	2,965,481
Top 100	934	78,990	50,358	24,945	3,087,820

Sources: Newspaper Advertising Bureau: Audit Bureau of Circulations, September 1991; S.R.D.S., February 1991.

Selected Consumer Publications

Circulation and Rates (1991)	Circulation Rate Base (000)	1-Time Rate	
		4-Color Page	B/W Page
General Editorial			
Ebony	1,750	38,103	28,204
Life	1,700	69,820	54,110
Modern Maturity	22,450	218,215	196,940
National Enquirer	4,000	49,800	39,500
National Geographic	9,472	139,280	107,140
Parade	34,120	451,000	365,000
People	3,150	91,165	70,730
Prevention	3,000	36,750	31,955
Reader's Digest	16,250	131,000	112,660
Smithsonian	2,100	53,100	35,400
Star	3,500	40,300	33,450
USA Weekend	15,000	193,875	176,550
Entertainment Guides			
Cable Guide	11,000	$ 85,155	$ 65,785
TV Guide	15,800	117,350	99,700

(continued)

PRINT MEDIA *continued*

Circulation and Rates (1991)	Circulation Rate Base (000)	1-Time Rate	
		4-Color Page	B/W Page
News & Business			
Money	1,800	73,580	47,430
Newsweek	3,100	108,050	69,455
Time	4,000	128,000	85,000
U.S. News & World Report	2,150	72,400	48,500
Wall Street Journal (Nat'l.)	1,935	N/A	105,352
Women's			
Cosmopolitan	2,500	$ 64,045	$ 47,590
Family Circle	5,000	89,805	75,470
First for Women	2,500	30,795	26,170
Good Housekeeping	5,000	112,995	90,055
Ladies' Home Journal	5,000	84,900	71,300
McCall's	5,000	83,315	70,615
Redbook	3,800	75,820	57,340
Woman's Day	4,600	79,600	66,495
Food/Home Service			
Better Homes & Gardens	8,000	136,500	112,980
Country Living	1,700	51,920	37,950
Southern Living	2,275	60,440	42,870
Fashion & Bride			
Glamour	2,000	60,000	42,580
Baby Care			
The First Year of Life	3,200	118,970	87,423
Parents	1,725	52,160	40,740
Youth			
Scholastic Magazine Teen Network (Fall 91)	3,000	45,065	36,055
Seventeen	1,750	42,750	29,500
Men's			
Penthouse	2,000	31,355	27,970
Playboy	3,400	68,545	48,940
Sports & Automotive			
Field & Stream	2,000	62,790	41,735
Outdoor Life	1,500	42,660	29,390
Sports Illustrated	3,150	120,950	79,115
Mechanics/Science/Technical			
Popular Mechanics	1,600	54,065	38,095
Popular Science	1,800	45,400	32,005

Sources: S.R.D.S., September 1991; ABC Publisher's Statements, June 1991.

Sources of Advertising and Marketing Communication Management Information

- American Advertising Federation
1101 Vermont Ave., N.W., Suite 500
Washington, D.C. 20005
(800-999-2231) FAX 202-898-0159

- American Business Press
675 3rd Avenue
New York, New York 10017
(212-661-6360) FAX 212-370-0736

- Association of National Advertisers
155 E. 44th Street, 33rd Floor
New York, New York 10017
(212-697-5950) FAX 212-661-8057

- Business/Professional Advertising
Association
901 N. Washington Street, Suite 206
Alexandria, Virginia 22314
(703-683-2722) FAX 703-683-3788

- Leading National Advertisers
11 W. 42nd Street
New York, New York 10036
(212-789-1400) FAX 212-789-3636

- National Association of Broadcasters
1771 N Street, N.W.
Washington, D.C. 20036
(202-429-5300) FAX 202-775-3520

- Radio Advertising Bureau
303 Park Avenue South
New York, New York 10017
(212-599-6666) FAX 212-254-8713

- Television Bureau of Advertising
477 Madison Avenue, 10th Floor
New York, New York 10022
(212-486-1111) FAX 212-793-5631

- American Association of Advertising
Agencies
666 Third Avenue
New York, New York 10017
(212-682-2500) FAX 212-682-8136

- American Marketing Association
250 S. Wacker Drive, Suite 200
Chicago, Illinois 60606
(312-648-0536) FAX 312-993-7542

- AdWeek Directories
1515 Broadway
New York, New York 10036
(212-764-7300) FAX 212-536-5294

- Direct Marketing Educational Foundation
6 East 43rd Street
New York, New York 10017
(212-768-7277) FAX 212-599-1268

- Magazine Publishers Association
575 Lexington Avenue, Suite 540
New York, New York 10022
(212-752-0055) FAX 212-888-4217

- Newspaper Association of America
11600 Sunrise Valley Drive
Reston, Virginia 22091
(703-648-1000) FAX 703-620-4557

- Standard Rate & Data Service
304 Glendview
Wilmette, Illinois 60091
(708-256-6067) FAX 708-441-2400

- Yellow Pages Publishers Association
340 East Big Beaver Road, 5th Floor
Troy, Michigan 48083
(313-680-9239) FAX 313-680-1251

Additional sources of information include the following journals and trade magazines:
Advertising Age, AdWeek, Business Marketing, Journal of Advertising, Journal of Advertising Research, Journal of Marketing, Madison Avenue, Marketing News, Marketing Communications, and *Marketing & Media Decisions.*

Index

ADVERTISING AND MARKETING
COMMUNICATION MANAGEMENT